THE DAWN OF ASTROLOGY

The Dawn of Astrology
A Cultural History of Western Astrology

VOLUME 1: THE ANCIENT AND CLASSICAL WORLDS

Nicholas Campion

continuum

Hambledon Continuum is an imprint of Continuum Books
Continuum UK, The Tower Building, 11 York Road, London SE1 7NX
Continuum US, 80 Maiden Lane, Suite 704, New York, NY 10038

www.continuumbooks.com

First published 2008

British Library Cataloguing-in-Publication Data
A catalogue record for this book is available from the British Library.

ISBN 978 1 84725 214 2

Typeset by Pindar NZ (Egan Reid), Auckland, New Zealand
Printed and bound by MPG Books Ltd, Cornwall, Great Britain

Contents

CONTENTS

Illustrations

Between Pages 180 and 181

Acknowledgements

I would like to thank Kathleen Quigley for her role in the gestation of this project, Tony Morris for his inspiration and decade-long patience, and Crystal Addey, Roger Beck, Chris Brennan, Joseph Crane, Ronnie Gale Dreyer, Demetra George, Gary Gomes, Dorian Greenbaum, Rob Hand, Herman Hunger, Lee Lehman, B.V.K. Sastry and Ed Wright for their comments on the manuscript and, lastly, my students in the Sophia Centre at Bath Spa University and at Kepler College for their constant stimulation.

Introduction

> No one has ever heard of a collective that did not mobilize heaven and
> earth in its composition, along with bodies and souls, property and law,
> gods and ancestors, powers and beliefs, beast and fictional beings ... Such
> is the ancient anthropological matrix, the one we have never abandoned.[1]

In the modern West astrology is an accepted if, in some quarters, controversial feature of popular culture. In some parts of the world, such as India, it remains as much a part of the prevailing worldview as it was thousands of years ago, evidence of continuity between the contemporary world and a time when it was universally accepted that the heavens revealed meaning to humanity. In the West, perhaps 70 per cent of the adult population reads horoscope columns. The language of birth-signs is ubiquitous. Most people, well over 90 per cent, know what zodiac sign contained the sun at their birth and a significant number, probably between 40 and 50 per cent, identify with their zodiacal character. Astrology's use in the political sphere is less than it was before the seventeenth century. President Reagan's well-known use of astrology was the exception rather than the norm. Similarly, its application to finance is restricted. Yet, the fact that it occurs at all is a matter of high historical interest: how did a pre-Christian, pre-modern way of understanding humanity's place in the world survive into the twenty-first century?

This book attempts to locate the origins in the ancient world of the astrology practised in the medieval and modern West. It cannot aim to be definitive, for historical scholarship in astrology is still at a rudimentary stage; there are thousands of Babylonian cuneiform tablets which have never been catalogued, let alone translated, an unknown quantity of which may include material about the stars, while most Greek astrological texts have either not been translated or, if they have, have not been properly studied. However, I have included areas which are normally excluded from histories of astrology, including evidence of interest in the stars from prehistory, and Egyptian and Jewish cultures, as well Babylonian astrology, which has all too often been ignored in spite of its huge importance. I have considered Greek philosophy, without which it is impossible to understand the ideological framework within which astrology prospered in the classical world. I have, though, made little mention of India, whose astrology is linked to the West, but which followed a different trajectory and is awaiting authoritative treatment. Nor could I consider China, Japan, or the other cultures, such as those in the Americas, whose astrology was completely isolated from the West. This is, then a history of Western astrology – and a cultural history at that; I have considered technical developments only in as much as they provide a framework for our understanding of changing views of humanity's relationship with the sky.

First, some definitions: 'astronomy', from the Greek, is simply translated as the law of the stars; 'astrology' as the word (*logos*) of the stars. Equally, *logos* as reason, mind or logic of the stars might take us closer to astrology's origins in a context in which the entire cosmos was thought to be a single, living entity all of whose constituent parts, from the psychic to the physical, and from gods, to planets, people, plants and minerals, were interdependent and interlinked. To adopt a useful distinction between astronomy and astrology, the former is the study of the physical universe, the latter of the psychic (in both its soulful and psychological senses) cosmos. But, cosmos itself comes with its own set of meanings. The Greek word *kosmos* may be translated as 'adornment', in which sense it is the root of our word cosmetic. It was an adornment because it was beautiful, harmonious and, in spite of the unpleasantness which could afflict human life, essentially good. Cosmos, in this traditional sense, is a subjective thing. It is beautiful, and beauty is in the eye of the beholder, not as an external observer, but as a participant in cosmos itself. One cannot stand outside cosmos: to study it is to study one's self. As a living creature, humanity is created in the image of cosmos, and by gazing at it, sees itself. This, briefly paraphrased, is the worldview formalized in the literature of classical Greece, though with older antecedents, and articulated precisely in a practical form in the astrology of the Greek-speaking world.

The split between the two words, astronomy and astrology, is a feature of the modern West; in the classical world, their meanings overlapped. To the Greek scholar Claudius Ptolemy, writing in the second century CE, there were two forms of astronomy, one which dealt with the movement of the stars, the other (which we would call astrology) with their effects or significance. From then until the seventeenth century, the two words were interchangeable. In 'King Lear', Shakespeare had Edgar refer to his brother Edmund, who had been posing as an astrologer, as a 'sectary astronomical'. Other terms Shakespeare might have used include mathematician (the astronomer Johannes Kepler studied astrology as part of his duties as 'Imperial Mathematician') or Chaldean (both astrology and astronomy were commonly traced to Mesopotamia). Nor do most non-Western countries employ different words to distinguish traditional astronomy from astrology. In India both are *jyotish*, the 'science of light'. In Japan they are *onmyōdō*, the 'yin-yang way'.

The separation between the words astronomy and astrology in any history which deals with the pre-modern West, earlier than the seventeenth century, therefore runs the risk of being anachronistic, being more concerned with modern assumptions than ancient ones. Various solutions have been proposed to this problem. Edgar Laird suggested the term 'star study', Roger Beck 'star talk'.[2] For working purposes though, we need a modern definition of astrology which will enable us to discuss its manifestations in different cultures and which extends, in conventional modern terms, from the scientific at one extreme, to the overtly religious at the other. Astrology is therefore both the study of the ways in which significance for life on earth is located in celestial objects and the resulting practices. It may be speculative, but it can also be operative; it involves not only myth and ritual, but also action. It depends on rationales as various as divine intervention, celestial influence or the notion of the sky as a script to be read for signs. It functions through horoscopes, calendars, talismans and purification rituals. It can claim that the future is entirely knowable or essentially unknowable, that the world is predetermined or open to manipulation. It can function through divination – communication with divine entities – or the correlation of terrestrial events with celestial patterns. It may emphasize the inner or the outer, either one's character or the events of one's life, and can be applied to ultimate spiritual truths – the ascent of the soul to the stars – or to the trivia of domestic life, runaway slaves and lost treasure.

Out of this enormous range of styles and applications, we need to distinguish two other useful categories. Natural astrology assumes only that the stars and planets exert a general influence on terrestrial affairs, that the future may be only loosely forecast, and that astrology can say little or nothing about the specifics of human affairs. Judicial astrology, which found its ultimate expression in the development of the horoscope sometime between the fifth and second centuries BCE, assumes that the astrologer can reach precise judgements about matters ranging from the ebb and flow of political events to the details of individual lives. As the narrative of this book unfolds, the distinction between these two ways of perceiving the human relationship with the heavens will become apparent.

But the discussion will always be plagued by problems of definition. So let me end by facing the problem with one last set of controversial terms: science, religion and magic. Ancient astrology has been defined as all of these, yet these categories are frequently treated by historians and anthropologists, as much as modern scientists, as if they are hermetically sealed. From a historical perspective they quite clearly overlap and can often not be distinguished. So let me explain how I am using these terms. Religion I define quite conventionally as the worship of, or ritual interaction with, divine beings or anthropomorphized natural forces – nature conceived of as having personality. Magic is the deliberate attempt to engage with, manipulate or control the future, while science is either the practice of a discipline with its own rules, or an understanding of the world as primarily governed by natural processes as opposed to divine intervention.

For Wendy

1

Distant Echoes: Origins of Astrology

'Moon makes baby come' ... When the moon is
full the woman knows her time is near.[1]

Astrology is marked by the search for meaning in the sky, amongst the stars and planets and in the sun and moon. It deals with the effects of the heavenly bodies, their role as divine messengers, as seasonal markers and heralds of night or day, and the dangers of darkness and the liberation that comes with the dawn. It presents the sky as a source of awe, wonder and meaning, as a sacred canopy which shelters the earth below.[2] We have little idea of its origins, at least, little more than we have about the origins of human thought as a whole. The entire area is ripe for speculation. At a certain point in human evolution though, our ancestors developed the ability to consciously evaluate and reflect on the natural world, to identify cause and effect, to understand that the day begins because the sun rises and darkness falls when it disappears. Some time after this momentous event, perhaps tens or hundreds of thousands of years later, human beings began to believe that celestial events revealed a deeper meaning, purpose or intent, governed, perhaps by gods and goddesses, or some supreme cosmic order. The natural world was divine, alive, possessed of personality. This much is plausible – and supported by everything we know of ancient and pre-modern cultures.

The debate on the earliest origins of astrology is distorted by what is still a very influential theory on the history of religion, what we now know as the 'primitive error' hypothesis. This model was argued persuasively by Sir Edward Tylor (1832–1917), one of the founders of Victorian anthropology. Having atheistic tendencies, he assumed that religion arose from mistaken attempts to explain psychological experiences, such as dreams and trances, as well as natural phenomena, from the weather to day and night, birth and death. And so, for Tylor, the search for such causes in the sky was a fundamental error.[3] Astrology itself, he believed, was intimately bound up with this primitive misunderstanding of the universe. Tylor's younger colleague, Sir James Frazer, gave the theory an evolutionary twist by arguing that human intellectual development passes through three stages: magic, religion and science; all are attempts to formulate laws to explain and manipulate natural behaviour, but only science is correct – and magic and religion are patently false.[4] Frazer did not deal specifically with astrology, unlike Tylor, but it clearly belongs to his magical and religious periods and constitutes a form of primitive error. Both Tylor's and Frazer's tidy models of human cultural evolution have long since been abandoned by anthropologists and historians of religion, but they remain current, as accounts of astrology's origins, having been adopted by astrology's sceptical scientific critics. Other historians in the late eighteenth and early nineteenth centuries were fixated by the belief that all religion originated not just in awe of the sky, but in veneration of the sun. The theory found favour with Enlightenment radicals in France in the 1780s, such as Charles Dupuis, was enthusiastically adopted by atheists in England and France, and achieved academic status in the work of Max Müller, the great orientalist. Müller argued that religion progressed from fear of the environment, to awe of the sky and worship of the sun.[5] Once language developed, Müller argued, the sun was given different names – Christ, Krishna, Hercules, Zeus and so on – and people imagined, wrongly, that different names indicated different gods. Religion, then was, in Müller's words, a disease of language, an argument which won influential support in the nineteenth century, along with the view that religion was solar in origin.[6]

Once we have put such rhetoric to one side, though, two questions remain, for neither of which there is anything like a clear answer. First, when did human beings develop a symbolic consciousness? When, in other words, might they have concluded that the sun, a physical object, either was, or represented, a deity, an intangible being, force or presence.[7] Second, when were they able to articulate causal connections between the sun, heat and light, and the moon and the tides? And when did they actually articulate the relationship between the presence of the sun and the blessed light of dawn?

The archaeological record suggests that human beings were making tools and other artefacts anywhere between one and a half and three million years ago. In the African plains, successive generations of *Homo habilis* learnt how to craft and refine the sharp stone tools which enabled them to fight off predators, hunt prey and perhaps use animals for survival or ritual purposes, exploiting their skins for protection or decoration. This tool-making revolution coincided with a rapid increase in *habilis*'s brain size. Which came first is impossible to say. It is likely, though, that the birth of astronomy – and astrology in the sense of the search for meaning in the sky – followed. Perhaps it was *habilis*'s expanded brain that allowed consciousness of the environment as something distinct from the self, that there is an 'out there' which is distinct from the 'in here'. The argument, simply, is that tool-making and language skills are ultimately dependent on the capacity of the brain to categorize, evaluate, abstract and model the processes and objects of the visual, perceptual world.[8] Where we find tools of sufficient technical sophistication then we might expect that their users found meaning and purpose in the sky. To be clear, tool-making in itself does not suggest an awareness of the sky, for the great apes and some monkeys have such skills. But it is the evolution of cognitive faculties that, perhaps over millions of years, followed these developments that prompted our ancestors to look at the world around them with new eyes. As soon as human beings realized that sunrise, the most dramatic event of the day, was necessarily connected to the experience of heat and light, they were doing astronomy, in the modern sense of the word. And, the moment they attached meaning to this phenomenon, they were well on the way to becoming astrologers. They may have been aware of the equation of light, the presence of the sun, with good; and darkness, the sun's absence, with hidden dangers. If the *habilis* tool-makers could engage in organized collective activity, it is perfectly reasonable to suggest that they may have participated in decorative, symbolic, ritual or religious acts. They may have made symbolic correspondences, perhaps between the sun's heat and fire, its colour and objects with red or gold colouring. Just when this happened is a matter of wild conjecture. Ultimately, the problem is one for evolutionary psychology, and for the complicated and uncertain attempt to work out what makes humans different from great apes. Until we discover that our nearest biological cousins count time or venerate the sun and moon, astronomy and astrology must remain the property of human beings. Archaeology is some help, but is always limited by the archaeologists' ability to interpret artefacts which may be heavily weathered and difficult to identify.

If our Stone Age observers lived close to the oceans – though not by inland seas such as the Mediterranean – they must have noticed that the moon was highest in the sky at high tides and on the horizon at low tide. This phenomenon is so obvious that one cannot be conscious and not notice it; it is just not possible to live either by the ocean or a major tidal inlet or river, for more than a month, and watch a clear sky, and not make the connection. A second round of observations after a longer period of time would reveal that the tidal rise and fall reaches its extremities at new and full moons. Any human who, in a temperate zone, articulated the fact that the absence of sunlight correlates with cold and darkness would also have been one small logical step away from also making the moon–tide connection. Once that small step was accomplished, Stone Age people would have inhabited a world characterized by a fundamental rhythmic order. So, even though we naturally have no prehistoric accounts of lunar control of the tides, the recognition of the link, and hence the origin of lunar astronomy, must have emerged as human beings began to consciously interpret the world around them.

The daily movement of the sun, its rising at dawn and setting at dusk, is the fundamental feature of human existence, a fact which is easy to forget as more and more of us crowd into densely populated, artificially lit, 24-hour cities. Even then we cannot escape the fact that our bodies are driven by internal clocks which largely operate on a daily cycle or that, quite simply, if the sun went out, life would cease. There is an argument which emerges from the 'nasty, brutish and short' school of thought, which holds that Stone Age life was so hard that no primitive hunter-gatherer would have been overawed by the wonder of the heavens, a luxury afforded only to the inhabitants of more comfortable, later times.[9] Instead, the theory runs, astronomy would have originated as a means of pure survival, of knowing, in temperate climates, when it was going to be hot or cold, when summer could be anticipated and preparations made for winter.

Each of us contains an internal representation of the solar day, which drives our physiological circadian – daily – rhythms. So ubiquitous are such rhythms that they are a signature of life on earth. To pre-urban societies the alternation of night and day is the essential regulator of human activity. To those for whom the stars are divine powers, the repetitive alternation between night and day is critical to their entire way of living and dying, their sense of identity and survival. The increasing evidence for existence of biological body clocks suggests that their connection with the sun and moon is, in some way, hardwired, into our physical beings, and the experience of migrating birds who navigate by the stars implies that some automatic response to the heavens is likely. It is more likely though, that the very experience of living so close to the edge, on the boundary of life and death, could have heightened Stone Age people's wonder at the rising of the sun with its welcome light and warming rays.[10]

Within the last 100,000 years, the situation becomes a little clearer, and we can begin to look at the question through considering what might be plausible. If anatomically modern human beings were alive 80,000 years ago, that rather suggests that they were psychologically modern as well. To judge from the ethnographic evidence gleaned from the surviving 'primitive' tribes in the twenty-first century, they are as smart, witty, intelligent, capable, emotional, generous and needy as any educated Western city-dweller. The whole notion of 'primitive' as a moral or intellectual condition needs to be well and truly abandoned. With that in mind we can turn to the best framework for understanding ancient humanity's relationship with the sky, Lucien Lévy-Bruhl's *participation-mystique*.[11] Essentially, Lévy-Bruhl argued, for the pre-modern mind (which he referred to as 'primitive'), the world is conceived as an integrated set of living beings, in which there is no difference between the psychic and physical (so dreams are as real as the material world), all objects may have 'agency' (in other words they may play an active part in the unfolding of events), and 'human' society is not confined to people, but includes animals, plants, stones and stars, with whom individuals may have a personal relationship. While arguments that early humans observed the stars because they either needed to herd their animals, plant their crops (in the Neolithic period), placate natural forces or worship divine powers, may have some truth, they are all functional and reductionist, seeking single, useful explanations whilst ignoring the bigger picture. Crucial to this idea is the concept of respect. One respects the earth because it is one's mother, an animal because it may be a reborn ancestor, and the stars because they are messengers, guardians and protectors.[12] The prevailing myth was what we would call ecological. David Abram understood this when he defined humanity's natural environment, the totality of inner and outer experience, as the 'life-world'.[13] For Sean Kane, the interpreters of this experience were the 'myth-tellers'. These were the people who carried collective wisdom, revealing it in the form of allegorical stories about the world and the sky.

To identify the development of astrology – or astronomy – as due to functional requirements, such as navigation is useful. But it misses the point that myth-making, storytelling and meaning-creating activities are also functional. Human beings cannot function without meaning, and this is actually the primary level at which social cohesion is created.

We have evidence of intricately worked tools in southern Africa dating to around 70,000 BCE and, if our tool-making hypothesis is correct, these artisans had the awareness to regard the sky as a source of meaning. Evidence from around the same time in Europe indicates that ceremonial burials were conducted by Neanderthals, suggesting an emerging religious consciousness, and that human beings with sufficient capacity to watch the stars had spread over vast distances. If Neanderthals were taking the trouble to cover their dead with red ochre in shallow graves, as we know they were, then it is likely that they were also aware of the full moon and in awe of the rising sun. It is also not unreasonable to ask whether red ochre may have represented the sun, even if there can never be definitive proof. At the Neanderthal burial at La Chapelle-aux-Saints in the Dordogne, the body was orientated east–west; the simple existence of a corpse laid to rest in line with the rising and setting sun is our first glimpse of a tradition of solar religion which survived until recent times in the Christian practice of orientating church doors to the west.

Astrology itself arises from more than any physical, machine-like connection between humans and the heavens. Its close relationship with ancient religion implies a numinous awe of the heavens, which may, some argue, be a universal human attribute.[14] Nobody, it is said, can gaze at a magnificent sky without being moved by it. But, if we are moved by watching the sun rise, is it because we like a pretty view, or is it due to the presence of some pattern which has been integral to our development as a species? Has, for example, the alternation of night and day given us dialectical thought, the tendency to thing in terms of opposites, spatially of up and down, morally of good and evil? The philosopher Ernst Cassirer pursued this line when he noted how, in all peoples and in all religions, creation begins with the creation of light, a simple but speculative observation.[15] The natural-survival hypothesis, which claims that early people looked to the stars for security, or to construct calendars to regulate their lives, runs alongside the numinous-awe school, which argues that our ancestors looked to the heavens as a theatrical backdrop for their religious yearnings; the sun and moon were not just the regulators of time, but had to be worshipped and appeased.

The notion that the origins of religion have anything to do with the sky is now confined to the odd maverick, such as the archaeologist Jacquetta Hawkes. Hawkes, famous in the 1960s for her scepticism concerning Stonehenge's possible role as an observatory, allowed herself a brief moment of poetic speculation on just when our hominid ancestors began to look at the sun. It must have been back in east Africa, she reasons, when the fossil record shows that the earliest humans were walking on two legs and making tools around three million years ago, that they began to notice the sun as a separate powerful force in their lives. She wrote:

Now at last mind was dawning, raised between sun and earth … In that dawn of mind, sunrise and sunset, if not the sun itself, seem likely to have been among the first things to have been named by the first men. Even such a being as Oldoway Man [Olduvai man, from the Olduvai Gorge in Kenya], one of the earliest known hominids … must always have been very much aware of the passage of the sun across the gorge where he lived. He may conceivably even have used the lips stretched over his ape-like snout to frame sound to express its coming and going. if so, then here already was a step in creation through *logos* – the separation of day and night.[16]

While sun-as-god theorists such as Dupuis and Müller overstated the case, it is frankly difficult to see how any religion could have emerged which ignored the sun and moon. It has become all too easy for modern city-dwellers to forget that, if one lives outside, or at least without electric light, the sun and moon are stunning, unavoidable features of everyday existence. The continued devotion of Jews, Muslims, Christians, Buddhists and Hindus to sacred calendars, based on strict observation of the sun and moon, suggests that the astral element in modern mainstream religion is still deep, if largely forgotten. For Jews and Muslims the first sight of the rising new moon is the key feature of the divinely ordained ritual month, even if Christianity forgets its connection with the stars.

The further north or south of the equator that our ancestors roamed, the more they would have been aware that the sun is lower in the sky for one part of the year and higher in the other. As soon as any settled community, perhaps of cave-dwellers, decided that it was necessary, perhaps for religious purposes, to observe the sun's rising or setting against the background of a sacred mountain, they would have quickly become aware of the progressive movement of its rising and setting points along the horizon. To the Palaeolithic inhabitants of northern Europe and Asia, the point at which the sun rose every day would have marched left along the horizon – or north in our terms – until it approached the point at which it was highest in the sky at midday. It would then have slowed, stopped and gradually changed its direction. Our Stone Age observers would then have noticed the sun speeding up again until it began to reach its most rightward – or southerly – location. As the midday sun was lowest, weakest and coldest, it would then have stopped and the process would have begun again. Just when it was realized that the sun's movements were subject to annual as well as daily patterns – in other words, when there is such a thing as a year – we cannot say. In north-western Europe it was certainly by 5000 BCE, though common sense, if we can appeal to such a concept, suggests that it must have been very much earlier.

A similar process would have been attempted with the moon. Although its cycles are more complex, it would have been longer before any regular patterns were noticed beyond the approximately 29-day alternation between full moons – or new moons – the synodic month. Generations of modern Westerners, who have never experienced a dark sky, will never have experienced the drama of high full moon. Yet under the right conditions the moon casts sufficient light to read by, and certainly more than enough for Palaeolithic nomads to travel and hunt by. For those for whom the moon fulfilled a religious role the night of the full moon would have been a time of heightened activity. In the words of the English nursery rhyme: 'Boys and girls come out to play, the moon doth shine as bright as day'.

The moon's appearance is easy to record – all one has to do is look at the sky every night. Even the movements of the stars are simple to plot. Any Stone Age artisan who watched the stars for a single night would have also noticed one important fact – that, while some of the stars rise and set, others rotate around a point in the sky in a huge circle. That point, in the northern hemisphere, is north, a fact of monumental significance. Once discovered it would have allowed migrating hunters to fix their direction exactly, to move north in the spring and expect the approaching winter in the autumn. It would also allow them to move east and west by keeping the north point to their left or right. While we cannot say with certainty that Palaeolithic humans navigated by the stars, to deny the possibility is just not consistent with their other achievements. And, it is consistent with all other evidence that the fact that the point in the sky around which the stars rotated and allowed travellers to find their way, which would have been seen as purposeful, perhaps placed there for a reason, and certainly intended to be of assistance.

Our ability to find evidence in the material record is seriously hampered by the fact that, apart from obvious stone axes, the earlier the date the more difficult it is to work out whether a stone or bone was deliberately shaped or accidentally weathered. Some evidence does exist in the form of animal bones with carved notches. The earliest, the so-called Bilzinsleben artefact produced by *Homo erectus* seems to have been carved around 350,000–250,000 BCE and appears to contain 28 notches, a figure always suggestive of the days in a sidereal lunar month – the time it takes for the moon to return to the same set of stars.[17] Naturally, we have to be cautious about anything so old, as its markings could well be the result of natural weathering. But there is no theoretical problem with the existence of calendars so early. If people could make tools and hunt they could count and, if they could count, they could keep simple calendars. In fact, it would be astonishing if they did not. It is simply not credible that a community of humans sufficiently conscious to make artefacts would not be deeply impressed by the moon's dramatic appearance when full, intrigued by its disappearance around 14 days later and fascinated by the fact that the period between the two events is always the same.

There is then a huge gap in the evidence until around 30,000 BCE, around the time when our direct ancestor, *Homo sapiens*, was beginning to migrate into Europe and western Asia, squeezing out the unfortunate and soon-to-be extinct Neanderthals. Dozens of notched bones have been found across Europe, with other examples from Australia and Africa, while there may be thousands more which have been excavated but never analysed.[18] While most archaeological digs have taken place in Europe, we are clearly dealing with a universal phenomenon. A baboon's thigh bone, discovered in the Lebembo mountains bordering

Swaziland and dated to 35,000 BCE, contains 29 notches, suggesting that it may have been a counter for the synodic month (from new moon to new moon) of 29.53 days. One of the most well-known artefacts, the Ishango bone, was discovered on the shores of Lake Edward in east Africa, on the boundary of Zaire and Uganda, and seems to have been carved around between 23,000 and 18,000 BCE by a member of a small fishing community. It contains several rows of notches, two of which add up to 30 which, like the Labembo bone, may have been lunar counters, while the third consists of 48 notches, not exactly a lunar number, though there have been attempts to discern another 12 notches to complete the lunar pattern. In Australia a diprotodon tooth dated to around 18,000 BCE and carved with 28 notches, perhaps representing the days of the lunar month, can be seen in the Museum of Victoria in Adelaide.[19] A reindeer bone from Czechoslovakia apparently indicated the moon's waxing and waning phases while a mammoth tusk from Gontzi in the Ukraine may have represented the moon's phases over four months. It is possible that not all the astronomical periods noted are lunar. Some may be solar, others planetary. Others may well have documented events which we know were to be important in the refined astrology of second-millennium BCE Mesopotamia, such as days when the sun was red at dawn, or obscured by clouds. These, though, are, and will always be, impossible to decipher in retrospect.

The evidence of the bones is reinforced by a series of cave paintings. The illustrations on the rock walls of Canchal de Mahoma in Spain are dated to around 10,000–8000 BCE and include 29 marks, some of them suitably crescent-shaped suggesting 'a precisely observed lunar sequence', while another Spanish painting, from Abri de las Vinas, consisted of 30 marks with the outline of a human figure which Alexander Marshak interpreted as a 'god'.[20] If the critical problem with the supposed calendar bones is our analysis of the notches, which may be either eroded or confused with natural cracks, with paintings the problem extends to intent: even if an astronomical message is obvious to us, how do we know it was what the artist had in mind? However, the view that what were previously regarded simply as 'ritual objects' are Palaeolithic calendars is difficult to challenge. They offer us a picture of a society which was organizing itself around time, exactly as we do today. This suggests in turn some sort of political order. It is unlikely the calendar bones were created by ancient astronomers working in isolation from their societies: the concept of the disinterested scientist, interested only in the search for objective truth, is essentially peculiar to modern Western society. We must assume that the Palaeolithic calendar-makers had a social role, either exerting direct religious and political authority or contributing to the power of others. Even if we imagine some Stone Age idyll in which collective decisions were taken through democracy or consensus, the calendar-makers clearly had a focal role. Only they could tell when the moon was full and when it would disappear and hence when appropriate rituals and observances should be held. In this role they were technocrats. If they had any view that the moon was divine or represented a superior, creative force to be worshipped, they were priestesses or priests. And, if they were concerned either to divine the future or elect auspicious moments for new enterprises, they were astrologers. Above all, they were myth-tellers.

We know a little about the Stone Age calendar-makers. From 40,000 BCE we find large quantities of jewellery indicating an ability to produce finely crafted objects for pleasure, adornment and attraction rather than for any directly practical function. And, after 35,000 or 30,000 BCE, when Europe entered the Upper Palaeolithic period, and certainly by 27,000 BCE, humans were constructing huts of skin, mammoth bone, clay and stone, burying their dead with ritual and ceremony and sculpting animal and human figurines from ivory and clay. It is one of these, the so-called 'Venus of Laussel' that gives us the best evidence of the religious function of Palaeolithic astronomy and the calendar bones and paintings.[21]

This most famous of the many female 'goddess' figurines which survive from the Palaeolithic period was discovered in the Dordogne in France and dated to the Upper Perigordian period, perhaps around 20,000 BCE. The figure is a bas-relief of a large-breasted, wide-hipped female about 43cm (17in) high, standing with one hand covering her belly, a gesture which may indicate pregnancy, and most certainly fertility, birth and reverence for the creation of life. The particular interest attached to this carving though, is that the woman is holding a crescent-shaped object incised with 13 clear notches. This object appears to be an animal horn, perhaps for drinking, but the crescent shape is suggestive of the moon; there may have been multiple symbolic references reflective of a range of ritual uses. The notches may represent the nights when the moon is visible between its first crescent appearance and the full moon, or they might represent the months of the lunar year: each solar year includes either 12 or 13 new crescent moons. The use of red ochre, a practice shared with the Neanderthals, may be indicative of menstruation but might also point plausibly to solar imagery and it has been suggested that the figure's head is either the sun or full moon. Perhaps she was a sky goddess who ruled over, or represented, both the sun and the moon. Maybe she was a great mother who presided over heaven and earth. The horn's 13 notches suggest that here we have a deity who presided over the calendar, who ruled both time and, from her fertile appearance, gestation, birth and growth. She is at once a sky goddess and a nature goddess. She is, perhaps, both subject to the mathematical regularity of the lunar cycle and in control of it. If this sounds like a paradox then it is one we can easily live with: the future astrologers of Babylon lived happily with the entirely contradictory notions that the planets at one and the same time moved in predictable patterns and could be manipulated by their deities to send omens. Astral religion is partly concerned with submission to powerful cosmic deities but, in Babylon and Egypt, was to be obsessed with the need to keep time on its proper course: this is the basis of all calendar keeping. Taken together the Venus figurine and the calendar bones may be evidence of a magical, political, astral theology, in which the management of time was crucial to society's smooth functioning. The keeping of calendars would also have allowed the use of astrology as an attempt to leap ahead, to anticipate the gods' and goddesses' intentions or, in later times, to extrapolate celestial cycles into the future, and thus to gain protection, avert the worst indications of dangerous times, and enhance the best portents of auspicious periods.

It is highly doubtful whether the goddess of Laussel existed in isolation. She merely happens to be the surviving representative of a rich calendrical mythology. Or rather, we should say, human life was tied to the natural environment which itself included the stars as much as plants, stones and animals. There was, it seems a high regard for the powers of the sky, a celestial theology in which human life was tied to the heavens. A simple, archaic astrology, as embodied in the goddess figurine, was part of a wider ecological religion.

A central argument in the web of theories concerning women's contribution to early human culture is biological – the approximate, though not exact, correlation between the menstrual cycle and the moon's synodic period – from new moon to new moon. The seminal work in the 1980s was Penelope Shuttle and Peter Redgrove's *The Wise Wound*, which presented menstruation as something magical, and collated the evidence linking menstrual to lunar cycles. Their work served as the partial inspiration for the current core text, Chris Knight's *Blood Relations: Menstruation and the Origins of Culture* (1991). Knight's essential thesis is that the lunar calendar originated as a means of measuring female fertility, with all its social, political, economic and religious implications. Knight argues primarily from a Marxist perspective, citing Marx's commonplace observation that 'in the final analysis, all forms of economics can be reduced to an economics of time. Likewise, society must divide up its time purposefully in order to achieve a production suited to its general needs.'[22]

This is really to state the obvious, that, before the recent advent of the '24-hour society', the timing of most human activities was generally determined by the sun during the day with the moon playing its own nocturnal and monthly roles. Many of Knight's observations are equally uncontroversial. That the menstrual cycle approximates to the lunar rhythm, and that it therefore interferes in sexual and other activities is not open to dispute. It is possible to harness a range of recent and contemporary anthropological evidence to show that in non-urban societies the moon's connection with fertility is widely assumed even if many scientists dispute it. In 1971 Jane Goodale described aboriginal practices on Melville Island in northern Australia: 'As soon as a woman knows she is pregnant, she starts to "follow moon". "Moon makes baby come", I was told. When the moon is full the woman knows her time is near.'[23]

From a possible lunar astronomy/astrology we might therefore gradually move to a stellar one, a step which would have happened perhaps when sky-watchers became intrigued by the fact that the moon can be tracked by its passage past particular stars. However, we should be wary of assuming any such general pattern. On the other hand, given the apparent irregularity of the moon's cycle it is equally likely that the first stars to be accorded significance were those which rose or set shortly after dusk or before dawn, and these would therefore have been hailed as heralds of day or night. As calendar markers they would also have measured the solar year, marking the sun's annual journey. There is some slight evidence in this respect dating to the Magdalenian period and the cave paintings of Lascaux in France, dating to around 15,000 BCE. Just above the neck of the largest of the aurochs (the now-extinct bulls), which has a length of 5.5m, are six spots. These are very likely the six most visible stars of the Pleiades, the star cluster which tradition later attached to the shoulder of Taurus, the Bull, while further dots on the bull's face may be the Hyades, another star cluster now included in Taurus.[24] Given that the paintings had a ritual purpose, being often created in caves far too deep for habitation, that some exhibit seasonal use, and that the Pleiades are unique in being the only star cluster easily visible to the naked eye, it is certain that we are looking at an image of profound astronomical and astrological significance. In 15,000 BCE the Pleiades would have been setting when the sun rose in the spring, and rising at dawn in the autumn. The sun's proximity to them therefore heralded both the lush times of summer and the harsh ones of winter. The Lascaux paintings offer our clearest evidence yet of a Palaeolithic astral religion and a solar calendar as well as the earliest visual evidence for the existence of a zodiacal constellation. Fashions in the interpretation of cave paintings change but the very fact they often occur in deep, inaccessible places, suggests a profound religious function. They may be plausibly seen as liminal, as boundaries between this world and an invisible one, linked to shamanistic rituals in which the participants became one with the image on the cave wall, and perhaps a world beyond it.[25] Our hypothetical initiate at Lascaux might have intended to become one with the bull, but may also have wished to unite with, or travel to the stars. In which case the Lascaux image becomes our earliest evidence of travel, even if only in the imagination, to the stars.

The Pleiades feature elsewhere in Palaeolithic astronomy. There is a remarkable similarity between stories about them found as far apart as North America, Europe and Australia. All these accounts link the Pleiades to myths of seven sisters (though occasionally brothers) and explain the fact that, often, only six are easily visible with stories to explain how one disappeared or fell to earth.[26] In both classical Greece and Australian Aboriginal tales, the sisters are perpetually chased through the sky by the stars we recognize as the constellation Orion the Hunter. Perhaps the best indications of the nature of old Stone Age astronomy may come from the Australian Aborigines, mainly because they may embody a continuous tradition back to perhaps 40,000 BCE. There the sky contains seasonal messages, but also stories with social messages. One story which is performed in some areas for a girl's first menstruation, concerns the pursuit and rape of one of the seven sisters (the Pleiades) by Njiru (Orion), and may contain warnings about such abuse (Njiru's penis is bitten off by a dog, although it then comes to life and continues the chase) or expressions of sexual fear or fantasy.[27] But there is variety in a central theme: in some areas the three stars of Orion's belt are fishermen and the Pleiades are their happily married wives.

Unless we accept a gigantic coincidence, there are only two conclusions. Either the inhabitants of all three continents independently recognized an archetypal quality in the stars, or the observation and myths of the Pleiades predated the migration of Palaeolithic hunters both to America and Australia.[28] That in turn gives us a latest possible date for the formation of the Pleiades mythology in the date for the migration of the Aborigines. And that, of course remains a field of considerable argument, given that an Aboriginal site dated to 176,000–117,000 BCE by one archaeologist might be dated to 7000–6000 BCE by another.[29] So, for the sake of argument we might say that the Pleiades myths were established by 30,000 BCE, perhaps later but equally likely, much earlier. Either way, it has been argued that there are significant parallels between Aboriginal and Middle Eastern myth, as between, for example, the threatening Tiamat of Sumer, and the looming 'Presence' of the Aboriginal night sky.[30] Of course, a cognitive psychologist might say our brains are 'hard-wired' to recognize certain patterns, a Jungian analytical psychologist that we recognize certain universal truths.[31]

And then there is the strange case of the Great Bear. This constellation, of which the stars of the Big Dipper, are probably the most familiar in the sky, is recognized as a bear both in northern Europe and amongst many native North Americans. Its power was derived from its proximity to the north point of the sky, rotating around it every night (at least, in the northern hemisphere) and playing a part as a celestial guide. The Micmac Indians of Canada's Maritime Provinces tell a story in which the stars' seasonal passage across the sky is an analogy for the bear's hibernation in winter and waking in spring. It is generally regarded as unlikely that the indigenous Americans borrowed the Bear, and perhaps Boötes and Corona Borealis, from early European explorers, leaving the possibility that it must have crossed into Alaska with migrants across the Bering Straits, an event dated at no later than 10,000 BCE, perhaps several thousand years earlier.[32] As a testimony to the enduring power of these stars, there is a tradition of bear myth and shamanic ritual which has survived, as folklore, into modern Europe and may stretch back tens of thousands of years.[33] We can never be entirely sure that such stories were not incorporated by Native American people after contact with the first European settlers and missionaries, from the mid-sixteenth century onwards. This is not to belittle Native American wisdom but rather to acknowledge that it, like European culture, is open to fresh ideas. The evidence is often frustratingly inconclusive. The notion of a mythic link from Europe to North America was first proposed by the folklorist Charles G. Leland, who travelled amongst the Algonquin Indians, collecting stories, poems and songs which he published in 1884.[34] One is a beautiful evocation of the shamanic relationship between the Algonquin and the sky.

> We are the stars which sing,
> We sing with our light;
> We are the birds of fire,
> We fly over the sky.

Our light is a voice.
We make a road for spirits,
For the spirits to pass over.
Among us are three hunters
Who chase a bear;
There never was a time
When they were not hunting.
We look down on the mountains.
This is the Song of the Stars.[35]

The whole tone of this invocation suggests the existence of the possibility of a journey between earth and stars which is similar to those found in classical literature. The bear may not have been the only celestial animal once revered as a religious totem across northern Europe and Asia. In Anatolia, for example, other animal images have been interpreted as stars or constellations while images of bulls and stags dated to the fourth millennium BCE in Italy have been associated with the sun and imaginatively described as a 'fusion of sexual and solar energy' and as examples of the formation of primitive zodiacs.[36] The obvious problem here, though, is a logical fallacy: the stars of Taurus may be represented by a bull, but that does not mean that all bull images represent the stars of Taurus.

Although certain bright stars, such as Sirius and Aldebaran, and asterisms – small star groups – such as the Pleiades would be recognized by any culture with even a passing interest in the night sky, that does not necessarily imply a wholesale mapping of the sky. We know from non-literate societies that the absence of writing is no bar to the transmission of detailed information, such as epic poems.[37] There is an alternative school of thought which holds that, as societies become more complex, so do their views of the sky.[38] Whereas Palaeolithic, Neolithic and agrarian societies had no need of such precision and therefore no need to concoct precise constellations, urban societies required detailed calendars and ever more precise systems of celestial divination. Either way, the cosmos was a mirror of political and social order.

Then there is the problem of how exactly the constellations were identified. Much later, how did the Mesopotamians portray one particular group of stars as a crab, another as a bull? The popular approach, a familiar one from children's books, has been appropriately characterized as the 'picture-book paradigm' which projects back a modern, whimsical view of the constellations and a view of astronomy as a recreation for amateurs.[39] Shepherds, according to this view, lay on their backs at night and made up various stories about the stars. The creation of the constellations then happened by chance, as some sort of random accumulation of stories. This theory has survived in the popular imagination even though it was condemned by Franz Cumont as an illusion and consigned to the 'realm of dreams' as long ago as 1911. What Cumont objected to though, was not the idea that ancient people saw pictures in the sky, but that ordinary people did so. In his view it was the elite, the priests, who held this function. 'Inspired ...

with superstitious fear', he wrote, 'they believed that in the complicated pattern of the stars, which gleamed in the night, they could recognise fantastic shapes of polymorphous monsters, of strange objects, of sacred animals, of imaginary personages.' [40] However, given that the Taurean Bull appears to have featured on the caves of Lascaux well over 10,000 years before the Babylonian constellations emerge blinking into human consciousness, and that all societies with a clear view of the sky have devised constellations, projecting images into the sky just seems to be something that people do. Perhaps it is a way for our brains to make sense of the world just as we classify, regulate and label everything else we can see. Most likely the shamanistic priesthood of the third millennium BCE inherited a system that had been evolving over thousands of years. Some constellations, such as the Bull, seem to have come from a shared tradition while others may have been their own invention. Ursa Major, the Bear of the forest-dwelling north Europeans and north Americans was, to the technologically advanced Sumerians, a Wagon.

By the end of the last Ice Age we can identify the earliest signs of a recognizable physical astronomy and astral theology. In the Near East, sometime around 8000 BCE, perhaps earlier, the earliest farmers were tilling their fields of wheat, the first urbanites were creating cities at Catal Huyuk in central Turkey and Jericho. Copper mining had perhaps begun already, encouraging trade across the region. But it was in western Europe that we have identified the richest remains of a culture which, some have argued, unambiguously went to extraordinary lengths to observe and measure the movements of the heavens.

2

Prehistory: Myths and Megaliths

Every age has the Stonehenge it deserves – or desires.[1]

It is clear that early humans had developed a close relationship with the heavenly bodies during the Old Stone Age, certainly by the upper Palaeolithic, after about 40,000 years ago. But it is difficult to trace the development of astronomical thought – or astrological attitudes – until the appearance of megalithic culture (from the Greek: *mega*, 'great', and *lith*, 'stone'), characterized by its great stone monuments, sometime around 3000 BCE. Neolithic culture, characterized by urban communities and the cultivation of crops, appeared in eastern Turkey, Syria and Palestine around 8000 BCE, and it is difficult to imagine such societies functioning without sacred and agricultural calendars or celestial deities and omens. But non-literate cultures leave no written records, a problem which is compounded by the lack of clear archaeological evidence. The most intense evidence for an astronomically based culture is therefore found in north-western Europe.

The prevailing assumption that megalithic culture was centred in north-western Europe is partly a consequence of the fact that the greatest, most accessible and well-known sites – Stonehenge, Avebury and Carnac – are in Britain and France, and that they naturally attracted the first archaeological interest. The awareness of megalithic culture amongst archaeologists, combined with the latest surveying techniques, has resulted in a small industry in which sites are discovered and astronomical significance is identified. However, research is producing a series of discoveries in the east. For example, it has recently been claimed that at Metsamor in Armenia, carvings which have been provisionally interpreted as solar or other celestial symbols can be dated to 7000 BCE, that the site functioned as an observatory by 5000 BCE and that three viewing platforms were carved out of the rock between 2800 and 2500 BCE.[2] Such work remains controversial. While it is reasonable to assume the existence of astronomically significant sites, there is a tendency to over-interpret specific locations.[3]

One of the most extravagant of recent claims identifies a huge Bronze Age pyramid, consisting of a complex of shrines and temples on top of a stepped hillside, and predating the pyramids at Giza by 300 years, at Lugansk in the Ukraine. The hilltop covered three-quarters of a square mile and was, the archaeologists claimed, in use for 2,000 years. Viktor Kochko, the excavation's leader, claimed that 'people lived in the surrounding valleys and climbed up to it (the top if the hill) to carry out their ceremonies. They had a pagan cult that bowed down to the sun, as did the ancestors of the Slavs'.[4] There is a problem with the spate of headline-attracting discoveries though; a tendency to convert provisional evidence into firm conclusions which may not be supported by later research. And, while such discoveries are adding to the picture, the British Isles remain the most heavily studied region.

From shortly before 3000 BCE, parts of the British Isles were witness to an immense programme of ritual architecture and construction, originally of earth and wood, later of stone. These are the tangible remains of a society which produced a Stone Age astronomy, which was capable of measuring the positions of the sun and, in all probability, the moon and stars, with as great a precision as naked-eye observation allows. There are arguments as to the extent of this astronomy: was it, for example, concerned simply with the fundamentals of solar and lunar periods – solstices and new and full moons? Or did the builders pay attention to particular stars and were they capable of measuring eclipses? These questions will never be answered to everyone's satisfaction for the evidence requires modern judgements concerning the builders' skill but, most of all, their intentions. The megalith builders left no writing, so we can only enter their minds through the awesome remains they left behind.

Indirect supporting evidence of the builders' intentions may be found from more recent folk-astronomical practices or from the projection back of later oral or literary traditions, yet our understanding of megalithic cosmology remains almost exclusively dependent on the archaeological evidence. It follows that, while methods of excavating and recording data may be increasingly rigorous, the conclusions reached are often highly subjective and depend on modern assumptions about the past.

The appearance of megalithic culture in north-western Europe is quite extraordinary, if we trace its origins prior to the use of stones, to the earliest earth ditch-and-bank monuments, there appears to have been a change of relationship with the land. One answer may lie in the submergence of 'Dogger Land', the region between Britain, Denmark and the north European coast which now lies under the North Sea. Around 10,000 BCE Dogger Land was probably, given the uncertainties of current archaeological knowledge, a focus of human activity. By 8000 BCE water from the melting ice sheets was encroaching at a speed of around 200m a year, and, sometime around 6000 BCE, the land bridge between south-east England and France was finally severed. The inundation of Dogger Land would have resulted in the migration of its inhabitants to the surrounding higher ground of Britain, northern France, Germany and Scandinavia. These displaced populations would then have been confined to a smaller area of land than previously, resulting in intensified social relationships. The loss of a relationship with previously occupied land would have been apocalyptic in scope: at 200m a year the water would have moved fast enough to have made it difficult to establish settled communities and there would have been repeated disruption over the period of inundation. It is fair enough to assume that this disruption in the 'life-world' would have required some re-evaluation of late Mesolithic humanity's understanding of the cosmic forces or beings who dominated nature. The extent and enduring power of the folk-memory of the floods, testimony to the intensity of the experience, which greeted the end of the last Ice Age are preserved in the global reach of deluge myths, of which we have examples from almost every part of the world.[5] The biblical story is the best known in Western culture. In the famous tale in the book of Genesis, humanity sins and the cosmos, directed by a wrathful God, takes its revenge and only the righteous Noah, and his family survive. Perhaps the appearance of fixed marks in the landscape, whose function seems to have been to locate the dead to particular places which were, in turn, aligned with the sun or, possibly, other celestial bodies, was a similar response to the crisis induced by catastrophically rising sea levels. These, were, of course, experienced not just in the area around the North Sea, but globally, in all coastal areas. Unfortunately the use of stones gives us only an approximate idea of when the monument-erecting society began. The discovery of Seahenge, a circle of wooden markers, off the east coast of England and dated, with remarkable accuracy to 2049 BCE, has opened our eyes to the possibility that megalithic remains survived precisely because they were made of stone, while other, earlier, monuments have been lost for good.[6] But how should we read the shift from Palaeolithic to Neolithic cosmology? Mark Edmonds is clear on the matter; time became an organized entity:

> Talk of Neolithic cultures has, in its turn given way to a view of the period as an economic entity, associated with a switch from hunting and gathering to food production. More recently still, interest has shifted towards a view of the periods as a time that saw the development of new ways of thinking about the land, people and even time itself.[7]

Peoples' experiences of their environments give rise to, and ultimately embody, their cosmologies, the structure they use to understand and explain their world. Jude Currivan has identified two forms of cosmology, one 'shamanistic', which presumes an inherently intrinsically uncertain cosmos and the other 'geomantic', which discerns an innate underlying order and eternal cycles, and encourages anthropocentric thought and a spatial and temporal ordering of the physical world. The geomantic worldview, significantly, legitimizes the 'altering of the Earth' by the digging of ditches and erection of monuments.[8] As Currivan identified a shift from shamanistic to geomantic cosmology so, for Sean Kane, the shift to the Neolithic, represented the beginning of a progressive shift away from the purity of the Palaeolithic myth-teller, who occupied a space in which the human being was at one with nature. Planting crops, scratching the earth, erecting monuments and reading the stars represented a move away from Eden.[9] Yet, he insisted, under the skin of a Neolithic astronomer, as much as a Greek astrologer, the myth-teller could still be found.

The sky-based features of north European Neolithic religion were exactly matched by an equal reverence for the earth. In an echo of the Old Stone Age use of caves as locations for contacting the other world, Neolithic people dug ditches, often very deep ones, which seem to have functioned as portals to other worlds, liminal points at which the gods, goddesses or mysterious powers of the living earth might be contacted.[10] Perhaps these powers were released over or into the pilgrim, initiate or worshipper who entered the ditch. Maybe the ancestors were contacted or the future revealed, an argument which has come into higher focus as the emphasis at sites such as Stonehenge has shifted to the winter solstice, the symbol of death, rather than the summer solstice. The intimate relationship between a fascination for the sky and the earth is not a hard one to fathom in an environment in which the sun's annual journey so clearly controlled the life of the earth; in winter it was covered in death, in summer abundance. One thing we do know is that these ditches were not defensive, as they were to be in the Iron Age settlements of 2,000 years later. Indeed, the fragmentary nature of some of the earthworks has led to their designation as 'interrupted enclosures'.[11]

The location of Neolithic monuments and megalithic stones in Britain, for which we have the most information, is often obvious, sometimes discrete or curious.[12] One particularly dramatic long barrow, a stone and earth tomb, at Nymphsfield, located on the western escarpment of the English Cotswold hills, is poised above the flood plain of the river Severn, facing the hills of Wales on the far horizon. To the west it presents a dramatic view of the setting stars, presenting a panoramic view of the heavens and undoubtedly was imbued with immense ritual power at key celestial moments. Approached from below, by pilgrims from the river valley, it would have stood out as a clear marker on the skyline. But it is not so much the site of the barrow which is significant, as the view from it, which would have offered a sense of almost direct contact with the sky.

As Mark Edmonds eloquently observed, 'people wove a constellation of mean- ings and histories into these houses [tombs]. Like a church of the Middle Ages, they were places where personal loss could be acknowledged and where a sense of kinship and community could be grounded in an ancestral and cosmological order.'[13] Such places were sources of authority and social context. They drew attention to the rising and setting of the sun or moon, mapping cycles, histories and stories in the sky, provided a locus for shamanic initiations or communication with the ancestors, scenes of rites of passage or the enactment of myth, at some time open to all or at others, perhaps, to the few. Important events at tombs could even implicate cycles and histories mapped out across the sky. We come to the question, though, whether the land was sacred, in the sense of being alive and/or populated by invisible beings, or whether the site's characteristic of Currivan's geomantic cosmology represented a shift between, as Mircea Eliade would have called them, two zones, the sacred and the profane. The former, in his view, would have been connected to an eternal, transcendent, absolute reality, the latter not.[14]

Some of the most important sites were designed to be approached, emphasizing their role as the final point of a pilgrimage or ritual procession. Stonehenge might be approached first from the river Kennet and then via the so-called avenue, a path marked out by two raised banks, and would only have become visible as the faithful reached the final phase of the journey. Other monuments were located in low-lying settings, recalling an earth-based, rather than sky-centred function. Of these the most mysterious is the massive earth mound at Silbury, about 20 miles north of Stonehenge and the largest monument of its kind in the world. Clearly a sacred hill rather than a tomb, its base lies in a valley, while its platform top reaches approximately the same height as the surrounding plateau. If the builders had wished to construct a high viewing point, they would have started from a high foundation, not a low one. They may have wished to connect with the sky but, from a point whose moist fertility is clearly more redolent of the folds of an earth mother than the expanse of a sky mother – or father.

Although the earliest known sites in north-western Europe consist of earth mounds, earth banks and ditches (henges) and wooden constructions, stone came into use in the centuries before 2000 BCE. This megalithic culture flourished within the Neolithic or New Stone Age, the period in which the hunter-gatherer lifestyle gave way to the first settled agrarian communities. The thousands of surviving sites from single standing stones to avenues and circles are the ritual remains of a major shift in human culture, as human beings ceased being wanderers and entered a stable relationship to a fixed piece of land. As the relationship with space changed, so did that with time. Time and space meet, though, in the calendar, the technology needed to enable humans to negotiate their relationship with the two in the construction of calendars. Calendars provide two functions. One is secular, the ordered arrangement of business and, to a lesser extent, agricultural affairs. The other is sacred, the proper celebration of religious ritual on a daily, monthly and annual basis. In most pre-modern cultures, observation of the calendar is far more than a matter of paying the gods their dues, or respecting natural forces, but a necessity if the divine will is to be done, earth is to be in harmony with heaven and human society is to be prosperous and peaceful. However, the problems that calendar-makers have always faced is how to reconcile the differing cycles of the sun, moon and stars. Compensation for this uncertainty could be found in the use of ritual as a means of reinforcing social cohesion.

The most ancient known human remains at Stonehenge are dated to around 8000 BCE, when southern England was still covered in subarctic tundra and around the time that the melting ice caps and rising sea levels finally submerged the bridge between Britain and France. The evidence consists of post-holes which are currently covered by tarmac in English Heritage's official car park.[15] Their purpose is unknown, although three of them seem to be in a roughly east–west alignment. Were these used for astronomical sight lines? They are, at the very least, intriguing evidence of a human presence on Salisbury Plain 5,000 years before the major building programme at Stonehenge and, at most are an indication that this may be one of the oldest known sacred sites in the world. Of the intervening period we know little.

However, in 2003 German archaeologists made a stunning find at Goszek, a small town in the German state of Saxony-Anhalt, which drove the date of organized ritual astronomy/astrology back to almost 2,000 years before the first earth and ditch construction at Stonehenge. The Goszek site, which is dated to between 5000 and 4800 BCE, consisted of several concentric rings of posts. Three gates in the outermost circle led to progressively narrower entrances in the inner rings, suggesting restricted entry to the central, ritual area, perhaps a holy of holies, or a point of contact with the invisible world. The presence of human remains is suggestive of burial, and the orientation of the southern most gates to sunrise and sunset on the winter solstice, the shortest day, confirms the existence of a 'solar state', a society whose religious and political ideology was founded, at least in part, on its relationship to the sun. Undoubtedly there were also lunar connections – it is just not reasonable to assume that such profound attention to the sun was not matched by devotion to the full moon. But, whether lunar measures were built into the fabric of the Goszek henge, or observed at other sites, is not clear. We can be sure, though, that religion – in the sense of veneration of superior forces – was significant, as was magic – by which I mean the intentional participation in, or manipulation of, the powers of the natural and supernatural worlds. Such astrology – and we must call it that – was embodied. It was based firmly in the perception and experience of the observer, his or her physical location in a ritual space, linking directly with the sun as it rose and set on either its summer or, more likely, winter solstice – the day of its death and resurrection.

Other early evidence of megalithic astronomy – in the sense of the use of stones as timepieces – is now found in the Middle East. In 1998 the discovery of an astronomically aligned set of stones was announced at Nabta Playa, a former oasis in western Egypt, about 100km west of the Nile, dated back to around 4500–4000 BCE.[16] The site itself may have been occupied, if intermittently, from as early as 8000 down to 3500 BCE, by which time lower levels of rainfall were encouraging the return of the desert. While the Neolithic farmers of the Boyne Valley and Salisbury Plain were marking out their calendar using wood and rope, at Napta Playa the representatives of a lakeside pastoral community were laying out what may be regarded as the oldest known astronomically aligned site in the world.[17] The monument consists of a set of sandstone blocks, some recumbent, others standing, arranged in an egg-shaped circle, much like many of the British sites. The stones were transported a short distance – half a kilometre or more, and erected in alluvial deposits around the playa (or lake). Two gaps in the stones suggest the existence of sight lines, one of which would have presented a view of the rising solstice sun around 4000 BCE, the latter phase of the Neolithic and the beginning of the pre-dynastic period, when the distinctive Egyptian civilization begins to emerge. While the stones at Nabta may represent an innovation, they could equally well be the most visible remains of a much earlier tradition of solar worship and calendar construction.

There is no other evidence, apart from the surveyors' measurements, to support the astronomical interpretation of Nabta Playa, although it is doubtful whether we really need one: the Egyptians' later fascination with the sun must have come from somewhere and probably had a much longer history than even this find would suggest. This is perfectly plausible. One writer speculates that the Nabta Playa circle 'may thus have integrated the temporal cycles of the sun with the recurrent cycles of the life-giving waters as a kind of cosmic clock tied to the underlying principles of life and death'.[18] Perhaps it was a model for the monumental temples of dynastic Egypt. As Ronald Wells wrote, rather extravagantly, 'almost all of Egyptian astronomy and religion' are derived from the observation of the solstices, the points at which the great god Ra stands still and then reverses his march along the horizon.[19] Certainly it was during the wet period in which Nabta Playa flourished that the seasonal–lunar calendar may have developed that we later encounter in the Old Kingdom Fourth Dynasty.[20]

Nabta Playa's return, along with other lakes in what is now the Sahara, to desert around 3000 BCE may well have precipitated a migration of the inhabitants to the Nile Valley, acting as a catalyst for the development of pre-dynastic society.[21] Either way, Nabta Playa was not just an ancestor of the Egyptian solar state but an heir, with Stonehenge and Goszek, to a shared tradition.

There was also, around the same time, a thriving Stone Age culture on the island of Malta, which would have been on any trader's sea route from the Middle East to the Atlantic, between around 3600 and 2500 BCE, and of which the impressive temples at Hagar Qim and Mnajdra, constructed from massive stone blocks, are the most famous legacy. And, at these sites, stellar alignments have been identified. Mnajdra appears to be aligned with the heliacal (pre-dawn) rising of the Pleiades, evoking images of the same stars as those painted in the cave at Lascaux, while a series of horizontal notches have been interpreted as measuring the interval between the rising of other bright stars, such as the three stars of Orion's belt. A carving at the nearby site at Tarxien is normally interpreted as a bull over a pig with 13 suckling piglets, while an alternative, and quite reasonable, explanation portrays it as a bull, a heifer and markers for 13 lunar months.[22] The ancient sites on Malta are actually some of the most mysterious to be found anywhere. Trackways across the limestone surface are marked by deep grooves suggesting major transport but of what, we have no idea. That the tracks end at the edge of steep cliffs only deepens the mystery. The goddess figurines found in the temples are massive. Some are both obese and almost 5ft high, considerably larger than many of the tiny and delicate Palaeolithic goddesses, such as the Venus of Laussel, and are evidence of a deep religious culture. Prior to the warming of the climate at the end of the last Ice Age, Malta had been connected to mainland Italy via Sicily so the Maltese temples may represent less a first flowering of Neolithic magnificence than a direct link back to Palaeolithic astral religion. The evidence is fragmentary but sufficient to suggest a continuous thread. The Maltese temples are currently thought to be contemporaneous with the pre-dynastic period in Egypt. Their demise, in turn, coincided with the height of the Old Kingdom, which we know possessed a profound astral theology and was responsible for the construction of the pyramids at Giza. However, the weight of evidence for the existence of an early astronomy or astrology takes us westward towards the Atlantic seaboard and the megalithic sites that are scattered across the landscape from southern Spain to Brittany, Ireland, western England, Wales and Scotland.

The megalithic culture of north-western Europe flourished for approximately 1,500 years, from around 3000 BCE to 1500 BCE, when climate change resulted in a shift from Mediterranean conditions and clear skies to wetter, cloudier weather. However, the building of barrows – tombs constructed with great stones, earth mounds and, often, astronomical orientations – began much earlier, around 4500 BCE and the last changes at various sites may be dated to around 1300 BCE. Within this 3,000-year period there were major cultural shifts, such as the introduction of stone monuments after 3000 BCE, while Stonehenge itself went through phases of construction – and reconstruction.[23] It is also wrong to think either in terms of either a universal culture or local fragmentation, as if these two were incompatible. The evidence for widespread existence of common solar, lunar and sky religions and knowledge of basic calendar construction over much of Europe is quite compatible with a wide variety of local variations over time and space.

Until the 1960s the consensus was that Stonehenge was built by migrants from the Mediterranean or Middle East. The notion of the diffusion of civilization from the fertile crescent of Iraq, Syria and Palestine to the barbarian regions of Europe was too entrenched for any other possibility to be countenanced. Stonehenge itself entered the literate world's consciousness in the writings of the Greek historian Diodorus of Sicily in the first century BCE and in a passage attributed to Hecateus of Abdera, who lived around 330 BCE. He tells us that:

> This [island] is in the far North, and it is inhabited by people called the Hyperboreans from their location beyond Boreas, the North Wind. The story goes that Leto [mother of the solar deity, Apollo] was born there. It is for this reason that Apollo is honoured above all the gods. There are men who serve as priests of Apollo because this god is worshipped everyday with continuous singing and is held in exceptional honour. There is also in the island a precinct sacred to Apollo and suitably imposing, and a notable spherical temple decorated with many offerings. There is also a community sacred to this god, where most of the inhabitants are trained to play the lyre and do so continuously in the temple, worshipping the god with singing … Men called Boreads are in charge of this city and over the sacred precinct … The account is also given that the god visits the island every nineteen years, the period in which the return of the stars to the same place in the heavens is accomplished.[24]

The reference to Apollo suggests the solar functions long associated with the monument while the 'god' is usually thought to be the moon on account of its connection to the 19-year phases; in the so-called Metonic cycle the sun and moon return to the same regions of the sky on the same day of the year after exactly 19 years. Or it may refer to the 18.61-year period during which the moon oscillates between most northerly and southerly setting points on the horizon.

The argument about whether the megalith builders measured such points runs to the heart of the debates on Neolithic astronomy. Whatever the significance given to the number 19, if this passage does refer to Stonehenge, and there is a general consensus that it does, it is evidence of an unbroken oral tradition in Britain, surviving well into Celtic times, which had preserved a memory of the monument's function and importance and, if we are to take Hecateus' words at face value, its ritual use. Diodorus' statement provides us with a prima facie case of knowledge, at the very least, that Stonehenge's function overlapped with the development of druidic astrology. Or, at least, that there was a memory of its former role.

The history of Stonehenge in the last three centuries and, to a certain extent, of megalithic research more recently, is partly the history of changing political needs and cultural fashions.[25] Surveyed in the 1610s by Inigo Jones, the 1730s by William Stukeley and the 1900s by Norman Lockyer, it moved progressively from a Roman sun temple, to a druid sun temple and finally to the location of precise stellar alignments similar to those supposedly found at Egyptian temples.[26] What all had in common was the assumption that the inspiration for the site must have come from the civilized Near East or Mediterranean. This 'diffusionist' model remained strong, the most plausible explanation, it was thought, of how such great achievements could have occurred in a land of savage barbarians. In his 1956 classic *Stonehenge*, R.J.C. Atkinson, whose digs at the site were the most comprehensive ever conducted, announced that Stonehenge 'stands as a symbol, as St Paul's Cathedral may stand for a later age, of the first incorporation of Britain, however transitory, within the orbit of the Mediterranean world, the cradle of European civilisation'.[27] Yet, in the 1960s, improved dating methods pushed the dating of the earliest earthworks at Stonehenge back to before 3000 BCE, almost 1,500 years earlier than Lockyer's date: archaeological evidence overturned astronomical. It became clear that the British stone circles could not be explained as poor copies of Near Eastern originals and the diffusion model was overturned. Suddenly there seemed to be multiple 'cradles' of Western civilization with a rival to the Middle East now established in the north west. Given the patchy condition of current knowledge, and the rate that archaeological knowledge is changing, it would be naive indeed to make any assumptions about the origins or transmission of megalithic astronomical knowledge.

The scale of the megalithic enterprise, though, extended far beyond Stonehenge or even southern England. The estimate of the number of stone rings in the British Isles is as high as 900, though it is much greater if single standing stones are included. In areas where stone was unavailable, wood was the basic material, as it was at Seahenge. Even where stone was plentiful, wood was also a significant part of megalithic structures, which means that many sites may have been lost. The Stonehenge post-holes may represent one isolated example of a widespread, now forgotten culture. Earth was also a construction material, and the largest prehistoric monument in the world is the great mound of Silbury Hill, a short walk from Avebury. Equally famous is the gigantic mound at Newgrange near

Dublin, which is dated to 3200 BCE, and is significant for the window above the main entrance, through which, as at Maes Howe, the neolithic settlement in the Orkney Islands, the light of the rising sun beams into the inner chamber, at the heart of the mound, at the winter solstice.[28] This provides the most impressive evidence that, in the late Neolithic period, the sun was given a central place in the religious rites surrounding death. It may be possible to describe Stonehenge as an observatory or computer, as if it had no numinous significance, but not Newgrange. Although it was carefully designed so that the light of the winter-solstice sun shone through the roof box into the inner sanctum, after the entrance was deliberately blocked, no living human could have seen this. The function was therefore entirely religious, concerned with the link between the visible and invisible worlds. Religion, of course, is also a matter of politics and social relationships; somehow, the land, the sacred space at the heart of the mound and whatever was inside it, whether bones or magical objects, received the power of the sun at the crucial moment on the boundary of light and dark, life and death. As a solar monument Newgrange was complemented by the so-called 'Calendar Stone' at Knowth, not far from the great mound, which contains, along with other markings, a sequence of, according to most assessments, 29 symbols, suggesting a lunar calendar. We cannot say for certain whether the Knowth stone was contemporaneous with Newgrange, but the tradition that each represented undoubtedly overlapped.

Avebury may be the largest stone circle, but its neighbour, Stonehenge, is more famous. Its solar alignments – particularly its orientation to the summer and winter solstices – are well known. Although there was continuous activity in the Stonehenge region from 3700 BCE and on the actual site from around 3200 BCE, the coincidence of the monument's eventual rise to importance with the decline of Avebury suggests some sort of cultural change. Whether this was the result of local power struggles, divine instructions received via oracular means, or a shift of religious emphasis from the moon to the sun we do not know, but all three are possibilities. The same goes for a possible shift from lunar to solar observation during the later Neolithic, perhaps around the middle of the third millennium BCE.[29] It is perfectly feasible, in terms of what we know about religious cosmology in many cultures, that the religious leaders of the time concluded from their divination that Stonehenge was a more auspicious site than Avebury. Reference to more recent practices provide the supporting evidence: in 1782 the Burmese capital was transferred from Ava to Amarapoura on astrological advice.[30] In the same year the Thai capital was moved to Bangkok, suggesting that the Thai court astrologers were observing the identical omens as the Burmese. The astrology practised in south-east Asia in the eighteenth century was far more complex than anything which might have been known to the megalith builders, but that is not the point. The lesson is that divination can, and has been, used to make critical decisions about the location of important sites.

The current state of our knowledge indicates that the bluestones, the first stones to be erected, were erected at Stonehenge after 2100 BCE, around 1,000 years after the first ditch-and-bank circle. The well-known sarsen trilithons – the giant stones with lintels, were installed soon after and represent a different design, imposed on the earlier pattern. The very fact that the bluestones appear to have been imported from west Wales on a tortuous journey which modern enthusiasts have been unable to replicate is a testimony to the huge feat of organization required to construct the site and the devotion of its adherents to the task. The transportation of the bluestones from Preselli in south Wales is, perhaps, the greatest mystery in megalithic history. Of the current experts only Aubrey Burl follows the logical solution, which is that the stones had been deposited on Salisbury Plain by Ice Age glaciation; there are accounts of bluestones being found on the plain not associated with Stonehenge, and one fragment survives in Salisbury Museum.[31] We would surely have expected more to have survived, although in such a heavily cultivated area it is not beyond the bounds of possibility that 5,000 years of farming could have destroyed them all. Worse, the geological consensus is that there is virtually no chance that the stones could have been picked up by a glacier in west Wales and transported almost due east to Salisbury Plain.[32]

This leaves us with a substantial and unanswered question: why on earth did the megalith builders go to such extraordinary lengths to transport the stones over such a hazardous and difficult route when there were better sources of stone close at hand, especially since a recent attempt to transport just one stone was only rescued from complete farce with the aid of trucks, divers and other modern aids unknown in the Stone Age.

Adding to the mystery is the problem of the sheer expense of collective energy required to construct such sites. One estimate for the amount of time required to construct Stonehenge is thirty million man-hours, ten times the already immense effort required to build Silbury Hill.[33] There also appears to have been changing fashions in the use of such sites. Stonehenge appears to have fallen out of use in the early third millennium, and renewed interest in the site – and parallel decline of Avebury – coincided with a major technological revolution – the arrival of the Bronze Age in Britain around 2100 BCE. What we can say with certainty is that the sarsen stones at Avebury were left in their rough state while those at Stonehenge, erected perhaps just 200 years later, were dressed. If changes in architecture are pointers to shifts in a society's intellectual outlook then this was a profound one and offers substantial evidence that megalithic culture was subject to major cultural shifts. But its meaning is long lost. Whatever the detail, the transport of the bluestones is the key problem of megalithic culture. Only when the reason why such an incredible feat was undertaken is satisfactorily explained will we come close to understanding the religious and political context of Neolithic culture.

It is difficult to separate our understanding of this ancient culture from the seminal studies of the 1960s and 70s. The most dramatic theories concerning the astronomical function of the megalithic sites were proposed in the 1960s by two men, the engineer Alexander Thom and astronomer Gerald Hawkins

The first was by Gerald Hawkins, who argued that the stone circles were an astronomical 'computer' capable of accurately predicting eclipses.[34] Hawkins was followed closely by Thom, who claimed that apparently rudely laid-out stone circles were constructed according to the exact principles of Euclidean geometry and contained precise solar, lunar and stellar alignments.[35] Conveniently for them, Hawkins' and Thom's books were published in 1965 and 1967 respectively just before the peak in two of the 1960s major contributions to popular culture: the birth of the 'alternative' society and the space race. Between them, psychedelic drugs and the space race – the Apollo moon landing was in 1969 – created an environment in which Stonehenge was seen either as a sort of embryonic NASA base or an alternative, hippy cathedral. Thom's and Hawkins' work appeared to substantiate ideas, already promoted by groups such as modern druid orders, that the megalith builders belonged to an intellectually sophisticated, spiritually enlightened golden age. From this perspective, the people who erected the standing stones of the British Isles were no longer the savages of archaeological imagination. They were closer to Rousseau's myth of the noble savage, the primitive holder of natural wisdom, untouched by the modern world, which has been central to the romanticization of prehistoric Britain. But, for the astronomer Fred Hoyle, who refined Hawkins's work, the megalith builders had a modern image. Called in by the archaeologists to comment on – and hopefully refute – Hawkins's work, Hoyle instead simplified the eclipse-predicting computer model, and identified its builders as forerunners of NASA scientists.[36] For the romantics of the alternative society Hoyle's ancient scientists were more than the possessors of a lost technology; they were mystics, high priests and priestesses who provided an example of an alternative lifestyle to a modern world dominated by science, suburbs and wage-slavery. The mythology surrounding Stonehenge – along with that long associated with the Egyptian pyramids and, more recently, the Mayan and Aztec monuments in central America, provides part of the cultural context within which modern astrology and alternative cosmology flourishes. The history of Stonehenge is therefore more than just the story of the development of the monument, in as much as our limited resources enable us to reconstruct it, but is an account of competing and evolving narratives of its function, and their cultural context and contemporary impact. To understand Stonehenge we have to navigate our way through its role as a contested landscape, the site of competing claims by historians, archaeologists, astronomers, sceptics, golden-agers, druids, eco-pagans and tourist companies.[37]

The fundamental astronomical feature at Stonehenge is its alignment with sunrise on the shortest and longest days – the winter and summer solstices. Although only the longest day is celebrated by modern druids and their pagan fellow-travellers, the evidence of Goszek and Newgrange suggests that the shortest day may have been most important to Neolithic people. Goszek's structure also suggests that the lunar 'standstills', the extreme northerly and southerly points on the horizon at which it rises and sets were also observed. It is likely that the cycles of major stars were also marked although it is impossible to reconstruct which ones or when. There is just one remarkable artefact which offers some sort of indication of how the astronomers at Stonehenge might have worked. In 1999 treasure hunters near the town of Nebra in eastern Germany discovered a disc about 32cm in diameter and made of bronze.[38] This fact alone is enough to date it to the very end of the period of Stonehenge's active use; it appears to have been constructed around 1600 BCE. An apparently random group of dots, which may or may not be stars, includes one group which, it has been argued might be the Pleiades. It would not be at all surprising if they were. But the disc's most intriguing feature are two long crescent shapes of around 80° each. If we were to measure the distance between sunrise on the shortest and longest days at Nebra, then the result would be very close – 82.7° to be precise. This rather suggests that the disc is the earliest known astronomical instrument and was part of a system, including probable horizon markers, used to observe the sun's passage from its dimmest, coldest extreme to its brightest and hottest, and to magically participate in both.

Many of the problems with which we struggle in order to comprehend the nature of prehistoric society's relationship with the sky involve the nature of evidence and methodology, what questions are asked and how they are answered. There is a simple distinction between 'alignment', suggesting exact relationships between stones and stars as proposed by Thom, and 'orientation', implying a general direction as in Christian churches which are generally arranged on an east–west axis but not to the rising sun in a particular day. Like churches, the Tholos tombs in Andalucia are designed with a general orientation to the east though not a precise uniform alignment.[39] The inspiration for Lockyer's work was his observation that churches were traditionally oriented to the rising sun on their saint's feast day; and Stukeley made a similar point about pagan temples. Moving away from questions of orientation or alignment, astronomically significant sites may have been based on a symbolic relationship with the sky. A recent example comes from the Basque country where *sarobes*, celestially oriented eight-stone circles (possibly conceived of as octagons) were until recent times used as seats of government and religious rites. Both functions received authority from the *sarobe*'s function within a 'cosmological network of social practices and beliefs'.[40]

To understand fully the nature of Neolithic astronomy, we have to understand a world in which heaven and earth, visible and invisible worlds were intimately connected. Barry Cunliffe, who takes an ultra-cautious line on the existence of Neolithic astronomy, regards it as natural that some observations would have been made: 'In a simple agrarian society', he concludes, 'it is no surprise to find that the community was concerned to chart the course of the seasons.'[41] Aubrey Burl, who is not prone to flights of fancy, writes poetically that the first earthwork at Stonehenge was 'thrown up by natives the descendants of the adaptable and inventive families of earlier generations, the short-lived members of an increasingly hierarchical society, people living in an age when the axe and skulls of oxen were cult objects and when the mundane drudgery of farming was enriched and sustained by elaborate rites of death involving the moon'.[42] The rough lives of the ancient Britons, he implies, were ameliorated by a religion which took them beyond the material world to the next and away from their oppressive lives to the sky. We have a picture of astral religion emerging as a compensatory activity, of astronomy being born in the alienation of humanity from nature. This is an essentially negative model, though. It is more likely that there was a positive interaction between humans and the entire natural environment, the 'life-world'. Currivan's shamanistic cosmology would have facilitated contact with the heavenly environment, a geomantic one with the earth.[43] Shamanism itself radically repositions humanity as an active participant in natural forces rather than a helpless victim and provides a more useful model for understanding the possible uses of megalithic sites as liminal zones, boundary zones between the visible and invisible worlds, between this existence and the 'other'.

The prevailing popular conception of Neolithic cosmological religion, as expressed most forcefully by modern druids is that it was based around sun worship. In the nineteenth century a new slant was given by students of comparative religion who saw the presumed archaic solar religion as the origin of not only all religion, but most mythology in which, it was thought, the motif of the perpetually dying god was seen as a metaphor for the sun's seasonal journey.[44] Aubrey Burl, whose descriptions of megalithic culture are among the most eloquent, has argued that it is probably more correct to see stone circles as concerned with a cult of death, and that astronomical orientations should be seen as secondary to religious concerns.[45] In his opinion, and in contrast to Hoyle, 'sorcery rather than science gave vitality to the rings'.[46] He speculated that a stone circle might have been 'a place where axes and gifts were exchanged, a place where annual gatherings were held, a place to which the bodies of the dead were brought before burial, but, above all a place that was the symbol of the cosmos, the living world made everlasting in stone, its circle the shape of the skyline, its North point the token of the unchangingness of life, a microcosm of the world in stone, the most sacred of places to its men and women'.[47] Burl's opinion is in line with realistic views of the Neolithic people as engaged in intimate relationship with the total environment. If this description sounds suspiciously like the accounts of Native American sacred geography then that is hardly surprising; from the seventeenth century Native Americans were used as visual models for ancient Celts, while the use of modern anthropological examples to make assumptions about the Neolithic is perfect acceptable. However, this type of comparison is hardly new; in 1649 Aubrey used the Native Americans as a model for the druids.[48] The use of the classic Mayan theocracy as a model for the proposed 'astronomer priests of Britain',[49] suggesting that there was a universal priestly caste, is subject to serious criticism[50] on the grounds that it implies that megalithic society was homogenous and centralized. More democratic comparisons find favour though, and the Plains Indians' Sun Dance, the apocalyptic ritual which coincided with the collapse of their culture at the end of the nineteenth century, provides a possible analogy for what might have taken place at British stone circles. Aubrey Burl put it succinctly: 'Besides the sun, other powers of the earth and sky, the thunder, the stars, mother earth, and the four cardinal directions, were represented in song, dance and painting', while the result 'structured the personality of the young, renewed the personality of the old, opened the mind's windows to a noble world-view'.[51] Certainly, it is interesting to make comparisons between Avebury and Gambian stone circles but, if we do no more than project current examples back to the past, then we can never really be sure that we are closer to understanding the megalith builders.[52] We are also rather close to the New Age version of the past, which conservative archaeologists regard with far more horror than they do the astronomers'. At the 1974 gathering at Stonehenge, the first of a series of anarchic free festivals, the core of the campers, the 'Wallies of Wessex', embraced a theology that drew its inspiration from 'the sun, of course, God, Jesus, Buddha, Allah, the earth, the environment, and Oglolala, the mystic poet of the Sioux tribe'.[53]

Just as we can never be sure whether our views of Neolithic astronomy are accurate, so we can never be certain that modern views are essentially different to the prehistoric. Clive Ruggles, who is heavily sympathetic to the idea that the astronomical presence in the material culture of the Neolithic is likely to be metaphorical rather than literal, considers that 'what has been bequeathed to us is a set of more esoteric – and perhaps ultimately far more interesting – associations between the ceremonial architecture of life and death and the sun and moon, associations that manifest aspects of otherwise largely unfathomable systems of prehistoric thought'.[54] His views are worth setting out in detail. He considers that:

Ironically in view of the 'science v. symbolism' debates in archaeoastronomy in the early 1980s, answers are not to be found by searching for proto-Western science but in the very symbolism that was once seen as its antithesis. If we see non-Western systems of thought as substituting (superstitious) myth, ritual and ceremony for (rational) explanation, we fail to recognize that the conceptual structures underlying them themselves constitute mechanisms for explanation that are perfectly logical and coherent in their own terms. Correspondences such as that between the Barasana Caterpillar Jaguar constellation and earthly caterpillars, have explanatory power within a non-Western world-view, and symbolic expressions of such correspondences – such as that between quartz and moon-light – possess the power to express perceived reality in such a framework.[55]

This is the fundamental astrological worldview – that all things are linked by what would once have been seen as essential, inner connections, but which would now more often be considered symbolic. This conclusion may have significance for other areas of the history of astronomy, assuming that we can take modern astrology and make certain generalizations about ancient astrology, and about megalithic culture. Ruggles argues that we can, writing:

Why should the archaeologist, and in particular the student of Neolithic and Bronze Age Wessex, be interested in the perception of astronomical phenomena? A general answer is that in many, if not virtually all, non-Western world-views celestial phenomena are not separated from terrestrial ones, but form part of an integrated whole with complex interconnections. The association may often be viewed as closer in nature to modern astrology than modern astronomy.[56]

Meaning, in some contexts, may be more important than measurement.

By 1800 BCE the Neolithic period in Britain was coming to an end and the emerging metalworking Bronze Age revolution was represented by what we know as the Wessex Culture. This, it appears, was dominated by a wealthy aristocracy, the evidence for which is found in solitary and lavish burials in distinctive round barrows, in contrast to the collective long-barrow burials of their Neolithic predecessors. The Wessex Culture's trade in artefacts – and hence ideas – extended to Ireland, central Europe, Crete and Greece, suggesting there was no barrier to a trade in ideas.[57]

The Bronze Age may have displaced one way of representing cosmology – in tone – but brought another. Bronze, it seems, was prized because it resembled the sun. It was also an alloy – of tin and copper (or sometimes zinc) – suggesting that it had special properties, being the result of the magical fusion of two other substances – what would later be known as alchemy. The earliest bronze objects tend to be decorative and appear to have had ritual rather than functional uses, and the workers who could produce such artefacts were, in a sense, working in a cosmological industry. There is also evidence that iron technology was known during the Bronze Age but was suppressed, only making its appearance when supplies of tin became scarce, lead was substituted, and the quality of copper ore declined. That is, while iron is normally, now, considered to have been superior to bronze because of its hardness, at the time bronze was thought better because if its celestial resonance. Our knowledge of just how such technologies spread changes with each new archaeological discovery. Recent evidence includes the 'Gundestrup' bronze cauldron found in Denmark and probably from the second century BCE, which portrays hunting scenes reminiscent of Persian art, and the discovery of Celtic remains in the Gobi Desert.

The question remains then, as to whether the megalith builders or their Bronze Age successors practised a form of technical astrology. We can be confident that they observed rituals designed to bring the Great Bear down to earth, or told stories concerning Orion's hunt of the Pleiades. Further evidence, though, comes from central Europe, the heartland of the Celts, and has been identified by Peter Beresford Ellis.[58] The written accounts are late, but may represent earlier traditions. The following, though, is the essence of the case which, like all etymological speculation, as much as archaeological, needs to be taken cautiously but does open up potentially valuable new lines of evidence. A gloss on an eighth-century CE Irish manuscript held in Wurzburg in which the Irish word *budh* was glossed in Latin both as the name for Mercury 'all victorious', 'gift of teaching', 'accomplished', 'enlightened', 'exalted' and 'virtue'. The earliest known Irish name for the month of July was *boidhmis*, the month of *boidh*, or month of knowledge or enlightenment, while Orion's Belt was called *Buaile an Bhodaigh*, the belt of enlightenment, and one Old Irish term for cosmology is *budh na saoghal*, literally 'world knowledge'. On the basis that the first wave of written Irish texts represent much earlier oral wisdom, we can assume that Mercury was already *Budh* in the first millennium BCE; in Sanskrit *budh* means 'to know', 'to enlighten' (its past participle is *buddha*). In early versions of the Vedas as well as in modern Indian astrology, the planet Mercury is also known as *Budh*. Now, for Mercury to be *Budh* in both Ireland and India in the eighth century BCE is either one of those meaningless etymological coincidences which occasionally cause confusion, or suggests either that there may have been direct communication between the two cultures in the preceding centuries or that both were heirs to a common Indo-European tradition dating back to before 3000 BCE. Given that there is no evidence to support the former contention, the latter is the more likely. The conclusion, which has to be tentative and requires further confirmation, is that, in Indo-European culture prior to the great wave of megalith construction, the planet Mercury possessed the associations with knowledge and wisdom which it still has in modern astrology.

Who would have held this knowledge? We have evidence from France, Germany and Switzerland of the existence of a priestly class in the form of four examples of conical gold hats decorated with astronomical symbols, which seem to have possessed some profound cosmic and ritual significance. One is covered in 1,739 suns and moons which, close analysis revealed, represent the Metonic cycle, named after the Greek astronomer Meton, who supposedly discovered it around 430 BCE, and which allows the prediction of eclipses through recording the repetition of solar and lunar cycles.[59] That there is evidence of similar hats, now unfortunately lost, having been found in Ireland in the seventeenth and eighteenth centuries, suggests that the priests or priestesses who wore them formed part of a priesthood which was recognized across northern Europe and held knowledge which emerged out of the world of the megalith builders. The people who wore these hats may also have been those who devised the so-called 'Coligny calendar', a remarkable artefact which dates, in our surviving example, from the first century BCE. It appears, though, to have been much older: the original calculations on which it is based were made no later than 550 BCE and perhaps as early as 1150 BCE, suggesting a tradition which dated back for some centuries even before then.[60] Unless, of course, it was calibrated in 550 BCE, and retrospectively projected back for 600 years. The calendar was engraved on bronze plates and discovered in 1897.[61] Although it used Roman lettering, the language is Celtic.[62] At first sight, the calendar covered 30 years but on closer inspection a different pattern emerges. It was divided into 16 columns, each of four months, pointing to a five-year cycle of 62 lunar months plus 2 intercalary months, part of a larger 19-year cycle presumably the same Metonic cycle as appears on the pointed gold hats. The year appears to have consisted of 12 lunar months plus an intercalary month to make up the extra days. The year began at Samhain, the beginning of November, which was followed by the three other quarter festivals, Imbolc, Beltaine and Lugnasad. Each unit of time possessed a quality. The year was divided into two halves – the dark half began at Samhain and the light half at Beltaine. Months were also divided into light and dark halves, while it is self-evident that night and day would have mirrored the same dualistic structure. Days might be lucky or unlucky while 30-day months were good ('MAT') and 29-day ones were bad ('ANM'). It has also been argued that the calculations bear a striking relationship to Hindu calendar computations.[63] If this is true then, as with Mercury's apparent Indian–Irish connections, we are looking back over 5,000 years to a common Indo-European tradition. In this case the Celtic, Hindu and Mesopotamian astrologies – and cosmologies – may be heirs to a single tradition. However, that is where our knowledge stops.

There is no doubt as to the Coligny calendar's function. Unlike modern calendars it was not concerned with the orderly arranging of events, but their success. We have to assume that the function of druidic astronomy and the Coligny calendar was astrological, either to elect auspicious moments or to predict the future.[64] We may also assume a continuity with megalithic culture – just. For the good of the community it was necessary that important acts, the planting of seed in spring, the bringing in of the herds in autumn, the inauguration of a ruler or the launch of a war, should take place on the most auspicious day possible. By controlling the calendar and the secrets of time, the druids therefore constituted the effective ruling class. They were also clearly astrologers, although there is no evidence in the calendar of interest in the planets. It was sufficient that their political cosmology be based on the movements of the sun and the moon, a feature which links them intimately to megalithic astronomy. Their worldview, though, shared similar features with other ancient beliefs. The world was populated by invisible beings, from nature spirits to the creator deities, who controlled the natural world and had to be placated. To observe the correct order of the sun and the moon was therefore a religious obligation as well as a very necessary survival strategy.[65] We have to consider one other area of human activity that is usually associated with calendars – ritual, perhaps involving the kind of contact with other realms that is the hallmark of shamanism.[66] If we talk about Neolithic – or Bronze Age astronomy or astrology then we should put aside ideas of astronomers examining the universe in a disinterested manner, or astrologers reading the stars as an end in itself. Great ceremonies would have accompanied critical points in the calendar and, if insight was gained into the state of the cosmos, present or future, then action would have been required, perhaps pilgrimage, purification or sacrifice.

There is a severe gap in our knowledge between the gold hats and the earlier date for the calibration of the Coligny calendar and the arrival of Celtic culture, with its druidic priesthood, perhaps in the second and first centuries BCE. There is also a simple problem which afflicts any attempt to understand the Celtic world; we cannot decide from a modern perspective exactly who the Celts were. The term *Keltoi* is first used by Herodotus in the fifth century to describe people living along the banks of the Danube, while in the first century BCE the great Roman conqueror Julius Caesar claimed that the Celts were just one of the many peoples living in Gaul.[67] The concept of the Celt might itself be an artefact, the result of the way in which Mediterranean Greeks looked at their northern neighbours. However, we do know that there was an expansion of the so-called La Tène, metalworking culture, artistic styles from the area of Germany north of Switzerland to both east and west from the fifth century. Whether this meant that the people who had this technology migrated, or that the technology itself was borrowed, we do not know. However, either solution points also to a possible movement of ideas. We have also found late first-millennium inscriptions in the same script in northern Italy, southern France and Spain. Linking all this evidence enables us to identify a culture which extended from Spain and the British Isles through France, Germany, northern Italy, much of central Europe down to the Bosporus and through into modern Turkey. If ideas travel with language and technology, then we have a cultural sphere of vast extent which, in the first century BCE, connected northern Europe with the Roman and Greek worlds, and Irish druids with the Chaldeans – the astrologers – of the eastern Mediterranean. Such connections are perfectly plausible; as early as the eighth century BCE, 700 years earlier, Homer had used both the north European and Babylonian designations, Bear and Chariot, for the same constellation.[68]

One core religious doctrine shared by druids with Greek Pythagoreans – and Indians – was reincarnation. But, of any cosmological similarities, we have little idea. We do know that druidic astronomers were highly respected, for many classical scholars refer to their skill, and we must assume that they were aware of the developments taking place in astrology through their trading links between Britain and the eastern Mediterranean.[69] A number of Celts, such as the first-century BCE poet Virgil, achieved prominence in the Roman world. But, it was not until the time of Christ that we hear of a druid visiting the east, when the arrival in Athens of a druid named Abaris was recorded by the geographer Strabo. Abaris created quite a stir among the Greeks, and no doubt they would have exchanged opinions on astronomy and its uses, including as a backdrop for divinatory techniques.

Much of the little we know about the druids has been handed down to us by Julius Ceasar. Writing in the first century BCE he claimed that, although the druids of Gaul – and the British Isles – had developed a system of writing for ordinary record keeping, their 20-year religious training was entirely oral. It was considered that sacred teachings should be committed to memory. Clearly, they were concerned with the physical and moral structure of the cosmos. In a famous passage which other classical authors, such as Pliny and Lucan, paraphrased, Caesar also reported that the druids had much to say 'about the heavenly bodies and their movements, the size of the universe and of the earth, the physical constitution of the world, and the power and properties of the gods'.[70] Tantalizingly, he gives us no other details on this score. However, if we examine

Caesar's account of the meanings given to the druidic planetary deities there is a distinct eastern Mediterranean flavour. Apollo (the sun), as in Greece, was the god of healing, Mercury, like the Greek Hermes, was associated with travel, trade and the arts, which would have included writing, and Minerva, as with the Roman Venus was the goddess of artistic and creative enterprise, Jupiter, as in Greece, Rome and Babylon was the ruler of heaven and Mars was the ruler of war, the god to whom vows were taken before battle. Was this Caesar's interpretation, a mistaken projection of the Roman pantheon on druidic cosmology? Or was he identifying genuine Greek imports into the Celtic world? Or, perhaps, a wide-spread, shared tradition? We have to assume that any exchange of ideas between the two, though, was mutual. If ideas flowed in one direction, the likelihood is that they travelled in the other. It would be surprising if they did not.

The development of Neolithic astronomy and astrology, and its legacy in the Bronze Age, is the direct consequence of what we might call an 'environmental theology', in which the prevailing ideology rooted society entirely in the physical environment – and its metaphysical extension into the invisible world of gods and goddesses. The sharp distinction between physical and metaphysical realms is, of course, a modern one which would have made no sense. If we extend this notion of the absolute unity of physical and metaphysical into cosmology and politics then we have a cosmic state, to describe societies in which the earthly system is thought to be inseparable from the celestial.[71] When political power is vested in the sky deities, or in a sky goddess or god, then we have a republic of heaven.

3

The Mesopotamian Cosmos: The Marriage of Heaven and Earth

> He raised his hands to Utu, the God of Justice and beseeched
> him ... Utu, you are a just god, a merciful god, Let me
> escape from my demons; Do not let them hold me.[1]

The ancient cosmic states of northern Europe were the losers in the battle for historical recognition. Their rich oral traditions were capable of carrying huge amounts of complex information from generation to generation but, where literacy spreads, it overwhelms cultures in which the transmission of learning depends on memory. So, in the third millennium BCE, while the megalith builders of France, Britain and Ireland were constructing the most impressive, lasting monuments of a highly organized, deeply motivated astral theology, the inhabitants of China, India, Mesopotamia, Asia Minor and Egypt invented writing.

The earliest evidence of a tradition of astrology as a highly organized and codified system of reading meaning into the sky emerged in the lowland, lush river valleys of Sumer, what is now southern Iraq. This was a region in which the absence of stone means that there can be no trace of megalithic monuments, but it is unlikely that the Mesopotamians' view of the sky developed in isolation. The evidence from the Egyptian stone circle at Nabta Playa does suggest that megalithic culture was part of a wider cosmological-cultural sphere which extended from north-western Europe to the eastern Mediterranean. Recent evidence concerning similar sites in Palestine has already extended our knowledge into western Asia, suggesting that megalithic culture was indeed more widespread than previously thought.[2] That certain Egyptian pyramids and some Mesopotamian temples appear to have been aligned with the sky, in both cases to the north celestial pole, suggests shared traditions between those two regions.[3] And, since this practice extends through the, admittedly much later, temples of India and southeast Asia, as far east as the great temples of Angkor Wat in Cambodia, we may suspect some common appeal of that part of the sky. Mesopotamian culture did not exist in isolation, even if it did possess certain distinctive qualities.

There are conflicting tendencies in cuneiform scholarship. For most of the twentieth century, scholars attempted to extrapolate conclusions from sparse textual evidence in order to reconstruct a coherent and comprehensive picture of a supposed Mesopotamian worldview. More recent scholarship has retreated from such ambitions, emphasizing the problem of sources: how can we truly reconstruct the Mesopotamians' universe when we have only a handful of tablets which tell us how they thought? We know that the people who lived along the banks of the Tigris and Euphrates developed a complex way of relating their lives to the sky but, of theoretical statements, there is little trace. We are not even sure which stars are referred to in some of the main texts.[4] Then, aside from obvious translation problems, there is the question of whether the mass of surviving tablets, which date from the Assyrian period in the ninth to seventh centuries, can be used to infer calendar ceremonies, astronomical rituals and astrological practices from earlier periods. As an example of the difficulties we encounter, we could examine the first line from the Sumerian myth of the descent of Inanna–Ishtar – tutelary goddess of the planet Venus, to the underworld, probably dating to before 2000 BCE. In modern English the epic's words are rendered as 'From the Great Above she set her mind to the Great Below'.[5] Now, the word translated as 'mind' means both 'ear' and 'wisdom' in Sumerian, and the translators quite reasonably inferred that the best modern fit is 'mind'. But the problems we face in trying to penetrate the Sumerian model of the cosmos are obvious. Much of what we believe about what the Mesopotamians believed therefore depends on our own intelligent reconstruction, rather than their own words.

All the current evidence, in the form of written records, indicates that it was the astrology which emerged in Mesopotamia which, revised and reformed with Persian, Greek and Egyptian intervention between around 500 and 100 BCE, which ultimately produced the characteristically complex forms of horoscope interpretation still practised in the modern world. And this astrology, it seems, emerged directly out of the central priority of the cosmic state; the need to maintain a harmonious relationship between heavens and earth, to please one's tutelary gods and goddesses, to observe the seasons and maintain political stability and economic prosperity.[6] If human society, politics and religion were absolutely interdependent then the immediate political problem for the authorities became one of how the intimate relationship with the cosmos should be managed, how Lévy-Bruhl's *participation-mystique* could be more effectively implemented for the common good. One crucial step was the development of a sacred calendar, and the observation of the associated rituals was to be both individual and national duty. The major ceremonies were state occasions but there could be as many minor observations as, say, in modern Indian religion. Individuals themselves could attend the temple at sacred moments to venerate a particular deity. The calendar was the means by which the need to observe divine order was achieved and evidently underpinned a culture in which gods and goddesses, whether conceived as natural forces or supernatural entities, issued instructions and made their wishes plain through the wind, the rain and the stars; theology was environmental. Astrology as we know it was the complex system by which divine language, as spoken through the environment, the sky and divinities, might be decoded and acted on.

It is easy to imagine that, over a 3,000-year time span, the entire Mesopotamian region was characterized by a single set of cultural norms. However, while there are distinct elements of continuity, such as the use of cuneiform script on clay tablets, or the belief in a pantheon of gods and goddesses who spoke to humanity through omens, there were also enough political upheavals to make us wary of generalizations. There were also some periods, such as the seventh century, which have left us large numbers of records relating to the use of astrology, while evidence from both earlier and later periods is often scarce, sometimes non-existent. We cannot assume that the Mesopotamian worldview was a constant. The early period, after 3000 BCE was dominated by independent city states, divided between the southern region, Sumer, and Akkad, which was to the north. Pressures towards unity and centralization were irresistible and, shortly after 2400 BCE, one of the first great rulers known to history, Sargon the Great established the first Akkadian Empire, which dominated the region for two centuries. At its greatest extent, Sargon's realm extended into Iran and Syria. In the west, the Akkadians had access to the Mediterranean trade and, to the east, their merchant ships would have sailed from the Persian Gulf to India, to the magnificent urban civilization that flourished in the Indus Valley. Following a century of disintegration, the Sumerian city of Ur – 'Ur of the Chaldees', legendary home of Abraham – took over the Akkadians' imperial mantle. The city's achievements were considerable. The first emperor, Ur-nammu (c.2060–2043 BCE) created the oldest known law code, while his son, Shulgi (c.2042–1995), ruled a state roughly the same size as modern Iraq, a huge area by ancient standards. The first Babylonian Empire is famous for the law code, representing another peak of centralization and cultural patronage issued by the Emperor Hammurabi, who ruled from around 1728 to 1686. The following dynasty, the Kassite, was notable for its alliance with Egypt, around 1400 BCE, a reminder that we should never imagine that the cultures of the ancient world existed in isolation; trading links between the different states of the Middle East were vital, and diplomatic contacts frequently vigorous. The rise of the Assyrians, based in the north, began after 1400 BCE and, after a number of periods of advance and retreat, the Assyrian state entered a period of supremacy which lasted from the ninth to late seventh centuries, included the brief occupation of Egypt and has left us our most substantial evidence for the nature and use of astrology at the highest levels of politics. The Assyrians were replaced in turn by the second, or Neo-Babylonian Empire, reviled in the Old Testament for its transportation of the Jews into exile. In 539, in an episode the Old Testament attributed to divine retribution for its treatment of the chosen people, the city of Babylon itself was conquered by the Persians. The Persian Empire in turn extended across a vast expanse of Asia, from Afghanistan and the Indian frontier in the east, to Egypt and the borders of Greece in the west. With the victories of Alexander the Great, who entered Babylon in 332, Mesopotamian culture finally entered its terminal decline, though its astrology, mathematical astronomy and cosmic religion survived, often disguised, in the Greek world. From there it became a part of the heritage of Western culture.

Mesopotamian astronomy possessed one overarching function: the improvement and eventual perfection of astrology's role in managing the state; astrology's grand narrative was the preservation of stability and order. Mesopotamian civilization adhered to the belief that the terrestrial, physical and human worlds were so intimately connected to the celestial, intangible and divine realms as to effectively constitute a single entity. As in medieval Europe, authority in Mesopotamia was divided between the religious hierarchy based in the temple, which appears to have owned large tracts of land, and political power, which was exercised by the *en*, literally 'lord' or 'king'. The Mesopotamian system was at once profoundly autocratic, yet depended on consensus. The gods and goddesses took their decisions in their democratic assembly yet, because they could be transmitted through celestial patterns, the king himself had little choice but to respect the astrologers' shifting interpretations of the divine council. Actually, even though the king had the power to dismiss or punish astrologers who gave him poor advice, it is a debatable point as to who was the master – them or him. A weak ruler, perhaps, might be portrayed as a mere functionary, waiting to execute the orders communicated to him from the divine council through its diviners. The ambivalent relationship between church and state in medieval Europe might offer a suitable comparison; ecclesiastical and political authorities were polarized sources of power and, while a strong king controlled the church, a weak one could be dominated by it.

In Mesopotamia true authority, though, was vested in the god and goddesses who, the *Enuma Elish*, the creation myth (named after the epic's opening lines, 'When above'), tells us, had moulded the first humans out of clay as their servants.[7] Although the surviving versions of the epic date from the Assyrian and New Babylonian periods, from the seventh century onwards, in its earliest form the epic may date from the Old Babylonian period, around 1800 BCE. Its mythical tale of divine evolution climaxes with the rise to absolute power of Marduk, Babylon's proprietary god, and earlier stages in the epic, prior to Marduk's appearance, may well represent Sumerian or even earlier cosmologies. After the rise of Assyria, Marduk shared his supreme position with Assur, the Assyrian national god. In the Persian period, from 539 to 332 BCE both were replaced by Ahura-Mazda, the Zoroastrian god of light. One theory, proposed by Bartel van der Waerden, holds that the story of Mesopotamian astral theology is of the gradual, though uneven, march from divine pluralism, from the many gods and goddesses, to the supremacy of the one.[8] And, he argued, as religion gradually progressed from localized polytheism to universal monotheism, so astrology also became more systematized, eventually, as it made the transition to Greece in the fourth century BCE, providing systematic answers to universal problems. Yet, concepts of religious evolution from animism to polytheism and monotheism have been criticized for their assumption that there is such a thing as a natural progression in religious belief. We should not imagine that polytheistic societies have no concept of a supreme unity. From the example of India, it is quite clear that they do, and that the 'many' are easily contained within the 'one'. As a telling example, the Babylonian deities' evolution from water, the single source, is compelling evidence of an underlying monism. And, then, the Babylonian gods could be seen as powers of a higher god, as Nabu and Ninurta were, or as Marduk, the chief Babylonian deity, or Assur, encompassed other gods.[9] Neither should we imagine that monotheistic religions banished the pagan deities. Rather, like Christianity, they converted them into angels, saints and demons. But what this process does involve is a diminution of the power of most divinities, apart from the supreme god. To try to identify a smooth pattern in the history of religion is a risky enterprise, yet, as we shall see, Van der Waerden's theory does provide a plausible explanation one of the major developments in astrology's evolution.

The gods and goddesses of Mesopotamia were creators of everything; people, animals, plants, stones. And, in return, their grateful children, human beings, worshipped them. The deities operated democratically, taking decisions through their divine assembly, where they met to discuss their plans for the future. The diviners then identified their heavenly parents' intentions through messages, often warnings (*omina* in Latin), which could be transmitted through a huge variety of methods. Messages might be sent via the natural environment, thunder, lightning or the flight of birds, or through dreams, or the examination of animal entrails (an expensive option, for most people could hardly afford to sacrifice their animals at will), or via almost any suitable ritual practice or chance occurrence. There was little, if anything, that was not potentially the basis of an omen, or which might be a source of knowledge about the present or advice about the future. Gradually, over the second millennium BCE, astrology appears to have grown in importance. As it did so, it required increasing dedication to the observation of planetary and stellar patterns, and ultimately, by the seventh century BCE, if not earlier, their extrapolation into the future.

It was not, strictly speaking, the temple, or even the monarchy, which owned the land, but the city's tutelary deity; and not the king who ruled, but the presiding god or goddess. In Babylon the divine ruler, at least from the early second millennium onwards, was Marduk, the god connected to the planet Jupiter. In the *Enuma Elish* he was the son of Ea, but in another suggested etymology, the name Marduk is derived from the Sumerian Amar-Utu, meaning 'calf of Utu', the sun; literally, the presiding god of Babylon was the son of the sun god. And so, a tradition in which the sun and kingship were identified with each other began. In the rituals of sacred kingship, the monarch's right to rule was sanctified by the blessing of the priests and his duty was ultimately to protect the people on behalf of the presiding deity.[10] One of the region's most important cities, Uruk, was the property of Inanna (Ishtar), the most powerful goddess, a creator and destroyer who has come down to us in a sanitized form as the goddess of love, the Roman Venus.

The Sumerian universe was made up of *an-ki*, heaven and earth; the Sumerian *an.ki.nigin.na* translates as 'the entire universe', and the equivalent *kippat šamê u erseti*, 'the totality (or circumference) of heaven and earth'.[11] The earth itself was flat and heaven was conceived of as being enclosed top and bottom by a solid vault, arranged in different layers, made of stone, of which the lowest, made of jasper, had the stars drawn on it.[12] Separating heaven and earth, holding them apart, was *lil*, air, out of which the stars and planets were created. So far this is a naturalistic cosmology. But there was also a cosmogony, in which natural evolution was converted into the genealogy of gods and goddesses, their relationships, rivalries, marriages and offspring. In the beginning, we are told in the *Enuma Elish*, the universe consisted of three entities, Mummu, Apsû (fresh water) and Tiâmat (salt water) or 'she who gave birth to them all'. The ensuing process of reproduction resulted in the creation of the first generation of gods, including Anu, the sky, and Ea (Sumerian Enki), the god of subterranean fresh water. Inevitably, generational tensions developed as children fell out with their parents. These culminated in a cosmic struggle, which was won by the younger generation. The subsequent birth of Marduk, together with a further series of gods and goddesses, resulted in further generational conflicts, which were resolved after a final, apocalyptic battle. Tiâmat, the original goddess, who had by then been demonized and become a terrifying monster, was vanquished, and Marduk's eternal rule was established.

It is tempting to see the myth as an imaginative account of the region's religious evolution beginning with the worship of the 'mother', Tiâmat, or perhaps a trinity of Tiâmat, Apsû and Mummu. It is possible that there was a time when Anu ruled the universe as sole king, but Sumerian religion generally recognized the trinity of Anu, Ea and Enlil (the air), sometimes with the addition of Ninhursaga, the goddess of the earth, forming a quaternary of creator deities. Around the middle of the third millennium it appears that four creator deities were recognized: An (heaven), Ki (earth), Enki (sea) and Enlil (air); along with the three astral deities: Nanna or Sin (the moon), Utu (the sun) and Inanna (Venus). All seven may have been those who were said to 'decree the fates'.[13]

When we come to the technical fabric of Mesopotamian cosmology, it is difficult to generalize over a 3,000-year period, but, it is clear that all parts of the cosmos were linked to each other, so that each star or region of the sky might have a terrestrial counterpart, and vice versa.[14] As political centralization proceeded, so the stars were co-opted into the emerging bureaucratic political order. Individual fixed stars offered a natural frame of reference for locating planetary position and it appears that, by the Old Babylonian period, perhaps by 1800 BCE, a system had been established which grouped stars according to the calendar; three groups of 12 stars were arranged in three paths across the sky, one based on the celestial equator, one north of it and the other south.[15] The central zone was ruled by Anu (heaven/the stars), the northern by Enlil (the air), and the southern by Ea (earth/water). The *Enuma Elish* gave its seal of approval to a vertical three-layered system, the air and heaven above and the earth in the middle, floating on a gigantic ocean. But a simple division into horizontal regions does not necessarily point to an exclusively hierarchical order in physical geography. The separation of the sky into the three paths and their relationship to the three regions of Elam (east, the way of Ea), Akkad (centre, the way of Enlil) and Amurru (west, the way of Anu), also suggests that all things in the universe could be divided into three categories, either vertically or horizontally.

According to the fifth tablet of the *Enuma Elish*, after Marduk had vanquished the forces of chaos in the universe:

> He fashioned the stations for the great gods,
> The stars, their likeness he set up, the constellations.
> He fixed the year, drew the boundary lines.
> Set up three stars for each of the twelve months.
> After he drew up the designs for the year.
> He set fast the station of Nibiru [Jupiter?] to fix their bands,
> so that none would transgress or be neglectful at all,
> he set the station of Enlil and Ea with it.
> Then he opened the gates on the two sides,
> strengthened the bolts on the left and right.[16]

The gods and goddesses were an integral part of the natural world in the sense that they inhabited it, occupying the same space as human beings, but invisibly. Divinity was, to an extent, transcendent in that it ruled the natural world, but also immanent, in that it was inside nature and acted through it. It was both separate from the material world, in the sense it that was invisible and intangible, yet part of it, for even the gods and goddesses emerged out of the primaeval water. Essentially, the entire world was alive, active and intelligent; there was no more a concept of a distinction between animate and inanimate objects than in the Palaeolithic 'life-world'; Thorkild Jacobsen wrote that, for the Mesopotamians, 'Salt and Grain are thus not the inanimate substances for which we know them. They are alive, have personality and a will of their own.'[17] They had what we would call agency, the capacity to affect their surroundings. This, of course, is the basis of magic. Relations between humans and the rain, the sun, the sky, their animals and crops were essentially social. They were also political and, for that matter, religious.

From the belief that the world was alive, it followed logically that all the most powerful Mesopotamian deities could be perceived through the natural environment. Of the trinity of male creator gods, An, or Anu, ruled the sky; Ea, or Enki (lord of the Earth), ruled the earth and oceans; and Enlil (lord of the air) ruled the wind. But, in the sense that the entire world was 'alive', the wind was not just 'ruled' by Enlil, or acted as a means for him to express himself, but *was* Enlil, as Ea *was* the ocean. But neither could the gods be tied down to their particular rulerships. Sin, for example, was the moon, but was also much more than the moon. He was the god who made the heavens work in ordered mathematical ways, so that the sacred calendar could be created and faithful humans would know when to worship. The gods and goddesses both 'ruled' sky, earth, air and water and actually were these things.

In a similar fashion, human society was absolutely integrated with the physical world and was therefore likely to operate along similar principles, growing, contracting and even dying, like the seasons. The Mesopotamians' primary experience would have included the perception of immutable regular patterns, the rhythms of the sun and the seasons, and the endless fluctuation between darkness and light, heat and cold. But there was a paradox, one which runs to the heart of Mesopotamian astrology and which was never resolved; the immutable order which was perceived in the regular patterns of sun, moon and stars and, to an extent, the planets, was at odds with the belief that the gods were continuously manipulating the natural world, sending spontaneous communications and producing the enormous diversity that meant that the exact same details were rarely if ever repeated. If, in a sense, a god or goddess *was* a natural phenomenon, then he or she was subject to, bound by, the rules which described the daily and annual fluctuations of that phenomenon. For astrology, this meant that, while the sun rose with the same stars on the same day of the year, every year, whether it rose close to one planet or another was a much less certain matter. Other details were completely unpredictable. Sometimes the sun might appear golden in the morning, at others it might be red or obscured by clouds.[18] The complex astrology which was developed in Mesopotamia was a means of exploiting this uncertainty in order to better manage the future, and the dialectical relationship between the known and the unknown has remained the basis of astrological thought until the present day. Prediction, often erroneously thought to be astrology's primary purpose, was essentially a subsidiary function to arranging matters so that the best possible future might be secured; the entire enterprise was deeply rational. And by rational, I do not rely on the word's modern colloquial sense of 'based on scientific evidence', but on the more accurate sense of the product of reason, of a coherently thought-out set of ideas about how the world works, and the means of managing such a world for the common good.

The search for the origins of astrology confronts us with two problems. The first is where exactly Mesopotamian divination came from, and whether it is a universal human practice with roots, perhaps in Stone Age shamanism. The second is when the Mesopotamians' view of the sky developed, and whether the notion that humanity participated in a dialogue with celestial powers was also widespread. The answers lie buried in the immense 5,000-year period between the origins of urban culture and agriculture in the Near East and the development of writing, not to mention the 20,000 years that separates the development of agriculture from the earliest known lunar calendars. Leo Oppenheim's opinion was that the religion of third-millennium BCE Sumer was underpinned by an earlier Near Eastern formulation which reveals the existence of what he called 'an age-old pre-deistic deterministic concept of life' which he considered was conducive to the development of astrology.[19] We should not assume that astrology itself is inherently deterministic; it can develop in opposition to determinism, seeking ways to manage the future rather than submit to it. Yet, the view of astrology emerging from a religious consciousness which was deeply embedded in a sense of unavoidable cosmic order is a plausible one.

It is unlikely that there was no preliterate tradition of astrology in Mesopotamia, although we should distinguish the complex deductive divination of which we have full accounts in the Assyrian period, and which may have been an elite practice, from folkloric traditions based on the much simpler observations of the solar cycle, or in dramatic celestial events such as meteor storms. It is probable that complex practices developed out of simple methods designed to give yes/no answers to specific questions. We do know that astrology evolved into a systematized science – in the sense of an elaborate rule-based system with its own internal logic – by 1000 BCE. By then it covered nearly all observable celestial phenomena, permitting detailed predictions of unanticipated events and giving detailed answers to precise questions. Celestially, it is probable that the sun was first used to solve particular problems. We know that oracular questions were put to the sun god Shamash in the Assyrian period, after the eighth century BCE; perhaps here is the distant echo of a practice which had motivated the megalith builders.

It seems clear that political imperatives made the development of divination a matter of urgency, for, as society became more complex, so decision-making processes grew more complicated. One contentious theory, borne out of nostalgic Marxist dreams of a long-lost primitive paradise, argues that the first, preliterate Sumerian states, perhaps in the fourth millennium, were governed by a sort of consensual democracy, of which the celestial divine assembly was a mythical reflection.[20] In this picture of an imagined past, divination would have provided the means to break through awkward arguments and administrative log-jams. This is not really so surprising. After all, most societies have mechanisms for asking their divinities what they should do; this is the very essence of religion's political function. By 2400 BCE, if not earlier, the theory runs, this hypothetical theocratic democracy (if it ever really existed) had given way to sacred kingship, an institution which took on different forms in each Middle Eastern culture. The contrast with Egyptian culture is instructive. Whereas the Egyptian pharaoh was himself divine, god made flesh, embodied by the sun and stars, in Mesopotamia the monarch was but a human servant of the goddesses and gods, subject to their orders. The physical hierarchy of earth and heaven was reflected in a political order in which the king was subordinate to the divine council, headed by Enlil, or to Marduk. Even the mightiest emperor was a slave to divine will, and herein lay divination's use; it enabled the king to maintain the harmony between earth and heaven.[21] The practical result of this cosmic task was to everyone's benefit. Society as a whole lived in accord with celestial patterns and political stability was preserved. The king's most significant quality, more important, perhaps, than military prowess, was the wisdom necessary to navigate his way through the world of omens, dreams and oracles, to understand and heed the advice of his diviners. If he could perform the correct ritual action at the appropriate moment then peace would be preserved. Kingship was a sacred office and divination was no mere optional accessory: nor was it a luxury or an idle superstition. It was as central a part of the political machinery as the computer in the modern age. In short, the state could not function without it.

The reasons why one sky-obsessed culture should develop a complex form of astrology, and another might not, may be found partly in environmental factors. In the Near East the greatest contrast is between Egyptian culture, which developed a highly codified astral theology, and Mesopotamian, which made the leap from the use of the stars as religious objects to their application to detailed forecasting and political management. It is true that both cultures believed that the stars offered a means of communication between the divine and humanity, and that they applied this knowledge to political management, but Mesopotamian astrology is essentially an extrapolation from astral religion, and is distinguished by its complexity. Whether Egypt did take any steps towards a Babylonian-style astrology prior to the sixth century BCE is at present a matter of debate. The most obvious natural difference between the two cultures is found in Mesopotamia's essential physical insecurity:[22] Mesopotamia had no natural boundaries, was surrounded by hostile enemies, and the flooding of the rivers on which its agriculture depended was erratic. By contrast, Egypt was well protected by desert, had few neighbours, least of all ones that could pose a threat, and could rely totally on the Nile's annual flood. Metaphysically, the pharaoh was god, but the Mesopotamian monarch was a mere mortal, frail flesh and blood, a creation and servant of the gods like any other man. While plausible, though, we should not overstate the environmental case. The Nile flood, contrary to myth, could fail, with catastrophic results, and the Egyptians' devotion to their astral religion is prima facie evidence of their projection of their own insecurity onto the heavens. The argument that astrology originated in some sort of existential insecurity is actually very similar to recent notions that astrology appeals to individuals who are unable to cope with the modern world, evidence of a form of psychological weakness.[23] The insecurity hypothesis fails on the general grounds that, if insecurity is part of the general human condition, then it must be as responsible for the development of science as it is for religion or superstition. If a society is insecure, every one of its beliefs and actions must be a consequence.

The origins of the 12-month Mesopotamian calendar are lost but are presumably Palaeolithic; the only way to calculate a calendar which roughly approximates the lunar to solar cycle is to divide the solar year into 12 segments, as any Stone Age observer would know.[24] However, 12 complete cycles from new moon to full and back again lasts 11 days less than a solar year, so a completely lunar calendar quickly moves out of sequence with the solar year – which is what still happens to the Islamic calendar and why the holy month of Ramadan moves through the seasons from year to year. The Mesopotamian solution was to intercalate, or add, an extra month when necessary. The sources are too fragmentary to allow us to identify any universal system by which this was done although, in view of the devotion to the divine order, it would be surprising if there were none. There is some evidence, from much later, around 500 BCE, of the use of the so-called Metonic cycle, which enabled the system to be recalibrated by adding seven months every 19 years, but we have no clear idea of when this practice began.

The Mesopotamian calendar's mythical origin is set out in Tablet V of the *Enuma Elish*. The cuneiform text describes how Marduk, fresh from his triumph over Tiâmat, set out to create a new cosmic order, in which he would rule in heaven just as the Babylonian emperor reigned on earth. Marduk ordered the moon to mark out its synodic period – from new moon to new moon – with a hint (the tablets are broken) that its crucial phases signified the moments when he communicated destiny to the watching astrologers. Translated into English in the style of the King James Bible, the passage tells us that, 'the moon he caused to shine forth; the night he entrusted (to her). He appointed her, the ornament of the night, to make known the days.'[25] This, from almost 4,000 years ago, is the earliest known account of the moon's motion.

Each month began, we believe, with the rising of the crescent moon and, if all was in order, the new moon's first appearance after the spring equinox marked the beginning of the first month, Nisan. The rising of the crescent moon in Nisan also signified the beginning of the greatest of the calendar festivals, the Akitu or Zagmug, which included, over the space of 12 days, a ritual recital of the *Enuma Elish*, and the reading of the destinies for the coming year. The great calendar festivals were rituals in which the entire society participated in the unfolding life of the cosmic state. The entire community was enrolled in the attempt to work with the divine will, as expressed at a particular time and place, such as the temple at the new moon, to ensure that a menace was averted, a promise fulfilled and peace, stability and order maintained. The Akitu and *Enuma Elish*, the ritual and the myth, established in written form the great cosmological theological motifs of Western religion; apocalyptic battles followed by everlasting kingdoms, the divine descent to the underworld accompanied by repentance and followed by forgiveness, resurrection and salvation, and all associated with the spring equinox. The recitation of the *Enuma Elish*, of the transformation of chaos into cosmos, was a magical act, providing a context for humanity's repetitive participation in the ordering of the universe. When we call this a cosmic drama we should be taken literally; the dating of the Akitu was defined by the location of the sun and moon and it provided, once the joy of resurrection had taken place, a chance for the wisest men of the state to peer into the stars for signs of the future. Cosmos – order – is restored through the act of redemption and cosmos, not chaos, enables divination to take place.

During the festival, death was vanquished, chaos defeated, order restored and kingship renewed. The first four days were taken up with preparations and purification. In the Old Babylonian version, Marduk's death was commemorated on the 5th day with great popular commotion and prayers to him as manifest as a heavenly body. The first determination of destiny, when the character of the coming year was established, took place on the 8th day when the gods gathered and bestowed their combined power on Marduk. On the 11th day the divine assembly gathered once again for the second determination of destiny, announcing their decisions and intentions for their human subjects over the coming year; the entrail diviners and astrologers would have been on hand to interpret the assembly's wishes. Failure to observe the festivals resulted in the withdrawal of divine favour and the threat of national decline or destruction.[26] The sack of Babylon, a traumatic event which took place in the early seventh century BCE, was later attributed partly to a breakdown in the divination system in which, we are told, people 'kept answering each other "yes" for "no" '. More importantly, though, the disaster was a direct result of the abandonment of the sacred rites, the neglect of the Akitu and the plunder of the magnificent fittings of the Esagila, Marduk's temple in Babylon. The belief that to ignore the respectful observation of the cycles of time is potentially disastrous exactly parallels biblical accounts of the Children of Israel's repeated abandonment of Yahweh, their failure to observe the proper timing of festivals and their subsequent enslavement. The concept that time can come unstuck, that for events to happen at the 'wrong' time is inauspicious, was an enduring one that was taken for granted until the Renaissance. It is a core problem to be resolved in Shakespeare's tragedies. As Hamlet despairs, 'time is out of joint'.[27] Or, as the Roman writer Seneca warned, striking an apocalyptic tone, 'deviation by nature from her established order in the world suffices for the destruction of the race'.[28]

Although the correct observation of the Akitu was central to the smooth functioning of the state, there were smaller festivals throughout the year. Regular monthly feasts were held on the day of the new moon as well as the 7th, 15th and last day of each month. Each month might also have a characteristic festival, which might last several days, to judge from Sumerian names such as 'the Month of the Eating of the Barley of Ningirsu' or 'the Month of the Eating of the Gazelles'.[29] As long as such festivals were commemorated at exactly the right time, there was a good chance that the gods and goddesses would smile on their subjects and order would be maintained. Once human and divine patterns of time became dislocated then disaster would ensue. *The Lamentation Over the Destruction of Sumer and Ur*, which commemorates Ur's destruction under King Ibi-Sin (2028–2004 BCE), begins with the decision of every deity who counted, including Anu, Enlil, Nintu, Enki (Ea) Inanna (Venus) and Utu (the sun god), to 'overturn the (appointed) time, to forsake the (preordained) plans, the storms gather to strike like a flood, to overturn the (divine) decrees of Sumer … to destroy the city, to destroy the temple … to take away the kingship from the land … to break up the unity of the people of Nanna (the moon god)'.[30]

When one moves from reading the universe into acting with it, one performs magic: an act in one part of space or time results in an equivalent event in another part. In this idealized, abstract system, it was clear that disaster could result if astronomical phenomena occurred on the wrong day, upsetting the entire system. The seriousness with which such a possibility was regarded was illustrated in the astrological reports from the seventh century BCE. In one, the Assyrian astrologer Balasi advised the king that if the new moon occurs in the 1st or the full moon is seen on the 14th, then 'the land will become happy', but if the full moon took place on the 12th, which is theoretically impossible in a lunar calendar, then 'business will diminish … a strong enemy will oppress the land'

and, even though 'the king of Akkad [i.e., Assyria] will bring about the downfall of his enemy', the prognosis is 'bad for Akkad … good for Elam and the Westland (Amurru)', in other words, favourable for Babylon's hostile neighbours.[31]

The Mesopotamian political project was profoundly religious but also rational. Having produced a reasonable explanatory version of their universe, the state's philosophers set out to turn it to practical advantage through a perfectly logical procedure, to negotiate with their political lords. There was no problem with the notion of being deeply religious and highly rational. The idea that these two are opposites is a by-product of modern secularism which obscured the manner in which religion can function as an ordering principle which emerges logically out of a reasonable worldview.

The distinction between science and religion as two explanatory models is one which only makes sense in the modern West but, as applied to Mesopotamian astrology, it is not a matter of either/or but of both: astrology was clearly scientific in its analytical and experimental rigour. It posed hypotheses which could be tested and sought to explain humanity's relationships with the natural environment. Mesopotamian cosmology, though, differed from modern science in its purely descriptive nature. It had no need of complex explanatory models to explain the origins of the cosmos for these were provided by the cosmogony of the *Enuma Elish*, in which the gods emerged out of water, moulded human beings out of clay and obligated them to serve their creators.[32] Astrology was religious in the sense that it involved gods and goddesses, rituals, sacrifice and worship, but these beliefs and practices were all part of the scientific model. The evidence for the gods' existence was found in the workings of the everyday world: when the wind blew, something had to make it blow, and that thing was naturally its controlling force, the lord of the air, Enlil. And if a ritual to a god averted danger then that was prima facie evidence that the ritual had worked. If it failed then, as with any good scientific practice, one had to try again or think again, refining and adjusting the procedures.

But, above and beyond the question of whether astrology was religious or scientific is its linguistic nature. Its political purposes could not be achieved unless a two-way communication could be maintained with the divine council in heaven. The movement of the stars was understood as *šitir šamê*, the 'writing of heaven'.[33] The world, it was thought, could be 'read' and understood in a logical manner, an idea which remained a constant in divination, astrology and magic until well into the Renaissance, when it began its gradual evolution into modern science.

Modern scholars have retrospectively divided Babylonian divination into two forms, known respectively as intuitive, natural, unprovoked or inspired on the one hand; and inductive, artificial, operational, deductive or provoked on the other.[34] The former relies on spontaneous messages from the gods, as in dreams, while in the latter specific techniques are employed to solicit an answer, as in extispicy, the casting of lots or the pouring of oil into water. Astrology seems to cross the boundaries between the two. It was unprovoked in the sense that the astrologers had to wait for the gods to send omens, and if the omen did not come there was nothing the astrologer could say, but it developed an interpretative procedure as complex as extispicy and, eventually, much more so.

However, while it is clear from the records that accumulated empirical observations, matching political events to astronomical patterns, were significant in compiling the omen literature, a profoundly anti-empirical trend is also evident in the omen literature, and we have examples of predictions for events which could never have been observed – such as for eclipses on the 19th, 20th and 21st days of the month, which in a lunar calendar are clearly impossible. A lunar eclipse has to occur on the full moon, which would usually be the 14th day. The same anomalies occur in extispicy – entrail divination – where we find omens for animals with up to ten gall bladders.[35] However, if we assume that the omens were not mistakes, but represented a coherent pattern of thought, then it is likely that observation was thought to reveal only a part of the divine will. Abstract systematization, based on the assumption that there was an ideal way for the world to operate, might reveal every possibility, every single conceivable event, whether an eclipse on the 'wrong' day or an animal with multiple gall bladders.[36] This theory, in which virtually the entire celestial divinatory corpus was constructed by working by analogies on the basis of theoretical models, has been extensively developed by David Brown, who has named it the 'EAE Paradigm', after the Assyrian omen collection known as the *Enuma Anu Enlil*.[37] According to this model, Mesopotamian astrology dealt less with what *is*, than with what *ought to be*. It projected theoretical frameworks on to the heavens, which were then read in line with these expectations. The ultimate and enduring product of the EAE paradigm, from the fifth century BCE onwards, was the zodiac. For the sake of comparison, Brown contrasts the EAE paradigm with the Prediction of Celestial Phenomenon, or PCP Paradigm, which prioritized the prediction and observation of actual celestial positions, especially from the seventh century BCE onwards, and which was to lead naturally to the search for empirical evidence for astrology. Astrology's entire purpose, prior to the development of the birth chart, was to tell the ruler not what was going to happen, but what they should do. Astrology could certainly be predictive but it was primarily managerial, designed to influence the future by manipulating the present. It was above all intentional – encouraging the king to develop an intent, based on the astrologers' ability to decipher divine intentions. Whatever might be imagined might occur, and whatever could be observed was influenced by, or related to, things which could not be seen. Babylonian cosmologists, like their modern descendants, filled in the gaps between their knowledge with speculation. However, Brown's hypothesis should not rule out the possibility that theoretical speculations were not supported by centuries of empirical observations. As P.J. Huber noticed, the 'almost unbelievable coincidence' that no fewer than three transitions of reign in the Akkadian dynasty, from 2381 to 2200 BCE, were preceded by an eclipse of the kind later recorded as indicating the death of the king of Akkad in the *Enuma Anu Enlil*.[38]

The concept of astrological omens as signs, in which there was no causal connection between star and event, was complemented by a theory of influences. Nobody lives in a world without influence and, if one's total environment included the sky, then it follows that heat, wind, rain and light, all of which originated in the sky, were part of the total picture.[39] The process is clear. The diviner might be asking the celestial bodies for signs, but the celestial deity influences the present and future through an act of will. In a context in which there was no distinction between the material and the mental, psychic worlds, any influence which depends on an act of will must also be physical. Divine intent could be experienced through the weather or through other people, through flood, drought or invasion by one's enemies. The problem becomes acute if we are considering the connection between stars and amulets, objects constructed for magical protection or healing. Did the stars share some essential 'sympathy' with the object, a copper bracelet, for example, or a herbal potion? Or did the star somehow irradiate matter, influencing its ability to physically affect its human user? The evidence is frankly unclear, and both of these explanations might have made perfect sense to the ancient mind.

As it stands we have just one explicit rationale for astrology – one which, has survived until the present time – the simple proposition that all is one. In the words of the *Diviners Manual*, the 'signs on earth just as those in the sky give us signals. Sky and earth both produce portents though appearing separately, they are not separate (because) sky and earth are related.'[40] The relationship between heaven and earth was equal and reciprocal. If anything was possible in heaven, anything must also be possible on earth. Past experience was only a partial guide to the future, and the astronomical omens recorded so far might represent only a small part of the total number of possible variations. *The Diviners Manual* dates from the first millennium BCE, but its cosmology is found in so many cultures, from the Chinese to the Meso-American, that it can be regarded as a universal attribute of sky-revering societies, rather than peculiar to any time or place. So we can assume it was with these thoughts in mind that the astrologers of 2000 BCE set out to refine and elaborate their art.

There is one further consequence of the reciprocal relationship between heaven and earth: if the celestial deities could influence the earth then humans might, with sufficient skill, influence those deities. After all, the gods and goddesses themselves evolved out of the natural world. But that is not all. If there is no difference between the natural and what we would call the supernatural worlds, members of the former, even when relatively powerless, can engage in the latter. And this belief in participation, that people might influence stars or, better to say, the cosmos, just as stars influenced people, was to later emerge as one of the mainstays of ancient astrology.

4

Mesopotamian Astrology: The Writing of Heaven

> Sun-god of Heaven, my Lord! That omen which the Moon-god gave
> – if he found fault with me, accept ye, Sun-god of Heaven and (all)
> ye gods, these substitutes that I have given and let me go free.[1]

It was the astrologers of the classical world who attributed the origin of their discipline to 'ancient wise men, that is the Chaldeans', as the Babylonian astrologers were called.[2] In the Christian world the knowledge that astrology originated in Mesopotamia was obvious to any reader of the Old Testament, the Chaldeans being familiar in the Middle Ages from the book of Daniel, in which the term is synonymous with 'magician' and 'enchanter' as well as 'astrologer'.[3] In the sixteenth century the astrologer John Dee, one of the most notable scholars in Elizabethan England, saw Chaldean, a language with which he cannot have been familiar, as one component in his planned reconstruction of the original language – including the language of cosmology – of humanity.[4]

The earliest examples of astrological practices in Mesopotamia have been traced to the late third millennium, but the evidence is fragmentary and the arguments about their nature polarized. There are a number of examples of astrological omens inscribed in clay tablets dated to the reigns of a series of the most important monarchs of the period, although there are arguments about whether they are genuinely contemporary accounts, or later reconstructions, intended to illustrate the sky's enduring role in history and politics.[5] This is a plausible argument and is consistent with later astrological practice. It would also conform to the long tradition of prophetic texts written after the events which they prophesy, an example related to Babylonian history being the Old Testament book of Daniel. There is actually a problem with almost all textual sources for Mesopotamian astrology; the majority of our earliest surviving texts date from the seventh-century BCE omen series, the *Enuma Anu Enlil*. This is not a problem unique to Mesopotamian history, but afflicts our attempts to understand ancient wisdom as a whole; we need only think of the problems of dating the books of the Old Testament.

One tablet, which has a reasonable claim to being genuinely early, apparently dates from the reign of Sargon, ruler of Akkad from around 2334 to 2279 BCE. It reads simply: 'When the planet Venus ... an omen of Sargon, of the King of the four quarters ... When the planet Venus ... so it is an omen of Sargon'.[6] The clear implication is that a record was kept of the correlation of Venus' significant astronomical phases with important events in the king's life. Each correlation was then codified as an omen so that Sargon could be prepared for similar occurrences whenever the planetary pattern was repeated. This is only natural for the planet was, after all, the visible representative in the sky of Inanna, the queen of heaven. In the cosmic hierarchy, when Inanna spoke, the king obeyed.

The priestesses were, as we may expect, important. We know of one, Enheduanna, who seems to have been a high priestess of Nanna, or Suen, the moon god, as well as daughter of Sargon himself. She was the author of 42 extant hymns to Inanna, which survive only from the Old Babylonian period, around 500 years after her death.[7] We can get a flavour of the devotion with which the goddess was regarded from a hymn which was written to venerate the goddess when Venus appeared after sunset as herald of night:

> At the end of the day, the Radiant Star, the Great Light that fills the sky,
> The Lady of the Evening appears in the heavens.
> The people in all the lands lift their eyes to her.
> The men purify themselves; the women cleanse themselves.
> The ox in his yoke lows to her.
> The sheep stir up the dust in their fold.
> All the living creatures of the steppe,
> The four footed creatures of the high steppe
> The lush gardens and orchards, the green reeds and trees,
> The fish of the deep and the birds in the heavens –
> My Lady makes them all hurry to their sleeping places.
> The living creatures and the numerous people of Sumer kneel before her.
> Those chosen by the old woman prepare great platters of food and drink for her.
> The Lady refreshes herself in the land.
> There is great joy in Sumer.
> The young man makes love with his beloved.[8]

We can imagine the scene as priestesses of Inanna welcomed the rising of her planet, Venus, as night fell and the air was filled with singing, music and incense. This was the religious context within which the astrologers set to work on their deeply rational attempt to identify the divine will.

By the late third millennium, if not earlier, the sun, moon and the five planets each seem to have been allocated to a deity. Inanna, or Ishtar, queen of heaven, was given the planet Venus, as well as the richest mythological tradition. The core drama in Inanna's life was her love affair with Dumuzi, or Tammuz, the shepherd-king, his betrayal and death, and her descent through the seven gates of the underworld to rescue him, shedding an item of jewellery or clothing at every one, with all its agony and passion.[9] Inanna's descent was commemorated in rituals which may have been at once solemn and hysterical not unlike those in which statues of the Virgin Mary as queen of heaven are carried in procession in Catholic Easter parades.[10] The climax of the procession was the statue's arrival at the palace, at which point it actually was the goddess. It was alive. As we read in one letter, 'tomorrow Shatru-Ishtar will arrive early from Milqia and enter before the king … How will the king, my lord, fall under the gaze of Ishtar?'[11] The question was far from pointless. The priest had to know whether the king wished to enter the chamber before the statue or after. The choreography had to be conducted impeccably and the king, taking on the spirit of Dumuzi, the goddess's lover, had to make his wishes known. We can imagine the scene, alternatively despairing and joyful, in the sacred precinct of Inanna's temple, the Eanna, as priests, priestesses, singers, dancers and musicians, created an atmosphere of sublime religious devotion. In its earliest form the rituals probably included an act of sacred sexual intercourse between the high priestess, representing Inanna, and the king, embodying Dumuzi. In the story of *Enmerkar and Ensuhkesdanna*, the king of Arrata boasts that he will lie with Inanna on her 'adorned bed', communing with her 'face to face', to which his rival suitor, Enmerkar, king of Uruk, boasts that he will lie with the goddess on the 'splendid bed … which is strewn with pure plants' for no less than 30 hours.[12] Inanna was a prodigious cosmic force, capable of making love for 30 hours. She was both a spiritual power who appeared in dreams, and a physical one who aroused passion, desire and fertility. Through her physical union with the king she endowed him with the power to reign for another year and her love and bounty were conveyed to the entire natural world. The rivers flowed, plants bloomed and the harvests were rich. The tale had a profound emotional appeal and the worship of Tammuz was widespread; in the sixth century BCE, the prophet Ezekiel angrily denounced the Jewish women who wept and wailed at the annual commemoration of his death.[13]

The appeal of 'seven-ness' in mythology is profound, in that the number may relate to the seven creator deities, or the sun, moon and planets, or, perhaps, to a quarter of the lunar phase (the Babylonian calendar did not identify the week), we may suspect an analogy with ritual space and deified time. Through the number's connection with the sun, moon and planets, we may imagine a celestial journey, though one which descends to the darkness rather than the light. The notion of a descent through seven gates is strangely evocative of the much later Hellenistic notion of an ascent to heaven through seven planetary spheres, suggesting that there may have been some corresponding, and still to be found, Sumerian notion of an ascent to the stars. Inanna certainly possessed seven temples in seven cities, and prepared herself for her descent with seven *me*, or protective powers.[14]

The planets were distinguished from the other stars by their erratic movements, and were known in Sumerian as the *udu.idim.mes*, or wild sheep (Akkadian: *bibbu*). The modern term planet being derived from the Greek word for 'wanderer', the Babylonians also knew them, at least by the late second millennium, as 'keeps changing its position and crosses the sky', 'together six gods who have the same positions, (and) who touch the stars of the sky and keep changing their positions' or 'keep changing their positions and their glow [and] touch [the stars of the sky]'.[15] If the stars and the solar and lunar calendar represented order in the Mesopotamian cosmos, then the planets crossed the boundary between order and disorder. They lay at the heart of the dialectical relationship between the shamanistic and geomantic cosmologies that gave Mesopotamian cosmology its practical application. The sacred calendar, governed by the cycles of sun and moon was to be respected at the risk of the breakdown of political and social order, yet the constant variation in their visual appearance encouraged diversity. Similarly Venus was strictly tied to its 5-year cycle, Ishtar retained the ability to speak to her earthly subjects through minor variations in the planet's movements.

Each planet provided a tool for its presiding deity to communicate with his or her subjects through its changing appearance and shifting location. As a planet moved or changed its appearance, so the divine intent was adjusted. Examples from the Assyrian period include the following; if the moon 'becomes late at an inappropriate time and does not become visible', it warns of 'attack of a ruling city'; if it was observed on the 16th of the month it favoured the king of Subartu or, if it was surrounded by a halo through which another planet could be seen then, the omen warned, 'robbers will rage'.[16]

One of the oldest of the Sumerian celestial divinities was the moon god, Nanna or Suen, a name later contracted to Sin, by which the moon is generally known in the cuneiform texts. The names may have had different meanings. Nanna may have referred specifically to the full moon and Suen to the new, crescent moon, for which there also appears to be a third name, Asim-babbar, the new light. One Sumerian hymn praised Nanna as 'you, who, perfect in lordliness, wear a right crown, awesome visage, noble brow, pure shape full of loveliness! Your grandeur lies imposed on all lands! Your glory falls over the clear skies! Your great nimbus is fraught with holy dread.'[17] Nanna was the presiding god of the third dynasty of Ur, where he was the object of great veneration. His festivals were celebrated on the 1st, 7th and 15th of the month and, when the moon was invisible, at the new moon, he was believed to have gone to the netherworld to judge the dead, along with Utu, the sun, and special offerings were made to help him in his task. As an indication of Sin's importance, much later, 14 tablets in the eighth-century BCE Assyrian omen collection, the *Enuma Anu Enlil* were devoted to the moon's appearance and a further 8 to lunar eclipses, which were thought to represent a demonic attack on the moon. Aside from the *Enuma Anu Enlil*, about half of the astrological reports related to the Assyrian emperors deal with lunar phenomena. The reasons are obvious, for the moon is the second brightest celestial object after the sun, it possesses the fastest and most dramatic cycle, moving rapidly from one phase to another and, unlike the sun, can be tracked at night and hence form relationships with the stars, visibly passing through constellations.

The sun was known in Sumerian as Utu, meaning 'bright', and in Akkadian as Shamash. Both are the names of solar deities but the two words could mean either the visible body or the hidden power within it – the god. Utu has been described as the 'power in light, the foe of darkness and deeds of darkness' a god who dispensed justice across the natural and supernatural realms.[18] In this role he anticipated the Greek Apollo's role as the god to whom oracles were addressed, presiding over the art and science of divination from entrails.

None of the other planets seem to have commanded nearly the same attention in astrological omens as the sun, moon and Venus. That is even the case for Marduk, whose theological status was made clear in the creation epic, the *Enuma Elish*: it was he who gave the other celestial deities their roles, and hence his hand might be seen behind, for example, the hundreds of omens devoted to the moon. He might always be ready with a blessing; one Assyrian astrologer wrote to the king: 'We kept watch, we saw the moon. May Nabu and Marduk bless the king my lord!'[19] Saturn, the faintest and slowest moving of the planets, was sometimes referred to as the god Ninurta in the texts, but also as *udu.idim.sag. us* (Akkadian: *kajamanu*) meaning 'the steady' or 'the stable planet', and had no single tablet dedicated to it in the *Enuma Anu Enlil* and only 25 mentions in the surviving reports to the Assyrian emperors. This does not necessarily imply a lack of power, but the sheer absence of variety in its appearance and location meant that, on purely functional grounds, it was far less useful than, say, the moon, as a source of omens. In this sense, astrology was pragmatic. It worked with the material at hand, which might not reflect theological priorities.

Mars, assuming its later astrological character, was invariably responsible for evil omens, being associated with Nergal, a god of the underworld, forest fires, fever, plague and war. The planet's malefic tendencies were heightened when it was bright, diminished when it was faint, and when it was at its reddest it might signify prosperity, but also an epidemic of plague. Mercury was usually identified as the planet of Nabu, the son of Shamash, and therefore seems to be connected to the crown prince. In one Assyrian text Mercury's approach to Regulus, the 'king-star' warned of an attempt by the heir to seize the throne.[20] The logic was clear; as the celestial signifiers of crown prince and king moved closer, so their earthly counterparts were heading for a collision. As the scribe of the gods, Nabu was given the important task of writing the destinies, announcing divine intentions to the diviners and astrologers, and he consequently joined Ea and Marduk as a god of wisdom.

With the exception of Marduk, a god who only rose to prominence under the first Babylonian Empire, after 1800 BCE, we have no idea when these associations were made, nor whether they had evolved over thousands of years, or were a deliberate invention by an organized priesthood. When they were first outlined, though, is less important than the fact that the entire natural environment provided the principal means of communication between humanity and the pantheon of invisible gods and goddesses.

The religious imperative in Mesopotamian astrology was persistent and profound, and rituals and prayers could be addressed to any divinity who possessed stellar associations, often at times determined by the moon's synodic cycle – at the new or full moons. A notably poetic incantation we know as the *Prayer to the Gods of the Night*, survives from the Assyrian period but probably dates back to the Old Babylonian Empire, before 1600 BCE. In this text, as they prayed for inspiration, the astrologers would have asked:

> Stand by me, O Gods of the Night!
> Heed my words, O Gods of destinies,
> Anu, Enlil, Ea, and all the great gods!
> I call to you, Delebat (i.e., Venus), Lady of battles (or Lady of the silence [of the
>   night]),
> I call to you, O Night, bride (veiled by?) Anu.
> Pleiades, stand on my right, Kidney-star, stand on my left![21]

The most elaborate prayers were those designated as 'lifting of the hand', describing the gesture to be performed, with hands raised up to heaven. From Assyrian tablets we know of such prayers, which might be addressed to the Arrow Star (Sirius, the brightest star in the sky after the planets), the Pleiades, the True Shepherd of Anu (Orion) and the Wagon (Ursa Major). One Old Babylonian prayer, probably from the eighteenth or seventeenth century BCE, lists ten constellations by name, most of which were ones that the sun passed through, suggesting some religious significance attached to the sun. In one tradition it seems that the entrail diviner would recite the prayer late at night, prior to performing the divinatory act at dawn, as the sun – and the sun god – rose and restored light to human understanding. The diviner was not alone, but was accompanied by the stars and constellations, the living beings who acted as his or her advisers.

Our earliest surviving account of the practical use of astrology to manage the state, occurs in the *Dream of Gudea*, the *en* (lord) of the city state of Lagash around 2000 BCE.[22] The story features the goddess Nanshe (also known as Nisaba), who may have been an antecedent of the scribe god Nabu (Mercury). Nanshe was said to measure heaven and earth, to know the secrets of calculation and, together with Suen, or Sin, the moon god, to 'count the days'. Nanshe's associated functions as goddess of grain and as the expert on accounting and the fair management of resources, hint at both the practical uses of astronomy in agriculture and the benefits of a well-regulated calendar in maintaining social order. Her temple in the city of Eresh was called the *e-mul-mul*, the 'House of Stars', and she was the owner of a lapis lazuli tablet which is known variously as the *dub mul-an* or *dub mul-an-ku*, 'the tablet with the stars of the heavens' or 'the tablet with the stars of the pure heavens'. This she consulted by placing it on her knees.

The story of the dream, of which we have a very full account, reveals with dramatic force the interplay of natural, divine, earthly and heavenly forces which were believed to regulate Mesopotamian society and which provided a rationale for the development of divination and the rise of astrology. The episode commences with the decision by Enlil, the leader of the divine assembly, to restrict the Tigris's annual rise, an order carried out by Ningirsu (later associated with the planet Saturn). The people of Lagash understood immediately that this break in the natural rhythm had alerted them to a divine warning – a threat of impending drought. But what, exactly, was required? It was incumbent on Gudea, as the intermediary between heaven and earth, to ascertain exactly what was needed. Once Gudea had announced his intention to open a dialogue by making a sacrifice, Ningirsu sent him a dream. Still unsure of the correct course of action, Gudea sought advice from Nanshe who in turn consulted her tablet of stars, and on this basis she drew the plan of a temple which Gudea was instructed to build for Ningirsu. There may well be further celestial imagery in the dream, for Ningirsu appeared as a sphinx-like figure with the lower parts of a flood wave and surrounded by lions. It is tempting to identify these as symbols of Leo and Aquarius, the constellations then occupied by the sun at the summer and winter solstices, the longest and shortest days of the year. But most important was the belief that, by taking action and constructing the temple, Enlil and Ningirsu would be placated, and a worse disaster then the Tigris's failure to flood would be averted. Actually, what we have here is not unlike an early protection racket, in which, the citizens of Lagash seek security by inviting the local bully to come and live with them, identifying his interests with theirs. He, for his part, will protect them if they build him a suitably palatial residence.

The story of Gudea's dream offers us a template of what was to be astrology's major function until the fifth century BCE, to simultaneously guarantee the harmonious function and survival of the state while at the same time gaining military and political advantage over its rivals. Once fate had been identified, it could be amended and astrology, whether practised by the king or his subjects, was essentially participatory. It can only be understood in the context of a cosmic state in which it provided a vehicle through which both monarchs and people could negotiate the future with their celestial rulers. They were engaged in a dialogue with destiny. And another important point needs to be stressed: although affairs of state were all mediated via the king in a system which, as far as his subjects were concerned, was fundamentally autocratic, anyone, rich or poor, high or low, male or female, might communicate directly with the celestial deities. Astrology was at once pluralistic and a feature of the prevailing vernacular religion, the religious beliefs and practices of ordinary people, irrespective of temples, priesthoods and theological dogma.

Our next set of surviving astrological tablets, four sets of omens from eclipses, date from some time around 1800 BCE, when the Babylonians were building one of the first great centralized empires of the ancient world, and are further evidence of the systematization of the relationship between sky and state.[23] Assuming that these tablets are genuine, the codification process appears to have moved beyond the realms of criminal and civil law and into natural law in a coordinated attempt to collate all that was known about the rules and regulations laid down by the gods. The significance of eclipses in terms of the desirability and location of the signified events were calculated in relation to its date, approximate time (evening, middle watch or morning watch), duration, magnitude and direction of the apparent movement of the sun's shadow across the lunar disc. There were different schemes, and evidently a lack of proper systematization, indicating either disagreement amongst the astrologers, or developments based upon observation of the political events which followed the eclipse. In one version, the upper part of the moon indicated Akkad and the north, the left was the east and Gutium, the right was the west and Anmurru, while the lower quadrant was the south and Elam. By observing where the eclipse began and ended, the astrologers could tell what region was signified by the disruptive events which were bound to follow. Even the wind was important. One omen surviving from an Assyrian version reads 'If an eclipse falls on the 15th of the intercalary Addaru and the east wind blows: the crops will thrive'.[24] The consequences could also be personal. If an eclipse were to fall one day earlier and the moon appear yellow, then 'the people [will sell] their children for money'.[25]

The most substantial evidence for the existence of a sophisticated Old Babylonian astrology is found in the Venus tablet of Ammisaduqa.[26] Ammisaduqa was Hammurabi's great-great-grandson and the tablet was composed in his reign, probably in 1651, though possibly as late as 1531 BCE. Once again, though, it survives only in the *Enuma Anu Enlil* and sceptics doubt whether it genuinely dates from this period. The majority of scholars, though, accept that it does indeed date from the mid-second millennium. Although the Venus tablet is at present one of a kind, the existence of both earlier fragments and possible omen collections for Mars, Jupiter or the other planets cannot be ruled out.[27] The tablet is a collection of 59 omens based on the first and last visibilities of Venus, each of which will occur twice in one of the planet's 584-day synodic cycles. The pattern is constructed by the regularity of Venus' relationship with the sun; as the two bodies draw close Venus becomes invisible, obscured by the sun's light and, as they part, the planet reappears again. Venus' visual appearance is the most dramatic of any of the planets. It oscillates between being a bright morning star, rising before the sun, and an equally striking evening star, appearing after dusk. That it was understood that Venus as morning and evening star was the same body is striking, for this is by no means obvious; a thousand years later the Greeks attributed the discovery that the two stars were one and the same to one of their sixth-century philosophers, Parmenides or Pythagoras. In each case, whether as morning or evening star, at its maximum distance from the sun, there are moments when Venus will briefly be the only visible star in the sky, dominating the heavens as a brilliant point of light. It is these periods that are separated by 584 days. In between each phase the planet passes by the sun, becomes invisible and so disappears. Equally significant is the fact that five 584-day Venus cycles are completed in 8 years to the day, an observation which was recognized from the third millennium onwards in the use of an eight-pointed star as Inanna's emblem. Even if Ammisaduqa's astrologers were unable to compute Venus' position on any particular day, they knew that it was subject to an overall regular rhythm.[28] The conclusion, which has never been properly discussed, is that the messages that the goddess might send must conform to some sort of periodic pattern. If so, Inanna – or Ishtar – might be worshipped as queen of heaven, but there was clearly some limit set to her powers.

The Venus tablet, may be the first written evidence of the subjection of divine power to natural, mathematical or cosmic law, however we want to describe it and, even if the idea conflicts with most other assumptions about Mesopotamian knowledge of the sky, the tablet's significance is critical for our understanding of divination and Mesopotamian religion. If even Inanna, queen of heaven and one of the greatest of celestial deities, was subject to an overarching order, a universe which even the gods and goddesses inhabited in a mathematically regulated system, it is impossible for us to imagine divination as operating on the basis of spontaneous communication by capricious deities who decide to reward or punish human beings on a whim. Instead, we again have a picture of divination as an organized attempt to harmonize with the rhythms and cycles of a natural world in which deities should be understood less as superior versions of human beings, with all their strengths and faults, and more living, natural forces. The world was subject to a mathematical order, a kind of machine of destiny. True, there was great attention to the varieties of natural phenomena, but always within a greater order represented. So, the sun rose every day and the moon was full every month, events which provided the basis of the ritual calendar. But the moon might be surrounded by a halo or the sun, rarely, eclipsed. There was therefore a tension between absolute, unavoidable order on the one hand, and the endless variety of the detail of daily life on the other. Both could give rise to omens, but it was the tension between the two that underpinned the Mesopotamians' ability to negotiate their future. The process was almost dialectical, with the opposition between order and disorder allowing the development of a third point through which the way might be found to a better future.

There is one other consistent feature of Mesopotamian astrology which is evident in the Venus tablet. That is the knowledge that the predictable patterns of the universe enable the codification of all possible correlations between astronomical event and terrestrial prediction. The universe may be alive, but it was not populated by the capricious deities of Homer, but by gods and goddesses who emerged from nature and whose lives were as regulated by natural cycles as were those of human beings. The fact that periodicity in the planets was observed is acknowledged by historians of astronomy, but there is no corresponding recognition of its significance by historians of religion.[29]

The omens in the Venus tablet are grouped into the eight-year cycles which measure the planet's return to the exact position it held on the same day eight years earlier. The first omen, which is typical in the information it gives, sets the tone:

In month XI, 15th day, Venus in the west disappeared, 3 days in the sky it stayed away, and in month XI, 18th day, Venus in the east became visible: springs will open, Adad his rain, Ea his floods will bring, king to king messages of reconciliation will send.

In Month VIII, 11th day, Venus in the east disappeared; 2 months 7 [or 8] days in the sky it stayed away, and in month X, 19th day, Venus in the west became visible: the harvest of the land will prosper.[30]

This observation was made in late winter, following the full moon (the 14th day) in the eleventh month. The 3-day period represents the shortest possible time that Venus might be invisible, following its last appearance in the west as morning star and its reappearance in the east as evening star. Analysed carefully, the omen reveals information about Babylonian astronomy, astrology and politics. Given that the purpose of the omens was to correlate astronomical patterns with terrestrial events, the tablets have a historical function. The Babylonians had a historical consciousness, a sense of the development of their society over time, together with a belief that the historical process was subject to the same rhythms as the stars, and an understanding that the earthly political hierarchy was subordinate to a divine state.

Mesopotamian astrology remained an integral part of religious ritual and practice. There was no reason why it should not in a context in which no distinction was made between religion and the rest of human life or the natural world. However, the tendency to codification of all possibilities in the universe, whether psychic and spiritual or physical, is a clear indication of what the sociologist Max Weber called disenchantment. In Weber's terms this is characterized by the loss of awareness of a living, magic world, by a dead, materialistic universe.[31] Weber regarded disenchantment as a modern phenomenon and blamed a combination of the Protestant Reformation of the sixteenth century and the scientific revolution of the seventeenth to nineteenth centuries. However, the progressive subordination of the Mesopotamian celestial deities to mathematical laws and the codification of astronomical omens into a form which inclined more and more to the notion of the world as a huge machine can be seen as, in Weber's terms, disenchanting. More recently Paul Ricoeur argued that, as writing replaces the direct experience of the world, something intangible is lost and humanity is trapped in what he called 'a divorce … between truthfulness and consolation'.[32] We do not need to agree with the inference in Weber and Ricoeur's statements, that there was some sort of decline in authenticity, for us to recognize that an edifice was being constructed over shamanic experience of the sky, one which assisted in the making of collective decisions in complex societies. But we should avoid golden-age narratives: disenchantment is not necessarily retrogressive.

The dominant focus of all astral divination, as the above examples make clear, was the state, politics and economics, the latter largely dependent on the weather and a successful harvest. The paradox of absolute order on the one hand and endless variety on the other has stood at the heart of astrology to the present day.

The basis of omen divination as a mathematically based, logical way of thinking was that an event in one part of space indicates an equivalent movement somewhere else. The fundamental process was one of circumstantial association. There is a clear logic which argues that, if event y correlates with sign x, then when x next appears, y will happen. If we again remove the gods from the equation then there is no causal direct link between x and y, or between sign (*ittu*) and prediction (*parassu*).[33] Although the gods caused both the omen and the succeeding event, there was no cause and effect relationship between the two. In modern terms there may be no apparent connection between the sign and the signified event. To the Babylonian mind they could be connected because the world was a single, living whole.

Astrological practice operated through the analysis of all phenomena in terms of dualities or binary opposites, such as up–down, above–below, in front of–behind, left–right, bright–faint, punctual–early/late and so on.[34] Babylonian astrology was scientific in the sense that it relied on a deductive methodology and logical inferences made on the basis of empirical observation, but emphatically not because it posited a set of physical relationships between stars and society. However, there is an additional factor to consider – divine intent. The development of modern science was marked by the replacing of the gods – or God – that is, 'imaginary representations of "intentional" causes by unintentional and inevitable relationships'.[35] By removing the intentions of the gods from the equation, we are left with the inevitable relationship between present omen and future event, between astronomical observation and political action. Astrology then emerges as an abstract, logical, almost scientific means of managing the world. In astrology, modern science began its gradual, uneven development out of religion.

There were a number of crucial considerations which allowed the astrologers to read the planetary signs. These included its position, which indicated the terrestrial region at which the omen was directed and the nature of the predicted event (being in Scorpio could mean an attack by scorpions), and time (whether of night or of the month), or direction, which might indicate the location of the event. In addition there was the question of whether the phenomena were, according to the best predictions, on time, which was favourable, or early or late, which was distinctly unfavourable. It is difficult, if not impossible, to establish consistent meanings for each planet, but it is possible to establish certain criteria according to which planetary meanings may have been constructed.[36] These might be theological, linking names of deities to planets (although we cannot say why, for example, Marduk was attached to Jupiter in the first place), by visual associations (the sun, the brightest planet is then linked to Saturn, the dimmest; Saturn was the 'steady, constant planet', apparently because it was the slowest moving). Such links represented the earliest known move towards the classical 'great chain of being', in which every single thing that existed in the cosmos, from archangels to emotions, and from parts of the body to planets and precious stones, were locked into a system of vertical and horizontal correspondences.[37] Thus, in one of a number of competing systems, Akkad, containing the city of Babylon itself, corresponded to the planet Mars, the constellation Cancer, the moon's right hemisphere, every 4th day of the month, and the first, fifth and ninth months.[38]

The omens were customarily written in two sections: an 'if'-clause, or protasis, followed by a 'then'-clause, or apodosis. In other words, the examination was followed by the diagnosis. We have examples surviving from the Assyrian period:

'If Venus stands in the crown of the Moon: the king's land will revolt against him';
'If Venus stands in the middle of the Moon's horn: women will have difficulty
giving birth'; or, particular importantly for paranoid rulers, 'If Venus stands
inside the Moon, the king's son will rise to make a revolt'.[39] Some astrological
reports read like predictions which cannot be avoided. The Assyrian astrologer
Akkullanu warned the emperor that, if the sun and moon were seen together on
the 16th of the month then he would be shut in his palace for a month while his
enemies marched through his territories. There seemed to be little that could
be done to avoid this unless of course, the sun and moon failed to appear at the
same time.

Yet, we can also see the entire astrological process as consisting of three phases,
of which the first is the measurement or observation of celestial phenomena
and the second their interpretation or diagnosis. The third is the consequent
action, the prescription, for there is no point in predicting the future unless it
can be changed. The prophylactic rituals, designed to alter divine intentions,
were known as *namburbi*. *Namburbu* means 'loosing', so we have the sense of
a future fate being loosened.[40] These rituals were part appeal to the gods, part
magical procedure designed to manipulate the cosmos along with 'hand-lifting'
prayers recited before the stars or creating with parallel identities, as in the rite of
the substitute king. The prescribed activity might be practical or ritual, or both.
In one surviving example from the Assyrian period, the astrologer Munnabitu
wrote to the emperor that:

> If on the 16th day the moon and sun are seen together: one king will send messages of
> hostility to another; the king will be shut up in his palace for the length [of a month] …
> The [ki]ng must not become negligent about these observations of the Mo[on]; let the
> king perform either a namburbi or [so]me ritual which is pertinent to it.[41]

What looks at first sight like a series of predictions are better seen as instructions
which are not open to negotiation. A *namburbu* might also be performed if it
appeared that the celestial order was breaking down We have examples of the
remedies applied when Marduk's own planet, Jupiter, breached its order by
remaining visible for 5 days longer than expected. The astrologer Mar-Ishtar
reported to the Assyrian emperor that the planet appeared on the 6th of Simanu
(third month), close to the constellation Orion and in the way of Anu, and each
of these three factors carried its own warning. These were reported together with
the advice to perform the relevant *namburbu*. However, the planet then remained
visible for another 4 days, an omen so bad that no ritual could appease divine
wrath, and all communication with heaven was broken off. The astrologer Mar
Ishtar predicted that:

> Bright things will become dull, clear things confused; rain and floods will cease, grass
> will be slain, (all) the countries will be thrown into confusion; the gods will not listen
> to pra[yers], nor will they ac[ccept] supplications, nor will they an[swer] the queries of
> the haruspices.[42]

Emphasis also was put on purification. One prayer to a river, perhaps the Tigris or Euphrates, begs for assistance:

> You, River, are creator of all things. I so-and-so, son of so-and-so, whose god is so-and-so, because evil signs and portents have repeatedly taken place against me, am terrified, afraid and in dread ... May the evil of those things be erased from my person, may the evil of those things be dissipated from my person ... River, that those who see me may forever sing your praise! Take that evil away! Take it down to your depths![43]

The priority was to match each omen prediction with a possible action which would enhance desirable outcomes and avoid undesirable ones. The belief that destiny could be altered at any moment is made clear in a tablet known as the *Advice to a Prince*, probably written between 1000 and 700 BCE. The first three lines read: 'If a king does not heed justice, his people will be thrown into chaos, and his land will be devastated. If he does not heed the justice of his land, Ea, king of destinies, will alter his destiny and will not cease from hostilely pursuing him.'[44] The inference, the foundation, in part of the theory of monarchy down to modern times, was that, if the king failed to fulfil his duty, to look after his subjects, the gods' children – they would be justified in rebellion. An unjust king will break the link between people and the divine, his subjects will rebel and the gods will not come to his rescue. That is why the best omen possible was that the king would 'stay in his truth', 'widen his understanding' or 'stay in his righteousness'.[45] If the king was wise, the country would prosper. There was, though, an endless paradox in Mesopotamian thought, and that was that the actions which were themselves to be undertaken to manipulate the world possessed their own auspicious and inauspicious times. The negotiation of destiny was a two-way process, but one in which humanity was always a supplicant, appealing to the divine council as a higher authority. The reconciliation of the duty to obey divine orders, while, at the same time, taking an active stance, meant that the problem of free-will was a delicate and rather slippery one. The timing was crucial and, if a *namburbi* was performed on an inauspicious day, it might be ineffective. As one astrologer insisted,

> Concerning the apotropaic ritual against evil of any kind, about which the king wrote to me 'Perform it tomorrow' – the day is not propitious. We shall prepare it on the 25th and perform it on the 26th.[46]

There is an inference here that time is the organizing principle, a notion which presents us with certain problems for our understanding of Mesopotamian astrology. The issue is this: if the pertinent god or goddess was genuinely in control, and their vanity, pride or compassion could be appealed to as if they were genuinely anthropomorphic deities, then the ritual could have been performed at any moment. Yet this appears not to be the case. Divinity is clearly constrained by time which itself seems almost to be deified; some times are inherently more favourable than others.

The kind of 'pertinent' ritual, with its attendant actions and incantations, which would have been required is set out in great detail in a Hittite tablet, probably from the mid-second millennium. The text provides instructions on the necessary action in the case of an evil omen from the moon and success depends on the moon god accepting a substitute. The text described a solution to the problem of evil:

> The king goes up the sanctuary [and speaks as follows: 'That] omen which thou gavest, I Moon-god – if thou foundest fault with me [and] wishedst to behold with thine own eyes [the sinner's] *abasement*, [see, I the king,] have come in person [to thy *sanctuary*] and have [given] thee these substitutes. Consider the [substitu]tion! Let these die! But let them die!'[47]

The substitute, though, does not always have to be killed. In another version, the substitute for the moon god's wrath, the tablet tells us, must be a healthy slave, who is subject to a full coronation ceremony, anointed with oil, clad in the royal robes, given a royal name and crowned. The prisoner is then released while the king bathes at dawn or sacrifices a sheep under the open sky and appeals to the sun god. The entire process, it seems, could stretch over two days. A letter from the astrologer Mar Istar suggested that a substitute be allowed to sit on the throne for 100 days before meeting his fate – his death.[48] The question of the *namburbi* is a crucial one, for it goes to the heart of the question of whether Babylonian astrology possessed notions of causality and fate similar to those which supposedly characterized later Greek astrology. The standard view is expressed by Francesca Rochberg, who argues that the very existence of the *namburbi* tradition indicates that there was no concept of fate.[49] However, the contrast with a supposedly deterministic Greek astrology can be a misleading one, for Greek views of fate came in different forms, but generally suggested that it could be negotiated. Negotiation of the future, then, does not deny concepts of either fate or causality; if there is to be a dialogue with destiny, there has to be a destiny with which one can engage.

Did the Mesopotamians possess a theoretical concept of fate? If they did, it was subtle and complex, and is little understood.[50] Leo Oppenheim has suggested that there may have been an underlying unifying principle at work expressed in the Sumerian words *nam* (Akkadian *simtu*) and *me*, though the idea is not popular with scholars in the field. We cannot be sure of these words' exact meaning, nor even if they were distinct, and we should be extremely cautious about either interpreting them or assuming any relationship between them. *Nam* may have equated with 'destiny' or 'essence', thought not necessarily in a fixed, predetermined sense. *Me* may have been the activating feature appropriate for each *nam* and required for its proper functioning, but, in the absence of definitive statements from the cuneiform texts themselves, it may be misleading to assume that the Mesopotamians conceptualized and categorized fate as the Greeks were to do. Yet they still had some idea that not only were they subject to an order defined by the gods, but that the gods were also subject to the same order by virtue of their manifestation in the natural order. In the Sumerian hymn, *Inanna and the God of Wisdom* the goddess lists the *me* conferred on her by Enlil. Oppenheim sees these as essentially including all her physical and psychological characteristics, the qualities which make her who she is and determine what she is able to do. Kramer sees them as protective powers, more like talismans than inherent qualities.[51] Yet the meaning is still not clear. The epic of Inanna's descent records that 'she gathered together the seven *me*' as if they were powers or objects one could possess, but that, having received the '*me* of the underworld', she could not return, as if in acquiring the *me*, her destiny had changed.[52]

The important point though, is not whether we can find an exact modern translation for Mesopotamian terminology, but that the Sumerians may have possessed a concept of 'fate' which was all-embracing, and was bound up with the concept of purpose, and a belief that the future had to be fulfilled, or we may say, negotiated, through a separate active principle. Destiny derived from a dialogue between heaven and humanity, between ideal and earthly realms and passivity in the face of the future was not an option. As Henri Frankfort said, for the ancient Mesopotamians, 'to live meant to act'.[53] And then, of course, astrology as a system of reading the sky, cannot be separated from the calendar rituals, which were a means of living in conformity with the sky.

It is often said that, at least until the fifth century BCE, astrology was practised exclusively on behalf of the king. This is true to the extent that the surviving texts list omen interpretations which are concerned with state business or affairs which affected the whole community, such as the weather. The correspondence from the astrologers also consists entirely of letters and reports to the monarch. However, it is hardly reasonable to assume that, in a land in which the stars were divine, the mass of the population paid no attention to them. It is just not realistic to assume that a particularly high or bright full moon neither inspired numinous awe nor conveyed messages about one's present or future conduct, nor warnings about good or ill fortune. In fact, anybody might pray to the stars. To avert evil from a baby one should pray to Ninmah, most likely Venus as pre-dawn star – as herald of day – as 'mistress of all lands'. For good measure, this was then to be followed by a prayer to the sun as it rose, bathing the land in its healing rays. Lovers might also turn to Venus, as could anyone with relationship problems. In one ritual the supplicant was instructed to ease his or her amorous problems by burning 12 figurines on an altar dedicated to the goddess Ishtar. One might also secure celestial protection by adopting the name of a favoured celestial deity. Those especially faithful to Venus might take auspicious names such as Ina-niphiša-alsiš, meaning 'I called to her at her rising', guaranteeing the goddess' protection.[54] The faithful would be further protected if they took care to observe the sacred order as manifested in fortunate and unfortunate days. The man who made love on the seventh day of the seventh month offended the stars of the Wagon (the Plough), which were often associated with Venus, and was punished with impotence, or at least a serious loss of libido.[55]

Other prayers which are either Old Babylonian or older, were addressed to the sky in the hope of securing reliable portents through dreams, a favourite method of divination. In one, the dreamer would pray to the constellation of the Wagon. The following version dates from the Assyrian period and asks for advice on the success of a journey:

> O Wagon star, heavenly Wagon!
> Whose yoke is Ninurta [Saturn], whose pole is Marduk [Jupiter],
> Whose side-pieces are the two heavenly daughters of Anu.
> She rises towards Assur, you turn towards Babylon.
> Without you the dying man does not die and the healthy man cannot go on his journey.
> If I am to succeed on this journey I am undertaking, let them give me something [in my dream].
> If I am not to succeed on this journey I am undertaking, let them accept something from me [in my dream].[56]

That this prayer shared the same four lines as several others suggests that there was a standard invocation which could be adapted to different circumstances. One asked for a dream which would reveal whether another person, not the dreamer but presumably someone close to them, would recover from illness. Ordinary people could use the stars as a source of knowledge, through an astrology of prayer and psychic communication rather than the logical reading of codified omens. Such activities contain the residue of the ancient traditions of shamanistic cosmology, the ecstatic journey to the heavens. These practices were not set in stone and were subject to constant adaptation. One priest, writing to the Assyrian emperor in the eight or seventh century, instructed his lord to conduct a complicated ritual when Venus passed through the great gate and descended into the canal – presumably passing behind a ceremonial viewing point and then appearing to set over the water. But, he added dismissively: 'this is not a ritual; this is nothing. It is not ancient – your father introduced it.'[57] Clearly, the conservative Babylonian priesthood valued antiquity as a source of authenticity but the Assyrian emperor, lord of the four quarters – and all he surveyed – saw no reason why he should not create his own rituals.

Astrology appears to have been regarded as a valuable aid to the management of the state by the neighbouring states to Mesopotamia. Astrological texts derived from Babylonian material and dating from the fourteenth to the thirteenth centuries BCE have been excavated at Bogkazköi, the Hittite capital in Asia Minor, and Ugarit, the great trading centre on the Lebanese coast.[58] From there, word would have travelled to wherever the city's commercial links were strongest, as ideas naturally follow trade. But whether there were significant philosophical contacts with Egypt is another question. It was around the fifteenth century that we find the first depictions of planets in the astronomical ceilings of New Kingdom tombs; the earliest is dated to around 1473 BCE. There were certainly close economic and political encounters between Egyptians and Mesopotamians. Egyptian armies conquered Palestine, extending into southern Syria, in around 1483 BCE, 10 years before the first known astronomical ceiling, and controlled it for a hundred years until rebellion during Akhenaten's reign, around 1379 to 1362. They reoccupied the region under Seti I, who came to the throne in about 1319, and remained in control until around 1200. Throughout this period Ugarit was a major centre of civilization, devising its own script, producing great literature and trading with Mycenae, the centre of Greek civilization. It is likely that Ugarit acted as the cultural, as well as financial, entrepôt in which Egyptians, Greeks and Babylonians met – and the former began to take an interest in the latter's very practical application of cosmology. The city was certainly in the perfect location to perform such a role.

To the east, contacts with India cannot be ruled out on the grounds that trading contacts from the third millennium onwards imply an exchange of ideas, or at least the possibility of such an exchange. But there was an indigenous Indian tradition of astrology which may have included reciprocal links with Mesopotamia dating back to the third millennium, and was essentially, at once, sacred and managerial.[59] It was considered one of the *vedangas*, the seven pillars necessary to understand the *Vedas*, and the kind of astrology practised was primarily concerned with ritual and purification. The *Vedas*, the sacred texts which, in their written form, appear to date from the late second millennium, perhaps around 1200 BCE (although we have no way of knowing how old any prior oral tradition may have been), contained rules for the timing of sacred rituals.[60] Such rules are, though, often opaque to the outsider, and the Vedic hymns are concerned more with reverence for the sun, and fascination with the numbers seven and 12, planets and months respectively, and with 360 – the number of days in an ideal year, as in Egypt – and 720, than with astronomical detail or astrological rules. In the *Rig Veda*, we read, 'Seven horses draw the seven who ride on the seven wheeled chariot', while the 'twelve-spoked wheel of Order rolls around the sky and never ages'.[61] The *nakshatras*, or 27 lunar mansions, an alternative to the solar zodiac, also appear to have been an Indian invention.[62] Whether there is any connection between the Indian scheme and the 28 Chinese lunar divisions, the *Hsiu*, is not known. The Chinese version is dated to around the fourteenth century BCE by Joseph Needham but, with remarkable accuracy to 3300 BCE plus or minus 480 years by Brad Schaeffer, who argues for good measure, on astronomical grounds alone, that the Indian system is later than, and therefore possibly derived from, the Chinese.[63] Indian scholars would certainly not share this conclusion, and there are inherent weaknesses in using astronomical arguments in isolation from other historical evidence. But it is certainly the case that Babylonian material has been found in Indian texts.[64]

There may also have been a further diffusion from India to central Asia and China. The possibility of some reciprocal influence of India on Mesopotamia, or even of China on India, has been given only slight attention, but cannot be ruled out in view of the antiquity of the Indus Valley civilization and its proximity to the Tigris–Euphrates culture. Trading relations between the Persian Gulf and the Indus Valley must have included ideas as well as artefacts. The evidence, though, is proving elusive. What is without doubt, though, is that, for any culture which adhered to the concept of the cosmic state, of the interaction of earthly and heavenly realms, astrology would have been regarded as an indispensable aid to wealth, prosperity and power.

5

The Assyrians and Persians: Revolution and Reformation

(Things?) will(?) be good before you.[1]

Babylonian astrology proved irresistible. Offering as it did, a means of participating in the unfolding of cosmic destinies, rather than merely surrendering to fate, it provided ordinary people with a means of making decisions about their futures and rulers with a way of gaining advantage over their rivals. As a method of managing the state it was indispensable. Aside from their apparent exclusion from any role in choosing the king, the astrologers had a wide-ranging remit to comment on any matter of significance.

By the late first millennium, the scribes were at work compiling two major collections of astronomical and astrological material, both of which survive in versions dating to the eighth century. The first, the *Mul Apin*, contained some astrological information but was devoted mainly to setting out the astronomical framework, such as the 36 stars and the 18 lunar constellations, within which divination might take place.[2] The astrological statements in the *Mul Apin* are few, and tend to be confined to simple statements about politics or the weather. Some are obvious. When the sun is in the path of Ea, in the months of Kislimu, Tebetu and Shabatu, or months nine to eleven, roughly November to January, it will be cold.[3] Other forecasts are reassuring: 'if on the 1st of Nisan [the new moon following the spring equinox, coinciding with the beginning of the Akitu], the Stars and the Moon are in conjunction, this year is normal'.[4]

The second of the two texts, the *Enuma Anu Enlil* (named after the opening words, 'When the gods Anu and Enlil'), includes the Venus tablet of Ammisaduqa as well as around 54 other tablets containing up to 7,000 omens, a vast collection designed to cover every possible eventuality.[5] An indication of the prevailing astronomical priorities are revealed in a breakdown of the topics covered. Twenty-two tablets cover the moon, while a further eighteen concern the sun. Of the remainder, five relate to Venus, perhaps four to Mars, two to Jupiter three to omens from thunder and lightning and only one to the Pleiades. There are some puzzles here. The apparent absence of specialized tablets for Mercury and Saturn suggests a lack of attention paid to the planets as opposed to solar and lunar phenomena. The small proportion of material paying attention to Jupiter is most mysterious in view of the fact that Marduk, the planet's god, was Babylon's presiding deity. The full text, though, has not been recovered, and may never now be found.

The astrology of the *Enuma Anu Enlil* and the *Mul Apin* tends to make little distinction in terms of astrological significance between the planets and the brightest stars, such as Sirius, or the most prominent constellations, such as Orion or Ursa Major, even though the significance of individual stars and planets was clearly demarcated. Attention was paid to a planet's colour and brightness and careful observations were made of acronycal rising (the last visible rising in the evening after sunset), heliacal rising (first visible appearance on the eastern horizon before sunrise) and heliacal setting (the last visible setting after sunset). Shooting stars and comets were judged according to their direction in which they flew. As an example of the range of observations made and the advice offered to the king, a sample of reports submitted by the Babylonian astrologer Asheradu the Older included the following:

> If a meteor which is like a torch flashes from the east and sets in the west: the troops of the enemy will fall in battle; Satu[rn] became visible [in]side of Leo. If Leo is dark: for three years, [li]ons and wo[lves] will kill people and cut off traffic with the [Wes]tland; [If J]upiter is red at its appearance: there will be [abun]dance in Akkad.[6]

Each planet possessed a range of associations with deities, colours, times of the year and with each other. Of particular interest are the *asar nisirti*, or *bit nisirti*, literally 'house' or 'place of the secret'.[7] A planet in its *bit nisirti* may have been privy to the divine council's secret intentions, and by revealing these to the astrologers it enabled them to negotiate a favourable conclusion. For example, we read that 'if Venus reaches the place of the *nisirtu*, there will be good luck'.[8]

The three paths of Ea, Anu and Enlil failed to survive the end of cuneiform script in the first century CE, and the rise of Greek as the international language of astrology after the fourth century BCE. Instead the zodiac, the system of 12 constellations based on the ecliptic, the sun's apparent annual path through the sky, became the central organizational model.[9] Its development is far from clear, yet the first step towards the development of a solar zodiac involved the moon, which can usually, except when it is full, and therefore bright, be plotted against its background stars. The account of the 36 stars in the *Mul Apin* was accompanied by what is, in effect, a lunar zodiac, a list of the 18 constellations 'which stood in the path of the moon':[10]

> Mul.Mul – The Stars (i.e., the Pleiades)
> Mul GALENA – The Bull of Heaven (Taurus)
> Mul SIPA.ZI.AN.NA – The True Shepherd of Anu (Orion)
> Mul SU.GI – The Old Man (Perseus)
> Mul GAM – The Crook (Auriga)
> Mul MAS.TAB.BAGAL.GAL – The Great Twins (Gemini)
> Mul AL.LUL – The Crab (Cancer)
> Mul UR.GU.LA – The Lion (Leo)
> Mul AB.SIN – The Furrow (Virgo)

Mul Zi-ba-ni-tu – The Scales (Libra)
Mul GIR.TAB – The Scorpion (Scorpio)
Mul Pa-bil-sag – The god Pabilsag (Sagittarius)
Mul SUHUR.MAS – The Goat-Fish (Capricorn)
Mul GU.LA – The Great One (Aquarius)
Mul KUN mes – The Tails (Pisces)
Mul SIM.MAH – The Swallow (SW Pisces)
Mul A-nu-ni-tu – The goddess Anunitu
Mul HUN.GA – The Hired Man (Aries)

This list seems to be a clear attempt to formulate a lunar zodiac based on visible constellations, a much simpler enterprise than the creation of a star-based solar zodiac for the perfectly obvious reason that when the sun is in the sky the stars are invisible. However, in that it includes most of the later zodiac signs, the *Mul Apin* list clearly represents a stage towards the formulation of a solar zodiac and most of the future zodiac signs are identified. The space later occupied by the Sagittarian archer was allocated to Pabilsag, a son of Enlil, sometimes associated with Ninurta/Ningirsu, the god linked in turn to the planet Saturn. Anunitu, meanwhile, was a goddess associated with childbirth and may have been connected with Inanna (Venus). The Hired Man is identified as Dumuzi, the antediluvian shepherd god/king, so there may have been a smooth transition from the Mesopotamian shepherd to the Greek Arien ram.[11] Aquarius, the 'Great One', represented Ea, who was often pictured accompanied by waves, giving us the later water-bearer.

Most of our records of the actual use of astrology, date from the ascendancy of the Assyrians in the eighth to the seventh centuries BCE. The Assyrians ran one of the most efficient fighting machines of the ancient world and acquired the largest empire seen so far, extending from the fringes of Persia in the east to the boundaries of Asia Minor in the north and, briefly, Egypt in the west. As great imperialists, the Assyrians were also inveterate codifiers and without the Emperor Ashurbanipal's order to his scholars to collect all of existing astrological *omina* into the *Enuma Anu Enlil* our knowledge of Mesopotamian astrology would have been slight.

Babylon had fallen to the mighty Assyrian Emperor Tiglath-Pileser III in 728 and his successor, Sargon II (721–705 BCE), was the first of the new line of Assyrian monarchs who we know took an astrologer on his military campaigns, as we are told in a description of his successful eighth campaign.

At the exalted command of Nabû (Mercury) and Marduk (Jupiter), who had moved on a path in a stellar station for starting my campaign, and besides, as a favourable sign for seizing power, Magur ('the boat' = the moon), lord of the tiara (made an eclipse that) lasted one watch, to herald the destruction of Gutium. Upon the precious approval of the warrior Shamash (the sun), who wrote encouraging omens on the exta that he would walk at my side ... I mustered my army.[12]

The logic was impeccable; Mercury's movements revealed the mind of Nabû, the successor to Nisaba as possessor of the tablet of heaven, while Jupiter's position indicated the thoughts of Marduk, the proprietary god of Babylon. Sin, the moon god, confirmed his colleague's intentions, and lastly Shamash, the solar deity, indicated his agreement by giving a positive answer to a question posed via extispicy. The gods' intentions would have been clarified against previous events listed in the omen literature, and Sargon would have been informed that a majority of the divine council had approved his action. One can only imagine the effect on the Assyrian army, equipped not only with its superior numbers and technology, but with the knowledge that heaven was on its side. With the sanction of the stars the Assyrian campaign assumed the character of a military jihad, or holy war, and Sargon's success no doubt convinced him that astrology was an essential tool in his political and military arsenal.

Sargon's lessons were not lost on his successors, Sennacherib (704–681), Esarhaddon (680–669) and Ashurbanipal (668–627), all of whom maintained astrologers who effectively formed a political class, submitting reports and letters, offering the best possible advice on the basis of their observations.[13] These paint a portrait of a society in which the scribes maintained their personal relationships with each other and with the king, offering sometimes contradictory advice on astronomical observations and astrological predictions, finding excuses for their mistakes and claiming due credit for their successes. As with modern political advisers, there were rivalries and occasionally blazing rows over who knew what – and when they knew it. In one incident, which took place in the last year of his reign, Esarhaddon, was informed by an astrologer that Nabu – Mercury – was rising and due to be visible after dusk in the following month.[14] The emperor, wisely, decided to check and wrote to another astrologer, Ishtar-shumu-eresh, who replied that Mercury had risen, denouncing his colleague by quoting an old proverb: 'An ignorant one frustrates the judge, an uneducated one makes the mighty worry'.[15] He then went on to discus Venus. Unfortunately Esarhaddon thought that Ishtar-shumu-eresh had claimed that Venus was rising. He ran a further check, calling in two other royal astrologers, Nabu-ahhe-eriba and Balasi, who denounced their rival. Nabu-ahhe-eriba was the most vitriolic, writing:

> He who wrote to the king ... is a vile man, a dullard and a cheat ... Venus is not yet visible ... Who is this person that so deceitfully sends such reports to the king ... Tomorrow they should let me glance over them, every single one of them ... Why does someone tell lies and boast about these matters? If he does not know, he should keep his mouth shut.[16]

According to Balasi, the affair reached a climax on 28 March 669 BCE. A furious row ensued when Ishtar-shumu-eresh and Nabu-ahhe-eriba met in the royal palace, and was only settled when both men went outside after dark and agreed on what planets were visible – and which were not. When astrologers seriously failed to please they could be neglected or even sacked. Adad-shumu-usur was reduced to begging: 'As a father I am your servant', he wrote, 'O king, my lord, may I see your face as those who are acceptable. Alas! I am dying for want of food. I am forced to beg like a dog.'[17] We know of another, Tabia, who was reduced to writing a begging letter to the king claiming he was starving and another who received short shift when he made the same complaint: he was told to go out and make bricks for a living.[18]

The astrologers of the Assyrian era seem to have constituted a civil service, but not in the modern sense. They appear to have been hereditary, the practice passing from father to son, and were also astronomers and priests. The best analogy might be to regard them as a scholarly caste whose duties might be wide-ranging. It was precisely those elements in astronomy which were unpredictable which preoccupied the Babylonians for, if the cycles of the sun, the moon and the seasons represented the endlessly repeating rhythms of fate, rich variety in natural and celestial phenomena offered a chance to negotiate with fate by opening a dialogue with the gods. Astronomy was directed exclusively to goals which were theological and political. Yet uncertainty remained. As one astrologer wrote to the emperor,

> Concerning the solar eclipse about which the king wrote to me: 'Will it or will it not take place? Send definite word!' An eclipse of the sun, like one of the moon, never escapes me; should it not be clear to me and should I have failed (to observe it), I would not find out about it. Now since it is the month to watch the sun and the king is in open country, for that reason I write to the king: 'The king should pay attention, whether it occurs or not'.[19]

It is clear that the astronomers were unable to accurately predict solar eclipses: we have no direct evidence that any ancient astronomer ever did. It is possible, though, that they did not consider the obstruction of the sun's light by the moon as necessarily more important than by clouds, which themselves could indicate dramatic consequences. One solar omen reads: 'If a cloudbank to the left of the sun flickers like a ... torch, a city of the enemy will be besieged and the ... will be destroyed/desecrated' and another: 'If a cloudbank lies in front of the sun: the king of the world's reign will be long-lasting'.[20] The reason for what would look to many people like a reversal of priorities is found in Mesopotamian religion: an omen revealed by clouds might be sent by Enlil, one of the three creator gods and the originator of kingship, while one indicated by the moon was sent by Sin, a god of great importance, but not quite as powerful as Enlil. It might be argued, perhaps, that on purely theological grounds, that a cloud might be a more significant celestial factor than the moon, and while the latter may be predictable, the former is not.

Throughout, the Assyrian monarchs' astrologers worked from standard interpretations of what might be expected in every possible situation, based on a combination of observation of what happened last time the same alignment took place, using records, even if reconstructed ones, going back 1,500 years to

Sargon, as well as the unwritten 'oral tradition of the masters' (about which we know nothing), all within the overall context of the theoretical framework.[21] With knowledge of the past, the future could be controlled: 'If the Pleiades enter the moon and come out to the north: Akkad will become happy; the king of Akkad will become strong and have no rival', 'If Adad [the storm god] thunders in Tishri [month seven]; there will be hostility in the land' and 'If Jupiter passes to the right of Venus: a strong one will conquer the land of the Guti in battle'.[22] It is clear that the oracular tradition – direct communication with the sky – remained strong, and questions were customarily put to Shamash, the solar deity and oracle god. We have a collection of such questions which were framed with remarkable detail. Affairs of state were regularly addressed, including official appointments and military matters. One question, which must have been of immense importance at the time, concerned Assyrian actions against the Egyptians. On behalf of the emperor, the mighty Esarhaddon, the astrologer, asked Shamash whether he should 'plan and go with men, horses, and an army as great as he wishes, to the city Ashkelon, whether, as long as he stays and sets up camp in the district of Ashkelon, the troops of … or Egyptian troops, or … troops will come to wage war against Esarhaddon, king of Assyria, and whether they will fight against each other'.[23] This was a matter clearly of great strategic risk, and from which it was thought he might not return. On another occasion Esarhaddon needed to know whether the Egyptian Pharaoh Necho, who would also, ironically, have been guided by the Egyptian sun god, was intending to attack the chief Assyrian eunuch who was then on a diplomatic mission.[24] Shamash, as god of light, dispensed knowledge and wisdom – with enlightenment. The text does not record Shamash's answer but we assume that Esarhaddon was successful and his faith in his astrologers was confirmed.

Having made their observations, the astrologers' first task was to report their findings to the king and offer whatever advice they felt necessary. They might hope that the gods and goddesses would offer them assistance so they could avoid Tabia's fate, but the demands for increased accuracy could ultimately be achieved by plotting the relationships between celestial events with political, social and economic data. Political necessity heightened the need for accuracy of forecasting and observation and resulted in a renewed attempt to perfect astrology's predictive powers.

This vigorous astrological culture produced pressure for intellectual innovation and the period from the eighth to the fifth centuries witnessed a scientific revolution, perhaps comparable to that which transformed European thought from around 1500 to 1700, from Copernicus to Newton. David Brown has summed this ideological shift as the gradual movement from what he termed the *Enuma Anu Enil*, or EAE, paradigm, which prioritized theoretical models, to the Prediction of Celestial Phenomenon, or PCP paradigm, which focused on prediction and observation of actual celestial positions.[25] The distinction between the two paradigms is particularly useful and will, as we shall see be effective in understanding some of the distinctions in Greek cosmology and

Hellenistic astrology; simply, different perceptions of the sky may equate to competing traditions and, ultimately, ideological positions.

The Babylonian scribes began to keep comprehensive accounts of lunar eclipses, beginning in 747 BCE, in the reign of Nabonassar, records which were later used by the Greeks.[26] Around the same time they began to keep records of celestial and terrestrial events known as 'regular watching', or diaries, followed by the compilation of goal year texts and almanacs, which tabulated planetary positions for regular dates, mathematical models for the calculation of planetary positions in advance, and the development of so-called horoscopic astrology – planetary omens based on the date of birth – and the invention of astrological techniques which no longer required direct observation.[27]

The scientific revolution, if that is the right term, had one effect on the complexity of astrological predictions. Astrologers were finally able to predict the planetary positions on which their forecasts were based. A second-order prediction was introduced which itself was later, in the second century CE, to be distinguished from whatever personal or political readings resulted and was to evolve.[28] Eventually, in the modern period, the prediction of planetary positions was to become dislocated from the traditional search for meaning and the management of society, and became astronomy.

The compilation of the diaries began in around 750 BCE and constitutes one of the most astonishing achievements in the history of science. They were kept almost continuously for over 700 years; our surviving records run for over 600 years from 652 to 47 BCE. Their purpose is not clear, although, as the compilers were the temple scribes who were also reproducing copies of the *Enuma Anu Enlil*, we must assume an astrological purpose. One possibility, which is in line with later astrological history, particularly developments during the astronomical revolution of the sixteenth to seventeenth centuries, is that they represented an attempt to create an empirically based astrology, that is, one based on observation, not on theoretical frameworks, and which would make up for the uncertainties and mistakes which afflicted the astrologers' professional lives.[29] If this was the case, then the aim was the proper understanding of the relationship between celestial phenomena and political and economic affairs. The typical diary entry contains information on the moon, the planets, solstices and equinoxes, Sirius, meteors, comets, the weather, commodity prices, river levels and historical events. Typical was tablet 332, which reported that: 'Month VI ... Night of the 27th, clouds were in the sky, gusty wind. The 27th, rising of Jupiter ... Venus was 3 cubits below gamma Virginis ... That month, the equivalent for 1 shekel of silver was; barley ... Venus, Mercury and Mars were in Virgo; Saturn was in Aquarius'.[30] The resulting database would have been intended to provide a comprehensive means of managing the world in line with the best available evidence. The fact that these records were produced through the centuries of collapse of the Assyrian Empire, the rise and fall of its Babylonian and Persian successors and the establishment of the Hellenistic Seleucid state is a remarkable testimony to the continuity of astrological scholarship, regardless of political upheavals. As a single intellectual enterprise, there is nothing in the modern world to match the astrologers' dedication.

The three principal priorities of second-millennium astronomy had been fairly straightforward: to record the rising and setting of stars and planets, and to quantify and calculate such phenomena as the length of lunar visibility in the beginning, middle and end of the month and the length of day through the year. The diaries, though, suggest that there was a feeling that astrology's religious context, its deities and rituals, was not working, and that the world needed to be understood on its own terms. The diaries also give us our clearest indication that the Mesopotamian calendar was based on the rising of the new moon. They regularly began their commentaries on a particular month with a statement whether the preceding month had 29 or 30 days (which had already been a matter of concern in Assyrian times), and noted the time difference from sunset to moonset on the evening of the first night.[31] However, if they represented an attempt to gather empirical data on which the state might be better organized, the diaries were an intellectual cul-de-sac, one which was abandoned until the sixteenth century CE, 2,000 years later. Their conclusions may have been incorporated as standard predictions in the texts of the first centuries CE, although his has not yet been established, but the attempt to create an empirical astrology itself failed completely; with a few exceptions, the Greeks were to prefer theoretical models to the evidence of empirical observation.

It might be that the success of the Assyrian regime encouraged the diaries' compilation. It may equally be the case that the empire's collapse in 612 BCE, when the capital, Nineveh, fell, concentrated the astrologers' minds on the maintenance of stability and the need to perfect astrology's ability to predict and avert political crises. The relationship between intellectual endeavour and political change is a complex one. It seems that the bulk of extant astrological reports to the emperors ceased about 30 years before the fall of Assyria and, while there might be later examples, we lack the ability to date them with any certainty. The reason for this apparent ending of court astrology is unclear.[32] It has even been suggested that astrology's public role as an aide to political management and decision making came to an abrupt end. If this is true then one reason could be that the new astronomical accuracy destroyed astrology's theological premise – that the stars and planets could be manipulated at will by the gods and goddesses.[33] Although this argument is put forward with confidence by some scholars, it remains no more than speculation based on the mistaken premise that astrology and astronomy are necessarily at loggerheads. An alternative point of view proposes that the astrologer's ability to predict astronomical events with certainty can only have reinforced their position. So what explains this apparent lack of interest in astrology from the political authorities? The possibility of religious objections seems unlikely. Nebuchadnezzar II, one of the greatest of the Neo-Babylonian rulers who replaced the Assyrians, reconstructed an expanded Esagila – Marduk's temple in Babylon – and there is no theological reason why he should have been hostile to astrology. Biblical tradition, recorded in Daniel, records that the Neo-Babylonian monarchs consulted astrologers as regularly as their predecessors; in the famous passage summoning Daniel, we are told that 'the king called out for the enchanters, astrologers, and diviners to be brought'.[34] We can only assume that, if astrologers remained as powerful at court as under the Assyrians, then the records have either been destroyed or are still languishing in some unexcavated site.

The lack of sources is particularly frustrating, as it is clear that the Persian period saw perhaps the most important developments in first-millennium astrology; the development of the 12-sign zodiac and the birth chart – lists of planetary positions for the day or, later, moment, of birth. Or, to be clear, the earliest surviving evidence of the zodiac and birth charts dates from the Persian period. The Persians occupied Babylon in 539, an event immortalized in the book of Daniel in the story of Belshazzar's feast; as the corrupt Babylonian court was indulging in the pleasures of the flesh, its nemesis and the Jews' avenger, the Persians, swept in and destroyed it. The Jewish prophets welcomed the Persian invasion, for it was to restore their liberty, and they were profoundly influenced by their new rulers' religion, Zoroastrianism.[35] The distinctive feature of Zoroastrian religion was its view of the material world as a theatre of war in which good, represented by the god of light, Ahura-Mazda, or Ormazd, was engaged in a perpetual struggle with evil in the form of the god of darkness, Angra-Mainyu or Ahriman. This universal conflict was to become one of the primary mythical motifs of Christianity. It provided the character of Satan as an independent rival to God, which was absent from Judaism, and, in its theory that the struggle between opposing forces divided history into a succession of distinct periods, laid the foundation for a series of Western theories of history down to Karl Marx.[36] It was also believed that the world or, at least, the world in its recognizable form, was to come to an end with the triumph of good over evil but that, in the meantime it was essential for each individual to make the moral choice to support Ahura-Mazda and do good, and so bring about Angra-Mainyu's defeat. Those who made the right choice would be rewarded with eternal life in the Zoroastrian heaven, while evildoers would be punished by being dispatched to hell. The Zoroastrian emphasis on individual responsibility and moral choice may have been the cause of a certain antipathy to Babylonian astrology with its polytheism and, to some eyes, perhaps, its amoral fatalism. True, the dialogue with destiny was at the heart of the astrological perspective, but it was within the context of an entire religious cosmology which strict Zoroastrians found potentially offensive. We also have to consider the problem of why the recorded astrological tradition in Mesopotamia was at least 1,800 years old before we see the first evidence of the consistent recording of planetary positions at birth. It is certainly tempting to see the appearance of, first, nativity omens and then birth charts, under Persian rule in the fifth century BCE, as evidence of a heightened Zoroastrian concern with individual destiny. This, at any rate is the argument made by Bartel van der Waerden.[37] There is one small piece of textual support in the much later claim that Zoroaster was the first to identify the zodiac, but this is no more likely than the Jewish claim that Abraham invented astrology.[38] Van der Waerden's theory has an appeal in that it relates an apparent seminal moment in the development of astrology to wider religious and political changes. However, it cannot account for the seventh-century revolution, including the development of calculation methods and the beginning of the compilation of the diaries. There are two other problems; first, if firm evidence is found of earlier use of the zodiac or birth charts, the religious theory collapses and, second, our knowledge of Zoroastrianism at this time is just too flimsy. We cannot even be sure that the early Persian emperors were Zoroastrians. The theory of a religious framework for the development of astrology is therefore tempting, but needs to be placed to one side and labelled as speculative.

However, there may have been a two-way flow of ideas. Early Zoroastrianism anticipated an eschaton, a glorious end of the world, which was to be imminent, certainly in the near future. However, once the Persian rulers became world-emperors a certain conservatism crept into official thinking. Perhaps the end of the established order could be postponed. Perhaps it could be put off until the distant future. And so it may have been under the influence of astrological conceptions of time that the life of the world was fixed in the *Bundahishn*, the sacred scripture, at 12,000 years, generally divided into 1,000-year periods.[39]

The Persians' occupation of Mesopotamia did, though, have a more tangible impact on the world of the astrologers. It is also at this time that a new class of astrologers emerged into the historical record, in addition to the temple scribes of Mesopotamia. These were the magi, who arrived in Babylon with the city's Persian conqueror, Cyrus (559–530). These new astrologers' fame is attested by the well-known version of Christ's nativity recorded in Matthew's Gospel, in which the first individuals to venerate Christ, were Persian priest-astrologers.[40] The Gospel writer's clear intent was to gain credibility for Christ's claim to be the son of God by linking it with the most renowned astrologers of the time, who would surely have known the mind of heaven. The magi actually made their earliest literary appearance half a millennium before Matthew's Gospel in Herodotus' *Histories*, where they are dream interpreters at the court of the Persian Emperor Cyrus, playing very much the same role as the prophet Daniel.[41] Herodotus tells us little about them except that they are priests who make a special point of indiscriminately killing anything, with the exception of dogs and men, with their bare hands. Their treachery was displayed when they seized the throne temporarily while the Emperor Cambyses was on his campaign of conquest in Egypt after 525 BCE and, on one occasion, they ritually buried nine boys and nine girls alive in order to propitiate the deities of a river which they successfully crossed at a place called Nine Ways.[42] Herodotus' response to such practices seems to have been that their perpetrators, being Persians were barbarians, so what else could one expect?

Herodotus' most detailed account of the magi's activities concerned Xerxes' invasion of Greece in 480, an assault which came perilously close to defeating the combined forces of the city states, but ended in the final failure of Persia's push to the west. His account, much like the story of Gudea, involves a combination of dream interpretation and astrology. Xerxes' decision to invade was influenced by two dreams even though, as Herodotus makes clear, conflict was inevitable once the Greeks had rejected the Persians' high-handed demand for tribute. The magi were finally called in to interpret the third dream (we are not told if they were employed for the first two) in which Xerxes had imagined himself crowned with an olive, which branches which spread over the entire earth before vanishing. The magi told Xerxes that he was therefore destined to rule the entire world. [43] However, to get to Greece the Persian army, with all its infantry, cavalry and support units, had to cross the Hellespont, the narrow stretch of water separating Asia from Europe. Herodotus tells us what happened next:

> No sooner had the troops begun to move than the sun vanished from his place in the sky and it grew dark as night, though the weather was perfectly clear and cloudless. Xerxes, deeply troubled, asked the Magi to interpret this strange phenomenon, and was given to understand that God meant to foretell to the Greeks the eclipse of their cities – for it was the sun which gave warning of the future to Greece, just as the moon did to Persia. Having heard this, Herodotus tells us, 'Xerxes continued the march in high spirits'.[44]

The emperor later confirmed his future good fortune with a homage to the sun. We are told that at dawn he stood and faced the sun, praying for success as he poured wine into the sea from a golden goblet which he then threw into the water with a golden bowl and a short Persian sword. So prepared, he invaded Greece and, in spite of some notable successes, including the occupation of Athens, the campaign ultimately ended in failure. The magi, as Herodotus makes clear, were wrong on both accounts. They had misinterpreted both the emperor's dream and a solar eclipse, out of the eagerness to flatter their monarch. Or perhaps they calculated, quite reasonably, that the tiny Greek city states could never resist a full-scale Persian invasion. In this assumption they were almost right. But, in the final analysis, Herodotus had no time for diviners of any sort. He tells us how the professionals read the Delphic oracle as advising the Greeks to accept defeat, while the Athenian statesman Themistocles, argued successfully that it recommended that they stand and fight, which turned out to be the successful course of action.[45] The politician was right, the diviners wrong. The magi's historical reputation, though, was saved by the Jewish author Philo, writing in the first century CE. Unlike Herodotus, he reported that the magi stood out from the barbarians amongst whom they lived. 'Among the Persians', he wrote, 'there is the body of the Magi, who, investigating the works of nature for the purpose of becoming acquainted with the truth, so at their leisure become initiated themselves and initiate others in the divine virtues by their very clear explanations.'[46] Presumably Philo's benevolent opinion was shared widely enough for the writer of Matthew's Gospel to consider the use of magi in the nativity story to be a positive bonus for Christianity's reputation.

Zoroastrianism no more existed as a hermetically sealed set of dogma than did any other religion and it appears that its encounter with astrology may have produced a heresy known as Zurvanism.[47] Zurvan was venerated as the God of Time. He was pre-existent and as such was the supreme creator and must, by implication have been the father of Ahura-Mazda and Angra-Mainyu. He also corresponds to Kâla, or deified time in the *Vedas*, of whom we read,

> Time, the steed runs with seven reins, thousand eyed, eagles, rich in seed ... all the beings (worlds) are his wheels. With seven wheels does this Time ride ... Time, the first god, now hastens onwards ... Time begot yonder heaven ... Time created the earth, in Time the sun burns.[48]

But, while the good and evil twins embodied the chaotic disorder which seemed to be humanity's lot, Zurvan was the universe as order. He was the relentless unfolding of time as day follows night and night day, as the stars and planets ran through their courses. Perhaps because of this, Zurvanism appears to have offered a natural and safe home to astrologers. The concept of an order of time itself may have been the natural result of astrology's drift from a conversation with the gods to the plotting of the natural order which is evident in the diaries. While a causal connection cannot be established between religious developments and the cosmological revolution, the encounter between the Babylonian astrologers and the Zoroastrian state was followed by a remarkable series of tablets which indicate an apparent shift in attitudes to the heavens. From the identification of the 12-sign zodiac in 475 BCE, to the use of planets in zodiac signs in 419, and the earliest known example of a birth chart in 410 BCE, the current evidence suggests that the fifth century saw a shift in astrology's underlying rationale, a further decline in the role of capricious deities, and a rise in the notion of cosmic order. If this shift took place within the context of a wider ideological adjustment, Zurvanism provides a likely candidate. Even though belief in repetitive celestial order is evident in the Venus tablet, and even though the seventh century had also seen evidence of an intellectual revolution in the form of the diaries, a hundred years before the Persian conquest, that does not rule out Zoroastrian influence in the fifth century. In this case, the fusion of the diaries' empiricism with the radical theology of Zurvanism laid the foundations for modern astrology.

The earliest evidence for the existence of the zodiac actually occurs on a lunar tablet dated to 475 BCE, while the tablet of 419 BCE, the first known ephemeris, gives the positions of planets in the signs, almost certainly as an aid to drawing up birth charts.[49] The tablet reads, 'Nisannu. Jupiter and Venus at the beginning of Gemini, Mars in Leo, Saturn in Pisces. 19th day: Mercury's evening star setting in Taurus. Addaru 2. Jupiter at the beginning of Cancer, Venus in Aries, Saturn, Mars, and Mercury invisible'.[50] The zodiac signs evolved as a system of measurement, but were also assigned astrological meanings. More than this, they were the 'mighty powers' of the universe, presiding over the unfolding of destiny.[51] An additional advantage, though, was to be the ability to tabulate planetary positions in terms of zodiac degrees. The 12 signs did not replace the three ways or constellations, but could be used alongside them. One tablet, dated to 164 BCE, records that Halley's Comet had been 'seen in the east in the path of Anu in the area of Pleiades and Taurus, to the west … and passed along in the path of Ea'.[52] The three ways, though, unlike the zodiac, never made the journey west to be taken up by later Hellenistic astrology.

The process by which the establishment of a constellational lunar zodiac and the attribution of astrological meaning to stars or groups of stars, led to the creation of the 12-sign zodiac is not clear. Certainly planetary meanings depended partly on their position in relation to the stars, and the *Enuma Anu Enlil* contains omens such as: 'If Mars approaches the Scorpion: there will be a breach in the palace of the prince'.[53] However, we cannot be sure whether the crucial factor here was Mars' position in the sky, or whether the constellation Scorpio was thought to contain meaning in the same sense as a Greek zodiac sign was to do. The astrological letters and reports contain similar observations, referring to stars as well as constellations, suggesting that in the eighth century there was still no neat and all-encompassing division of the sky into distinct regions. However, the transformation of constellations into zodiac signs represents a substantial conceptual shift from stars, physical points of light gathered in untidy groups, towards zones of the sky arranged in a neat sequence. The equal-sized signs of the Mesopotamian zodiac were no longer identical with the constellations, with their untidy boundaries, but were a kind of tidied-up, conceptualized version of them, a bureaucrat's dream. There was still some fluidity, though, and the boundaries of the zodiac did not coincide with those adopted in the early Christian era. Tables of moon positions from the fourth to second centuries BCE locate the spring equinox at 8° or 10° Aries rather than at 0° Aries as it does in later Western astrology.

The construction of a solar zodiac may have been the eventual consequence of the development of the 18 lunar constellations. However, it is by no means such a logical exercise for, when the sun is visible, the stars are not. It therefore makes no sense, in a strictly observational astronomy, to describe the sun's location according to its position amongst the stars. The importance of twelve-ness as a division of time is not at issue, though. In the primaeval battle recorded in the *Enuma Elish* the monster Tiamat creates 11 creatures to fight with her, including a few who share identities with constellations, including 'the great lion, the mad dog, and the Scorpion-man'.[54] Certainly Marduk's creation of the constellations and 12 months in the *Enuma Elish* points to an Old Babylonian recognition that twelve-ness is important for space and time.[55] However, while the existence of a 12-month year is not open to question, there is no other evidence that the 12 zodiac signs were identified prior to the fifth century.

There were undoubtedly practical imperatives for the creation of a solar zodiac – the need to take celestial omens for daytime births – or religious motives – the increasing importance of solar deities – but we have no explicit statements to this effect. Once again, we encounter the perennial problem of sources, and the possibility that somewhere a cache of letters from astrologers to the emperors Nebuchadrezzar or Cyrus are waiting to be discovered. The scribes continued to make copies of the *Enuma Anu Enlil* well into the Greek Seleucid period, and to record their observations in the astronomical diaries, the latter into the first century BCE, though there may have been breaks in both. The overall picture suggests that astrology lost none of its intellectual vigour, and, as we have seen, its apparent absence from court, at least in the Persian period, may be a result of the emperors' Zoroastrian distaste for the Babylonian pantheon. Whatever the reason, out of this period emerged the form of divination or prognostication which has since, more than any other, been associated with the term astrology – the prediction of destiny on the basis of planetary positions at birth.

The remarkable length of time that separated the earliest signs of a written astrological tradition from the first birth chart – around 1,800 years – requires some explanation. Unfortunately, none is forthcoming. The astrologers' emphasis on affairs of state is not a sufficient explanation, for we would have expected to find some sort of record of the heavens for the birth of a prince. Would any king, keen to hear from his astrologers about his prospects from day to day, not ask them about the planets on the day of the birth of an heir? The available evidence suggests they did not. This is in spite of the fact that omens from unusual or deformed animal births were taken from early in the second millennium and collected in the *Summa Izbu*, or that birth was surrounded with mystery. In the third millennium, gestation and birth were periods fraught with the danger of bad influences. Nintur or Ninhursaga, the midwife goddess, included in her role the ability, 'to give birth to kings, to tie on the rightful tiara, to give birth to lords, to place the crown on (their) heads', but not, apparently, to send any celestial omen of goodwill.[56] The *Enuma Anu Enlil* shows some concern with personal affairs but only in a generalized sense. Amongst the Venus omens we find the following somewhat pessimistic examples, none of them capable of being related to specific individuals.

> If Venus becomes visible at daylight: men's wives will not stay with their husbands but run after their men.
> If Venus rises in the morning and does not set … the Lamaštu demon will seize infants.
> If Venus at dawn rises at sunrise, at nightfall at sunset: father will expel his son, mother will bar her door to her daughter.[57]

By the fifth century, we find evidence of standardized statements, so-called 'Nativity Omens' clearly designed to assess a child's prospects at birth. These read: 'If a child is born and Jupiter comes forth …'.[58] The significant feature of these omens in terms of the development of astrological meanings, is that the personalities of the planets appear to have become standardized into their later Hellenistic forms. Venus is benevolent, Jupiter confers wealth, Mars brings a hot temper and Saturn signifies restrictions. A form of standardization has developed which is unknown from the *Enuma Anu Enlil*. The tablets are broken but there also seem to have been predictions for standard periods, such as 40 years of age, the first time that such an idea occurs in the astrological literature.

We do not know how far back the birth-omen tradition dates, so we have to work with the assumption that it is, as the texts indicate, a fifth-century innovation. The earliest known birth charts, which survive as lists of planetary positions with fragments of interpretation, date from 410 BCE. Of these, one, calculated for 29 April 410 BCE, and cast for the 'son of Shuna-usur, one of Shuma-iddina, descendant of Dēkē' gives the following planetary positions; moon 'below the horn of the Scorpion (that is, Libra), Jupiter in Pisces, Venus in Taurus, Saturn in Cancer and Mars in Gemini'. Mercury was invisible, being too close to the sun to be seen, and so was ignored. The sun itself was not mentioned. This is followed by the momentous, optimistic prediction '(Things?) will(?) be good before you'.[59] Apart from its status as the earliest known astrological prediction made on the basis of planetary positions at birth, the text presents us with the question as to whether we can reconstruct the premises on which an astrologer reached his positive conclusion. The only way to get to this conclusion is to extrapolate back from later Hellenistic astrology in which the two great 'benefic' planets, Jupiter and Venus, were strongly placed in Pisces and Taurus respectively, signs which they ruled, and Saturn, the most destructive planet, was seriously weakened in Cancer, opposite its rulership in Capricorn.[60] It seems that the Hellenistic system of exaltations, which linked planets to zodiac signs, was of Babylonian origin, so is this first horoscope evidence of a Babylonian origin of planetary rulership of zodiac signs, however tenuous? Although fragmentary, the text goes on to define future periods, mentioning eight-year and 12-year periods, themselves suggestive of forecasts made on the basis of Jupiter's 12-year passage through the zodiac and Venus's familiar eight-year cycle. The other intriguing feature of this birth chart is that it includes information taken directly from a diary entry for the relevant dates indicating a respect for empirical observation.[61] The significance though, of the need to compute planets in advance for an event – birth – which might take place during daylight hours, was that astrology was no longer primarily devoted to the visible night sky. It began to be abstracted from the visible world, paying attention to stars and planets which were unseen while the sun was above the horizon.

There is then a gap of almost 150 years before the next known birth chart, cast for a child born in 263 BCE. Why the gap should be so long is not clear.[62] Either we are looking at a practice which was still rare, or we are dependent on the accidental nature of archaeology; we only know about what we have found. A slightly later chart, set for a birth in 263 BCE is particularly notable as the first to include planetary position recorded by degree, indicating an increasing concern with mathematical precision. It also includes the sun as well as Venus, which was close to the sun and hence invisible, indicating that the astrologer may have been working from tables of positions computed in advance, rather then direct observation. More important for our understanding of the individual's relationship with the cosmos, though, there are indications of a substantial predictive system of remarkable precision. The text reads: 'The wealth which he had in his youth(?) will not [remain(?)]. The 36th year ... he will have wealth. His days will be long (in number). His wife, whom people will seduce(?) in his presence, will ...'.[63] The reference to the thirty-sixth year as prosperous is intriguing; to the Greek astrologers of the first century CE Jupiter was 'the greater benefic', the planet whose presence encouraged good fortune. Perhaps three of the benevolent planet's 12-year cycles might bring great favour to this young child. Another point we should note is the remarkable precision – people will not just seduce his wife, but do so in his presence. Normally this kind of detail is characteristic of the Hellenistic astrology of the Greek-speaking world, which is not really evident until later. There is, though, no evidence yet of the notion of an inherent personality, imprinted in the baby from birth; this was to appear later, probably from the second century BCE onwards to judge from the evidence in the surviving Hellenistic texts. But there was a distinct sense that each infant came into this world with a path to tread, experiencing a series of opportunities or obstacles which coincided with planetary patterns. As the Greek philosopher Plato, who was deeply influenced by what he knew of Babylonian opinions about the sky, said, the planets are the keepers of time.[64] So they were also the markers of the key stages in life. The evidence is scarce but we can state with confidence that, under Greek rule – Alexander had conquered Babylon in 332 BCE – the astrologers were working with a system of astrology which was routinely applied to individuals and whose complexity was approaching the intricate, labyrinthine interpretative routines known from the surviving Greek texts of the first century CE onwards.

The city of Babylon itself began to stagnate in the last years of the Persian Empire and their successors, the Greek Seleucids and Iranian Parthians, who conquered the region in the 140s and 130s, moved their capitals to the new cities of Seleucia and Ctesiphon respectively. Sometime around 280 BCE Berossus, a priest of Bel – Marduk – moved to the Aegean island of Kos, there to teach astrology, along with Babylonian culture, to the Greeks. With this, the innovative energy in both Babylonian astronomy and astrology moved decisively to the west, to the Hellenistic world of the eastern Mediterranean: Greece and Egypt. Yet Babylon remained a hub for astrologers, as the birth chart of 263 BCE demonstrates. Five further surviving birth charts, all cast in Babylon, date from between 89 and 69 BCE, while a number of cuneiform astronomical almanacs, listing the information necessary to compute birth charts, date from between 31/32 and 74/75 CE.[65] Babylonian astrology, as David Brown has pointed out, survived into the Christian era.[66] Yet, as cuneiform script died out, the Mesopotamian tradition spread both directly and via its more complex, Hellenistic form. It passed to Persian astrologers, speaking Pahlavi, and from there it entered India, merging with the indigenous tradition. Of Persian astrology itself, we have almost no trace for a further seven centuries, when a vigorous literary tradition surfaced in the Arabic texts of the Islamic world. Instead, it is to the Greek-speaking world that the literary record passes. And there, it was to absorb the intensity of the Egyptian temple tradition.

6

Egypt: The Kingdom of the Sun

I am Re, I am Atum, I am the Lord of Everlasting,
I am the beam which upholds eternity.[1]

Egypt's enduring role in the Western imagination has been institutionalized not only in dozens of horror films, or in art deco design and architecture, but in the pivotal position of a pyramid capped by the magical eye of Horus in the seal of the USA – and on the American dollar bill.[2] The dominant images of ancient Egypt are of monumental mystery and incredible continuity; similar styles of religious and cosmic imagery seem to have endured for around 3,000 years. There is some truth in these suppositions. In Egypt the megalithic astronomy of Nabta Playa found a magnificent and enduring legacy in the celestial religion of the pharaohs, in complete contrast to northern Europe where the penchant for massive monuments completely died out as the Neolithic mindset gave way to the metalworkers of the Bronze Age.

The temples at sites such as Karnak and the pyramids at Giza are indeed testimony to a profound religious consciousness and the mystery is real – the Egyptian priesthood appears to have favoured oral teachings over written accounts of their beliefs with the exception of texts found inside tombs, where nobody but the dead could read them. There was also a strong sense of continuity and the old gods and goddesses were still worshipped well into the Christian era, three millennia after the Great Pyramid. In spite of this continuity, though, it is misleading, to imagine that there is a single, orthodox Egyptian cosmology which remains unchanged for thousands of years. Instead, there was a multiplicity of deities and explanatory myths.

Political unification in the Nile Valley appears to have taken place around 2850 BCE and the Old Kingdom, to which we owe the pyramids, flourished from around 2615 to 1991 BCE. We know that at this time the state was locked into an intense relationship with the sky in which the function of the priesthood and the divine monarchy was to maintain the bond between the heavens and earth, and in which key figures in the pantheon, particularly the sun and moon, were located in the sky. The coming of the New Kingdom in around 1570 BCE seems to have coincided with a cosmological revolution for which the evidence is first complete representations of the sky including, for the first time, the planets, the solar-monotheistic revolution of Akhenaten around 1379–1362, and then the first hints of divination from the stars. Astrology of the Babylonian variety was first introduced around 500 BCE under Persian influence, perhaps a little earlier.

Throughout, though, the Egyptians' religious system is best described as cosmotheism, a term which can apply equally well to the Babylonians, and which suggests that the cosmos itself is the object of worship.[3] The state, then, can be described as a cosmotheocracy. Even though there was a multitude of deities in the Egyptian system, each had a function and a place in the cosmic order, so much so that it was the cosmos itself, the spinning of the stars, the daily movement of the sun, the monthly changes of the moon and the annual shift of the seasons which was the ultimate focus of religious ritual.

The Egyptians had an extraordinarily rich astral theology in which the entire universe was a single cosmic state. Mortals were confined to the physical surface of the earth and the immortals, whether gods or the souls of the dead, occupied the heavens where they were represented by the sun, moon and stars.[4] Egyptian astronomy may have had little mathematical content but it was absolutely integral to the ritual management of the state's politics and religion: the king was god and god was king – and both were stars.[5] The Egyptian cosmos was alive, it was at once sexual and spiritual, physical and religious, enchanted, magical and scientific: it failed to recognize any of our modern distinctions between different ways of perceiving the world and relating to the universe. And, at its core, the Egyptian cosmos was moral. The judgement of the dead in a form which was to be adapted, along with Persian notions of good and evil, by Christianity, offered a view of the starry realm as a reward for ethical behaviour. After death each soul was sent to stand trial and its heart weighed in a set of scales which contained a feather. If the heart was the heavier, the soul was guilty; if the lighter, it was innocent.

The origins of Egypt's astral theology, like Babylon's, predates writing. Moreover, when the Egyptians did write they failed to offer justifications of their beliefs so speculation flourishes. Many authors, academics included, present ideas for which there is no evidence as if they are fact. For example, the suggestion that the prehistoric population of Egypt failed to personalize the heavenly bodies because they were remote is clearly nonsense, for remoteness never prevented other cultures from personalizing the stars, besides which, apart from the fact that the stars were untouchable, nobody had any idea how far away they were.[6] Similarly, Otto Neugebauer, one of the most influential scholars in the history of ancient science, denied that the Egyptians possessed an exact mathematical astronomy.[7] This is only partially true. Egyptian astronomy was not concerned with whether one planet was moving at a particular speed, or with deriving mathematical formulae to calculate its future position. What worried the Egyptians was when the sun was going to rise, a matter of considerable importance if the associated rituals were to be conducted in the proper sequence.

Egyptian astronomy was primarily observational in practice and religious in intent: the motions of the stars were the movements of the gods and goddesses so by watching the sky they were the observers of a divine drama – and, through their rituals, the priests became active participants. Much the same applies to

Egyptian culture. Explanatory models were provided by the creation myths and poetic accounts of the sun's daily descent into night. As far as we can tell, they never seem to have been concerned with such matters as the duration of planetary cycles, which preoccupied the Babylonians, or the mathematical and geometrical explanations for their motions, which fascinated the Greeks, at least not until the wholesale import of Babylonian and Greek culture after 331 BCE.

Our sources for Egyptian cosmology are sparse, but what we do have is sufficient to paint a picture of a world in which there was a universal order and in which the human relationship with the cosmos was essentially participatory and spiritual. Whereas the Babylonians took omens before they acted, for the Egyptians the action was the primary task – to time one's sacred rituals precisely according to the rising of particular stars. The oldest sources are the Pyramid Texts, mostly inscriptions on the walls of tombs in pyramids, depicting the view of the afterlife and the Pharaoh's ascent into the sky after death.[8] The Coffin Texts, magical funerary spells typically inscribed on coffin lids (but also on tomb walls, chests, papyri and mummies) belonging to court officials, date to the Old Kingdom, but are primarily a Middle Kingdom (c.2030–c.1640) phenomenon.[9] They suggest a democratization of access to the afterlife, broadening the exclusiveness of the Pyramid Texts and placed an emphasis on Osiris rather than the sun as ruler of the dead. Re, the sun god, lost little of his political power, though, and in the New Kingdom, after 1570 BCE, he came close to overwhelming all other gods. The third set of texts were known to the Egyptians as *The Book of Coming* [or *Going*] *Forth By Day*, known more familiarly to us as *The Book of the Dead*.[10] These texts, mainly from the New Kingdom, were carved either on the dead person's sarcophagus, or on papyri which were buried with them, and consist of charms, spells and utterances which were designed to help the deceased on their way, guiding them through the perils of the underworld. Our fourth set of sources are the astronomical ceilings, highly schematic portrayals of the heavens which survive from early New Kingdom tombs, again, those of high court officials. The one thing which all these documents and images have in common is that they are associated with death – and the hoped-for salvation which follows. However, we have to be clear about what we mean by death. In a situation in which the physical body is merely a vehicle for an immortal soul, it is the soul's relationship with the stars which is crucial. In later astral religions, such as the Mithraic Mysteries, which were to flourish in the Roman Empire, the key rituals were designed to prepare the initiate, while alive, for the inevitable journey to the stars after death. It seems plausible, then, that given the Egyptians' preoccupation with the sky, the funereal texts may also be read as descriptions of ecstatic rites to be conducted in life, in which the king, shaman-like, travelled to the sun and stars, literally so in the mind of him and his priests, in order to maintain the link between heaven and earth.[11] Collectively, these texts establish for the first time in written form the belief, which may be many thousands of years old, and which has certainly lasted until the present day, that one's spiritual destiny is connected to the stars. And this is critical for our understanding of

Western astrology; while the Babylonians devised a technical system for reading the sky and interpreting divine intentions, the Egyptians provided a meaning and purpose in which the rationale was one's own, individual connection with the stars.

Although the earliest texts included in the *Book of the Dead* are dated to after 2400 BCE, some indicate a much earlier tradition. Pyramid Text utterance 662, for example, tells the dead king to cast the sand from his face, as he might have done when buried in the desert, as was the custom in the pre-dynastic period, before 3100 BCE,[12] indicating a probable lineage back to the megalithic Nabta Playa culture. The purpose of such texts though, appears to have been to engage humans in negotiation with the gods, perhaps even to control them. Ivan Edwards wrote that 'in all matters concerning their religion, the Egyptians placed considerable reliance on the magic power of the written word. They believed that, by using the correct formulas, they could impose their will upon the gods.'[13] This is probably an overstatement. It would be hubris to imagine that one could impose one's will upon the gods. More likely, the Egyptians were attempting to enter into a state of spiritual unity with them. There may be a difference then, with the Babylonian attempt to establish just what the gods and goddesses intended.

Inasmuch as the pharaoh and his queen appear to have had a particular connection with the heavens, it seems that the Egyptian state was a counterpart to, or an integral part of, the heavenly realm. The sky itself was the goddess Nut, typically portrayed as a naked woman arched over the earth, her feet touching one horizon, her hands the other. From her union with Geb, the earth, came the great divinities of the Egyptian pantheon, Isis and Osiris, the celestial king and queen, Nebthet (Nephthys to the Greeks), a goddess of the dead, and their evil brother, Set. There were then a total of nine primary gods and goddesses, known after the centralization of local religious variations as the Great Ennead of Heliopolis. To this was added a Little Ennead under the leadership of Horus.[14] Osiris – and perhaps Isis – might have been pre-dynastic human rulers, much like the Sumerian Gilgamesh.[15]

The Egyptian sky was a theatrical backdrop against which was played the daily drama of death and resurrection, as the sun rose and set. That the same process took place on monthly and annual cycles only added to the richness of a powerful salvation theology. In what is one of the earliest known motifs of both the dying god and the eternal struggle of good and evil, Set, the personification of evil, killed Osiris, dismembered him into 14 or 16 parts (which it is tempting to see as the number of days either in half a sidereal lunar phase or half a synodic month) and scattered the parts throughout the country. Despite her grief, Isis, his sister and wife, was able to reunite the body and restore it to life just long enough to conceive a son, Hor (more commonly known by his Latin name, Horus), who then avenged his father's murder by vanquishing Set. The iconography of Isis and Horus as mother and child, and of Horus overcoming Seth, eventually found their way into Christianity as Mary and Jesus, the holy mother and child, and

Jesus and Satan, the deadly foes;[16] Isis was worshipped until the sixth century CE, overlapping with Christianity by half a millennium. In the Old Kingdom Osiris became the ruler of the netherworld, the *det* or *duat*: he was the judge of the dead and was identified with the constellation Sah (corresponding to the Greek Orion), in which form he ruled the night sky. The hieroglyph for *duat* was a star in a circle, the star being Osiris himself,[17] while Osiris himself is represented by the three stars of Orion's belt. His consort, Isis, became Sopdet, later Sothis, our Sirius, the brightest star in the sky: it rises and sets after Orion and so is its loyal companion, just as Isis was Osiris' faithful queen. Whereas Re, the solar deity, was regarded as a god of the living and closely associated with the priests of the religious centre at'Iwnw (usually abbreviated to On but better known by its Greek name, Heliopolis – city of the sun), Osiris had certain cult centres as god of the dead, but was worshipped throughout Egypt.[18] This fact is of more than theological interest, for, although Re ruled supreme in heaven and was very popular with certain dynasties, such as the fifth whose pharaohs were responsible for the pyramids at Giza, his priests were confined to Heliopolis. Meanwhile Osiris was accessible across the country, suggesting that the king exercised undisputed political control, as well as sharing responsibility (as a trinity with Isis and Osiris as Sirius and Orion) of regulating the seasons.[19] For this reason the Pyramid Texts may have been intended to incorporate Osirian elements in the funerary and shamanic rites, reinforcing the point that the pharaoh also ruled as the embodiment of Horus, an alternative representation of the sun to Re.[20] In life the pharaoh was Horus, the son – the Fourth Dynasty monarchs added 'Son of Re' to their royal titles – in death he became Osiris, the father.[21]

In practice, the pharaoh himself, sanctified by his relationship with the sky, was the universal monarch. The Old Kingdom monarchs became increasingly identified with the sun, the first signs of a tradition which was eventually bequeathed to the Roman emperors. In the tomb of Teti, a Sixth Dynasty pharaoh we are told that 'O Re ... thou art Teti and Teti is thou ... make Teti sound and Teti will make you sound'.[22] In sky terms, then, the pharaoh was Orion by night and the sun by day.

The Egyptians' relationship with the sky was intense, experiential and a matter of national survival as well as religious imperative. There are though, certain persistent themes and, even if Osiris ruled the night, the sun presided undisputed over the day and his daily journey was a permanent reminder of the eternal struggle between light and dark and perhaps the central feature of religious cosmology.

In one myth, Re impregnates his mother Nut each day, while in another he enters her mouth and travels though her body during the hours of darkness, and in both he is reborn at dawn – and, as both Osiris and Re were generated from Nut, they were, in effect, brothers. Usually the sun sails through the sky in a boat: in one Sixth Dynasty (*c*.2315–*c*.2175 BCE) text we read that 'thou embarkest therein (the sun's bark) like Re, thou sittest down on the throne of Re that thou mayest command the gods; for thou art Re who came forth from Nut, who brings forth Re every day'.[23] Alternatively, it was carried on the wings of a falcon, which excelled all other birds in its ability to fly to a great height,[24] or both traditions were combined. Pyramid Text utterance 488 tells us that 'you have grown wings as a great-breasted falcon, a hawk seen in the evening traversing the sky. May you cross the firmament by the waterway of Re-Harakhhti.'[25]

The sun was given different names to designate its various phases; rising it was known as Re or Ra and setting it was Atum, although originally both gods may have been regional deities of the whole solar cycle in their own right. The *Book of the Dead* spell 15 hails the sun as 'Re when you rise and Atum when you set'. The spell continues in a style which indicates spectacularly the reverence with which the sun was regarded:

> Hail to you, O Re, at your rising, O Atum-Horakhty! Your beauty is worshipped in my eyes when the sunshine comes into being over my breast. You proceed at your pleasure in your Night-bark, your heart is joyful with a fair wind in the Day-bark, being happy at crossing the sky with the blessed ones. All your foes are overthrown, the Unwearying Stars acclaim you, the Imperishable [circumpolar] Stars worship you when in the horizon of Manu, being happy at all times, and living and enduring as my lord ... How beautiful are your rising and your shining on the back of your mother Nut, you having appeared as King of the Gods.[26]

Re was Horakhty or Harakhte, meaning Horus of the horizon, or Atum-Harahkte as he sank over the western horizon. As the rising sun he was Khepri (literally 'scarab beetle' or 'he who becomes' – or the 'self-created'.[27] Both associations had a logic. Horus was represented as a falcon, a bird who flies high enough to carry the sun, while the dedication with which scarab beetles push balls of dung along the ground resembles the force with which the sun is moved across the sky – or the fact that the beetle 'emerges from its own substance and is reborn of itself'.[28] The goddess Sekhmet, the terrible ruler of war and battle, is not normally categorized as a solar deity, although the fact that her statues are crowned with a solar disc suggests that she was. Her lioness's head is intriguing, suggesting a link between the sun and the lion which was to be found in the Mesopotamian constellation of Leo, but otherwise not in Egyptian culture, and perhaps anticipating Leo's later, Greek, link with the sun. Horus is also a solar god, often identified with the Apollo of Greek myth. But in Egyptian, 'Hor' is consistent with the word 'sky'; thus Horus is depicted as a falcon-headed god, and, as a falcon, his two eyes are sometimes the sun (right eye) and moon (left eye).[29] After the loss of his left eye in the fight with Set, the eye of Horus is also called the Wadjet eye, and is present today in its depiction on the back of the American dollar bill. This was not an idle story but an astronomical allegory; if the left eye was the moon then its loss provided a narrative around which the mystery of the moon's monthly disappearance could be told.

The evolution of Egyptian astral religion in the Old Kingdom seems to represent some sort of centralization of various regional traditions as the state consolidated itself. The building of the pyramids at Giza, just outside modern Cairo, which appear to incorporate elements of both, may indicate the attempt to formulate an official national celestial theology with a priesthood based in the nearby city of Heliopolis.[30] The pyramids should be seen as a symbolic expression in stone of the state religion of the pharaohs and the priesthood of Heliopolis, exactly as a mosque embodies mystical Islamic principles or the cruciform shape of a Gothic cathedral the salvation through the cross which stands at the heart of Christianity. Our difficulty though, lies in working out how these principles were incorporated in the pyramids, given that the most magnificent examples, the three monumental Fourth Dynasty pyramids at Giza, including the Great Pyramid built by Pharaoh Khufu (Cheops) around 2480 BCE, contain no inscriptions.

The pyramid age began in the Third Dynasty with the step pyramid of Djoser, who reigned from 2630 to 2611 BCE, virtually ceased during the disintegration of the First Intermediate Period (Dynasties Eight to Eleven, c.2175–1991 BCE) and was revived, though on a lesser scale, during the prosperous and powerful Middle Kingdom Twelfth Dynasty (c.1991–1786 BCE). The New Kingdom (c.1570–332 BCE) pharaohs preferred to be interred in the ground and established a communal cemetery in the Valley of the Kings, in the south, near Luxor. The pyramid age therefore occupied a relatively brief portion of the entire 3,000-year civilization and the great period of construction at Giza lasted only a century. It represents a particular relationship to the cosmos, as specific in time and space, as say, one building phase at Stonehenge. Whether we accept Herodotus' statement that the Great Pyramid was built by 100,000 slaves over 30 years, or the more recent view that it was constructed by 20,000 paid artisans over 20 years, the pyramid's construction represents an astonishing collective devotion to a shared view of the relationship to the state to the cosmos.[31]

The statistics are truly awesome: Khufu's tomb consisted of 2.3 million 10-ton blocks and is 100m high, as tall as a fifty-storey building. The granite blocks, some as heavy as 60 tons were brought from Aswan, 1,000km away. It is the most convincing evidence we could have of a state which was immensely wealthy – to supply the necessary labour – and united – gangs of labourers arrived from all over the kingdom, and worked in teams depending on their locality.[32] Although there are no inscriptions on the Great Pyramid, simple archaeoastronomy reveals its role as a mediator between the stars and earth, the next life and this. When modern scholars did consider the pyramids' possible astronomical symbolism, they originally thought that it was exclusively solar.[33] In fact there is no reason why solar and stellar cults should not coexist and increasingly the Great Pyramid is seen as the embodiment of both.

It was not until 1963 that astronomer Virginia Trimble checked one of the four hitherto unexplained shafts which run in an upward diagonal fashion from the centre of the pyramid. Two start at each of the king's chamber and the queen's chamber, one pointing north, the other south. She found that the king's southern shaft pointed to the stars of Orion's belt around 2500 BCE.[34] The conclusion is that at the appropriate moment Khufu's soul would be able to travel to Orion, to be welcomed by the great king and judge Osiris. If Trimble was wrong then that tells us that the precise pyramid–star alignment hypothesis fails, but the fact that there is a general orientation with the cardinal directions sustains the notion of a direct relationship between the earthly state and the heavenly.[35] The evidence that temples were aligned with key points on the solar cycle, solstices and equinoxes, and bright stars, such as Sirius and Canopus, is persuasive.[36] We know from the Pyramid Texts, which first occur in the later, Fifth Dynasty pyramids, that the king mounted to heaven on the rays of the sun. Pyramid Text utterance 508 reads: 'I have trodden those thy rays as a ramp under my feet whereon I mount up to that my mother, the living Uraeus on the brow of Re', and utterance 523 tells us that 'may the sky make the sunlight strong for you, may you rise up to the sky as the Eye of Re'.[37] It is not difficult to argue that Orion could have fulfilled the same function at night as the sun in the day. The point was to journey to a corporeal, not an ethereal life, in the *duat* and the pyramids were the means by which this might happen.[38] The soul, the *ba*, might travel either to the sun's rising[39] or to Orion and achieve precisely the same result: immortality. This was no otherworldly religion though. The physical world existed in partnership with the other world, the *duat*, and, as Ed Krupp put it, Khufu's 'agenda was nothing less than the stability and continuity of the world, and he exerted celestial power to fulfil it'.[40] It is also likely that Khufu was deliberately elevating his own cult as representative of the sun (and Osiris) as a direct challenge to the priests of Re at Heliopolis, exactly as the heretic pharaoh Akhenaten was to do in the fourteenth century BCE. The Great Pyramid's remaining major stellar connection appears to be a link between the southern shaft of the queen's chamber with Sirius, the star of Isis, suggesting that the pyramid served both female and male aspects of the divine.[41]

It is also a simple fact that the Great Pyramid faces almost exactly due north, as was demonstrated by Sir Flinders Petrie in the late nineteenth century.[42] The match is astonishing: the north side's deviation from true north is out by 2' 28" of arc, a figure so small as to be scarcely noticeable, certainly not by anyone standing next to it. We do not know exactly how this was accomplished, although the simplest method is to observe the rotation of two selected stars around the celestial north pole. When one is directly above the other then the observer watching them is facing north.[43] The stellar alignment itself connects the north shaft from the king's chamber to Thuban, not an unusually bright star though, at the time, the closest thing the Egyptians had to a pole star.[44] While orientation to the solstices, or to the sun's general rising and setting points, are common both in Egypt and elsewhere, alignment to the cardinal points is less so, at least in Egypt. Not only that, but in Egypt itself only eight of the approximately ninety known pyramids have been surveyed, and even though those that have are all constructed to face the cardinal points, Egyptologists' resistance to astronomical investigations so far means that we have no data on any of the others.

The Egyptians were deeply concerned with the point of sky we know as the north celestial pole. It is the hub around which the night sky revolves and, while some stars rise and set every night, those close to the north celestial pole, such as the Big Dipper, never set, at least not when viewed from the northern hemisphere. To the Egyptians they were therefore the 'indestructibles', 'those who know no tiredness' or 'no destruction', perfect symbols of immortality.[45] They were the immortal pharaoh's kingdom; Pyramid Text spell 269 reads: 'He [Atum] assigns the king to those gods who are clever and wise, the Indestructible stars'.[46] To align a pyramid to this point of the sky was therefore to make a bold statement that whatever and whoever is connected with this building, namely the Egyptian state and its pharaoh, will live for ever. There is nothing remarkable about this: every empire suffers from the same conceit. In any case, the alignment of the king's northern shaft with the northern point removes all doubt. One caveat which has to be mentioned in the discussion of the shafts is that no other pyramid possesses them, so we cannot take a large sample and ask how many point at certain or, indeed, any, stars. However, the Great Pyramid is, by virtue of its gigantic size, a special case. Either way, it seems that Egyptian religion was directional: face east, to the rising sun and one is gazing at birth, look west, to the setting sun and one contemplates death, and stand with one's back to the south and front to the north and one is confronted with eternity.

In view of the central position the sun occupied in their religion, we would expect the Egyptians' temples to be constructed with fairly pronounced solar alignments. This is hardly a controversial suggestion – after all Christian churches are generally aligned with the east. The notion was apparently first suggested by the German Professor H. Nissen in 1885 and taken up in some detail by the same Norman Lockyer who was to go on and study the British megalithic sites.[47] However, we find the same conflict of methodologies operating as in the surveys of the pyramid and megaliths. Lockyer relied too heavily on astronomical data, assuming, a priori, that this would help in his stated goal – determining an exact chronology.[48] However, he came up with dates, such as a foundation of the first sun temple at Karnak of 3700 BCE,[49] as opposed to the probable date of c.1900 BCE, which defy the archaeological and textual evidence while, with a few exceptions such as E.A. Wallis Budge, the Egyptologists themselves were 'repelled by the intrusion of an outsider into their realm'.[50] However, Lockyer's assumption, that monuments such as the Great Temple of Amun-Re at Karnak might be aligned with the summer solstice sunrise are perfectly reasonable. It is known, for example, that the entrance pylons to many temples reflected the sun's diurnal cycle by incorporating into their design the hieroglyph *akhet*, 'horizon'.[51] The significance of the horizon can hardly be overestimated. It was the boundary between the world of the living and the dead. When the sun set the world went into mourning and when it was reborn there was joy. It was like Easter and Christmas every day. On this basis Richard Wilkinson embarks on a flight of fancy concerning the temple's function:

The temple, stood at the nexus of the three spheres of heaven, earth and the netherworld; and it served as a kind of portal by which gods and men might pass from one realm to another. In the same way that the temple pylon functioned symbolically as an *akhet* or 'horizon' in terms of the solar cycle, so the whole temple functioned as a kind of temporal and spatial *akhet*. Just as the physical horizon is the interface between heaven and earth – and in terms of the setting sun between today and tomorrow, the present and future, this world and the beyond – so the temple, of whatever type, was regarded as an *akhet* or interface between these spheres or realms, and was often described as such.[52]

The temple was more than a place of worship. By embodying in its very structure the measures of time and space, balancing the certain present and the uncertain future, it solidified the relationship between the divine and earthly states and facilitated, if not guaranteed, the maintenance of order and security. However, in spite of the widely accepted inclusion of cosmological principles in the Egyptian temple, Egyptologists ignored Lockyer's ideas and it was left first to Paul Barguet and then the astronomers Gerald Hawkins, fresh from formulating his eclipse theories at Stonehenge, and Ed Krupp to repeat Lockyer's claims, rejecting some but confirming others.[53] Hawkins, for example, concluded that what Lockyer calculated was a summer-solstice alignment at Karnak was in fact a winter one, while contradicting certain of Lockyer's other claims. Ed Krupp's 1982 survey, meanwhile has confirmed the existence of winter-solstice alignments at a series of major sites, such as Karnak, as well as the mortuary temple of Hatshepsut, near Luxor.[54] However, as students of north-western European megaliths have discovered, it is sometimes misleading to look for precise solstice or equinox alignments. Some sites may be oriented to the sun on other significant days. Thus, while the chapel of Re-Horakhty at Abu Simbel is aligned to the winter-solstice sunrise, the main temple is oriented to sunrise on 22 October and 18 February in our era; October 22 may have corresponded to New Year's day in *c.*1250 BCE, the jubilee year of Ramesses II, the builder.[55] At dawn on the appropriate day, in a deeply religious event reminiscent of Newgrange, the sun's rays would have fallen on three statues in the temple's inner sanctuary – two of solar deities, Amun-Re and Re-Horakhty, and one of their earthly representative, Ramesses II himself. The fourth statue, of the underworld god Ptah, remains untouched. Thus, we assume would the heavenly life-giving power of the sun have been harnessed in the service of the earthly state. Considering all the evidence, Ed Krupp concludes that there was probably a shift from the Old Kingdom, when temples may have been oriented, like the pyramids, to the cardinal points, to the New Kingdom, when solstice alignments seem more likely. Also, as solar chapels are mainly on the north sides of temples, while mortuary chapels are generally on the south, and winter-solstice sunrise takes place in the north-east and winter-solstice sunrise in the south-east, then the north-east may 'be a place of renewal (and) the south-east may represent a place of light's triumph over darkness'.[56] Recent statistical analysis has for the first time demonstrated the alignments of Egyptian temples, but has reminded us the land is as important as the sky; the orientation of temples in the south indicated that their gates tended to face the Nile and the primary solar orientation, similar to our current understanding of megalithic sites in northern Europe, was to the winter solstice.[57]

The sun god may have been the presiding deity of the Egyptian cosmic state, comparable to Shamash in Babylon. But there is clear contrast with Mesopotamia where, to judge from the number of omens devoted to it, the moon, Sin, steadily assumed a greater prominence. The moon was represented in the Egyptian celestial kingdom by Thoth, who was pictured either as an ibis-headed man surmounted by a crescent moon, or as a dog-headed ape, a strange combination which, perhaps, represents the union of two archaic traditions. Strictly speaking Thoth was the guardian of the moon, which was described as the left eye of Horus, and always needed defending from the monsters of darkness on its nocturnal journey – as did the sun.[58] As an ally of Isis and Horus in the struggle against Seth, he became Osiris' chief minister and was charged with measuring time, much like the Babylonian god Sin; his importance was recognized when the first month of the year was named in his honour, Thoth. A host of other talents were the natural consequence of Thoth's ability to count and measure; he was the clerk, herald and arbiter of the gods, resolving disputes between them and announcing Osiris' verdict on the dead, kept a complete inventory of all natural resources and property, and invented every one of the arts and sciences including surveying, medicine and music. It was Thoth, who by speaking, brought apparently inanimate objects to life.

Thoth also invented writing – and therefore magic. The reason why the one implied the creation of the other is simple: words contain the power of the beings, ideas or objects thy represent, which is why the texts we find on the inside of tombs are interpreted less as pleas to the gods to accept the soul of the deceased than as a form of magical technology designed to facilitate the soul's journey to the *duat*.[59] This was an understanding of the way language works which lasted well into the European Renaissance and still survives in esoteric traditions such as the Jewish Kabbalah. In short, Thoth had complete knowledge and wisdom, which is why the Greeks were later to identify him not with the moon but with their Hermes, the teacher of divine philosophy and god of the planet Mercury.

There appear to have been other moon gods, apart from Thoth, probably the heirs to pre-dynastic regional traditions. One was Seshat or Seshata, Thoth's consort and collaborator in many of his functions, such as writing and record keeping. She was also known as the 'mistress of the house of architects' in which role she helped the king to determine the axis of a new temple with the aid of the stars, marking out the four angles of the building with stakes,[60] not unlike the Sumerian Nanshe: the coincidence of two celestial temple-building goddesses might point to an earlier tradition of female astronomers. We do not know, though, whether Seshat was invented to be Thoth's partner, or whether she was a previously independent goddess who was linked to him in the process of syncretization which may have accompanied the consolidation of the Old Kingdom.

The Theban god Khonsu (or Khons or Khensu), himself appears to have been a regional lunar deity who only assumed national popularity when Thebes became the capital of the New Kingdom, after around 1570 BCE. His name is derived from the verb 'to cross over' giving the word the meaning 'He who traverses [the sky]';[61] like the sun he travelled across the sky in a barque. Khonsu had a time-keeping role, like Thoth, but without the latter's political power, though the ninth month of the year, Pachon, does seem to have been named after him. With his prominence in the New Kingdom, he became renowned as a healer and exorcist under the name Kons Hor, and was represented as a man with a falcon's head surmounted by a disc in a crescent moon. He never, though, came close to equalling the sun's political authority, which reached its highest point in the reign of the controversial New Kingdom Pharaoh Akhenaten – 'The-glory-of-Aten' (c.1379–c.1362 BCE).[62]

Akhenaten originally came to the throne as Amenophis IV ('Amen-is-satisfied'), named after Amen, or Amun, the supreme god of the priesthood of Thebes, the New Kingdom capital. Early in his reign he instituted a religious reformation in which the cult of Re-Harakhte was set up as a direct rival to Amun, and was represented by the 'Aten (or Aton) of Day', that is, 'the solar disk whence issues the light of day'.[63] He was not content though, to favour the sun in a particular form and was determined to suppress the worship of gods other than Re-Harakhte manifested in Aten, and it is this that is responsible for the myth that he was a proto-monotheist. However, that he saw himself as the earthly part of a trinity consisting of Re-Harakhte, the primordial god and father, and Aten, his physical manifestation in the sky, suggests that his theological break with previous pharaohs was far from substantial. That he constructed a new capital at Akhet-Aten ('Horizon of Aten') and that only he was allowed to worship the new supreme god (and that the rest of the population was ordered to worship him as the representative of Aten) suggests that he might, alternatively, have been using the religion to attack the power of the priesthood in the style of many a Reformation prince, and that his elevation of his own divinity prefigured the Roman emperors' manipulation of solar religion to maintain their power, even if his beliefs were utterly sincere. That Amun had already been syncretized with Ra as Amun-Ra points to a tendency, evident so often when religious pluralism encounters political centralization, to unify and simplify the pantheon. That Aten had already been elevated to the pantheon by Akhenaten's predecessors indicates that his revolution did not come out of thin air. But it was part of a struggle between political power-centres – the court and the temple – and evolving cosmologies.

7

Egypt: The Stars and the Soul

Hereditary prince and count, sole companion, wise in the
sacred writings, who observes everything observable in
heaven and earth, clear-eyed in observing the stars.[1]

The Egyptian sky was at one with the land, and life on earth flourished all the
more if it was harmonized with life in the heavens. The belief that the Egyptians
did not possess a precise mathematical astronomy in the modern sense is strictly
correct, but misses the point that the sky provided a set of visual images which
provided meaning for life on earth, as well as a series of structures and living
beings which enabled auspicious moments of time to be identified, the state to
be managed and souls to travel through space. As such, divisions of the sky were
both particular and imbued with numinous significance. The whole sky was
divided into constellations. The most important group were the 36 which are
generally known to us by the Greek word decan, though they were known to early
Egyptologists as diagonal calendars or, more properly 'star clocks'. These were
used to record the time, a critical process if nocturnal religious rituals were to
be conducted at the divinely sanctioned moments.[2] They make their appearance
in drawings and texts on 12 coffin lids surviving from the Tenth Dynasty
onwards, before 2100 BCE, perhaps by 2400 BCE, and may have been the result
of deliberate invention, similar to the Old Kingdom calendar reforms, rather
than a long evolution.[3] What we find are 36 constellations listed graphically in
36 columns of 12 lines each, arranged in diagonals.[4] Detailed illustrations of the
decans also appear on the astronomical ceilings of Senmut around 1473 BCE
and the pharaohs Seti I, around 1300 BCE, and Rameses IV, around 1170 BCE,
and were recently discovered on the pre-Ptolemaic monuments excavated in
the Mediterranean off Alexandria.[5] Each of the decans, probably beginning
with Sirius, was invisible for 70 days, and was given a 10-day period of special
significance (a decade) following its period of invisibility and rebirth from the
duat. To reduce the decans to mere time-keepers is to obscure their significance
though, and there is no reason to doubt the literal claim that a star dies and a
star lives every 10 days;[6] to measure time was to observe the endless drama of
death and resurrection, of life and immortality, the endlessly alternating triumph
of darkness and light. Collectively they appear to have been arranged in a band
which appears to have been just south of the ecliptic, the sun's apparent path
through the sky. Thus they were led by Isis (who was associated with Sirius) on
a path set out by Re. There were 12 decans visible in the course of one night, the

origin of our 12 hours; in all of the texts, none of which survives from earlier than the New Kingdom, which document the sun's nocturnal journey through the *duat*, it is divided into 12 regions and it is tempting to speculate that it is a spatial analogue of the 12-month year. In this sense, the decans have been compared to a Christian advent calendar, marking the time until the triumphant reappearance of Sirius.[7] These are reasonable assumptions although the texts do not tell us this. The earliest reference to hours occurs in the very first Pyramid Text from Unas' pyramid, in which we are told that the sun 'clears the night and dispatches the hours'.[8]

It is likely that the decan system evolved from direct observation of stellar risings to more systematized measurement of equal periods, hinted at in the tomb of the official Amenemhet (in the reign of Amenhotep I, 1545–1525 BCE), who has been called the 'first astronomer we can name in ancient Egypt'.[9] Certainly we know that mechanical clocks were being invented – the earliest surviving water clock dates from the reign of Amenhotep III (1397–1360 BCE). One outstanding question is the extent to which Egyptian astronomy was influenced by other Near Eastern cultures. The problem though, may be a consequence of the sheer lack of source material. It is inconceivable that Egyptian priests had no access in the second millennium to the knowledge and systems of Mesopotamia, and the use of 36 stars by both cultures suggests a common origin in the third millennium or earlier. It is just not realistic to assume that cultures which traded in artefacts never came into contact with each others' ideas.[10] The Greeks were later to borrow 12-hour nights from the Egyptians, sexagesimal counting from the Babylonians and bequeath us our modern days of 24 60-minute hours.

It seems likely that the 36 decans may have been represented spatially in the Egyptian state, as well as in the sky. In the fifth century the Greek historian Herodotus tells us that the Egyptian Mediterranean coast was exactly 3,600 stades (420 miles) in length. Herodotus also tells us that that during the reign of the 12 kings, a memorial had been constructed featuring a sacred lake, Lake Moeris, the circumference of which was 3,600 stades. The lake was positioned next to the labyrinth of 12 covered courts, six of which faced south and six of which faced north, and contained in its centre two pyramids, each 600ft high. If each of these pyramids stood on a square base whose sides measured the same as the height, as did the Pyramid of Cheops, their volume would be 72 million square feet. The labyrinth itself contained 3,000 rooms, half above ground half below, in similar fashion to the pyramids, half of which were submerged below the sacred lake, connecting underworld to overworld.[11] Given that Herodotus' information about former times is often wrong, he may, nevertheless, have been reporting a genuine belief in his time that earthly dimensions mirrored celestial ones.

The earliest surviving complete catalogue of the universe was compiled around 1100 BCE by Amenope, a scribe of sacred books in the House of Life. He intended it to comprise everything made up of 'heaven with its affairs, earth and what is in it, what the mountains belch forth, what is watered by the flood, all things upon which Re has shone, all that is grown on the back of earth'.[12]

Amenope began his catalogue with 'sky', followed by 'sun', 'moon' and 'star'. He then listed five constellations, only two of which can be identified. We can identify *Sah* (Orion), a man running while looking over his shoulder, from the characteristic three stars of its belt, which figure on Osiris' crown, and *Mshtyw* or *Meskhetiu*, the seven stars of the Big Dipper which the Egyptians saw as an ox-leg, or sometimes as a whole bull.[13] That Amenope mentions neither any other constellations nor planets has been used to suggest that such celestial affairs may have been of far less importance to 'the ancient Egyptian than the terrestrial matters with which he was intimately involved'.[14] However, the fact that he also ignores Sirius suggests that either the catalogue is incomplete or that Amenope's possible personal disinterest in the sky was not representative of Egyptian culture as a whole.

As far as we can tell, aside from the decans, a total of about 25 constellations were recognized and represented by animal and human figures in an abundance of sacred texts. There was the crocodile, the lion, a hippopotamus and a bull's leg. It is also possible that their importance was related to regional and chronological variations in religious practice. Also, because representations of the Egyptian sky are always artistic or symbolic, or 'inaccurate',[15] we have only been able to reconstruct three constellations with any certainty. The few detailed pictures we have, such as those on the New Kingdom ceilings of Senmut and Seti I, also show significant variations.[16] We can assume that all the constellations were north of the ecliptic although we do not know whether they were all circumpolar – 'indestructible'.

The one other Egyptian constellation we can identify with any certainty is Sopdet, later Sothis (Sirius), which appears to be part of a star grouping pictured as a recumbent cow. We are just not sure what the groups of stars are represented by *Rrt* or *Reret*, the hippopotamus, *Nht*, the ape, the crocodile or the spearing god, although there have been some tentative suggestions. The little crocodile might be Cancer and the man normally positioned in front of it could be Gemini while the scorpion could approximate to Virgo and the hippopotamus might be our Draco.[17] The lion might be Leo though the majority disagree, while the sheep might occupy part of Capricorn and Aquarius.[18] It is also possible that the sky was divided in two by the Milky Way, the 'Winding' or 'Shifting Waterway', rather than by the ecliptic, the sun's path, as was later to be the case,[19] or that the Milky Way was itself the goddess Nut, with her mouth, near Gemini, swallowing the sun as it crosses the Milky Way.[20]

We have no idea whether the constellations fulfilled a divinatory role although it must be unlikely that no religious or political significance was attached to a planetary transit, say, or the passage of a comet through a particular group of stars. It is difficult to imagine that, for Old Kingdom cosmologists, the colour of the sun or the shape of the moon had no significance, but the fact is that we have no hint of divination from the stars until the Twentieth Dynasty, the era of the Ramesses.[21] Whether this was a period in which the monarchs were weak, leaving the priesthood of Amun-Re to control the state, is unclear. Whether there was some influence from the Babylonians is also not known, though by no means impossible. Two of the powerful pharaohs who established the New Kingdom in the mid-second millennium, Tuthmosis II (1512–1504) and Tuthmosis III (1504–1450) launched a campaign of conquest in Syria which extended their domains up to the Euphrates. At this point it is almost certain that the lands they ruled had already adopted the astrological practices developed at Babylon, and would have been familiar with the Mesopotamians' political cosmology. Although the empire collapsed under Akhenaten (1379–1362), control of part of Palestine and Syria was reasserted by Ramesses I, who came to the throne around 1319, and then lasted for around a century.

That the coming of the New Kingdom appears to have coincided with a cosmological revolution of which Akhenaten's reform was perhaps an extreme manifestation is also suggested by the fact that the planets also appear for the first time. Our earliest known portrayal of the planets (excluding Mars) is found in a painting in the tomb of Senmut, a high official in Queen Hatshepsut's court at Thebes around 1473 BCE. Other notable examples come from the tombs of the great imperial pharaohs Amenhotep III (c.1417–1379 BCE), Seti I (c.1319–1304 BCE), Ramesses II (1304–1237 BCE) and Ramesses III (c.1188–1156 BCE). The Egyptians knew the planets as 'stars that know no rest' and identified three (if not all) of them, Mars, Saturn and Jupiter, with Horus.[22] Jupiter was 'Horus who bounds the two lands' or 'Horus who illuminates the two lands' and, later, 'Horus who opens mystery', Saturn was 'Horus, bull of the sky' or just 'Horus the bull'. Mars was 'Horus of the horizon' or 'Horus the red', and while the last name is obviously purely descriptive, the first two suggest religious significance and all three suggest that they were aspects of the sun god – or, perhaps the universal god manifested in the sun. Pictorially, on the latest monuments, all three included some elements of a falcon's body. Mars, for example, might be a falcon with a human head or a serpent's tail, Saturn may be bull-headed with a human or falcon body and Jupiter might be completely falcon or have a human head.

One of Venus' names, 'Crosser' or 'Star which crosses', might refer to its habit, like Mercury of moving back and forth about the sun, but we cannot be sure. According to Parker, we cannot even be certain whether the Egyptians knew that Venus as morning and evening star was one body, although it is probable that they did by the end of the second millennium; nor do we know why they portrayed it as a heron. Later she was known as the 'Morning Star' and given human form, occasionally two-headed or two-faced and sometimes falcon-headed implying a link with Horus. Faulkner, however, argues from the Pyramid Texts which identify the pharaoh as both 'Morning Star' and 'Lone Star', that the former was Venus before dawn and the latter Venus after dusk.[23] Mercury's name, *Sbg(w)*, or *Sebeg(u)*, has not been translated, although an inscription of Ramesses VI (1148–1138 BCE): 'Set in the evening twilight, a god in the morning twilight' also points to a religious role, as well as to a recognition that the planet is a single body, in spite of its distinct evening and morning phases.[24] More importantly, though, the fact that the planet was auspicious at its heliacal rising

– just before dawn – and ominous at dusk, points to an undeniable divinatory role. It is one of the few indications we have of a possible planetary astrology in the late second millennium.

If we ask whether the Egyptians, prior to the Hellenistic period, before 331 BCE, used astrology, then the question largely depends on our meaning of the term. If we see astrology as the complex system for analysing past, present and future developed in Mesopotamia then, on present evidence, the answer should be no. Claims that the Egyptians possessed a sophisticated astrology tend to confuse pre-Ptolemaic Egypt with the introduction of astrology in the Hellenistic period.[25] However, if we take a liberal definition of astrology as being the attempt to communicate with the celestial deities, then the answer may be a considered yes. Ed Krupp points out that if the *akhet*, the horizon, was so important in Egyptian hieroglyphics and temple facades, some must have been watching it 'for signs of cosmic order'.[26] We know that dawn was the trigger for profound religious ritual, in which case Egyptian religion was hardly different to the later Christianity or Islam, and that the rising of Sirius must have been observed with great care for the regulation of the civil year. What we do not know, though, is whether the variations in horizon phenomena, which were to be so central to Mesopotamian astrology, were regarded as significant. Did it matter what colour the sun was when it rose, and was the nature of the preceding decan significant for the quality of the times? We may consider it likely that they were, but we do not know how. Were there astrologers? There was certainly a class of priest known as the *imy-wnwt*, variously translated as 'hour-watcher', 'observer' or 'astronomer'. One Eighteenth Dynasty (1550–1295 BCE) tomb, famous for its decorative scenes of daily life, belonged to a man called Nahkt whose titles included 'Scribe' and 'Hour watching priest of Amun'.[27] The chief priest of Heliopolis' titles, 'Chief of the secrets of heaven', of 'Chief of the astronomers' in a modern translation, and his cloak of stars, imply that he was certainly more than a mere time-keeper and that he held a crucial role in interpreting the heavens as well as timing them.

We know that Imhotep, the Middle Kingdom priest was known as the 'Chief of the observers',[28] but we do not know whether he watched for the sun, the stars or both, or whether he was concerned solely with the time they rose, or drew conclusions based on their varying appearances. If he did the latter then he was, in our terms, an astrologer. If he was obliged only to time religious ceremonies then we would normally consider him a time-keeper or calendar-maker, though we should remember that in medieval and Renaissance Europe one of the astrologers' principal activities was to elect auspicious moments for important events, a function they retain in modern Hinduism. The distinction between what is and what is not astrological is a fluid one.

There are arguments, based on the fact that Egypt was a relatively secure society, that it was unlikely to have developed a form of astrology: if the future was certain, the theory runs, what is the point in predicting it, in contrast to the insecure Mesopotamians' supposed obsession with the future?[29] Thus Gregg de Young concludes cautiously that 'in general, it seems that the Egyptians were less likely than other ancient peoples to perceive evil omens in celestial events ... We can only speculate what the Egyptian scribes might have said in interpreting a lunar eclipse'.[30]

There is a school of thought which attributes the origins of all Western astrology to the Egyptians, and it is difficult to separate the idea that this was so from the belief that it should be so. There is a degree of confusion due to the fact that the Greeks and Romans believed that astrology was devised by the seventh-century BCE Pharaoh Nechepso and his priest, Petosiris (who, in fact lived much later), though the textbook which bears their name was probably composed around 150 BCE.[31] There were two kings on whom Nechepso might have been based. The first, Neko I, was placed on the throne as a challenge to the existing pharaoh, the Ethiopian Tanwetamani, by the Assyrian Emperor Esarhaddon, though he was a puppet who never exerted undisputed power. His grandson, Neko II (609–594) was also an Assyrian ally, and was notable for his attempt to build the first 'Suez canal'. He also extended Egyptian rule into northern Syria where his imperial ambitions brought him into direct conflict with the resurgent Babylonians under Nebuchadnezzar. He was driven back after suffering a defeat at the great battle of Carchemish in 605.[32] Such details aside, there is no reason, from the astrological standpoint, why the authors of the second-century text should have used either Neko, grandfather or grandson, as the model for Nechepso, except for the Assyrian connection. The obvious inference is that some tradition was preserved of Neko I or II having introduced astrology from the Assyrian court to the Egyptian.

Although the actual Assyrian occupation of Egypt in 671–651 BCE was brief, the Emperor Esarhaddon, was receiving constant advice from his astrologers; not only does the bulk of the astrologers' reports and letters from Babylon date from Esarhaddon's reign, but a very large amount dates from 670 and 669, the two years after he struck Egypt with massive force.[33] After 1,000 years of intermittent military contact the Egyptians must have had no knowledge of Babylonian practices, even if they saw no need to imitate them. Yet, the Assyrians commanded the mightiest military machine of the time and were using astrology on a daily basis in order to direct their affairs. It has to be considered likely that any monarch who was both their ally and wished to emulate their success, would take an interest in the means by which they conquered and maintained their dominions, in other words, astrology, the peculiar code by which the Assyrians ascertained their deities' wishes and maintained the harmony of their lands with the heavens

Reasonable arguments for the Egyptian origins of Western astrology are made on the grounds that, as the country's religion depended so much on the perceived intimacy between divinity and celestial phenomena, as well as the timing of some of those phenomena, it can be argued that those phenomena were used to divine the gods' and goddesses' wishes.[34] What we are lacking in the extant Egyptian material, though, is the corpus of prognostications from the stars that we should really consider an essential part of astrology.

The only textual confirmation that the hour-watchers might have been astrologers, dates from the early Ptolemaic period. A statue of the hour-watcher and astronomer (*wnwnw*) Senty, perhaps from the third or second centuries BCE, describes his duties as including 'announcing to man his future, telling him about his youth and death', as well as assessing the right time to conduct important rituals, keep the calendar and observe the stars.[35] An inscription on the statue of one of Senty's colleagues, Harkhebi, a priest of Selket (or Serket), the scorpion goddess, details his duties:

> Hereditary prince and count, sole companion, wise in the sacred writings, who observes everything observable in heaven and earth, clear-eyed in observing the stars, among which there is no erring; who announces rising and setting at their times, with the gods who foretell the future, for which he purified himself when Akh (one of the decans) rose heliacally beside Benu (Venus) from earth and he contented the lands with his utterances (predictions?); who observes the culmination of every star in the sky, who knows the heliacal risings of every ... in a good year, and who foretells the heliacal rising of Sothis at the beginning of the year. He observes her (Sothis) on the day of her first festival, knowledgeable in her course at the times of designating therein, observing what she does daily, all that she has foretold is in his charge; knowing the northing and southing of the sun, announcing all its wonders (omina?) and appointing for them a time (?), he declares when they have occurred, coming at their times; who divides the hours for the two times (day and night) without going into error at night ... knowledgeable in everything which is seen in the sky, for which he has waited, skilled with respect to their conjunction(s) and their regular movement(s); who does not disclose (anything) at all after judgment, discreet with all he has seen.[36]

The text informs us that Harkhebi was required both to watch the heavens very closely in order to arrange sacred festivals and to forecast the future. Forecasting the future was itself a sacred act – hence he purified himself at the appropriate moment – when Venus rose with Akh. He was also a close and trusted adviser of the king. His religious and political functions were the same as those of a Babylonian astrologer even if his divinatory techniques were different. Although Egypt was by then under Greek rule, attempting to discern the influence of Graeco-Roman astrology in Senty's duties is unconvincing:[37] it was Graeco-Roman astrology that borrowed from Egypt. Similarly, the suggestion that the 'astrological flavouring' of Harkhebi's text is Babylonian in origin has no basis;[38] there is nothing in the inscription particular to Babylonian astrology. This is not to say that neither man had been influenced by either Babylonian or Greek practices, only that the attempt to claim that this was so on the basis of the inscriptions on their statues is unsustainable and may have more to do with the attempt to preserve the theory that there was no native astrology in pharaonic Egypt.

At present, our earliest conclusive evidence of the exchange of astronomical and astrological ideas between Egypt and the east dates from the Persian period, after the conquest by the Persian Emperor Cambyses in 525 BCE. There was a constant cultural exchange over the entire empire over the following century, bringing Ionian Greeks into contact with Indians and Babylonians, and Egyptians into contact with both, anticipating the similar mixing of cultures after Alexander's conquests, 200 years later. A vivid illustration is provided by the Greek philosopher Pythagoras, one of the most influential figures in what was to become Western mysticism, who, tradition holds, studied in Babylon, Egypt and with the druids of Gaul. There is no reason to doubt such claims – all he had to do was hitch a ride with some merchants. And he was born in around 586 BCE, decades before the Persian ascendancy.

It is known that Egyptian priests visited Persia. We know of one, Udjeharresnet, who was ordered by Darius I (521–486 BCE) to return to Egypt and reform the Houses of Life, the temple centres in which religious and medical texts were written: it may have been through him that Babylonian astrological ideas first reached Egypt.[39] We have two texts surviving in copies from the Roman period, the second or third centuries CE, but which clearly date to the fifth or sixth centuries BCE.[40] The first, Text A, which has survived only in fragments, is a compendium of predictions based on eclipses of the sun and moon consisting of two systems, I and II. That it fails to mention Egyptian constellations suggests that it is not native and that it does not mention the Babylonian zodiac indicates that it is probably derived from texts dating to the sixth century. Although there is no exact comparison with any Babylonian system, the similarities are sufficient to suggest a derivation from eclipse omens contained in the *Enuma Anu Enlil*, dating from the eight century BCE, and old Babylonian eclipse tablets dating back to perhaps 1700 BCE.[41] The surviving omens, which are all from system II, read remarkably like Babylonian omens, structured clearly with an 'if' clause and a 'then' clause. For example the most complete passage reads:

> If the sun be eclipsed in [I Peret], since the month belongs to the Amorite, it means: the chief [of the Amorite shall ...] occur in the entire land.[42]

An example of a lunar eclipse omen contains slightly more information:

> If [the moon be eclipsed in II Shimu, (since) the month belongs to <Egypt>] it [means]: The chief of the land named shall be captured. The army shall fall to [battle]-weapo[ns].[43]

Our surviving copies of Texts A and B, dated to the second or third centuries CE, were used in a major astrological compendium from the fifth-century CE, Hephaistio of Thebes' *Apotelematics*. Although Hephaistio's rules for the interpretation of eclipses are applied to the zodiac, and contain elements of Babylonian astrology not included in our surviving copies of Texts A and B, such as the winds, it is clear that they are an adaptation of the Egyptian system – and also that they show significant disagreement with the Greek canon on eclipse interpretation as set out by Ptolemy in the second century CE. Hephaistio recorded that, 'if the Sun has undergone eclipse in the first hour in Sagittarius, the Cretan tribe will have war'.[44] Hephaistio would have perhaps been relying on second-century CE copies of the second-century BCE texts by Nechepso and Petosiris, the 'ancient Egyptians' who he credits as his source, themselves copies of perhaps sixth-century BCE Egyptian adaptations of Babylonian originals. He is dealing with a written tradition which may by then have been around 2,000 years old.

It is clear though, that by the time Text B was written, there were competing traditions (unless these are later insertions). Text B concerns other material familiar from Babylonian originals: about 20 omens derived from happenings in or near the disc of the full moon such as its colour and conjunctions with other stars. A typical extract reads:

> Another. If you see the disk coloured completely, its scent (?) red downward in it, there being one black disk on its right and another black disk on its left, [you are to] say about it: Enmity shall happen (in) [the entire land] – another version: the land of Egypt – and king shall approach king [...] Great fighting shall happen (in) Egypt. Barley and emmer (shall) be plentiful and every harvest likewise with respect to every ploughing and every field (in) the entire land. Good things and satisfaction shall occur everywhere, so that they quarrel, they drink ... and they eat the knife.[45]

In the fifth century Hephaistio gave the rules laid down by Nechepso and Petosiris for interpreting the colour of the moon. He tells us that:

> The ancient Egyptians recorded the effects that arise from eclipses, most of which we mention briefly as follows. For total eclipses, the colour black signifies the death of the ruler and depression and famine and change: red, affliction of the land; whitish, famine and death for the herds; purple, war and famine; gold-like, pestilence and death.[46]

We also have evidence from shortly before Alexander's invasion in 332/1 BCE, that the decans had astrological meanings. We also know that the decans were incorporated into both Hellenistic-Egyptian and Indian horoscopic astrology (the latter as 'drekkana') after 300 BCE and were to be particularly significant in medieval and Renaissance European astrology where, as one of the five 'essential dignities', they were capable of revealing the strength of a particular planet and hence the likely outcome of the events it signified. In the Hermetic astrology of the first century BCE, they maintained their early significance, regulating the motion of the planets on behalf of the fixed stars, and 'holding all things together and watching over the good order of all things', including of course, human history: 'The force which works in all events that befall men collectively comes from the decans, for instance, overthrows of kingdoms, revolts of cities, famines, pestilences, overflowings of the sea, earthquakes'.[47] In the Hermetic cosmic state, the decans acted as the supreme administrative tier, implementing divine decisions in earth, using the seven planets as their intermediaries, though they had by now become divorced from the rising stars, and were divisions of the zodiac signs into three.[48] Their last appearance in the classical world is in the Hymn to the Sun written by the Roman Emperor Julian in 362 CE, where they are apparently connected to the three ways of Ea, Anu and Enlil, the Babylonian division of the sky into three, suggesting a fusion of Egyptian and Babylonian traditions.[49]

The textual evidence for the hour-watchers, the omens from Hephaistio, and the meanings ascribed to the decans are all frustratingly late. Whether the hour-watchers had the roles outlined for Harkhebi in the Old Kingdom, we have no idea. And we have no more clues as to whether the Old Kingdom decans possessed individual meanings, let alone those evident in the texts of the first century BCE, nor whether the omens preserved by Hephaistio include elements of an indigenous astrology which might have predated the Persian invasion. But we do know where the Egyptians influenced the development of astrology; the oral traditions of the temples, their solar religion, notions of cosmic order, belief that their society was a model of heaven and that the soul may travel to the stars all played their part in shaping the astrology of the Greek and Roman worlds.

8

The Hebrews: Prophets and Planets

'And on that day,' says the Lord God, 'I will make the sun go
down at noon, and darken the earth in broad daylight'.[1]

The most complex cosmologies in the ancient Middle East 3,000 years ago
were those of Egypt and Mesopotamia. Perched between these two societies,
and frequently fought over by them, was the narrow strip which came to be,
perhaps more than other, associated with heaven – the Holy Land, Palestine,
the cradle of three of the major religious traditions of the modern world.
The earliest archaeological evidence that the people of Palestine shared their
Egyptian and Mesopotamian neighbours' fascination with the sky dates from
the Neolithic period, around 5500 to 4500 BCE.[2] A large, recently excavated,
apparently religious, complex in the Negev Desert which is dated to around 4700
to 4200 BCE, at least 1,000 years before Newgrange, appears to have been generally
oriented to the cardinal points – north, south, east and west – and containing a
'cult area' in the westernmost corner, which would therefore be inclined to the
setting sun. Sixteen pointed standing stones suggest that megalithic culture, while
so distinctive in north-western Europe, may have extended across the Middle East
but could, in many cases, have been obscured by later development. There are
though, surviving examples of standing-stone complexes, positioned in various
significant alignments, such as to the cardinal points, and in association with
symbols such as stars and apparently lunar crescents as late as 1600 BCE at Hazor
in northern Israel, and Gezer. Visual evidence further supports the proposition
that the Stone and Bronze Age religion of the area was strongly celestial. A wall
painting at a site just to the east of the River Jordan, and which dates from the
Chalcolithic period, around 4500 to 3500 BCE, displays an eight-pointed star
1.84m in diameter. That the Mesopotamians were representing Inanna, goddess
of the planet Venus, as an eight-pointed star in the third millennium, suggests
that this is also a symbol for the planet. And, if so, that the star was surrounded by
images of masks, animals and temples may testify to the existence of a profound
religious sensibility around the planet's brilliant appearance at dawn and dusk.
That other images showed the sun and moon rising above mountains suggests
the horizon was being watched for significant solar and lunar phases exactly as
at Stonehenge. There is also plentiful evidence of the occupation of 'high places'
in the second millennium BCE (and well into the first) – the open-air, hilltop
ritual sites which were to be repeatedly denounced by the prophets and which,
in the first century BCE, were, according to the Roman writer Cicero, bases for

astrological observation.[3] Whether they were used for celestial observation during the Stone Age is not attested, but hilltop sacred sites have an obvious astronomical purpose. That one such site, dated to the second millennium, was Megiddo, which lends its name to the mythical battle, Armageddon, is suggestive of the intimate links between apocalyptic beliefs and crises in the sky. One passage, from much later, in Judges, which may echo the mentality of the builders of the site at Megiddo, suggests that the stars coordinated with human society, when they fought a heavenly war alongside the struggle between the Jews and the Canaanites, a conflict which actually included a battle at Megiddo. The text, which anticipates the use of apocalyptic omens later in the Old Testament, reports that 'From heaven fought the stars. From their courses they fought against Sisera.'[4]

The form of distinctive monotheism and religious nationalism which evolved in this area during the first half of the first millennium eventually developed into the early phases of Judaism. The historical and prophetic books of the Old Testament provide evidence for how this religion emerged in reaction both to foreign domination and to competing ideologies in their native traditions, asserting its distinctiveness in part by attacking its oppressors' and enemies' alien cosmologies. Eventually, the biblical prophets' fierce loyalty to the god Yahweh, and their angry denunciation of astral religion and Babylonian astrologers, was to find its way into early Judaism and Christianity and has decisively shaped Western attitudes, including scientific opinions, to the heavens to the present day. The prophets' version of religious thought and practice is often taken as the norm yet, if we examine the practice of Jewish society as a whole, a different picture emerges. We find a culture which shared the astral religion of its neighbours and gradually absorbed the astrology coming from the north, from the Hittites and Syrians; the prophets represented only one strand in Jewish society which emerges as pluralistic, frequently divided and often at war with itself. Although, it is clear that certain beliefs were imported, we should not imagine that early Jewish religion was distinctive from indigenous Canaanite beliefs. The latest scholarship suggests that they were one and the same, that Jewish religion shared the polytheistic, astral inclinations of Near Eastern cosmology in general.[5] Furthermore, the polytheistic tradition survived down to the last centuries BCE, by which time gods had been accommodated to monotheism and converted into angels, as in the apocryphal second-century BCE text, *1 Enoch*.

There were two rival cosmologies within Jewish culture. In the first, which has come down to us as the standard model, the one supreme God was simultaneously the creator of the stars and could be represented, quite possibly under Egyptian influence, as the sun.[6] But worship of, or divination from, the stars was forbidden. It was only in the sixth century BCE that the prophets began to deny the existence of other gods, and the doctrine of the existence of only one God, emerged. In the second, which thrived in the independent Jewish states from the tenth century BCE until the final conquest by Babylon in the sixth century, there was a widespread adoption of Mesopotamian astrology and astral worship. This model revived from around the third century onwards and, by the first century BCE we find the adoption of Babylonian astrological texts to fit Jewish models and, later, the incorporation of zodiacs in synagogue design. The entire process is extremely difficult to trace, partly because our major literary source, the Old Testament, survives only in versions which were finalized after the captivity in Babylon from 586 to 539 BCE. There are also other questions of cultural transmission and the direct experience of first Babylonian and then Persian religious beliefs, decisively coloured prophetic cosmology, and we can never be sure how far this process obscures earlier beliefs. It does seem, though, that the Old Testament represents a narrow strand of Jewish thought, and the practices and beliefs condemned by the prophets may have been favoured by the majority.

We can construct a picture of the physical cosmos from various Old Testament passages. The universe was divided into three parts: heaven, earth, and underworld, with the sky as a hard dome with storehouses for rain, snow and hail on either side. Where the dome met the earth, it rested on pillars, or mountains, which had roots extending deep into the earth. The earth itself was a flat disc, resting on water, which explained where springs came from.[7] The totality of the universe is represented by the phrase *shamayim ve-aretz*, 'heaven and earth'. *Olam*, which represents 'world' or 'universe' in rabbinic literature, means 'long-time' or, by extension, 'eternity' in the Bible and up to c.500 CE, God is spoken of as *melekh ha-olam*, 'King of the universe', or 'King of eternity'.[8] Traces of this all-powerful order, though, are found in the earliest sources. The political hierarchy in ancient Israel in the first millennium BCE functioned much like that of Mesopotamia: it was a cosmic state in which God and the celestial bureaucracy of angels occupied a superior place to humanity, with the animals and the natural world below. This much is evident from God's declaration in the creation myth: 'Let us make man in our image, after our likeness; and let them have dominion over the fish of the air, and over the cattle, and over all the earth, and over every creeping thing that creeps upon the earth'.[9] This, of course, is the classic manifesto of Christian political cosmology in which, while the earth exists to be disposed of by humanity at will, ultimate political power resides with God, the invisible, supernatural overlord. And so the superiority of Israelite political cosmology, in its biblical form, was asserted over all its rivals.

The continuity in many cosmological ideas from the earliest Hebrew tradition at the end of the second millennium, down to the Christianity of the first century, reflects that of Mesopotamia. As in Babylonian cosmic geography, in which all earthly things were copies of heavenly models, the key institutions of the earthly state were modelled on heavenly originals; the anonymous first-century CE author of the Epistle to the Hebrews described the temple in Jerusalem as a copy of heaven exactly as the Esagila, the home of Marduk in Babylon, was a representation of a heavenly original.[10] That early Hebrew cosmology drew on Mesopotamian originals is well attested.[11] The greatest example, of course, was the transposition of the deluge narrative in the Epic of Gilgamesh to Noah's flood.

The core cosmological–theological doctrine of the Jewish prophets was the physical location of one all-powerful god in the sky. He was, like the Mesopotamian deity Anu, a sky god. As Isaiah put it: 'heaven is my throne and the earth is my footstool'.[12] In later biblical tradition Yahweh himself, the supreme creator god, exerted total authority without the restraining influences suffered by Anu, Ea, Adad, Enlil, Marduk and Assur, the chief gods of Sumer, Akkad, Babylon and Assyria. It is clear that Mesopotamian religious eclecticism – the habit of recognizing all male creator gods as essentially equal – supported the democratic traditions of the pre-monarchical primitive democracy. Hebrew henotheism, on the other hand, banned the worship of other gods (while not denying their existence) and allowed for no democracy in heaven.[13] However, far from replacing the individual gods of Mesopotamia, Yahweh was a synthesis of their different functions. The prophets' problem was one of nationalism more than theology. It was not that other gods did not exist, simply that they should not be worshipped. Therefore, for the strict Yahwists, the Hebrew God, Yahweh had to fulfil the functions of every other god, which is presumably why he was thought to be more powerful than his rivals.

Like Anu, the Sumerian sky god, Yahweh lived within his own creation, yet was in some senses above it. As in Mesopotamia, the prophets maintained the notion of the physical world as a medium through which divine intentions were made known, and dialogue with humanity initiated. The movement of the stars was perceived as a language, as revealing the word of God. As we read in the Psalms: 'The heavens are telling the glory of God, and the firmament proclaims his handiwork'.[14] Yet Yahweh also appeared as the god of the sun, the most important of the stars. He moved the sun and stars, but he also shone like the sun.[15] According to Habakkuk, 'his glory covered the heavens, and the earth was full of his praise. His brightness was like the light, rays flashed from his hand.'[16] For the author of *1 Enoch*, in the second century BCE, the throne of god was 'like the shining sun'.[17] He was thus exactly identical to the Egyptian god Amon-Re who was both supreme creator and represented by the sun-disc, at once above creation and within it, simultaneously transcendent and immanent.[18]

But, in common with Egyptian deities such as Atum or Nun, the father of the gods, Yahweh was the creator of the stars rather than one of them; Amos tells us that he made the Pleiades and Orion.[19] The evolutionary process which took place in Jewish religion over the first millennium BCE was focused on the emergence of one particular point of view in which the role of the creator Yahweh, was privileged over all other gods and goddesses. This tendency has come to be seen as normative of Israelite religion, whereas the historical sources make it clear that it represented only one school of thought. If Jewish religion was the religion practised by the Jews then, in its popular form, it relied heavily on the standard astral theology of Mesopotamia and the Near East. It is clear that astral religion and astrology were a consistent feature of Jewish life and religion from earliest times.[20]

The origins of Jewish monotheism itself are obscure.[21] An Egyptian ancestry was identified by James Breasted and enthusiastically taken up and popularized by Freud in 1939 in his *Moses and Monotheism*.[22] Briefly, the theory holds that, during their period of slavery in Egypt, the Jews adopted Akhenaten's solar monotheism and took it back to Palestine with them after the exodus. The problem with this argument, of course, is that it depends on the literal historicity of the captivity, and so it is no longer taken seriously. However, the direct link between Jewish slaves and a sun-worshipping pharaoh is not necessary for there to be some connection. Transmission could easily have been possible via the normal travelling and trading links. Besides, the common assumption that Akhenaten's religious reform was uniquely monotheistic ignores the essential monotheism which lies at the heart of many apparently polytheistic systems, that the host of lesser gods and goddesses can be seen as manifestations of the one creator. But, then, neither do we need any evidence of transmission; it is quite normal for the sun to be nominated as the supreme deity, and an Egyptian influence is not necessary.

The entire dispute between monotheism and polytheism is largely the consequence of Christianity's – and Judaism's – political need to assert itself over all other religions, and to find legitimate, often retrospectively applied, theological reasons to do so; it is difficult, if not impossible, to argue that medieval Catholicism, with all its saints and angels, was any less polytheistic or more monotheistic than, say, Hinduism, with its thousands of minor deities. Most Middle Eastern cultures tended to practise some form of syncretism; they adopted each other's deities, either on theological grounds – they recognized their essential similarity regardless of their different names – or pragmatic – the precautionary principle dictated that it was safer to respect all known deities and one god was not necessarily entirely separate from another. Thus, Enlil, the originator of earthly kingship, played a role which tended to merge with that of Marduk, the supreme king, who was himself venerated as the 'Enlil of the gods'.[23]

However, the evidence for some connection between biblical monotheism and Egyptian solar religion, particularly to Akhenaten's reforms is tantalizing, especially as there is no need to assume the literal truth of the captivity or exodus. The Egyptians conquered Palestine around 1483 BCE and controlled it for 100 years until a rebellion which actually took place during Akhenaten's reign, between *c.*1379 and 1362. The Egyptians re-occupied the area under Seti I, who reigned from *c.*1319 to 1304, and controlled the area for the next century, until about 1200 BCE. The iconography of Canaanite deities in the late second millennium reflects the collision of Egyptian with Mesopotamian culture, and statues of gods and goddesses survive in the distinctive styles of both societies, with the familiar headdresses of the former or the curly hair of the latter. We have to assume that, where styles of religious imagery travel, so do notions of theological cosmology, of gods, goddesses and their relationship to the stars.[24]

The prolonged struggle between the monotheistic prophets and polytheistic 'idol worshippers', which is such a feature of Old Testament history, may be portrayed as the unresolved struggle between Egyptian and Babylonian cosmologies, between the monotheistic elements of the former and the astral theology of the latter. That there was a permanent tension between the nationalist cult of Yahweh and the more liberal, eclectic, instincts which frequently domi-nated the royal household is beyond doubt. Yet the two cosmologies are not entirely incompatible, and that of the prophets provides its own theological path to the practice of astrology; a sacred calendar based strictly on exact observations of the sun and moon, simple celestial omens and a social structure organized to reflect the 12 months of the year, in other words, the passage of the sun through one life cycle.

It was said of Yahweh that 'he changes times and seasons, he removes kings and sets up kings'.[25] This passage, with its tone reflective of Sumerian political theory, occurs in Daniel, and was therefore written after the release from the Babylonian captivity, most likely in the mid-second century BCE, but the same idea occurs in earlier texts. It implies that political life operates according to the same laws of growth and decay as any other realm in the cosmic state. Strict Yahwist monotheism was built largely on one basic law: that disobedience to Yahweh would be punished and obedience rewarded.

The fundamental fact of Hebrew ritual life was the observation of the solar and lunar cycles. Passover, the most important ritual moment of the year, commenced as the full moon rose over the eastern horizon on the 14th day of the first month, corresponding to Nisan in the Babylonian calendar.[26] A second major seven-day festival was held in the autumn, commencing on the 15th day of the seventh month, which corresponded to the full moon in the month of Tishri, which also takes its name from the Babylonian month.[27] The use of the Babylonian calendar is in itself sufficient evidence of the extensive borrowing from Mesopotamian culture. The preparations for each festival began on the 10th of the month, with strict observances proceeding for 7 days after the full moon, making a total of 12 days, exactly as in the Akitu. Whereas the Babylonian festival was held at the new moon, the Hebrew ritual hinged around the full moon; the Babylonian ritual celebrated Marduk's death and resurrection, while the Hebrew, carrying overtones of death and resurrection of the people, saw Yahweh triumphant.[28] Each festival represented a ritual return to the beginning of time, a conscious and cyclical return to the primaeval order, before history became disrupted by disorder.[29] Both major annual festivals, while probably originally agricultural, located the Israelites and their god within history and nature. The spring festival, focusing on the Passover, marked the connection with the major point in Israelite history: the liberation from Egypt, which signified the collective national rebirth of nature after winter. The autumn festival was an anchor to the agricultural year, to seasonal rather than historical cycles. Such fine distinctions aside, though, the parallels between the Babylonian and biblical festivals are sufficient to argue for Yahweh as a form of Marduk, and that biblical monotheism may have emerged in the east as much as the west. Even Tammuz, Inanna's dead lover, was worshipped at the temple in Jerusalem by Israelite women, at least if Ezekiel's denunciation of what he regarded as an abomination can be believed.[30] Evidence of transmission is clear, but the significance of the festival for individuals is more significant. They enabled the participants to become an active co-creator in the unfolding cosmic drama, shaping the future via an encounter with God's divine law, or the gods, engaging with the heavens as a manifestation of the perfect order. As God repeatedly declares in Genesis 1, his creation was good.

As in Babylon, the ritual year marked the integration of history and individual, cosmos and state, creation and society, in an ever-repeating pattern. The purpose of the Yahweh cult was to honour the creator by ensuring human participation in the preservation of the cyclic seasons of nature, thus ensuring their continuation into the future. For the believer history must be managed, and the means whereby this might be accomplished lay in obedience to the cosmic order and, if the specified rituals were actively observed, the survival of the state would be guaranteed for another year. Yahweh, it was hoped, would be encouraged to keep his promise to Noah that 'while the earth remains, seedtime and harvest, cold and heat, summer and winter, day and night, shall not cease' and if, for any reason, the festivals were not kept, it would be the nation of Israel that would cease.[31] The preservation of order was the supreme requirement of both individual and state and explains why the prophets resisted and demonized Babylonian planetary astrology. For the Babylonians the endless variations in planetary movements and appearance represented a chance to negotiate and modify the fixed order embodied in solar and lunar cycles, but in the eyes of the prophets such variety undermined that divine order. Planetary anarchy represented not a path to a better future but a dire warning of disintegration. The worst crime that any star could commit, exactly as in Babylon, was to fail 'to come out at the proper time', as the second-century BCE *1 Enoch* put it.[32] Any star which acted independently of Yahweh thus broke the vital lines of communication between the celestial king and his agents, the kings on earth, as well as with the people themselves.

Yet, the situation was not really quite so simple. The problem appears to have arisen only if a planet defied God's order. While this order was revealed to humanity via the regular cycles of the sun and moon, and the ritual calendar, his intentions were communicated daily with his prophets and anyone else who cared to listen through omens which included celestial 'signs and wonders'.[33] This form of rudimentary astrology occurs in most of the prophetic works. One of the biblical prophets' major concerns was the coming of the 'Day of Yahweh', God's promised destruction of all those evil people who had slipped from his true path and his subsequent creation of a new world. All apocalyptic Christianity down to the present day takes its cue ultimately from the prophets, Ezekiel, Isaiah, Amos and the rest, so its power is as strong as ever, even if it often takes secular forms. The notion that the world can die and be reborn is one of the great motivating engines of Western society. The Israelite God, exactly like his Mesopotamian counterparts, spoke through omens, and the question of whether he was part of the natural environment, or above and apart from it, is less important than the fact that he was expected to announce coming events through natural omens, including celestial ones. One verse points to eclipses as the main warning sign: ' "And on that day," says the Lord God, "I will make the sun go down at noon, and darken the earth in broad daylight" ', though 'falling' stars, perhaps meteorites or comets, also feature.[34] Such texts were to provide the justification for an entire strand of astrology which continued into the modern period. Within this context it is not surprising to find the boundary between watching for omens and veneration of the sun itself becoming blurred. When God was compared to the sun and moon, worshippers in the temple hailed the rising sun, as they would have done in Egypt, it becomes quite plausible that the temple was actually constructed by Solomon in response to a solar eclipse, to thank God for sparing his children.[35]

The representation of Hebrew society itself as a manifestation of the solar cycle occurs first in Joseph's famous dream, in which the sun and moon, together with 11 stars, bow down to him, the twelfth.[36] The implication is quite clear: Joseph's brothers were stars, or might be compared to stars. Simply, then, the 12 tribes are stars, though whether this is a metaphor for the 12 months or whether they were identified with constellations we do not know: the explicit identification of the tribes with the zodiac signs occurs much later – after the first century CE. The notion of a spatial division into twelve-ness followed the Children of Israel from their exile in Egypt. The first oasis reached by the Israelites after the crossing of the Red Sea, was Elim, a settlement, we read, which contained 12 springs and 70 palm trees.[37]

The division of the land conquered by the Israelites after the exodus into 12 sections, one for each tribe, was a means of organizing political geography as a mirror of the celestial cosmic state. Both, however, are directly adapted from the Israelites' camp outlined in Numbers, in which the tribes were arranged in a square of four groups of three. The most important section, including Moses and Aaron was, with the tabernacle and the 'tent of meeting', aligned towards the sunrise. Eventually this became the model for the New Jerusalem of Revelation.[38] Nor was it unique. The system of the division of administrative units into 12 occurred elsewhere, for example, in fifth-century Athens and in northern Italy, where Etruscan culture was organized into 12 cities as 'a religious rather than a political union'.[39]

The actual worship of the sun was denounced in Ezekiel, who describes men standing in the temple, venerating the east, though he was living in Babylon and attacking a practice which he assumed had provoked God into surrendering his people to the Babylonian captivity.[40] It is not exactly clear why he should be surprised that devout Jews should gaze at the sun; the Sabbath, the most holy of days, always began 'at the moment that the sun's disc stands distant from the gate [of the Temple] by the length of its own diameter'.[41] That worship 'of the sun or the moon or any of the host of heaven' was considered a serious problem was reflected in its prohibition in Deuteronomy, the proscribed penalty for conviction on the evidence of two witnesses being death by stoning.[42] There is an allusion to a possible solar – or lunar – ritual in Job, which we know of through the prophet's condemnation: 'if I have looked at the sun when it shone, or the moon moving in splendour, and my heart has been secretly enticed, and my mouth has kissed my hand'.[43] If Yahweh had indeed been worshipped as the sun, this could explain later accounts of the worship of Saturn during the long period in the wilderness, when the Children of Israel are said to have wandered in Sinai following the exodus. Saturn, referred to as Kaiwan, Kiyyun or Rephan, was described by Amos as 'the star of your god', prompting comparison with Babylon, where Saturn was described as the star of the sun.[44]

The second of the Jewish cosmologies, incorporating Mesopotamian astral theology, was favoured at the court of the legendary King Solomon, who reigned from 970 to 931. There is also no direct evidence that astrology should not have been practised at his court – but every reason to assume that it was if he regarded himself as a great king. To consult the stars was what kings did if they were to receive divine instructions which is, of course, why the prophets condemned the practice. Astrological texts derived from Babylonian material and dating from the fourteenth to the thirteenth centuries BCE have been excavated at Ugarit, on the Lebanese coast, by far the most important commercial centre on the eastern Mediterranean coast, so they could easily have reached Jerusalem.[45]

Solomon favoured polytheism, at least in the last years of his reign, as did his wives, who included Egyptian and Hittite princesses; amongst the altars he set up was one to Venus as the Sidonian Ashtoreth.[46] As 'Lucifer', the light-bearer, Venus was detested by the prophets: Isaiah, taunting the king of Babylon, perhaps addressing him as Marduk, chief of the divine assembly, and certainly using the imagery of Ishtar, declared:

> How are you fallen from heaven,
> O Day Star, son of Dawn!
> How you are cut down to the ground,
> You who laid the nations low!
> You said in your heart,
> 'I will ascend to heaven;
> above the stars of God
> I will set my throne on high;
> I will sit on the mount of assembly in the far north;
> I will ascend above the heights of the clouds,
> I will make myself like the Most High.'
> But you are brought down to Sheol, to the depths of the Pit.[47]

This passage was to become the model for the defeat of Satan in Revelation, condemned as he was to lie in a pit for 1,000 years after Christ's second coming.[48] Furious with Solomon, God decided to punish the Hebrews by dividing the kingdom in two. The crisis erupted when Rehoboam, Solomon's son and designated successor, on hearing pleas to abandon his father's oppressive policies, announced that he was going to intensify them. In the resulting unrest Jeroboam, who had been in exile in Egypt, returned in 931 to become the founder of Israel, consisting of ten tribes with its capital at Samaria.

Rehoboam was left as the ruler of the smaller southern kingdom, Judah. The split was bitter and the Israelite state was involved in sporadic wars with Judah, which was reduced to vassal status by Joash (798–782 BCE), as well as with its powerful northern neighbours, Syria and Assyria. Divine punishment made no difference to political policy and, while Rehoboam followed Solomon in favouring astral polytheism in Judah, Jeroboam also established it as the state religion of Israel as a deliberate act of policy. His reasons were purely pragmatic. He calculated that by undermining the power of the temple in Jerusalem, which remained under Rehoboam's control, he could eat away further at his rival's power base, a scheme which suggests that astral worship, which he was proposing as an alternative, was the popular religion of the time. To counter the power of the temple, Jeroboam set up a magnificent shrine with two gold calves, and instituted a national festival on the 15th day of the eighth month, Marcheshvan corresponding to the full moon in Taurus.[49] The coincidence of the calves and the festival suggests that the calves may have been Taurean symbols; though, with Egyptian influences in mind, he may have been thinking of the goddess Hathor. More obvious though, is the Canaanite connection; the bull was the traditional image of the Western Semitic god El. From then on, in both Judah and Israel, astral religion was likely a major component of the royal religious system, with the prophets confined to a protesting role, leading reform movements, which were often frustrated but occasionally successful, as when Elisha encouraged the general Jehu to lead a rebellion in 841.

Even though the prophets Amos and Hosea denounced the decadence and corruption of the powerful Jeroboam II (783–748 BCE), such reformers gradually lost ground to the astral theologians. Astral religion appears to have been consistently popular amongst the ruling class. Typical was Zechariah, king of Israel for just one year (754–753 BCE), who 'did what was evil in the sight of the Lord', code for 'worshipped other gods'.[50] The end came for Israel around 725/3, when Hoshea rebelled against his overlord, the Assyrian emperor Shalmaneser V (725–722), who deposed him and annexed the kingdom. As any restraining prophetic influence was effectively removed, traditional polytheism flourished. The Israelites, we read, constructed altars on 'high places', worshipped 'all the host of heaven', practised sorcery and divination and sacrificed their children. They also adopted various planetary gods as city-rulers: 'The men of Cuth', for example, made Nergal, the Babylonian Mars, their tutelary deity.[51]

In Judah the situation was much the same, although the Yahwist prophets seem to have had more influence in and around Jerusalem where the temple, their power base, was located. It was in Judah that the most influential denunciation of astrologers was issued by Isaiah. In a text still cited regularly by Christian opponents of astrology, he declared,

You are wearied with your many counsels;
let them stand forth and save you,
those who divide the heavens,
who gaze at the stars,
who at the new moons predict
what shall befall you.
Behold, they are like stubble,
the fire consumes them;
they cannot deliver themselves
from the power of the flame.[52]

Although some kings, such as Rehoboam's immediate successor, Asa (911–871), attacked astral religion, their task was an uphill one. Asa had to exile his grandmother, Maacah, who had commissioned a particularly 'abominable' image of Asherah, a version of Ishtar as queen of heaven. But he was obliged to leave the 'high places', the hilltop shrines, intact, lacking the power to enforce religious orthodoxy. A century and a half later, Hezekiah (714–686) renewed the attack and reasserted strict Yahwistic monotheism, going so far as to break the Nehushtan, the bronze serpent reputedly made by Moses.[53] His attempted reformation, though, came to an end with his death. His successor, Manasseh (685–641) reverted to established policy and erected altars to Baal ('lord', 'master'), a prominent god sometimes associated with the sun or weather, and Asherah, his consort, both in the temple and on the 'high places'. Manasseh also practised soothsaying and augury, dealt with wizards and mediums and 'worshipped all the host of heaven', including the moon and sun, in whose honour solar chariots were set up at the entrance to the temple. It is unlikely that, if he had any aspiration to imitate the Assyrian emperors, he did not also employ astrologers. He was restoring the older, non-Yahwistic practices that Hezekiah in his Yahwistic zeal tried to eradicate. The Yahwists could not let these forms of astral religions go unchallenged, for their claim was that Yahweh alone controlled the cosmos. Any inroad by the astral religious ideas was a challenge to Yahweh's, and their, superiority and control. Manasseh's successor, Amon (640–639) followed the same practices.[54] But evidence of a profound religious struggle in Jewish society is found under his successor, Josiah (639–609), who turned back to strict monotheism. Like Asa and Hezekiah, he attacked the shrines of the astral religion, destroyed the altars to Baal and Asherah in Jerusalem and elsewhere, removed the 'idolatrous' priests who had burned incense to Baal, the sun, moon, the constellations and all the host of the heavens, and removed the male cult prostitutes, who seem to have been associated with Asherah. However, like previous reformations, Josiah's was brief and unsuccessful; he had the power of the Jerusalem priesthood behind him, but not the majority of the population.

Two centuries after Isaiah's attack on the astrologers, around the end of Judah's existence, or perhaps during the Babylonian captivity, Jeremiah issued a further, condemnation. It has an air of desperation about it, as if the battle to save the Judaean people for Yahweh has been lost:

> Thus saith the Lord,
> 'Learn not the way of the nations,
> nor be dismayed at the signs of the heavens
> because the nations are dismayed at them,
> for the customs of the peoples are false.'[55]

Jeremiah's problem was not with celestial omens, for this was how Yahweh spoke, but with celestial and other signs sent by rival gods. His words, though, like those of the other prophets, had little effect and Josiah's successors, all of whom were caught on the front line between Egypt and Assyria and were puppets of one or the other imperial power, maintained the pagan status quo until the Babylonians formally annexed the kingdom in 586 BCE. From then on the region was under the rule successively of the Babylonians, Persians and Greeks who, even though the Persian Emperor Cyrus allowed the Judaean exiles to return to Jerusalem and rebuild the temple, worshipped gods other than Yahweh. This practice appears also among Jews, naturally enough, and the bitter tension between strict Yahwists and the polytheists or henotheists continued. The last great struggle was triggered by the installation of a statue of the Greek Zeus Olympius in the temple by the Hellenized Jewish priesthood in 167 BCE. The priests no doubt understood that the supreme male god whom they worshipped was also revered in other cultures under different names, but this particular incident provoked a massive fundamentalist revolt against the Greek Seleucid monarchy of Antiochus IV.[56]

By the time, though, that the independent state was re-established, in 165 BCE, strict Yahwistic religion had experienced an intense encounter with Persian Zoroastrianism, with which it found certain shared sympathies, including a profound antipathy to Babylonian astral religion. Astrology itself was also profoundly influenced by developments within Zoroastrianism after the sixth century BCE, and it was in this context that post-exilic Judaism emerges, thoroughly familiar with astrological discourse. Throughout the last two centuries BCE and the first two centuries CE, Jewish thinkers were in a dialogue with their Greek, Persian and Roman neighbours and, where they had a problem with astrological cosmology, it was only over the superiority of their god over others.[57] There were even Jews who identified themselves as pagans, setting a precedent for some later Christians.[58] Religious boundaries were important for some people, irrelevant for others.

The Babylonian 'Tablets of Destiny', in which the future was inscribed in the *Enuma Elish*, and which hark back to Nanshe's tablet of stars, made a relatively late appearance in the Hebrew scriptures. In *1 Enoch*, probably compiled in the second century BCE, we finally meet the concept of the 'Tablets of Heaven', which contain all that is written 'for the generations of eternity'.[59] Moreover, the most explicit early Jewish reference occurs in one of the Qumran scrolls, *The Epochs of*

Time (*The Ages of Creation*), probably written in the first century CE, and which has survived only in fragments:

> As regards God's having set a fixed epoch for the [occurrence of everything past] and future, (the fact is that) before He created [the angels] He determined what [they] were to do [in their several epochs], epoch by epoch. Moreover, this was engraved on (heavenly) tablets [and duly prescribed] for the respective epochs in which they were to bear rule.[60]

Astrology's relationship with determinism, though, is far from straightforward. In all forms of astrology the future is to be negotiated, even in instances in which the physical future is unavoidable and the negotiation takes place only in the realm of the soul. The close encounter with Hellenistic philosophy following Alexander's conquest in 332 BCE brought the language of Platonism and the Stoics into common usage amongst educated Jews and other peoples of the Near East. Concepts such as *heimarmenê* and *tyche* became familiar as did the discussion of whether heavenly signs accompanied corresponding events as signs – *sêmeia* – or were responsible for them as *poiêtikoi*.[61]

Claims were even made that astrology was itself a Jewish invention. According to the *Jewish Antiquities*, written by the first-century CE historian Josephus, the children of Seth, the son of Adam, 'were the inventors of that peculiar sort of wisdom which is concerned with the heavenly bodies and their order'. Their knowledge of this and other things, he claimed, had been inscribed on two pillars, one of brick and one of stone, so that they would survive the future destructions of the world by fire and water. It was Abraham, Josephus continued, who was the first to publish this idea. It was when he was still resident at Ur that Abraham wrestled with the idea that the irregular motions of the planets 'contribute to the happiness of men'. His conclusion was that they do so, but only as agents of the one true God, an idea that he took with him to the Holy Land.[62] For a section of first-century CE Jewry, Abraham's break with polytheism was therefore not to be understood as a rejection of astrology but as the creation of an astrology which was compatible with monotheism. To accomplish this, an astrology-friendly historiography was necessary. Astrological symbolism stood at the heart of many aspects of the iconography of first-century Judaism; Josephus tells us that the menorah, the seven lamps of the sacred candelabra indicated the seven planets, and the twelve loaves on the table the zodiac. The Platonic Jewish writer Philo of Alexandria, also in the first century, described the zodiacal imagery on the breastplate worn by the high priest, its purpose being that, when he entered the holy of holies, he might become the whole world, which might then enter with him and share his prayers.[63] The law of correspondences, on which such practices were based was universally accepted; it was part of the natural worldview of the time. Such principles were established by Philo in his treatises 'On the Creation' and 'Concerning the World', which are essentially a reworking of Plato's *Timaeus* in the light of Genesis; God created the world, but he did so as a geometer, endowing the heavenly bodies with both mathematical harmony, numerological significance, and with their all-important role as signs (Gen. 1.14).[64]

Philo's Jewish Platonism was responsible for a cosmology in which monotheism and astrology were to survive and flourish in both a Jewish and Christian context. His God is a God of reason, who can be approached through the thirst of knowledge. This, in turn can be inspired by the heavens, just as the constellation of the Bear enables mariners to discover new lands. But also, he claims, that the eye is to the body as the mind is to the soul; as the mind receives God so the eye receives the light of the stars, and both can confer wisdom. He continues, in his treatise 'On Providence', that all things in heaven, including the stars, exist as a result of providence, which is why eclipses are omens of the death of kings or the destruction of cities.[65] However God, being the Platonic Good, is shorn of the vengeful qualities of Yahweh, and the evil consequences of omens are no longer the direct result of divine punishment but of the unfortunate mixing of elements, in other words, natural causes. Such disruption might originate with God, being part of his creation, but it is sufficiently removed from him for him to avoid responsibility. His attempt to solve the problem of astrological causation in a monotheistic cosmos led Philo to a formula which was to save astrology in Christian Europe and, along the way, solved the problem of evil. This formula was picked up in the fifth century CE by Augustine, who accepted the reality of celestial influences but rejected any role of the stars in the soul. Writing in his *Confessions* he claimed that 'all this wholesome advice [the astrologers] labour to destroy when they say "The cause of your sin is inevitably fixed in the heavens" ... all this in order that a man ... may regard himself as blameless, while the creator and Ordainer of heaven and the stars must bear the blame of our ills and misfortunes'.[66]

Philo's discussion of the stars was theoretical but, elsewhere, practical solutions to living with the stars were being sought. Astrological notions run through the scriptures of the time.[67] Hermetic and magical ideas are particularly strong in the apocryphal *Testament of Solomon*, most likely composed in the first century CE, perhaps a little later. The most distinctive feature of this text is its grim view of the cosmos, shared by the Gnostics, which becomes a hostile and malevolent place whose awfulness is only mitigated by angelic forces, whose task is to obstruct the celestial bodies' power to cause harm. The seven planetary powers were brutal, deceptive and oppressive, and their destructive power was restrained only by the presence of seven benevolent angels. The Egyptian decans make an appearance in this text as 'the thirty-six elements, man-shaped, bull-shaped, bird-faced, animal-faced, sphinx-faced, serpent-shaped'.[68] Importantly for medical diagnosis and treatment, they cause physical problems – the first two cause headaches, the third damages the eyes, and so on – for which charms and remedies, which are not included, are prescribed. More controversial perhaps, was the demonology of the kind which occurs in the text, which relates how Solomon learns the relationship of demons to stars so that he can gain control over them, Drawing on claims of Solomon's knowledge of the natural world,[69] the *Testament of Solomon* extends his wisdom to celestial realms. The text relates how demons were causing trouble during the building of the temple. One, called Ornias, used to take half the pay and rations of a young overseer, who was wasting away. Solomon interrogated Ornias and asked him which sign of the zodiac he lay under. Ornias replied that he was under Aquarius and was responsible for suffocating 'those who lie under the Water-pourer, who because of their lust for women have called upon the sign of the Virgin'.[70] Ornias was no servant of evil, though. His mission was a deeply moral one; he was the offspring of the archangel known as the Power of God and could be restrained by another archangel, Uriel. Solomon then established that a second demon, Asmodeus, was linked to the Great Bear. Returning to Ornias he asked how exactly the demons operate. Ornias told him that, when they fly amongst the stars, they hear the decrees of God and, on their own initiative, implement them in a destructive manner. They are too exhausted to ascend to heaven, as great men do, and fall to earth as shooting stars or lightning. This astronomical detail aside, we have here a Babylonian model for astrological causation and a Platonic recipe for its solution. The creator is actively intervening, like Marduk or Sin or Ishtar, even if souls are ascending to the stars through the planetary spheres of the Platonic cosmos. But the demons fly around in the lower levels of the cosmos, unlike wise men, who escape evil by flying to the stars.[71]

Such secrets might be revealed to adepts who travelled, like Er in Plato's *Republic*, to the heavens. The most famous was Enoch, whose celestial journey takes him through a heavenly realm which is at once constructed according to a beautiful, perfect order, particularly constructed according to the calendrical numbers 7 and 12, but also populated by demons of the kind Solomon encountered. These were the fallen angels who taught men the knowledge of the 'eternal secrets which were made in heaven', including Baraqiel and Tamiel who taught astrology and astronomy, Kokabel, who instructed men in the reading of portents, and Asradel who taught the path of the moon, meaning the regulation of the calendar.[72] The heavens were perfectly ordered, yet that order deviated into supernatural conflict, according to *1 Enoch* and the *Testament of Solomon*, or into natural decay according to Philo. Yet, whatever one's view, a knowledge of either demonic links to the stars or natural forecasting might help one negotiate the future, stave off crisis and preserve harmony.

The most explicitly astrological Jewish text is the *Treatise of Shem*, which is difficult to date, but like other such documents may survive in a version from the first to the third centuries CE, but be composed of earlier material. It is essentially a perpetual almanac which determines the prospects for the coming year depending on what zodiac sign it begins in, presumably the rising sign, or *horoscopos*, at the spring equinox. The predictions are remarkably specific. For example: 'If the year begins in Virgo: Everyone whose name contains Yudhs or Sentakth, and Beth and Nun, will be deceased and robbed, and will flee from his home … and the first grain will not prosper … but the last grain will be harvested … and produce will be expensive in Hauran and Bithynia … and dates will be abundant, but dried peas will be reduced in value'.[73] The emphasis on weather and finance in all 12 chapters suggests that this may have been a compilation from the centuries of empirical research such as that evident in the Babylonian astrological diaries, together with some letter symbolism attached to the Greek or Hebrew meaning of one's name.

The end of exile and the formulation of a still recognizable Jewish religion in the latter centuries BCE, saw a partial resolution of Yahwist opposition to Babylonian astrology by its adaptation to monotheism, hardly a difficult step as God had always spoken in celestial signs. The difference now was that the link between astrology and astrolatry, astral religion, had been broken, a step of immense significance for astrology's future survival.

The restoration of the independent monarchy in 160 BCE, saw a full return by the new Hasmonaean dynasty to the astrological practices which had flourished amongst the kings of Israel and Judah until the exile, this time without worrying about denunciation by the prophets. The new kings explicitly identified themselves with the messianic prophecy of the oracle of Balaam, that 'a star shall come forth out of Israel' and vanquish all the nation's enemies.[74] Alexander Jannaeus, who reigned from 103 to 76 BCE minted a series of coins bearing stars either with eight points, which might suggest Venus, or six, and with or without a circle. Alexander had been born in 126 BCE, a year which saw a triple conjunction of Jupiter and Saturn, always a brilliant event in the sky, and, by placing a star on his coins he was declaring his messianic credentials. Herod the Great, who ruled from 37 to 35/4 BCE, and is notorious for his massacre of the innocents, also identified himself as the fulfilment of the prophecy that 'a star shall come forth out of Jacob and sceptre shall rise out of Israel'.[75] The latter part of his reign coincided with the next triple Jupiter–Saturn conjunction and it may be argued that the slaughter not just of his known enemies, but his wife and sons, was a sort of namburbi, a ritual response to a planetary warning that he should remove all threats to his throne. That the final act of Jewish resistance to foreign domination, the Bar-Kochba revolt of 134 CE coincided with the next triple conjunction in the series points to a consistent messianic theme. That Bar Kokhba means 'son of the star' reinforces the point. And that the Roman Emperor Hadrian, himself an astrologer, destroyed Jerusalem and rebuilt it as the city of Aelia Capitolina, a sanctuary for Jupiter, points to an awareness on both sides that the military conflict was also fought in the heavens.

The heavens' failure to support the Jewish rebels, though, along with the disaster which followed their defeat was not blamed on the stars. How could it be if they were mere signs, the messengers? Astrology, by now a part of mainstream culture across the word from Rome to India, was not to be challenged except by philosophical sceptics. Its incorporation into religious architecture is confirmed by the presence of mosaic zodiacs in a series of synagogues dating from perhaps the Byzantine era, often with Sol Invictus, the Roman sun god, at the centre.[76] Such images mark the visual highpoint of the paganizing tendencies within Jewish religion which had flourished in Alexandria since the second century BCE.

There was no longer a high priest with vestments which embodied zodiacal imagery, but all could now share in its cosmic power. In the rabbinical texts scholars debated whether, for example, it was the *mazal* (star) of the day or the hour that determined people's fate.[77] They did so within a context now shaped by Aristotelian cosmology, in which the stars could act as influences rather than just as signs. Yet, even then, fate could be negotiated by pious behaviour and one who followed the law would never be subject to the dictates of the planets. Above all, according to Rabbi Yohanan, *Ein mazal le'Israel* (there is no star for Israel); only God can directly determine the future of the Children of Israel.[78] In one sense the Yahwist prophets had lost the struggle for the control of Jewish cosmology, for astrology had become a normal part of the majority worldview. Yet, seen from a different perspective, the strict Yahwists had won. For their problem had never been with astrology as such, as a matter of divine communication, otherwise they could not have contemplated the possibility of celestial omens. Rather, they objected to an astrology which was part and parcel of astral polytheism. This was the problem they solved, with the aid of Platonic philosophy and Zoroastrian monotheism. The astrology which emerged among some segments of the Jewish world by the Hellenistic period was technically no different to its Babylonian or Greek counterparts, but it was being refined through a robust debate within the Jewish community and was now reconciled with a cosmos ruled by the one true God.

9

Greece: Homer, Hesiod and the Heavens

> There he made the earth and there the sky and the
> sea and the inexhaustible blazing sun and the moon
> rounding full and there the constellations.[1]

Greece occupies a special place at the heart of European culture which no other ancient civilization can rival. The standard formula is still that set out by H.A.L. Fisher in 1935. In the opening section of his *History of Europe*, he announced: 'We Europeans are the children of Hellas'.[2] Whereas Egypt was regarded as a source of ineffable wisdom by Renaissance thinkers, to the Enlightenment radicals of eighteenth-century Europe, Greece became the source of all that was best about Western life – scientific inquiry, rational thought, civic virtue and democratic ideals. These ideas achieved a tangible form in the neo-classical architecture of the great Western cities, from St Petersburg to Paris, London and Washington DC. The history of the ancient world was appropriated into the service of shoring up of modern Western identity. Egypt and Babylon, meanwhile still suffer from the West's lingering distaste for the East, the victims of Edward Said's 'orientalism', the provocative theory according to which the Islamic and Asian worlds are perceived as corrupt, tyrannical and exotic, and the source of absolutely no worthwhile contribution to Western civilization.[3] This view, in which the origin and authenticity of current forms of Western social and political organization are located exclusively in one civilization, and not in its neighbours, is still widespread, though increasingly challenged by the limited band of scholars who specialize in non-Western cultures.

By the early twentieth century, when the intellectual achievements of Mesopotamian civilization were becoming apparent, the standard model of Greece's unique contribution to learning was revised, but only to a limited extent. While it was conceded that the Greeks might have borrowed from their eastern neighbours to the extent that, for example, in the fourth century BCE, they adopted Babylonian names for the planets, all that was of value in science and astronomy, it was argued, was still unique to the Greeks. As Peter Kingsley, who is heavily critical of orthodox Western Hellenophilia – love of all things Greek – put it: 'myths on the subject of a single self-enclosed Greek world still abound in the scholarly imagination'.[4] Worse, many twentieth-century scholars believed that astrology, which the Greeks had clearly imported from Babylon, was a sort of intellectual sickness, a cultural virus which infected the otherwise noble Greek psyche.[5] Some writers have spoken of a veritable 'flood of cosmic religion' overwhelming the Greek world, carrying astrology with it.[6] The narrative of heroic Greeks and decadent Babylonians, Persians and Egyptians is nonsense, but is remarkably difficult to shift. In one recent book, the Greeks' supposed 'craving' for novelty is contrasted with the 'monolithic, eternal, empires of Babylon and Egypt'.[7]

Yet, the orientalist position, which is still found in the history of science, is becoming increasingly difficult to sustain when the evidence is allowed to speak.[8] In particular it is clear that, while Greek culture did achieve a distinctive personality and was undoubtedly home to a series of remarkable philosophers, it did not exist in isolation from its more ancient neighbours. Its great achievements in philosophy, science and rationalism were not developed as a reaction against the superstition of its neighbours, but by appropriating and developing their existing worldviews. As Walter Burkert has argued, we should abandon the view that the Greeks marched the whole way from *mythos* to *logos*, from superstition to reason, in isolation from their eastern neighbours.[9] The lingering view amongst historians of science, that cosmology, as distinct from celestial religion and mythology, developed in Greece, still has strong support, but the relationship between the Greeks and Babylonians defies simplification.[10] We can trace oriental influences in Greece from the Mycenean period in the late second millennium onwards. We have a few artefacts as evidence, such as a ninth-century northern Syrian bronze plaque portraying Adad, found in a sanctuary to the goddess Hera at Samos.[11] Such contacts continued over the following centuries. There is no reason to doubt, for example, as Western scholars have done, the accounts that Pythagoras, the great sixth-century BCE philosopher, studied in Babylon and Egypt and with the Celts.[12] From then exchanges continue until, in the third century BCE, Greek mathematicians borrowed Babylonian methods for calculating planetary positions.[13] In the fifth century BCE, Herodotus himself reported that the 12-hour day and the *gnomon* (for taking astronomical measurements) had been imported from Babylon, adding for good measure that geometry was probably Egyptian.[14] If David Brown's PCP and EAE paradigms represent different ways of seeing the universe, the products of psychological inclinations as much as cultural tendencies, the need to distinguish Greek from Babylonian astrology on racial, regional or philosophical grounds disappears. Both paradigms are evident in the astrologies of both cultures. But, before we proceed, we need to quote G.E.R. Lloyd, a pioneering student of the Greek belief system who wisely wrote: 'any attempt to offer generalisations concerning Greek speculative thought as a whole must be deemed hazardous'.[15] With that warning, generalization is the only way to proceed.

Very little is known about Greek attitudes to the stars before the first millennium, though there is, naturally enough, plenty of speculation. For example, Jane Harrison, early in the twentieth century, identified a pure strain of ethical, archaic, celestial–seasonal religion, the worship of the *eniautos daimon*, the god who died and was reborn every year, and which she believed predated the degenerate deities of the Olympian pantheon.[16] But Harrison's theories rely on a chronological sequence which cannot be sustained. Some theories are perfectly reasonable, such as the identification of solar imagery in Minoan art of the mid-second millennium BCE. Visual artefacts always lend themselves to competing interpretations and it is in the very nature of symbols that they possess levels of meaning, but a plausible argument can be made that the swastika and horse-chariot motifs which appear on Minoan pottery are indeed representations of the sun.[17] It would, after all, be astonishing if any Mediterranean society with a visual art did not possess solar symbols. It is no more surprising to find lunar symbolism – images of the apparent worship of the crescent moon.[18] There is also some evidence of orientations to the sun and moon, and perhaps stars, suggesting a shared tradition with the megalithic builders; Minoan civilization flourished as megalithic culture was entering its last phase. One example is found at the palace at Knossos, where the so-called 'Corridor of the House Tablets' appears to face the rising sun on the autumn equinox.[19] However, Minoan society was in terminal decline by the late second millennium and its cosmological traditions were lost when its cities disappeared: Knossos, the capital was abandoned around 1400 BCE. Speculation then seeps into the vacuum left by our absence of knowledge.

One literary theory sees Homer's epic poem, the *Iliad*, dating in the form we have it now from the eighth century BCE, as a mirror of the heavens which can, in parts, be traced back to the ninth millennium.[20] Greek states, Trojan regiments and the heroes on either side are all, it is claimed, representatives of stars and constellations. The basic premise is not in itself impossible, given that this was the period when the earliest known Near Eastern cities were founded, but it is far too ambitious too argue such a case on the basis of one text. Besides, if one puts one's mind to it, almost any work of literature can be read as a celestial allegory and, in themselves, such readings tell us nothing about the author's intentions. They fall into the familiar category of imagined history, the quest for ancient origins based on the premise that antiquity equals authenticity. Only stories with a basic seven- or twelve-fold structure can be assumed to have a celestial connection, even if it is not spelled out. The 12 labours of Hercules, would have been understood to be an allegory of the sun's journey through the sky, even though none of the stories suggest a neat passage through the constellations; if there is a pattern to Hercules' struggle, it is a monthly, not a zodiacal one.[21] Similarly, claims that the Greeks devised the zodiac as a single exercise lack credibility, even if they did refine it.[22] The evidence that the zodiac developed in Mesopotamia is just far too strong; when the Greeks needed an organized system of constellations, they did not have far to look. More credible are theories that Greek temples were aligned with either the rising of particular stars or, at least with the rising and setting sun.[23]

The earliest accounts of an early religious, magical astrological tradition in Greece date only from the first-century CE Roman poet Lucan, although they have the whiff of prehistoric custom. Lucan recorded how the sorceresses of Thessaly, in northern Greece, used their magical powers to draw down the moon:

Magic the starry lamps from heaven can tear,
And shoot them gleaming through the dusky air;
Can blot fair Cynthia's countenance serene,
And poison with foul spells the silver queen ...
Held by the charming song, she strives in vain,
And labours with the long pursuing pain;
Till down, and downward still, compell'd to come,
On hallow'd herbs she sheds her fatal foam.[24]

Lucan was certainly using his poetic skills to embellish, but there is no reason why there should not have been such a magical tradition. The sorceresses sang to the moon in what was clearly an arduous ritual, and induced the planet, or the god or goddess associated with it, to impregnate herbs with their healing, or perhaps destructive, power. They also, it seems from the second line, were able to summon up shooting stars. Actually, while we may consider such practices magical, they were also natural. In the first or second centuries CE, the Roman writer Plutarch reported the Stoic view that the moon's watery nature is fed by evaporation, a 'sweet and mild exhalation' from springs and lakes.[25] If it is observed that water comes down as rain and rises as steam and, if it is assumed that the world can be manipulated by will, then it is logical to assume that the wider generative power of the moon can be turned to advantage. Sometimes it is difficult to distinguish religious beliefs from purely functional ones. When the Spartans delayed their march to face the Persians at the battle of Marathon in 490 BCE until the moon was full, was that because they thought it was a fortunate omen, or because they wished to draw down its power, or just that they needed its light – or all three?[26]

The oracle was a crucial feature of the Greek city state, an important source of advice for traditional custom, the interpretation of sacred law or a preview of the future.[27] Yet, this rarely or never seems to have required asking the stars for advice. One of the few indications of a possibly archaic, formal, astrological tradition in Greece occurs in Plutarch's biographical account of King Agis IV of Sparta (244–240 BCE) who, by all accounts, was a reformer. Though Agis reigned in the late third century, the practice Plutarch describes is so unusual that it is tempting, like Lucan's astral sorceresses, to see it as a survivor from a much earlier age. He tells us that:

It was the custom for the Ephori [magistrates] every ninth year, on a clear star-light night, when there was no moon, to sit down, and in silence observe the heavens. If a star happened to shoot from one part of them to another, they pronounced the kings guilty of some crime against the gods, and suspended them till they were re-established by an oracle from Delphi or Olympia.[28]

On the occasion in question the omen was used to topple Leonidas, Agis' aristocratic rival and co-ruler, who had introduced the oriental despotic style of rule that he had witnessed, and admired, at the court of the Seleucids, the Greek rulers of Syria and Mesopotamia. Agis, the reformer, appointed the radical leader Lysander as a magistrate. Lysander then convened his colleagues for a night of star-watching. When a sign from heaven duly appeared – we are not told what it was – Lysander put Leonidas on trial for having had two children by an Asiatic woman, an act considered a serious crime for any true descendant of Hercules. Heaven may have spoken, but it did not do so decisively, and Leonidas was restored in the following year, after Lysander's term of office had expired. Agis himself was executed by the landowners after he attempted a radical redistribution of land. The promise of heaven was fulfilled, but the revolution was unsuccessful. The celestial omen could not trump the Spartan political process and the strict limit on terms of office. While the Spartan story apparently relates to earlier practices, it is an example of the use of the astrological omen in the sense defined by Patrick Curry – it is local and spontaneous – it is not democratic.[29] Its political context, like Assyrian astrology, is autocratic. We cannot be sure whether the Spartan practice was the legacy of a lost, archaic Greek omen astrology, but it certainly has that feel; the Babylonian astrology of the time, which would have been practised at the Seleucid court, was vastly more complex. The use of the stars to manage the political process through, in this case, an attempted coup d'état, was impressive, but the chaotic and unpredictable astrological procedure is more redolent of the open-ended dialogue involved in Gudea's dream than the systematized proto-horoscopes already being used in Babylon; Agis' cosmic assault on Leonides took place about 40 years after Berossus started his teaching to Greek students on Kos.

We know that, 500 years before the clash between Leonidas and Agis, when Homer was composing his epic accounts of the Trojan wars, the Greeks were absorbing astronomical notions from both the north and the east – Homer recognized the stars of the Plough both as the north European Bear and the Babylonian Wagon. The fact that the *Iliad*'s description of the stars on Achilles' shield appears to be taken directly from the Babylonian *Hymn to the Gods of the Night* also suggests that cuneiform material was already being translated into Greek, even if in small quantities.[30] With his usual poetic skill, Homer described the intricate decorative scenes depicted on the shield that the god Hephaestus forged for Achilles:

> There he made the earth and there the sky and the sea and the inexhaustible blazing sun and the moon rounding full and there the constellations, all that crown the heavens, the Pleiades and the Hyades, Orion in all his power too and the Great Bear, that mankind also calls the Wagon, she wheels on her axis always fixed, watching the Hunter, and she alone is denied a plunge in the wash of the Ocean.[31]

The last sentence is a reference to the Bear's circumpolar status – as seen in the northern hemisphere it forever circles the pole and never sets; in Egyptian celestial theology it was one of the Immortals, the imperishable stars which were spared the nightly struggle with darkness. More important, though, as evidence of Greece's location on a crossroads in the trade routes of ideas rather than artefacts, is Homer's simultaneous use of the northern European Bear and the Sumerian Wagon to describe the same stars, testimony to the fact that, even though the Mesopotamian literary tradition was eventually to be dominant, the northern oral tradition was as accessible. In cosmological terms, Homer's Greece was a melting pot, a meeting point between two worlds.

The question of Mesopotamian links with the Greek world may be approached on two levels, the general and the specific. Oriental influence on Greece via trade and religion is not a matter of dispute, and has been well documented as far as the Assyrian period, during which Homer lived, is concerned.[32] The trade in ideas would have followed the same route as that in artefacts. It just happens to be far more difficult to trace. There are, though, specific instances, for example, images identified as Assyrian 'solar motifs' being copied in Greek art. Spiral decorations and winged figures, evocative of representations of not just Assur, the chief Assyrian god, but also Amon-Re, Shamash and Ahura-Mazda, have been found in Greece as well as further afield, in Etruria.[33] The conclusion is that either such images had a shared origin, or that they were spreading west as the Assyrians' military success created a wider cultural zone of Near Eastern influence.

To put these reciprocal contacts into their wider context, in the eighth century the mighty Assyrian Empire was reaching its peak; it occupied the entire Mediterranean coast of Palestine, Syria and, briefly, Egypt, dominating Greek merchants' trading relationships with the east. The Babylonian astrologers themselves constituted a bureaucratic caste with a crucial decision-making role in the state, and their cosmology began to move west as ideas followed the trade routes; their skill in converting their understanding of the cosmic state into the success of their political masters was evident. Whatever the reason, we know that Babylonian cosmology was on the move at the highest level. Homer's acquaintance with the *Hymn to the Gods of the Night* was matched by his younger contemporary Hesiod's familiarity with the *Enuma Elish*. Either Hesiod read the *Enuma Elish* or both were heir to an archaic Neolithic tradition.[34]

It was Hesiod who, in his *Theogony*, provided the earliest written account of the Greek creation myth in which the world emerged from a primeval Chaos, open, unbounded space, which gave birth to Earth, Eros and Night. From Night was born Air and Day and from Earth, Ouranos, the starry heaven, which was to be the home of the gods. As in the *Enuma Elish*, the deities of the *Theogony* indulged in generational wars as, in succession, first Cronos overthrew Ouranos and then Zeus, playing the same role as Marduk in Babylon, rebelled against Cronos. He then elaborated the myths of the gods and goddesses which were the basis for all future written accounts, although he never attempted to link individual divinities to the stars and planets. Only Ouranos, the starry heaven, had a celestial presence. There is a curious lack of celestial detail in Hesiod's work. The *Homeric Hymns*, ascribed to Homer, if not actually written by him, seem completely unconcerned with any divine, starry associations. The Hymn to Apollo, the Olympian sun god, for example, makes no absolute reference to the physical sun itself. It is assumed that the gods can travel through the sky if they wish, but the narrative is detached from any attempt to either measure or attribute meanings to celestial bodies. To be sure, Apollo is impressive: 'as he goes through the house of Zeus [the sky]', we read, 'the gods tremble before him and all spring up when he draws near'.[35] The Homeric hymns are actually not hymns in any modern sense at all. They are accounts, which include references to song, of the activities of the gods and goddesses. They have none of the power of say, the Mesopotamian hymns to Ishtar, which are both overtly tied to a heavenly body – in this case, Venus – and exude a religious passion of exquisite power.

The Greek heavens were not seen as a repository of detailed religious power to the same extent as the Egyptian and Mesopotamian skies. They functioned as a stage set for mythical drama, but little more. Even Ouranos was never the object of worship. The Greek deities were mainly earth-bound, based on Olympus, the sacred mountain, even if they could change their form and fly. Only the repetition of the number 12, as in the 12 gods and goddesses of Olympus, suggests a calendar connection between deities and sky, although nowhere is this spelt out, at least not until the beginning of first century CE in the *Astronomica*, an extended astrological poem composed by the Roman writer Marcus Manilius.

Hesiod's work on the stars, the *Astronomiae*, reveals an attitude to the stars which was based neither in the need for precise measurement and meaning, as in Babylon, nor religious power, as in Egypt, but in a view of the sky as a theatrical backdrop to human affairs. The lines between humanity and divinity were blurred. Gods might consort with humans, as Zeus did on so many occasions, while humans might ascend to the stars. The *Astronomiae* survives only in fragments, but they are sufficient to indicate that the celestial fabric of Geek mythology, if not religion, can be traced at least to the eighth century, if not much earlier; apparently archaic myths, such as Orion's pursuit of the Pleiades, are only hinted at in the surviving text – he offends Merope, one of the Pleiades, with his drunkenness. The unanswerable question is whether Hesiod was inventing stories or transcribing much earlier ones. The story of Orion, for example, the son of Euryale, daughter of King Minos of Crete, and Poseidon, as set out by Hesiod, evokes the classic mythic structure identified in ancient stories.[36] Born a human with supernatural powers – he could walk, Christ-like, on water – he was an adventurer who suffered from all-too human flaws such as a violent temper and a penchant for drunkenness. He was blinded and reduced to beggary as a punishment for his debauchery, but was healed by the sun, whom he met in the east. He then became a hunter and decided to destroy every living creature. To prevent this calamity, Earth sent a giant scorpion to kill him. Artemis and Leo, Orion's hunting companions prayed to Zeus, who raised him to the sky, becoming the constellation named after him, while the scorpion was placed opposite. The hero's life, in Orion's case, unfolds according to certain standard models. He is half divine and half human, born with great power but a tragically flawed personality, he repeatedly brings disaster on himself but is saved by the kindness of others. What would people discover from hearing this story? There is a clear moral lesson: that bad behaviour leads to punishment, but that salvation is always available from the gods. From a literary perspective we have an early example of celestial journey literature – Orion meets Helios and is healed. But also, and this is important if we are to understand the origin of later ideas about the soul and the stars, Orion ascends to the sky where he becomes one with the stars.

Cosmological references run through a number of the heroic myths. The Theseus epic offers a clear example. The hero's most famous escapade was his visit to Crete to slaughter the Minotaur (a Taurean symbol?) and save the 14 young Athenians – seven youths and seven maidens, who were sent as sacrifices every ninth year.[37] Seven would have been read at the time as equivalent to the number of planets and the ninth year, as in the story of Leonidas and Agis, was the year which followed the eighth – the year in which the Sun, Moon and Venus all arrived back at their starting positions on the same day. This is not stated in the original accounts, but it is a plausible explanation. The problem with such accounts, of course, is that in their written form they are relatively late. Plutarch, to whom we owe the canonical written form of the Theseus story, lived from around 46 to 120 CE.

It is unclear to what extent archaic Greek myths were generally attached to constellations, which stories may have been deliberately created by reference to particular stars and whether there was a process of evolution between Homer, Hesiod and the extensive, surviving account in the *Phaenomena* of the Macedonian court poet Aratus of Soli, 500 years later.[38] The sun itself was personified as Helios, often pictured driving a chariot pulled by four horses representing the four quarters of the year. Even though Apollo, the god of solar light, was to take a more important role, Helios was worshipped at religious centres across Greece, from Corinth and Athens to the island of Rhodes, which was sacred to him. He was, like Apollo, the all-seeing, who could peer into men's hearts and knew their every thought, not unlike Shamash, who exposed crimes and misdemeanours. Apollo, like Shamash, was the oracle god, to whom one addressed pleas for the answers to one's problems. In both cultures the sun was the embodiment of wisdom. Helios' eldest sister was Selene, the moon, whose golden crown illuminated the starry night. The most famous story told of Selene was of her love for her eternally sleeping lover, Endymion; as her rays caressed him so she looked down over every sleeping mortal. Helios' other celestial sister was Eos, or Aurora, the dawn. She in her turn had two sons, Eosphoros, or Phosphoros, who represented the planet Venus as morning star, rising brilliantly just before sunrise, and Hesperos, who was Venus as evening star, appearing as a splendid sight after sunset. Of any other planetary deities we hear nothing.

We turn to Hesiod's only other (with the *Theogony*) surviving work, *Works and Days*, for indications of an astrological mentality. *Works and Days* is unique for its time, though was to be influential on later literature, such as Virgil's *Georgics*, in the first century BCE. It combined a theory of history with specific rules for aligning one's life to the stars in a style which combines the individual with the universal. It was the first of a series of works which are best known from the late fifth century onwards, the *parapegmata*, a style of astrological work comparable to the Babylonian diaries, correlating mainly meteorological phenomena with the stars, and the *Mul Apin*.[39] Hesiod also provided the broader political framework in which all future political astrology was to thrive, outlining a five-stage theory of historical periodization in which the key to the entire process of historical degeneration was to be found in the steady decline of individual moral standards – the increasing tendency for human nature to deviate from the utopian bliss of the original Golden Race through the successive Silver, Bronze, Heroic and Iron Races. The moral cycle which determined such decline is summed up by the Greek word *hybris*, the belief that excessive pride is followed by eventual personal disaster, as in the story of Orion. If decline was partly caused by human beings, exacerbated by their alienation from heaven, it follows that they also have the power to reintegrate themselves with the cosmos and attempt to restore some sort of harmony. One solution to the historical problem which faced the Iron Race, was to encourage as far as possible a life of self-discipline – obedience to the sacred calendar and reverence for ordinances of 'starry heaven'.[40] The best the people of this race could hope for was that the threatened future disaster would be averted, but never far away was the longing for a return to the primaeval paradise. Hesiod's theory, together with a closely related account outlined in the Old Testament book of Daniel, became a core feature of European apocalyptic thought down to the seventeenth century. In this context astrology's ultimate use as a grand narrative was to watch the heavens in order to avert political and social collapse by maintaining humanity's harmonious link with the cosmos.[41]

Following the introduction to the history of the world, and how it came to its current sorry state, the greater part of *Works and Days* is given over to ordinances on correct behaviour for individuals, a guide to cosmic etiquette. It seems to have been either influenced by, or part of a common tradition with, Babylonian, and perhaps Egyptian, *hemerologies* – rules on fortunate and unfortunate days.[42] It offered sensible and concise advice on how the honest citizen might most efficiently maximize the potential of constructive strife and minimize the impact of its destructive opposite by seeking heavenly signs.[43] Each action had its appropriate moment: when a thing was done was as important as what was done. On the simplest level the wise farmer would plant, tend and harvest his crops at the correct season and on the most propitious day. The harvest should begin when the Pleiades are rising with the sun, in early May, and ploughing when they are setting with the sun, in November. In September, 'when Orion and Sirius are come into Midheaven, and rosy fingered Dawn sees Arcturus, then cut off all grape clusters ... and bring them home'.[44] Sailors were also subject to the common-sense rules dictated by the solar year: 'Fifty days after the solstice, when the season of wearisome heat is come to an end, is the right time for men to go sailing'.[45] Each day possessed its own quality, which derived in part from its position within the lunar calendar. The 13th of the waning month, for example, was better for planting than sowing, being the 26th of the lunar month and hence the date when the moon ceased to be visible in the sky. Other dates appear to have had a supernatural significance, the observation of celestial position having a clear sacred as well as natural relevance: 'Do not stand upright facing the sun when you make water, but remember to do this when he has set and towards his rising'.[46] In other words, if you must urinate during the day, do it with your back to the sun. Other aphorisms assumed a religious significance later; it is difficult not to connect the Pleiades' disappearance from the night sky for 40 days with Jewish traditions that the prophet withdraws to the desert for a 40-day cleansing period.[47] To call *Works and Days* a farming calendar, as many scholars have done, is to reduce its significance, to extract it from its context in a cosmos, characterized by the divine order which, as the *Theogony* made clear, superseded the primaeval chaos.[48] *Works and Days'* pragmatic, common-sense language is little different in spirit to that of the more naturalistic tendencies in Babylonian divination, and is clearly couched within a numinous context in which the good citizen's overwhelming duty was respect for the immortal gods. Correct timing was rooted in the religious observance that time and space were intimately integrated in a single organic whole. Above all, it was considered vital to show due respect to the gods and avoid the offence which would be committed if the natural order, which they had created for humanity's benefit, was ignored or abused: 'That man is happy and lucky in them who knows all these things and does his work without offending the deathless gods, who discerns the omens of birds and avoids transgression'.[49]

Taken together, Hesiod's two great surviving works, the *Theogony* and *Works and Days*, represent a comprehensive attempt to describe the origin of the universe and a theory of history, while outlining a code of conduct for each individual in relation to the stars. Now, Hesiod's work survives in fragments and is not always systematic. *Works and Days* in particular is a conflation of two works – one on historical periodization, the other on precise rules for living in harmony with the cosmos. But it remains tempting to see his ideas as adding up to a grand theory of everything. We might have imagined that his designation of the sky as divine and the stars as vital markers of proper behaviour, would have encouraged the development of astronomical knowledge. Yet, while he codified existing theories of the origin of the universe and the nature of history, it was to be around another 300 years before the Greeks became concerned either with measuring the positions of the stars more exactly, or with allocating planets to their gods and goddesses. Instead they developed a fascination with investigating the physical and psychic structure and processes of the universe in a way which is not evident in the surviving literature of either Egypt or Mesopotamia. The Greek philosophers did, it is true, draw on precedents established in those cultures, and their insistence that the dynamics of natural behaviour could be understood independently of direct divine intervention may have been eased by the Greek pantheon's largely chthonic, earth-based, nature. There appears, in other words, to have been a smooth transition from religion to what we would understand as philosophy – speculation on the nature of the cosmos – and from Mesopotamian culture to Greek, rather than a revolutionary break.[50] All such discussions, though, need to be quite clear, that philosophy, for the thinkers we are concerned with here, was close to what we would call theology and their speculation was closer to revelation.[51]

In Herodotus' account, from the sixth century BCE, the Greeks learnt geometry from the Egyptians, but astronomy, including the 12-hour day, from the Babylonians.[52] In spite of the fact that the Greeks had a sophisticated oracular tradition, which included, as in Babylon, their solar deity, Apollo as oracle god, and that the Homeric hymns include divine omens, they appear initially to have had little interest in astral divination beyond the Spartan practices related in Plutarch's tale of Agis.[53] Hesiod aside, their interest in cosmology was in models and explanations (though within a context set by deity) rather than in its day-to-day practical applications.

Greek thought is conventionally divided into two phases by the relationship to the Athenian philosopher Socrates (c.470–399 BCE). Those before Socrates, the Presocratics, were generally concerned with grand questions of existence, eternity and the structure of the cosmos. Socrates argued that we cannot know such things until we can define what we are talking about, and so is held responsible for developing rational methods of investigation which depend on continual, critical re-examination of the terms of the inquiry. Of course, he stood on the shoulders of his predecessors, but his contribution should never be underestimated. As we shall see, Socrates' student Plato brought together the Presocratics' universal concerns with Socrates' intellectual method to create a synthesis that established a foundation for Western cosmology until the seventeenth century.

The first Greek astronomer, leaving Hesiod aside, and Presocratic thinker, is usually said to have been Thales, who was born in Miletus on the southern Aegean coast of Asia Minor in around 640 BCE, possibly to a family of Phoenician priest-kings. He was Greek, but we need to understand the political geography of his world. He lived on the fringes of an empire in which astrology was a central part of managing politics and relationships with divine powers. Ashurbanipal was creating his great library at Nineveh, Assyrian astrology, as a political tool, had reached its height and the Babylonian astrologers had begun to compile the diaries. He cannot have been unaware of the developments in Babylonian celestial culture. Thales is famous for two reasons. Firstly he argued that the *arche*, the fundamental substance of which the universe is made, is water. While modern classical scholars have often portrayed this as a mighty intellectual breakthrough, initiating the Greek study of the universe as a physical construct, it is equally probable that Thales was familiar with the Babylonian origin myth in which, as the *Enuma Elish* tells us, creation began when salt water mixed with fresh water.[54] Certainly, if Hesiod was familiar with the Babylonian theogony, there is no reason why Thales should not have been. He was certainly influenced by Hesiod's naturalism, that, even if the cosmos was divine, it still made sense to focus on natural phenomena on their own terms. The attempt to portray Thales as the originator of Greek naturalism, as opposed to a student of Babylonian supernaturalism, is unconvincing.

The most famous story told about Thales is that he predicted a solar eclipse whose effect was to halt a battle between the Medes and the Lydians, probably in 585 BCE, and bring their six-year war to an end. The event was one of rare drama. 'The armies had already engaged', Herodotus tells us, 'when day was suddenly turned into night' and the armies, presumably stricken by panic, put down their arms and ceased fighting.[55] Scholars argue over this incident, unable to accept that a Greek could have made such a forecast.[56] Some accept that it would have been perfectly possible for Thales to have obtained Babylonian eclipse data and to have made a correct prediction, but others cling to the outmoded notion that Greek culture owed nothing to Near Eastern ideas. Given that Babylonian eclipse *omina* had spread to Syria and Turkey by around 1500 BCE, it would be somewhat surprising if Thales was not operating within a Babylonian framework.[57] As it is, we do not know whether he predicted the date of the eclipse or just the year. To predict the likely date of a solar eclipse is not difficult once the underlying pattern has been identified, but to identify the locations from which it can be clearly seen is extremely difficult. It is therefore quite plausible that, on the basis of Babylonian information, he predicted the possibility of an eclipse. Exactly what Thales did or did not do, though, is not really the point. The fact is that the story was told by Herodotus and has ever since been regarded as a model of what is often viewed as the greatest strength of astrologers up until the advent of modern astronomy – their ability to predict celestial events. Thales also, and this is crucial for the development of Greek cosmology, is said to have visited Egypt. There he studied how land on the banks of the Nile was delineated (which was crucial if boundaries were to be reinstated following the annual flood), took his knowledge back to Greece and, legend continues, founded geometry, the science of measuring the earth.

Over the next 200 years, a succession of Greek philosophers set out a series of speculative explanations for how the universe worked and what exactly it was made of that eventually laid the foundation of the worldview accepted in Europe until the sixteenth century.[58] They also compiled specific written accounts of the metaphysical processes that underpin the visible world, and which were to provide a coherent model of celestial causation which still provides astrology's central rationale. Most of these early texts are lost but, given that what we know of Greek cosmology of the seventh and sixth centuries BCE is largely reconstructed from later fragments, it seems that major strides were made in the formulation of a cosmos which could operate according to impersonal laws rather than the whims of gods and goddesses. Our problem, of course, is that our knowledge of Greek thought under the so-called Presocratics is filtered not just through the modern West's belief that Greek philosophy represented the progressive rejection of oriental superstition and discovery of reason, but distortions were incorporated into later accounts of this early work by other Greek philosophers.

The emerging consensus holds that such early philosophers are better seen as poets and their ideological affiliation as much closer to Near Eastern religion than has previously been believed.[59] The best way to see the Greek philosophers' achievement, as far as astronomy and astrology are concerned, is as an elaboration of existing theories, a search for the detail which would sustain, explain and embellish the understanding of the human condition in the context of a universe which was alive and intelligent. True, there were philosophers who moved close to materialism and atheism, but their work had no, or very little, impact on attitudes to the heavens.

It is customary to divide the philosophers following Thales into two groups, the Ionians, after Ionia in Asia Minor, who took their cue from Thales, and were supposedly primarily interested in natural causes, and the Eleatics, after Elea in southern Italy, and who were allegedly more concerned with what we would regard as metaphysics, or 'super-naturalism'. Such distinctions are difficult to sustain, based as they are on much later fragments and secondary accounts of now lost works. Neither should we imagine that the two schools were necessarily regarded popularly as mutually exclusive. Naturalism and supernaturalism could operate happily together. A story was told, admittedly, 500 years later, by Plutarch, of how the Athenian leader Pericles (c.495–429 BCE) was brought the head of a ram which had not two horns but one – and that growing out of the middle of its head. Anaxagoras (c.500–428 BCE), one of the finest thinkers of his day, and generally classed as a naturalistic Ionian, dissected the skull and revealed its deformity as a perfectly normal phenomenon. Meanwhile the well-known soothsayer, Lampo, prophesied that the head's appearance indicated that the current split between two parties, led by Pericles and Thucydides respectively, would be resolved. Plutarch brings his story to a close in which both approaches were right: 'This procured Anaxagoras great honour with the spectators; and Lampo was no less honoured for his prediction, when, soon after, upon the fall of Thucydides, the administration was put entirely in the hands of Pericles'.[60]

Thales' student, Anaximander, who lived from around 601 to 546/6 BCE, postulated the existence of the *apeiron*, the 'Unlimited', a boundless reservoir, from which all things come and to which all things return.[61] He may also have been the originator of the idea, only finally overturned by Galileo in the 1610s, that the heavenly bodies travel in their own spheres around the earth.[62] Whatever the origin of this idea, by providing a spatial cosmology in which the planets formed a sequence, progressing from the earth to the stars, it offered a map of the terrain between heaven and earth which was to decisively mould later ideas of humanity's relationship with God. Anaximander also, though, believed that the world is enclosed by an upturned bowl surrounded by fire, and that the stars are holes which enable us to glimpse the furnace on the other side; the notion of the heavens as a bowl was Babylonian, although more likely supporting water than fire.

Anaximenes, who flourished around 550 BCE and may have been Anaximander's student, apparently took a different point of view, and argued that the stars were not holes at all, but points nailed to the celestial dome which, he thought was crystal, a condensation of air into ice, a fair explanation, lacking other options, of where hail came from.[63] This ingenious model explained both how the planets were held in place by physical support, and why they could still be visible, crystal being transparent. The idea, though is not original. In the Old Testament we read that 'over the heads of the living creatures there was the likeness of a firmament, shining like crystal, spread out above their heads'.[64] Anaximander's slightly younger contemporary Xenophon (*c*.580/70–475/2 BCE), not to be confused with the later historian, was born in Colophon in Asia Minor, later moving to the western fringe of the Greek world, the colony of Elea in southern Italy; he is now regarded as the first of the 'Eleatic' philosophers. Xenophon was notable as the exponent of one idea: the doctrine of a single universal creator, a clear challenge to Hesiod's polytheism. We know little about Xenophon's god aside from one later comment from Aristotle who reported that 'Xenophanes, the first ... to postulate a unity ... made nothing clear ... but with his eye on the whole heaven he says that the One is god'.[65] It is tempting to see Persian influences at work in view of Xenophon's birthplace: Colophon was on the western boundary of the Persian Empire, and was absorbed into it in 546 BCE, so Xenophon's monotheism was conceived in a context in which Zoroastrianism was a familiar part of the religious environment. And behind Zoraoastrianism, of course, lay Assyrian and Babylonian religion with its suggestions that the one encompasses the many, as Nabu and Ninurta could be portrayed as powers of Marduk, or Assur, like Zeus, encompassed other gods.[66] The Persian god, according to the Zoroastrian creation myth, was a marvellous, transcendent being. He was 'supreme in omniscience and goodness, and unrivalled in splendour', he occupied the place of 'endless light' and was 'independent of unlimited time'.[67] He was above and beyond the often venal concerns of petty Greek deities, even of Zeus. There was also, it has to be said, a tendency within Greek religion, and later classical paganism generally, to identify a supreme heavenly ruler.[68] Inscriptions have been found which are dedicated to Zeus Hypistios, 'Zeus the Highest God' and Theos Hypistos, the 'Highest God'. The worship of Zeus Soter, or 'saviour', appears to have been instituted after the Persian wars. The reservation of monotheism as a special category for Judaism, Christianity and Islam at once underplays the doctrines of essential unity which underpin many pagan faiths, and ignores those religions' multiplicity of invisible spiritual beings.

Aristotle may have been dissatisfied at what he regarded as Xenophon's lack of clarity, but the notion that the 'whole heaven' is one and is God, was, perhaps, the seminal cosmological statement of the Western esoteric tradition – that the entire cosmos, is one, divine, and therefore a living, interdependent whole. Even Xenophon's lack of clarity was to have huge consequences for Western thought, including astrology. Far from being a failure on his part to supply the kind of detail that Aristotle required, uncertainty was to be the starting point for philosophical scepticism, the notion that one can never make any statement of absolute truth.

Discussing the limits of human knowledge, Xenophon drew on the idea of religion, of humanity's relationship with the divine, as a mystery, compromising his supposed monotheism along the way; his supreme unity multiplied into many gods. 'No man knows, or ever will know', he argued, 'the truth about the gods and about everything I speak of; for even if one chanced to say the complete truth, yet oneself knows it not'.[69] Strictly, a cosmos in which a multiplicity of deities emerges out of a unity is henotheism, rather than monotheistic. But that distinction aside, what really matters for the future development of astrology is his theory of knowledge. All, Xenophon adds, is covered in 'seeming', meaning imagination or illusion. Two competing approaches to knowledge were opened by Xenophon's thought, to which all Western philosophy is indebted; either the entire universe is one and therefore knowable, or its essential truth is concealed and it is therefore unknowable. And, from these arguments, all future arguments about the scope of astrology, and the extent to which we can understand and analyse the sky, were to flow. For those philosophers, from the first century BCE onwards, for whom astrology was a topic of concern, the boundary they trod between faith and scepticism allowed them to assume a basic logic in which they accepted astrology's assumption of cosmic unity, but doubted its ability to make prognostications about the world. Whereas the Babylonian astrologers inhabited a universe of uncertainty, desperately trying to make sense of signs sent by celestial deities, the Greek philosophers began to provide models for this uncertainty which, paradoxically, as we shall see, were to allow astrologers to aspire to certainty.

The philosophical edifice of speculative cosmology was further complicated by Heraclitus of Ephesus, who died sometime after 480 BCE. The unifying principle in Heraclitus' universe was the *logos*, technically translated as 'measure' or 'proportion', though as it appears in the opening passage of English translations of John's Gospel as the 'Word', and can equally mean 'reason' or 'mind'. If we assume that *logos* is mind, then the cosmos was governed by a fundamental, divine, intelligent order. Certainty, order was crucial. The sun, Heraclitus wrote, 'will not overstep his measures' and, if by any chance it did, then the Erinyes, the infernal deities whose job was to punish those who broke their oaths, would find out.[70] Heraclitus was no more prepared to tolerate celestial bodies which departed from their allotted path than were the Hebrew prophets. This essential order was divided into pairs of opposites, an idea which, like belief in the one creator, seems to have been influenced by the Persian notion of the cosmic struggle between light and dark, and good and evil. 'God', Heraclitus wrote, 'is day night, winter summer, war peace, satiety hunger'.[71] Yet, while Zoroastrian cosmology anticipated a final triumph of light over darkness, Heraclitus envisaged a perpetual dialectical process in which all opposites could be reconciled, a notion summed up in his famous phrase, 'the path up and down is one and the same'.[72] The process can be seen as rhythmic, or cyclical, with a constant separation of unity into opposites, which later come back together in an eternal return. The notion of order, though, was pervasive and, introducing another component into an emerging, systematic cosmology, Heraclitus applied it to the individual life, writing that 'Man's character is his daimon', a word which, in this context has been translated as 'personal destiny'.[73] Simply, in this sense, one's life, character and personality are intimately bound up with one's place in the cosmos. However, the word has divine associations: Hesiod records that, when the people of the Golden Race died, they became daimones, a word translated either as 'pure spirit', good beings who acted as guardians for human beings.[74]

Heraclitus left unanswered the question of how far one's ethical behaviour carried rewards in the afterlife. The general view was that good behaviour counted for no more after death than did, say, political achievement. Homer's account of Odysseus' visit to the underworld is indicative of the early Greek view of the afterlife. The great poet told how the victor of the Trojan War encountered his mother, a virtuous and noble figure, together with Agamemnon, the greatest of all kings, and found that both were trapped underground in the same miserable world of shades and darkness as individuals who had lived a poor or immoral existence. Most depressing of all were the words of Achilles, the *Iliad*'s greatest warrior. In spite of his magnificent life in the overworld, in the underworld he was no better than the lowliest person. 'By god', he tells Odysseus, 'I'd rather slave on earth for another man – some dirt poor tenant farmer who scrapes to keep alive – than rule down here over all the breathless dead'.[75] The Homeric soul had nothing to look forward to except an eternity bound to the earth and, unlike Egypt, for example, Hesiod's starry heavens played no part in humanity's immortal future.

The focus on the sky as a source of enlightenment, truth or salvation finds support in the teachings of Parmenides, an Eleatic philosopher who was probably born around 515 BCE, so was in his twenties when Heraclitus died.[76] He visited Athens in around 450 BCE, and met the young Socrates, through whom his ideas would have been transmitted to Plato. Parmenides developed the notion of two paths, one to opinion and falsehood, corresponding to darkness and night, and the other to absolute truth, day and light. Truth, though, Parmenides reveals in an allegory of his ascent to heaven on a solar chariot, is available only to those who can transcend the limits imposed by ordinary existence.

Beginning in the sixth century, we become aware of a possibly reforming trend in Greek religion which goes under the name of Orphism, after its key iconic figure, the mythical Orpheus, famous for his ability to charm wild animals with his exquisite lyre playing.[77] We know little of Orphism's origins, and there is a fair amount of disagreement. It may have been archaic, or its teaching may have been formulated in the fourth century BCE. It certainly veered towards monotheism in the sense of a supreme God, Zeus, encompassing all others.[78] But, if Orphic teachings are genuinely sixth-century, it is tempting to see possible Indian connections in view of certain key doctrines regarding the soul, particularly reincarnation – the transmigration of souls in which, though successive incarnations, the soul might occupy a stone or an animal as much as a human; there are certainly Egyptian and Phoenician parallels.[79] This marks a substantial break with the literal, dismal Homeric view of the soul's destination as a gloomy subterranean existence. Equally important was the introduction for the first time of a notion of personal salvation, of what Plato was to call 'remissions of sins and purifications for deeds of injustice', of rewards for the virtuous and punishment – 'terrible things' – for those who have neglected the gods.[80] This was a development of immense significance. When the soul's ultimate destination was moved from the earth to the sky and the mechanism for salvation was projected onto the stars, the foundation was laid for all those Middle Eastern religions which located heaven, and salvation, in the sky. The celestial tradition proved persistent and, in the second century CE, Lucian claimed that it was Orpheus who taught astrology to the Greeks. He played a lyre, the poet added, whose sweet sound charmed the wild beasts, and whose seven strings represented the seven planets.[81] From the Orphic point of view, it was not the celestial order's brilliant mathematical power which required respect, but the harmony and beauty it embodied, and the feelings it aroused, emotions which were later to be idealized as Platonic love, in the sense that love of wisdom, including knowledge of the cosmos, was a quality of the soul.[82] This much is public knowledge. But one of the keys to Orphism was its secrecy: only the initiated were privy to its truths.

Orphic teaching was to play a major part in the work of Pythagoras, a man widely considered to have been one of the most influential philosophers of all time.[83] We know that Pythagoras was born on the Aegean island of Samos sometime between 586 and 570 BCE although many of the details of his life are uncertain. As a young man he probably knew both Thales and Anaximander and it is said that he also studied in Egypt and, after the capture of Egypt by the Persians in 525 BCE, and in Babylon, where he was taken as a prisoner. He is also said to have studied with the druids, an idea that is quite plausible considering that the Celtic world extended down to Italy and Greece. Suggestions of cultural mixing are reinforced by the fact that druids, like the Orphics, believed in reincarnation. Julius Caesar said that the belief that they would live again made the Celts braver in battle.[84] Around 518 BCE Pythagoras returned to his home on Samos and, both there and in other parts of Greece, he used his time visiting religious shrines and teaching mathematics, combining religious initiation with a quest for the origin and nature of the universe. From Samos he emigrated to Croton, the Greek colony in southern Italy, which became the base for the Brotherhood, the group of disciples which congregated around him, eager to hear his message of salvation though a mixture of wisdom and morality.

We do know that the Pythagoreans observed a code of secrecy which placed a ban on the propagation of Pythagorean teachings outside the order. True initiates abstained from eating meat, grew their hair and nails, held all their goods in common and observed a series of taboos which made for a strict lifestyle. They were not unlike *saddhus*, Indian holy beggars, though they lived in a monastic environment. In the context of Greek religion, as Orphics, they represented a reformed branch of the worship of Dionysus but, although they rejected the Bacchic revels of the Dionysians, they still appear to have used a mixture of wine and opium to achieve transcendent states. As Orphism taught that the body is a prison in which the soul is preserved until it has paid its penalty, so the rituals and lifestyle of Pythagoreanism were designed to purify the body and so assist in the liberation of the soul.

The concept that the earth is a sphere is sometimes also attributed to Pythagoras; this was not a simple geographical observation, but a religious one; the perfect solid is spherical, and the entire living cosmos is a sphere. He may also be responsible for the use of the word *kosmos*, meaning 'world-order' (although some say this, as well as the concept of the spherical universe is due to Parmenides, who was born after Pythagoras, around 515 BCE). *Kosmos* can also be translated as 'order' or 'adornment', the root of the modern 'cosmetic'; the Pythagorean cosmos is, simply, beautiful. It is not the same as the Latin universe, which implies order, but not beauty and harmony.[85] Unfortunately for us, as a subscriber to Orphic traditions of secrecy, Pythagoras left no written accounts of his teaching, so we have to glean what we can about him from later versions, and our knowledge is necessarily fragmentary. What survives, though, is enough to piece together a coherent picture of a harmonious cosmos based on soul and number; the physical cosmos is embedded in soul and measured by number. Pythagoras' enduring contribution to cosmology lay in his theory that number and numerical relationships, or harmonies, were the basis of the universe, that the universe could be explained through number, and that therefore each number contains a meaning beyond the literal representation of a particular quantity.[86] According to this system, the number one represents the quality of 'one-ness', or the One out of which all creation emerges; two represents the clash of 'duality'; three the harmonious synthesis of the two; and four the emergence into physical form. The process by which this process takes place is the 'decad', based on the idea that $1+2+3+4=10$. The procedure was as follows: the number one gives a single point, representing the One, the Unlimited; add a second point and the two can be linked by a straight line; add a third point and we can draw a triangle, a two-dimensional plane figure; finally, when a fourth point is added we can create a solid four-dimensional figure consisting of the four elements – a pyramid. This simple mathematical principle was extended into a set of geometrical propositions which accounted for the process by which Anaximander's 'Unlimited' produced the material world. In an application of the theory of eternal return, the system then turned in on itself and the 'ten' reverted to the 'one', for the whole process to begin again. The notion of the universe as a mathematical, geometrical construct was henceforth to be central to classical philosophy, survived in the near east after the fall of Rome and re-entered Europe in the twelfth century, surviving until the early seventeenth century. All human life, from physiology to morality was given geometrical analogies, in a structure which provided, and continues to provide, a rationale for the systematic interpretation of the horoscope according to mathematical principles.

The consideration of mathematical harmonies led naturally to musical ones, and Pythagoras is usually also credited with the discovery of the basics of acoustics, the numerical ratios, or harmonies, underlying the musical scale, although the stories of Orpheus' seven-stringed lyre suggest a much earlier, long-standing tradition. As each planet rushed through space in its own geometrical relationship to the earth, it made a sound. Together, these sounds produced the celestial harmony of the spheres. Influenced by this view, Plato was to express the proportions of the cosmos in terms of the musical scale in the *Timaeus*. In the seventeenth century Johannes Kepler made the 'music of the spheres' the basis of his entire cosmology, and one of his greatest works was *Harmonices Mundi*, the Harmony of the World. The whole principle was that, as long as human beings successfully lived in tune with the celestial harmonies, peace and order would be maintained. The notion was a commonplace in the Renaissance and Kepler's contemporary, William Shakespeare, had Ulysses say, in *Troilus and Cressida*, 'Take but degrees away, untune that string, and hard what discord follows.'[87]

Empedocles, who may have lived from around 495 to 435 BCE, and was of a later generation to Pythagoras, Xenophon and Heraclitus, contributed significantly to the cosmological discourse. He seems to have been influenced by Parmenides' dialectic, and perhaps by Persian dualism, arguing that all historical, natural and individual processes in the cosmos oscillate between two opposites, strife and love; whenever one of these reaches universal dominance then the cosmos unravels in a version of the eternal return, only to be created again in an inevitable cycle of creation and decay.[88] There was a clear apocalyptic narrative here which was to later feed into astrological accounts of the life and death of the universe. However, Empedocles' major contribution to Western cosmology was his apparent solution of the problem which had been bothering philosophers since Thales: was water the fundamental material of the cosmos, or was it fire, perhaps, or earth, or air? Empedocles declared that it was all four, to whom he gave the divine names Zeus, Hera, Aidoneus and Nestis, corresponding, in some accounts, to fire, air, earth and water.[89] We need to sound a note of caution here. Empedocles' work has been subject to later interpretations and possible misinterpretations. He was a poet and his work was couched allegorically, in terms of the religious understanding of the time. What precisely he meant by the four deities he picked, and how he understood their relationships with the four elements, or what the elements exactly were, has been called into question.[90] However, for the purpose of understanding the development of later astrological ideas, it is those later readings of Empedocles, however erroneous, that are crucial. And, for the purposes of later commentators, Empedocles' version of the four elements, as they came to be known, were to be accepted, almost without question, as the fundamental building blocks of all physical matter for the next 2,000 years, until the seventeenth century. As such, they were, from the early centuries CE on, fundamental to the astrological worldview. Even now, they have a resonance, having been adapted and incorporated by the psychologist C.G. Jung in the metaphysical structure of analytical psychology.[91] But, and Jung understood this, matter did not exist without mind, and Aristotle himself said that, according to Empedocles, each of the elements *is* soul.[92] The separation between matter and psyche is a modern fantasy which meant nothing to the Greeks. As Jane Themis pointed out, the seasons, with their physical experience of rain, sun and wind, were alive and were worshipped.[93] This is why Empedocles and his fellow philosophers were described by Culianu, with deliberate reference to the word's use in non-Western societies, as 'medicine-men', physicians and seers, concerned with visionary journeys through the cosmos as much as fascination with its structure.[94]

The Greek philosophers were theorists. This does not mean that they were not practitioners. They quite clearly were, and the development of the idea of the philosophical lifestyle, lived in harmony with the cosmos, was central to their work. They were also as concerned as the Babylonian astrologers with abstract models, with what David Brown called the 'EAE paradigm', but they differed in that they were moving from models which depended on many gods, to one which required only a single creator. In their own way, too, the Babylonians had to adjust to the Zoroastrianism of their Persian rulers, and the emerging Greek philosophical monotheism should be seen as part of an international trend. When Babylonian astrology was imported into the Greek world in the third and second centuries, it was incorporated into the theoretical foundations laid down by the Presocratics. However, the observational imperative was maintained. For some, astrology had to be based on empirical observation and seasonal cycles. We have just a few hints that the pragmatic, naturalistic astrology of *Works and Days*, Brown's 'PCP Paradigm' – the reliance on the empirical prediction of celestial phenomena and related events – was continuing.

By the early fifth century, Hesiod's 'cosmic man', whose life was ideally to be tied to the stars not through any concept of influence, but on account of their role as seasonal time-keepers, was taken up by Hippocrates. Hippocrates' universe was a materialist version of the Babylonian cosmos in which humanity is constantly surrounded by invisible agents, but without their individual divinity; the air was no longer Enlil, the storm god, just plain, simple air. Humanity was an integral part of the world of the four elements and, as the seasons changed, indicated by the rising and setting of different stars, so the balance of fire, air, earth and water shifted. Disease was caused first by an imbalance between the body's own elemental system and the environment, but the cause of such daily change was astronomy.[95] In such a context it became critical to measure the seasons accurately: one's health – and perhaps death – depended on it. Describing the diagnosis and treatment of disease, he wrote,

> If it be thought that all this belongs to meteorology, he will find out on second thoughts, that the contribution of astronomy to medicine is not a very small one, but a very great one indeed. For with the seasons man's diseases, like other objective organs, suffer change.[96]

In general, Hippocrates argued that humans consisted of four main components. In one text, the *Nature of Man* he asserted that people were a mixture of four

Empedoclean elements (fire, air, earth and water), four qualities (moist, dry, hot and cold), and four substances (blood, phlegm, yellow bile and black bile).[97] There are many inconsistencies throughout his work, which may be evidence of a 'school' of Hippocrates, with different authors, perhaps students, attributing their work to the master. However, in *Airs, Waters and Places*, a seasonal model was outlined, which was to become standard in medieval medicine:

Season	Quality	Substance
Winter	Cold	Phlegm
Spring	Moist and Warm	Blood
Summer	Dry and Warm	Yellow Bile
Autumn	Dry	Black Bile

There was a dynamic process underlying this pattern in which each humour achieves dominance in turn. In Hippocrates' physical rationale, phlegm is dominant in winter because it is colder to the touch than blood or bile. Blood assumes its greatest strength in spring when people are most likely to haemorrhage, and suffer from hot, red complaints – typically fevers. In summer, when yellow bile is dominant, blood is still strong and phlegm is at its weakest point. Blood is then at its weakest in Autumn. Each season then has its expected weather which is related to the stars, as well as age and sex. For example:

> If at the rising of the Dog Star stormy rain occurs and the Etesian winds blow, there is hope that the distempers will cease and that the Autumn will be healthy. Otherwise there is danger lest deaths occur among the women and children, and least of all among the old men.[98]

The sky clearly was recognized as a source of practical benefit. By around 450 BCE the outlines had been established of the medical astrology which was later to dominate European medicine for half a millennium, from the twelfth to seventeenth centuries, and in which precise astronomical measurement was a matter of life and death. It is important to understand that the Hippocratic project was explicitly anti-magical. It was not practising an astrology of the kind that was designed to draw down the moon, as one text, *On the Sacred Disease* (epilepsy), argued:

> If these people claim to know how to draw down the moon, cause an eclipse of the sun, make storms and fine weather, rain and drought, to make the sea too rough for sailing or the land infertile, and all the rest of their nonsense, then, whether they claim to be able to do it by rites or by some other knowledge of practice, they seem to be impious rogues.[99]

The PCP paradigm had its own momentum and, just when Hippocrates was writing, the Greeks began to write astronomical and meteorological diaries called *parapegmata*, a programme which continued for about 300 years. The early *parapegmata* mention two astronomers, Meton and Euctemon, who made observations in Thrace, Macedonia, the Cyclades and Athens, apparently using the signs of the zodiac to describe planetary positions, only a few decades after the zodiac's first appearance in Babylon.[100] Whatever the Greek star-watchers were doing in the fifth century, they were in touch with Babylonian colleagues. As in Babylon, this work was of religious benefit in the reorganization of the calendar. Months and days were sacred to deities, and the correct observation of festivals at the right time was as essential to collective welfare as it was to the Babylonians, Egyptians or Jews.[101] It was crucial to civic religion, to the health of the polis. The festival of Kronos was on the 12th day of the first Athenian month, Hekatombaion (mid-July to mid-August), and the god was hardly likely to be pleased if state or personal sacrifices took place on the wrong date.[102] The whole Athenian calendar was therefore reformed and revised at the end of the fifth century, all the better for Athenian life to harmonize with the celestial. It was in this context that the Athenian philosopher Plato was to draw together a series of existing strands in Greek thought, laying the foundations for Western astronomy and astrology until the seventeenth century.

10

Greece: The Platonic Revolution

Wherefore we ought to fly away from earth to heaven as quickly as we
can; and to fly away is to become like God, as far as this is possible;
and to become like him, is to become holy, just, and wise.[1]

By the beginning of the fourth century BCE a series of significant currents in
Greek cosmology were being pulled together by the Athenian philosopher Plato,
the towering figure in Western thought until modern times. Even in the twenty-
first century Plato's philosophy overshadows Western thought from political
theory to pure mathematics, abstract art and New Age mysticism. It has been
said that all Western philosophy is a footnote to Plato and his equally famous
student, Aristotle. Whatever the truth of this, and a strong case can be made,
Plato is certainly the formative influence in Western attitudes to the heavens. He
decisively shaped astronomy, in terms of an understanding of the physical nature
of the sky, and all subsequent debates about astrology's validity have taken place
in the context of the arguments he outlined regarding the nature of knowledge,
and the difficulty of knowing anything for certain. He determined the shape
of European cosmology, establishing a dogma that was only finally shattered
when Galileo peered through his telescope in 1609, but has echoes down to the
present day. One thing, though, needs to be understood about Plato's cosmos; it
was moral. It was embedded in psyche. It had soul and personality.[2] And it is this
that provided a, if not the, rationale for astrology as it left behind the capricious
world of the Babylonian pantheon. Plato laid the foundations for a universe
which could be trusted.

Plato was born into an aristocratic Athenian family around the year 428 BCE,
and died around the age of 80 in 348. His school in Athens, the Academy,
survived, with interruptions, for 1,000 years, until the year 529 CE. It was closed,
not because there was a lack of demand for its teachings, but because the
Emperor Justinian was seized by a righteous, if futile, desire to bring an end to
all pagan learning. The Christian monarch's attempt to suppress Platonism was,
though, too little, too late, for Plato's ideas had long since penetrated Christian
theology. They were present at the new religion's foundation and many of the
most influential Christian Church Fathers, including St Augustine who laid the
foundations for medieval attitudes to astrology in the early fourth century CE,
had received a classical education, including instruction in Platonic thought.
Augustine famously said that the Platonists were the only pagans with whom
one could have an intelligent conversation.[3]

Plato's worldview was profoundly shaped by his despair at the collapse of an imagined perfect old order – Hesiod's golden age. Dismayed by the wars between the city states – he was born during the first Peloponnesian War of 431 to 421 and was a teenager during the second war, from 414 to 404 – and hostile to the two most familiar political alternatives, tyranny and democracy, he advocated the creation of a new form of state which was to be based on the harmonization of the social and political order with the laws discerned in the cosmos by Pythagoras. His goal was to import the Babylonian cosmic state, but remodel it in line with the dominant trends in Greek cosmology, a cosmos which was alive, intelligent, ordered and mathematical. His vision was all-embracing. He imagined a utopia in which there would be no room for error, in which the sun, as Parmenides warned, would never exceed its limits and the full moon, as the Babylonian astrologers feared, would never fall on the wrong day. It was not as if he was starting from scratch. There appears to have been a general orientation of Greek temples from east to west, to the rising and setting sun, though there are notable exceptions, such as the temple of Apollo at Bassae which faces north–south, and the measurements are loose.[4] But, either way, the notion that one should align one's earthly state with the celestial was not unknown.

Plato was profoundly influenced by his teacher, Socrates, in a number of crucial respects.[5] Most important, perhaps was the ethical argument that went as follows: the soul is more important than the body and individual actions should therefore be designed to benefit the soul; the happy life is a fulfilled life, the fulfilled life is a virtuous life and the virtuous life benefits the soul. Therefore morality shuns revenge, emphasizes non-violence, elevates service to one's fellows and depends on a cosmically sanctified self-interest rather than worship of capricious gods. For this radical break with tradition, Socrates was put to death. However, as we shall see, concern with the well-being of the soul was, from the third century BCE onwards, to be one of the central features of Greek astrology.

Plato's cosmology was set out primarily in two of his most important dialogues, the *Timaeus*, in which he outlined the creation and structure of the cosmos, and the *Republic*, which formulated the rules for the perfect cosmic state. Supporting material for correct governance was provided in the *Laws*, while one shorter text, the *Epinomis*, provided additional astronomical material.[6] Other dialogues, including the *Symposium*, *Phaedo* and *Phaedrus*, discussed the theory of knowledge, vital if one was to know one's place in the cosmos, and explored the soul's relationship with the stars. All Plato's works were written down as dialogues between two or more characters, who debated the finer points of cosmology, the soul, the state and the stars. It is often difficult to disentangle his own ideas from the general debate and we can never be sure if we have identified his 'real' thoughts. Where Plato was trying out ideas, his followers saw a system and 'Platonism', which itself comes in different varieties, was created. However, that said, there is a broad consensus as to the nature of Platonic thought. Simply, he believed that the material, phenomenal world inhabited by humanity may be seen as an illusion resting in a real world consisting of 'soul', conceived as thoughtful, intelligent, benevolent reason, and emanating from the mind of a creator, a remote, impersonal God, best conceived of as a creative intelligence, the source of reason and good (itself defined as stability and order) and described by words such as father or maker and constructor of the universe.[7] The Platonic God did not answer prayer or intervene in the world on a whim; he (although we should probably avoid gender stereotypes) was a remote, rational and benevolent creator. This is a generalization and we struggle to find the right words, and separate later traditions from what Plato himself meant; to say that the physical world is an illusion does not mean that it is not 'real', for we quite clearly experience it as such and, in the *Timaeus*, the body of the world is created before its soul. The stars and planets assumed importance because they revealed the creator. It was not quite as the Psalmist put it – 'the heavens are telling the glory of God, and the firmament proclaims his handiwork'[8] – but it was similar. For Plato, the planets had been placed in the sky for the 'determining and preserving of the numbers of Time', to identify the creator's unfolding Ideas.[9] Time in the Platonic cosmos was, in a sense familiar to our modern Einsteinian world, less a means of measuring the passage of events than an organizing principle. For Plato, the order of the heavens was a mirror of divine reason, an assumption which made the study of astronomy so important. His God was almost Zurvanite in his distance from humanity and the argument may be made that his new cosmology hinged around the importation of Persian theology. The Persian conquest of Greece had failed but the Zoroastrian God of time proved irresistible. And, while Platonists were not star-worshippers, at least not until the late Roman Empire, they did revere the mathematical beauty of the regular movements of the celestial bodies.

There is some anecdotal evidence that Babylonian astrologers were visiting Greece by the late fifth century, and that Greek scholars were interested in Babylonian astrology, prior to Plato, as one would expect from such inquisitive individuals.[10] Plato observed the way in which Babylonian astrology was applied to political problems and realized that, in simple practical terms, the Babylonians had far more knowledge of the heavens than the Greeks. For this reason he, or his followers, recommended the introduction into Greece of Egyptian and Babylonian planetary deities.[11] But, even though he thought that astrology was, in principle, a valuable aid to the management of the state, his attitude to contemporary Babylonian astrology itself was quite dismissive, mainly because he thought it lacked the mathematical models which, he believed, were essential if it was it be genuinely useful. Plato was no fan of the PCP paradigm. He saw no point in empirically correlating celestial patterns with events and expecting a pattern to be identified from the data. He was an exponent of the EAE paradigm; theory was everything. Without theoretical models, Plato believed, astrology could only provide alarming predictions of the things to come:

But the choric dances of these same stars and their crossings one of another, and the relative reversals and progressions of their orbits, and which of the gods meet in their conjunctions, and how many are in opposition, and behind which and at what times they severally pass behind one another and are hidden from our view, and again re-appearing send upon men unable to calculate alarming portents of the things which shall come to pass hereafter, – to describe all this without an inspection of models of these movements would be labour in vain.[12]

But, in theory, he regarded it as important that a true understanding of the cosmos was vital to the wise ruler. Using a nautical analogy, he wrote that 'the true pilot must give his attention to the time of the year, the seasons, the sky, the winds, the stars, and all that pertains to the art, if he is to be a true ruler of a ship'.[13] In the same passage he laughed at people who just gaze at the stars, by which he means the unthinking observation of which he thought the Babylonians were guilty. Plato's anger at the deficiencies of Babylonian astrology was not unprecedented. It appears to have been part of an irritation felt by the Athenian elite against the ignorance of those who lived in fear of celestial omens, illustrated by a story told about Pericles, the Athenian leader, by his former rival, the historian Thucydides. At the outbreak of the Peloponnesian War in 431 BCE, Pericles was preparing to set sail with a vast fleet of 150 ships when, the Roman biographer Plutarch tells us, a solar eclipse took place. 'The sudden darkness', he reports, 'was looked upon as an unfavourable omen, and threw [the Athenian troops] into the greatest consternation'.[14] Pericles took his cloak, used it to shield his pilot from the sun and then asked why this should be any more threatening than the eclipse. Reassured by their leader's wisdom, the Athenian fleet set sail. Plato may not have shared Pericles' position exactly, for he valued the oracle as both a traditional Greek institution and path to truth. But he undoubtedly regarded Babylonian astrology as worthless.

Plato's attack was mirrored by his students. Eudoxus, the most brilliant astronomer of his time, attacked the Babylonians for casting birth charts; he had been born in 408 BCE, two years after the earliest known example.[15] Significantly, neither Plato nor Eudoxus attacked astrology as such, only its practice. But that is a minor consideration. Plato's words, tucked away in the *Timaeus* and rarely noticed by historians, are a triumphal assertion of the belief that the universe can be explained within abstract frameworks. They constitute the core statement in all subsequent European astronomy, down to the seventeenth century, and much of the science. They assert the primacy of theory over observation, claiming that what is observed and experienced – that, as the Babylonians thought, certain celestial movements coincide with alarming events – cannot be trusted. No evidence, no data can make sense without a philosophically correct explanation and, if a phenomenon does not fit the expected mathematical formula, it should be disregarded. The Platonic project was therefore clear – to create a mathematical astronomy which could provide an accurate basis for astrology, predict 'better' and 'worse' births, stave off social decline and postpone political collapse for as long as possible. Plato's grand task was nothing less than to manage world history.

There is no doubt that Babylonian astrology was reaching Plato and his students as is evident from the naming of the planet. Prior to Plato, only Venus had a standard name; Homer called it Eosphoros when it was the morning star, visible just before dawn, and Hesperos when it was an evening star, visible just after dusk. In Hesiod's *Theogony*, only Helios (the sun), Selene (the moon) and Eospheros were named.[16] In the *Timaeus*, the planets were placed in the following order: moon, sun, 'Morning Star' (Eospheros, or Venus), 'The star called sacred to Hermes' or 'Star of Hermes' (Mercury), and, by inference (they were not named) Mars, Jupiter and Saturn; only one planet, Mercury, was given a divine association.[17] The precise matching of Greek planets to Babylonian deities occurred first in the *Epinomis* so, depending on that work's authorship, may have been due to Plato's student Philip of Opus rather than the master himself, though it is also attributed to the Pythagoreans.[18] Saturn, the planet special to Ninurta, became the 'star of Kronos', while Jupiter, sacred to Marduk, the tutelary deity of Babylon, became the 'star of Zeus', the king of the Greek gods. The warlike Nergal was a natural equivalent to the Greek Ares and so the planet Mars became the 'star of Ares'. Aphrodite, he concluded, was naturally the Greek equivalent of Ishtar, so was given the planet Venus, while Nabu, the Babylonian scribe, was an obvious fit for Hermes, the messenger of the Greek pantheon, who was allocated the planet Mercury. All these connections are obvious except for the link of Ninurta, 'the trustworthy farmer of Enlil', to Kronos, lord of the golden race.[19] The *Epinomis* also paid explicit tribute to the Syrian and also, incidentally, Egyptian, origins of astronomy and strongly advocated the introduction of their planetary deities. This was a risky enterprise and he exposed himself to a serious charge of atheism on the grounds that he failed to honour the traditional gods and instead focused on the divinity of the stars. He believed, though, that the Greeks would naturally improve whatever the foreigners had started.[20]

However, the Babylonian astrologers were, ironically, working hard to create just such a framework, the evidence for which is found in their systematic division of the sky into 12 equal sections and the instruction of degrees to measure celestial positions. Nevertheless, Plato's effective provision of a comprehensive cosmological and philosophical manifesto for astrology provided the gateway for its wholesale introduction into the Greek world. So great was his impact on both astronomy and astrology that we should talk of a Platonic revolution to rival the Copernican revolution which, in the sixteenth century, was to set the scene for the modern world by placing the sun, rather than the earth, at the centre of the universe. That the cosmos was regulated by divinely determined, perfect mathematical and geometrical ratios dictated the course of European astronomy until Newton. Plato's cosmos was a single, living, divine entity, in which all parts were inextricably linked to all others. That it was, in itself, divine, rather than created by God as a purely external agent was to provide Christian theology with a crucial dimension from classical times onwards, one in which the world's problems were no longer a product of the Fall, of Adam and Eve's original sin, but of its distance from the perfect, divine source. The path to salvation therefore lay not necessarily through faith alone, but through reason and, in terms of cosmic geography, the way to heaven was charted via the stars. At one level astronomers might peer into the mind of God, or initiates plot a path to heaven while, at the other, astrologers could make statements of astonishing detail about the nature and course of the individual life. Plato was actually the first in a long line of Western astrological reformers, of whom the last was Johannes Kepler in the seventeenth century, who reacted against what they saw as the chaos of the astrology inherited from the East. The result of every phase of astrological reform except for the most recent, in the twentieth century, was a massive boost in astronomical research, the purpose of which was to refine and hone the practical application of astrology to daily concerns.

In his quest for universal truth, Plato drew together all the previous philosophical currents except those which regarded matter as the primary cause of everything. He had no time for the atomists, for example, who thought that, once they had established what the smallest particle of matter was, the world's existence might be explained. By contrast, he was deeply influenced by Heraclitus and Parmenides, borrowing the sceptical notion that no significant knowledge could come from direct observation of the natural world, leaving abstract thought as the only path to wisdom. He was to formalize what the Babylonian astrologers had always known – that absolute knowledge is available, but human fallibility means that their forecasts are often technically wrong.

From Pythagoras he adopted reincarnation and the mathematical universe arranged in musical harmonies. From his teacher Socrates, he learnt that philosophy should concern itself with values and with the nature of the cosmos rather than with its physical composition; it followed, and this was a cardinal tenet of Platonic cosmology, that every man and woman is ultimately responsible for their own actions. Also embedded within Plato's cosmogony was a notion which it is now easy to take for granted, but was a revolutionary shift away from the conventions of Hesiodic, Babylonian and Egyptian creation myths. Life no longer emerged out of a primeval chaos or water or egg, but from Xenophon's supreme creator, the creative mind and father of all. But this was not the external creator God of later Christian theology. The entire universe was itself alive, divine and intelligent as, therefore, were individual parts of it, including the planets. In a sense, the cosmos *was* God.

And from these core beliefs are drawn the fundamental features of Plato's political theology. Firstly, if the universe is governed by mathematical laws, then it functions like a vast machine which, like Newton's some 2000 years later, is essentially deterministic. Freedom, then, is essentially a state of mind. It is for this reason that Karl Popper, in the latter part of the twentieth century, berated Plato as the intellectual ancestor of modern authoritarianism, especially Marxism. He identified political Platonism, the belief in the benevolent dictatorship of the philosopher, as the source of tyranny in the modern world. There are ambiguities in Plato's thought, though, and his counter statement, drawn from his teacher, Socrates, that we are all responsible for our own lives, exists alongside the predetermined universe as a permanent paradox which Popper termed historicism; most theories that the future is broadly predetermined, Popper noticed, require the believer to actively strive to create that future, a philosophy which he termed activism. As the Marxist prepares for the inevitable revolution by forming a revolutionary vanguard, he argued, the Platonic philosopher rides the predetermined cycles of politics and history by administering the state in perfect accord with celestial harmonies. The astrologer, having predicted the future, can influence its outcome; 'all astrology', Popper wrote (meaning Platonic astrology), 'involves the apparently somewhat contradictory conception that the knowledge of our fate may help us influence this fate'.[21] From Plato onwards, the Babylonian notion of an astrology of signs, in which the onus is on the astrologer to read divine messages, can be distinguished from an astrology of celestial order, in which astrology becomes a means of describing the processes to which all people, from kings to the lowliest peasant, are subject. Although their ideologies differ, both approaches to astrology were designed to manage the state. Plato would not necessarily have recognized the two as distinct, for he regarded oracles as a vital means of reading the divine will. But the distinction between the two theoretical models was later to be increasingly important in arguments over astrology's validity. The Platonic model, with its assumption of universal order, was no more nor less free than the conventional Greek cosmos, with its pantheon of competing gods and goddesses, and the astrology it spawned was to allow for human participation, exactly as did the Babylonian. As Popper argued, Platonism made human participation in the cosmic drama a necessity. In this sense, the Platonic cosmos actually enhanced human freedom in that one's destiny was to be influenced by one's own actions rather than by the whims of deities who were under no obligation to accept the sacrifices and offerings made to them.

For Plato, the stars and planets represented the world soul, the universal intelligence. Astrology as *astro-logos* became, in the hands of his successors, a rational construct for interpreting the mind of the universe, or divine providence. There was a shift of emphasis from the Babylonian concept of multiple deities, but only a slight one. Plato's reverence for the universe as a single entity did not blind him to the power of individual gods and goddesses speaking through the stars. His system may have been monist in that it emerged from a single creator, but the world itself was pluralist.

Platonism was to infuse Christianity, offering an alternative perspective on the human relationship with the divine which was somewhat more optimistic than the gloomy view, derived from pessimistic readings of the expulsion of Adam and Eve from Eden, in which humanity was alienated from God and mired in sin. Plato had no problem with Greek tradition. He accepted the standard cosmogony set out by Hesiod, including the birth of the gods and goddesses within a framework in which chaos gave way to ordered cosmos.[22] But, into the picture comes Xenophon's God, and the gods and goddesses of the Greek pantheon were allocated a reduced status as his agents.

As creator, God does not create matter *ex nihilo*, out of nothing, but brings order to existing chaos, although, he does not create a universe outside himself, like the God of Genesis. Instead the universe emanates out of him, as he thinks. First the world soul, universal consciousness, emerges and then physical existence materializes out of soul. If God is reason, and the whole universe shares in his divine nature, then it follows both that we contain a little of this original divine nature, even if enclosed in a body driven by raw passion and gut instinct, and that our path back to God is therefore through the use of reason and philosophical contemplation and, and this is critical for the history of both astronomy and astrology, through the stars.

And this is the essential point – that the mathematical motion of the universe is predetermined, but the motion of the soul; the psyche is not. It can choose. It is in a participatory relationship with the divine. The cosmos is a moral as well as mathematical entity, and the order evident in the regular patterns of sun, moon and stars is matched by disorder and variety. Cosmos never entirely does away with chaos. But while, Plato, like the Hebrew prophets, fears chaos, the random-ness which allows for ecstatic contact with the divine is of enormous value. So is the indeterminacy which allows the individual to make moral choices.

From Heraclitus Plato adopted two modes of existence, 'Being' (influenced by Parmenides' Way of Truth) and 'Becoming' (influenced by Parmenides' Way of Seeing). God himself inhabits the condition of Being, in which everything is eternal, perfect, motionless, good and true. Being contains the models (like every architect, God needs a set of plans) on which everything we know is based. Plato called these Ideas, though they are also known as 'ideal forms', or 'types' or 'archetypes'. His Ideas precede action; the belief that consciousness precedes matter is the origin of idealism, the belief in a perfect world. As a Pythagorean, Plato believed that such Ideas could only be expressed as numbers, or as geometrical forms. A Platonic 'Idea' is not a mental construct as we would have it, but a pre-existent essence, that which makes a thing exactly what it is as opposed to something else. The basic concept is that the essences which define things pre-exist any instances of the things themselves. Thus the essence of 'treeness' pre-exists any actual tree. The terms 'essence' and 'substance' are variously used to describe the idea that there is a layer of reality underlying the visible world. So Plato's philosophy provides the foundation for the still-influential 'essentialist' or 'substantialist' strand in Western thought.

As soon as God begins the creation, Becoming comes into existence. In Becoming everything is in Heraclitus' state of constant flux, literally always becoming something else, while remaining as a copy of the original Idea. Plato is replicating, in different language, the distinction between the sacred and the profane that Eliade has argued is fundamental to the religious experience.[23] Without necessarily agreeing with the idea, Heraclitus and Plato were sufficiently close to the Indian notion that the material world is essentially an illusion for us to suspect that both were influenced by earlier contacts between Greece and India at the Persian court. As Plato put it: 'You must suppose, then … that there are these two powers of which I have spoken, and that one of them is supreme over everything in the intelligible world, the other over everything in the visible world – I won't say in the physical universe or you will think I'm playing with words. At any rate you understand there are these two orders of things, the visible and the intelligible'.[24] There was an unchangeable (intelligble) world you cannot see, and a changeable (visible) one you can.

There is undeniably a form of dualism in Plato's thought, but we need to understand that his is not the absolute mind–body split that entered Western thought with Descartes. He was, instead, concerned with the interplay of inter-linked poles of existence. Mind is real for Plato, but so is body. Platonic dualism is written into the fabric of the universe. While he believed that movement was necessarily a bad thing because it resulted in change, decline and falsehood, and that perfect bodies remained utterly motionless, less movement was better than more. The stars, which appeared to hold exactly the same position in relation to each other, even though they appeared to rotate around the earth once a day, were representatives of cosmic order, as was their daily movement from east to west. The planets also moved from east to west every day, so shared in some of that stellar perfection, but over longer periods of anything from a month in the case of the moon to 29 years for Saturn, they wandered (the Greek word planet literally means wanderer) north and south, slowed down, stopped and even appeared to travel backwards. Even the sun, which has the most predictable motion, was constantly changing colour. It was these variations which formed the bridge between heavenly order and terrestrial chaos.

Plato is insistent that naturalistic causes do not explain the ordering and motions of the planets.[25] Instead, and in spite of appearances, he claimed that the planets moved according to perfect circular patterns, based on geometrical structures. He later added that the fact that the planets follow such erratic courses reinforces the need to understand celestial motions, pray reverently at the proper times and avoid blasphemy.[26] The Hebrew Prophets would have agreed.

Plato believed that all physical things were made of mixtures of the four Empedoclean solids – fire, air, earth and water – structured according to the four physical solids that could be created from triangles.[27] Plato also adopted the Pythagorean doctrine that the distances between the planets and the earth are musical sequences. Each of the planetary spheres has a siren who is borne round on the sphere and sings one note as she does so, the total of eight notes blending into a single harmony.[28] Mathematically, then the Platonic cosmos is geometrical and musical. But there is more.

The moral structure of the universe was based on the premise that the world emanated from the mind of God. The initial phase involved the development of the world soul, out of which matter itself was created. In spatial terms, the cosmos, though inherently perfect, therefore became ever more degenerate as it became more distant from the creator. The fixed stars, whose appearance never changed were most divine, being closest to God, while the planets became steadily less divine as the crystal spheres on which they revolved moved closer to the earth in the order Saturn, Jupiter, Mars, Mercury, Venus, the sun and, lastly, the moon, whose rapidly changing appearance was proof of its profound imperfection. Eventually we arrive at the earth, which is round and held at the centre of the universe by the whole system.[29] The earth is perfectly still, but everything is in a constant state of decline, as witnessed by both individual disease and death and the sickness which Plato saw all around him in the body politic; only the soul retains a link with God. But the situation was not as bad as it seemed. Even corrupt matter was an emanation of the Nous, the divine mind. As such it partook of the good. The assumption of an essentially good universe was to shape Christian cosmology and eventually was to find echoes in eighteenth-century notions of the perfectibility of man.

The planetary spheres themselves revolved on the Spindle of Necessity, which extended from the poles up through the planetary spheres to the stars. Around the spindle were clustered the three *moirae*, the 'Destinies and ruthless avenging Fates', who, according to Hesiod, 'give men at their birth both evil and good to have; and they pursue the transgressions of men and of gods'.[30] Plato had them singing as they spun fate; Lachesis sang of the past, Clotho of the present and Atropos of the things still to come. The task of the musician, a profession Plato deeply admired, was to bring that harmony alive.[31]

The whole structure could also account for all events on earth. Everything that takes place must have a cause but these were arranged in a hierarchy. God, the good, is the 'first', or 'final' cause, which initiated all change in the cosmos, while the motions of the stars and planets, were 'auxiliary' or 'secondary' causes which 'God employs as his ministers in perfecting, so far as possible, the Form of the Most Good'.[32] Therefore, while the planets act as physical causes in terms of the manipulation of the four elements, this process is subordinate to the metaphysical causes emanating from God and the universe's divine, intelligent, rational nature. As expressed by the Stoics in the following centuries, 'the orderly succession of causes wherein cause is linked to cause and each cause of itself produces an effect'.[33] The implication was that astrology could reveal, via the planets, God's will. However, nothing was so simple.

Plato's theory of knowledge is critical for a proper understanding of his attitudes to astrology. There is a clear paradox in his attitude to knowledge gained from the sky, which is underpinned by the contrast between Being and Becoming. The former, which is eternal and true, is perceived through reason, meaning the study of theoretical and abstract principles, while the latter, which can yield only opinion, can never yield reliable information.[34] In the world of Becoming everything is in a state of change. We change from minute to minute, physically and psychologically. Our knowledge also changes. We forget some things and learn others. The divine by contrast is unchanging.[35]

On the one hand the stars were part of the changing, visible, universe and so astrology could never provide accurate information by tracking their movements, which was the Babylonians' fundamental error. As Plato put it, 'the region above the heaven was never worthily sung by any poet'.[36] This cosmic dualism led direct to an apparent schism in human knowledge. For those who could not see beyond their own senses, and were trapped in the world of Becoming, there was no possibility of truth.[37] And here lies another of Plato's contributions to Western thought – scepticism. Under ordinary circumstances, in this material world, there could be no true knowledge, and the only respectable position was doubt. The consequence, in the following centuries, was that the most serious attacks on astrology were launched by Platonists. Plato himself explained human ignorance though one of his best-known myths, in which human beings are likened to cave-dwellers who are gazing at the wall, imagining that their shadows, cast by a fire on the wall, are reality.[38] However, ignorance is not unavoidable and, once the individual has emerged from the cave, he will begin to 'contemplate the appearances of heavens and heaven itself' – the night sky. Progressively the soul begins to turn away from darkness and to learn to see the shining truth, the essence, the good, that is the true nature of the cosmos.[39] Literally, the cycles of the stars and planets from day to day and year to year reveal the revolutions of 'Reason in the Heaven', teaching humanity not just about the external heavens, but themselves as embodiments of the cosmos.[40] Taken together, Plato's description of the stars as markers of time, causes, paths to God and sources of information about humanity provide a persuasive rationale for astrology.

Even so, Plato never directly says what form of astrology he is proposing in order to replace what he sees as the chaotic Babylonian version. He is clear that, as with all forms of knowledge, it must employ absolute reason, not rely only on observation.[41] But the clues are contained throughout his texts. The collective astrology which had been used to manage the Mesopotamian cosmic state was now to be used as an organizing framework rather than a predictive tool. The individual astrology which had recently emerged in Babylon was to be used not for working out one's destiny. In fact, one should not even use it all. Instead by studying the mathematical principles, geometrical forms and musical harmonies, and by gazing at the sky, one would take one's soul closer to God, to the divine mind and, in the process, distinguish between reality and the shadows on the cave wall.[42]

In spite of Plato's respect for the East, there was a certain nationalism in his position, and his rejection of Babylonian astrology was contradicted by a respect for native Greek oracles, which he saw as vital to the smooth running of the state, as well as a powerful source of truth. He had the highest respect for the political advice received from the great oracles, mentioning specifically Delphi, Dodona or Ammon (note the Egyptian influence – Ammon was the Egyptian solar deity Amon or Amun, equated by the Greeks with Zeus: his oracle was in Egypt). He argued that such advice, whether from 'visions' or 'inspiration from heaven' should no more be altered than should rules derived from sacred numbers.[43] He was the first thinker we know of to introduce a typology of divination, dividing it into two forms, which he attributed to Socrates.[44] The first, mantic prophecy, was the product of frenzy or inspired madness, as found in the oracles, such as Delphi. He preferred to call this variety manic, rather than mantic, on the grounds that true madness could take one close to the divine. From this he distinguished augury, based on rational methods, such as the observation of birds and signs and their interpretation in line with established rules. Why he could not include Babylonian astrology within such rational divination is not clear.

Given Plato's concern with the theory of astrology and his rejection of the practice, at least as it was known in Babylon, it was down to later generations to adapt these arguments to take positions either for or against the kind of detailed astrology which claimed to make precise prognostications. It was also left to future philosophers to draw out of his teachings certain principles which were to be crucial to the practice of magic down to the Renaissance. The first of these was the idea that knowledge is possessed by the soul before birth and that the educational process therefore depends on 'remembering' what has been forgotten. The child's mind is not a *tabula rasa*, an empty slate to be filled with knowledge, but a soul to be awakened.[45] Crucially, images could be used as an *aide memoire*, to recover this lost knowledge and enable the soul to, once again, see God.[46] The magical image then becomes an icon, less a portrayal of a divine figure, than a gateway to it. And here, to contradict earlier assertions about the Platonic theory of knowledge, we have to add that events in the temporal world may help the soul recollect knowledge of the divine. The second of Plato's contributions to the later development of magic was that the magician, as a philosopher, must lead a good, moral, ascetic life, in which physical passions are curbed and pleasurable indulgence rejected.[47] Not only does this path lead to happiness, but it enables the soul to see the good, the eternal truth. Without this, magic could not work. Simply, the cosmos was essentially good, magic depended on manipulating the cosmos and this could only be achieved by good people for good ends. This was a matter of simple fact. Piety was essential. As *Timaeus* records, 'all men who possess even a small share of good sense call upon God always at the outset of every undertaking'.[48] To be sure, we have many ancient examples of magic being used to curse one's neighbours, rivals or enemies, at least to judge from the talismans thrown into such sites as the hot springs the Romans used at Bath. But, as a tradition of high magic developed, Platonic theory dictated that to inflict a curse was, as a matter of principle, impossible. It was from this notion of magic as a means of liberating the soul that a tradition developed in the classical word known as theurgy – god-work – as opposed to theology – god-study. When the Greek world wholeheartedly adopted astrology in the second century BCE, it was to take two forms. One, inherited from Babylon was to concentrate on the management and prediction of Becoming via the use of horoscopes. The other, theurgical, was to concentrate on enabling the soul to reconnect with the divine. This was no less practical in intent than horoscopic astrology, but its goal was different.

Observation of the sacred calendar was central to the secure and ordered functioning of the state. Plato set down the perfect education for the good citizen. This included enough mathematics to understand the motions of the sun, moon and stars in order to calculate the calendar 'so that the seasons, with their respective sacrifices and feasts, may each be assigned its due position by being held as nature dictates, and that they may create fresh liveliness and alertness in the State, and may pay their due honours to the gods, and may render the citizen more intelligent about these matters'.[49]

Plato's political astrology was to be applied to the service of the state with authoritarian rigour. The entire organization of the state and politics should, he insisted, be deliberately arranged to conform to the same mathematical principles which regulated the motions of the stars and planets. Solar and lunar cycles, rounded to 360 and 30 days respectively (perhaps borrowed from the Egyptian calendar, or from the *Mul Apin*), were critical: the state was to be governed by a council of 360 members, of whom 30 should govern for a month of 30 days at a time.[50] In the *Laws* the state was a microcosm of the celestial order and, in the *Republic*, the soul was a microcosm of the ideal political system. This was not an astrology of prediction but of political control, closer to the Egyptian model than the Babylonian. But, as a Heraclitian, Plato knew that perfection was a state to be aspired to rather than attained. Life was rhythmic and, if perfection could ever be achieved, it would be instantly lost. He dealt with such problems in his analysis of political and historical patterns, the cyclical rise and fall of states and the birth and decay of societies. All such cycles were contained within a cosmic cycle, which he adapted from Empedocles, in which the planets and stars all returned to the location they occupied at their creation. When then this happened one 'Great Year' would end and other begin.[51] The cosmos would come to an end and be reborn. He offered no other details. Later commentators assumed that the apocalyptic moment would arrive when all the planets occupied the first degree of Aries, the beginning of the zodiac. But all Plato did was set out in his typically obscure manner an elaborate code, the so called 'nuptial number', which specified the length of time it took for the whole cycle to take place. From the fifth-century CE philosopher Proclus onwards, this number has been given as 36,000 years, although it was not until the 1890s that the figure was actually justified on the basis of Plato's text.[52] Of what Plato really thought, or even whether he believed that the number could be specified, we have no idea. What we do know, is that the doctrine which came to be known as *apokatastasis*, the periodic destruction of the world, was to justify the subsequent development of astrology as a means of forecasting global crises including, in the Christian world, the second coming. As Paul Ricoeur put it, the beginning and the end are tied together in a manner which suggests to the collective imagination, a triumph of concordance over discordance.[53]

Plato's view of the afterlife was a compromise between Greek and Egyptian beliefs. He retained Hades, the subterranean world of shades, but allowed the good to ascend to the stars. The virtuous and those who have loved the philosophical life go to heaven after death, 'raised up into a heavenly place by justice', while the others go to the 'places of correction under the earth'.[54] As the Vedas put it 'the seers, thinking holy thoughts, mount him (Time)'.[55] The shift of the immortal soul's home from the underworld to heaven has survived in writing for the first time in Plato's works and represents one of the most dramatic innovations of Greek philosophy. As Plato, said, the 'soul ... traverses the whole heaven'.[56] This is plausibly a democratization of Egyptian cosmology in which only the pharaoh and his queen had a guaranteed spiritual presence in the stars; for Plato, in spite of his elitist instincts, every soul belonged in the starry heavens. There may also be some correspondence with Indian beliefs about salvation in the sky: 'That I do know of thee', the Atharva-Veda intones, 'O immortal, where thy march is upon the sky, where thy habitation is in the highest heaven'.[57] Along with Pythagoras' articulation of the mathematically ordered universe, this also represents the most significant Greek contribution to astrology, distinguishing it from its Babylonian origins. The descent of the soul from the stars leads naturally to an astrology that is deigned to analyse one's moral character and spiritual destiny.[58] In terms of human freedom, the universe was polarized between reason, which might lead humanity back to God, and necessity, the passions, instincts, desires and needs which are part and parcel of physical existence. In the coming centuries, astrology developed as the practical tool which might make this possible.

Plato's spiritual cosmology, set out in the so-called Myth of Er in book X of the *Republic*, established a model for the relationship between the soul and the stars which was to become one of the mainsprings of religious arguments in the Roman world, provided a huge problem for medieval theologians and provided a rationale for astrology which is still evident in the number of New Age astrology books which include the words 'spirit' and 'soul' in their titles. It also established a literary tradition in which it is taken for granted that, whether literally or metaphorically, the soul descends from and will ascend to, the stars.[59] The moral, and this is vital to understanding Plato's views on the correct life-style, was that the just soul benefits after death, and that a virtuous life, lived in harmony with the cosmos as part of the divine, therefore brings rewards. Er himself, the central character in the story, was a soldier who was killed in battle and later revived, but not before surviving in the afterlife for the cosmologically significant period of 12 days.

In the *Timaeus* we read that when God made the stars he fashioned a soul for each one, and so the eighth sphere, that of the stars, is the natural home of humanity in its original, perfect condition. '[God] showed them [the souls] the nature of the Universe, and declared unto them the laws of destiny.'[60] When each soul was implanted in a star it grew into the most god-fearing of living creatures, but, when implanted into a human body, a struggle began in which each soul was tasked to overcome the body's physical passions.

The Myth of Er fleshes out this model. Before birth, Plato tells us, each soul is paraded before Lachesis to choose from a number of lots, or 'patterns of lives', which are taken from her lap and scattered on the ground. Each soul then chooses a life and it is in this act that all future responsibility lies; once the life has been chosen, nobody and nothing else, neither the gods nor any fate, can be blamed for any misfortune that the individual suffers. The souls are then taken before Lachesis again, where each chooses its 'genius' or 'daimon', defined as 'the guardian of his life and the fulfiller of his choice'.[61] Guardian angel might be a modern equivalent. But, we have to understand, the element of choice was crucial; no matter how far life's circumstances might seem to be fated, they were the consequence of a voluntary act.

Plato was issuing a direct challenge to the view, common in literal readings of Homer, that individuals often cannot be held responsible for what they do, that whatever goes right or wrong is ultimately the fault of some god or goddess who is toying with them for their own amusement.[62] Now, the daimon is a spiritual entity but, in the Myth of Er it becomes bound up with the choice of one's life on earth, which explains the word's translation as 'personal destiny'.[63] If the daimon determined the individual character, then we do have some control over our moral choices, independent of external, and often capricious powers, acting through chance or fate. Whereas the heroic mentality, as conventionally portrayed by Homer, was morally helpless and often the architect of its own tragedy, for Plato, moral or prudent behaviour might lead to a fortunate future. The two positions are not mutually exclusive, but we can discern a difference of emphasis. The Platonic view embedded into the emerging cosmological discourse a philosophical basis for the view that, in the astrological universe, the future depends on the individual's successful negotiation with the universe rather than as in Mesopotamia, one's obedience to individual deities. The notion was found much later in the words Shakespeare put into the mouth of Julius Caesar: 'The fault, dear Brutus, is not in our stars, but in ourselves, that we are underlings'.[64] Although the gods had been removed from the equation, the principle was Babylonian. As Heraclitus had said of the greatest oracle in the Greek world, 'the lord whose oracle is in Delphi neither speaks out nor conceals, but gives a sign'.[65] That is, there is no direct instruction to be followed but a sign to read. The Babylonian hypothesis is maintained – wise individuals can read the signs and steer themselves to a successful future – but the cosmos itself, rather than Marduk, say, or Ishtar, becomes the 'thou', the entity with whom individual dialogue takes place.

Back to the Myth of Er, the daimon then leads the soul to Clotho, who ratifies the chosen life, and finally to Atropos, who spins the web of the chosen destiny. And, when its destiny has been finally sealed, the soul passes under the throne of Necessity and is escorted to the arid heat of the Plain of Oblivion, where it drinks the water of the River of Forgetfulness and promptly falls asleep. Then, in the middle of the night, each soul moves to its birth, falling to earth like a shooting star. It followed that each soul had to descend to the earth through the planets, a point of immense significance for both the astrology and religion of the classical world. As Er's journey showed, the route back to the stars was also through the planetary spheres. Now, Plato never developed the astrological implication of this story but if, as he argued, the soul travelled to and from heaven via the planetary spheres, the position of the planets at such moments, should indicate the nature of the enterprise. This was to be the model developed by his successors.

Plato's ideas on the soul changed in his various writings. However, as with his cosmology, we can generalize. The human being consisted of four different parts, the body and a soul divided into three; the divine unfolded in stages, first through soul and mind, and finally through its self-realization in physical form. In the *Phaedrus* Plato attributed to Socrates a threefold structure metaphorically represented by a charioteer and his two horses.[66] The highest part was the rational soul, mind or intellect, which discerns what is true, judges what is real and makes rational decisions. Next was the spirited soul, the active part, the will, whose function was to carry out what reason has decided. Last, and lowest, was the appetitive soul, the seat of emotion and desire, which needed to be restrained by the higher, rational soul. The division of the soul into different functions was to have immense consequences for the future of classical and medieval cosmology for, it was concluded by Plato's successors, if the soul came from the stars, and was ultimately, like all things in the cosmos, divine, then different types of soul would have distinct relationships both with God and the stars. Later forms of Platonic philosophy generally held that there were two types of soul, but the question about their connection with the stars remained. Again, without making any statements of detail, Plato argued that, in general, if the body and all three parts of the soul are balanced in each individual, then the state will function smoothly.[67] For the Platonic astrologer, political stability therefore follows on directly from individual harmony which, in turn, might in theory be deduced from knowledge of the heavens. Plato's theory of soul takes us to the heart of the development of astrology in the Greek world.[68] The concept of the entire universe as alive and resting in soul, or psyche, enabled Plato to see the cosmos as psychological in the modern sense, as having personality, driven by manners, habits, opinions, desires, pleasures, pains or fears.[69] But then this, of course, was how the megalith builders or Palaeolithic calendar-makers would also have understood it.

Plato himself was deeply concerned by the whole question of what he called 'better' and 'worse' births. He believed that children born at the appropriate season and phase of the planetary cycles would be 'better' and more likely to grow into upright, virtuous citizens and hinted that it would be possible to breed such people, a matter which could be achieved if couples married and hence conceived at the right time.[70] Those who were not would be more likely to grow into selfish, decadent adults and, as their number grew, society would slip into terminal decline. However, he never actually specified when children should be born and when they should not. He set out a theoretical framework, but made no steps to elaborate it.

Every human being contains something of the divine, is made of the same stuff as the rest of the universe, and is linked to a star. The task of the incarnated soul is then to lead a just and righteous life. Those who succumb to the passions of the flesh, to greed, jealousy, lust and anger are condemned to be reincarnated as women. And, if they still give in to their baser instincts, they will be reincarnated as whatever sort of animal best reflects their bestial behaviour.

The question, then, was how the individual could avoid this fate. Plato explained this clearly. The universe had come into existence as a compound of 'reason', the attribute of God, and 'necessity', the attribute of physical existence.[71] To give in to physical passion is to be subject to necessity. To control such passions helps the individual return to reason. It is clear that the incarnated souls choose their own lives and therefore cannot blame God, fortune or the gods for their misfortunes: 'The blame is he who chooses: God is blameless'.[72] Those who care for their souls and turn their backs on the demands of the body gain communion with the gods after death.[73]

For the Babylonians what we would understand as fate, as an external ordering principle, appears to have been expressed primarily through the needs and desires of the gods and goddesses, though we may, perhaps, perceive a hint of a sense of personal destiny in *nam* and *šimtu*.[74] In Greece, in spite of the continued importance attached to the dialogue with the divine through oracles, the balance tilted towards the sense of fate as an organizing principle – although in different forms. The concept first appears with Hesiod, who personified *moira* as a goddess and the word could mean one's share or portion; after a battle, for example, a soldier would receive his *moira* of the booty. It might also mean one's lifespan, and hence the individual's relationship with fate as a metaphysical concept in which one life might be fortunate, another less so. Typically a temple of Zeus would have two urns outside it, one with good *moira* and one with bad. Only the gods were entitled to a life of exclusively good *moira*, while humans were dealt good and bad in arbitrary mixtures. The three *moirae* appeared at a child's birth and an adult's marriage and death and, in that even the gods were subject to *moira*, the decrees of the three *moirae* were more powerful than those of Zeus himself.

All living creatures are subject to *ananke*, or necessity, broadly speaking the unavoidable laws of physical existence. How far this extends into the events of our lives though, is another matter. *Ananke* may oblige us to eat and drink, but does it force us to go to war? This is where *pronoia*, or foreknowledge, comes in, for if we are capable of perceiving the future then we can negotiate with it. The key was to avoid *agnoia*, or ignorance. From a Platonic perspective, divination was a means of breaking through the confusion inherent in Becoming, and perceiving the truths contained within Being. By the first century BCE, and perhaps earlier, degrees of the zodiac were known as *moirae*, so the world which had formerly denoted one's fate as in one's share or portion of land, one's physical circumstances, described one's share of the heavens – or the share that the heaven's had in the individual's fate. The virtue of astrology is that, if the planets are recognized as the agents both of providence, *heimarmene*, and *ananke*, as they become when the soul descends through the planetary spheres, then knowledge of their movements naturally enables the astrologer to antici- pate future possibilities and evade or enhance them, depending on preference. Only the third form of fate, *tyche* or chance, was unpredictable, a wild card in the pack. Greek astrology may have been more complex technically than

Babylonian but the negotiation with destiny remained its primary ideological inspiration.

While the existence of a fate determined before birth could not be denied, one's relationship to it might be modified precisely because the entire edifice is rational. This model of human affairs was to pervade Hellenistic thought. The complications were spelt out by Julius Firmicus Maternus in the fourth century, almost 800 years after Plato, as the classical world was drawing to its close.

> But there are some who agree with us to a certain extent and admit that Fate and Fortune have a certain power, which they call *heimarmene*. But they attribute to it a different character which contradicts the law of the necessity of Fate. Thus they appear to maintain which is possible and not possible at the same time.
>
> They claim that this thing which they call *heimarmene* is connected to mankind and all living things by a certain relationship … They claim that we are subject to Fate, that is, to Chance, for attaining the end of life. Thus by the law of Fate they claim one end – that is, dissolution – destroys us and all living beings. But all the things that pertain to our daily lives they say are in our power. What we do while we are alive belongs to us; only our death belongs to Chance or Fate.[75]

There is a logic in the Platonic cosmology which leads directly to a theory of education, which runs like this. If human beings emanate out of the divine then they are themselves divine, even if enclosed in matter, and the rational soul is the means by which the relationship between human and divine can be maintained. Learning then becomes a matter of remembering what one once knew, but have forgotten.[76] But, as we have seen, knowledge gleaned from the visible, material world is unreliable. Plato is therefore the patron saint of scepticism; in astrological terms, the present may be manageable but the future is essentially unknowable. The first major assault on astrology in the ancient world was to come from within Platonism and was penned by Carneades, head of the Academy in the second century BCE. Yet, the parallel belief – that, if we only search hard enough, Being will reveal the perfect order which underlies, and is obscured by, the apparent confusion of Becoming – still provides the quasi-religious motive for much modern science: every psychologist engaged in the search for the laws of human behaviour and every cosmologist who dreams of discovering the grand single unifying theory of everything is, without even recognizing it, a worshipper at the Platonic shrine. In Plato's moral universe the entire cosmos is 'alive' in the sense that it is an extension of God's mind – and when Stephen Hawking famously said that his goal was to know the mind of God he was part of a noble tradition. The distinction is that in Plato's cosmology, which remained the dominant model in Europe until the seventeenth century, the universe was held together by the world soul, the Latin *Anima mundi*, as a living organizing principle. In the disenchanted, de-animated mythology of modern astronomy the world soul has been replaced by the unified field theory, the supposed principle which underpins the known nuclear and electromagnetic forces and reconciles classical and quantum physics.

If, in political terms, Plato's dualism was represented by the conflict between the virtues of order and the perils of disintegration, which brings him into line with Near Eastern cosmology as applied in Egypt, Palestine and Mesopotamia, the fundamental formula was that celestial order equals political order. If there is a difference between them it is that, while the equation must be inferred from Babylonian tablets and Egyptian hieroglyphs, Plato goes to great lengths to make it absolutely explicit. Whereas the Babylonian astrologers of the previous centuries appear never to have faced the paradox of a universe in which, on the one hand, the planets were being manipulated by their gods and goddesses while, on the other, it was clearly subject to identifiable and regular patterns, Plato shifted the cosmos decisively towards universal laws. He retained space for divination based on both dramatic portents sent by the gods and traditional methods of inquiry, such as the casting of lots or the inspiration oracles of Delphi and other cult centres. Yet, nowhere did he allow for the gods to speak individually through the stars or planets.

The decisive step from theoretical principles to causal mechanics was taken by Plato's most eminent student, Aristotle. He did, though, preserve the divine universe and *Anima mundi* as organizing principles. Whereas for Plato the mathematical nature of the cosmos could only be understood through pure number and musical harmonies, Aristotle, with convincing prose and great detail, added the mechanics without which Plato's cosmology was too heavily reliant on speculation. He was not the only student of Plato to do this: the brilliant mathematician Eudoxus of Cnidus (*c*.400–*c*.347 BCE) did the same, but his writings have been lost, while Aristotle's survived.

However, both Eudoxus and Aristotle continued and developed Plato's fundamental errors concerning the physical structure of the cosmos. Plato, having little regard for material evidence as opposed to theoretical principles, insisted that all celestial motion was fundamentally cyclical on the grounds that perfect objects, such as planets, could only move in a perfect direction – in a circle. While this insight did lead to the correct assumption that the earth is not flat but spherical, and that no sailor would ever fall off the edge, it also led to the fundamental problem of how to explain the erratic motions of the planets which, only a small amount of observation reveals, speed up, slow down, reverse their direction and wobble from high in the sky to low. Plato had already suggested that each planet moved through its own circular sphere, but his explanation of their movements was confined to their musical ratios. Yet, he did issue a call to arms to those who might perfect his system.

It was Eudoxus who saved Plato's system by devising a complex system of 27 spheres; one for the stars, three each for the sun and moon and four for each of the five planets. The planets' erratic motions could therefore be shown to be evidence of a perfect order which only became apparent when one had established the correct, perfect, model. The system still failed to satisfy, though, and Callippus of Cyzicus (*c*.370–300) increased the number of spheres to 34 while Aristotle brought the total up to 55.[77] Even though Heraclides of Pontus (*c.*388–*c.*315) tried to abandon the spherical system by proposing that it was the Earth that rotated, not the stars, and that Venus and Mercury orbited the sun rather than the earth, the symmetry of Plato's perfectly harmonious universe proved irresistible. Even when the brilliant Aristarchus of Samos (*c.*310–230) went further and argued, correctly, that the earth not only rotates but orbits the sun, the tide of Platonic orthodoxy was unstoppable. Apollonius of Perga (*c.*240–*c.*190) refined the spheres into the so-called epicycle-deferent system, in which larger spheres were mixed with epicycles, or smaller wheels which would spin the planets around. Hipparchus of Nicaea (*c.*190–*c.*120), the author of the earliest surviving Greek star catalogue, gave the system his blessing and Claudius Ptolemy (*c.*100–*c.*178 CE), the Alexandrian geographer, astronomer and astrologer, included the model in his *Mathematike Syntaxis* (*System of Mathematics*), the book which was to become the canonical text of medieval European astronomy. This Platonic–Ptolemaic cosmology was accepted without question in medieval and Renaissance Europe where it became the principal rationale for astrology and a causal mechanism by which God's divine will might influence human life.

Aristotle himself refined Plato's concept of causes, retaining the idea that, while God, as prime mover, initiated the entire creation, the planets, played the role of Platonic 'secondary' causes, mediating and qualifying his ideas as they moved through the planetary spheres to the earth. Aristotle talks of the creator, God, as the prime mover, the being who initiates all motion and hence creation. Describing God is the Pythagorean number One, he declared that, 'the prime mover, which is immoveable, is one both in formula and number', and 'the first principle and primary reality [God] is immoveable, both essentially and accidentally, but it excites the primary form of motion, which is one and eternal', by which he meant the circular motion of the stars.[78] Soul itself was a means not just of cognition but of movement.[79] That the cosmos is intelligent is therefore an essential part of understanding the mechanics of planetary movement. And, if motion is the primary cause of change in earthly things, then the sun's movement through the sky was the immediate cause of the origination and destruction of earthly things.[80].

Crucially for astrology, following Plato, the Aristotelian planets are secondary causes, transmitting the will, reason or mathematical logic of the prime mover to earth, via the influence of the planets. In spite of his failure ever to mention astrology, there could be no better justification of its use to work back up the planetary spheres and examine the disposition of the planets at any given moment to gain insights into God's greater plan. In Aristotle's cosmos, just as in Plato's, space as well as time possessed a moral quality. Again, following his teacher, Aristotle equated goodness with stillness, while motion, leading to change, was always related to decline and the loss of perfection. Motion was the Greek equivalent of the Fall in Jewish mythology, the force which kept man from God, the cause of all human ills. Essentially God, the good, inhabited the space beyond the fixed stars and was absolutely motionless. The stars, moving yet keeping their fixed order, were almost perfect, but not quite. The five planets, beginning with Saturn, the slowest moving and hence most perfect, then became progressively more degenerate until Venus and Mercury, and were analogous to man in that they only needed a limited number of improvements to return to the good. The sun and moon, being farthest from God, were most imperfect, while the Earth, the home of corruption and decay, lay inert at the centre of the whole system. The three bodies, sun, moon and earth, were analogous to plants and animals in that they had no hope whatsoever of returning to God. Aristotle's reworking of Plato was equally moral. Like Plato he identified the universe as alive and divine in some readings of his work, and located the ultimate application of his astronomical theories, at least as far as humans are concerned, in the correct management of politics. However, technical questions remained. The immediately obvious problem with this apparently pleasing system is that, if the earth is motionless, it must be perfect, which was the complete opposite of what Aristotle believed. However, this did not become a serious issue for philosophers until the thirteenth century, when it became one piece on the intellectual jigsaw that eventually persuaded Nicolas Copernicus that the sun, rather than the earth, is the true heart of the cosmos.

The whole equation of descent through the planetary spheres with moral decline was, though, to chime with Plato's concerns about social and political degeneration and a profound pessimism concerning the rottenness of physical life which was a distinctive feature of the Hermetic and Gnostic cosmologies which were soon to gestate in Egypt. In this sense Aristotle provided the justification for what was later to be a profound religious opposition to astrology. However, his positive impact on astrology's future development was also immense. His writings were discovered by Islamic scholars in the tenth century and then transmitted to medieval Europe in the twelfth and thirteenth, where they provided a challenge to the established intellectual order not unlike that of Marxism in the nineteenth and twentieth centuries. They also established the notion that physical and moral existence was intricately connected with the cosmos and provided a rationale for astrology which persisted until the seventeenth century. It is often said that Sir Isaac Newton ushered in the modern era with his discovery that the universe is a vast clockwork machine, a model in the heavens for industrialization on earth. Yet, over 2,000 years earlier, Aristotle had given the mechanical universe its most polished form. For both men the universe was created by a God who gave it its initial impetus and then waited for it to unfold. The difference between the two was that, in Newton's cosmos, God withdrew beyond the stars and in Aristotle's he was inseparable from it, threaded throughout its entire fabric.

One of the most appealing features of Aristotle's cosmology was his creation of a coherent system of causation which for the first time provided a convincing alternative to the Homeric pantheon. The constant interference of capricious gods and goddesses in human existence was replaced by the actual underlying processes which Aristotle believed accounted for the emergence of Plato's Ideas into physical existence. Nothing, he argued happened at random, except for meaningless coincidence.[81] Aristotle classified causes into four categories which he believed could answer the 'why' of an object's existence: the formal cause was an object's form, Idea or archetype; the material cause was the matter from which an object is made; the efficient cause was the object's maker, ultimately God, and the final cause was its use or purpose.

God, in Aristotle's scheme could be the 'efficient' cause, or the maker of an object. Normally this might be a potter, carpenter or stonemason – but what was God except the divine architect? The 'formal' cause was the Ideal Form, in Plato's cosmology, which was the object's essence. Thus, the formal cause of a tree is the tree's essential Idea, in other words 'treeness'. If we extend this to the planets then the formal cause of the moon is 'moon-ness'. This 'moon-ness' may also be the formal cause of everything else with which the moon is linked which, in the Middle Ages, came to include fleshy fruits, people with round faces, women, fishermen, ports, crystals, silver and Mondays. The movements of the planets were therefore in later classical and medieval astrology to provide a comprehensive explanatory model for, literally, everything, although many preferred to make exceptions for all affairs deemed properly covered by religion. The material cause, although being essentially the matter from which the object is made, was essentially dynamic. If everything, according to Empedocles, was made of either fire, air, water or earth, and if, as Heraclitus said, all was in a constant state of flux then, matter was always moving. However such motion was never random – there was always a natural place for each piece of matter to end up. Fire goes up, because its natural function is to return to heaven; Air goes up, but not as high as fire; while water goes down, as is evident from rain, but always rests on earth, which sinks to the bottom of water. This sense of the entire world being on a journey to somewhere else leads us to Aristotle's final cause – the object's purpose, the thing that it is growing into. It is actually a simple concept when applied to plants where the simplest example is that an acorn always, if it grows, becomes an oak tree, never an elephant. This has become a remarkably enduring metaphor, proving a rationale for medieval astrology and still informing esoteric thought.[82] As Aristotle put it, animals do not see in order that they may have sight, but they have sight that they may see.[83] The universe is essentially purposeful. As far as people are concerned the issue is more complex. A baby grows into an adult, but what is the adult's final cause? We can generalize and say that human beings naturally want to be healthy, but what of individuals? Does a poor man have the same final cause as a king? The key, for astrologers, as we shall see, was to adapt the concept of the daimon, link it to the stars, as Plato had done and, over the next two centuries, develop an astrology which dealt with what we might be rather than what we must be. In fact, the notion that the planets at birth denote not what we are but who we might be is an essential part of modern popular astrology.[84] The modern human potential movement, with its doctrine that human beings are all in the process of becoming something else, a something which, in a sense they were born with, is essentially an Aristotelian phenomenon.

Aristotle's four distinct causes provided a theoretical framework for astrology, one in which the planets could be used to describe an individual's life in terms of their purpose and function, rather than as signs of divine pleasure or anger. The two philosophies, Babylonian and Aristotelian, might overlap, and frequently did, but the concept of astrology as a means of communicating with the divine was henceforth always to be contrasted with an astrology which dealt with real, natural processes, seen as integral to the physical universe. In medieval and Renaissance terms, Aristotelian astrology was to be a part of Natural Philosophy and, in modern terms, we might consider it to be a fit subject of scientific enquiry. However, what made it particularly appealing to the European Middle Ages was the fact that it always retained God as the first cause and it could therefore be successfully integrated into the Christian cosmos. It was also essentially conservative, carrying, as it did, the notion that everything, and therefore everyone, should occupy their appropriate place in the social and political hierarchy. Discussing the effect of birth on social and political status, Aristotle concluded: 'That one should command and another obey is both necessary and expedient. Indeed some things are so divided right from birth, some to rule, some to be ruled'.[85]

While modern astrology has retained some archaic concepts, its use of Aristotelian mechanics is often misunderstood. The astrological use of the word 'cause' is derived from Aristotle, yet is rarely, if ever, used, to denote 'cause and effect' in the modern sense. This is not to say that modern astrologers know what the word means when they use it, just that it does not mean simply that when a planet moves it necessarily exerts a direct influence on humanity. The word 'influence' is similarly misunderstood. Aristotle distinguished three varieties of 'influence', celestial motions, which transmitted light and heat, celestial light, which produced day and night, and *influentiae*, which explained terrestrial processes such as the formation of metals in the earth, magnetism and the tides. So, while 'influence' has remained the standard astrological term for accounting for planetary relationships with the earth, it does not mean some sort of influence, such as gravity, by an individual planet on the earth, Rather, in the classical sense, it is a matter of the entire disposition of the cosmos at any one time. Like Plato, Aristotle believed that the whole cosmos is a single living unit in which the stars and planets, though not gods, are in a constant relationship with themselves and with humanity, exactly as in a human body.[86] Once this was understood he said, unexpected events should no longer be surprising. Aristotle actually opens the way to celestial determinism more completely than Plato, who insisted that the philosophical lifestyle could aid the return to God. Yet he dealt only briefly with one of Plato's major concerns – the issue of birth at the right moment. He only once stated that some people are born to rule, others to obey yet, given the state of the world at the time, this was hardly a controversial statement.

Aristotle himself had always mixed at the highest level. His father was personal physician to Amyntas II of Macedon and in 342, when he was 52, he returned to become tutor to the future Alexander the Great; Alexander's father Philip dominated Athens for most of the 340s, finally conquering it in 338 and, when Alexander ascended the Macedonian throne in 336, Aristotle returned to Athens in a position of considerable influence. The medieval belief that Aristotle was Alexander's astrologer was a myth, though one with significance for European monarchs. He was thought to have been the author of the most popular book of advice for kings, the so called *Secret of Secrets*, which included recommendations on the use of astrology. Such assumptions were perfectly understandable, for Aristotle generally used the term astrology to describe what Socrates, Plato and other cosmologists were defining as astronomy – the strict measurement of the positions and motions and the stars and planets. However, possible evidence of some astrological interest on Aristotle's part is suggested by the fact that, after Alexander conquered Babylon in 336, his gift to this old teacher was a set of Babylonian eclipse records. And this was as powerful a symbol as we could have of the coming marriage of two traditions which had for so long flirted with each other, but were about to blend into an entirely new set of teachings about the relationship between humanity and the stars.

11

The Hellenistic World: The Zodiac

For (Zeus) it was who set the signs on heaven, and marked
out the constellations, and for the year devised what stars
chiefly should give men right signs of the seasons.[1]

It was the Macedonian King Alexander the Great's conquest of Mesopotamia in
331, and his subjugation of Asia up to the borders of northern India, that brought
Greek culture into intimate contact with the cultures of Syria, Babylon, Persia and
central Asia, as well as Egypt. The Greek world itself extended from Asia Minor to
the western Mediterranean, to the coasts of France and Spain, and Greek became
an international language from Marseilles to the Indus Valley, occupying very
much the same position as English in the modern world. If one wanted one's
work to reach an international readership, it had to be composed in Greek and,
even though its decline took over 300 years, cuneiform script gradually lost its
importance as a language of intellectual communication. The Hellenistic era,
characterized by this extraordinary spread of the language, featured a remarkable
intensification of the cultural encounters already established at the Persian court,
together with a smooth flow of cosmological ideas between Egyptian priests,
Babylonian astrologers and Greek philosophers, with druids at the western
extreme and Buddhists and Hindus at the eastern limit of a circulating current
of ideas. The transmission of astrology from cuneiform to Greek was part of
this process of cultural mixing.[2] From Homer's account of the constellations
on Achilles' shield down to the astronomical computation techniques of the
fourth and third centuries, Babylonian astronomy made its way to the West. The
picture, when it arrived in the Greek world, appears to be one of complexity in
which different forms of astrology emerged, some naturalistic, others magic.
Some assumed a Pythagorean cosmos ruled by number, others maintained direct
observation of the sky. One might use it to locate a lost slave or find one's way
to God and, by the first century CE, astrology could suit any purpose required
of it. The problem was that, while Plato set a task for his students – to create a
suitable model of the cosmos according to which astrology might fulfil a truly
useful social and spiritual purpose – his attitude to astrology has to be inferred
from his discussions of the theory of knowledge in general. As a consequence,
two varieties of astrology were to emerge by the first century BCE, both of
which could find a place within Platonic teachings. One required the reading
of horoscopes in order to establish precise details about the past, present and
future. The other was theurgic – from theurgy meaning, literally, 'god-work' – and

emphasized the soul's ascent to the stars.[3] Both were practical and they were by
no means mutually exclusive; theurgy could make use of horoscopes, but did
not have to. Theurgists could equally be dismissive of horoscopic astrologers'
claims to make precise judgements. But the key to theurgic astrology was to be
the astrologers' quest not for knowledge, but personal transformation; in that,
in Orphic cosmology and Platonic philosophy, the individual contained a spark
of the divine, the astrological discourse was converted from human supplicant
to divine power, as in Mesopotamia, to a dialogue between two aspects of
the divine.

The critical and self-conscious qualities of Greek science from the fourth
century onwards, including its astronomy and astrology, has been attributed,
at least in part, to the traditions of radical debate in Greek city-state politics.[4]
Scientific thought may have imitated political behaviour, or perhaps politics
provided a framework for intellectual inquiry to develop. But, given the importance of the oracular tradition to political decision making, we may also
identify a process in which astrology gradually assumed greater significance,
alongside oracles, as an instrument of state, as in Mesopotamia. It is these very
traditions though, which make it difficult to generalize about Greek astrology.
One distinction, identified by Jim Tester, relied on different approaches to
the extent to which necessity could be evaded or negotiated, and suggests a
contrast between a 'hard' deterministic astrology as opposed to a 'soft' version
in which individual freedom of action was much greater.[5] Tester assumed
that 'hard' astrology, characterized by chains of cause and effect, was fundamentally Greek, and 'soft' as a matter of celestial signs, was characteristically
Babylonian.

That the Greeks were receptive to astrology is suggested by one anecdote told
by Cicero about the Macedonian invasion of Persia in 330 BCE. We are told that a
pre-dawn eclipse of the moon in Leo indicated that the Persians would be defeated
and Darius, the Persian emperor killed – exactly as happened.[6] Presumably this
slant was placed on the eclipse by the winners – the Macedonians. History has not
recorded whether the Persian astrologers forecast victory for their monarch.

The growing encounter between the Greek invaders and Babylonian astrology
was dramatized by the first-century BCE historian Diodorus Siculus as a warning
against the perils of scepticism. He began his story with a vivid account of
Alexander's meeting with a group of astrologers who intercepted him some way
from the city.

When [Alexander] was 303 stades from Babylon, the so-called Chaldeans – who have
obtained the highest reputation in astrology being accustomed to predict the future
on the basis of age-old observations – chose from their midst the oldest and most
experienced men, because they knew through the prediction of the stars that the king's
[Alexander's] death would occur in Babylon, and instructed [those men] to reveal to
the king the danger and to urge him to enter the city not at all, no matter from what
direction. He might, however, escape the danger, if he would rebuild the tomb of Belus

[Marduk] which had been destroyed by the Persians if he then approached the city on the planned route.[7]

Alexander, naturally enough, suspected that the astrologers had a simple political agenda – to keep him out of the city. His doubts were strengthened by arguments couched in terms of Greek scepticism – that if events are ordained by fate they are unknowable and, if they are not, there is no need to pay any attention to them. The irony, of course, is that the Babylonian astrologers agreed with the latter proposition, which is precisely why they told Alexander he could avoid his fate by entering the city from the right direction and restoring the temple of Marduk, bringing himself under the god's protection. Effectively, they were instructing him to enact a *namburbu*, a ritual to ward off evil. Alexander survived and went on to lead his army on an epic journey through Afghanistan into India, apparently defying the astrologers. Yet the prophecy came true when he returned to the city on his way back to the west; he died in Babylon, perhaps poisoned, on 13 June 323. Diodorus' moral tale may be fictionalized. There is certainly a neat narrative of a type familiar in Greek mythology, in which a prediction is initially defied but cannot be avoided.

But we have to assume some encounter between Alexander and the astrologers. It is just not realistic to imagine that he could have avoided them, used as they were to access to the highest levels of the state. A similar dramatized story – probably based on a kernel of truth but moulded into a moral allegory was told of Seleucus Nicator, one of Alexander's greatest commanders and his successor as ruler of Mesopotamia and Persia, when he decided to move his capital from Babylon to the new city, named after him, of Seleucia. When Seleucus, we are told, asked the astrologers, described in the later accounts as magi, for the most auspicious time at which to lay the foundations for his capital they tricked him and chose an unlucky hour. However, fate intervened and the builders began early by mistake, unwittingly choosing a fortunate moment. The second-century CE Alexandrian historian, Appian, couched the astrologers' response in unlikely Stoic terminology. According to him they admitted their devious plan and conceded: 'That which is fated, O king … neither man nor city can change, for there is a fate for cities, as well as for men!'[8] But, whether this incident happened or not, we do not know. If it did, details of the astrologers' work have been lost. However, the point of this story is that fate, in the Stoic sense, will defy human attempts to change it. The workmen at the site began to lay their foundations early and the heralds attempted to stop them, but failed. Instead of the inauspicious hour selected by the scribes of the *Enuma Anu Enlil*, fate selected a moment full of promise and Seleucia became a great city while Babylon's decline accelerated. From his standpoint 400 years later, Appian read the story as the clash between two astrologies, two ways of relating to the cosmos; one in which fate is negotiated and the other in which it is accepted.

The earliest surviving documentary evidence of Greek use of astrology actually dates from half a century later. It is a birth chart which was calculated not for a king, but for a commoner, inscribed on a cuneiform tablet and set for a baby named Aristokrates, who was born on the morning of 3 June 235 BCE.[9] But whether the child was Greek or merely had a Greek name, we do not know. The problem is simple: as Greek became the educated language of Asia Minor, Syria, Mesopotamia and Egypt, the distinction between who was or was not Greek becomes a distinctly difficult one to answer. However, we may assume he was Greek and that the astrologer who cast Aristokrates' chart was Babylonian, for he wrote in cuneiform on a clay tablet. We should also bear in mind that this was almost 50 years after Berossus began teaching, and astrological material may have been making its way from the Greek-speaking world to Babylon. We just do not know. Aristokrates' parents may have been Babylonians or Persians who had taken a Greek name for their son. But, if they were Greeks, they may have been merchants or civil servants, taking part in the Hellenization of the Middle East. If they were from a Stoic, Pythagorean or Platonic background, or were initiates of a mystery cult, going to a Babylonian astrologer would have been an essential consequence of their philosophical worldview. We know that Aristokrates was born with the sun in Gemini and the moon in Leo, for the details of the planetary positions for his birth are listed. Sufficient technical and interpretative details are given for us to deduce some features of the astrology practised in third-century Mesopotamia. We know that planets could be located in the signs of the zodiac with great precision – by degree – that planets might be strong or weak depending on the sign they occupied and that, as in the medieval and modern tradition, Gemini ruled brothers and Taurus was fertile.

Clearly, astrology had an appeal to the Greeks. It could not be otherwise in a culture in which influential philosophers and religious schools preached the unity of humanity with the cosmos. The Babylonian perception, though, was that its culture was at risk from creeping Hellenization. One astrologer who felt this way was a priest from the temple of Bel – or Marduk – at Babylon. At least, this was the story recorded by the Roman writer Vitruvius (c.50 BCE – 26 CE). Berossus, we are told, set out to teach Babylonian culture to the Greeks on its own terms. As part of his mission, sometime in the early third century he set up a school on the Aegean island of Kos, an appropriate choice since it was the site of Hippocrates' great medical school and the Asclepion, a healing sanctuary sacred to Asclepios, son of Apollo.[10] Kos had been organized as part of the 'Islander's league', a group of Aegean islands, by Antigonos Monophthalmos in 315/314 BCE, but came under the control of the Ptolemaic kings of Egypt by 'the late 290s or early 280s'.[11] Berossus' choice was either particularly shrewd or a happy coincidence; his school was both based in a historic centre of learning and directly tied to the emerging intellectual hub in Egypt.

The evidence suggests that Babylon remained a hub of traditional activity – the continued copying of the *Enuma Anu Enlil* – and innovation – the creation and development of birth charts, until the first century. Yet the focus of both astronomical and astrological invocation shifted to Alexandria in the second century BCE. The reason was the creation of the Great Library of Alexandria, a massive project initiated by the Greek Pharaoh Ptolemy I, who took over control of Egypt when Alexander's empire was divided amongst his generals. We know that the library was fully operational under his son, Ptolemy II (282–246 BCE) and, when he asked Callimachus, famous for updating the *Homeric Hymns*, to compile a catalogue, it was found to contain 490,000 papyrus rolls, which must have contained pretty much the entire knowledge and literature of the Mediterranean and Middle East. The second librarian, Eratosthenes (*c.*285/80–*c.*194 BCE) was the astronomical genius who measured, remarkably accurately, the circumference of the earth, disposing of any lingering notions that it might be flat.

The coincidence of timing between the library's foundation and Berossus' arrival on Kos may itself be significant. The library's first head was Zenodotus, himself a student of the scholar and poet Philetas of Kos, who was born around 320 BCE, so he would have been around 40 when the teaching of Babylonian astrology began. By that time Philetas was in Alexandria, where he was appointed tutor to the young prince, the future Ptolemy II. Kos, along with the rest of the Dodecanese was part of the Ptolemaic realm so it made sense for there to be close connections between Kos and Alexandria, and hence a direct channel of astrological material to Alexandria. There is certain evidence for this assumption, or for other direct channels from Babylon to Alexandria. One of the most complicated astronomical achievements of the second century was the invention, by the Alexandrian astronomer Hypsicles, of a mathematical method for calculating the exact degree of the zodiac sign ascending over the eastern horizon; in fact, Hypsicles' work was derived from Babylonian systems which had themselves been well established by the previous century.[12] There was no technical reason at all why the Babylonian astrologers could not have cast proper horoscopes, with an ascending degree. And, given that they could, they probably did.

Like so many early sources, Berossus' great book, the *Babyloniaca*, a compendium of Babylonian thought in which the astrological sections were included and written around 280 BCE, has come down to us only in fragments. Just one paragraph on astrology has survived, and that only because it was paraphrased by the Roman writer Seneca. In a passage clearly related to Platonic and Stoic theories that great periods of history were separated by planetary conjunctions, Berossus claimed that, when all seven planets meet in Capricorn, the world is destroyed by water and, when they combine in Cancer, it is consumed by fire.[13] This particular piece of apocalyptic cosmology became a feature of Roman astrological historiography. Pliny believed the prophecy was coming true when Vesuvius exploded in 79 CE, and the Jewish historian Josephus believed it provided confirmation of the story of Noah's flood.[14] From Pliny, Berossus' theory became a commonplace of medieval historiography and was last cited by Louis Le Roy, Regius Professor at the Collège de France in his *Of the Interchangeable Course or Variety of Things in the Whole World*, a universal history which appeared in English in 1594.

Berossus' mission to the Greek world met with a receptive audience. Theophrastus (*c*.370–*c*.285 BCE), the head of Aristotle's school, apparently admired the Chaldeans' skill in predicting the weather and public and private affairs.[15] The source is unreliable – the Platonic philosopher Proclus around 600 years later – but it is not implausible. In any event, there is evidence that, by 290–250 BCE, Greek astrologers were spreading the word. Apollonius of Myndus was followed by two others, Antipater and Achinapolus, who are said to have repeated the Babylonian rules for predicting a person's fate from the date of conception rather than birth. The problem, is, though, that we know little about these writers or their dates. One, Critodemus, wrote two influential works, now lost, which we know only by their names, the revelatory *Horasis* ('Vision') and *Pinax* ('Table').[16] However, while Critodemus is reputed to have been one of Berossus' notable students, he may equally have worked in the first century BCE.[17] Although these writers are obscure and their texts are lost, they were known to the Roman world; the second-century CE astrologer Vettius Valens appears to have been familiar with Critodemus' work, and the *Pinax* was quoted by the fourth-century astrologer Hephaistion of Thebes. As an example of the deterministic logic of a life subject to necessity, according to Critodemus, if the sun or moon are in the last degrees of a zodiac sign, life will be short; an individual born when Saturn and Mars are strong and the sun and moon are in the eighth house, will be eaten by wild dogs.[18] Of other known astrological texts from the period, none survive. The astrological work apparently written by one of the greatest astronomers, Hipparchus (*c*.190–*c*.126 BCE) has now disappeared without trace, though was used by astrologers up to the fourth century, at least.[19] Even the five books on divination written by the Greek philosopher Posidonius (*c*.135–50 BCE), who is credited with taking astrology to Rome, have been lost, as has the influential work attributed to the seventh-century BCE Pharaoh Nechepso and the fourth-century priest Petosiris, but now assumed to have been composed sometime around 150 BCE. One work, quoted by Nechepso and Petosiris, is only known by its name, the *Salmeschoiniaka*, a word which may be translated roughly as 'Pictures'. The transitional texts that might connect Berossus to Vettius Valens and Claudius Ptolemy, in the second century CE, are known only in fragments. Worse, any texts which might reveal the development of the complex rules which developed in the third and second centuries BCE have completely disappeared. Three hundred years of astrological belief, thought and practice has virtually disappeared and we are left with later texts which, we have to assume, represent the astrology that developed between Berossus' arrival on Kos and the beginning of the Christian era.

Yet, from now on we should talk about Hellenistic astrology as opposed to Greek. The language in which most astrological texts were composed was Greek, but they were products of a cultural climate which intimately connected Babylon to Greece and Egypt.

We can assume that Greek-speaking astrologers in the first century BCE, by which time astrology had reached its heights of complexity, were in constant communication with their Babylonian colleagues. As Vitruvius, wrote in the first century BCE:

> The rest which relates to astrology, and the effects produced upon human life by the twelve signs, the five planets, the sun and the moon, must be left to the discussions of the Chaldeans, whose profession it is to cast nativities, and by means of the configurations of the stars to explain the past and the future. The talent, the ingenuity, and reputation of those who come from the country of the Chaldeans, is manifest from the discoveries they have left us in writing.[20]

Chaldean could be a generic term for astrologer, but there seems no reason to doubt that Vitruvius was referring to practitioners who came from Babylon or Uruk.

Most of Berossus' astrology may be lost but, if we assume that he was familiar with the whole body of Babylonian astrology, he would have taught the entire system of omen reading from the *Enuma Anu Enlil*, may have emphasized the compilation of empirical observations, as in the diaries, and would certainly have taught the use of both birth and conception charts. He would have used the mathematically precise zodiac of twelve 30° signs and he would also, as is clear from the surviving birth charts, have understood the fundamental meanings of the planets and zodiac signs, and, perhaps, the basics of the relationship between the two. It is also apparent that the planets at birth could be used to make predictions by extrapolating them into the future, probably by using long-range planetary cycles. If fate was still negotiable, then it seems that one could now prepare for events which might not take place for 10, 20 or 30 years.

Scholarly attraction to astrology was, though, far from universal. Carneades (c.214–129 BCE), head of the Platonic Academy, adapted his master's view that knowledge from physical observation was impossible, and doubted that any knowledge of anything was possible. All that was left was doubt. There was therefore nothing useful to be learnt from astrology. Other philosophers who departed from the Platonic–Aristotelian tradition, such as the Atomists, appear to have little interest in it, either for or against. Lucretius, for example, the first-century BCE Roman thinker, never mentioned astrology in his extensive writings on the nature of the cosmos. Clearly, it was of no interest to him.

Although Greeks, such as the parents of Aristokrates, commissioned cuneiform birth charts, there is no surviving, recognized horoscope which is conventionally classified as Greek until the so-called coronation horoscope of King Antiochus I of Commagene, a small kingdom in what is now south-west Turkey.[21] Although part of the Greek world in the first century BCE, in the seventh it had been the northern boundary of the Assyrian, so its rulers were no strangers to the royal use of astrology. The horoscope is, in fact, a monumental carving on the summit of Nimrud Dag, a mountain peak 7,000ft above sea level. It portrays a lion – Leo – with a series of stars and it appears to represent the date, probably deliberately chosen, when Commagene was reorganized as a Roman client state by Pompey in 62 BCE. The main feature is a carving of a lion covered by 19 stars, most likely the stars attributed to Leo by Eratosthenes and inscriptions to Zeus, Apollo and Hercules. Analysis of the monument suggests that, if it is set for a particular date, the moon, Mercury and Venus – and perhaps Jupiter, appropriately enough as the star of Zeus – were in Leo, the royal sign. It is not actually clear why this monument should be regarded as a Greek horoscope other than that Commagene was now in the Hellenistic world. Its characterization as a 'Greek' horoscope by Neugebauer and van Hoesen, the authorities in the field, is a fundamental error and, to be fair to them they acknowledge other interpretations. However, they argue that the evidence that it is a horoscope is the crescent shape, perhaps a new moon, on the lion's chest. Unfortunately, the crescent moon was a standard representation of the Babylonian god Sin on countless reliefs and boundary stones; if Nimrud Dag is a horoscope, then why not all the Babylonian carvings? The Nimrud Dag relief may well be set for a particular date but it is best seen as a giant talisman designed to call down the blessings of heaven on an auspicious day and, as such, resembles the Babylonian boundary stones, of which a large number portrayed celestial images, typically the sun, moon and Venus. Its true antecedent is the monumental Hittite ceremonial site at Yazilikaya, a gigantic site dedicated to the harmony of heaven and earth, dating from around 1500 BCE.[22] Antiochus is better seen as the heir to Ammisaduqa, Ashurbanipal and Esarhaddon, great rulers who sought allies in the stars.

On the grand scale, the encounter between Greece and Babylon was embodied in the marriage between the Platonic concept of the single, living cosmos and the Babylonian zodiac. Nowhere did Plato himself mention the zodiac, although he must have been familiar with it. There is some evidence that two of his immediate predecessors, the astronomers Meton and Euctemon, may have been using the signs of the zodiac to describe the sun's position in the 430s.[23] Plato himself did declare that the fifth of the solid shapes on which the cosmos was based was the 12-faced dodecahedron, which he considered to be the most perfect because it was closest to the sphere and so used by God to decorate the universe; the modern assumption is that he meant the zodiac signs or constellations.[24] But we can never be sure whether references to twelve-ness refer to the 12 Olympian deities, or their presumed cosmological relationship with the 12 months.[25] Whether Plato knew about the zodiac, though, is not a matter of great significance. Far more important is the power it attracted when it was transferred from the Babylonian measuring system and medium for reading divine communications, to a living feature of the Platonic cosmos. From a Platonic sense, the images which represented the zodiac signs, or constellations, were more than mere pictures. They were more like religious icons which possessed numinous power, indicating the different manner in which parts of the sky were actually alive. The zodiac becomes a projection into the sky of the archetypes, the birth chart a map of the disposition of archetypes at the moment of incarnation.

The word's roots certainly point in this direction. *Zōion* translates as animal but *zōios* as living, while *zōidiacos* may therefore mean either 'circle of animals'

1. Venus of Laussel, Museum of Aquitaine, Bordeaux

he 'Venus of Laussel', dating from around 20,000 BCE and discovered in the Dordogne in southern
ance, is not an image of Venus, but is usually interpreted as a divine female figure. The thirteen
otches and crescent shape of the drinking horn point to a lunar connection and the hand on
e stomach suggests fertility. The 'Venus' may therefore be an image of a stone-age Moon-
rtility goddess. *(Marshak, Alexander,* The Roots of Civilisation, *Mt. Kisco, New York and London:*
oyer Bell Ltd., 1991, pp. 334, 5. Peabody Museum of Archaeology and Ethnology, 2005.16.22.1).

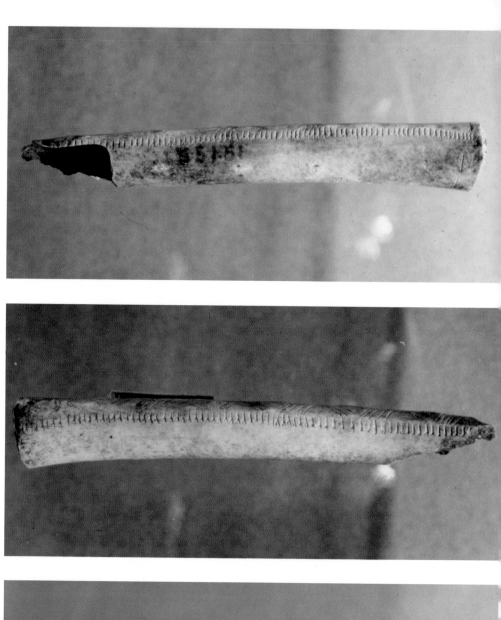
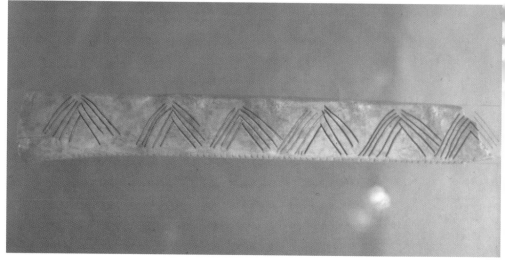

Opposite page (top to bottom): 2. Paleolithic eagle bones inscribed with possibly lunar notation, *c.* 11,000–13,000 BCE

An increasing number of animal and bird remains, such as these eagle bones dating from around 10,000–20,000 BCE, are interpreted as lunar calendars. A few earlier examples, from as long ago as 250,000–350,000 BCE are more suspect as it is impossible to tell whether the markings are artifical or the resut of natural weathering. *(Marshak, Alexander,* The Roots of Civilisation, *Mt. Kisco, New York and London: Moyer Bell Ltd., 1991, p. 148. Peabody Museum of Archaeology and Ethnology, 2005.16.795-6-11).*

Above: 3. Stonehenge, megalithic circle, late 3rd millenium BC, Salisbury Plain

Stonehenge, the most iconic of all sky-related neolithic sites, was part of a vast ritual landscape in southern England from around 3000–1500 BCE. Astronomical interpretations of the monument link it to the measurement of eclipses, lunar phases and the risng and setting of particular stars, but there is considerable disagreement and the consensus is only that it was aligned with the midwinter sun (not the midsummer sun as modern pagans believe). *(The Art Archive/Alfredo Dagli Orti, ref. AA341514).*

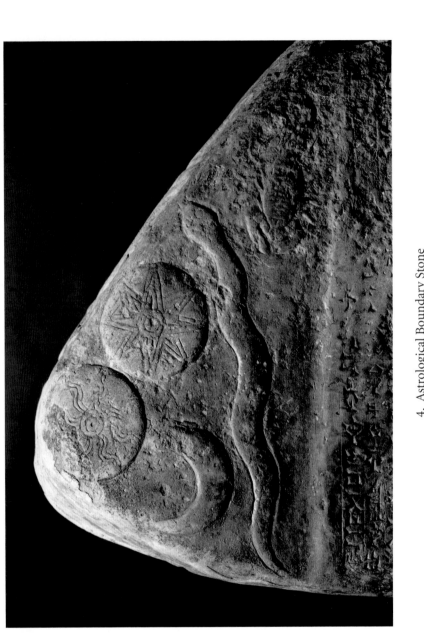

4. Astrological Boundary Stone

Boundary stones from the Assyrian period frequently depicted astrological images. This example showing the Sun, Moon and Venus with the constellations of Hydra and Scorpio. The function is unclear but it may mark a particular moment coinciding with a Sun-Moon-Venus conjunction in Scorpio, signifying the blessing of heaven for a particular division of terrestrial space. (*Hunger, Hermann, Astrological Reports to Assyrian Kings, Helsinki: Helsinki University Press, 1992, p. 134, British Museum, 90827 ©The Trustees of the British Museum.*)

5. Babylonian Birth Chart

We know that the interpretation of planets in the zodiac signs at the position of birth was used to analyse a child's destiny from the fifth century BCE. This cuneiform birth chart is dated to 2–5 February 298 BCE. The text shows that the Sun, Venus and Mercury were in Aquarius, Mars in Capricorn, Jupiter in Leo and Saturn in Aries. The Moon was probably in Sagittarius. (*Rochberg, Francesca, Babylonian Horoscopes, Philadelphia: American Philosophical Society 1998, p. 58. British Museum 32376 ©The Trustees of the British Museum*).

6. Great Pyramid

Astronomical theories about the great pyramid rang
from its shape (like sun rays shining through a cloud)
the orientation of its shafts to Sirius, the brightest of th
fixed stars, sacred to the goddess Isis, and the three sta
of Orion's belt, sacred to Isis' consort, Osiris. The on
certainty, though, is the pyramid's almost exact alignmer
to the cardinal points (East-West, North-South), suggestir
a relationship with celestial immortality (the stars whic
circle the celestial north pole never set, that is, never die
(*With kind permission of Danista Appadoo*).

7. Circular Horoscope Diagram

A rare example of a circular horoscope diagram dating from the reign of Tiberius, probab
between 15–18 CE. The ascendant (*horoscopos*) is to the left. The signs of the zodiac are writte
in long hand beginning with Taurus on the ascendant, followed in an anti-clockwise direction I
Gemini (Didimoi), Cancer, and so on. The names of the planets are also in long hand. For examp
Kronos (Saturn) is clearly written to the right-hand side, outside the circle; the Sun and Ma
were in Libra, Moon in Taurus, Saturn and Jupiter in Sagittarius and Venus in Scorpio. Accordir
to the astrologers of the time, the locations of the benevolent Venus and unfortunate Mars ar
Saturn were weak, but benign Jupiter was strong. With two unfortunate planets weak and or
fortunate planet strong, the balance of probabilities would be auspicious. The Moon in its ow
sign, Taurus, is further evidence that the child's soul, had in terms of Platonic philosophy, chos
a fortunate incarnation. (*Neugebauer, Otto and H.B. van Hoesen,* Greek Horoscopes, *Philadelph
The American Philosophical Society 1959, p. 18*).

8. Square Horoscope Diagram

Example of a square horoscope diagram dated to 28 October 497, during the reign of the easte
emperor Anastasius I, towards the end of the classical period, and almost two centuries aft
Christianity became the state religion of the Roman Empire. The use of the shorthand planeta
and zodiacal glyphs is now evident. The ascendant *(horoscopos)* is to the left in Aquarius. Th
Sun, Mercury and Venus are in Scorpio, Mars in Leo, Jupiter in Virgo and Saturn in Aries. Th
square format is still used by Indian astrologers. (*Neugebauer, Otto and H.B. van Hoesen,* Gre
Horoscopes, *Philadelphia: The American Philosophical Society 1959, p. 156*).

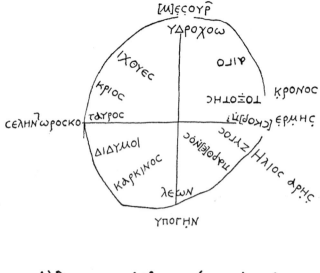

Diagram labels (clockwise from top):
[Μ]ΕΣΟΥΡ̄
ΥΔΡΟΧΟΟΥ
ΔΙΟ
ΚΡΟΝΟΣ
ΤΟΞΟΤΗΣ
διὰ [ΣΚΟΡΠΙ] ΕΡΜΗΣ
ΖΥΓΟΣ / ΗΛΙΟΣ ΑΡΗΣ
[ΠΑΡΘ]ΕΝΟΣ
ΛΕΩΝ
ΥΠΟΓΗΝ
ΚΑΡΚΙΝΟΣ
ΔΙΔΥΜΟΙ
ΣΕΛΗΝ ωροσκο ΤΑΥΡΟΣ
ΚΡΙΟΣ
ΙΧΘΥΕΣ

ἀμφορ' ὅρ᾿ τα· λι δ᾿ ἀμαρ τι λίω· τούτο γὰρ καὶ ὁ θαυμάσιος
ὁ μηρος αἰρι τι μέρος διάφρι· ὁ δι᾿ διος τα μετ᾿ χια
καιρο θοίο· καὶ ἀλλαχοῦ· σὺν γὰρ θδω ζ᾿ πήλο νθρόρ :–
τὸ δε σχῆ μα τοῦ θε μα :–

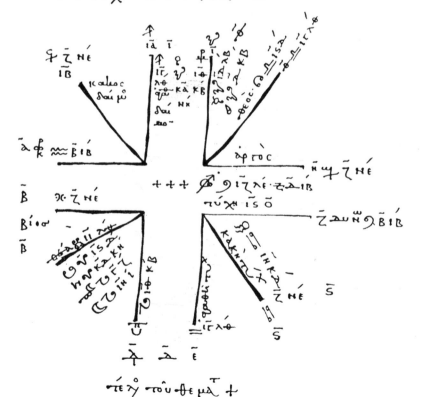

πε γ᾿ τοῦ θε μα τ +

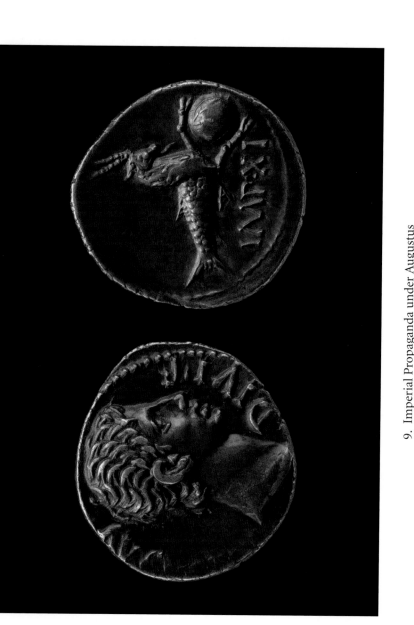

9. Imperial Propaganda under Augustus

The emperor Augustus' (27 BCE–14 CE) promotion of his own messianic status involved him in the manipulation of astrology for propaganda purposes. He minted coins showing Capricorn, the sign containing the Moon at his birth on 23 September 63 BCE. The most likely reason was that Saturn, Capricorn's ruling planet was, as Cronos, the ruler of the mythical Golden Age outlined in Hesiod's *Works and Days*. (*British Museum C465* ©*The Trustees of the British Museum*) or 'circle of life'. It has been suggested that the zodiac may be 'a place for life', the 'seat of the soul' or the 'temple of the spirit' in the sense that, as an image, a zodiac sign contains, or is, the same as the divine essence it represents, just as a Christian icon may, in some senses, embody the divine.[26] The earliest known use of the word *zōidion* was by the historian Herodotus, around 500 BCE, and clearly meant a carved image. The second known instance, by Aristotle, was in the modern meaning of zodiac as a band of constellations and also most likely, given Aristotle's belief that the universe was divine, 'aliveness' or 'image where aliveness dwells'.

The technical development of the zodiac was another matter. Following Homer and Hesiod, there do appear to have been further discussions of the constellations beginning with a shadowy sixth-century astronomer called Cleostratus, even perhaps by Thales and Anaximander, but all are lost.[27] The earliest undisputed treatises on the constellations were composed by Plato's student, Eudoxus of Cnidus (406–355 BCE), in 366 BCE as 'handbooks' for a globe on which the constellations were mapped. Eudoxus' globe, like his treatises, has not survived, but may have been the model for the later and more famous globe held aloft by the Farnese Atlas exhibited in the Museo Archeologico Nazionale in Athens. Eudoxus' interest in astrology, to judge from his surviving work, was strictly meteorological, in the style of Hesiod. A work attributed to the Stoic philosopher Geminus of Rhodes (*c.*110–40 BCE) paraphrased Eudoxus' work, along with that of Euctemon: 'On the 7th day (of Taurus): for Eudoxus, there is rain. On the 8th day: For Euctemon, Capella arises [in the mornng]: fair weather or driving rain from the south'.[28] Even though it is now lost, Eudoxus' text assumed importance as the basis of the earliest surviving Greek treatise on the constellations, the *Phaenomena*, composed by the Stoic philosopher Aratus of Soloi (315–250? BCE), mathematician, poet and astronomer at the court of the Macedonian King Antigonus around 270 BCE. Aratus' work was a combination of description of the sky and the constellations' location, and weather prediction. He seems to have been either uninterested in, or unaware of any mythology associated with the constellations beyond the most basic connections – such as that the constellation of Argo was related to the story of Jason and the Argonauts.[29] He did include information on the rising, setting and seasonal significance of 48 constellations together with extensive meteorological omens which indicate a clear continuation of the Hesiodic tradition:

> Mark as the Sun is rising or setting, whether the clouds ... blush (on North or South or both), nor make the observation in careless mood. For when in both sides at once those clouds gird the Sun, low down on the horizon, there is no lingering of the storm that comes from Zeus.[30]

From Aratus' work we can reconstruct Eudoxus' original text, at least in outline, and it seems that he was using the *Mul Apin*. It also appears that the Greeks adopted 19 constellations from the Babylonians, renamed and gave new mythologies to 12, invented a further 12 and retained the archaic constellation, the Bear.[31] The two major fifth-century innovations were the Piscean Fish, which replaced two Babylonian constellations, Mul KUN mes (The Tails) and Mul SIM.MAH (The Swallow), and the Arien Ram, which took the place of the Babylonian Mul HUN-GA (The Hired Man). The Ram may well be an adaptation of the Hired Man, which, in the *Mul Apin*, was associated with Tammuz, the mythical Sumerian shepherd king; it is conceivable that the Greeks dropped the shepherd and kept the sheep. It is likely, though, that this tidying up took place in Babylon under Persian rule, and that Meton and Euctemon simply adopted the neat, 12-sign zodiac as a ready-made system. Once the zodiac had been Hellenized, Babylonian astrologers themselves adopted it and started teaching it back to the Greeks.

Aratus' work hit the right note and became a popular classic. It inspired a score of Greek imitations, Roman translations (including one by Cicero in the first century CE) and a celebrated eighth-century illustrated version, the *Aratea*, and was influential on the great Roman poet Ovid (43 BCE – 17 CE), whose poem *Fasti*, was composed in the context of the Emperor Augustus' use of the cosmos to boost his family fortunes.[32] Aratus' importance though, is that his work gives us a date for the Greek importation of the zodiac from Mesopotamia – before Eudoxus' *Phaenomena*, so either before Plato or during his lifetime. Much of the mythology of the zodiac signs appears to have been assembled by Eratosthenes of Cyrene (*c.*285/80–*c.*194 BCE), who was summoned by Ptolemy III in 245 BCE to become head librarian of the library at Alexandria, and is most famous for his remarkable measurement of the earth's circumference to within 1 per cent of the true figure. However, yet again, his work, the *Catasterismi*, is lost and survives only in fragments recorded by later transcribers.[33] The contrast between Eratosthenes and Aratus, though, does suggest two distinct, if overlapping, components in the Greek adaptation of the zodiac, a naturalistic one represented by Aratus and a mythological one represented by Eratosthenes; both may be traced to Hesiod, the former to *Works and Days* and the latter, perhaps, to the *Astronomia*. It is clear though, that the Greeks sometimes borrowed and sometimes innovated. As Ed Krupp put it, some star myths, 'read like astronomical allegory and are reasonably relevant and consistent. Others seem arbitrary and off-the-wall and sound like after-the-fact efforts to assimilate symbols that belonged to someone else'.[34]

Babylonians and Greeks were mixing freely, so much so that the labels may be meaningless. The problem is illustrated by the case of Sudines; he was a Babylonian who was renowned both as an astronomer and diviner, spent time at the court of the Greek King Attalus I of Pergamum around 250 BCE, and was sufficiently versed in Greek culture to compose a commentary on Aratus' *Phaenomena*. A further process took place in Egypt where there was a transitional period in which the Hellenized Babylonian constellations were used alongside ancient Egyptian asterisms and the 36 decans.

The earliest surviving evidence of a Babylonian zodiac in Egypt is a carving in a temple at Esna, probably dating to the reign of Ptolemy III Euergetes (246–221 BCE), and includes a combination of Babylonian images with Egyptian decans and northern constellations.[35] More famous is the monumental carving from Dendera dating to some time before 30 BCE. Now in the Louvre, but originally from the roof of the East Osiris Chapel in the temple of Hathor at Dendera, 'Dendera E', as it is known, also incorporates ancient Egyptian constellations such as the ox leg and the Hippopotamus as well as Orion and Sothis, suggesting an attempt, if an ultimately unsuccessful one, to merge the two systems rather than replace one by the other.[36] The Babylonian component features the planets in their own zodiac signs, the significance of which may be found in later texts. The Roman astrologer Julius Firmicus Maternus, writing in the fourth century CE, described a birth chart for the universe in which all the planets were in their exaltations. He relates that he copied the chart from a book called *Myriogenesis* by the Alexandrian hermetic writer Aesculapius, but said the doctrine owed as much to the other teachers, Petosiris, Nechepso and Hanubius. The purpose of the chart was purely symbolic – to show all the planets in their most perfect positions as an inspirational model for the perfect human life. According to Firmicus, 'the divine wise men of old invented this birthchart of the universe so that it would be an example for astrologers to follow in the charts of men'.[37] The Dendera E zodiac seems to be an image of the living cosmos at its most perfect, a moral lesson in right living to all who gaze upon it. But as an image, it did not just represent something that was alive, it was itself alive.

A second zodiac, 'Dendera B', was carved in the reign of Tiberius (14–37 CE) in a slightly different format to Dendera E and with slight variations, but in a form which makes it easier to locate the Egyptian constellations in relation to the Babylonian, the point being that the two systems were combined. The Egyptian constellations were soon dropped in favour of the 12 Babylonian–Greek versions and the 36 decans settled into being exact 10° segments of the ecliptic, rather than groups of stars, and were incorporated as one-third portions of the zodiac signs. Even though the main Egyptian constellations were abandoned, first-century CE astrology included Egyptian techniques or concepts even though, apart from the decans, and due to traditions of temple secrecy, it is almost impossible to say what these might have been.

The meanings of the zodiac signs were worked out sometime between the fifth and first centuries BCE, perhaps in a gradual process, possibly in a series of innovative steps. What we do know is that, in the literature of the first and second centuries CE, they are recognizably the same as in any modern text. From the second-century astrologer Vettius Valens we have the following descriptions:[38] Aries was assertive and signified leaders, Taurus solid and prosperous, Geminis liked to talk, Cancerians (and here we are not so close to the modern stereotype) were fond of pleasure and entertaining, Virgos were modest and methodical, Librans like justice and promote the welfare of others, Scorpio is treacherous and secretive, Sagittarius good and generous, Capricorn is hardworking and good at planning, Aquarius (again, unlike the modern version) deceitful and treacherous, and Pisces changeable and popular. And here, from 2,000 years ago, we have a series of character descriptions that constitute the world's oldest psychological model and which remains the most widely known form of personality analysis.

12

The Hellenistic World: Scepticism and Salvation

> To Heaven, a god perceptible by sense, is committed the
> administration of all bodies; and the growth and decay
> of bodies fall under the charge of Sun and Moon.[1]

For the Babylonians, the core rationale of astrology had been the need to placate capricious gods and goddesses. Astrology's transfer to the Hellenistic world saw a shift away from a universe populated by multiple personalities towards a cosmos conceived of as a single living body. The core justification of early classical astrology then shifted towards a notion of cosmic sympathy, an idea closely identified with the Stoics, but embedded in the works of Plato and Aristotle. It is believed that all phenomena, divine and material, are linked together by 'sympathetic' powers or energies. They are linked not just symbolically or metaphorically, but in themselves, in their very essences.[2] The vertical and horizontal relationships established between all things connected in this manner has been termed the 'Great Chain of Being', and was to become one of the basic tools for analysing the operation of the cosmos until the seventeenth century.[3] Sometimes the term 'correspondence' is used instead of sympathy. In cosmic terms there was a closely knit structure that binds together the energies deriving from the sun, the planets and the stars. Often these are spoken in terms of 'light.' The chain maintained affinities between the most disparate areas of the natural realm – each animal, plant and part of the human body corresponded to a particular planet or god. This god or planet can be manipulated in order to influence change, providing the precise procedures and formulae are known. Each animal, plant and part of the human body, and any one part of the system, can be affected if an influence is exerted, via words or deeds, on a part to which it is connected. This is the basis of magic.

There was to be no single orthodoxy in Greek cosmology. Aristarchus (c.310–230 BCE) argued that the sun, not the earth was the centre of the universe, while Lucretius postulated the existence of atoms as the basis of all things and completely dispensed with the entire structure of Platonic cosmology, from its fixed planetary spheres to its teachings on soul and mind.[4] But such ideas appealed only to a minority. Most philosophers accepted the nested planetary spheres supported by both Plato and Aristotle, and leaned either towards the supernaturalism of the former or the naturalism of the latter. We have to remember that Hellenistic astronomy – after 300 BCE – existed within a philosophical context largely defined by Pythagoras, Plato and Aristotle – that the dominant cosmology both assumed a divine, living cosmos and had a direct practical application in astrology. But there was no single application. Plato's theory of knowledge allowed his successors to take radically different approaches to the amount of detail astrology could provide. And his practical emphasis on the need to harmonize one's life with the cosmos left different possible routes for achieving this. Was it enough to live the life of an aesthetic scholar, as he seemed to suggest, contemplating the wonder of the heavens and studying the abstract rules of mathematical astronomy? Or, as much of his work implied, should one take active steps to reintegrate one's soul with the divine, a task which, whether literally or figuratively, requires a journey through the planets?[5]

While Plato and Aristotle provided all the philosophical rationale that astrology required if it was to function independently of Babylonian religion and capricious planetary deities, their work was refined by Zeno of Citium, the founder of Stoicism. While he taught at Athens, Zeno was a prime example of the interrelationship between Greek and non-Greek worlds in the formulation of the West's philosophical foundations. Reputedly a Phoenician from the city of Citium in Cyprus, he moved to Athens around 311 BCE and, at first, studied at the Platonic Academy, but was to be heavily influenced by Cynicism. The Cynics, who had much in common with Platonism's more puritanical inclinations and devout cosmic piety, argued that only virtuous action leads to happiness, most pleasures therefore being useless. Zeno adopted from Plato the notion that nature, the entire universe, is controlled by *logos*, reason, which is itself identified with God and is manifested through fate, described as necessity and/or providence.[6] A number of conclusions flow from this simple proposition. The first, and most important, is that whatever occurs in this world must take place in accord with divine reason. As Zeno reasoned, in the divine, organic, interdependent Platonic world, nothing can possibly take place independently of divine reason. The wise man understands this and therefore, knowing that events are unavoidable, realizes that the only solution is to live in harmony with nature, accept what happens and lead a virtuous life. As the first-century astrologer Manilous wrote: 'Yet this too is the gift of fate; the will to learn fate's laws'.[7] There is no point in wishing the world is other than it is, because this is impossible and the virtuous man is not only wise, but noble and brave, for he knows that pain and death are not evils. The second is that all things are linked. The Stoics are often thought to be responsible for the doctrine of sympathy by which all things connected through similar essences even though the notion of such associations between stars, stone, plans, people, periods of time – and everything – was, though, a consequence of Platonic thought and an essential part of Mesopotamian magic.[8]

Stoicism is not exactly passive, for the self-discipline involved in leading a virtuous life and avoiding the pleasures of ordinary men is considerable. The well-known aphorism, 'the wise man rules his stars' is the classic statement of the Stoic position. Strictly speaking, freedom, for the Stoic, was a strictly internal affair – the freedom to accept necessity. Necessity was not a crude force, but a means of activating a sequence of connections, or sympathies between things, a world-controlling breath.[9] And, necessity was to carry a number of Stoics to positions of extraordinary power. The Roman scholar Seneca the Younger (4 BCE – 65 CE), for example, was political advisor to the Emperor Nero from 54–62 CE, a period, before Nero's personal rule, which is remembered as one of particularly good government, while Marcus Aurelius, author of the famous *Meditations*, was actually emperor himself from 161–180 CE. For Marcus, inspired by Plato, there were various ways to cope with the flood of necessary events which flowed from the 'primal cause' – to contemplate the heavens: 'Survey the circling stars', he wrote, 'as though yourself were in mid-course with them. Often picture the changing and re-changing dance of the elements. Visions of this kind purge away the dross of our earth-bound life'.[10] One's soul could be cleansed by an imaginative union with the stars. Seneca issued the classic prescription for the Stoic lifestyle when he wrote that we should live every day as if it were our last but, if God grants us another day we should live it joyfully. He quoted from Virgil's *Aeneid*: 'I have lived; I have completed now the course that fortune long ago allotted me'.[11] Popperian historicism, with its reconciliation of predetermination and with the pressing need for individual action, is the best way to understand the Stoic position. Seneca or Marcus Aurelius were obliged to actively rule in a fair and just manner, because this was what necessity required. Seneca, for good measure, added: 'Superstition is an idiotic heresy; it fears those it should love: it dishonours those it worships. For what difference does it make whether you deny the gods or bring them into disrepute'.[12]

The Stoic attitude to astrology, though, shared the same complex attitude as the Platonic, which is natural considering that Zeno owed so much to Plato. Although, like Platonists, some Stoics argued that true knowledge could be achieved if one had a clear enough mind, others were also influenced by the same sceptical tendencies. The sceptical Platonist Carneades, head of the academy until his death in 129 BCE, launched the first major philosophical attack on astrology. His arguments, though lost, were repeated by the Stoic Cicero (106–43 BCE) and formed the basis of all critiques of astrology down to the present day. He was the first to raise the twins problem: if two babies are born at the same time, how can they have different destinies? Yet most Stoics found astrology to be a reliable guide to the dictates of necessity. Along with Platonism, Stoicism was the main philosophical host which carried astrology throughout the classical world, giving it an intelligent, rational voice. Cicero's own teacher, Posidonius (135–50 BCE), is reputed to have been largely responsible for introducing astrology to the Roman world, although his work is almost entirely lost and no astrological fragments from his extensive writings survive. Although the Stoic school in Athens itself appears to have closed sometime around the year 216 CE, its assumptions had by then already proved amenable to many Christian theologians as part of their general acceptance of Platonic teachings, and whose writings carried then into medieval Europe where they gave meaning to notions of cosmological order. Already, though, Antiochus of Ascalon, head of the Platonic Academy from 86–68 BCE, taught a philosophy based on the agreement between Plato,

Aristotle and Zeno. If Stoicism contributed one teaching in favour of astrology to this mix of teachings, it was that everything in the universe obeys the same set of laws, whether planets or people, in contrast to the Platonic–Aristotelian idea that life on earth was fundamentally corrupt and lacking in the perfection which was such a feature of the planetary and stellar realms. It was therefore, in theory, a simple matter to use the planets to comment on the human condition. There is a comparison to be made between this essentially egalitarian view of a law-based cosmos and astronomical developments in Babylon, particularly the evidence from the *ephemeredes*, the mathematical tables, which suggests that the astrologers had acquired the ability to predict solar and lunar eclipses and upcoming planetary positions according to reliable formulae.

The development of practical astrology in Hellenistic Egypt from the third century onwards took place within the context of a venture which carried Platonic philosophy in an overtly religious direction. Beginning probably in the second century BCE and perhaps, given re-editing, copying and additions, ending in the first or second centuries CE, a group of Egyptian, or Egyptian-based, scribes produced a set of texts known to us collectively as the *Corpus Hermeticum*.[13] The texts were ascribed to Hermes Trismegistus (literally Hermes thrice-great, or 'the greatest') and constructed in classic Greek style as dialogues with other characters, such as Asclepius, the patron of medicine, Ammon, the solar god, and Tat, or Thoth, the Egyptian moon god. The texts assumed considerable fame across the Roman world. Around 200 CE the Christian writer Clement of Alexandria mentioned 'forty-two books of Hermes' which were considered indispensable for the rituals of Egyptian priests; the list, four of whose items he calls 'the astrological books of Hermes' resembles a description of sacred writings inscribed in the second century BCE on the wall of an Egyptian temple in Edfu.[14] Although, for the most part, lost to the Latin world, and therefore Western Europe, after the disintegration of the Roman Empire in the fifth century, the texts survived in the Greek-speaking East. Both there and in Persia they may well have received further additions, though not enough to distort the essential message. Eventually they were brought to the West from Constantinople in the fifteenth century. And when they were finally translated into Latin by the Florentine scholar Marsilio Ficino in the 1450s, they caused a cultural earthquake, taking the Italian Renaissance in a distinctly pagan direction, and laying the foundations for Western esotericism and occultism down to the present day. Their explicit purpose was to provide the believer with 'a way of achieving knowledge of the Divine'.[15] In this sense the Hermetic texts should be seen as part of the wider current of Gnosticism, the belief that humanity could achieve direct, intimate, knowledge of, or union with, the divine.[16] This is the summation, the practical end result, of Platonic cosmology.

The Hermetic texts do not represent a complete break with previous Greek religion. The notion of the single creator was inherent in the Derveni Papyrus and the ascent of the soul was explicit in Plato. However, Luther Martin suggested that Hermeticism's 'discursive strategy', particularly its reliance on necessity, represented a reversal of the assumptions of previous beliefs.[17] He identified a sequence in which the feminine principle of nature was mythologized as the benevolent Earth Mother, then as the transformative principle Tyche or Fortuna, and finally as the oppressive, chaotic masculine Heimarmene, transcendent and above nature, rather than in it. The difficulty with such models, as with van der Waerden's evolutionary theory of Mesopotamian religion and astrology, is that they reduce an essentially untidy set of complex relations to a neat evolutionary pattern.

The *Corpus Hermeticum* is the direct written record of a period of remarkable religious syncretism, a blending of Greek and Egyptian religious traditions, iconography and practice. It is a work of textual archaeology which takes us back to the spiritual ferment which produced the Christian worldview. For Walter Scott, who translated the corpus into English in the 1920s, the *Hermetica* gives us 'a glimpse into one of the many workshops in which Christianity was fashioned'.[18] While, in the first and second centuries CE, Egyptian Hermeticists were few in number in relation to Christians, they may have had a disproportionate influence on the vital theological debates on questions of Christian theology in Alexandria. However, Hermeticism and Christianity were more than rivals, they were heirs to a shared tradition. While the *Hermetica* probably did not borrow from the New Testament, there are a significant number of parallels, enough to suggest that either the New Testament borrowed from the *Hermetica* or, perhaps, that they emerged from a shared religious environment. We can make a plausible argument that, away from the more truculent and aggressive wings of the early Christian movement, followers of Jesus and Hermes were talking to each other. In first-century CE Alexandria, Hellenized, Greek-educated Jews, who were a primary target for Christian evangelists, had read Plato, were familiar with both the Septuagint, the Greek-language Old Testament and teachings of the death and resurrection of Osiris.

The bulk of the Hermetic texts are theological, setting out a rationale for the use of astrology without setting out any technical rules. Book I, which lays out the creation myth, sets the tone. It was composed as a prophetic message from Poimandres, 'the Mind of the Sovereignty' (that is, of God, the *logos* of John's Gospel). The word has also been provocatively translated from the Greek as 'Shepherd of Men', suggesting common imagery with Christianity and Christ's role as the shepherd, or of the emblematic descent of both Poimandres and Christ from Tammuz, the Sumerian Shepherd-King.[19] There is a long-standing and popular tradition that supports this translation. However, an alternative emphasizes Poimandres' traditional Egyptian identity as 'P-eime n-re', or 'knowledge of Re'.[20] However, whether Poimandres was a form of Re, or Christ, or both, the Hermetic texts are clearly a product of their time. In what reads like a combination of the Platonism of John's Gospel, the cosmogony of Genesis 1 and Egyptian or Syrian solar religion, Poimandres first reveals to Hermes a marvellous 'joyous' light. He then describes its meaning: 'That light ... is I, even Mind, the first God, who was before the watery substance which appeared out of the darkness; and the word which came forth from the light is son of God'.[21] The human condition can also be seen as a marriage of the rival creation myths of *Timaeus* and Genesis in that humanity was not only furthest away from the light but actually mired in darkness and 'lamentation'. 'Kosmos', we are told, 'is one mass of evil, even as God is one mass of good'.[22] Hermeticism's purpose was to adapt Platonic cosmology to provide an escape route from evil, a means of salvation.

The Hermetic view of humanity was one of appalling pessimism. At the extreme its black fatalism anticipated the grimmest forms of Calvinism. The material body has no room for God. Instead, it is 'hemmed in and gripped by evil, – by pains and griefs, desires and angry passions, delusions and foolish thoughts'.[23] All was not lost, though, and Hermeticism offered an essentially Platonic path to salvation, recognizing the inner divine and the possibility of a return to the light via the planetary spheres. Poimandres continued, giving Hermes a set of instructions for salvation: look 'at what you yourself have in you'; he ordered, 'for in you too, the word is son, and the mind is father of the word ... Now fix your thought upon the Light ... and learn to know it'.[24] 'He who has recognised himself', that is, acknowledged the divinity within, then 'enters into the Good'.[25] They key to cosmological salvation lay in self-understanding. However, it seems that not everyone was capable of achieving self-knowledge. Although Hermes' conversation with Poimandres, the shepherd, seems to indicate that Nous, divine mind, is a quality of being human, we are then told that it is an external power, like the grace of God, perhaps, which will come to the aid of the pious, leaving the evil, the worthless and ungodly to their miserable fate.[26] For those virtuous individuals who are blessed with Nous, the way back to God is through the planetary spheres.[27] The soul's shedding of seven human qualities at each planetary sphere may be the origin of the seven cardinal sins.[28] At any rate, at each one, the vices associated with that planet are shed, in a pastiche of Inanna's shedding of her jewellery and clothing on her descent to the underworld. As the soul passes the moon it sheds growth and decay, Mercury trickery, Venus deceit, the sun the qualities of being a ruler, Mars daring and recklessness, Jupiter greed, and Saturn falsehood. At the eighth sphere, that of the stars, the soul begins to praise God, and is encouraged by the sound of voices from the higher levels. Finally the soul ascends to God and, in the logical climax of Platonic theology, it is reunited with God. In fact, it becomes God. It is difficult to overstate the importance of this conclusion, indeed the whole of book I. It leaves absolutely no doubt that Christianity emerged out of a broad religious context and should be seen as an extension of certain Platonic notions, including the belief that the soul has an urge to ascend to heaven. But, at the same time, it was sufficiently cautious, and perhaps true to its Jewish legacy, to deny that the soul could become God. Such notions became the province of the Gnostic Christians, and were later declared heretical and stamped out.

Hermetic theology and cosmology was strongly Platonic, but with deep Stoic overtones, especially an overwhelming sense of the power of unavoidable necessity, those parts of life which are essential to being human, including disease, misfortune and death. The universe was structured in three main divisions. There was one supreme God, the father of all, the supreme creator who, 'in making all things, makes himself'. From God the entire universe emanated, first into the 'intelligible' world of ideas and then the 'sensible' world – the material, visible world accessible to our senses. God's benevolent powers flow through these worlds to the sun, the demiurge ('craftsman'), the creator of our world, 'a mighty deity ... who is posted in the midst of the universe and watches over all things done on earth by men', and without whom there would be no physical life.[29] The demiurge then operated through the cosmos, the eight spheres on which the stars and planets rotated, the planet-gods and the daimons they ruled. Men were, in turn subject to the daimons, 'who mould all things on earth'.[30]

The divine powers that bind this closely knit cosmos together may be spoken of as light or 'energies'. They are derived from the sun, planets and stars and exert an influence on all bodies, animate and inanimate. The entire spectrum of life, change, decay and creation is derived from them. That includes every human activity from the simple functions necessary for survival to the arts, sciences and philosophy, from individual affairs to the rise and fall of kings and empires. But all such events, being part of the Platonic world of Becoming, were essentially illusory for, being constantly subject to change they could never be truly known. Only the 'absolute and unmixed Good ... not fouled by matter, nor muffled in body', is real.[31]

This all left humanity in a somewhat ambivalent position, both distant from God and separated from him by the daimons and planet-gods, yet, in that everything that God makes is itself God, all creation is an inseparable part of him. This problem of simultaneous intimacy and alienation was resolved by the simple formula that it is the physical body, together with those parts of the soul which are subject to physical desires, that are dominated by daimons and gods. Eventually, in the thirteenth century, the formula in which the body is subject to the stars but the soul to God, was to carve out a legitimate place for astrology in Catholic theology. Meanwhile, the rational soul, if the individual takes the right choices, is in direct contact with God. Elaborating Plato's Myth of Er, the texts tell us that:

> The planets replace one another from moment to moment; they do not go on working without change, but succeed one another in rotation. These daemons then make their way through the body, and enter the two irrational parts of the soul;[32] and each daemon perverts the soul in a different way, according to his special mode of action. But the rational part of the soul remains free from the dominion of the daemons, and fit to receive God in itself. If then the rational part of a man's soul is illumined by a ray of light from God, for that [in] man the working of the daemons is brought to nought; for no daemon and no god has power against a single ray of the light of God.[33]

This passage, whose message is mirrored elsewhere throughout the rest of the Hermetic texts, is of absolutely critical importance in the development of Western cosmology. Plato's benevolent daimons are converted into the malicious demons of Christianity. The planets occupy a double role. On the one hand, through their responsibility for the daimons, they are co-opted into the essentially oppressive system and release, via the rational soul, is only possible through the light of God. On the other, in that they surround the sun, through which God's light is transmitted, they partake in his glory.[34] The implications for astrology are therefore as ambiguous as they are in Plato's original teachings: are the planets evil, and is astrology therefore to be avoided, or are they good, and is it to be encouraged?

The planets, meanwhile, were the 'Administrators'.[35] Book I sets out the predicament of humanity, born with an immortal soul but a frail body:

> Man had got from the structure of the heavens the character of the seven Administrators … He is mortal by reason of his body; he is immortal by reason of the Man of eternal substance. He is immortal and has all things in his power; yet he suffers the lot of a mortal, being subject to Destiny (*Heimarmene*). He is exalted above the structure of the heavens; yet he is born a slave of destiny.[36]

The individual's sacred task is therefore to acquire self-knowledge and move closer to the divine, escaping the brute dictates of physical necessity and attempt to live in line with cosmically sanctioned providence or destiny.[37] The immortal soul incarnates in the physical body, birth and death being illusions that represent each individual's brief sojourn in the material world. Although people forget their prior existence, God still speaks to them via dreams, the flights of birds, the entrails of animals and the movement of the heavens. The visible world is God in motion. The world is God and God is the world. This is the ultimate rationale for astrology:

> And it is not too difficult, my son, to contemplate the God in thought, or even if you will, to see him. Look at the order of the Kosmos; look at the necessity which governs all that is presented to our sight, and the providence shown in things that have been, and in things which come to be; look at matter filled to the full with life, and see this great god in movement, with all things that are contained in him.[38]

Hermes continues: 'It is the lot of men to live their lives and pass away according to the destiny determined by the gods who circle in the heavens', the stars and planets.[39] This is Aristotle spiritualized. It is embryonic science with God included. It is, in fact the very conception of modern science that was precious to Newton and prevailed until atheism gained the upper hand in scientific circles in the late nineteenth century. And because each human was the microcosm, an exact model of the universe, the grand spiritual scheme could be applied to anyone's life.

The planets' cyclical motions were read in the context of a Zurvanite struggle between good and evil, with each celestial body supporting a rival faction.

The sun sets in array the troop or, rather, troops of demons, which are many and changing, arrayed under the regiments of stars, an equal number of them for each star. Thus deployed, they follow the orders of a particular star, and they are good and evil According to their natures – their energies, that is. For energy is the essence of a demon. Some of them, however, are mixtures of good and evil.[40]

The details of each person's chosen destiny might therefore be revealed exactly in their birth chart, particularly on the *horoscopoi, pantomorphos* or rising decan.[41] The process was set out in terms of the manifestation of the Platonic archetypes, each of which is eternal and unchanging but manifests in a completely different form as each decan rises. The varieties, or 'copies', in which each archetype appears in human life are 'as numerous and different as are the moments in the revolution of the sphere of heaven'.[42] With this philosophy in mind, the Hermetic astrologer could provide a service which was as profoundly religious as that of any priest, but was designed to enhance the individual's freedom to make moral choices, rather than worship a supreme being. The route to salvation was one of reason rather than faith.

The Hermetic teachings existed in that schizophrenic space created by Plato in which the entire cosmos is good but human society, even though contained within, and containing, the good, is a place of misery from which the only escape is through the philosophical life and preparation for death – and the longed-for ascent through the stars;[43] the world is a miserable place, a prison. So awful is it that most people are incapable of receiving the 'good'.[44] The prisoner is the architect of his own imprisonment, but the true philosopher practises dying, and death is to be welcomed because it leads naturally to rebirth. Is this what Plato really meant, though? Did he really think that the body imprisoned the soul, or did it guard and protect it? It depends how we understand the Greek.[45] The goal of Hermetic astrology was to take the soul to heaven, avoiding the perils which might still await the unjust in the underworld.[46] Astrological prognostication could help with this process; as Ptolemy wrote; one of the justifications he provides for astronomical prognostication is that it 'calms the soul … and prepares it to meet with calm and steadfastness whatever comes'.[47]

Hermetic astrology could therefore be intensely moral. One late classical work which appealed directly to the Hermetic teachings, the *Liber Hermetis*, which dates in its present form to the early fourth century CE, though it contains much earlier material, gives the astrological indicators for female promiscuity.[48] A woman born with Venus in Capricorn, Mars in Libra and Saturn and the moon in Cancer slept with her own stepchild; another with a similar configuration slept with her father after her mother died. Such behaviour was not inevitable. By recognizing the tendency it might be avoided. In fact, it must be avoided, for the people who give in to the carnal desires and physical pleasures, are denied immortality condemned to wander in the darkness of the material world, suffering the perpetual cycle of birth and death.[49] In Platonic cosmology the woman who gave in to such behaviour would be reincarnated as whichever sort of animal most closely resembled her bestial behaviour, but if she resisted it she might be born again as a man, one level up the ladder of existence. According to Hermetic logic, in the man's body the reborn soul would then have to pay attention to its horoscope in order to come closer to God and avoid the terrible fate of returning as a woman next time round. Hermes sets out 12 vices, related to the zodiac, which constitute the 'irrational torments of matter' in the prison of the body, which must be overcome if rebirth is to take the soul closer to God, and provides an invocation by which each vice is replaced by a virtue.[50]

A text such as the *Liber Hermetis* appears at first sight to be deeply amoral in its cool descriptions of what planetary patterns point to which sorts of human activity. Yet the apparently non-judgemental tone of the sample astrological prognostications can only be understood within the context of Hermeticism as a profoundly moral path to salvation. Astrology, to the Hermeticist, was an essential part of the injunction to know one's self, to escape this miserable world and return to God. The greatest evil, beyond anything else imaginable, is ignorance of God, and 'there is one road that leads to the Beautiful [or Good], and that is piety joined with knowledge of God'.[51]

Each planet has a certain number of daimons under its command and planetary patterns at birth therefore determine the nature of the daimons that enter the body, including the two parts of the irrational soul, those that experience desire and repugnance. However, the daimons are unable to enter the rational soul which therefore remains free and able to 'receive god into itself'.[52] The human who gives way to physical desire and the daimons is subject to destiny, but he who opens his contact with God transcends it and is free from *heimarmene*. Essentially, then the good daimons of Plato's *Republic* become the evil demons of Christian mythology, no longer a central part of human life, but a destructive force to be overcome. Even one ray of the light of God, the divine and incorporeal light of mind, is enough to defeat any daimon or planet–god, but only a few men can ever actually make the supreme effort required to open their rational souls to the good. Most will remain subject to their desires and the fate spun by the decans, stars and planets.[53] Even then there are choices to be made at every moment: 'Men', Hermes relates, 'are subject to Destiny by reason of the forces at work in their birth, but are subject to Penal Justice by reason of their errors in the conduct of life'.[54] The individual navigation of fate was as urgent as in Mesopotamia but conducted in the light of different notions of cosmological order.[55] Destiny was the 'seed', which could be read through the birth chart, necessity was the process by which all results follow from causes and might, perhaps, have been read through ongoing planetary transits, while order, the interweaving of events in temporal succession, was the meeting of destiny and necessity as people interacted with their environment. All three were ordained by God. Yet, a fourth form of fate, if we can call it that, was intermingled with all material things. Uncertainty, and therefore an ever-present opportunity for individuals to make moral choices, pervaded the otherwise mathematically predetermined universe. Magic becomes the means by which determinism is evaded. Thus the increasing sense that the cosmic order is unavoidable stimulates a corresponding need to circumvent that determinism.

The implications for astrology, astral magic and planet worship are quite ambiguous. Ideally astrology is only permissible if it is seen as a means of releasing one's self from the planetary gods and daimons who are obstructing the individual's view of God. The worship of the planetary gods themselves could only act as a distraction from the primary task – to return to God – and hence enhance the sway of evil in this miserable world. Yet there also seems to have been a pragmatism resulting from the realization that few men would ever actually achieve union with the divine. For them even worship of planetary idols was acceptable, for at least they were reflections of the archetypes and hence of God, even if indirectly.[56] The Jewish Gnostics went further. Unable to explain why their God repeatedly abandoned them to oppression they concluded that their creator, Yahweh, was fundamentally wicked.

Plato's legacy was diverging into different forms by the first century BCE, and a very different strand was represented by the Roman politician and philosopher Cicero (106–43 BCE). His work is crucial because, in the absence of surviving texts from the first century BCE, he gives us the fullest account of astrological thought and practice at this crucial moment. He was no disinterested observer, though: he took Platonism in a different direction to the *Corpus Hermeticum*. The soul's ascent to the stars was very real for him, though a matter of reasoned knowledge rather than salvation from sin. But he regarded any possibility of detailed astrological knowledge as ridiculous. His authorities in this respect were Carneades (c.213–129 BCE), the founder of the 'New' Academy, which took Plato's teachings in a distinctly sceptical direction, and Panaetius (c.185–109 BCE), the head of the Stoic school. Astrology's defenders fought back against the sceptics. Panaetius' own student Posidonius (c.135–c.50 BCE), who was famous for his 52-volume history of Rome and belief that the Roman republic represented the universal state dreamt of by the Stoics – and hence that it was ordained by fate to rule the world – grappled with the problem of why two apparently unrelated men might be struck down by disease at the same time. The answer was obvious, within the logic of astrology, at least to Posidonius: they must have been both conceived and born at the same time.[57] Men whose philosophical stance was in other ways identical could disagree sharply over the issue of astrology. Just as Posidonius contradicted his teacher, Panaetius, so Cicero, who was profoundly influenced by Posidonius, emerged as astrology's foremost critic.

Much of what we know about astrology's arrival in Rome, and the reception it received, is gleaned from Cicero's *De divinatione*, an examination of all forms of divination. Cicero's theological work, *De natura deorum*, was finished in 45 BCE and he started work on *De divinatione*, which is closely related, immediately: we know that it was begun before Caesar's assassination and completed soon after. In *De natura deorum* Cicero made it quite clear that the cosmos, was beautiful, harmonious, intelligent, rational, ordered and imbued with mind, soul and purpose.[58] This was standard Platonic–Stoic cosmology. His task in *De divinatione* was to discuss first the problem of whether, if the cosmos was perfectly ordered, and if it contained gods, they sent signs to humanity via natural and supernatural events, including the movement of the stars. Secondly, he was concerned with the specific details of the use, universal in the Mediterranean world and Near East at the time, of divination, including astrology, to advise on political strategy. The book is structured as a dialogue between Cicero and his brother Quintus. Drawing on debates which had been current in Greek thought for the previous 300 years, Quintus puts the case in favour of divination while Cicero, following the scepticism of the New Academy, held that certain knowledge was impossible and that the best that could be hoped for was an assessment of probabilities. Given that major political decisions as well as theological debates might hinge on whether the gods spoke through the stars or not, the discussion, particularly of astrology, possessed a clear and immediate political purpose: to evaluate to what extent the principles of the cosmic state should be applied at Rome.[59]

It is difficult to escape the conclusion that Cicero's objections to astrology, while rooted in the Platonic scepticism of the New Academy, also had an element of republican snobbery about them. As a member of the College of Augurs he was aware that certain divinatory practices were engrafted onto the Roman constitution, but he considered state-controlled divination to be necessary for the maintenance of civil order; those outside state control were, by inference, a threat to public order. In short, he believed that religious practices should serve political functions.[60] Into his brother's mouth he put the claim that the best regulated states, particularly Athens and Sparta, were those in which divination was a central part of government.[61] There is also an element of dissembling in some of his arguments against astrology which suggests that he was engaged in the prosecution of a case whose conclusion was foregone. That said, De divinatione is by far the richest account of both astrology and divination we have from this time. While, as we are several times reminded, divination was practised by all known peoples up to the highest level, and that it was therefore a central decision-making tool in the ancient cosmic state, it is also clear that the Roman state was heir to the intellectual creativity of Athens and home to a philosophical pluralism in which any religious belief or ideology could be practised – given that due deference was paid to the emperor.

Cicero's scepticism actually enabled him to analyse and define divination as a whole, as well as astrology in particular, which he quite clearly regarded as one of its branches. He had Quintus define divination as 'the foreseeing and foretelling of events considered as happening by chance'.[62] He considered the theoretical arguments for its veracity: on the one hand if the gods exist then they must want to speak to us but, on the other, they have far more interesting things to bother about than us mere mortals. But then again, he argued, perhaps nature can give us signs without divine intervention while, even if the gods exist, the power to talk to them might be a special one which they have not conferred on humanity as a whole. Quintus also adapts Plato's distinction in the Phaedrus between rational and 'manic' prophecy, offering a division of divination into two forms which remains a major template for the analysis of ancient forms of prophecy and prediction.[63] The first he called 'artificial', or 'by art', an insight into the meaning of our modern word. This, he insisted, required the analysis of empirical or observed data and proceeded by clear rules of deduction. Entrail divination was artificial, as was astrology. The second was defined as 'natural' in that it proceeded from human nature unmediated by external data. Prime examples of natural divination included dreams, 'mental excitement' and 'frenzy'. The famous oracle at Delphi would have been classed by Cicero as 'natural'. There is a parallel here with the modern functional classification of Babylonian omens as 'provoked' or 'unprovoked' – resulting either from a divinatory procedure or sent by the gods. Except, of course, that, from the point of view of the diviner, all messages were sent by gods and goddesses. In the context of later developments, though, we can identify a 'natural' divination which should include astrology in the sense that it is based on general influences. The concept that Mars, as a planet with a hot, dry nature, can be responsible for fevers and drought, is clearly astrological but requires no divinatory constructs and no horoscopes.

Astrology, for Cicero, itself was a '*scientia*', best translated as a discipline or form of knowledge with its own rules; based on regular observation of the paths and movements of the stars and requiring knowledge of mathematics,[64] a description which somewhat contradicts the definition of divination as predicting events brought about by chance and so somewhat closer to the notion of an ordered cosmos regulated by 'laws of nature'.[65] We are though, given, a complete account of the different theories of astrology current at the time, ranging from atmospheric pressure to the divine will.[66] In Cicero's account, the Chaldeans believed that the zodiac possessed a force which varied according to the movements of the stars and planets and the angular separation between them, which sounds rather more Aristotelian than Babylonian; either he was describing Greeks as Chaldeans, which was normal usage for the time, or the Babylonian astrologers he encountered were appropriating Greek physics.[67] This force then affects the physical environment and hence both the general disposition and specific destinies of children born under particular patterns. This is the first indication in the discussion of astrology of the concept of planetary influence as a rationale for astrology. We are also introduced to the idea that there might be gods whose task is to direct the affairs of individual men, presumably Platonic daimons, and to the Stoic doctrine that 'the universe was so created that certain results would be preceded by certain signs, which are given sometimes by entrails and by birds, sometimes by lightning, by portents, and by stars, sometimes by dreams and sometimes by utterances of persons in a frenzy'.[68]

Quintus takes his cue mainly from Stoic thought. He argues essentially that, if the gods exist, they must, of necessity, speak through the stars, an extension of Babylonian astral theology into classical thought. As an example, he cited a lunar eclipse in Leo which preceded, and hence was a sign of, Alexander the Great's defeat of the Persians in 332. From Posidonius he takes the typically Stoic argument that all things happen according to fate, itself defined as 'an orderly succession of causes wherein cause is linked to causes and each cause of itself produces an effect'.[69] It follows that to know the cause is to know the effect, to know how the stars move is to predict their future. Although observation of the relation between cause and effect means that the future can be predicted,[70] ultimately each cause is joined to each other cause across space and time in a complex web more akin to the Hindu law of karma than to simple notions of single causes producing similar effects. If one accepts the connections between stars and the state, there are major consequences for politics as well as for individuals. Aristotle meets Babylon in Quintus' summation of first-century BCE cosmology: the heavens cause and influence life on earth, but it is up to the astrologers to read the signs which those causes and influences reveal. This comprehensive approach attracted some high-profile adherents. In the following century, Plutarch made it clear that events which are explicable in natural terms may still be regarded as omens: 'the clattering of brass quoits', he wrote, 'the light of beacons, and the shadow of a sun-dial, have all of them their proper causes, and yet each has another signification'.[71]

It is also clear that there was no concept of a precise distinction between 'influences' caused by atmospheric conditions in the heavens on the one hand, and divine warnings on the other: both nature and the gods sent signs and humanity's job was to make sense of them – if it can. Nor does there seem to be any idea of stars and planets acting as independent causal agents: divinatory signs may 'make manifest', 'portend', 'intimate' and 'predict', but they do not reveal independent 'causes'.[72] There may even be a sense in which astrology is poetry. Cicero reports the sympathetic argument that diviners approach the divine spirit of the gods in very much the same way as scholars do when they interpret the poets: 'Men capable of correctly interpreting all these signs of the future seem to approach very near to the divine spirit of the gods whose wills they interpret, just as scholars do when they interpret the poets'.[73] But, as a system of warnings, astrology can also function metaphorically through dreams, and Cicero gives a practical example taken from the famous dream of the Roman King Tarquin the Proud.[74] This included the lines, 'the blazing star of day [the sun] reversed its course and glided to the right by pathway new', which were interpreted in a manner that would have been familiar to the Babylonian scribes. First, the sun's change of direction indicated an imminent change in the state; second its movement from left to right (east to west) was so auspicious that it indicated Rome's eventual rise to global supremacy, following the rising sun. A similar example was cited from the Persian Emperor Cyrus who, we are told, 'dreamed that the sun was at his feet'.[75] Three times he tried to grasp it and each time it turned away, escaped him and disappeared. The magi were called in and told him that this meant that he would rule for 30 years, 10 years for each time he tried to grasp the sun, which is exactly what happened. These examples may feature celestial symbolism from dreams rather than astrology as such, but point to a tradition that can be traced directly back to the dream of Gudea, joining Sumer to Rome.

Astrology emerges in Quintus' description as a practice justified by a spectrum of ideological and religious positions. There was no single rationale or set of truth claims. Cicero replied to Quintus with a critique of astrology which was to form the basis of all subsequent sceptical (as opposed to strictly theological) criticism of astrology down to the present day and which includes the first philosophical separation of astronomy from astrology in the ancient world. Astronomical positions, Cicero argued, could be foreseen because they were based on the laws of nature, but no such law could allow astrologers to make precise judgements, to predict who, for example, might inherit an estate. He cited incorrect predictions made by astrologers for Roman generals, including Julius Caesar, argued that the planets are too distant to exert a measurable effect, and asked about the role of heredity – why people born at the same time have different lives. He pointed out that people born with physical defects might be healed by medicine, thus overruling the stars, and that the thousands of soldiers who died when Hannibal annihilated the Roman army at Cannae in 216 BCE must have been born with different horoscopes – and yet all died at the same time. He asked whether all people who had the same profession were born under the same stars (a question already answered, if unsatisfactorily, by Posidonius) and why astrologers did not take cultural or climatic influences into account.

Cicero's criticism of astrology begs a number of questions. What astrologers really said, we are not told; all we are given is Cicero's version. His attack on astrology was entirely political in nature; the issue is not whether astrology is effective, or even whether it has a rational basis, but whether it should be permitted. And the reason why is clear: astrologers were generally regarded by the Roman authorities as a politically destabilizing influence and Cicero believed that divination should be controlled by the state and used to promote political order. He may have supported the constitution against budding tyrants like Julius Caesar and Mark Antony, but his ideology drew on Plato's kingdom of the philosophers, in which the elite told the masses what was good for them. And astrologers, coming to Rome with their oriental ideas, predicting a future beyond the control of the Roman Senate, was bad for them. Cicero's attack on astrology is less an attempt to deal with any real issues it might have raised than a lawyer's trick designed to undermine a rival political theology. So complete was his denunciation of astrology that he even denied any possible connection between the moon and the tides.

Cicero's political concerns were far more than a matter of armchair chatter. He was actively engaged in Roman politics and, as a young man, joined the army under the command of Pompeius Strabo, the father of the future Pompey the Great. He was deeply involved in public affairs for the rest of his life, as a supporter of Pompey until the latter's death in 48 BCE. Pompey engineered his recall to Rome in 57 BCE, after a brief period of exile, and he became a trenchant defender of constitutional values against dictatorship. He was, for a time, effective head of the government in Rome. He welcomed Caesar's assassination in 44 BCE and became a leader of the opposition to Mark Antony. Although he expected protection from Octavian, the future Emperor Augustus, when Octavian made peace with Antony in 43 BCE, he was caught attempting to escape and executed.

The eventual tragedy of his own political life contrasted with Cicero's thoughts on the ideal state, directly influenced by Plato, were set down in the *Republic*, written in 54 BCE when he was at the height of his political powers. The critical astronomical passage occurred in book VI in which the famous general Scipio Aemilianus had a dream in which, in an early form of 'celestial journey' literature, he was escorted through the stars by his grandfather, Scipio Africanus the Elder, a legendary hero on account of his defeat of the Carthaginians and conquest of Spain.[76] While the passage is designed to encourage the younger Scipio (and by inference all Romans) in the pursuit of patriotism and a virtuous and humble life, it is directly inspired by the Myth of Er in book X of Plato's *Republic*. This set out the doctrine of the descent of the soul through the planetary spheres before birth and its return by the same route after death. Most important from the astrological point was his exposition (through Scipio's words) of a spiritual universe, modelled on Plato's, in which the human soul is made of fire and hence derived from the stars. As all substances must return to their natural place, the soul must, logic dictates, return to the stars. Politicians, he believed, may accomplish this goal by ruling justly in line with God's will, while philosophers and musicians can do it by imitating the music of the spheres, the sounds the planets make as they rush through the sky.

Although Cicero, being an admirer of Roman tradition, would not have relished the comparison, the doctrines of the descent and ascent of the soul though the planetary spheres were central to the astral theologies emerging at the same time from Egypt in the Gnostic texts and the mystical treatises ascribed to Hermes. The passage was preserved by the Neoplatonic philosopher Macrobius, who wrote an influential commentary on it around 400 CE[77] and its discussion on the relation between the soul and the stars thus survived into the Middle Ages. Notably, a poetic summary of it occurs in Geoffrey Chaucer's *Parliament of Fowls*, written around 1382. The effect was to reinforce the idea, current in medieval Europe, that astronomy possessed significant spiritual implications and political applications.

Taken together, the arguments against astrology in *De divinatione*, and in favour of the spiritual nature of the cosmos in the *Dream of Scipio* fall into context. Astrology is attacked because it is subversive and Cicero can find no way to control astrologers on behalf of the Roman state. Plato's political theology, though, in which rulers have a unique relationship with God and a spiritual connection with the stars, as future emperors were to find, lent itself obviously to political control.

Cicero was no doubt the cause of great irritation amongst the astrologers of the Augustan age and his arguments were answered by both his contemporaries and successors. His friend and ally in the service of Pompey, the astrologer and Pythagorean philosopher Nigidius Figulus, reputedly the second most learned man in Rome (after Varro), was one of the first. He responded to the problem of why twins often have separate lives. He came up with the metaphor of the potter's wheel, which earned him his nickname (a *figulus* was a potter). [78] He demonstrated that if you spin a potter's wheel very fast you can drop two ink spots apparently on the same place, but on stopping the wheel they are found to be in very different places. Thus two babies might be born apparently very close together, but experience quite distinct lives.

The voice of the classical scholar against astrology was almost silent after Cicero. From the second century onwards his rational criticisms were taken up by Christian evangelists and subordinated in a larger superstition that astrology was demonic and anti-Christian. Only one other major critique of astrology was published – by Sextus Empericus (160–210 CE), around 200 years later. Sextus argued that astrological forecasts are equally useless whether the future is predetermined, in which case we can do nothing about it, or not, in which case we can alter the future ourselves, rendering astrology futile. [79] But Sextus was very much the arch-sceptic: nothing made sense to him. He even argued that music was nonsense on the grounds that it is based on time intervals and time does not exist. [80] It was Cicero's work which was to open the way to astrology at Rome; even if one could not trust horoscopes, nobody doubted that the soul was tied to the stars. And, if this was accepted, the visit to the astrologer was never far away.

We only have to read Marcus Manilius' words to see how the Platonic teachings could lead to the casting of horoscopes. The deity pervades the whole of the cosmos, including nature, and by contemplating it, especially the stars, we can know him, And, because we are made in his image, we know ourselves:

> We perceive our creator, of whom we are part, and rise to the stars, whose children we are. Can one doubt that a divinity dwells within our breasts and that our souls return to the heaven whence they came ... why wonder that men can comprehend heaven, when heaven exists in their very beings and each one is in a smaller likeness the image of God himself? [81]

Manilius' rationale, that humanity is a cosmos in miniature, a microcosm of the heavenly macrocosm, became one of the most enduring justifications for astrology.

13

Hellenistic Astrology: Signs and Influences

The mind of man has the power to leave its proper abode
and penetrate the innermost treasures of the sky.[1]

The astrological cosmos was a systematization of the Babylonian cosmic state
in which each planetary deity had its own precise set of functions, established
according to certain set rules However, time, in the Platonic universe, was central
to the reflection of divine reason in the visible cosmos, so each horoscope, distinct
from all others for being cast for a different moment, varied the planets' precise
relationships. The planets were like ministers, or perhaps courtiers, in the palace
of the Platonic creator; 'administrator' was the term used in the Hermetic texts.[2]
As living beings, in the Aristotelian sense, the planets are at home, in terms of
their relationship to the world soul, in the signs of the zodiac to which they each
have a particular connection.[3]

An examination of the astrology of the Greek world presents us with the need
for certain clarifications. For one thing, all that the relevant texts necessarily have
in common is that they were written in Greek, the educated language of the
Hellenistic world and the Roman Empire. Because the geographical area was
so extensive, some writers prefer the term Hellenistic astrology, to Greek, indicating that the prevailing culture combined schools of thought from Egypt and
Mesopotamia, as well as from Greece. Whichever way we phrase it, though, there
is inevitably a potentially misleading tendency to assume a fundamental unity of
theory and practice, rather than diversity.

There were four fundamental factors from which the astrologers of the Greek
world constructed astrological meanings and analysed the earthly condition of
the soul.[4] The first two were the planets and the 12 zodiac signs we encountered
in fifth-century Babylon. The two others are, as yet, unknown in the cuneiform
literature. The first is the *horoscopos*, or horoscope, the zodiac degree rising in
the east for the moment of the event for which the omens are being taken and
the other is the system of 12 'places' or 'houses' in modern astrology, each of
which denoted a different area of life or activity.[5] We know that the Babylonian
astrologers had the ability to calculate the *horoscopos* in the third century, for
Hypsicles, the Alexandrian astronomer who gave the formula, used a Babylonian
system. However the earliest surviving example is from Egypt and dates to 4 BCE:
Scorpio was rising, on which basis the astrologer considerately advised the need
for care for 40 days.[6] However, an intriguing passage attributed to the second-
century BCE work, the *Salmeschioniaka*, gives rules for interpreting the Egyptian

decans in relation to the *horoscopos*; the seventeenth, which rises in the west, deals with wives and marriage, the twenty-fifth, which culminates at noon, signifies sickness, and so on.[7] It is tempting to see Egyptian concern with the Akhet and horizon events as one origin of the *horoscopes*, in which case the ascending degree at an individual's birth becomes the sacred point, the liminal zone which the Egyptian priests watched for signs of the daily salvation, the rising of the sun. And so the individual becomes a participant in the cosmic drama. In fact, the *horoscopos* became a standard feature, along with other significant points through which the destiny chosen in the soul's current incarnation could be anticipated, including the Lots of Fortune, Eros, Daimon and Necessity, names which anchor technical astrology firmly in Platonic thought.[8]

Although the horoscope was, strictly speaking, just one degree, in modern convention the horoscope is the entire diagram of the heavens for a particular place and time so, for clarity, we need to use the modern term 'ascendant' to describe the Greek *horoscopos*. The use of the ascendant was linked to the development of a whole additional interpretative structure based on the 12 houses, the divisions of the sky often based on the diurnal circle, which represented different areas of life, such as marriage, friends, enemies and public success.[9] The houses enabled the astrologer to convert segments of sky into tangible information about an individual's life, reading sections of space as an encoded diagram of human potential. Whereas the zodiac sign indicated the planet's strength, the house pointed to the areas of activity over which it ruled. This enabled an interpretative logic which could, at a simple level, be followed quite easily. For example, if the sun was in Scorpio, it was in the sign of Mars, Scorpio's ruling planet.[10] If it was then in the second house, then Mars is the landlord – or Hermetic administrator – so to speak, of the second estate and was obliged to provide hospitality for the sun. If Mars is then in one if its own signs, Aries or Scorpio, it is then strong.

There is something distinctly odd about the system of places, or, in modern terms, houses. The system ran counterclockwise with the first house being that which contained the *horoscopos*, or ascendant. This means that the twelfth contained the sun either at dawn or soon afterwards. Now, in the orthodox cosmology of the time, this was a moment of profound celebration, as light, life and hope banished darkness, fear and death. Yet the twelfth house was that of the bad daimon, of toil, enemies and misfortunes. This rather suggests that the house system was an idealized scheme, an embodiment of the EAE paradigm, in which the cosmos was judged by the manner in which it conformed to a projected, abstract system, rather than to any observation of the sky or systematic correlations between celestial patterns and terrestrial events.

The most remarkable evidence for the sophistication of the technical culture that surrounded astrology by the second century is the so-called Antikythera mechanism, named after the island near Crete where it was discovered in a shipwreck in 1901. The mechanism, which has been attributed to Geminus of Rhodes, contained 37 gear wheels which were capable of predicting the sun and the moon, including eclipses and Hipparchus' recently discovered lunar irregularities, and the planets. Some historians believe that the mechanism was unique, an implausible position which assumes that there were not even any prototypes, let alone copies. The evidence that it was one of a series is provided in a passage written by Cicero in around 45 BCE, apparently describing a similar device. Cicero's friend, the Stoic philosopher and astrologer Posidonius, had 'recently made a globe which in its revolution shows the movements of the sun and stars and planets, by day and night, just as they appear in the sky'.[11] If the Antikythera mechanism was dated to around 150–100 BCE, and Cicero died in 50 or 51 BCE, having recently described a similar machine, this suggests that it was one of a series of sophisticated devices designed for the general purpose of observing the unfolding of divine providence, and the specific function of casting horoscopes.

There are a number of sources for Greek horoscopes, chiefly around one hundred used for teaching purposes in Vettius Valens' second-century textbook, *The Anthology*, dating up to the late second century; and 68 discovered on a rubbish pile in Oxyrhynchus, a provincial capital in Roman Egypt, and dating up to the fifth century.[12] It is evident from these sources that horoscopes could be calculated for different purposes. There were some which were clearly set for a birth. However, there are others which are labelled *katarche*, and set the moment in which a new initiative is launched.[13] From the Greek for *katā* (down) and *arche* (first point), the word implies the drawing down of heavenly potential and, in the earliest literary references, was commonly applied first to the launching of ships and then to the launching of virtually anything. The earliest known instance would appear to be Babylonian – the selection of the supposedly favourable hour to lay the foundations of Seleucia.[14] From such horoscopes the Greeks derived what was known to medieval Europeans as *elections*, the deliberate use of astrology to select auspicious moments to begin new enterprises. We need to clarify, though, a difference between charts we might know as *inceptions*, set to analyse an event which was not actively selected, and the deliberate election of auspicious moments. Both of these may be included under the general term *katarche*, but such developments are difficult to date, and we cannot be sure whether such a distinction was made at the time. Certainly, Antiochus I's monumental inscription at Nimrud Dag is a *katarche* in spirit, whether or not it used the technical rules apparent in later classical texts. So was Esarhaddon's decision to fight a battle at an auspicious time, or Gudea's foundation of a temple to Ningirsu. Greek astrology continued its Babylonian forerunner's dual function, which was both to nominate auspicious moments and inquire into future prospects. In this sense we cannot be sure if the reading for the horoscope for 4 BCE, 'take care for 40 days', was set for a birth, or was in response to a question, such as, perhaps, 'will my child live?' The use of *interrogations* (horary charts to modern astrologers), horoscopes cast in order to answer specific questions about the success or failure of a particular enterprise, may date to the second century but the evidence is disputed.[15] The problem, of course, is that some early fragments consist only of listings of planets and we have no idea whether they refer to a birth, the launch of a new venture or a question about the success of an existing one. Either way, three examples from surviving horoscopes from the late fifth century make the variety of topics clear; one, in the days before fast communication, concerned a ship which was late arriving in Smyrna and was feared lost; another asked whether a small lion would be tamed, and a third was for the proclamation of Leontius, a rebel emperor.[16] In the event, the cargo of ostrich feathers, plain papyrus, cooking implements and medical supplies was safe, the lion was tamed and Leontius' rebellion was defeated.

Technically, the astrology revealed in the texts of the first and second centuries, rested on foundations which are evident in the cuneiform birth charts, particularly the zodiac and planet–zodiac sign relationships, but the range of interpretative possibilities reached scales of incredible intricacy. To begin with, the astrologer would consider whether the chart was set for night or day, each of which would bring different rules. A diurnal chart emphasized the sun, a nocturnal one the moon, in a system known as 'sect' which may have been an astrological application of the Persian battle of dark against light, or the Egyptian struggle between night and day. There was then a complex system in which, for example, a planet in Aries, Leo or Sagittarius might be ruled by the sun in a diurnal chart and Jupiter in a nocturnal one, with Saturn as a secondary, co-ruler regardless of the time. The location of the sun, Jupiter and Saturn would then need to be considered to provide further information.

The construction of astrological meaning depended partly on the systematization of Babylonian material into an intricate system which took its cue from the Pythagorean perception that the cosmos is constructed on the basis of number. The astrological cosmos was mathematical, and mathematics was a path to divine truth as well as mundane reality. Abstract points could have as much astrological significance as observed planets. For example, the Lots, abstract points which may be calculated by adding the position of two celestial positions and subtracting a third, make their first appearance – probably in Nechepso–Petosiris.[17]

It became the custom amongst Greek-speaking astrologers, as among Greek philosophers in general, to attribute their wisdom to the Egyptians.[18] Nechepso–Petosiris became a vital and much-quoted source for the astrologers of the Roman world, so much so that some came to the completely mistaken conclusion that the Egyptians invented astrology. However, Babylonian influences are also immediately apparent in fragments cited by later authors; in the first century, Dorotheus claimed to have travelled to Babylon.[19] The style of some omens, though adapted to Egyptian circumstances, was clearly Babylonian in inspiration. One combines predictions based on the transit of the moon and planets through the zodiac with omens taken from the heliacal rising of Sirius which raises an interesting question: had the Egyptians long taken omens at Sirius' heliacal rising, or did they only begin to do so once the Babylonians had given them the idea that this might be done? One typical passage reads:

If it [Sirius] rises when Jupiter is in Sagittarius: The king of Egypt will rule over his country. An enemy will be [his and] he will escape from them again. Many men will rebel against the king. An inundation which is proper is that which comes to Egypt. Seed (and) grain (?) will be high as to price (in) money, which is ... The burial of a god will occur in Egypt ... [will come] up to Egypt and they will go away again.[20]

A later Greek text, perhaps from the second century or later but attributed to Zoroaster in order to give it authority, was a brontologion, analysing thunder in a style which indicates both Egyptian and Babylonian influences. It started with the beginning of the Egyptian year – the rising of Sirius and then considered the zodiac sign containing the moon. For example, thunder when the moon is in Aries indicates unrest and disturbance, in Taurus, a plague of locusts, failure of wheat and barley harvest, and happiness at court but oppression in the east.[21] Babylonian astrology, of the observational kind, rather than reliant on tables, survived right through the Hellenistic period; in the late fourth century, Hephaistio of Thebes, wrote about the colours of eclipses and comets as well as such gems as, 'if a short cloud-like line is observed making a section from the star (Sirius) to the east, and if the extremity of the line should be fiery', a lesser ruler will overcome a stronger one.[22]

Around 50 demotic (Egyptian language) horoscopes are known, the earliest of those that have been published dating from 39 BCE and the latest the birth charts in the tombs of two brothers who died in 141 and 148 CE.[23] The continuation of the iconography of the second millennium is clear in the portrayal of the planets in ways very similar to those in the tomb of Senmut, around 1,600 years earlier: Jupiter, Saturn and Mars are all falcons with outstretched wings, though Saturn has a bull's head and Mars three serpent's heads and a serpent's tail. Mercury is a falcon with the head of Set (suggesting an ominous reading) while Venus was a god with two heads. Both Sirius and Orion are also included, representing Isis and Osiris, along with other characters. Also from the Roman period, one astronomical treatise, Papyrus Carlsberg 1 contains a commentary on the cosmologies found in the tombs of Seti I and Rameses IV, while Papyrus Carlsberg 9 repeated the 25-year cycle.[24] Other surviving texts, such as the Stobart Tablets, a planetary ephemeris for 16 BCE–133 CE, were written in Egyptian but contain Greek or Babylonian material.

A separate strand of thought, which was to be directly applicable to political forecasting in medieval Europe, emphasized the planets' physical natures in an Aristotelian sense, but had no time for detailed astrological judgement. The naturalistic perspective was set out in the first century CE by the Roman scholar Pliny the Elder (23/4–79 CE), whose Naturalis Historia set the standard for investigation of the natural world and remained an authoritative text in Europe up until the scientific revolution of the seventeenth century. Like Cicero, Pliny was a devout Platonist and his regard for the sun as 'the soul, or more precisely the mind, of the whole world ... glorious and pre-eminent, all-seeing and even all-hearing',[25] suggests Hermetic influence. His belief that, not only is God distant but that it is a mark of weakness even to try to discover his form, points to some Gnostic parallels. Yet he mocks polytheism, including the planetary deities, as the 'height of folly ... the mad fancies of children' and ridicules the invocation of fortune and belief in chance and oracles as 'pitiable'.[26] Yet, it is undeniable that the planets, moving as they do through the Aristotelian ether, or 'vapour', have physical qualities which exert a material influence; Saturn is cold and frozen, Jupiter warmer and Mars positively hot, while Venus is 'the cause of the birth of all things upon earth' and 'scatters a general dew' at its rising which stimulates the sexual organs.[27] The sun and moon speak for themselves, the former being hot and the latter moist. The significance of Pliny's work for astrology was not so great in the first century, for he was merely stating the obvious consequence of elemental theory and Aristotelian cosmology, while denouncing the use of astrology for detailed prognostication. Yet, if astrology is partly a matter of planetary influences then the *Naturalis Historia* was to be a Trojan horse for astrology in medieval Europe. Such was Pliny's authority that no educated medieval Christian could deny the reality of general planetary influences.

The picture emerges of multiple points of astrological transmission in the second and first centuries BCE. In the first century BCE Mesopotamia and Syria were still home to the unbroken astrological tradition dating back 2,000 years to the kings of Sumer. We know this because Cicero tells us as much in his *De divinatione*. Cicero tells us that the Chaldeans, the astrologers of either the Babylonian tradition or race, were active in Syria and well known for their knowledge of the stars and impressive intellectual qualities.[28] The magi, the Persian priesthood, were also active throughout the Middle East and met regularly in sacred places, including hilltops, to conduct divinatory exercises, which we assume would have included astrological consultations. Such practices may have been inseparable from the soothsaying, interpretation of oracles, lightning and prodigies which were an integral part of political decision making in the Mediterranean and Middle East.[29]

We have one astrological text which is incomplete and may date from the first century BCE, though it may be later, such is the state of uncertainty.[30] However, from the early first to early second century CE we have four substantial texts. The earliest complete, reliably dated text is Marcus Manilius' *Astronomica*, written in Latin during the reign of Augustus. Dorotheus of Sidon's *Carmen Astrologicum* ('*Pentateuch*' in Greek) probably dates from around the second half of the first century, though it contains possibly later Persian and Arabic interpolations, apparently including rules for reading interrogations. Vettius Valens' *Anthology*, an extensive set of rules with case notes composed in the mid to late second century; and Claudius Ptolemy's *Tetrabiblos* (properly known as the *Apotelematika*) a work of immense importance which was written in Alexandria around 120 CE and was to become one of the core texts of medieval and Renaissance astrology. The last of the surviving classical astrological texts were the idiosyncratic *Mathesis*, written in Latin, not Greek, by Julius Firmicus Maternus, dated to the mid-fourth century, probably 338 and the *Apotelesmatics*, composed by Hephaistio of Thebes after 381. Parts of others works by Paul of Alexandria, a contemporary of Hephaistio, and Rhetorius (491–518) also survive. It is clear from all these works that there are competing traditions although, between them, they contain the major techniques and principles of astrological interpretation down to the twentieth century. Ptolemy's work, though, arguably had the greatest effect over the long run, through the medieval period, due in part to his reputation as an astronomer, as well as his general reputation as the great classical authority on astronomy and geography, as much as in the text's own merits. His astronomical work, the *Syntaxis*, was so highly regarded that European scholars borrowed the Arabic name for it, *Almagest* – the 'greatest' or 'majestic'. He was frequently confused with the royal Ptolemies and pictured wearing a crown. Between them, Ptolemy and Vettius Valens give us a rich impression of practical astrology in the second century CE. The earliest surviving manuscript of the *Tetrabiblos* is actually from the thirteenth century, over a thousand years after it was written, but we assume that we have a fair representation of the original.[31]

Ptolemy was born around 70 CE, and lived in Alexandria in a scholarly environment in which Gnostics, Hermeticists and members of various mystery schools were moving astrology in practical directions, dominated by their view of the cosmos as a stage set for the struggle of good against evil. In this context the stars were not useful for the prediction of the future so much as for personal salvation. However, stung by the savage criticisms of astrology launched by Carneades and Cicero, Ptolemy set out to present it as reasonable by straddling the line between Plato and Aristotle.[32] From the former he took orthodox notions concerning the soul, to which Cicero could not possibly have objected. From the latter, he adopted a concern with a world in which nature, through such primary qualities such as hot, cold, wet and dry, really mattered. One of Ptolemy's priorities was to answer astrology's critics, most likely Cicero, although he did not mention the Roman sceptic by name. But, in spite of this, he appears to have adapted Cicero's division of divination into two parts by presenting astronomy, as he called it, as consisting of two parts, a distinction which endured until the seventeenth century. The first was the calculation of the movements of the stars and planets, which he covered in the *Almagest*, while the second was the investigation of the changes these movements bring out, which he described in the *Tetrabiblos*.[33] It was all supposed to be very rational and devoid of magical and religious overtones. Ptolemy's astrology is often understood as the logical conclusion of the supposed process of secularization that found its origins in Thales' search for the material foundation of the cosmos and was given its sophisticated mechanical form by Aristotle. We talk about Ptolemy providing a 'scientific' basis for astrology, not in the Babylonian sense that it was a discipline with its own rules, but by providing natural causes.[34] He resisted the spiritualizing trends of Hermeticism and Mithraism, which preserved astrology's overt religious dimension. However, there is a dislocation between the naturalistic features of Ptolemy's cosmology and his astrology. The latter, however he saw it, is a highly codified divinatory system, based on abstract conceptions of a mathematically ordered cosmos ultimately derived from Pythagoras.

But to propose a theory of natural influence as a response to Cicero's attack on astrology was not a smart move. Cicero had already pointed out that, even if celestial influences might influence people, it was unrealistic to suggest that they could affect bricks and mortar; Ptolemy might have been better to appeal to doctrines of celestial signification. Besides, natural influence only works so far as a rationale. When Ptolemy writes that 'Mars brings about blindness from a bow, a thrust, iron or burning', we see Stoic doctrines of 'sympathy', that Mars 'sympathizes with' in some way shares the same essence as, violent blows, heat and iron.[35] Yet, he also appears to have found the dogmatic tone of contemporary astrology, highly Stoic as it was, deeply unsatisfactory. This was the kind of text he would have encountered:

> If you wish to compute the lot of brothers, count from the degree of Saturn to Jupiter and add to it the degrees of the ascendant [by day] and subtract it from the ascendant [by night]; wherever it comes to, then [there is] the lot of brothers.[36]

Ptolemy clearly regarded such Pythagorean complexity as completely reasonable – astrologers long ago accepted that everything in the cosmos could be reduced to numerical ciphers. But he wished to see a basis for astrology which acknowledged that human beings are embodied, walking, living, breathing creatures, more than collections of numbers, or souls enduring a period of earthly imprisonment. Because Ptolemy adopted the standard Aristotelian divisions of knowledge into physics, mathematics and theology, and used the moon's effect on the tides as a naturalistic rationale for astrology, he is retrospectively classified as an Aristotelian, rather than a 'Platonist', as if these descriptions are mutually exclusive.[37] They are not, and Ptolemy, as we shall see, specifically appealed to Plato. It may be that his work evolved over time, but what we have to consider is his historical impact, and for that his body of work has to be read as a whole. True, he saw the Aristotelian cosmos as providing a framework for astrological mechanics: 'a certain power emanating from the eternal etheric substance', he reasoned, became increasingly varied in its form as it descended through the planetary spheres, entering a world of every-greater changeability.[38] Whereas Valens introduced the planets by describing their associations in the chain of being, Ptolemy followed the naturalistic tradition represented by Pliny in describing their natural qualities. Mars was hot and dry, Venus warm and moist and Saturn cold and dry, for example.[39] From this developed an entire rationale for astrological influence. Antiochus of Athens, who probably lived in the late second century, explained the propensity of Saturn and Venus to produce childlessness, because Saturn cooled Venus, preventing fertility.[40] But, it is a complete mistake to imagine that the naturalistic rationale necessarily produced the astrological judgement. We can go back to the fifth-century BCE Babylonian tablets to find that Venus was favourable and Saturn sick and constrained.[41]

Besides, the decidedly un-Aristotelian Manilius had identified Saturn's 'native ice' and Venus' relationship to love.[42]

The *Tetrabiblos* develops into a series of rules for horoscope interpretation which may be seen as an elaboration of the procedures clearly developing in fifth- and fourth-century BCE Mesopotamia, but does not depend on Aristotelian cosmology. This is an important distinction: Aristotelian naturalism provided a rationale for astrology – it was part of an attempt to locate it in a secular context – but it was not necessary for the rules of interpretation. Ptolemy brought the abstracting, theorizing, model-building tendencies of Babylonian astrology to Greece, but gave them a naturalistic justification which meant he hoped that it was difficult to challenge them. He was the great preserver of the mindset of Babylonian astrology and, in spite of his devotion to the measurement of the stars, to David Browns's EAE paradigm, the location of all phenomena in a theoretical framework. Ptolemy's exposition of the significance of eclipses, to take one example, is based on mathematical abstractions as far removed from empirical observation as were the Babylonian omens for eclipses on the 21st day.[43]

Ptolemy is frequently described as a Stoic, the very embodiment of determinism. And to an extent he was, though in a diluted form; he was deeply influenced by the combined Platonic–Aristotelian–Stoic philosophy advocated by Antiochus of Ascalon, head of the Academy in the first century. While all change on earth might be explained in terms of natural forces, higher up the causal chain the planets' movements, he claimed 'were eternally performed in accordance with divine unchangeable destiny'.[44] Yet, in an absolutely fated world, astrology had no purpose, so for any astrologer Stoic determinism had to be tempered by at least some Platonic belief that the future was negotiable.

Ptolemy's exposition of the correct procedures for reading horoscopes was complex, devoid of practical examples and, in spite of a clear attempt to be encyclopaedic, apparently lacking any section on *katarche*, the use of astrology to select auspicious moments for new initiatives (although the rules he set out could easily be adapted to the management of the future). Neither did he include interrogations but, as we have seen, there are suggestions that their use may not have been current in the second century. But, considering that selection of auspicious moments was one of the principal appeals of astrology to its most powerful political patrons, certainly from Antiochus of Commagene onwards, perhaps much earlier, it is not entirely clear why he omitted explicit instructions on its use. After all, the whole notion of manipulating the natural world by harmonizing with celestial influences and order, fits perfectly with the Aristotelian, naturalistic dimension of Ptolemy's worldview. One explanation might be that he was too much of a Stoic to regard astrology as anything other than a means of reading a pre-ordained future. This is true – in part. He did write that foreknowledge of predetermined events calms the soul; by knowing that the future is inevitable, one accepts it with grace. However, in the same passage, he also argued that the only point in forecasting the future was to change it and that, in any case, some events were due to chance.[45] So, in his discussion of

Egyptian medical astrology he argued that 'they would never have devised certain means of averting or warding off … the universal and particular conditions that come or are present by reason of the ambient, if they had any idea that the future cannot be moved and changed'.[46] There was no point in astrology unless the future could be changed. It remained managerial and participatory, and the astrologer adopted the role of co-creator, but the locus of participation had changed. No longer was the astrologer a supplicant pleading a case before capricious gods and goddesses before whom he was relatively powerless. Instead he was participating, as a humanist, in the creation of the future. Ptolemy's divinatory act did not involve talking to divinities. But, as in Babylon, it allowed an act of will which might, it was hoped, control the cosmos.[47] There were, to be sure, astrologers who apparently accepted complete Stoic determinism, down to the merest detail, including most of Ptolemy's contemporaries in fact, including Vettius Valens. One was Julius Firmicus Maternus in the early fourth century, but in his defence of his position, he made it clear that others, perhaps the majority, believed that only death was subject to fate, leaving the rest of life negotiable.[48]

Ptolemy does seem to have made a deliberate attempt to mitigate the Pythagorean determinism of much of the astrology of his time, in which the mathematical movement of astrological factors trapped the individual not just in a clockwork cosmos, but a vast series of cogs, the existential prison envisioned by Hermetic pessimists. The Aristotelian in Ptolemy sought a path to freedom. He naturalised the *katarche* as a 'seed' moment, in which all origins can be understood on their own terms – as natural.[49] He was not the first to use this metaphor. The seed in the Hermetic texts was sown by destiny and gave rise to all succeeding events, while Manilius spoke of the construction of the universe from its component seeds.[50] Again, he straddled the boundary between Plato and Aristotle. He took Aristotle's formal cause – that a thing can only be, or grow into, what it is – and final cause – that a thing is already what it is to grow into – and spoke of the process as if he were a farmer. In astrological terms the astrologer was able to assess the amount of 'Venus-ness' or 'Mars-ness' in a horoscope.

The adaptation of the Aristotelian scheme to astrology, though, has a major consequence in that astrology explicitly focuses on just one level of the hierarchy of descending Aristotelian influences. In Ptolemy's scheme the sub-lunar level was given a greater emphasis, and climatic and cultural influences were considered crucial additions to the intelligent understanding of natal astrology. Quite simply, each individual should be understood within their culture, and that culture itself depending on geography and weather. Thus, by implication, although Ptolemy did not spell this out, two people born with very similar horoscopes but in different locations would have different lives. Within such a scheme astrological truth claims are relative rather than absolute.

The adoption of a theory of influences gave astrology a mechanism but had virtually no discernible impact on the process of interpretation. The qualities of the planets alone – their degrees of heat, cold and moisture – merely added another layer to their existing roles. Judicial astrology remained an abstract structure, a set of thought processes through which the astrologer reached a rational judgement of affairs. Its closest relationship was to pure mathematics, except that in the Platonic and Pythagorean tradition each number converted into a state of Being or Becoming. Whatever complex formula the astrologer constructed could therefore convert into a conclusion such as 'the child is yours', 'your ship will arrive on Tuesday' or 'you should take these herbs for that complaint'. The gradual shift from residual Babylonian polytheism to Persian and then Platonic, Aristotelian and Stoic monotheism was far more important, for all planets and zodiac signs became symbols of the One, cogs in the machine and stepping stones to either worldly success or spiritual salvation.

In Ptolemy's scheme of causation, the divine manifests successfully through the stars, planets, climate, geography and culture.[51] In other words, the promise of one's natal horoscope might vary if one lived in a mountainous climate or a coastal plain, in the cold north or the tropics. This is common sense. Ptolemy set out the causal position comprehensively, arguing that:

> The stars likewise (as well the fixed stars as the planets), in performing their revolutions, produce many impressions on the Ambient. They cause heats, winds, and storms, to the influence of which earthly things are conformably subjected. And, further, the mutual configurations of all these heavenly bodies, by commingling the influence with which each is separately invested, produce a multiplicity of changes.[52]

However human intervention does not actually reduce the level of causality, for human action itself becomes another cause:

> It must not be imagined that all things happen to mankind, as though every individual circumstance were ordained by divine decree and some indissoluble supernal cause; nor is it to be thought that all events are shown to proceed from one single inevitable fate, without being influenced by the interposition of any other agency.[53]

That the stars move along mathematically defined paths should not lead to the mistaken conclusion that human life is similarly determined. Ptolemy explicitly rejects any assumption that human beings have no control over their lives and triumphantly asserts, as a classical humanist should, a spirit of freedom. He was not so far from the consensus on such matters. Manilius, for example, wrote that: 'Now nature holds no mysteries for us; we have surveyed it in its entirety and are masters of the conquered sky'.[54]

Ptolemy's task in Lucien Lévy-Bruhl's terms, was to restore some of the initiative in the *participation-mystique* to humanity, to locate humanity in nature and qualify the Stoic position that participation lay in adjusting one's attitude to a world that was beyond one's control. Ptolemy attempted to straddle the gap that Cicero had opened between divination by nature and by art. Although he succeeded in the sense that the *Tetrabiblos'* naturalism and absence of any religious doctrines was to make it the ideal foundational text for the astrology which flourished alongside Christian theology in medieval Europe, the difficulty of reconciling his theoretical divinatory structure with a cosmology based on observable influences has been the cause of much subsequent criticism of astrology. Many critics could accept the notion of a cosmos bound together by physical influences which might form the basis of general forecasts without accepting that astrologers might then go on to make detailed statements about such matters as length of life.

While Ptolemy's naturalism is seductive, it only tells part of the picture. Matter was still intimately connected to soul and he was clearly exploring the numinous, the realm of psyche. His naturalistic rationale for astrology was embedded in a Platonic view of the cosmos as ensouled. Divinity stood at the heart of Ptolemy's cosmology, through what he imagined, in his cautious way, as divinity, was the 'first cause of the first motion of the universe', impersonal and remote, like an 'invisible and motionless deity'.[55] His goal, he wrote, was to 'strive for a noble and disciplined disposition ... to devote most of our time to intellectual matters, and especially those to which the epithet "mathematical" is particularly applied'.[56] He wholeheartedly accepted Plato's sceptical theory of knowledge, that the material world is unreliable and only abstract thought could be a certain guide to truth, and saw the end of astronomy as a love of contemplation of the eternal. Prediction on a material basis had to be uncertain due to changes in the natural sphere. Whatever the configuration of the stars might indicate, any prediction had to take into account whether a person was young or old, lived in a cold climate or warm – or was even a person, rather than an animal. This, to Ptolemy, was simple common sense. Astrology, he maintained, is therefore conjectural and inherently unreliable, at least when compared to astronomy. And, in this, he was simply facing the same problem that had troubled the Babylonian astrologers in their correspondence with the Assyrian emperors. But, even when astrology was wrong, Ptolemy maintained, it still reveals the beauty of the universe.[57] That he was not averse to putting forth evidence from observation does not lessen his Platonic credentials. For example, Plato said that the world was spherical because the sphere was the most perfect shape. But Ptolemy needed simple observation to confirm Plato's logic. The stars, he reasoned, rose in the west, moved overhead in a vast arc, set in the west and then began the process again the next evening.[58]

Ptolemy's preferred model of the soul was Plato's standard threefold division arranged in hierarchical order as rational, emotional and 'cupidinous'.[59] Self-control of the latter two, through the aesthetic, philosophical lifestyle, is necessary if the former is to achieve its full potential. The rational soul is subject to a division into seven qualities, in a clear, but undefined, analogy with the planets, which are not mentioned explicitly, all of which are varieties of sharp, critical thinking, experience and wisdom. The soul is then embedded, in Pythagorean style, in a series of mathematical formulae and musical scales related to the zodiac signs and planets.[60] The rising of Mercury and Venus, for example, relates to a particular sound, a perfect harmony which, if one could hear it, would represent the perfect contemplation of the divine. There is, though, no exact translation of this model into astrological correspondences. He set out rules for identifying the condition of the soul, or *psyche*, in a manner which we would describe as psychological, though, in his astrological example, he was concerned only with two levels of the soul, rather than three.[61] The condition of the rational soul was to be determined by the placing of Mercury, the 'star of Hermes', and the irrational by the moon, planet of emotional changeability, and the stars linked to her. We have to understand that, in the Stoic conception, which was undoubtedly an influence on Ptolemy, animals were compelled to action by a movement in the soul/psyche called the *hormê* – an impulse or drive.[62] There is a kind of celestial mechanics at work here, but one which can only be understood within a theory of extended consciousness, in which the movement of a planet is connected with a disturbance in the individual soul, and with a consequent tendency to action. The distinction between a planet's psychic or psychological, and physical function may be one which we observe, but is not related to the essential nature of the cosmos, in which the two are absolutely interrelated. When Mars dominated the soul, Ptolemy argued, the individual would display the planet's qualities, whether negative or positive, either blind aggression or great courage. When Venus was dominant, the soul had the characteristics of that planet, whether pleasant, affectionate and charming or 'careless, erotic, effeminate, womanish, timid ... depraved and meriting reproach'.[63] Although he did not discuss it, Ptolemy clearly accepted that the soul's descent through the stars provided a convincing rationale for natal astrology. On this basis it was possible to work out not just an individual's character, but what profession they might take up, when they were likely to fall sick and therefore, using fine judgements, how long they might live. In other words, the *Tetrabiblos* was a practical manual to accompany the *Corpus Hermeticum* and the *Timaeus*, and provided a comprehensive means for analysing the kind of life the soul chose in the *Republic.*

Ptolemy was also deeply concerned with collective affairs and gave the rules for interpreting the future on the basis of the horoscope for the spring equinox – when the sun entered Aries on 21 March – or from eclipses. One of his major achievements, which formed a staple of medieval political astrology, was an adaptation of Babylonian cosmic geography. He took the more recent idea, found in Manilius, that countries conformed to the 12 zodiac signs and linked it to Babylonian astrology's characteristic division of the world into four quarters, each corresponding to different stars, planets and times of year. In his scheme, which was in common use in political astrology throughout the Middle Ages and Renaissance, Europe, north Africa, north Asia and southern Asia formed the four quarters, with a central zone of interlocking influences in the Middle East; India was Capricorn, Persia Taurus, Egypt Gemini, Palestine and Italy Leo, and Spain Sagittarius, while the warlike barbarians of England, France and Germany were ruled by Mars' sign, Aries.[64]

Ptolemy's work had one unintended consequence. His definition, whether by intent or through a misunderstanding of the zodiac as beginning with the sun's location on the spring equinox, was to cause problems in the future because, by tying the zodiac to the seasons, he cut its ties to the stars, which gradually moved away from the signs. The Babylonian zodiac consisted of 12 equally sized sectors, but it was tied to the stars – it was sidereal. Eudoxus had located the vernal equinox at 8° Aries.[65] In the first century Pliny had recorded that the sun on 21 March was at 8° Aries.[66] However, according to Ptolemy's calculations the gradual shift of the stars meant that the sun was now at 0° Aries on 21 March and his statement to this effect was taken by subsequent astrologers as an indication that the sun always occupied 0° Aries on the equinox regardless of the stars' movement.[67] This phenomenon, know as the precession of the equinoxes, displaces the Babylonian/Persian sidereal zodiac at a rate of one sign every 2,156 years from the Ptolemaic, 'tropical' zodiac. The sidereal zodiac remained in use in India while the tropical zodiac was gradually established as the norm in the West, the consequence being that the two systems have diverged. The dislocation of the zodiac signs from the constellations after which they were named has provided constant fuel for astrology's critics from the second-century Church Father Origen onwards. Ptolemy's contribution to astronomical mechanics was also, eventually, to cause huge problems for astrology. He added new complexity and authority to the Platonic belief that all heavenly motions were perfectly circular, tightening up Eudoxus' elaborate theory of cycles within spheres.

Ptolemy's slightly younger contemporary, Vettius Valens (c.120–175) was born in Antioch, Syria, and may have visited Alexandria, where he reportedly received formal astrological training, after which he became a professional astrologer, and proprietor of an astrological school. Between the years 150 and 175 CE, he wrote the *Anthology*, a work which provided a perfect contrast to the *Tetrabiblos*. There is no account of Ptolemy and Valens meeting and, whereas Ptolemy is often thought to have been an encyclopaedist, Valens was clearly a working astrologer and teacher. Eventually his work was transmitted to the Byzantines and from there to the Persians and the Islamic world, from where it re-entered medieval Europe; John Dee, astrologer to the English queen Elizabeth I, possessed a copy.

The *Anthology* is the most comprehensive source of Greek horoscopes: over a hundred are provided for the instruction of students. Yet, even though Valens was clearly an evangelist, he appears to adhere to the secret protocols of the Egyptian temple tradition. Having taken a risk by committing his work to the written word, he implores his reader several times throughout the *Anthology* to take an oath 'to keep these things secret, and not to impart them to the unlearned or the uninitiated', though he was clearly impatient with the convoluted language of the sources he was using.[68] There's a suggestion here of some affiliation with a mystery school, as opposed to Ptolemy's public scholarship.

The *Anthology* is logically organized, beginning with the basic structural features of horoscopic astrology such as planets and houses, describing an elaborate and complex technical structure which enabled astrological readings of great precision. Valens explained how to use the various time-lord systems, by which the future might be predicted with great precision, included a system of calculating houses, later named after the Neoplatonic philosopher Porphyry, and anchored the theoretical structure firmly in the natural world by relating the 'trigons' of zodiac signs to the four elements.[69] That the latter was not reported by Ptolemy suggests that it may have been a second-century innovation. But like Ptolemy, Valens seems to have at once advocated a Stoic theory of immutable fate, and allowed room for the individual to negotiate their relationship with it.

> But those occupied with the prognostication of the future and the truth, by gaining a soul free and not enslaved, think slightly of fortune, and do not obstinately persist in hope, and do not fear death, but spend their lives without disturbance by training the soul ahead of time to be confident, and neither rejoice excessively in the case of good nor are depressed in the case of foul, and are content with what is present. And those who are not in love with the impossible carry along that which is ordained, and being estranged from all pleasure or flattery, they are established as soldiers of fate.[70]

In spite of their contrasting styles, there is enough of an overlap between Ptolemy and Valens, for us to make certain generalizations about second-century astrology. Each zodiac sign was subject to multiple classifications, which served either as rationales for their meanings, or suggested links between them. The Babylonian system, in which signs separated by a third of the zodiac (such as Aries, Leo and Sagittarius) were in a friendly relationship, was developed so that opposite signs (such as Cancer and Capricorn) or those separated by a quarter of the zodiac (such as Gemini, Virgo, Sagittarius and Pisces) were in a difficult relationship. The signs were further subdivided into decans, which were also known as faces, terms, divisions of each sign into unequal thirds, and *dodekatemoria*, one-twelfth divisions inherited from the Babylonians (the word could also mean a twelfth part of the zodiac – one sign). All of these were ruled by planets which further complicated the web of relationships.

It is widely assumed, though, and with good reason, that the personalities of the astrological planets were imported from classical mythology. We have seen how the Platonic *Epinomis* converted the Babylonian deities to the Greek pantheon, but did the Olympian deities' mythological characters contribute to astrological meanings? The evidence suggests that they did, but only in general terms; they had no part in the construction of the rules of astrological interpretation and, with the exception of Manilius, the astrological authors do not refer to the Olympian gods and goddesses. But we can discern some relationship between the deities' personalities in myth and astrology. Homer described Hermes as a 'shrewd and coaxing schemer' and 'a tiny child steeped in crafty wiles' and had him declare 'to some men I will bring harm and to others benefit'.[71] He was fickle, unreliable and a compulsive if charming liar whose major Homeric story involved the theft of Apollo's cattle. His spirited manner won the solar deity's friendship and patronage, rather than his wrath, and the young god was rewarded by being made lord over all omen birds and messenger between Olympus and Hades. Only he could travel to the underworld and return unharmed. Accordingly he became a god of wisdom; as he correctly claimed, 'except for me, none of the Gods would know the inscrutable will of Zeus'.[72] His astrological character reflected this mix of qualities and Mercury ruled both those who 'know the heavens', the very heart of Platonic wisdom, on the one hand, and fraudsters on the other.[73] The planet's core meanings are clearly related to the Babylonian Nabu and were associated with commerce, clerical professions and intellectual activities, including omen reading. But, then, Hermes was also the god of the marketplace, which was often the location of his oracle, and was a patron of traders and merchants as well as ruling over all forms of writing and communication, from scribes to orators. Similarly Venus was loving, Mars warlike, Jupiter benevolent and Saturn restrictive, qualities which can be traced to Babylonian originals, even if they have been extended.[74] All these characteristics are still repeated in modern astrological texts.[75] Other attributions were added which can only be Greek. Saturn was linked to time, through word association, as Cronos (Saturn) was connected to *chronos*, or time (and hence, according to some writers, to the Zoroastrian Zurvan).[76] There were also relationships to the working out of fate: Saturn ruled ignorance (*agnoia*) and necessity (*ananke*), which together subjected people to an uncontrollable destiny, while the moon ruled *pronoia*, the foresight required to change one's future. And of course, for the Romans, there was a further conversion of Greek names into Latin: the star of Cronos became Saturn, the star of Zeus, Jupiter, the star of Ares, Mars, the star of Aphrodite, Venus and the star of Hermes, Mercury.

The one clear problem with the planets' shift from Babylon to Greece was the moon, which changed sex on its westward journey. The Greeks revered the moon as Diana, Artemis or Selene. While Selene was the actual moon disc; Hecate and Artemis were associated with the moon but distinct from the moon itself. Hecate is an older goddess who allied herself with Zeus against the Titans. She guarded flocks and ruled navigation, and conferred wealth, victory and wisdom, and was also associated with magic (especially witchcraft), murder, crossroads, tombs, dogs and Hades. Artemis, with whom Hecate was sometimes merged, was a wild huntress, goddess of night, nature and fertility. Like her brother Apollo, her weapon was the bow. In the most famous story about her she punished Actaeon for disturbing her bathing in the forest by turning him into a stag, to be devoured by his own dogs. The Roman Diana was a huntress, perhaps in honour of the full moon by whose light nocturnal animals could be trapped and was to become a romantic and vigorous figure in the European poetic imagination, as the 'Queen and huntress, chaste and fair'.[77] It is difficult to see, though, how the moon's divine attributes are evident in her astrological qualities except for her relationship with mothers; the two most influential surviving second-century texts, Vettius Valens' *Anthology* and Ptolemy's *Tetrabiblos*, almost ignore it in their opening sections on planetary qualities.[78] It was left to their contemporary, Plutarch, to give a list of its qualities, but then in strikingly non-mythical tones. Repeating what he knew of Egyptian theories of the moon, he contrasted it with the sun:

The moon, because it has light that is generative and productive of moisture, is kindly towards the young of animals and the burgeoning plants, whereas the sun by its untempered and pitiless heat, makes all growing and flourishing vegetation hot and parched, and through its blazing light, renders a large part of the earth uninhabitable. In fact the actions of the moon are like the actions of reason and perfect wisdom, whereas those of the sun are like beatings through violence and brute strength.[79]

The Babylonian scheme, again evident in the cuneiform birth charts, for giving planets benevolent (Venus and Jupiter) or malevolent (Mars and Saturn) qualities, and consider them to either rule, or be exalted in, certain signs, was extended. Planets acquired gender, in a further testimony to the notion of the cosmos as a living organism; the sun, Mars, Jupiter and Saturn were male, the moon and Venus were feminine (the Babylonian moon had been masculine) and Mercury was a hermaphrodite.

The planets might form relationships with each other depending on their geometrical relationship; those in signs opposite each other or separated by a quarter of the zodiac were in a difficult relationship (a square in medieval astrology), those in signs separated by a third or a sixth (a trine or a sextile in medieval astrology) were friendly. The principle was partly Pythagorean but also partly Aristotelian; in Latin the generic term for such links was aspect, from *aspecto/are*, to gaze or look at, so there was a transmission of light, or a sending of rays, from the planet which looked to that which was looked at. Again, we return to the notion of the cosmos as a living organism. The sense of the cosmos as imbued with personality was reinforced by Manilius, who analysed the mathematical relationship between zodiac signs, on which the interpretation of the horoscope was based, in terms of human relationships. Suggesting a link back to Pythagorean doctrines, he wrote: 'Between opposite signs there exist mostly hatred', he wrote, 'and to quadrate signs are mostly ascribed ties of kinship; ties of friendship to trigonal signs'.[80] One could go on. Adjacent signs, such as Aries and Taurus, or Taurus and Gemini, aid neighbours while alternate signs, such as Aries and Gemini or Taurus and Cancer, favour guests. Ptolemy, in particular, extended this idea from its Platonic roots, demonstrating how much he was the heir of Hesiod and Hippocrates, by dividing all things according to their qualities, of heat or cold, dryness or moisture; Mars was hot and dry, and Venus cold and moist. Like Hesiod, and like the Babylonians he used rising and setting planets; a planet which was visible before dawn and growing brighter from one day to the next was masculine and one which was visible after dusk was feminine. To a Pythagorean, of course, to be male was good and female bad, and even in the fourth century we find Firmicus Maternus writing: 'Venus on the ascendant by night [before dawn] will make men of divine intelligence, friends of emperors', while 'Venus on the ascendant by day [after dusk] makes the natives oversexed, unchaste, of ill repute'.[81]

Hesiodic naturalism and Hippocratic medicine found their fulfilment in Hellenistic astrology's concern with the estimation of vitality, from which it could be deduced whether a child was likely to survive or die, an important consideration in an age of high infant mortality. The whole interpretative chain depended on lines of association which enabled any object, thought or emotion to be given an astrological rulership. For example, working from first principles, if Mars was hot and dry (its colour, after all, has a reddish tinge), then it signifies fevers from a medical point of view, drought in weather prediction, hot-tempered people in psychological analysis and hence war, knives and blood. Even in the seventeenth century we find books which list every conceivable entity in the cosmos, from archangels to stones, linking them to zodiac signs and planets. The one area of astrological activity missing from both Ptolemy and Valens was the construction of magical talismans and amulets. These clearly existed, for we have beautiful examples of precious stones inscribed with planetary and zodiacal symbols.[82] One could, for example, attract a lover or curse a rival. The literary context for such amulets is found in a remarkable collection of texts we know collectively as the Greek Magical Papyri, and which date from the second to fifth centuries. What we have is but a fraction of the original. The Emperor Augustus burned 2,000 prophetic manuscripts when he became chief priest in 13 BCE, and the Christians later contributed to the destruction.[83] Those that do survive demonstrate astrology's active side. One reads:

> Orbit of the moon: Moon / in Virgo; anything is obtainable. In Libra; necromancy. In Scorpio: anything inflicting evil. In Sagittarius: an invocation or incantations / to the sun and moon. In Capricorn: say whatever you wish for best result. In Aquarius: for a love charm. Pisces: foreknowledge. / In Aries: fire divination or love charm. In Taurus: incantation to a lamp. Gemini: spell for winning favour. In Cancer: phylacteries. Leo: rings or binding spells.[84]

If such rules set up the interpretative guidelines, what did one actually do? One might take a laurel branch, inscribe the zodiac signs on the leaves with cinnabar, and crown oneself with it, or walk towards the sun at the fifth hour, wearing a cat's tail, reciting incantations, or to receive dreams mould an image of Selene, the moon goddess.[85] There was no area into which astrologers could not inquire. Their concerns were universal. Astrology became a means of applying the principles of the cosmic state to every aspect of human life. One could ask the cosmos about almost anything, from the best bargain in the market, the way to treat a runaway slave, or the appropriate moment to proclaim oneself emperor. In the second century CE, the satirist Juvenal mocked the typical, venal, Roman woman who 'wants to know why her jaundice-ridden mother takes so long dying (she's enquired about you already). When will she see off her sister, her uncles? Will her present lover survive her? (What greater boon could she ask of the Gods?)'.[86] He also had little respect for the astrologers' level of skill, suggesting that there were many who earned a living without bothering with the technicalities set out by Valens or Ptolemy. As the scope of concerns on which astrology could comment expanded, and the number of texts multiplied, it became clear that astrologers had different ways of working. They could comment on affairs of state, as their Babylonian antecedents had long done, or on individual lives, as had been the practice since the Persians. But they could also answer specific questions (as 'is my ship safe?' or 'will my lion be tamed?'), or elect auspicious moments for beginning enterprises. And, having inquired, they could, if they were not absolute Stoics, alter the future. Astrology, no more than any other discipline, existed in a vacuum and when it depended on the use of planetary deities to read character, understand the condition of one's soul or manage the future, it could not have functioned independently of a religious practice. In the Hellenistic world, as in Babylon, astrology invariably indicated action. One might have a talisman cast, make a sacrifice to the appropriate deity or, if one was emperor, have one's enemies rounded up. To act in such a way was to engage in what we would call magic: the management of the world with the aid of the supernatural. In some applications, such as *katarche*, the selection of auspicious moments, the astrological act was itself magical. But we should not understand magic in this sense to be somehow irrational. In a world in which the existence of a supernatural creator, archetypes and gods and goddesses, and a divine connection between God and the mind was taken for granted, astrology made perfect sense.

All our known classical astrological writers in the 700 years from Critodomus to Firmicus Maternus were men, and the role of women in Greek astrology is uncertain. Until recently it was assumed that women were also invisible in the Greek city state as a whole. This assumption suited nineteenth-century classicists who believed that, as in modern Europe, Greek women were confined to the home. Recent evidence, though has established convincingly the powerful role that priestesses held throughout Greek religion, and the vital role that the temple played in the state.[87] It follows that priestesses, distinguished and often from aristocratic families, would have played a significant role in articulating Greek cosmology or, at least, that part of it which dealt with humanity's relationship with the political hierarchy of the cosmic state, the Olympian gods and goddesses. Women's powerful religious role was carried over into early Christianity and was eclipsed only in the early medieval church, after the demise of classical paganism. The most powerful woman in Greek spiritual life from archaic times was the Pythia, who held court at the Oracle of Delphi, uttering riddles and prophecies from a cave, pointing to origins in the veneration of the living earth. But the sanctuary's dedication to Apollo, at least in the historic period, indicates respect for the sun as a source of truth and enlightenment. But, when astrology made its gradual appearance in Greece from the fifth century inwards, a division of labour appears to have taken place in the prophecy industry. Women retained their place of power in the temples. Oracles, whether run by men or women, continued to operate in a manner more suggestive of links with ecstatic shamanism than the rationalism of Babylonian astrology. The orthodox view of astrology in the Greek world is, then, that it operated in a secular milieu outside the temples. There is some truth in this. The gods and goddesses of astrology, while sharing the same

names as the Olympian deities, began to assume a different character. They
became part-actors in a cosmic drama dominated by the Platonic creator, aspects
of the divine mind. However, the notion of Hellenistic astrology as essentially
secularized is far from the truth. As Juvenal wrote in the second century CE:
'These astrologers' predictions come straight, it is believed, from Ammon's
oracular fountain'.[88] Women, whether a priestess or not, are certainly invisible
amongst both the astrological writers and the thinkers who provided the context
for the practice of astrology. One notable exception, the Platonic philosopher
Hypatia, lived in the fourth century CE, at the very end of the classical era, and
has become a symbol of the gradual death of the old order when, in 415, she
became a pagan martyr to a Christian mob in Alexandria. But there were others.
Proclus (412–485) himself, the foremost Platonic philosopher of his day learnt
divination and the practice of 'Chaldean prayer-meetings' and other 'mystic rites'
from Asclepigeneia, the daughter of Plutarch of Athens, his predecessor as head
of the Academy.[89]

A clear connection between astrology and the temple tradition survived in
Egypt, particularly the temples of the Hellenistic-Egyptian god Serapis, as well as
Isis. We have surviving texts from the second and third centuries which indicate
that the temples were visited for consultations and that the astrologers used boards
on which they placed the planets, represented by precious stones, to represent a
horoscope.[90] The boards appear to have been a standard part of the astrologer's
toolkit, for ones very similar to the Egyptian have been found in France.[91] A
similar system can still be seen in Indian temples. Their use could explain why we
have so few surviving diagrammatic representation of the horoscope, rather than
just listings of planetary position. There is a rare example of a circular diagram
in Greek, from Oxyrhynchus, set for sometime between the years 15 and 22 CE,
and a square one for 28 October 497, by which time the familiar symbols for
planets and zodiac signs had emerged.[92] The uncertainty of the dating of the
circular diagram is a testimony to the inaccuracy of the planetary positions, a
commentary on the problems of astronomical measurement even with the latest
calculation systems. The boards themselves might have been technically simpler
than the Antikythera mechanism, but their religious use was more apparent. We
have the following description of their use:

> A voice comes to you speaking. Let the stars be set upon the board in accordance with
> [their] nature except for the Sun and the Moon. And let the Sun be golden, the Moon
> silver, Kronos of obsidian, Ares or reddish onyx, Aphrodite lapis lazuli veined with gold,
> Hermes turquoise: let Zeus be of (whitish?) stone crystalline (?); and the horoscope, in
> accordance with (nature?).[93]

The provocative statement here is the mysterious mention of the 'voice'. Clearly,
the god was speaking. Serapis worship spread to Italy, where he was popular in
the third century, so it is likely that a tradition of temple-astrology flourished at
Rome. His chief sanctuary in Egypt, the Serapeum in Alexandria was destroyed in

anti-pagan persecutions inspired by the Emperor Theodosius, so we may assume that horoscopes of the type found at Oxyrhynchus were still being produced there until the late fourth or early fifth centuries.

To talk about a either 'Hellenistic' or 'Greek' astrology as if there was a single set of ideological assumptions and techniques is misleading. There were multiple points of creation, which originated in fifth-century BCE Mesopotamia, and extended the process of innovation. The most obvious feature that the different texts have in common is that they were written in Greek. Astrologers such as Ptolemy, Vettius Valens and Paulus Alexandrinus shared Platonic, Aristotelian and Stoic influences, though in different combinations. The *Corpus Hermeticum* was concerned with the soul's ascent to the stars, Valens with the meticulous detail of daily life, Manilius with the inner divine, and Ptolemy with the natural world. If there is a common thread running through Greek astrology, which may distinguish it from its Babylonian origins, it is of the universe itself as an organizing principle.

As a mathematical construct the birth chart, newly invented by the Babylonians, had become a means of examining the unfolding of the Platonic creator, the great mind out of which all humanity was thought to emerge. The planets were the sign of the movement of the world soul, beyond which lay eternal truths. Literally, as Plato put it, 'the cycles of the stars and planets from day to day and year to year reveal the revolutions of Reason in the Heaven'.[94] If the stars and planets were the writing of the gods and goddesses to the Babylonians, Plato took the assumption one step further: they were the thoughts of God.

14

Rome: The State, the Stars and Subversion

> The divine Mind is diffused throughout the whole body
> of the universe ... and rules and orders all things.[1]

The Romans left European culture with an abiding mythology, a belief in the possibility of a universal state. By establishing a realm which stretched from Scotland to Bulgaria and Spain to Turkey and surrounding it with walls and defensive positions, it established the dream both of European unity and the concept of firm boundaries between 'us' and 'them'. What lay outside was often of no value; it was barbarian. That the empire endured for five centuries in the west, and much longer in the east, ensured that its influence has proved enormous. In addition to the Latin language, Roman law and the Catholic church, the Romans, absorbing Greek philosophy, bequeathed the Europeans a set of contradictory attitudes to humanity's relationship with the universe which have been the cause of some of the most stubborn obstacles to development in Western astronomy as well as the engine for some of its greatest achievements.

Following the model set by the great Near Eastern empires, the Romans pursued an inclusive theology, absorbing their subject peoples' worldviews and celestial deities. As the imperial age dawned, and syncretism gradually overwhelmed lingering republican pride in the inherent superiority of Roman ideas, all gods and goddesses were accepted. Only militant Christians set themselves outside the Roman religious sphere, and that only until they were able to dominate it and exclude other groups. The epic struggle for supremacy between Christianity and classical paganism was in part a struggle for political supremacy, but also a subplot in a complex clash between competing views of the stars' role in salvation and the afterlife.

Our knowledge of the early history of Rome is a combination of later legend with our ability to reconstruct the probable history of a central Italian hilltop city from the early first millennium BCE onwards.[2] We can make a number of plausible assumptions. For a start there would have been cultural influences coming south from Etruscan civilization and, slightly more remote, the cultures of southern France and Germany, from the distant descendants of the makers of the Nebra sky disc. Rome's legendary founding date of 753 BCE is eight years before the accession of Tiglath Pileser III, who inaugurated the final and greatest phase of Assyrian expansion; the conquest of Egypt in 671 BCE, taking Babylonian astrologers to the Nile Valley, perhaps for the first time. We also know that, at this time, the Greek world was listening to its eastern neighbours and absorbing their myths; there was a smooth, if distant, line of communication between Rome and Babylon, even if one was an insignificant overgrown village and the other an ancient imperial capital. When, around 509 BCE, the Roman kings were overthrown, the northern Mediterranean coast was in the process of being colonized by Greeks, while Phoenicians were spreading along the African shore. The Pythagoreans were establishing their presence in the Italian south – Sicily appears to have been an important link – and, by the early fourth century BCE, the Gauls had replaced the Etruscans as the dominant power in the north, in the Po Valley; many north Italian towns have Celtic origins and, as soon as the Romans began their conquest of the north, they were subjugating people whose cosmology was represented in the Coligny calendar. When Alexander was invading Egypt, Mesopotamia and Persia in 332–330 BCE, Rome was occupying the whole of Italy, a task it completed by the year 282. And, as Rome clashed with competing states, so it would have encountered competing cosmologies. As the Romans' legions overwhelmed the Celts from the second century BCE onwards, they erased from history whatever astrology the Druid priesthood had either invented for themselves or inherited from the megalith builders. That is why the signs of the zodiac which appear in Western horoscope columns are mainly Babylonian, even if (in English, at any rate) they carry their Latin names, not Celtic or British or German ones.

The impact of Celtic wisdom on the Romans is hard to trace, for we have only scanty Roman accounts of druidic teachings, together with rare artefacts, such as the Coligny calendar. We know little about the celestial divinatory techniques which may have existed in pre-Roman Italy, although we know that the Etruscans, for example, practised lightning divination by dividing the sky into 16 segments.[3] In the early period we have little evidence of direct Roman interest in the stars, although there might have been broader cosmologies. For example, Rome's seven hills are more a cosmological reality than a geographical one. Nobody in the last centuries BCE could have claimed that their city was built on seven hills without making a very obvious statement – that it was related either to the seven planets or the seven days of the week. So pervasive was symbolism based on the number seven that this needed no further explanation. Any passing Phoenician trader, knowing that the world was surrounded by seven mountains – and that all wisdom had been taught by the seven sages – would have got the point: the Romans thought they were the centre of the universe. Naturally, sky gods assisted in the defence of republican Rome while heroes were projected into the sky; Castor and Pollux, the brightest stars in Gemini, fought for the city in battle, while Mars appeared in person to inspire the Romans.

The transfer of Babylonian and Hellenistic astrology to Rome was a natural consequence of the republic's expansion to encompass the entire Mediterranean region. The city's armies occupied the Mediterranean coast of Spain by 206 BCE, while further campaigns in the second century led to the conquest of most of Spain, Greece and the Greek states in Asia Minor; it was soon after this expansion that we find the first evidence for the practice of astrology in the city. The legions gained their first toehold in north Africa in 146 when Carthage fell and, by the late first century, they had occupied Egypt – the creative centre of Hellenistic science and mysticism – and Gaul. With this, Rome took under its direct authority the centres of virtually every known variety of teaching about the heavens.

Astrology's entry into Rome was not welcomed by some of its leading intellectuals, whose dismissive attitude was embedded in Platonic scepticism. Cicero described the relationship between the Chaldeans and their new rulers. He took great pleasure in reporting that the Chaldeans made a multitude of inaccurate predictions to the leading military leaders of his time – Crassus, Pompey and Julius Caesar – including the plainly wrong forecasts that all three would die of old age at home and in great glory; Cicero considered these predictions particularly ironic in view of Caesar's recent murder.[4] The problem, though, was a complex one for astrologers: how on earth can one ever predict an imminent violent end to a king or general's life without putting one's own life in danger? The result was a taboo against any prophecy concerning the emperor's life. In the fourth century Julius Firmicus Maternus, a senator from Sicily and enthusiastic astrologer, composed advice for trainee astrologers, declaring: 'Beware of replying to anyone asking about the condition of the Republic or the life of the Roman Emperor ... For it is not right, nor is it permitted that from wicked curiosity we learn anything about the condition of the Republic'.[5]

Our earliest surviving accounts of astrology at Rome are, in fact, highly critical and come from the pen of the poet Ennius (237–169 BCE), who despised those who sought answers in the heavens instead of the here and now, In a lost work, the *Iphigenia*, he had the Homeric hero Achilles complain of:

> The astral signs that are observed above,
> When goat or scorpion or Jove arise,
> Or other beasts; all gaze intent thereon,
> Nor ever see what lies before their feet![6]

Yet, there may be etymological evidence for serious contemplation of the sky in the language itself. Cramer speculated that the word '*considerare*' – inspect, consider, contemplate – which was in use by the mid-third century BCE, suggests a Stoic-like practice in which wisdom could be gained by gazing at the stars.[7] Ennius also provided data for the recording of eclipses back to the death of Romulus, who was supposed to have expired, Christ-like, during an eclipse. Ennius' purpose was sceptical – to show that the eclipses formed a natural sequence and that they could therefore not be omens sent by capricious gods. Cicero later cited Ennius' work together with the opinion that Romulus died because his time was up, not because of the eclipse.[8] Not even a naturalistic astrology was to survive his scrutiny. Ennius, though, had launched further attacks on astrologers, whom he clearly regarded as belonging to the lower orders. In his play *Telemon* he declared that:

> In fine, I say, I do not care a fig
> for Marsian augurs, village mountebanks,
> Astrologers who haunt the circus grounds,
> Or Isis-seers, or dream interpreters
> [who are] superstitious bards, soothsaying quacks,
> Averse to work, or mad or ruled by want,
> Directing others how to go, and yet
> What road to take they do not know themselves.[9]

Ennius could not have been more damning. Astrology was not worth considering because it arrived with migrants from the east; it was wrong because it was
foreign. Roman exclusivity was not yet ready to take on the broad-minded
syncretism that characterized the imperial age. All denunciations of ideas, beliefs
and practices, though, have a historical value precisely because they suggest that
the ideas being condemned were popular enough to merit censure. In 160 BCE
the orator Cato, who shared Ennius' views, composed a treatise on agriculture in
which he warned farm overseers that under no circumstances should they consult
Chaldeans.[10] We can imagine that his advice may have fallen on stony ground
if Italian farmers were already familiar with the sort of stellar farming calendar
outlined by Hesiod. And, if Cato is to be believed, astrologers were practising at
Rome at the very time that, across the sea in Alexandria, Nechepso–Petosiris,
one of the seminal texts of Hellenistic astrology, was being composed. And that
is hardly surprising, considering the popularity of the worship of Saturn in the
crisis-ridden heart of the Punic War in 217 BCE. A century later some people,
Cicero wrote, were so familiar with the rising, setting and revolutions of the
heavenly bodies that they knew in advance where they would be – and hence what
was likely to happen, doubtless because they had access to tables or mathematical
formulae originating from Babylonian scribes.[11]

Astrology's role at Rome was always to be problematic. In a society in which
the vast majority took the efficacy of divination for granted, and assumed that
the gods sent signs to those who could read them, there was really no way to
escape it. Yet it always remained something of a foreign import, regarded in
some senses as alien to the traditions of republican Rome. Worse, in common
with other varieties of soothsaying, it was outside state control. We therefore find
astrology becoming an aid to political decision making and imperial propaganda
from the earliest empire onwards while, at the same time, the astrologers were
repeatedly expelled from Rome. The pagan emperors' strictures against the
astrologers were to segue perfectly into the Christian emperors' prohibitions in
the fourth century, and for very much the same reason – the need to control the
flow of ideas. Whereas the tradition of political astrology in Mesopotamia had,
until the fifth century BCE, been conducted exclusively in the service of the state,
in Rome it became heir to that democratic instinct which the emperors never
managed to entirely banish. Nor did astrology have an easy ride in a society in
which educated atheism was not uncommon and intellectuals sceptical of the

existence of the gods had little time for a science apparently devoted to reading messages from those gods. Rome gives us the earliest surviving examples of sceptical attacks and satires directed against astrology itself, and most of the arguments used by modern critics to attack astrology are copied indirectly from the Roman originals. In Babylon, if astrology had got it wrong it had not been the astrology but the astrologer who was at fault. In the Roman world, even though it was pervasive, the value or efficacy of astrology as a whole was called into question.

Condemnation of astrologers deepened into the first full-scale expulsion from Rome and Roman Italy (accompanied by the members of the cult of Zeus Sabazios, who were also regarded as undesirable aliens[12]), in 139 BCE. An earlier expulsion of diviners dated to the early third century BCE, makes no mention of astrologers, suggesting that their arrival at Rome was after 275 BCE, perhaps, but in time for Ennius to mock them around 200 BCE.

The earliest known example of the use of astrology by Roman politicians – rather than by rebellious slaves – can be dated to 87 BCE when the generals Gaius Marius and Lucius Cornelius Cinna seized Rome. On the corpse of the defeated consul, Gnaius Octavius, was found 'the astrologic diagram that had lured him to his death'.[13] We are not told whether this was a horoscope or, as sounds more likely, a talisman bearing astrological inscriptions. Later, Sulla, Marius' great rival, is said to have brought a horoscope back from the east, where he had occupied Athens, which forecast the date of his death. Apparently he believed the prediction and, according to Plutarch's account, deliberately finished writing his memoirs shortly before the scheduled date in 78 BCE.[14] This may, of course, be a popular rumour, although not unlikely: closer to our own time we have the notable example of Sigmund Freud, who believed devoutly that the date of his death was fixed by numerology.[15] A coin minted in 44 BCE, sometime after Sulla's death, depicted the dream in which the goddess Luna, the moon, predicted victory over Marius, but this may reflect a later story.[16] And, when Cicero tells us, as part of his assault on astrology that, of the generation of generals who succeeded Sulla, Crassus, Pompey and Julius Caesar, all received astrological forecasts, he does not add whether they were actively solicited or offered by ambitious and publicity-seeking Chaldeans.[17]

Roman concern about astrology's potentially destabilizing effects on the body politic can only have been deepened by the case of Athenio, the leader of the briefly successful Sicilian slave revolt in the late second century BCE. The historian Diodorus tells us that Athenio was an 'expert astrologer', and his own predictions of success doubtless encouraged his followers.[18] Athenios' celestial skills, though, were no match for the disciplined ranks of the Roman legions; the rebellion failed and its leader was eventually killed in around 100 BCE. The expulsion of 139 BCE set the pattern for a policy which was to prove singularly ineffective and there were at least eight and possibly as many as thirteen decrees expelling astrologers from Rome or Italy from the death of Julius Caesar in 44 BCE to that of Marcus Aurelius in 180 CE.[19]

The astrologers were again expelled by Augustus in 11 CE and by Tiberius five years later, in 52 by Claudius, 69 by Vitellius and 70 by Vespasian. Eventually, in the fourth and fifth centuries, the control of astrology for purely political purposes – to control the flow of predictions – dovetailed with Christian prohibitions, and was successful. Clearly the authorities were struggling to hold back the inevitable and, as in so many attempts to prohibit private behaviour, they were doomed to failure. Astrology presented the guardians of Roman order and cultural purity with a number of problems. Tiberius' expulsion was linked to the banning of such unwanted foreign items as silk, a concern which may be surprising in view of his decadent reputation, although it may have been linked to resistance to foreign imports. Claudius' and Vitellius' prohibitions were based on the more conventional reason that the stars had been used to aid aristocratic conspiracies. In other words, there was no single reason to ban astrology and no consistent policy.

Legal sanction against astrology was supported by a continuing tradition of ridicule. Ennius' mockery of astrology was echoed by some notable satirists. In the mid-first century Petronius, a close friend of the emperor Nero and notorious decadent, ridiculed the zodiac signs in his *Satyricon*. Into the mouth of Trimalchio, his central character, Petronius placed a contemptuous version of each of the signs' characteristics; Ariens were muttonheads, Geminians 'do it both ways', Virgos are effeminate, Scorpios murderers, Aquarians are jugheads and Pisceans 'spit in public'.[20] With a last dig at the Stoics – he would have known Seneca well – he concluded wearily that the sky turns like a millstone, bring nothing but trouble and the endless round of birth and death. A hundred years later Juvenal sneered at the 'Chaldeans' but had most venom for the customers, mainly women, who combined a pathetic inability to take decisions for themselves with a chronic dependence on diviners of every sort.[21] Around the same time Apuleius told the story of a Chaldean stranger at Corinth, who was earning a handsome income by answering questions posed by the credulous.[22] Apuleius was gentler on astrology than Petronius and Juvenal. He was a Platonist – he wrote a guide to Plato's thought for those who were not ready to tackle the original works – and believed in the divinity of the stars. But he shared with his literary colleagues the elitist philosopher's disdain for the moneymaker. Clearly the astrology of the marketplace had separated itself from the temple and the philosophical schools.

It would be a mistake to regard astrology as exclusively a lower-class activity. Street fortune-tellers were clearly using astrology, but its attraction was evident at the highest reaches of society, amongst both politicians and thinkers. Cicero tells us that, of the Greek philosophers up to his day, only Epicurus was completely opposed to divination, while all the others were wholly or partially in favour of it. Of course, allowing oracles, as Cicero did, was not the same as acknowledging the use of astrology, which he did not. Highbrow debates, though, were of limited interest to astrology's most powerful patrons in the Roman world. Although the emperors attempted to proscribe the activities of individual astrologers, they actively co-opted it into their service as a natural extension of existing forms of political propaganda. It is but a short step from claiming, as Julius Caesar did, to be descended from the goddess Venus, to observing the movements of the planet Venus to gain political advantage. Diplomatic astrologers colluded in this system and tried to keep out of trouble by acknowledging their emperor's greatness. Wariness of the emperors' whims, expressed by Firmicus in the fourth century, was clearly evident at the beginning of the imperial period when Marcus Manilius, the author of the oldest extant astrological text in Latin, extolled the greatness of Libra and Capricorn, the signs containing the sun and moon when Augustus was born. Of Capricorn he asked 'what greater sign can he ever marvel at, since it was he that shone propitiously upon Augustus' birth?'[23] Writing about Libra, though, he excelled himself: 'blessed is he that is born under the equilibrium of the Balance. As judge he will set up scales weighted with life and death; he will impose the weight of his authority upon the world and make laws. Cities and kingdoms will tremble before him and be ruled by his command alone, whilst after his sojourn on earth jurisdiction in the sky will await him.'[24] More than that, he proclaimed that the divine Augustus had actually descended to earth and will one day ascend to heaven where he will rule alongside Jupiter, the king of Olympus himself,[25] a fascinating indication of the extent to which certain of the rhetoric and iconography of Christian political cosmology was to emerge seamlessly out of paganism; the evidence suggests that the *Astronomica* was completed in the first part of Tiberius' reign when Jesus would have been a young man. Over 300 years later Julius Firmicus Maternus himself, who converted to Christianity, removed the emperor entirely from the world on which astrology could legitimately comment. He converted the pragmatic need to avoid upsetting the emperor into a political theology which perfectly fitted the autocratic theocracy established by Diocletian, and anticipated medieval Caeseropapism – the doctrine of the unity of state and church. Like Christ, the emperor was above the stars. Firmicus justified his advice to astrologers not to inquire into the emperor's life with the following rationale:

> For the emperor alone is not subject to the cause of the stars and in his fate alone the stars have no power of decreeing. Since he is master of the whole universe, his destiny is governed by the judgement of the Highest God, since the whole world is subject to the power of the Emperor and he himself is also considered among the number of gods whom the Supreme Power has set up to create and conserve all things.[26]

The first detailed accounts of the relationship between politics and astrology follow the inauguration of the imperium by Augustus in 27 BCE. Two separate narrative strands run through the literature. On the one hand there are stories of the portents which accompanied the emperors' lives and, on the other, accounts of their own use of astrology itself. Accounts of the celestial portents which surrounded emperors' lives emerge out of the same literary tradition as the Gospel of Matthew's story of the Star of Bethlehem and the birth of Christ.

The notion of emperor as Messiah was part of imperial iconography from Augustus onwards and was legitimized in astrological texts: 'Augustus', Manilius wrote, decades before the same messianic theme was adopted by Christian apologists, 'has come down from heaven, and heaven one day will occupy'.[27] Imperial application of astrology as a political tool falls into two categories, which are not necessarily mutually exclusive. It was exploited either in order to manipulate public opinion, apparently cynically, or out of a deeply held belief that the heavenly spheres revealed the flow of time and the future, the very image, in Platonic terms, of the divine. There are also certain themes which recur during the tales of imperial astrology including such matters as the astrologer's correct forecast of his own or an emperor's death or the prediction that a somewhat unlikely candidate will become emperor; he then reacts with humility but eventually the prediction comes true. Also, sometimes further details were added by later authors – as Dio Cassius extended Tacitus' anecdotes – suggesting that the all-seeing astrologer was as useful a dramatic device for the imaginative chronicler as was the magician or sorcerer.

Augustus himself established the pattern by constructing one of the most effective personal myths in history. The first-century historian Suetonius Cassius detailed the portents surrounding the future emperor's birth in 63 BCE, including a prophecy of greatness by the senator and astrologer Publius Nigidius Figulus. Reconstructing the dramatic scene, he tells us that 'Augustus' birth coincided with the Senate's famous debate on the Catalinarian conspiracy, and when Octavius [Augustus' father] arrived late, because of Attia's confinement, Publius Nigidius Figulus the astrologer, hearing at what hour the child had been delivered, cried out: "the ruler of the world is now born"'. 'Everyone' he adds, as if there might be some doubt, 'believes this story'.[28] The infant Augustus took on the solar attributes of an Egyptian pharaoh when he was discovered one day 'lying on the top of a lofty tower, his face turned towards the rising sun', while apparently Attia, Augustus' mother, attempted to ingratiate the young boy with Julius Caesar, her uncle, by announcing that he had been engendered by Apollo himself:[29] he was none other than the son of the sun. Caesar duly adopted the youth as his own son and heir and, as soon as a suitable opportunity arrived, Augustus returned the favour by promoting his patron to divine status. This step was achieved immediately following Caesar's assassination in 44 BCE, when Augustus and Mark Antony had to move fast to seize control and neutralize the conspirators. The appearance of a comet which shone for seven days in the northern sky during Caesar's funeral games, organized by Augustus in honour of Mother Venus, was popularly viewed as Julius Caesar's soul on its way to join the immortal gods – the stars. This was not such a wild claim; Manilius wrote of the stars, in Platonic mode: 'Perhaps the souls of heroes, outstanding men deemed worthy of heaven, freed from the body and released from the globe of earth, pass hither and thither and, dwelling in a heaven that is their own, live the infinite years of paradise and enjoy celestial bliss'.[30] Augustus moved fast to place a statue of Caesar in the temple of Venus with a star above its head, gave the dead dictator his own feast day and named a month after him – July.[31] Privately, Augustus also interpreted the comet in messianic terms as 'having been born for his own sake and as containing his own birth within it';[32] the heavens had spoken to him personally.

There is also one account of the young Augustus – still known as Octavian – visiting an astrologer by the name of Theogenes, who lived at Apollonia.[33] Accompanied by his friend Agrippa, Augustus climbed the stairs to Theogenes' observatory where both young men were due to receive advice on their future careers. Agrippa went first and was given predictions of such incredibly good fortune that Augustus at first felt ashamed to reveal his time of birth in case his own future was found to be far less auspicious. At last he gave Theogenes the information necessary to cast his horoscope – with unexpectedly dramatic results. Theogenes, Suetonius tells us, rose from his chair and, without a word, threw himself at Augustus' feet. Whether this was actually how the consultation happened we will never know; if Theogenes knew that he was advising Julius Caesar's adopted son and heir, his action would be thoroughly reasonable. Whatever the truth, it is perhaps more likely that the story of Theogenes' recognition of Octavian's future greatness is of the same genre as the magi's adoration of Christ. It is a literary device designed to show that greatness was heaven-sent. The story is, though, credited with giving Augustus an enduring faith in his own destiny and sufficient confidence in astrology's messianic power to publish his horoscope once he was emperor – and to mint coins bearing Capricorn – his moon sign.[34] We might wonder why he chose Capricorn rather than Libra which, being ruled by benevolent Venus, was also linked to Julius Caesar. The answer is almost certainly that Capricorn was ruled by Saturn who, as the Greek Cronos, was the ruler of the past and future Age of the Golden Race, as set out in Hesiod's *Works and Days*.[35] Hesiod's prophetic scheme of history was current, having been reworked in the so-called Messianic Fourth Eclogue, composed by Virgil after 42 BCE and published around 37 BCE. This prophecy was to cause much confusion amongst later Christian writers, for some 30 years before Christ's birth it forecast the coming of the divine Child. In words with which any Hebrew prophet would instantly sympathize, Virgil proclaimed that 'the great line of the centuries begins anew. Now the Virgin returns, the reign of Saturn returns, now a new generation descends from heaven on high. Only do thou, pure Lucina, smile on the birth of the child, under whom the iron brood shall first cease, and a golden race spring up throughout the world. Thine own Apollo now is king.'[36] Later Virgil predicted the rule of a child, the son of Jupiter – Apollo – who will rule the earth and replace the old gods.[37] This messianic symbolism proved peculiarly effective, surviving into the Renaissance when Duke Cosimo I de Medici, the ruler of Florence, issued medals bearing Capricorn in a direct invocation of Augustus' example.[38]

Augustinian messianism was enclosed within the widespread assumption, inherited from Plato, that the cosmos would come to an end when all the stars and planets simultaneously returned to the point of their creation. The theory was set out in scholarly tones by Cicero: 'On the diverse motions of the planets', he intoned, 'the mathematicians have based what they call the Great Year, which is completed when the sun, moon and five planets all having finished their courses have returned to the same positions relative to one another. The length of this period is hotly debated, but it must necessarily be a fixed time.'[39] The theory was, of course, reinforced by Seneca's preservation of Berossus' belief that destruction by fire – *ekpyrosis* in Greek – accompanied conjunctions of all seven planets in Cancer, and by water when they met in Capricorn.[40] These ideas were repeated and appeared in Nigidius Figulus' lost first-century BCE text, *On the Gods*.[41] Pliny himself was convinced that the conflagration was imminent, and saw the evidence in the physical collapse of the average Roman as the biological cycle hit a trough: 'It is almost a matter of observation', he claimed, 'that with the entire human race the stature on the whole is becoming smaller daily, as the conflagration that is the crisis towards which the age is now verging is exhausting the fertility of the semen'.[42] In this atmosphere the eruption of Vesuvius and the catastrophic destruction of Pompeii and Herculaneum in 79 CE, in which Pliny himself died, were widely taken as an omen of the imminent world fire.

Augustus inaugurated a tradition in which astrology could be used not just to threaten Roman rulers, but to legitimize them. He established the template for the imperial use of astrology both to gain practical advantage in daily affairs and to construct the image of the emperor as a messianic figure, the representative of heaven on earth, increasingly taking on the trappings of Egyptian pharaohs. Tiberius, who succeeded Augustus in 14 CE, was reputedly an astrologer himself, having been taught, while in exile, by the philosopher Thrasyllus. As an example, of his skill, on one occasion he is said to have sent for the consul Servius Galba. After making polite small talk the emperor cut to the chase and announced, 'thou too, shalt one day have thy taste of Empire'.[43] Tiberius' prediction was fulfilled when Galba went on to reign briefly as successor to Nero in 68–69 CE. Thrasyllus himself was a figure of considerable importance, being the first scholar in the classical world to organize Plato's dialogues. So important was he that all subsequent editions of Plato's works are based on his version, although some scholars suspect that he introduced just a little more of a Pythagorean emphasis than Plato would have intended. He also wrote an astrological textbook known as the *Pinax* ('Table') which appears to have relied heavily on the lost texts of Hellenistic Egypt attributed to Nechepso and Petosiris, and Hermes. The *Pinax* was copied by later writers but is only known to us from fragments in the works of later astrologers, such as Porphyry in the third century and Hephaestio of Thebes in the fifth.[44] With his importance in the history of philosophy and his critical role at the Tiberian court, Thrasyllus was the Platonic astrologer *par excellence*, the scholar and diviner envisaged in the *Republic* as essential to the government of the ideal state.

According to Tacitus, Tiberius had been an inveterate consulter of astrologers during his life in exile on Rhodes, where he was sent to keep him out of Rome while Augustus was still alive. Apparently the chosen astrologer would be escorted into Tiberius' presence at his hilltop villa by a trusted, illiterate and very strong freedman. If Tiberius suspected that the unsuspecting astrologer was deceiving him, or just not up to the job, he would be hurled into the sea below, leaving no witness to what had been said. One would have imagined that the disappearance of so many astrologers might have prompted suspicions but, eventually, Thrasyllus' summons came. Tacitus tells us that Thrasyllus forecast Tiberius' future imperial honours so persuasively that Tiberius decided to set the astrologer a real test: could he anticipate his own destiny? 'Thrasyllus', we are told, 'consulted the position of the heavens and the aspect of the planets. Stricken with fear, he paused, hesitated, sank into meditation, following which he was shaken with fear and amazement. Breaking silence at last, he said, "I see the crisis of my fate. This very moment may be my last".'[45] Astonished at this display of prescience, rather than suspicious that Thrasyllus might be missing a number of his colleagues, Tiberius welcomed the philosopher as his lifelong confidante and court astrologer. According to Suetonius' version, Thrasyllus had already been working as Tiberius' astrologer and, when the risk of being thrown off the cliff presented itself he saved himself by pointing to a ship which had just appeared over the horizon and announced that it brought good news. When the boat docked it was found to carry a letter recalling Tiberius to Rome, and his faith in Thrasyllus' divinatory powers was restored.[46] Whichever version is true, or even if neither is, the story conveys the idea of astrologer as magus, the all-seeing and, literally, as life-saver. The theme of an astrologer falling down a cliff or a pit is encountered elsewhere. The sixth-century BCE philosopher Thales is said to have fallen down a cistern while looking at the stars, while Alexander the Great reputedly threw his natural father, the astrologer Nektanebos, into a pit, his crime being to study the heavens while remaining ignorant of the earth.[47] In the Thrasyllus story, a new twist was added – the astrologer was saved. Similarly the story that the astrologer Scribonius forecast an illustrious career for the infant Tiberius is too similar to Nigidius Figulus' prophecy of Augustus' future greatness to be taken literally.[48] Rather, it is part of the literary tradition in which astrologers were used to confirm the dictates of heaven. Astrologers not only wove a narrative about the sky – they were characters in it.

Tacitus' account of Thrasyllus' work for Tiberius on Rhodes also includes the colourful detail that the astrologer was employed to search his master's rivals' horoscopes for signs of an imperial future. It follows that, were such indications to be found, than the unfortunate individuals would be killed. The emperor Galba only survived because Tiberius was told he would die young, and so presented no immediate threat.

Astrology could be used to support state power, but also to subvert it. A notable use of the stars to undermine the emperor occurred in 16 CE, just two years into Tiberius' reign. The praetor Scribonius Libo, a man who was quite clearly out of his depth in the complex and unforgiving politics of imperial Rome, was drawn into a conspiracy against the emperor. The fact that he was Pompey's great-grandson had convinced him that he should have a glorious future, so he set out to consult a variety of astrologers, magicians and dream-interpreters in order to check his prospects.[49] Certainly, he thought, the heavens could offer advice on how he should maximize his options. Inevitably, Scribonius was betrayed and committed suicide. The authorities duly clamped down on the activities of freelance diviners, perhaps seizing a welcome opportunity to reassert central control over the forecasting business. An edict was passed expelling astrologers and magicians from Italy, though not Thrasyllus, of course. One, Lucius Pituanius, was hurled from the Tarpeian Rock and another, Publius Marcius, was beheaded outside the Esquiline Gate 'at the sound of the trumpet ... according to the form prescribed by ancient usage'.[50] We should never get so wrapped up in the sordid anecdotes though, that we forget the profound religious dimension to divination, for diviners spoke directly to the gods, bypassing the secular authorities. At the heart of the issue of popular astrology is then, the question of who exactly is allowed to communicate with the divine, a problem that was to cause immense problems for astrologers as the classical world drew to an end and Christianity became the religion of political choice.

Thrasyllus himself was extremely well connected; rumour has him marrying Aka, a daughter of Antiochus III of Commagene, a dynasty famous for its use of astrology. Tiberius Claudius Balbillus, who is generally thought to have been his son, became court astrologer after Thrasyllus died in 36 CE.[51] Balbillus served Claudius, Nero and Vespasian in this capacity, but was also a man of many parts. He was chief military engineer on the invasion of Britain in 43 CE and may also have been the same Balbillus who was prefect of Egypt for five years from 54 to 59 CE.[52] Like his father he composed an important astrological treatise. The *Astrologumena*, of which only a synopsis survives, deals mainly with the complex rules determining the stages and likely length of life, important matters if one was dealing with emperors and their rivals.[53]

An absence of evidence concerning the imperial use of astrology during the reign of the notorious Caligula, emperor from 37 to 41 CE, or of celestial portents indicating his future greatness may be a testimony to the shortness of his life, of the belief that the heavens could never have smiled on such a monster. It should also, though serve as a warning against exaggerating astrology's importance in the Roman state. It never became an accepted part of political decision making as it had been in Babylon, but rather occupied an ideological marketplace where it was in competition with other methods of divination, particularly augury and the officially sanctioned Sibylline Oracles, and was always susceptible to sceptical criticism. Perhaps, though, Caligula was aware of Thrasyllus' prediction to Tiberius that 'as for Gaius [i.e., Caligula], he has no more chance of becoming Emperor than of riding a horse dry-shod across the Gulf of Baiae', and hence ill-disposed to astrologers.[54] If the prediction was indeed public currency then Thrasyllus had saved himself by dying the year before Caligula assumed the purple and, as Suetonius tells, us defied his destiny by building a pontoon bridge across the gulf across which he rode in triumph.

Caligula's successor, Claudius also took measures to prohibit astrologers. His general attitude became clear in 45 CE, four years into his reign, when an eclipse of the sun was forecast for his birthday.[55] A consummate propagandist such as Augustus might have turned this to his advantage, but Claudius took the more standard view that it might encourage unrest, especially as it followed other difficult portents. Like the Athenian ruler, Pericles, he issued a proclamation setting out the astronomical reasons for the eclipse, the implication being that it could not be a bad omen. Actually, this incident tells us that astrology in first-century Rome was still seen as a matter of the gods interfering at will in the natural order, for, as Ptolemy was to argue, there is no inherent contradiction between an eclipse having a physical or mathematical explanation and still carrying an ominous significance. To extend the astronomical discussion, though, we are told that it was a matter of dispute at the time whether the sphere of the moon was directly below that of the sun, or whether Mercury and Venus were in between.

Astrology could also be used to denounce one's enemies. Agrippina, Claudius' niece and mother of Nero, used precisely this technique to dispose of Lollia, Caligula's widow, and her rival for the emperor's affections. She accused Lollia of 'traffic with Chaldeans' and, as if this were not enough, added that she had also consulted magicians and asked the image of the Clarion Apollo for information on the emperor's marriage.[56] Lollia was duly exiled and committed suicide rather than risk an extra-judicial execution, while Claudius passed a special law legitimizing incestuous uncle–niece marriages and made Agrippina his empress. Given that we have no idea what private communications may have passed between Claudius and Balbillus, the evidence suggests that the emperor was more likely to have trouble from astrologers than make use of them himself. In 52 CE one Furius Camillus Scribonius, a relation of the Scribonius who was executed by Tiberius, was exiled on a charge of making astrological enquiries concerning the emperor's death.[57] Scribonius the younger got off with a much lighter sentence than his predecessor, but the result was, as before, a general expulsion of astrologers from Italy. The senatorial decree was, however, 'drastic and impotent';[58] by all accounts little notice was taken and we have to assume that the prohibition of astrology in first-century Rome had about as much effect as the prohibition of alcohol in twentieth-century USA.

One anecdote from Suetonius hints at a deeper and more subtle use of divination, one more akin to the manipulation of the future practised by the Mesopotamian monarchs. We are told that Messalina, Claudius' first wife had planned to marry her lover Silius and place him on the throne, an incident in which Claudius is portrayed as an incompetent and helpless coward. However, it seems that Claudius had been warned of dangers to 'Messalina's husband' although we are not told if this was through astrological or other divinatory means.[59] By allowing the marriage to proceed Claudius had transferred the danger to Silius and, by then executing him, had cleverly satisfied the omens and preserved his own skin. In a sense, Claudius' use of Silius' disloyalty functioned as a *namburbu*, a Babylonian ritual designed to ward off an omen's evil consequences. Also true to the Babylonian tradition, when Claudius' death coincided with the appearance of a long-tailed star – a comet – was Suetonius' description of it as an omen, not a cause.[60]

Claudius' death also became the excuse for mockery by Seneca, the Stoic philosopher. Giving the time of the emperor's death as between 12 noon and 1 p.m. on 13 October 54, Seneca considers in turn the three planets which were crossing the mid-heaven (culminating) – the sun, Mercury and Venus. At noon, exactly as the sun culminated and began to move 'nearer to night than day' Claudius breathed his last, but Seneca had no time for polite obsequies. Mercury, which had preceded the sun had already taken one of the three fates aside and asked her to let the emperor die. 'Do let the astrologers tell the truth for once', he pleaded, 'since he became emperor they have never let a year pass, never a month, without laying him out for his burial. Yet it is no wonder if they are wrong, and no one knows his hour. Nobody ever believed he was really quite born [i.e., they thought he was a nobody]. Do what has to be done.'[61]

Seneca was a man of immense influence, He was Nero's political adviser for eight of his twelve years on the throne, from 54 to 62, having been his tutor since 49 CE. Claudius was allegedly poisoned by Nero's mother so Seneca was in a good position to say exactly what he pleased – at least until Nero forced him, in turn, to commit suicide in 65. Nero followed in the self-mythologizing tradition established by Augustus and was the first emperor to explicitly equate himself with the sun. He minted coins portraying himself wearing a crown consisting of a band around his head and long vertical rays – representing the solar disc, exploiting the iconography of Syrian or Egyptian monarchy. He called himself Helios Basileus – the 'sun-king' – and constructed a huge palace in Rome, the Golden House, as a cosmic setting for his solar magnificence. His heavenly identity was recognized by King Tiridates of Armenia who, in 65 CE, undertook a magnificent state visit to Rome to be crowned by Nero as a client king. Before the coronation Tiridates acknowledged Nero as his lord with the following words, evoking Plato's spindle of destiny: 'I have come to thee, my god, to worship thee as I do Mithras. The destiny thou spinnest for me shall be mine; for thou art my Fortune and my Fate.'[62] After the ceremony the two monarchs relaxed by watching a theatrical display in which the decorative centrepiece was an embroidered figure of Nero as the sun god, driving a chariot and surrounded by golden stars.

The actual use of astrology in Nero's reign though, could be every bit as sordid as in his predecessors'. At least one incident in Nero's reign smacks of the sort of police-state denunciation we encountered earlier. This case was engineered by an exile called Antitistius Sosianus, who had been punished for composing scurrilous verses about the emperor.[63] Aware of the honour paid to informers who fuelled Nero's desire for bloodshed Sosianus set out to search for victims. He noted that an astrologer on the same island, an Egyptian named Pammenes, was constantly receiving messengers and reasoned that these might be carrying incriminating information; Pammenes was fond of Agrippina, who by then was out of favour with her son. He intercepted a letter soliciting Pammenes' advice from a senator called Publius Anteius Rufus, stole the horoscope of a noted general, Marcus Ostorius Scapula, and used his purloined evidence to persuade Nero that the men were plotting against him. Antitistius ingratiated himself back into Nero's favour while his two unfortunate victims were obliged to commit suicide.

The most notorious astrological anecdote from Nero's reign relates to his murder of his mother which, had, it is claimed, been forecast at his birth and, if the prediction was indeed current during his life, rather than being a later fiction, may have been encouraged by the astrologers. The historian Dio Cassius tells us, when detailing the usual miraculous portents associated with imperial births, that just before dawn on the morning of Nero's birth, rays which appeared to be from the sun, though which could not have been cast by it, enveloped the infant in their light. An astrologer, who could have been working for Nero's mother, forecast from both this portent and the horoscope for the moment, that Nero would first become emperor and then kill his mother. On hearing this, Agrippina is said to have declared, in a spirit of maternal self-sacrifice, 'Let him kill me, only let him rule'.[64] When Claudius died and Nero's opportunity arrived, Agrippina relied on the astrologers to chose the most auspicious time, holding her position by issuing bulletins about the emperor's health and guarding strategic points until the most auspicious moment arrived. This came at noon on 13 October 54.[65] It is not clear how much work the astrologers really had to do, or even whether they chose the time for Agrippina to kill Claudius, for we do not know exactly how accurate their measurements of the planetary positions would have been, or even whether they calculated the ascendant. However, quite simply, they placed the sun, the celestial king, on the mid-heaven – as it always is at noon. In terms of solar religion, the king of heaven was at his most powerful, giving a blessing to his earthly representative, the new emperor. The moon, as the main female planet, the astrologers might have taken as representing Agrippina, may have been close to, or in the eighth house, ruling death. In this case it is possible that, if the prediction of Agrippina's death was indeed current, the astrologers were aware that they were incorporating the prophecy into their selection of the moment of Nero's proclamation. This is conjecture but, in the Stoic worldview this would have been a natural means of assisting Fate on its predetermined course.

For his part, though, Nero manipulated the future like a Babylonian monarch. The appearance of a comet was an evil omen, signifying the death of a person of outstanding importance and there was nobody more important than the emperor. Understandably alarmed, Nero sought Balbillus' advice. The astrologer observed that there was a way out and that 'monarchs usually avoided portents of this kind by executing their most prominent subjects and thus directing the wrath of heaven elsewhere',[66] as Claudius had done with Silius. Nero then resolved on a wholesale massacre of the Roman aristocracy, inaugurating the reign of terror which eventually brought about his downfall. He was confident though, of a long reign. To astrologers who had once told him that, if overthrown, he would be removed from the throne, he retorted 'a simple craft will keep a man from want', meaning he could always make a living playing the lyre. Others forecast that, if deposed, Nero would either regain the throne or find another one in the east, even Jerusalem, framing perhaps, their answer in the context of Jewish millenarianism.[67] The Oracle at Delphi, meanwhile, warned Nero to beware his 73rd year – 100 CE – encouraging him to look forward to a healthy old age. Yet, as often happens in divination narratives the prophesied event was technically incorrect while within the range of suggested possibilities. Nero did not die aged 73 but was deposed by a 73-year-old man, his successor, Galba. The heavens had contained true information about the future but the diviner, being human and fallible, living in Plato's cave, had been unable to read it correctly. This was precisely the kind of issue which technical advances in astrology, and related developments in astronomy, were designed to solve, so that the future could be understood precisely and error eliminated.

Even before Galba had established his own authority, though, the *ancien régime* fought back, exploiting the skills of a group of astrologers, including one called Ptolemy (not the famous Alexandrian writer), who were linked to Poppaea, Nero's wife. They selected Marcus Salvius Otho, one of Nero's dissolute friends, as their candidate, and urged him to depose Galba, which he did on 15 January 69. Tacitus, the historian who chronicled these events, was disgusted at this subterfuge and condemned the deceitful and manipulative astrologers as 'the worst possible tools for an Imperial consort'.[68] He need not have worried, for the very first sacrifice at Otho's inauguration was marked by threatening prodigies; there were reports of strange births in Etruria, an ox spoke in Etrurian and, in Rome, a superhuman figure rushed out of the temple of Juno.[69] Worse, on 3 January, two weeks before Otho's coup, a third successor to Nero had been proclaimed; the eight legions of the Rhine, unwilling to accept Galba, had saluted their general, Aulus Vitellius, as emperor. Just as they had with Galba, astrologers had early on predicted imperial honours for Vitellius, though we do not know if this falls into the class of retrospective portents which were always linked to great men, or whether astrologers made a habit of predicting future honours for every likely candidate for high office and potential future patron. Vitellius' reported response to the forecasts was dismissive, though perhaps more out of a sense of self-preservation than of lack of trust in the astrologers; sensibly, he had no wish to appear a threat to Nero. 'Certainly', he said of the astrologers, 'they know nothing when they say that even I shall become emperor'.[70] By all accounts Vitellius had as deep a belief in omens as did everyone at the time – aside from the insignificant band of philosophical sceptics. It was a given that the gods were in constant dialogue with humanity via both natural phenomena and abnormal occurrences, and there was no reason for a violent, drunken lecher like Vitellius to doubt it. To him, coping with the astrologers was a matter of clamping down on a potentially dangerous source of information and, even before he arrived in Rome, he sent an order ahead to banish them, requiring them to leave Italy by

1 October. The astrologers responded with defiance, issuing their own counter edict predicting the emperor's imminent demise: 'Decreed by all astrologers, in blessing on our state: Vitellius will be no more on the appointed date'.[71] Two lunar eclipses, a comet and the simultaneous appearance of two suns provided heaven's blessing for the astrologers' judgement.[72] The fact that, of the two suns, the one in the west was pale and weak while the one in the east was brilliant and powerful, was a sign that the new emperor, like the sun, would rise triumphantly in the east. Is this story apocryphal or does it reveal the tip of an iceberg of long-distance cooperation between astrologers who were selecting and deposing emperors? Vitellius' challenger, Vespasian, a legate in Judaea, was said to consult only the best astrologers and had previously favoured one known as Barbillus, almost certainly Nero's astrologer, Balbillus, who had died in 68.[73] Vespasian's assault on Vittellius was fought in heaven as well as on earth. The lunar eclipse which coincided with his rebellion was particularly ominous, coloured black, red and other terrifying colours, prompting fear amongst Vitellius' supporters. Vespasian's army itself, though known as the Gallic, had wintered in Syria and contained a high proportion of sun worshippers.[74] When the sun rose, according to Dio Cassius, Vespasian's soldiers 'greeted it according to their custom, with a great shout', causing panic amongst Vitellius' troops.[75] If the prophecy of an emperor arising in Judaea sounds today suspiciously like the Jewish prediction of the future Messiah, then it also appeared so at the time. Tacitus reported that the Jewish prophecy had been fulfilled in Vespasian; the Jewish Messiah was the Roman emperor.[76] As appropriate for heaven's new representative on earth, Vespasian's entry into Rome was greeted with messianic omens and portents, yet his first action, though was, like his predecessors, to banish the astrologers.[77] The reason was clear. It was not that astrologers were disreputable or despised or merely foreign: they were too powerful. The fate they saw, though, could never be broken and, when Vespasian's end came in 79, it, like Claudius' was heralded by a comet.[78] The emperor was *pontifex maximus*, chief priest and under no circumstances could he allow freelance diviners their own uncontrolled access to the gods: this is, in a nutshell, the pagan origin of the doctrine of papal infallibility, inherited by the bishops of Rome when they usurped the power of the emperor from the fifth century onwards.

Domitian, Vespasian's legendarily depraved younger son, kept up the practice of murdering those whose horoscopes indicated imperial potential and was in a state of permanent paranoia after astrological predictions had warned him of the exact hour and manner of his death.[79] In a vain attempt to demonstrate his defiance of the astrologers he challenged one, by the name of Ascletario, to predict the manner of his own death. On being told by the astrologer that he would be torn to pieces by dogs Domitian had him executed on the spot and ordered his funeral rites to be conducted with the greatest care. But destiny could not be defied and while the funeral was in progress a sudden gale scattered the funeral pyre and a pack of dogs savaged Ascletario's half-burned corpse.

Domitian's successor, Nerva, the first of the much admired 'good' emperors, escaped the emperor's wrath only because a sympathetic astrologer told Domitian that he, Nerva, was about to die anyway; the conspirators initially approached Nerva, before he succeeded Domitian in 96, partly because of the forecast that he would be emperor, so deliberately turning a prediction into a self-fulfilling prophecy.[80] When the time forecast for Domitian's death approached – the fifth hour on 18 September 96 – he became increasingly agitated. The previous day he had remarked to his companions that 'there will be blood on the Moon as she enters Aquarius, and a deed will be done for everyone to talk about throughout the entire world'.[81] At midnight he was so terrified that he jumped out of bed and, at dawn, he condemned to death a soothsayer who had predicted a change of government on the basis of some recent lightning. He then picked a wart on his forehead and made it bleed in the hope that this would satisfy destiny's need for blood. Eventually the emperor's servants lied and told him that it was the sixth hour, and that the moment of danger had passed. Domitian relaxed, went to take his morning bath and then, on being told that a man had called to see him on urgent business, hurried to his bedroom – where he was fatally stabbed in the groin. How do we interpret this story? There is no need to doubt that Domitian's death was predicted, for it is clear that such forecasts were a staple of Roman divination. In any case, the procedures of technical astrology explicitly included the rules for prediction of death. But was Suetonius, who tells this story, exaggerating the prediction's accuracy for dramatic effect, to demonstrate his own acceptance of astrology or to show that even the life of an emperor is subject to the immutable cosmic order of Stoicism?

Hadrian, another of the 'good' emperors, was himself, like Tiberius, an astrologer and was said to have correctly predicted his own death, which took place in 138. His ascent to the imperial honour was forecast by his great uncle, an amateur astrologer and distant relation of his predecessor, the emperor Trajan.[82] In his turn, Hadrian is said to have used astrology to select his successor, rather than kill his rivals as seemed to be the general custom.

Septimius Severus, who reigned from 193 to 211 was interested in astronomical measurements – he 'observed most accurately the variation of the sun's motion and the length of the days' when he was in Scotland – and had his birth chart painted on the ceiling of his palace, in the room where he held court, in order to impress his celestial destiny on his subjects.[83] He took the cunning precaution though, of concealing his *horoscopos*, or ascendant, lest anyone should turn this information against him. He also carried out a massive investigation into 'secret lore' while he was in Egypt and confiscated a large number of books, presumably including astrological texts, to prevent anyone else using them.[84] The astrological forecast for Severus' demise specified that he would die by the sword of a barbarian, which he took to mean a glorious death in battle. Destiny had a sense of irony though, and he was ingloriously assassinated by one of his own barbarian guards.

The emperors' use of astrology, together with fears that it might be used against them, continued throughout the rest of the imperial period down to

Constantine and Christianity's final entry into the political arena, after it was legalized in 313. At that point the two messianic strands in Roman culture, imperial and Christian, came together.

15

Christianity: A Star out of Jacob

Now when Jesus was born in Bethlehem of Judea in the days of
Herod the king, behold, wise men came from the East to Jerusalem,
saying, 'Where is he who has been born king of the Jews? For we
have seen his star in the East, and have come to worship him.'[1]

Early Christianity is conventionally regarded as a counter-cultural movement, a
sort of resistance front against the corruption of religious truth across the board
from the imperial cult to popular paganism and Jewish hypocrisy. It was indeed
to be radical in its assertion of political equality and the welcome it offered to
all, regardless of class, race and gender. However, the theological position is not
so clear-cut. First, Christianity emerged from a series of cosmological currents in
the first century which sought salvation in the sky and included Hermeticism.[2]
Second, it can be misleading to talk about the first Christians as if they were
a homogenous group. By the middle of the first century, probably less than
20 years after the likely date of the crucifixion, the first schism had separated
St Paul and the Hellenizers from the Jerusalem church, led by James, brother of
Jesus, which regarded the Jewish tradition as sacrosanct.[3] Even though there was
a tendency to reject many aspects of contemporary culture, including astrology,
the rhetoric does not always give a real picture of the complex situation. The
origins of Christianity in the mythology of what was to become the mainstream
church were unambiguously framed by messages from the stars. Christ's birth
was announced with majestic splendour by the star of Bethlehem and the homage
of a group of Persian magi, his death was accompanied by the terrible darkening
of the sky, an event regarded by many devout commentators since as an eclipse,
and his last act on earth was to ascend to heaven, which by inference lay in, or
beyond, the stars. Christianity is no less a sky religion than any other ancient
Near Eastern faith. It may even be more so in view of its rejection, like its Jewish
parent, of the classical and Near Eastern pantheon of earth- and water-based
divinities.

Conventional Christian cosmology was culled from Jewish sources, including
the Old Testament Scriptures, combined with an overlay of Persian dualism and a
strong element of Greek philosophy, mainly Stoicism and Platonism. The famous
phrase at the beginning of John's Gospel – 'In the beginning was the Word' (the
logos) – is the most dramatic evidence of the intrusion of the rational Greek
cosmos into early Christian thought.[4] The New Testament needs to be read in the
context of the religious developments taking place from the second century BCE

onwards, especially the development of Gnosticism and Hermeticism. One of the texts from the *Corpus Hermeticum*, the 'Poimandres', subtitled 'On the Power and Wisdom of God', was important because it was believed to have dated back to Moses and its philosophy appeared to link Graeco-Roman wisdom to the Holy Scriptures. This text's imagery resembles that in various Old and New Testament books. The use of the 'Word', *logos*, in John's Gospel is a case in point.

> Then from that Light, a certain Holy Word joined itself unto Nature, and out flew the pure and unmixed Fire from the moist Nature upward on high; it is exceeding Light, and Sharp, and Operative withal. And the Air which was also light, followed the Spirit and mounted up to Fire (from the Earth and the Water) insomuch that it seemed to hang and depend upon it.
>
> And the Earth and the Water stayed by themselves so mingled together, that the Earth could not be seen for the Water, but they were moved, because of the Spiritual Word that was carried upon them.[5]

Reading this passage, it is difficult not to be struck by the similarity of the prose with that of the King James Bible. That, though is hardly surprising, for the translations were roughly contemporaneous – the *Corpus Hermeticum* appeared in English 10 years after the authorized version of the Bible. Nevertheless the similarity is such that we are reminded that Christianity, Judaism and Hermeticism did not exist as self-contained bubbles. Hermeticism drew on Judaism, and Christianity was influenced by both. The overlap between them, of course, was provided by Platonism.

The political essence of Christian cosmology, though, remained Jewish. God created the entire universe, but unlike the Platonic and Aristotelian God, his creation is continuous and he is always ready to answer prayer and intervene in events either on his own initiative or at the request of the faithful. Also, in contrast to the Greek God he is transcendent and can move through the creation but is essentially above and separate to it. As he proclaimed in Isa. 66.1: 'Heaven is my throne and the earth is my footstool'. Matthew had Jesus announce that 'all authority in heaven and earth has been given to me' (Mt. 28.18), while St Paul added further detail: 'he [God] made him [Christ] sit at his right hand in the heavenly places, far above all rule and authority and power and dominion … not only in this age but also in that which is to come' (Eph. 1.20–21). Syncretism was out. Gone were the days when the Assyrians might venerate Marduk alongside Assur or the Greeks could merge Hermes with Thoth. The Christian cosmic state had one ruler, rather than the competing celestial leaders of conventional Near Eastern religion, although Persian influence was reflected in the cosmos's dualistic nature, polarized between God and Satan, the Christianized Ahriman, the Persian god of darkness, and good and evil, body and spirit, heaven and hell, eternal life and perpetual damnation. Humanity was alienated from God as a result of the Fall, Adam and Eve's expulsion from the Garden of Eden, but its purpose was to find a way back to him both individually and collectively, to worship and obey him, secure personal salvation and prepare the way for Christ's second coming.

However, Christianity's conception of the sky as a route to salvation can only be understood in the context of the cosmopolitan nature of first-century Jewish society. The concept of Palestine as some distant corner of the Roman Empire is nonsense, a myth which accompanies the equally false idea that there was an original pure Christianity. The area had been on the major trade routes between Egypt and Mesopotamia for thousands of years, since the Neolithic period, had been ruled for much of its history by Egyptians, Assyrians, Babylonians and Persians, and was host to around 100 Greek cities. There was no standard version of Jewish religion, which was represented at one extreme by the puritanical militancy of the prophets and at the other by an educated overlap with classical philosophy and paganism. One group, the Essenes, appear to have moved the Sabbath from Saturday to Sunday, almost certainly setting the precedent for the Christian choice of the sun's day as the holy day and others, as we know from the Dead Sea Scrolls, were adapting Babylonian astrology. The various 'horoscope' texts in the scrolls show strong Persian influence, attempting to divine the amount of dark and light in a man's character – or perhaps his soul. The most prominent astrologer in the region in the early days of Christianity's spread around the eastern Mediterranean who is known to us was Dorotheus of Sidon, whose *Carmen Astrologicum* was a major first-century compendium of astrological rules. Saint Paul himself travelled to Rome via Sidon in 59 CE, which does not mean that he knew of Dorotheus,[6] but as a Greek-educated Stoic he certainly knew all the relevant arguments for the stars and planets as instruments of fate, even if he disapproved. However, whatever St Paul thought, the legacy of the Jewish astrology of the last centuries BCE carried over into the world of the Christians, even if it is largely invisible in the Gospels.[7]

Aside from the Star of Bethlehem, the New Testament contains no specific astrological content. There are no statements in any Gospel or in Acts or the Epistles, either for astrology or against it. There are a number of passages with obviously mystical-cosmological significance, for example, in one moment of frustration at their obtuse failure to grasp his message, Jesus berated his disciples, setting them a numerological riddle:

Having eyes do you not see, and having ears do you not hear? And do you not remember? When I broke the five loaves for the five thousand, how many baskets of broken pieces did you take up?' They said unto him, 'Twelve'. 'And the seven for the four thousand, how many baskets of broken pieces did you take up?' And they said unto him, 'Seven'. And he said to them, 'Do you not yet understand?[8]

There is only one reasonable solution to this puzzle, which is that the numbers 7 and 12, two of the key ritual numbers in Hebrew and Near Eastern cosmological tradition, point to the totality of time. Seven can only be understood as the days of the creation and 12 as the number of tribes or, in astronomical terms the numbers of planets, months and zodiac signs. No intelligent audience of the first century can have been unaware of the cosmological significance of these numbers, particularly in the context of the mentality which produced the famous synagogue zodiacs of the first to fourth centuries.[9] As if the selection of the core 12 disciples was not obvious enough, Jesus also selected a further band of 72 disciples, this being the same as the number of countries in Ptolemy's scheme of zodiac politics, in which each country had a ruling sign of the zodiac.[10] Ptolemy's scheme may have been committed to writing in the second century, but it was both contemporaneous with the Gospels and shared a common cosmological tradition with them.

There also appears to have been a ritual connection between the number 12 and the numbers 7, 70 and 72. In Exodus the 12 leaders of the tribes were supplemented by 70 elders, a model Jesus followed when he appointed 70 additional disciples to supplement the original 12.[11] The 12 for their part required the entire body of disciples to select seven of their number to serve at table after the ascension.[12]

The theme of twelve-ness as a cosmological model for the structure of Jewish social and religious organization was made explicit when the 12 tribes' orientation to the sun was established.[13] Just as the 12 sons of Jacob, the fathers of the 12 tribes, found a parallel in the 12 sons of Ishmael so Jesus' disciples, his 12 executive deputies, were exactly mirrored in the 12 chief priests (Levites) who ministered to the 12 tribes in the Qumran sect, the writers of the Dead Sea Scrolls.[14] Authority in the Qumran sect, as in the earliest Christianity, lay with 12 lay elders who, according to the *War Rule*, were to play a vital role in the coming eschaton, the apocalyptic end of the world as set out in the Dead Sea Scrolls. These three groups of 12 fulfilled a function which was in essence exactly the same as that of Jesus' apostles, to prepare for the ending of the age. During the final battle between two conflicting sources, the Sons of Light on the one hand, and the Sons of Darkness in the other, the 12 tribal elders were to discharge their duties 'on the festivals, new moons, Sabbaths or weekdays', so ensuring the community's survival through harmonization with heavenly cycles.[15] We read that 'so long as these men exist in Israel, the deliberative council of the community (of Qumran) will rest securely on a basis of truth'.[16] Jesus would have understood the significance of twelve-ness and the Gospel writers would certainly have known it. It was not a matter of mystery or subtlety but public knowledge. When Jesus uses the numbers seven and 12 as the keys to his ministry, then, he is sending a clear cosmic message – that his preaching concerns the mystery of space and time, particularly his role in bringing a world age to an end and inaugurating the kingdom of God. He is, in the words of St John, 'the Alpha and the Omega, the beginning and the end'.[17]

The familiarity of early Christian thinkers with this kind of numerological thinking extended right through the classical period, into the fifth century when St Augustine provided the following Pythagorean analysis of biblical genealogy as a formula for understanding the relationship of sin to salvation.[18] First, he argued, the line of descent from Adam through Cain (the first murderer), ended after 11 generations with Namaah, whose name means 'pleasure', in effect, sin. Therefore sin, he reasoned, is represented by the number 11. The number of generations from Adam to Noah, who saved the human race and established a new order, meanwhile, was 10, which is therefore the number of the law. Then, he added the three sons of Noah, deducted the one who fell into sin, but kept the two who received Noah's blessing, then 10+2=12. The result was 12 which, Augustine tells us, is not only the number of both patriarchs and apostles, but is also, and here he borrows directly from the Pythagorean tradition, composed of the 'two parts of seven', four and three.[19]

The only overtly cosmological text in the New Testament, though, is the Revelation of St John, an imaginative work of grand proportions. Its repetition of the number seven – churches in Asia, spirits before the throne of God, the famous seals and, significantly, stars, ties Christian cosmology to the planets.[20] The woman with a crown of 12 stars and the tree with 12 kinds of fruit, one for each month for the 'healing of the nations' brings in the zodiac.[21] Meanwhile, the omens of the end of the world include eclipses – a blackened sun and blood-red moon – as well as stars falling to the earth, implicitly reinforcing the use of Babylonian-style astrology of celestial signs.[22]

There is only one explicit reference to astrology in the New Testament – the Star of Bethlehem story in Mt. 2.1–2. The story is also remarkably brief, considering the elaborate narratives which have been woven around it, and its ubiquitous presence in Christian iconography. The Revised Standard Version tells us only that 'when Jesus was born in Bethlehem of Judea in the days of Herod the king, behold, wise men came from the East to Jerusalem, saying, "Where is he who has been born king of the Jews? For we have seen his star in the East, and have come to worship him"'. Matthew continued with the astronomically impossible statement that 'the star which they had seen in the East went before them, till it came to rest over the place where the child was' (Mt. 2.9). So, here we have an astrology of signs, with no relation to the emerging astrology of influences. The familiar designation 'wise-men' is a translation of *magi*, the astral-priests of Persia, and was more accurately rendered as 'astrologers' in the New English Bible, published in the 1960s. The transformation of priests to kings, and the clarification of their number as three, were later medieval additions. Some versions even listed up to 12 wise men. Evangelical Christian tradition still holds that the star was a miraculous intervention; not a real star at all, in fact, but a brilliant light which led the wise men to the infant Christ, eventually stopping over the stable; any astrological connection is safely avoided.[23] However, the statement that the star appeared in the east and obviously acted as a sign has provided as an irresistible mystery for astronomers for hundreds of years. The most obvious solution to the story is that that star was a literary device intended by Matthew to persuade a readership used to tales of miraculous events surrounding the birth of great teachers, that Jesus was a great teacher whom they should take seriously. Matthew was, after all, a Hellenized Jew rebelling against the strict traditions of his own religion and engaged in a deliberate attempt to win over the pagan world. The presence of the Persian magi at Christ's birth is indeed suggestive of a literary borrowing from Zoroastrian ideas of the future saviour.

It was in this context that we find a series of astrological texts which were discovered as part of the Dead Sea Scrolls, probably from the first century CE, and which provide evidence for the kind of astrology which might have been familiar to a Jewish nationalist.[24] The omens appear to be of a style directly derived from Babylonian tradition from the *Enuma Anu Enlil*, based on thunder, the moon or lunar eclipses, sometimes adapted to specific Jewish circumstances. For example, 'if it thunders in the sign of Taurus, revolutions (in) the wor[ld]...', or 'if you saw the moon upright towards the south and its other horn inclined towards the north, let it be a sign for you: be careful of evil; trouble will go out from the south'.[25] Some texts appear to have been designed to be read at the new celebrations, exactly as would have happened when fates were taken at the *Akitu* in Babylon. The most intriguing texts are those which possess possible messianic associations. For example, the prediction that a great man will go out of the Sanhedrin when the moon is eclipsed in the middle of Nisan, which coincides with Passover, is evocative of later traditions that Christ's crucifixion, which immediately followed the Passover, was accompanied by an eclipse (though a solar one, which would have been impossible at the time).

The texts also include two or three so-called horoscopes. It is not clear, though, whether they are horoscopes in the sense that they are birth charts including a horoscope (ascendant) and houses in the Greek manner, or whether they are just birth omens. They deal partly with physical appearance and partly with spiritual condition but it is also unclear whether they are birth charts for individuals already born or who are yet to be born. One though, has been labelled the horoscope of the Messiah. Its apocalyptic tone is somewhat startling.

> His eyes are black and glowing. His beard is ... and it is ... His voice is gentle. His teeth are fine and well aligned ... His spirit consists of eight (parts) [in the House of Light, of] the second Column, and one [in the House of Darkness. And this is] his birthday on which he (is to be/was) born ... And his animal is ...[26]

The emphasis on light and dark may show the influence of what was by then the standard method of Hellenistic horoscope interpretation, which was to distinguish between horoscopes cast for the day and those for the night. It may also anticipate the third-century Christian heresy, Manichaeanism, which flourished in Persia and was to emphasize the same split. According to a later Arabic account, 'Mani said, "The origin of the world was [composed of] two elements, one of which was light and the other darkness. Each of them was separated from the other. Light is the great [element] and the first, but not in quantity. It is the deity, the King of the Gardens of Light' ".[27] The passage certainly reveals Zoroastrian influence and points to a possibly lost form of horoscopic interpretation in which the individual's location in the cosmic struggle of light against darkness is revealed.

The most well-known comment on the Star of Bethlehem as a physical entity was Johannes Kepler's in the seventeenth century, that it was a conjunction of Jupiter and Saturn – which could indicate the birth of kings – in Pisces in 7 BCE; the other major candidate is Halley's comet in 12 BCE which is, though, just too early to fit in with the Gospel narrative.[28] A break with standard astronomical reasoning was made by Michael Molnar in the 1990s. He argued that, if the magi were astrologers then the search for the star should focus on its astrological nature, rather than on whatever bright object might have appeared in the east.[29] There was therefore no reason at all why the 'star' need have been a significant astronomical event to anyone apart from astrologers. Indeed, there was no reason why it should even have been visible, which explains why Herod could not 'see' it.

Molnar's quest began with the purchase of a first-century CE coin minted in Antioch which depicted a ram, the Arien symbol, turning its neck to look backwards at a star which, he argues was a messianic icon dating back to prophecies that the Emperor Nero would recover his kingdom in the east.[30] In the second century Ptolemy claimed that Judaea was ruled by Aries so a textual case can be made that any 'king of the Jews' would have been represented by celestial events taking place in that sign. The date which comes closest to fulfilling the astrological criteria within the likely time frame for Christ's birth, 8–4 BCE, was 17 April 6 BCE. On this day Jupiter became visible, rising as 'spear-bearer', along with Saturn, for the Sun, which itself was exalted (strong) in Aries. Jupiter itself was Aries' 'triplicity' ruler (and therefore given additional importance, and was occulted by the moon, all of which, the theory runs, were indications within Hellenistic astrology of the birth of a great ruler or divine figure. The counter argument to Molnar's thesis is exactly the same as for previous theories – that it assumes the essential historicity of a nativity story which many would argue is just a means of impressing potential pagan converts.

One way or the other, though, the star presented a serious problem for early Christian polemics against astrology. Any form of astrology which was too closely linked to Christianity's polytheistic rivals was naturally deemed unacceptable. Yet here, in the nativity story, was a Babylonian-style celestial omen revealing the most significant event since the Fall, and it was astrologers themselves who were the first to recognize and venerate the infant redeemer. Why, then, should astrology be declared wrong?

While the Bethlehem star is an obvious astrological omen, anti-astrology Christians still managed to argue the reverse. So serious was the problem that the arguments begin in the first century, possibly before the story assumed its written form. For example, St Ignatius (c.35–c.107) who, as bishop of Antioch, presided over one of the key centres of the rising religion, argued that the star actually brought a final end to the old beliefs and practices. It was as if the light of God swept away a world of darkness. 'This was the reason', he wrote, 'why every form of magic began to be destroyed, every malignant spell to be broken, ignorance to be dethroned, and ancient empires to be overthrown'.[31] It was the star's very novelty – that it was both so much brighter than all the rest which in turn, formed a kind of heavenly choir around it – which itself pointed to the newness of the eternal life which was only available through Christ and not through any other kind of belief, including other versions of stellar salvation. Ignatius established the rationale for the star's inclusion in the nativity story, which was to become standard amongst Christian apologists. Saint Augustine discussed the problem of the star in the fifth century and, like his colleague, the Bishop of Constantinople, St John Chrysostom (*c.*347–407), he asserted that it was a new star that shone *because* Christ was born and its purpose was to point the way for the magi to find the Word of God.[32] It therefore represented the end of the old world, not an excuse to continue its false religious practices.

However, the arguments on astrology were subtle. Could the future be predicted in a situation in which God could change it from moment to moment? On the impossibility of predicting the second coming, humanity was mired in ignorance, as the writer of the Acts of the Apostles made clear in this report of an encounter between Jesus and his followers: 'So when they had come together, they asked him, "Lord, will you at this time restore the kingdom to Israel?" He said to them, "It is not for you to know times or seasons which the Father has fixed by his own authority".'[33] If, the anti-astrologers argued, Christ's return could not be predicted, then neither could anything else. The apocalypse itself would come 'like a thief in the night' and could not possibly be predicted.[34] Yet, there was a problem for those who thought that forecasting the future was impossible; the second coming was to be accompanied by celestial omens. Mark's Gospel contains the passage from which two distinct approaches to prediction might be taken. He begins by predicting that 'in those days, after that tribulation, the sun will be darkened, and the moon will not give its light, and the stars will be falling from heaven, and the powers in the heavens will be shaken'.[35] But he then adds: 'But of that day or hour no one knows, not even the angels in heaven, nor the Son, but only the Father. Take heed, watch, for you do not know when the time will come.'[36] There would be little in the way of advance warning, but signs would nevertheless be sent. The Acts of the Apostles elaborated:

> And I will show wonders in the heaven above
> And signs on the earth beneath,
> Blood, and fire, and vapour of smoke;
> The sun shall be turned into darkness
> And the moon into blood,
> Before the day of the Lord comes,
> the great and manifest day
> And it shall be that whoever calls on the name of the Lord shall be saved.[37]

This is a crucially significant passage. Astrology, by inference, is not a matter of treating the sick or finding runaway slaves, as the Hellenistic instruction manuals were implying. It was critical to one's chances of everlasting life. If such omens are sent sufficiently far in advance of Christ's *parousia*, his second coming, then there is time to repent for one's sins, to welcome the returning saviour and secure salvation. The difference is between an eternity in paradise in heaven and an infinity of torment in hell.

The evidence that such omens could be expected was provided by events surrounding the crucifixion. Matthew's account of the darkness that covered the earth for the three hours until Christ's death was widely interpreted as being a solar eclipse.[38] This was technically impossible for the crucifixion took place at the Passover, which was celebrated on the first or second full moon following the spring equinox, and eclipses of the sun can happen only at the new moon. There was, as it happens a lunar eclipse on 3 April 33, but lunar eclipses are only visible at night and do not make the day go dark. One solution was to argue that God can make a solar eclipse whenever he likes, whether the moon is new or full. This line was taken by Dionysius, the 'Pseudo-Areopagite', a prominent Neoplatonic Christian who flourished around 500, and claimed to have actually witnessed a solar eclipse – the 'moon fell into the sun', as he put it – on an impossible date, by which he meant not at a new moon.[39]

These debates continued well into the medieval world, through the Renaissance and Reformation. In the thirteenth century, John of Sacrobosco, the author of the medieval world's most authoritative astronomical commentary, concluded that 'it is also evident that, when the sun was eclipsed during the Passion and the same Passion occurred at full moon, that eclipse was not natural – nay, it was miraculous and contrary to nature, since a solar eclipse ought to occur at new moon or thereabouts. On which account Dionysius the Areopagite is reported to have said during the same Passion, "Either the God of nature suffers, or the mechanism of the universe (*machina mundi*) is dissolved".'[40] If human action, in this case the crucifixion of God's only son, is so terrible that God cannot bear the suffering, then the natural order breaks down. Under these circumstances an eclipse could well occur outside the appointed time, exactly as it could have done in ancient Sumer. Medieval theology preserved the reciprocal relationship between humanity and the stars, with the former influencing the latter as much as the latter signified the state of the former, which underpinned the Mesopotamian worldview. In a sense this was inevitable, for it had to find a way of coping with the astral omens which accompanied Christ's birth and death.

The story of the Star of Bethlehem was frequently directly linked with the prophecy from Numbers, 'I see Him, but not now; I behold Him, but not now; a Star shall come forth out of Jacob; and a Sceptre shall rise out of Israel'.[41] But, in claiming that Christ was fulfilling this passage, what did Christian apologists mean? Clearly there is a fine line between arguing that the prophecy was an omen of an open-ended future, and assuming that Christ's ministry was part of a plan that existed from the beginning of time, as suggested in the Qumran text, the *Epochs of Time*.[42] There is clearly an element of metaphor, of using a celestial body to make a point about terrestrial importance. In Revelation, St John has Christ say of himself, 'I am the root and offspring of David, the bright morning star'.[43] Yet, the notion of predetermination was reinforced in the early Christian texts. According to the Gospels, Jesus self-consciously fulfilled the various messianic prophecies, but it was also claimed that his existence and mission on earth had been determined even before the creation.[44] Saint Paul further refined the predestined framework by claiming that the Old Testament covenants between Yahweh and his human servants were themselves predestined and not the result of free moral choice.[45]

Yet Paul and all the early Christian writers retained an equal and opposite belief that individual choice was necessary for salvation, and vital for the correct management of history. This paradox between historical law and individual choice lay at the heart of Jewish and Christian millenarianism. Determinism sustained the millenarians on their path, offering them the certainty of eventual victory through the dark times of the Babylonian exile and repression at the hands of the Greeks and Romans. The language of the apocalyptic texts offered hope for the future and freedom from suffering. The practical consequence of the promise of the end of times was to liberate the faithful from the chains of time, in essence to free them from history. Jewish and Christian apocalyptic hysteria took its place amongst the liberation cults of the Near East and eastern Mediterranean, and added force to the notion that any unexpected astronomical event, a comet or eclipse, for example, might warn of divine judgement or the second coming.

In the Middle Ages the pro-astrology view consistently depended on the understanding that such omens can be anticipated, combining the religious power of Babylonian astrology with the predictive capabilities of the Greeks. Manuel Komnenos, Emperor of the Byzantine Empire from 1143–80, and a user of astrology for political decision making, took this view, arguing that 'the stars, by their different motions and manifestations, both in terms of their configuration and the zodiacal sign in which they appear, clearly indicate beforehand variations of great matters'.[46] From the thirteenth to the seventeenth centuries astrology was to be, with Scripture, the key means of predicting Christ's second coming.

It was politically essential for the Church Fathers, who were attempting to construct an image on earth of the single authority in heaven, to distinguish their new faith from all others, and astrology was to be swept up in the condemnation of pagan ritual. However, the theological position was unclear and the scriptural foundations of the steady polemic assault on astrology were weak.[47] The astrologers were, to an extent, let off the hook by the fact that the New Testament contains no condemnation of astrology. There were passages, however, which might be used against astrology in certain circumstances, such as the sweeping order: 'Do not swear at all, either by heaven, for it is the throne of God, or by the earth, for it is his footstool, or by Jerusalem, for it is the city of the great King'.[48] There were sections which could imply that the heavens could be a focus of evil, and therefore should not be trusted: Luke had Jesus say: 'I saw Satan fall like lightning from heaven'.[49] Then there was the prophecy that there would be no stars in the New Jerusalem and hence, by inference, no place for astrology. As Matthew prophesied, 'heaven and earth will pass away'.[50] The final age was to see the creation of a new heaven and a new earth, with no sun or moon, and hence no astrology. But then, there would be no need of astrology, for the future would be assured, the people would once again be in direct contact with the divine and there would therefore be no need of diviners nor of prophets to issue omens of the future. No longer would God talk through portents, oracles and dreams. And, as St Paul added: 'if any one is in Christ, he is a new creation'.[51] What price the casting of nativities, then? And if one of the implications of the story of the magi in the Gospel of Matthew was that Jesus was born under a specific astrological configuration and thus was, in a sense, under the control of the stars in some way, the answer, following St Paul, the leading ideologue of the first century, was that the born-again Christian was freed from the stars.

In public, Paul refused to acknowledge the usefulness of celestial movements at all, proclaiming in a celebrated passage that the second coming could not be predicted by 'signs and seasons'.[52] His one concession to the stars was to use them figuratively, his quotation from Aratus: 'in him we live and move and have our being', using the motion of the stars in the divine cosmos as an analogy for human beings' continual movement in society.[53] Whereas Paul, had absolutely nothing to say specifically about astrology, he did appear to differentiate, as an Aristotelian might, the natural from celestial worlds:

> There are celestial bodies and there are terrestrial bodies, but the glory of the celestial is one, and the glory of the celestial is another. There is one glory for the sun and another for the moon, and another glory for the stars, for one star differeth from another in glory.[54]

There was nothing here about the challenge posed by theories of planetary influence to God's omnipotence or the role played by demons in sending celestial omens, all arguments which were to be established in the following century.

From such unpromising material the Church Fathers, the theologians who shaped Christian doctrine in the Roman world had to fashion an anti-astrology position. Their fundamental position was that still held by the Roman Catholic Church, whose catechism, updated in 1994, states:

> All forms of divination are to be rejected: recourse to Satan or demons, conjuring up the dead or other practices falsely supposed to 'unveil' the future. Consulting horoscopes, astrology, palm reading, interpretation of omens and lots, the phenomena of clairvoyance, and recourse to mediums all conceal a desire for power over time, history, and, in the last analysis, other human beings, as well as a wish to conciliate hidden powers. They contradict the honor, respect, and loving fear that we owe to God alone.[55]

There was a fundamental problem for anti-astrology Christians. Not only did the Bethlehem star offer apparent vindication of astrology, but the New Testament contained no condemnations of it; sorcery and magic, yes, but astrology, no. The new dispensation ushered in by Jesus Christ had nothing to say about the matter. Even all the scriptural citations used to back the modern catechism are from Old Testament injunctions against star worship, rather than astrology as an interpretative system. The Church Fathers were in the same position, forced to rely on Old Testament texts to counter the apparently privileged role given to celestial omens in the New Testament. They also, though, had the example of anti-astrology Roman law to imitate and, in the year 120, the noted mathematician Aquila Ponticus was excommunicated from the church in Rome for his astrological heresies. Even though a war was fought by high-profile Christian polemicists against astrology, the lack of scriptural authority may, perhaps, be one reason why it was not until the fourth century that the prohibition of astrology was written into church law.

16

Rome: The Imperial Heaven

The universe is one and a single melody.[1]

If horoscopic astrology flourished at Rome, then so did the theurgic tradition, especially from the second century onwards. Its most well-known vehicle were the Mithraic mysteries, a formalized, ritual adaptation of the Hermetic belief that the soul abandoned certain earthly qualities as it ascended through the planetary spheres at death.[2] The function of the mysteries appears to have been to enable initiates to rehearse the ascent of the soul while living, so that, at death, the passage to heaven would be smoother. Mithras, or Mithra or Mitra, himself appears to have been known in India, Persia and Mesopotamia in the second millennium BCE, but the religion as it was known in the Roman Empire may be roughly contemporaneous with Christianity, to which, for a while, it was a serious rival. The mysteries may even have been deliberately devised in the kingdom of Commagene, from where they spread to the empire, appealing particularly to the army. This may have been a strength in terms of building a supportive atmosphere, but the exclusion of women proved fatal when Christianity appeared as a more egalitarian alternative, offering a more direct route to salvation. The mysteries remain, as the word suggests, mysterious, largely because we are dependent on secondary accounts and archaeological remains if we are to reconstruct a picture of their cosmology. The central iconography was the Tauroctony, in which Mithras was shown killing a bull, representing Taurus, and perhaps representing a memory of the era, before 2000 BCE, when the sun rose in the constellation Taurus at the spring equinox. Mithraism also has sufficient iconic similarities to suggest some identification with the Theseus myth, which was very popular at Rome and featured not just the hero's killing of the half-man/half-bull Cretan Minotaur, but the great fire-breathing bull which terrorized the citizens of Athens.[3]

This, at least, locates the origin of mysteries' symbolism as earlier than the earliest recorded literary astrological traditions, even if the dogma and rituals were much later. In the foreground were animals representing the 'summer' constellations – those close to the sun, and hence invisible in summer, but clearly visible in the winter night-sky, including Canis, the dog, Hydra, the serpent, Crater, the cup and Corvus, the raven. Last was a Scorpion, representing Scorpio, the opposite sign to Taurus. These two therefore framed the entire celestial mystery. Why the constellations between Sagittarius and Aries were ignored is not clear. Neither is it obvious why a practice with such heavenly interests was

conducted in temples – Mithraea – which resembled caves. Perhaps they evoked
Plato's parable of the cave. It is possible that they represented tombs. A little more
definite is our understanding of the initiatory sequence, which was reported by
St Jerome, in his jubilation at the destruction of a Mithraic sanctuary: Raven,
Bridegroom, Soldier, Lion, Perseus, Sun, Crab and Father.[4] There appear to be
different versions, though and, if these are linked to the planets then the sequence
appears to be:[5]

Pater (father)	Saturn
Heliodromus (sun-runner)	Sun
Perseus (Persian)	Moon
Leo (lion)	Jupiter
Miles (soldier)	Mars
Nymphus (bridegroom)	Venus
Corax (raven)	Mercury

This sequence does present us with technical problems. In the normal order
of planetary spheres, the so-called 'Chaldean Order', the soul would have
passed through the moon first, then Mercury, Venus, the sun, Mars, Jupiter and
Saturn.[6] To place the moon and sun immediately below Saturn suggests that
the sequence was allegorical and that the soul's ascent was figurative rather than
literal. It would have been no less real for that, but the emphasis would have
been on the soul's relation with the divine, rather than a journey through the
physical cosmos. Once the spiritual Saturn had been reached then the way was
clear for a return to the stars, and the freedom, bliss or ecstasy that awaited the
final glimpse of the divine. There is also evidence that initiates used technical
horoscopic astrology, but we would imagine of a type which could inform them
about the condition of their souls, rather than material advantage. Although
Mithras has been associated with Orion, or given responsibility for turning the
stars through the precession of the equinoxes, he is usually linked to the Sun.
Either he is the Sun, the brightest planet, or he is a solar deity and, through
him, is connected to Saturn, the dimmest; according to Ptolemy, the Persians
worshipped Saturn as 'Mithras–Helios'.[7] Imperial favour was found under
Marcus Aurelius (161–180 CE), who granted the mysteries civic immunities,
while his son Commodus (180–192) chose to become an initiate.

Throughout the empire the sun's role as a supreme god, or representative
of divinity, sustained imperial power.[8] Under the republic, from around the
fifth century BCE, the festival of Sol Indiges (the 'national' sun), dispenser of
agricultural fertility and one of the city's mythical ancestors, had been celebrated
on 9 August but it was with the ascent to power of the single ruler that the
sun, as the most distinctive body in the sky, assumed its political–theological

importance. With the rise of the empire, the sun became a political rather than agricultural deity, and was present in the here-and-now rather than the distant past. Augustus credited Apollo with his victory over Cleopatra and Mark Antony at Actium, but it was Nero who was the first to explicitly relate his authority to the brilliance of the sun, minting coins on which he was shown wearing a gold crown from which emanated sunbeams. The popularization of sun-worship at Rome seems to have been encouraged by Hadrian (117–138), who was responsible for the construction of the Pantheon, a magnificent temple to the seven planetary deities, and the largest surviving Roman building. From 158, in the reign of Antoninus Pius, we have the first known dedication to Sol Invictus, the unconquered sun – that is, the sun who was resurrected, born again at the winter solstice, conquering darkness and death. Septimus Severus (193–211), took such messianic imagery on himself, calling himself Invictus, and constructing a shrine to the seven planets, the Septizonia in which, it is suggested, he placed himself in the middle, like the sun or, perhaps, the central Hermetic sun. One emperor, Elagabalus, or Heliogabalus (218–222) was actually a priest of the Syrian sun god, although it was Aurelian (270–275), the son of a sun-priestess, who established Deus Sol Invictus, the Unconquered Sun, as Rome's supreme deity with a feast day on the winter solstice, 25 December. The worship of Sol Invictus and Mithras-as-Helios tended be blended together and became what Steve McCluskey has called an 'ornament' of imperial power.[9] As he pointed out, in the year 307 the Emperors Diocletian, Galerius and Licinus jointly dedicated a major Mithraeum at Carnuntium on the Danube border, as a sustainer of their imperium.[10] The last pagan emperor, Julian, who ruled for just two years from 361 to 363, restored the mysteries as an act of defiance against the new Christian orthodoxy.

If Mithraism appealed to the Roman soldier, it was paralleled by no less significant discussions amongst the philosophical elite about how, and whether, human life was connected to the stars. The wave of interest in Platonism of which Cicero was a part lasted until the second century and is known to modern scholars as Middle Platonism. One key feature of Middle Platonism was the search for common themes between Pythagoras, Plato and Aristotle. To simplify the resulting ideas Aristotle's divine mind was reconciled with Plato's world of Forms and Ideas and the whole system codified into a hierarchical trinity: God, the divine mind, the good, the One, derived from himself a second, subordinate mind, or God, which was able to begin the process of creation, beginning with the third part of the trinity, the *Anima mundi* or world soul. It was accepted that human souls were parts of the world soul which had descended to earth through the planetary spheres and become incarnated. As they passed through each sphere they forgot something of their origin but acquired the character of the respective planet – action from Mars, thought from Mercury and so on. Such ideas did not constitute a single dogma and different writers would disagree on the finer points of detail, but there was a broad consensus and a sympathy for astrology. However, there was now, unlike in Mesopotamia, no such single creature as astrology. Instead there were different astrologies with distinct philosophical and technical assumptions and we increasingly encounter complex positions, notably from the Neoplatonists.

We have to recognize that Neoplatonism, like Middle Platonism, is a nineteenth-century German category which would have made no sense at the time, and is somewhat artificial. On the other hand, it has become the standard way of talking about late classical Platonism. The Neoplatonists, beginning with their most charismatic figure, Plotinus (203–270 CE), continued the Middle Platonists' synthesizing tendencies, fusing Pythagoras, Plato, Aristotle and Hermes Trismegistus into a single system.[11]

Plotinus, who was born in Egypt, visited Mesopotamia in order to teach himself Eastern wisdom, and settled in Rome in 244, is actually regarded as the greatest Greek philosopher of late antiquity. He also, along with his famous student, Porphyry, appears to have been in contact with Indian teachings. We know that there were direct trading links between Rome and India and, even after they seemed to have declined, around 200 CE, indirect links remained strong. It seems that the strong similarities between Neoplatonism and Hindu thought – the belief in a single remote cosmic source of whom the universe was an emanation, the illusory nature of the material world, the pursuit of an aesthetic lifestyle – were sustained by scholarly connections which paralleled the trade routes.[12]

Plotinus' fundamental problem, one already addressed by Hermeticists, Mithraists and Christians, was how the individual soul might reach God. He confirmed the process by which the One gave rise to mind (*Nous*), soul (*Psyche*) nature (*Physis*), the principle of life and growth, and matter in a succession of stages, each of which was inferior to the one that preceded it. Human beings are microcosms, containing within themselves parts of matter, nature, soul and mind, and have two chances to ascend through the planetary spheres. Intellectual discipline, fuelled by love and enthusiasm, can take them back to the mind, but ecstatic experience, which Plotinus enjoyed on four occasions, can actually result in a brief reunion with the One. One might have thought that an acceptance of astrology was a natural extension of this philosophy. Certainly, in the single, unified, living universe, all things are linked to all others, so the stars may tell us something about human life. But not necessarily.

The essential Neoplatonic philosophy of astrology, as laid down by Plotinus in his tract *On Whether the Stars are Causes*, preserved the theory of Aristotelian influences but advocated an astrology of signs, rejecting Ptolemy's model of mathematically determined or regulated causes.[13] Of course, nothing is so simple, and even signs appear as a result of causes.[14] Plotinus' problem, with not just Ptolemaic astrology but with the entire edifice of Hellenistic astrology, was three-fold. First, it was theologically offensive to consider the planets as possible causes of disease, poverty and misfortune when the planets, in the Platonic *kosmos*, are essentially good. Secondly, to attempt to make precise predictions on the basis of exact planetary locations and the relationship between planets was manifestly ridiculous. Certainly, the human soul, moral character, emotions and behaviour were derived from the stars.[15] This had been shown by Plato in his Myth of Er and was not to be questioned. But to assume from this that the planets made us good or bad, lucky or unfortunate, as astrologers claimed, was nonsense. Plus, if planetary influences are used as a justification for such predictions then it needs to be remembered that, as influences descend to the earth they become diluted. A cold Saturnine influence will naturally have been moderated by Martian heat before it reaches the earth. Besides, Plotinus said, disagreeing with Ptolemy, there is no way that we can extrapolate from physical influences to assume a planetary role in the construction of personality. This is only common sense. Plotinus had no doubt that such general influences existed and he accepted without question the model set out by Pliny. However, he incorporated into astrology what can only be described as an 'uncertainty principle': some things do happen as a result of the movement of the heavens', he wrote, 'but others do not'.[16] And why not? In fact, his resistance to the idea that astrology was a universal answer to everything was because, ironically, he shared with Ptolemy the idea that, at the human level, the universe is multi-causal. The environment, one's life circumstances and archetypal nature, or formal cause, had something to do with it. If one is a man, one is a man with certain needs, instincts and priorities, and nothing the stars do will change that.[17] We need to understand the concept of causes a little better. In Latin a *causa* was a cause in the senses of a reason, purpose, sake, excuse, pretext, opportunity or connection; it could be active – one causes something – or it could be the link which describes the relationship between two things. Plato had said formal causes can exist by themselves but Aristotle argued that, in general, formal causes do not exist independently of their manifestation as material causes. The Neoplatonists solved this problem by tying Forms to Nous, the supreme mind, freeing them from the material cause. In Latin a *res* was a thing, but it was also matter, an affair, a transaction – that is, it was in a process, an object in, in Platonic terms, a state of becoming.

And then there is the little matter of chance, the apparent randomness of events which appear to fit no pattern, certainly not a planetary one. If the rational soul was inherently virtuous, vice arose from its chance encounters in the world.[18] Nor, even if we accept an astrology of signs, or indications, is astrology reliable. Some events may be signified, others not. And signs might come from anywhere. 'The wise man', Plotinus wrote, 'can learn about one thing from another'; he can find out things about a man from looking in his eyes; this, essentially, had been the Babylonian position. But the addition of the soul created uncertainty: those who lived through their animal souls would be subject to whatever planetary influences, or other fated pressures that came their way. But people who lived through their rational souls would not. This, around 500 years after Plato, is the logical conclusion of Plato's musings on the soul and the stars.[19] And Plotinus' formula was to be formalized in later Western astrology in the aphorism, the 'wise man rules his stars'. 'All happenings', he said, 'form a unity and are as it were spun together, in the cases of individuals as well as wholes'.[20]

Plotinus' position then, can only be understood in terms of the debates which took place in the first century BCE and the first and second centuries CE, in the context of Platonic scepticism and Aristotelian mechanics. Cicero, basing much of his work on Carneades, preserved the ensouled Platonic *kosmos*, but rejected both Hellenistic horoscopic astrology and its Babylonian antecedents. Pliny then joined the rejection of astrology but confirmed the existence of general planetary influences as central to the Aristotelian universe. Ptolemy then took this physical model and proposed it as a secular rationale for horoscopic astrology, attempting to counter Cicero's contempt for it as superstition. Plotinus takes a different position. Like Ptolemy he accepts Pliny's naturalism, but, unlike Ptolemy, he agreed with the broad thrust of Cicero's criticisms of Hellenistic horoscopic astrology and instead anchors his work in an astrology of signs, one inherited from Mesopotamia. 'Let us suppose', he wrote, 'that the stars are like characters always being written on the heavens'.[21] Like a Babylonian astrologer one can then read the divine script.

Plotinus' mechanism is simple: the universe is a single living creature which operates according to a rational order, and Platonic Ideas descend from the higher to lower levels tying the whole edifice together at the level of soul as well as matter. Astrology is no longer a matter of causes, or even of a mathematically rigid Ptolemaic code, but of reading the signs from one level of reality to form conclusions about another. He is quite clear about this and gives the example of a rich man. The planets, he says do not cause a man to be born wealthy, but they announce it. The actual causes of wealth are to be found in the sub-lunar sphere, in a man's parentage or culture. Indeed, the whole world is full of signs, so astrology, as in Mesopotamia, is just one possible form of divination. In addition, if influences are general and diluted, while signs require careful interpretation, astrologers cannot make specific predictions.

There was, though, a weakness in Plotinus' position, which is that, having rejected the rules and regulations of horoscopic astrology, he had no interpretative system to use along with his reformed version of the discipline. However, as his goal was neither to make predictions nor offer advice this was not a problem. His vision was salvation from the physical prison of life. His mission was to encourage those who were able to return to the One or, at least, to the Nous. In theory every human being might do this for all are microcosms, compounds of mind, soul and matter. But, in effect, many people are unsuited by means of their temperament; they are ignorant of that part of the soul outside the body, the one which can ascend to the stars. These are the people who are then controlled by destiny, unable to develop their reason, and are subject to planetary influences. (He leaves a space open here for a universal astrology, but only for the ignorant). Those who develop their rational soul will ascend to the stars, enter the world of Being, and reconnect with the divine. There is an essential body-hating, world-renouncing core to Plotinus' thought, one which is little different to that popular amongst the Christians whom he despised. His quarrel with them, especially with the Gnostics, was that they regarded the cosmos as inherently evil rather than good.[22]

But here Plotinus introduced another paradox which is not fully explored. One's moral character is acquired as the soul descends through the planetary spheres at birth, the implication being that some people may be inclined from birth to be able to transcend destiny, and others not. From Plotinus onwards, though, it is possible to identify two main currents in Western astrology, the Ptolemaic and the Plotinian. The former assumes that the astrologer acts as the impartial observer of a universe subject to an elaborate mathematical code, concentrates on external circumstances, and is able to make exact judgements concerning the time, date and location of events which are broadly predetermined. The latter elevates moral character above outer circumstances as the focus of astrological concern, severely limits astrology's ability to make precise judgements and is concerned with one's intellectual and spiritual development, aiming for knowledge of God.

These two positions can be clearly identified, but they were inevitably moderated. Plotinus' student, editor and biographer Porphyry (213–c.305) is reputed to be the author of an introduction to Ptolemy's *Tetrabiblos*, as was Proclus. However, there was no common Neoplatonic position on astrology. In a sense every Platonic position on astrology has to contain a certain internal contradiction; the descent of the soul through the planetary spheres suggests that astrology is a vital practical application of Platonic theorizing. Yet the sceptical view that all knowledge gleaned from the material world is likely to be false leads inevitably to doubts that astrologers can make detailed judgements on specific matters. Similarly the web of destiny spun by the three Fates as the soul moves down to earth suggests the future is predetermined, yet the individual need to return to the One requires a challenge to fate. Both Porphyry and Iamblichus agonize over exactly what balance one should take, trying desperately to find a third way between these poles. Both tend to be critical of contemporary astrology's technical determinism, the notion that one can read the future in the mathematical structure of the horoscope, yet have no more notion than Plotinus of how to create a more suitable interpretative framework.[23] Both, though, advocated the construction of astrological images, talismans created at an appropriate time from the relevant materials and continuing inscriptions designed to facilitate human contact with the divine.[24] Such practices mark out the Neoplatonists' character as, in part, descendants of the Hermeticists. Iamblichus himself identified Hermes as 'the God who presides over language ... formerly very properly considered as common to all priests',[25] laying the foundation for the notion of a pristine theology, a perennial wisdom which was once, before religion fragmented between different cultures, common to all humanity.

Like so many Platonists Porphyry was caught between astrology's undeniable logic – that the stars revealed divine intent and offered a potential means for the soul to return to the heavenly spheres – and scepticism – that the astrologers' precise claims are just difficult to swallow in a world in which no absolute knowledge is truly possible. He still managed to write a major commentary on Ptolemy's *Tetrabiblos*, and another on Aristotle, which was well known and widely read in the Middle Ages. One of Porphyry's shorter, and somewhat sceptical discussion of astrology, the *Epistle to the Egyptian Anebo*, was to prompt a huge response from another of the leading Neoplatonists, the Syrian-born Iamblichus, who died in around 330 CE. Iambliclus engineered a revolution in elite Platonic circles by rejecting the standard view, espoused by Plotinus and Porphyry, that the divine should be accessed through reason and logic.[26] Instead he looked to the popular traditions of magic current in religious Platonism, amongst the followers of the Hermetic teachings, and argued that divine wisdom could be understood both through omens and through theurgy – literally god-work – meaning ritual and magic. His *On the Mysteries* is, in effect, a theurgy of Neoplatonic astrology, a comprehensive rejection of what he saw as the stilted, precise, mistaken dogma of Hellenistic astrology.[27] Like Plotinus he asked how one planetary aspect can cause, or signify misfortune, another vice?[28] How can astrologers suppose that the daimon is revealed in the planet ruling the sign of the zodiac ascending at birth?[29] The study of astrology alone cannot achieve salvation though; only theurgy can achieve this. It was not enough to practise astrology, passively reading horoscopes and making forecasts, for humanity was inseparable from its supernatural dimension – its daimons and souls. Astrology could only be of practical value, he reasoned, if it was shorn of deterministic rules, and backed up by ritual acts and the active invocation of higher powers. Iamblichus was the major theoretician of magic in the ancient world. In fact, it is no understatement to call him the major philosopher of magic in the entire Western tradition. His works were known to the Arabs and rediscovered in the west when they were translated into Latin in the late fifteenth century, becoming a major influence on Renaissance thought, encouraging the notion that humanity was free to aspire to higher wisdom and control its own destiny. In his major work on magic, *On the Mysteries*, he insisted that 'only divination ... in uniting us with the gods, truly enables us to share in the life of the gods', in other words, liberates us from necessity.[30] But by the time that Iamblicus was setting out his pagan path to salvation, the Christians were on the way to theological control of the empire.

Between the dedication of the Mithraic temple at Carnuntium and Julian's failed attempt to re-establish the old solar religion, Constantine had legalized Christianity. This, he had done, as is well known, after he apparently received a heavenly sign prior to his last great battle, at Rome's Milvian Bridge on 28 October 312. There are different accounts of this story. It may even be a pastiche of the favour Aurelian conferred on Sol Invictus after winning a decisive victory at Emesa. Whatever the truth, later tradition has it that Constantine's vision was of the Christian Chi-Rho symbol, which a few years later appeared in Christian iconography. For Constantine it was but a short step from Sol Invictus to Christ; Christianity, with its extensive organization, offered a more effective monotheistic counterpart to the imperial throne than the sun. The worship of Sol Invictus as supreme state deity had manifestly failed to encourage political unity. Perhaps a merger of solar religion and Christianity would provide the religious power capable of ensuring political authority.

The final and most enduring act of imperial astrology is sometimes said to have been Constantine's use of astrology to choose the most auspicious date for the foundation of his new capital city at Constantinople in 330 CE, a story accepted by most writers of Byzantine history. Unfortunately, there are a number of competing contenders for the position of official Byzantine horoscope, some of them astronomically impossible, and the origin of the confusion appears to be a horoscope cast retrospectively by a tenth-century astrologer named Demophilus, probably around 990.[31] We read of a certain 'Praetextatus the hierophant' who assisted in the city's foundation, and might have been an astrologer, and it would not have been at all surprising for Constantine to have employed astrologers for he was, above all, a pragmatist and to have done so could have been a means of securing pagan support. However, it seems more likely that Demophilus was engaged in an astrological examination of Constantinople's history rather than an attempt to fabricate it.

Throughout the accounts of the many imperial uses of divination though, we find that astrology was not regarded as a unique source of knowledge. Exactly as in second-millennium BCE Babylon, it was one form of divination amongst many, and existed alongside such forms of communication with the gods as dream analysis and oracles, and techniques for manipulating the future such as an array of magical techniques and religious practices. And these techniques and the practises proved remarkably resistant to Christianity.

The Emperor Julian (360–363), who briefly restored the official pagan religion, was an enthusiastic follower of Iamblichus, whom he praised in his own *Hymn to the Sun*. Curiously, while the empire was being progressively Christianized, the Neoplatonists developed a taste for sun worship The last of the great classical Neoplatonists was Proclus (412–485) who achieved distinction as head of the Academy in Athens and as a prolific writer, and under whom the philosophy assumed a decidedly religious tone. Death, he taught was nothing more than the reunion of the fire of the soul with the divine fire of the stars and he prayed to the sun, the supreme fire, three times a day, asking for enlightenment and purification. His works included a series of Hymns including a famous one to the sun not as a god but as a great symbol of the divine, translated by Kenneth Guthrie in the 1920s with a mock-Shakespearian flourish:

> Hear golden Titan! King of mental fire,
> Ruler of light; to thee supreme belongs
> The splendid key of life's prolific fount;
> And from on high thou pour'st harmonic streams
> In rich abundance into matter's worlds.
> Hear! For high rais'd above th' aetherial plains,
> And in the world's bright middle orb thou reign'st
> Whilst all things by thy sov'reign power are fill'd
> With mind-exciting providential care.
> The starry fires surround thy vig'rous fire,

And ever in unweary'd ceaseless dance,
O'er earth wide bosom'ed, vivid dew diffuse.
By they perpetual and repeated course
The hours and seasons in succession rise.[32]

Proclus' death was heralded by celestial prodigies not unlike those which coincided with Christ's crucifixion: a solar eclipse in Capricorn (which, it was believed, was the gateway for departing souls) caused darkness in the daytime and the stars to shine. They also warned of the death of philosophy at the hands of Christianity.[33] The similarity between these prodigies and those at the crucifixion goes deeper than the fact that the sky grew dark; both events involved celestial signs, not causes in the Aristotelian sense. The parallels are more than coincidence. For the educated Roman citizen Neoplatonism fulfilled the needs satisfied by a monotheistic salvation religion, but it encouraged its adherents to study, think and read, rather than find everlasting life through blind faith.

The empire may have become officially Christian after 312 but classical paganism took about 200 years or more to die out. The transition was a long and complex one in which Christianity itself had difficulty in presenting a united face: Arians persecuted Catholics, Catholics hounded Gnostics and Christians sometimes allied with pagans in rebellion. Theodosius I (379–95), the last man to rule the entire empire before its disintegration in the west, was strongly anti-pagan, presided over a spate of violent assaults by Christians on pagan sacred sites and passed laws prohibiting pagan rites in 391 and 392. The worst violence of his reign occurred in Alexandria, where the bishop organized the destruction of the Serapeum, the temple of the Egyptian god Serapis and reputedly one of the most magnificent buildings in the empire. The direct consequence was a rebellion in 393 which, though led by a Christian, Eugenius, attracted widespread support from aristocratic pagans,[34] an illustration of the complexity of theological–political allegiances. In the western empire the senate retained strong pagan sympathies in contrast to the emperors, now based in Milan, for whom Christianity offered the best chance of holding the empire together. But, with its blessing from both the emperor and the Germanic kings who were moving into the empire, the rise of Christianity was unstoppable – and, with it, the end of cosmic pluralism.

17

Christianity: The Triumph of the Sun

The hope of heaven cannot exist with the abuse of heaven.[1]

The Christian polemic against astrology began in the early second century, when the New Testament was being formalized. The earliest major Christian polemicist to declare astrology incompatible with Christianity appears to have been Justin Martyr (c.100–c.165), a pagan thinker who converted around 130 and taught for a time in the church at Ephesus. He later opened a Christian school at Rome, for which crime he was beheaded with his disciples in the year 165, but not before he had continued the Pauline project – to move Christianity away from Judaism, appealing to Hellenistic culture by reconciling faith with reason and presenting the new religion as an acceptable part of the Roman world. This required a delicate balancing act in which the broad cosmology set out by Plato and Aristotle – the existence of the soul in an intimate relationship with a creator who caused all things to happen – was easily incorporated into Christian theology. There was also another strand of religious thought and practice which fed into Christianity; according to one theory it was Orphism, with its respect for the sun, messianic inclinations and ethical piety, which made Platonism palatable to the religion of St Paul.[2] But the notion of the universe as itself alive or divine was problematic and its logical conclusion, the worship of celestial divinities, was entirely unacceptable. As Paul had written: 'Give no offence to Jews or to Greeks', no more than to the church, but 'do not be mismatched with unbelievers … for what fellowship has light with darkness … what has a believer in common with an unbeliever?'[3] However, the problem was exactly where the line should be drawn between what could be considered legitimate and what was not. Astrology was to be generally condemned by leading theologians, but the arguments are weak, varying between rational criticisms and theological condemnation. We can read between the lines of the various polemics enough to suggest that a number, perhaps a large number, of ordinary Christians, had no objection to astrology.

Justin's theoretical and theological system was developed through a series of texts which made the case against the old faith and argued for the new. His *First Apology*, written around, 155 CE, was addressed to the Emperor Antoninus Pius and defended Christianity as the only rational faith. The *Dialogue with Trypho the Jew*, developed the Hellenizing theme, taking the *logos* and the God of the Old Testament, the creators of Platonic philosophy and Jewish teaching and arguing that they all shared the same identity. For good measure, he developed the idea that the Gentiles had taken the place of Israel as the chosen people. His narrative

worked on two levels, incorporating the internal paradox which was always to
undermine Christian attempts to outlaw astrology. Paganism and all its ways
were rejected, but Platonic teachings were broadly accepted because they added
a vital component to Christianity. By adopting Plato's advocacy of reason as a
path to the divine, Justin, and his fellow Hellenizers, enabled the new church to
attract intellectuals for whom blind faith was distinctly unappealing. But Plato
had also proposed that the creator's intent was expressed through the stars, which
were themselves divine.

Justin, though, held the line against astrology in his *Second Apology*, addressed
to the Roman Senate. Whatever the implications of Platonic cosmology, Justin
saw astrology as fatally tainted by its religious associations. There could be no
compromise with pagan practice. Justin's assault was extended by Tatian the
Syrian, who was born, as his name suggests, in Syria around 120 CE and became
a Christian in Rome in around 150–165. Tatian was no orthodox believer, though
and, in about 172, he returned to the east and founded the Encratites, a group who
took their ascetic practices to such extremes that they were considered possibly
heretical; Christianity itself was showing signs of increasing diversity. In Tatian's
major work, *Oratio ad Graecos – Address to the Greeks* – which was a passionate
defence of the antiquity and purity of Christianity combined with a violent attack
on Greek civilization, we see two separate strands of polemic; one which accepts
the 'best' of Greek culture as represented by Plato, and the other which denies it.
Tatian's attack on astrology, like Justin's belongs to the latter. His righteous anger
against astrology which, in his view, was demonic, was uncompromising: 'Men
became the subject of the demons' apostasy', he wrote, 'for they showed man a
chart of the constellations, and like dice players they introduced the factor of
fate … Murders and their victims, rich and poor, are children of fate, and every
nativity gave entertainment as in a theatre to the demons, among whom, like "the
blessed gods" of Homer, "unquenchable laughter arose".'[4] Somehow, the Platonic
daimon, a benevolent 'higher-self' in modern terms, had become the Christian
demon, a wholly malicious agent of Satan.

Tatian's allegation that astrology was taught by demons had scriptural
precedents. After all, the apocryphal Jewish text *1 Enoch* recorded how the
fallen angels taught humanity the various arts and sciences. The argument
struck a chord for, no matter what the defences put up by astrologers, however,
accurate their work or good their lives, they were still, according to Tatian,
in league with demonic powers. Tertullian (*c*.160–*c*.225), originally a pagan
lawyer from Carthage, was of the same opinion. His spiritual path was not
unlike Tatian's. He joined the Montanists, an apocalyptic movement which
forecast an imminent outpouring of the Holy Spirit and was then instrumental
in developing a particularly ascetic strain which disallowed second marriages,
condemned the rules on fasting as too lax and forbade flight from persecution.
We get some insight into second- and third-century astrology from these texts.
Tertullian himself engaged in arguments with at least one astrologer, for he
reported on the exchange. The astrologer had defended himself of charges of

idolatry, perhaps responding to Justin's *Second Apology*, but this defence was of no interest to Tertullian who responded that, even though the astrologer neither honoured idols nor 'inscribed [their names] on the heaven', 'one proposition I lay down: that those angels, the deserters of God [demons] … were likewise the discoverers of this curious art [astrology], on that account also condemned by God'.[5] The astrologers were damned if they worshipped demons and damned if they did not; as all astrology had been invented by demons, it did not matter how innocent one's intent or naturalistic one's rationale for the art. The practitioner of Ptolemaic rules was no less a victim of evil than a worshipper of Ishtar. There was no real theology, just a naked power-play between one group who claimed access to the absolute truth about the cosmos, and its older rival.

Even though Christian condemnation of astrology veered close to an assault on classical learning as a whole, such an approach remained difficult, if not impossible, to reconcile with the opposite strategy – winning converts through appealing to Hellenistic cosmology and blurring the distinctions between Christianity and philosophy. This often called for different strategies. Hippolytus, a contemporary of Tertullian and a presbyter at Rome, a man apparently of some importance (he was exiled to Sardinia in the persecution of the Emperor Maximinus in the 220s) adopted sceptical ridicule as his main approach. Hippolytus thought philosophy as whole, especially Platonism, was a dangerous competitor to Christianity, but that did not stop him copying his assault on astrology from the arch-sceptic Sextus Empiricus. Hippolytus mocked astrology's claims to psychological profiling, the notion that 'a person born in Leo should be irascible [like a lion] and that one born in Virgo moderate [like a virgin] or one born in Cancer wicked [like a crab]?'[6] Even so, the 'demonic' hypothesis remained the dominant one. Lactantius (*c*.240–*c*.320), a pagan and former teacher of rhetoric at Nicomedia, achieved considerable influence for his views as a result of his elevated position as tutor to Crispus, son of the emperor Constantine. Lactantius' seminal work, the *Divine Institutions* was addressed to educated Romans and, for the first time, set out in Latin rather than Greek, a systematic account of the Christian attitude to life, including the denunciation of astrology as demonic. The assault was continued by other polemicists, including Athanasius, after whom the creed was named. For him, writing in the 360s, astrology was nothing more than 'lying and contemptible'.[7]

The assault on astrology was not purely a matter of a struggle with pagans for humanity's eternal soul. Ridicule and condemnation were not enough. There was also a strong element of sophisticated Platonic scepticism, of which the major exponents were Clement (*c*.150–*c*.215), Bishop of Alexandria, and Origen (*c*.185–254), his successor as head of the influential catechetical school in Alexandria, an institution which aimed at the propagation of Christianity amongst the educated classes and was one of the key centres for the overlap with Neoplatonism. This should be seen as perfectly natural. If the standard cosmology of the times held that the planets moved through spheres situated between heaven and earth then it followed that righteous souls had to travel through them if they were to reach heaven. The stellar journey was an integral part of the path to salvation.

Clement spoke approvingly of Pythagoras, who said God is within the universe, not outside it, and Plato, who learnt geometry from the Egyptians and astronomy from the Babylonians. He went on to call God 'the measure of the truth of all existence' and cited Plato in his support: 'Now God, holding the beginning and end and middle of all existence, keeps an unswerving path, revolving according to nature'.[8] Clement's God was the impersonal Pythagorean–Platonic geometer married with the personal Jewish creator. That much was acceptable. But Clement's Platonism had major consequences, encouraging him to seriously blur the line set by Justin between what was and was not legitimate in pagan learning. His flirtation with heresy became explicit in his acceptance of the notion that the spiritual, or numinous, nature of the stars was present inside each human being, that 'there was of old implanted in man a certain fellowship with the heavens'.[9] His belief that knowledge, *gnosis*, or illumination, was the chief element in Christian perfection, was to take him into association with the Gnostics, the arch-heretics of the early Christian world.

But, like Cicero and Plotinus, Clement's acceptance of the soul's connection with the stars, did not lead to an acceptance of judicial astrology. Yet, precisely because it is well informed, Clement's critique does not fall into the simple astrology-is-demonic formula. This relative sophistication is the result of his respect for pagan learning, in which he was a little more liberal than Tatian and Justin. He was a devout Platonist, enamoured of classical culture, and he favoured an allegorical rather than literal reading of Scripture. He was interested in meaning rather than in literal rules. The major problem, he claimed, was not that astrologers are lined up with the forces of evil, but that they are ignorant. Clement's arguments are supported by a group of pseudo-Clementine writings, which may date to the first or second centuries.[10] Very usefully for our attempt to understand the cosmology of the first and second centuries, pseudo-Clement included some discussion of the possible mechanics of astrology – not that he was doing any more than reporting it as a neutral observer. He described a variety of moral Aristotelianism, or Platonism, in which the stars behaved not as autonomous powers, but as passive agents of divine will. They could be the servants of good but, when 'malignant power' was transferred into them, they became the agency through which man's lust was excited, the result being sin. Although Clement's arguments were cruder than Plotinus', it is likely that he was thinking along similar lines, that the animal soul is influenced by the stars but the rational soul is not. According to this model, sin was only 'provoked', not caused or produced by such celestially inspired lust. Whereas this model – that the stars influence us, but it is up to us how we respond – has been a staple of Western astrology since the thirteenth century – for Clement it was the fatal flaw in a system which to all intents and purposes was deterministic. Whatever astrologers say, he claimed, they couch both their explanations of past events and predictions of future ones, in terms which suggest certainty. Yet the human freedom to choose whether to sin – or live in virtue – meant that no event could be predicted before it happened, and that nor should any retrospective explanation for astrology be taken seriously. To test his claim that astrologers resorted to unreliable explanations after the event, seeking any planetary configuration to suit their argument, pseudo-Clement resorted to reason and proposed a simple controlled experiment. First, he told his father, go to an astrologer and tell them that he suffered at a particular period in his life. Such misfortune, pseudo-Clement predicted, would be explained according to the movements of the malefic planets, Mars and Saturn. Next, he told him to go to another astrologer and tell them that he experienced good fortune at the same period and wait for them to tell him that the benefic planets Venus and Jupiter were responsible. There is therefore no real validity in astrology, pseudo-Clement reasoned, and astrologers only check their horoscopes retrospectively to find a good fit for any event with the planets after the event. Worse, he said, there is an inconsistency between the rules of astrology and the stars' influence. For example, Venus and Jupiter are supposedly benefic planets yet can tempt us into adultery, a sin. Where is the benevolent result, then, if we end up burning in hell? Christian cosmology thus clashed inevitably with astrology's essential amorality. The path to salvation through the stars was irreconcilable with the path to salvation through Jesus.

Read closely, pseudo-Clement's writing offers us a valuable insight into the way in which commercial astrologers operated in the Roman Empire, and the dislocation between practice and philosophy. The major instructional texts by Valens, Ptolemy and the rest, took a serious view of the human condition and their sample prognostications can all be read as predictions of what happens when one lives through the emotional or animal souls, rather than the rational. What appears to be deterministic amorality is not necessarily so. Ptolemy, for example, was insistent that the future could be changed, so his negative reading of Venus as encouraging a venereal disposition can be read as much as a warning to those who fail to lead the Platonic lifestyle, rather than as an excuse for bad behaviour. The way in which the texts were written, though, removed any such sophistication and enabled astrologers to treat their clients as if their futures were absolutely fixed.

The real problem with all predictive systems, when we have left demons to one side, and whether one was an evangelical Christian or a sceptical Platonist, is that the future is completely and profoundly unknowable. When pseudo-Clement and his father were admitted to the public meeting, he actually talked to St Peter. Peter's response was that not even Jesus knew the signs of the end: only God, knows all things. Humanity only knows what is permitted at any given time. Clement argued that Jesus had revealed everything that he considered sufficient for human knowledge and anything else was either irrelevant or would be revealed as and when necessary. This is somewhat reminiscent of the sort of attitude espoused by St Jerome (c.347–420), whose lasting legacy was the translation of the Bible from Greek and Hebrew into Latin. 'Thus must a soul be educated which is to be a temple of God', he wrote, 'it must learn to hear nothing and to say nothing but what belongs to the fear of God'.[11] Plato's theory of knowledge had been reduced to, what to him would have appeared as a shocking reverence for ignorance as a virtue in itself. Nothing could be further from the enlightened Platonism which was still current at the time. As St Paul himself had written, 'Jews demand signs and Greeks seek wisdom, but we preach Christ crucified, a stumbling block to Jews and a folly to Gentiles'.[12] Yet Clement of Alexandria was himself a great scholar. The statement makes sense, though, in the context of Platonic scepticism: absolute knowledge is always impossible. And so we arrive at his compromise with Platonic cosmology. Technical astrology in the form of the calculation and interpretation of horoscopes may have been condemned for its determinism, but the living Platonic cosmos was widely accepted. Clement, for example, was happy to interpret Plato's Myth of Er as suggesting that the soul descends through the 12 signs of the zodiac before birth and then returns through them after death.[13]

That there was an overlap between the old cosmology and the new religion was also evident in the works of one of the most radical of mainstream theologians, Origen (c.185–254), successor to Clement as head of the catechetical school in Alexandria. Origen was a man of independent thought who angered Demetrius, his bishop, when he went to preach in Palestine, even though he was a mere layman. He was promptly recalled to Alexandria, though subsequently invited back to Palestine by the bishops there, who showed their respect for him by ordaining him as a priest. A furious Demetrius sacked Origen from both the school and the priesthood and sent him into exile. Origen promptly settled at Caeasarea, the Palestinian capital and a noted centre of learning, where he preached Christianity within a Neoplatonic cosmology.

Of all the Church Fathers, it was probably Origen who came closest to eroding the boundary Justin had set between Christian orthodoxy and astrology. He was even attacked for apparently supporting astrology, an assertion reported but discounted by Plotinus. Origin also found that the Jewish-Christian meaning of signs, as in the first chapter of Genesis, could be identified with the Platonic view as expressed by Plotinus, a position which can lead to support for an astrology in which the stars are signs rather than causes. The key to understanding the overlap between Origen and Plotinus, in spite of the former's anti-paganism and the latter's contempt for Christianity, is found in their common Platonic education; they shared a teacher in Ammonius Saccas (c.160–c.242), an enigmatic individual who seems to have been born a Christian but may have reverted to paganism and ran his own school of philosophy in Alexandria. Origen developed his argument that the stars are signs or indicators of events, rather than causes, in his commentary on the book of Genesis, dealing with the famous statement on the stars: 'Let them be for signs and for seasons'.[14] He well understood this, writing that 'we must maintain that the stars are not at all the agents of human affairs, but only signs', words which could have been written by Plotinus himself.[15] Origen also understood that wisdom might come from watching the changing seasons and the moving positions of the stars, but such wisdom was divinely inspired rather than derived from logic or empirical observation.[16] Such arguments could easily add to support for astrology but, like Plotinus – and Ptolemy – Origen defined astrology as necessarily based on an assumption that the stars were causes. It is almost as if he saw knowledge gained through 'signs' as somehow of lesser value, for all important things come into being through causes, as when God himself caused the world to come into being.[17] Above all, the cosmos was a sign of God's majesty, infused with his intelligence and being. Against this, Origen found horoscopic astrology just rather unlikely. His was a rational argument, rather than a denunciation of demonic manipulation. For example, he considered the idea that an individual's destiny is found not just in his or her own horoscope, but in those of his brothers and sisters.[18] The stars at their births, astrologers claimed, would reveal their siblings' lives, a claim which Origen just found rather unconvincing. His opposition to astrology, like Clement's, fell directly in the sceptical tradition arising out of the second-century BCE Platonism of the New Academy. Yet, like Cicero and Plotinus, he accepted without question the theory of the intelligent, living universe, inhabited by divine stars and planets. The marriage between Christianity and Platonism, with its own theory of an invisible, perfect world, as Justin and Tatian had found, was an easy one; Platonic doctrines of the ordered, harmonious, mathematically regulated universe provided the Church Fathers with a cosmology which demonstrated that God's creation was, above all good.[19] But this clearly made it difficult to hold the line against Christians who appeared to support, or even practise, astrology. That such individuals existed is suggested by Origen's irritation with those who pointed to Gen. 1.14 – 'Let the lights be for signs' – as a justification for astrology as a whole. Jews who relied on this verse would be unlikely to concern Origen; Christian astrologers would have posed far more of a problem. That he was concerned by a blurring of the lines between pagans and Christians is suggested by his refutation of the pagan philosopher Celsus' claim that worshipping Helios could be a step to worshipping the one true God.[20] Clearly, some people, whether they called themselves pagans or Christians, were doing just this.

In Christian moral cosmology, heaven was in the sky, the area between heaven and earth might be populated by angels, and hell was below, or in the centre of the earth. The visible, material world was populated by good and evil spirits which were constantly vying for human attention. But, like Clement, Origen also discussed the doctrine of the ascent of the soul through the planetary spheres. In each planetary sphere the soul, he believed attains a certain level of mind and understanding, a theory he shared with the *Corpus Hermeticum*. Once the appropriate level has been reached then the soul passes on to the next sphere and so on until it reaches its final abode – heaven.[21] The saints ascend to heaven, he wrote, via the planetary spheres and understand each one as they pass through it. Reincarnation, of course, posed a potential theological difficulty, but not an impossible one. As the keen reader of Plato would have observed, once the soul has begun its upward progress, it will not go down again.[22] It may be that there was some connection between Origen's respect for doctrines of the soul's

ascent through the stars and his contempt for horoscopic astrology; he was the
first critic to mention the dislocation between the zodiac signs, fixed as they
are to the seasons, and the constellations, which shift in relation to the seasons
according to the phenomenon known as precession of the equinoxes. But this
was a minor part of his cosmology. Origen's belief in the divinity of the stars
took Plato beyond the normally acceptable limit, and he had few followers and
many opponents in the emerging church. However, outside the tight constraints
of institutional orthodoxy, the Gnostics went further than Origen dared.

Gnosticism was a complex of religious movements, including Hermeticism
which developed between 100 BCE and 100 CE with roots in pagan, Platonic and
Jewish thought.[23] It also claimed to be based in the conventional mainstream
Christianity, drawing on a few enigmatic references in the writing of St Paul.[24]
Arguing that secret teachings were hidden within the Scriptures, the Gnostics
quoted Jesus from Luke and his rebuke to his audience: 'You hypocrites. You know
how to interpret the appearance of earth and sky; but why do you not know how
to interpret the present time?'[25] They backed this with a further account from
John, which was repeated for effect in Matthew: 'If I have told you earthly things
and you do not believe, how can you believe if I tell you heavenly things', and 'To
you it has been given to know the secrets of the kingdom of heaven, but to them
it has not been given'.[26] There was a cosmic code embedded in the Scriptures
and the Gnostics set out to elaborate it. This was actually a far from controversial
enterprise. Quite aside from Pythagorean numerology, every letter in the Hebrew
alphabet possessed a numerical equivalent which enabled parallel messages to
be read. Even though Christian Gnosticism became an important force in the
second century, until the 1940s most of our knowledge of Gnosticism came from
denunciations by Irenaeus, Tertullian and Hippolytus. In 1947 a remarkable
collection of Gnostic material was discovered at Nag Hammadi in Egypt that
point to the richness of its cosmology.

The essential feature of Gnosticism was that humanity is capable of direct
knowledge of God without the intercession of priests, a belief that naturally
took it into direct conflict with the emerging political hierarchies of the Catholic
Church. This idea, though, is not in itself dangerous. It is one shared with many
Reformation radicals and modern evangelical Christians. However, there were
other critical features of Gnostic dogma which the Catholics found completely
unpalatable, especially its combination of the Platonic and Jewish gods in a single
cosmology with two levels of divinity. At the top was the supreme God, the Platonic
creator, remote, distant and good. Much lower down was the God who created
the earth, with its imperfections, misfortune and evil, the Old Testament Yahweh,
the corrupt, arrogant, ignorant, brutal Yaldabaoth, described often by the Platonic
term 'demiurge'. Yahweh was, the texts tell us, the misconceived son of Sophia,
herself an aeon, or cosmic power, benevolent, but far removed from the supreme
creator. Everything in the world created by Yaldabaoth was rotten, and the only
hope for humanity was to survive through a life of austere asceticism until death
arrived and the soul was released and embarked on its return to the stars.

The most prominent exponent of Gnostic cosmology was Valentinus, who lived at Rome around 136–165 but left the Catholic Church after failing to be elected bishop. Valentinus was an influential figure who wrote the earliest commentary on John's Gospel and may have written the Gnostic *Gospel of Truth*; the Valentinians were the largest Gnostic group and the surviving account of his cosmology was provided by Irenaeus. Beneath the creator, the spiritual world (*pleroma*) contained 30 'aeons' or powers of time, corresponding to the 30 years of Christ's life after baptism, the 30 days of the lunar month and the degrees of one zodiac sign. Eighteen of these aeons corresponded to the 18 months between the resurrection and ascension while the remaining 12 related to Christ's age when he was discovered by the doctors of law in the temple, the apostles, the 12 months of his ministry, the months of the year and the signs of the zodiac. The complete system was based on the understanding that time and space were not only interdependent, but were moral. The *Apocryphon of John* records that, under Yaldaboath, were 12 equally brutal 'authorities', which we can assume are the zodiac signs although no exact correspondences are given and even kings, ruling over the seven heavens – or planetary spheres.[27]

Salvation was possible through Christ, another aeon, who had united himself with the human Jesus in order to bring humanity the saving knowledge (*gnosis*) of his origin and destiny. However, salvation was not open to everyone, at least, not without a struggle. In Valentinus' version, gnosis was only given to the spiritual men or *pneumatics*, who enter it through the pleroma. Other Christians (*psychics*) can attain only the middle realm of the demiurge through faith and works. The rest of humanity is damned. Others were not so pessimistic. The *Teachings of Silvanus*, which were insistent that the world was so full of deceit that nobody could be trusted, still accepted that the penetration of divine mind into humanity, which meant that humanity contained divinity, offered a means of escape.[28]

The Gnostics adopted the notion of *heimarmene*, 'universal fate', from the Stoics, and a certain determinism evident in the belief that salvation may only be available for some people, known as *pneumatikoi* or 'spiritual ones', suggests a use for astrology to determine in advance who might be saved, perhaps in a manner akin to the horoscopes in the Dead Sea Scrolls. The relationship between Gnosticism and astrology is far from straightforward and not necessarily favourable. The cosmogony set out in *The Apocryphon of John*, one of the major Nag Hammadi texts, documents the creation of the zodiac, the planets and the days of the year – the entirety of space and time – as part of the oppressive system created by the demiurge as what is in effect a physical prison for the soul. Any system of astrology is likely, from a Gnostic perspective, to be seen as an elevation of the soul's prison warders to a position they do not deserve. There are echoes here of the prophets' opinion that the planets' apparently erratic movements were evidence of disorder within God's ordered cosmos. The Letter of Jude had spoken of 'wandering stars for whom the nether gloom of darkness has been reserved for ever'.[29]

The obvious problem for the Gnostics was just how salvation should be achieved. Unlike devotees of the *Corpus Hermeticum* or the Mithraic mysteries, there was no chance of ascending through planetary spheres, which were essentially evil. This is where Christ, the light who is like the sun, comes in.[30] At his ascension Christ had risen through the planetary spheres without the evil powers that rules each one noticing, and as he did so, he neutralized them. The *Pistis Sophia* records, Christ's triumph:

> I came into the houses of the spheres shining exceedingly, there being no measure to the light which I had. And all the archons and all those who were in that sphere were agitated together. And they saw the great light which I had. And they looked upon my garment, they saw the mystery of their name within it. And they were increasingly agitated, and they were in great fear, saying: 'How, has the Lord of the All passed through us without our knowing?' And all their bonds were loosened, and their places and their ranks. And each one abandoned his rank.[31]

At a blow, Christ had defeated the evil powers of the planets. There was, then no reason for astrology, not even as an aid to salvation. Whether this myth is responsible for conventional Christian hostility to astrology is not evident in the works of the Church Fathers, although there is at least some indication that Christian anti-Gnostics shared Gnostic cosmology. The evidence is slight, but does exist in for example, an apparent statement from Tertullian that the soul spontaneously knows that God is good and man evil.[32] There may also be a tradition of seven demons, perhaps linked to the planets through their number rather than any precise correspondence, when Matthew speaks of the seven demons who were even more evil then the unclean spirit.[33] That the preceding verses evoke the wisdom of Solomon is suggestive of some connection with the malevolent celestial demons of the *Testament of Solomon*. But, of course, the texts are by no means conclusive.

However, other aspects of Gnostic cosmology did point to a possible support for astrology, especially its use of solar imagery to describe Christ. For example, Basilides, like Clement and Origen, a leading Alexandrian thinker in the second century, argued that Jesus was endowed with a heavenly light to summon the elect, who will ascend to the highest heaven, above the stars. Irenaeus responded, advocating an allegorical reading of Scripture and complaining that the Gnostics were too literal. He preferred to see the sun as a universal metaphor for God's teaching. The problem with this theory is that Christ, as the sun, was responsible for destroying astrology's rationale in the form of the power of the planetary spheres over humanity. True, some Gnostics were astrologers. Irenaeus, refers to one known as Mark as 'an idol-framer ... and portent-gazer, skill'd in the astrologers and wizard's art',[34] suggesting that he made talismans as well as casting horoscopes. We also know from St Augustine that the Manichaeans, of whom he was one as a young man, practised astrology. But Gnosticism's teaching that salvation could only be achieved through Christ was a more effective argument against the casting of horoscopes than the conventional arguments.

The critical difference between the Gnostic's cosmology on one side, and Neoplatonic versions on the other, was the way in which they interpreted Plato's legacy. The Gnostics were, supremely, heirs to Plato's pessimism, which they took to extreme lengths. They extended the corruption of earthly society to the entire visible universe, which they saw as fundamentally rotten. The Neoplatonists took completely the opposite view. They were the children of Plato's optimism, seeing the universe as essentially good. Their logic dictated that, if the physical cosmos had emanated out of the good then it simply must be inherently benevolent. The Gnostics avoided this logic by promoting Plato's God to a region so distant that humans had no realistic chance of direct contact with him. Between humanity and God stood the ignorant, brutal presence of Yaldabaoth. The consequences for life after death were critical. In the Neoplatonic cosmos the soul could travel freely through the planetary spheres, drawn to its natural home in the stars, shedding its earthly baggage on the way. The Gnostic soul, though was faced with planetary spheres ruled by malicious spirits whose task was to imprison and punish the innocent as much as the guilty. For strict Gnosticism the soul's only way to eternal life was somehow to bypass the planetary spheres, to find a path to eternal life which avoided any encounter with the planetary deities. And it was Christ who had shown the way, by ascending to heaven without the planetary spirits noticing, so breaking their power on behalf of all true believers.

Both Catholic and pagan Platonists, such as Plotinus, found Gnostic cosmology offensive on the grounds that it argued that the cosmos was essentially evil, whereas for them it was fundamentally good.[35] There was essentially a triangular debate between three groups, Catholics, Gnostics and pagans, concerning the nature of the cosmos. All were heirs to the Platonic tradition and all could be, to one degree or another hostile to astrology. If we could rank them on a scale then Catholics would be most antagonistic to astrology and pagans least so, but all advocated a cosmology, a living universe which could speak to humanity, which could only be seen as sympathetic to it. Even those Catholic theologians who condemned astrology as demonic therefore unwittingly nurtured it.

The critical moment in the relationship between solar religion and Christianity took place after the Battle of Milvian Bridge at Rome in the year 312, when Constantine defeated his last rival, Maxentius. Having apparently experienced a vision which may have solar or Christian overtones, or perhaps a combination of the two, Constantine chose the latter version and legalized Christianity, adopting it as the state religion. The two religions' adherents were encouraged to assimilate when Constantine proclaimed Sunday to be the Christian day of prayer in 321 and the celebration of Christ's birth was fixed for 25 December. In the heart of Constantinople Constantine installed a statue of himself as Apollo/Helios, with a crown whose radiating spokes were both sun's rays and the nails of the true cross. And, even though, the religious authorities were perturbed by the eagerness with which worshippers at St Peter's in Rome venerated the sun, they encouraged such acts by orienting the building, like most churches, to the east, the rising sun.[36] There is even a famous mosaic, dating from the second century, of Christ represented as the 'Sun of Righteousness' in the style of Helios riding the solar chariot.[37] As for Christmas Day, it was located on 25 December, the feast day of Sol Invictus, in the Calendar of Filocalus, an illuminated manuscript produced in 354 which mentioned both festivals. In the east a different tradition emerged; the birth of Christ was celebrated 12 days later, on 6 January, the Epiphany. As if solar monotheism was not enough, of course, the monotheistic strand in Greek religion, as evidenced in the reverence for Zeus Hypistos – the highest god – was still widespread.[38] Many pagans had to make only a slight adjustment to adapt to the new church. As Christ had prophesied, in the kingdom of heaven 'the righteous will shine like the sun in the kingdom of their Father'.[39] The boundary between metaphor and the literal truth – between Christ symbolized by the sun and Christ personified as the sun, is a fine one to tread and the subtlety is easily lost.

Solar imagery was enthusiastically married with Christian, but this did astrology no good. Saint Basil the Great (c.330–379), a Cappadocian hermit who was brought out of isolation to become bishop of Caesarea and lead the fight against the Arian heresy, also found himself discussing the subtleties of astrology rather than condemning the entire field outright.[40] He accepted the natural astrology derived from Hesiod and Aratus; if the sky is clear a few days after the new moon, he claimed, then good weather can be expected but, if the moon's horns are thick and red (as they would be if the air is hazy), then a storm is on the way. Basil acknowledged the pragmatic use of such astrology to farmers, as well as to sailors for whom it could be a matter of life and death. Astrology might also be divinely sanctioned in that 'the Lord has already foretold that the signs of the dissolution of the universe will appear in the sun, moon and stars': no good Christian could do any other than watch the sky for signs of the End. However, that the general condition of the world is indicated by divine omens or the pressure of the moon on the atmosphere does not suggest that individual destiny is revealed in the horoscope. This, Basil insists, is a ridiculous proposition, mainly on the grounds that the certainty and precision claimed by the astrologers is contradicted by many examples, as well as being inherently implausible. And, for good measure, he condemned Origen's belief in the divinity of the stars.

By Basil's time, Christian ideologues found that their absolutist view of the cosmic state had moved swiftly from the risk of severe persecution to unprecedented imperial favour. Eusebius, who preserved Origen's discussion of astrology in his *Preparation for the Gospel*, set out the foundation of Christian political cosmology, at least in its Byzantine form in his *Tricennalian Oration*, composed in 336. Enthused by Constantine's conversion, he argued that the emperor was now God's representative on earth, the pivotal link between the microcosm and the macrocosm.[41] The implication was that the kingdom of God was already realized and, with it, the prophecies in Revelation of a new heaven and a new earth. In these circumstances, astrology, tied to the old heaven and old earth, was irrelevant. Constantine's new state church was a marriage of Christianity, including its existing borrowings from astral religion, with Sol Invictus, the cult of the celestial king. However, while sun worship had historically always provided a friendly ideological home for astrology, when united with Christianity, the latter's rejection of stellar pluralism prevailed. The sun remained a symbol of divinity, but the planets were relegated to mere instruments of physical causality, embodiments of Pliny's natural history and the pressure on astrology intensified as theological imperatives reinforced the emperor's long-standing dislike of its unregulated practice.

Even though solar religion continued in a Christian guise, when religious devotion combined with political centralization, astrology found itself under assault from wider anti-pagan legislation. At first sight, there is little difference between some of the post-Constantine anti-astrology legislation and that which came before. When Constantius (337–360), in the year 357 outlawed divination and, the following year, threatened any astrologer found in his retinue with torture, whatever their rank, he was emulating the paranoia of his predecessors such as Tiberius, or the prohibitions of the early republic. He also appears to have suffered from a fear of the astrologers' power as much as from a righteous distaste for their beliefs. These and other laws were gathered together on the instructions of the eastern Emperor Theodosius II and issued in 438 in book 9 of the vast legal document known to us as the Theodosian Code.[42] In turn, this became the basis of the legal systems adopted in Ostrogothic Italy, under the great King Theodoric (493–526), as well as in Visigothic Spain, carrying prohibitions on astrology into early-medieval, Catholic Europe. As far as church law is concerned, although a late Arabic version of the decrees of the Council of Nicaea, convened by Constantine in 325, included a prohibition of astrology, it is the only source for that council which does.[43] The first clear condemnation was issued by the Council of Laodicea, called around the year 364 or 367 to update and codify canon law, and astrologers were barred from the priesthood: 'They who are of the priesthood or of the clergy shall not be magicians, enchanters, mathematicians, or astrologers'.[44] A century later, in 447, the Council of Toledo, organized to condemn the Gnostic heresy Priscilianism, declared it anathema to put faith in astrology.[45] And from there the ritual condemnations of astrology continued into the early medieval world, beginning with the Council of Braga, in 561.

When we consider the totality of the Christian world in the late Roman Empire, including the Gnostics, it is clear that there has never been a single Christian line on humanity's relationship with the stars any more than there has ever been a single Christianity. Fourth-century Christianity was marked by the existence of often violently opposed churches, from the Arians who regarded Christ as wholly human to the Gnostics who believed he was completely divine, of which the Catholics, who took a middle line between these two, were to emerge as dominant, thanks to their alliance with the Roman state. The great ideologue of the Catholic faith, its Lenin to St Paul's Marx, was St Augustine of Hippo, born Aurelianus Augustinus in the year 354. In his two great works, *Confessions*, written

around 397, and *City of God*, composed in 410, St Augustine established himself
as the foremost theologian of the medieval church. Augustine was essentially
faced with a serious problem of political cosmology: Rome had become Christian
yet, no sooner had it become so than it became the victim of divine retribution
in the form of barbarian invasion. All the Roman emperors since Constantine,
except Julian, had been Christian and yet, in the late fourth century, the empire
was in a state of almost perpetual crisis due to civil war between rival generals
and the pressure of the Germanic tribes. An emperor like Theodosius the Great
(379–395) might temporarily restore confidence in the Roman imperium but,
in 410, catastrophe struck with the sack of Rome, the eternal city itself, by the
Visigoths. If the *Confessions* was a proclamation that all humanity was wracked
by sin and that the only salvation was through God, the *City of God* was a political
treatise announcing that, if all authority lay with God, then the Roman emperors
were his instrument on earth. The empire was no longer the great beast of
Revelation, but the earthly manifestation of the kingdom of God.[46] This formula
was to be the foundation of political thought in the medieval world.[47] He gave
the church a firmly conservative identity as the ally rather than opponent of the
political order which was to be the basis of church–state relations through to
the early modern period – at least up to the upheavals of the Reformation. Such
was the urgency of the situation, though, that all other sources of power apart
from God and the emperor had to be stamped out. That included rival Christian
churches, including Arians and Gnostics, as well as pagan ideologies. The notion
that humanity might look to the stars for information about the future was
particularly dangerous and, although Augustine devoted only a small part of his
work to the denunciation of astrology, he was to have a major impact on attitudes
to both astrology and astronomy for the next 1,200 years.

The son of a pagan father and Catholic mother, Augustine had a good classical
education though, perhaps unique amongst classical philosophers, he failed to
learn Greek, which he disliked intensely, to any more than a rudimentary level.
He is remarkably frank about his dislike of Greek literature, even of Homer. At
the age of 19 he became a Christian, joining the Manichaeans, a Gnostic sect
which had adopted the Zoroastrian Persian cosmology in which the structure
and history of the universe was based on the perpetual struggle between light
(good) and darkness (evil).[48] As he later wrote: 'The Manichean books are full
of the most tedious fictions about the sky and the stars, the sun and the moon.'[49]
And, if this were not enough, their astronomical calculations were inaccurate!
To the Manichaeans Christ, rather than the Persian deity Ahura-Mazda, was the
representative of light. Augustine studied hard and clearly gained considerable
recognition for his philosophical work – he was appointed professor of rhetoric
at Milan. At the age of 28 he converted to Catholicism and, at the same time,
immersed himself in Socrates, Plato and the neo-Platonic philosophers, Plotinus
and Porphyry. He was baptized in 387 and in 391 he was ordained a priest in
Hippo, near Carthage in what is now Tunisia. He was appointed bishop of Hippo
on 395 and spent the rest of his life there.

Although Augustine personally challenged such elements of Neoplatonic cosmology as the divinity of the stars, lest anyone still support Clement and Origen, such was his authority that he established an unambiguously favourable attitude to Platonic cosmology within later medieval Christian culture. It seemed to him that Socrates' monotheism and reverence for intellectual purity and a virtuous life marked him out as a sort of proto-Christian.[50] As Plato followed and developed Socrates' worthy example, and argued that the world had been created by God, so both he and his followers as a whole were given the same sort of honorary Christian status as were the Jewish patriarchs, and he argued that only the Platonists were worthy of theological debate with Christians.[51] The difference between Socrates, Plato and other pagans was one of ethics; the philosophers believed in a virtuous lifestyle, combining right living with rational thought, whereas ordinary pagan worship was utterly amoral and bestial, with its ecstatic rites and, at extremes, self-mutilation.

Augustine had studied astrology during his time as a Manichaean and found that he had no theological objection to it because astrologers neither offered sacrifices nor prayed to spirits for assistance in their divination. However, his conversion to Catholicism resulted in a substantial change of heart. He now regarded God as the only supreme power in the universe, with direct authority over all creatures.[52] Astrology, which held that divine authority might be channelled via the stars, introduced what he considered to be a dangerous and democratic element which had to be stamped out. He was concerned both to crush pagan astrology and to head off the rise of a Christian astrology, which he clearly saw as a potential threat. His assault was two-pronged, relying on faith as a devout Christian, and reason, like a good philosopher. First he argued, as it had been traditional to do since Justin Martyr, that astrology was quite simply incompatible with Christianity and, second, like the more intelligent of the Church Fathers, he pointed out flaws in its logic.

In the *Confessions*, Augustine's personal renunciation of his previous sinful life, he claimed that to argue that God's authority could be exercised via the stars (a defence which was presumably current amongst Christian astrologers) caused theological offence, for it both limited God's power to intervene directly in human affairs and implicated him in the stars less admirable decisions.[53] It also absolved human beings from responsibility for their own actions and, ironically, pushed that guilt on to God who must, presumably, have instructed the stars to cause men to sin. In his view, then, astrology made God responsible for sin. This was, as it happens, a standard Gnostic position.

Augustine's problem with the Manichaeans was that they came too close to worshipping the sun and the moon, in other words, worshipping the creation rather than the creator,[54] a criticism of astrology which is repeated in evangelical Christian literature to this day. Theological arguments are unassailable. You either accept them or you do not but you cannot defeat them with logical or evidence. However, having allied astrology with a religious group – the Manichaeans – Augustine then set out to demolish it with reason, a risky enterprise. He widened his attack in the *City of God*, borrowing directly from Cicero by dealing at length with the issue of twins and how two babies born at the same time could have different lives.[55] He also tackled the problem of the apparent contradiction between the astrally determined fate inherent in an astrology of individual births on the one hand, with the assumption of free will inherent in the astrological election of auspicious moments – the practice of *katarche* – to begin new enterprises, on the other. In other words, astrology was damned if it denied free will and damned if it did not. Augustine was judge, jury and executioner. He also disingenuously questioned whether astrology applied to worms or trees, asking whether they could really all have their 'moments of nativity' and challenged the belief that the rise of the Roman Empire had been astrologically determined, rather than a consequence of God's favour. Even so, in book V, he had also sought allies amongst the pagans, appealing to them on the grounds that, if astrologers ascribed power over human affairs to the stars, they were challenging the authority of pagan deities as well as the Christian God. This argument, it has to be said, was unlikely to convince anyone, but no doubt he thought it worth a go. Augustine's attempts to use reason as a weapon against astrology were essentially weak: astrology already had replies for them. Besides, it was much too complex to be vulnerable to his caricature. There was no more a single astrology in the fourth century than there was a single Christianity, but Augustine had to pretend there was, otherwise there would be nothing to attack. He was on much stronger ground when he argued on the basis of his undeniably profound faith in the one true Catholic God; faith is irrefutable.

He did, though, deal with the competing philosophical problem faced by astrologers, addressing issues already raised by Clement and Origen. Were celestial phenomena signs, as the Babylonians believed, or causes, as Aristotelian cosmology suggested? It is clear from his argument that the insistence on an astrology of signs was still very strong and that this was being used by Christian apologists for astrology as a way of deflecting the criticism that if the stars were causes this detracted from God's authority. He decided that the astrologers themselves were being disingenuous when they made this argument. 'Now this is not the way the astrologers normally talk', he wrote, 'they would not say, for example, "This position of Mars signifies murder"; they say "it causes murder"'.[56]

In book VII he went on to ridicule the flawed logic behind the naming and meaning of the stellar divinities, pointing out contradictory claims, some mythical, some naturalistic and noting all the inconsistencies. Sometimes, he said, the morning star was allocated to the goddess Venus, at others to Juno.[57] It is clear that his knowledge of astrology was not great, in spite of his background, and his experience was far more with an astrology of an overtly religious, planet-worshipping nature, than one based in the Hellenistic texts.

Even though Augustine regarded the reasoning behind astrology as profoundly flawed he had no doubt that it worked, although he changed his mind on how. In the *Confessions* he argued that it appeared to work because of chance. Thus an astrological forecast appeared to be right in the same way as a volume of poetry might fall open at a page which was meaningful at that moment. In the *City of God*, he followed the familiar line established by Tatian, claiming that evil spirits fed correct predictions to astrologers.[58] In other words, if he had not convinced the supporters of astrology by reason, he may as well try and put the fear of God into them. Whichever reason was responsible for astrology's accuracy, to work as an astrologer was to practise deception.

Augustine's attack on astrology should be seen as an attempt to de-spiritualize the universe at the same time as he constructed a new moral cosmology. His respect for Plato did not allow him to retain the notion of the universe as a living creature. Instead, some parts of the world were no longer alive, and were distinguished from those which were.[59] The 'life-world', the concept of the human and the cosmic, the physical and psychic, as one living entity, which had provided the rationale for humanity's intimate connection with the stars, was severely disrupted, and humanity's alienation from nature was heightened, if not initiated.[60] Augustine's criticism of secular, liberal education[61] and advocacy of Scripture as the ultimate source of truth also left little room for classical astronomy, leaving the Genesis creation story as the basis of Catholic cosmology. Certainly he did praise Thales for his prediction of the eclipse of 585 BCE,[62] and he was as aware as anyone of the need to calculate the date of Easter correctly, a complicated astronomical procedure. He could, though, be reluctant to accord the physical study of the heavens any importance at all, pointing out that it is a waste of time to study astronomy since the stars are of no use in the quest for salvation.[63] Augustine's philosophy is clearly dominated by a combination of Scripture and Neoplatonism, which, between them, taught that all truth is based on faith and abstract reason rather than the false gods of evidence or observation. While his separation of astrology from astronomy was, therefore, of great significance, the effect of his teaching was to retard the development of astronomy in the Christian world until the seventeenth century.

Nor was Augustine's advocacy of human free will, which was so necessary for salvation, particularly convincing, contradicted as it was by his insistence that God must know the future, implying that human actions were predetermined. He was desperate to demolish the Stoics' belief in fate, for this was their unshakeable ideological justification for astrology. He argued that while God rules everything, human will is not in the order of causes and that God controls all powers but not all wills.[64] Augustine's dilemma was of his own making. He denied the pluralist universe of the astrologers in which the individual might negotiate with a series of cosmic powers, insisted that there was only one political authority in the universe with absolute power over past, present and future, and yet asserted that individuals could still decide their own futures. The result, of course, aside from the rationale he provided for the later emergence of Christian churches, like sixteenth-century Calvinism, which openly espoused predestination, was that the individual exercise of conscience and religion was circumscribed by the Christian emperor's absolute right to implement God's will. In this sense

Augustine's attack on astrology was the counterpart of his propaganda effort on behalf of a new political and religious absolutism. In the service of political order, he had engineered a cosmological *coup d'état*.

But, even Augustine could never challenge the belief that there was a link between life on earth and the stars. After all, Basil had noted the sense in weather lore. The sun's relation to the seasons, and the moon's to the tides were undeniable. But were they astrology? Augustine thought not, but reluctantly conceded that not just solar and lunar, but stellar, including planetary influences, had to be acknowledged:

> Now it could be maintained, without utter absurdity, that some influences from the stars have an effect on variations confined to the physical realm. We observe that the variation of the seasons depends on the approach and withdrawal of the sun, and the waxing and waning of the moon produces growth and diminution in certain species, such as sea-urchins and shell-fish, and also the marvellous variation of the tides.[65]

For Ptolemy the moon's effect on the tides was the fundamental rationale for a full-blown astrology of human character and destiny. Augustine himself, though, could not see the connection. In his view there was no way that one could logically move from the natural observation that there was a celestial correspondence with the seasons to the conclusion that human choice is subject to the disposition of the stars. His concession to natural astrology, or Cicero's divination from nature was, in terms of the fourth century, a statement of the obvious, for the reality of seasonal influences was not open to question. Even his concession that the stars might influence the body, though, was to prove a Trojan horse for astrology within the Christian world. If, for example, the moon was to be taken into account in medical treatment, then why should horoscopes not be cast?

Embedded in the midst of Augustine's vast work, and unnoticed in the wealth of material from the early Church Fathers condemning astrology, this single passage was to be one of the momentous for medieval astrology as well as astronomy, as we have seen. The theological objections to astrology can be reduced to two. The first was supernatural – demonic intervention. The second was deterministic – the argument that, no matter whether stars were signs or causes, astrology regarded the future as fixed and therefore denied God's power. However, if one were to combine a Ptolemaic, naturalistic hypothesis, rejecting the need for demonic involvement, with Plotinian indetermism, and accept that astrological forecasts are limited and do not restrict the future, astrology once again becomes legitimate. And this, resting in Augustine, is precisely what was to take place in the Middle Ages.

Augustine's acknowledgement of natural celestial influence was not to be Christianity's only concession to the astrological worldview. The church's compromise with pagan cosmology was also encouraged by fudges over the sacred calendar. Even though the theologians might protest, the boundaries between astrology and the prevailing culture were fluid. At the head of the church there was an attempt to appropriate and disguise popular veneration for the sun by celebrating Christ's birth on 25 December, the solstice and festival of the birth of Sol Invictus, the 'sun of righteousness'. We do not know when this happened but it was the practice in Rome by 336 CE, 24 years after Constantine legalized Christianity. That the emperor had already, in 321, ordered that Sunday, which everyone knew was sacred to the sun, should be a public holiday, suggests that the location of Christmas at the solstice had imperial approval. The new state Christianity was keenly absorbing the salvational doctrines of Near Eastern solar religion. Rather than trying to suppress solar worship, Constantine deliberately identified it with Christianity and so won approval for his emerging state church. Astrologers themselves saw which way the wind was blowing and set out to accommodate the new order. In 367 the bishop of Alexandria, Athanasius, after whom the creed is named, complained that astrologers were giving the stars saints' names.[66] A quarter of a century later, John Chrysostom, bishop of Constantinople, denounced Catholics who rejected the resurrection, 'adhere to superstitious observances ... omens and auguries', and 'fortify themselves with the horoscope'.[67]

It is also clear that astrologers throughout the classical period were using Gen. 1.14, 'Let the lights be for signs', as a justification for an astrology of signs, otherwise Basil and Origen would not have condemned what they saw as a clear abuse of Scripture.[68] Were these astrologers Christians or pagans making a mischievous use of the Bible? The truth is that prominent religious propagandists may frequently not be representative of the majority of their congregations. It may therefore be false to imagine that the Christian position on astrology, if there ever was such a thing, was embodied in the rhetoric of the Church Fathers. Out there in the real world, the majority of Christians would have been involved in any number of ideological, spiritual and lifestyle compromises with the Roman world.[69] This is hardly a controversial point of view. It is the core complaint of those many reformers who have railed against the Roman Church and those evangelicals who still regard the use of the sun's day and the festival of Sol Invictus as sacred Christian days as objectionable.[70]

The continuity between paganism and Christianity was facilitated not only by the preservation of Platonic cosmology by influential theologians, but by the blurring of boundaries amongst ordinary Christians.[71] The equation of any prominent deity with the sun was impossible to resist; some contemporaries looked to the Old Testament prophet Malachi, who prophesied the rising of the 'sun of righteousness' and identified it with Christ.[72]

While so many of the Church Fathers took a strict line on astrology, it is clear that, once Constantine had lifted the prohibitions on Christianity, many theologians began to take a more liberal line. One response to condemnations of astrology, though, was not to reject it but to Christianize it. This is the goal that Valentinian and Origen were delicately moving towards. The earliest known text conforms to the church's standard policy of making Christianity acceptable to pagans by appropriating their cosmology. The evidence appears in a sermon by

Bishop Zeno of Verona, who died in 380.[73] Zeno attempted to show the user and practitioners of astrology in his congregation not that their beliefs were wrong, just misplaced. Once born again in Christ they would, in effect be born again into a new set of zodiac signs, though with the old symbolism depaganized but intact. In the new system, Aries and Taurus represented Christ as sacrificial victim (lamb and calf, respectively), Gemini, the dual sign symbolized the two Testaments, Old and New, Cancer was vice, but Leo was the lion of Judah and Virgo, as the Virgin, brought forth Libra, Christ as bringer of justice.

The fourth-century Priscillianists, an ascetic movement originating in Spain and who appeared to have Manichaean, and possibly Gnostic, characteristics, identified the 12 signs with the 12 apostles. Priscillian himself was bishop of Avila, though this was insufficient to protect him against first exile and, in 386, execution on a charge of sorcery. Priscillianism was condemned at the Council of Toledo in 400, but survived until the Council of Braga in 563, when the guardians of orthodoxy had to condemn it again. The Nestorians, followers of Nestorius, who was briefly bishop of Constantinople before being deposed by the Emperor Theodosius II in 431, had no problem with astrology. Their preservation of it was even a factor in its survival after Justinian closed the Platonic Academy in Athens in 529 and Catholic orthodoxy suffocated astrology in the Greek world. Both Priscillian and Nestorius fell foul of the Catholic authorities, yet the movements they founded survived, in the case of Nestorianism, down to the present day in Iraq. The point is that the condemnation of astrology represented only the position of a small group of theologians who were involved in a perpetual power struggle for the control of official doctrine. After 312 they were backed by the emperors, for whom theological centralism was seen as essential to the effort to retain control of a disintegrating empire. Yet Christianity has always contained not just tensions between different theologies in senior levels of true hierarchy, but between official views of doctrine and vernacular religion, the practices and beliefs of the congregation. Lester Ness considers the position at Edessa, where the Nestorians had a major school (the patriarchal see was in Ctesiphon, on the Tigris, in what was then the Persian Empire). He argues that popular religion in Edessa was marked by 'pagan-mindedness' in which 'many Edessans went to church, but also practised magic, divination, and astrology'.[74] Although Edessa was formally Christian the nearby city of Harran remained firmly pagan, the last temple surviving until the eleventh century.[75] Even under Islamic domination it retained its planetary temples and use of the *Corpus Hermeticum* as a sacred text as an alternative to the Bible or Koran.

It is questionable whether merely legal sanction had a serious effect on the practice of astrology. When, in 409, as recorded in the Theodosian code, Theodosius II and his western counterpart, Honorius, required all astrologers to burn their books in the presence of a bishop or face exile, was any more notice taken than under the republic? It seems likely that inter-Christian rivalries were so bitter that they took precedence over the persecution of pagans. The Arians, who denied Christ's divinity, were strong well into the fourth century. Though, they suffered a powerful blow when the pro-Arian Emperor Valens was killed at the Battle of Adrianople on 378, the Goths and Lombards were both converted by Arian missionaries, and they remained a force until the eighth century. In the west, there is strong evidence that pagan sympathies remained strong in the Roman senate until the early fifth century and we know of two rebel emperors in the east who employed astrology to select the appropriate moments for their coronations – Basiliscus in 475 and Leontius in 484.[76] Clearly, as far as some of the most influential individuals in the empire were concerned, prohibitions on astrology were a matter of supreme irrelevance. The horoscopes for these two moments, though, are especially interesting for another reason. Both were so dire within the rules of Hellenistic astrology that they indicated certain failure, and any astrologer caught sabotaging his patron's chances on such a scale would certainly have faced appalling punishment.[77] On the other hand, the pre-dawn sky on both dates was especially auspicious, chiefly because, in each case, Venus was at its brightest. This is somewhat suggestive of a direct continuation of a visual, Babylonian astrology parallel with the horoscopic tradition. Ishtar was powerful, the astrologers would have reasoned, and the time, presumably supported by the appropriate rituals, for revolt had arrived – especially as the incumbent emperor, Zeno, was a Christian. We do not need to assume a survival of the *Enuma Anu Enlil* at this point, only that the sky and the appearance of the stars was the primary focus for astrological reasoning, rather than mathematical tables and horoscopes.

The most likely cause of the decline of astrology as the classical world drew to its close was less legal sanction than a shift in the nature of the prevailing world-myth as more people joined the new order. The Christian cosmos was as packed with invisible beings – angels and demons – as the pagan, but there were two major differences. First, authority was highly centralized in the one true God and his son, Jesus Christ, leaving the saints as mere agents of their power, rather than authorities in themselves. The stars and planets themselves also found their autonomy diminished as they ceased to have an effective role in salvation. The path to heaven was now purely metaphysical – direct through Christ – and the physical ascent through the stars was no longer literal. It was not even, as some readings of Plato allow, figurative. It was irrelevant. One view of this shift sees it as a liberation in which humanity was freed from the chains of fate and able, at last, to take a real, free moral stand. True, Christian morality, if correctly applied, was impressive. Yet we can equally argue that the decline of pluralism in the cosmos and the focusing of every prospect for salvation on Christ, inhibited human freedom. Ironically Tertullian was an exponent of this argument. 'They [astrologers]', Tertullian wrote, 'say that God is not to be feared; therefore all things are in their view free and unchecked'.[78] Such arguments are ultimately a matter of personal taste. But it is clear that astrology virtually disappeared in Western Europe because of the collapse in literacy, especially knowledge of Greek, as Germanic culture, with its rural rather than urban focus, combined with war and invasion, gradually undermined Roman culture from Britain to north

Africa, taking in France, Italy and Spain, through the fifth and sixth centuries. The disappearance of Roman culture was most extreme in the north – in Britain – and far more gradual around the Mediterranean, but even in Italy the ravages of looting armies extracted a huge cost. The incoming German tribes had their lunar months, lucky days, star lore and constellation stories, but horoscopic astrology, with its literary base and mathematical complexities, was not part of their culture.[79] They may have shared some of their cosmology with the classical world. In some Teutonic stories fate was spun by three Norns, suspiciously like the three Fates, and the universe turned on a spindle, of which the North Star was the spindle and Orion's belt the distaff. In parts of the West, cosmology returned to a state which would have been familiar to the megalith builders, even to the Palaeolithic lunar calendar makers.

In the eastern empire, whose cultural sphere, by the early sixth century had expanded to include Italy and eastern Spain, as well as north Africa, the situation is far less clear. Astrology undoubtedly lost its political clout and access to the highest levels of society. But there does seem to have been a literary continuity which was to connect with Persia to the east, and carry over into the lowering of Islamic culture in the eighth century. And we should not forget the Jews, whose intellectual culture preserved Neoplatonic ideas unobstructed by evangelical Christians' emotional obsession with salvation through Christ alone, let alone their chronic fear of demons. There is evidence, as yet unpublished, that Jews in southern Italy continued to innovate, devising new forms of technical astrology perhaps, and here we are on uncertain ground, contributing to the wider development of ideas of the ascent of the soul which appeared in medieval Kabbalah.

Christianity from its very origins incorporated elements of Platonic cosmology. It is not that Christianity began to compromise with pagan worldviews as it sought to win converts and move away from strict Jewish tradition. It did not have to, for the concept of such a tradition is itself a fiction. Judaism existed in a variety of forms, some of which had already been Hellenized, or had adapted Babylonian astrology. Thus the concept of an original pure Christianity which, in spite of the failings of many of its members, always maintained a doctrinal heart which was fundamentally opposed to pagan cosmology is fundamentally false. Platonism was the fifth column which smuggled into Christianity a geometrically ordered, mathematically meaningful, divinely animated cosmos in which astral influences and sympathies were taken for granted.[80] What the Church Fathers found unacceptable was judicial astrology, the casting of horoscopes, and in this sense they were the heirs of Platonic scepticism, of Carneades and Cicero, as much as of Old Testament denunciations of astrology. But did the new church banish the old magic or merely appropriate it. The radical point of view was put by Ronald Hutton who concluded in an interview in 2003: 'They [Christian priests] are there to produce magic, to go through the rituals which are needed to keep the community in a state of grace and harmony with the universe … The old gods and goddesses are swept away and the trinity and the saints are put in their place ... As far as we can tell people's relationship with religion didn't change a jot between paganism and Christianity.'[81] One set of myth-tellers had outmanoeuvred another but the magic remained. But in the new orthodoxy, the Sun, now revered as Christ, could no longer share power with the planets.

Afterword: Decline and Survival

> The Inexhaustible Power (of God) … keeps the immortal loves of
> the angels inviolate; and the luminous stars of heaven It keeps in
> all their ranks unchanged, and gives unto Eternity the power to
> be; and the temporal orbits It differentiates when they begin their
> circuits and brings together again when they return once more.[1]

By the fifth century CE, astrology had fractured into competing narratives and truth claims, which were often contradictory. Differences of opinion ranged from the extent to which the stars revealed the precise details of human life, or merely its general prospects, the need to evoke celestial divinities, and whether one's focus was on the trivia of daily life or the prospect of eternal salvation or the minutiae of technical prediction. There were two traditions; one, the elite, which tended to be literary, and the other, popular, which was mainly practice-based. But both went into a steep decline in Christian Europe from the fifth century onwards, under the combined pressure of theological intolerance and, in the western reaches of the former Roman Empire, the decline of literacy, particularly knowledge of Greek. But, amongst the elite, even though astrology fell out of favour, its philosophical context and cosmological rationale survived largely thanks to two men. One, ironically, was St Augustine, who conceded that planetary influences were real, even if he was bitterly opposed to the casting of horoscopes, which he thought was demonic. The other was a Neoplatonic Christian author in the late fifth century who wrote under the name Dionysius the Areopagite, and whose writings preserved the notion of a divine, perfectly ordered, meaningful cosmos, complete with its musical ratios, mathematical harmonies, planetary spheres and angelic orders. Adopting the name – and prestige – of one of St Paul's famous converts, Dionysius' cosmology, was to have a huge influence on later Christian thought.[2]

The Platonic Academy in Athens itself was never actually officially closed, but, in 529, the Emperor Justinian issued an edict denying pagan teachers stipends from the imperial treasury and ordering them to accept baptism at the risk of exile and confiscation of their property.[3] When he followed this financial measure with a letter forbidding the teaching of law and philosophy at Athens, the philosophers had no choice but to leave and the Academy, the last classical powerhouse of pagan cosmology, closed by default. Justinian acted not just because he was devout or because, like Constantine, he believed there should be just the one religion to serve the one empire, but very probably because the Academy was enjoying something of a revival under its energetic leader Damascius.[4] But, having begun the job, he had to complete it. Like a zealot, he then validated and reinforced all existing anti-pagan legislation, barring pagans from public service, forbidding heterodox children from inheriting property from orthodox parents and ordering the death penalty not just for pagans caught secretly practising, or Christians who lapsed, but even Christians who failed to break completely with paganism. Justinian was not opposed to teaching of the classics *per se*. Nobody with civilized pretensions could be. But he insisted that it be done by Christians who would put the right gloss on such debates as the eternity or perishability of the cosmos. His main concern, like the early emperors, was order, and he had no more time for those who failed to toe the official Catholic line than for pagans. Pagan teaching actually continued at Alexandria until late in the century, well after Justinian was dead, but the philosophers there learnt to keep a low profile and avoid antagonizing their Christian colleagues.

The Neoplatonic writers had a huge impact on Christian theology. In spite of their rivalry (for intellectuals, Neoplatonism offered an attractive alternative to Christian theology) and occasional angry exchanges (Porphyry launched a savage criticism of Christianity) the Platonic path to God was seen as deeply compatible with the Christian emphasis on salvation through faith. Besides, Plato had provided an entire rational cosmology which was absent in the Scriptures and which, for an educated Christian, compensated for the Bible's failure to deal with the mechanism and structure of the cosmos. Proclus' writings, were reworked, Christianized and promulgated by Dionysius the Areopagite, while one of the leading students of Ammonius, himself a student of Proclus, was the Monophysite Christian, John Philoponos. For many, quite simply, Platonism provided such a convincing bridge between paganism and Christianity that one's religious persuasion was of rather less significance than one's philosophical allegiance. And, wherever Platonism went, there one was likely to find astrology. One of the last notable Greek astrological tracts, *On Signs*, was composed around 550 by John of Lydia in Constantinople, where he had attended lectures by Proclus' student Agapius.

Safely Christianized, Plato's thought never completely died out in the eastern, Byzantine, empire, and was reintroduction to the Latin West 200 years later when Dionysius' work was translated into Latin by John Scotus Erigena (*c.*810–*c.*877), the great Irish scholar who worked at the Carolingian court. At Byzantium itself, Platonism received a new lease of life when it was revived by Psellus in the eleventh century, from where it was re-exported to Italy in the 1460s, providing one of the major catalysts for the Renaissance.

Yet, as Christianity smothered pagan pluralism in the Roman world, astrology was flourishing in Persia and the East. Possible traces of Babylonian or Persian astrology have been found in China and, by the eighth century, Hellenistic and Indian astrology, including the 12 zodiac signs and the meanings of the planets, had arrived in Japan, merging with indigenous practices.[5] But our main focus must be India, which witnessed a renewed flowering of civilization in the Gupta civilization. In the fourth and fifth centuries CE, Gupta astronomers knew, like the Greeks, the circumference of the earth. But their understanding of the cosmos also included knowledge of the heliocentric solar system, which the Greeks, under pressure from Plato and Aristotle, had discarded, and an understanding that the cosmos is unimaginably huge.[6] They had also imported Hellenistic horoscopic astrology, the story of which is set out in the *Yavanajataka* of Sphujidhvaja, the earliest major work of Indian horoscopic astrology, dating in its original form from 149–150 CE, though in its current version is from the next century – 269/70 CE. The provenance of this form of astrology is set out in the closing verses.

> Previously Yavanesvara (the lord of the Greeks), whose vision of the truth came by favor of the Sun and whose language is flawless, translated this ocean of words, this jewel-mine of horoscopy, which was guarded by its being written in his tongue (i.e., Greek), but the truth of which was seen by the foremost of kings (in the year) 71; (he translated) this science of genethlialogy for the instruction of the world by means of excellent words.[7]

The *Yavanajataka*'s indebtedness to the Greeks is not in doubt, and the testimony for this is itself Indian. *Yavanas* is Sanskrit for 'of the Greeks', while *Svara* is 'lord'. *Yavanesvara* would therefore seem to have been a Greek-speaking (I hesitate to use the word Greek, for he may have been an Egyptian or Syrian, or an educated member of any part of the Hellenistic world) astrologer, living in India. *Yavanajataka*, meanwhile translates as 'sayings of the Greeks'. The Indians appear to have welcomed the arrival of Greek texts such as the *Romaka Siddhanta* ('Doctrine of the Romans') and *Paulisa Siddhanta* ('Doctrine of Paul'), based on the works of the fourth-century astrologer Paul of Alexandria. The literary canon was extended by Minaraja, who composed his *Vrddhayanajataka* ('Great Greek astrology) around a hundred years after the *Yavanajataka*.[8] The greatest of all, though was Varāhamihira, whose dates, in spite of his fame, are uncertain; he may have lived any time between around 350 and 550 CE. More even than Sphujidhvaja, his comprehensive writings established the canonical form of Indian astrology to the present day. He wrote on the interpretation of birth charts, arrangements of marriages, planning of battles and divination of omens, as well as the astronomical and mathematical systems necessary to the work of the astrologer.[9]

The issue of Greek influence on Indian astrology is one of huge political significance for modern protagonists, wrapped up as they are either in notions of the West's inherent superiority or the assertion of the East's greater antiquity. Ramakrishna Bhat, in his introduction to his translation of Varāhamira's sixth-century compendium, the *Brhat Samhita*, has this to say:

> The bogey of Greek influence is laid to rest by the strong arguments of Swami Vivekānanda. He says: 'There may be, it is true. Some similarity between the Greek and Indian terms in astronomy and so forth, but the westerners have ignored the direct

Sanskrit etymology and sought for some far-fetched etymology from the Greek. That such shallow and biased learning has been manifested by many orientalists in the West is deplorable'.[10]

The orientalist position in the history of philosophy and science has been quite clear in its attribution of the origin of all Western knowledge of any value to the Greeks, so the Indians do have good cause for complaint. The dominant, orientalist, view is, though, being gradually demolished within the West by specialists in other cultures – Egyptologists, Sinologists, Indologists and cuneiform scholars. Yet, difficulties remain. The etymological arguments mentioned by Bhat, and on which varying claims depend, have yet to be resolved and there are considerable uncertainties. It may be demonstrated that the *Yavanajataka* contains direct transmission from the *Tetrabiblos*, but it is completely plausible, though impossible to demonstrate, that Hellenistic astrology benefited from imports from India in its formative years in the fourth to first centuries BCE. And, if we are seeking plausibility for connections between India and Greece, rather than direct evidence, then we have it in the form of the Persian emperors' gathering of scholars from all over their realm in the sixth century BCE, the syncretizing tendencies of Hellenistic culture, embracing as it did, the entire region from northern India to the western Mediterranean, and the evidence of parallels between Platonic and Buddhist thought.[11] The arguments about whether Greek or Indian astrology is older can therefore only be understood in a modern context in which to be Greek or Indian are categories shaped by 2000 years' worth of religious separation and three centuries of imperialism. These are not distinctions which would have made sense to the scholars of 2000 years ago, at least not in the sense that we understand them.

The final resolution to the argument, though, is that medieval Western astrology itself owes a huge debt to India. When, from the eighth century onwards, the Islamic world became the hub of a new Renaissance, its scholars drew on resources from the Hellenistic world, Persia and India. And it was this new synthesis which was, in the twelfth century, to be adopted with enthusiasm by the kings, bishops and intellectuals of Catholic Europe. The myth-tellers did not die out, but their cosmos was fragmented, their role uncertain. Some advocated a complex form of astrology. Others denied it. Multiple narratives had emerged, some of which bitterly denied each other's relevance. Yet, from their ancestors, the calendar-makers and shamans of the Stone Age, they carried the concept that the stars speak to humanity into the early modern world.

Notes

Notes to Introduction

1   Bruno Latour, *We Have Never Been Modern* (Cambridge, Mass. Harvard University Press, 2006 [1991]), p. 107.
2   Roger Beck, *The Religion of the Mithras Cult in the Roman Empire: Mysteries of the Unconquered Sun* (Oxford: Oxford University Press, 2006), esp. ch. 8; Edgar Laird, 'Christine de Pizan and Controversy Concerning Star Study in the Court of Charles V', *Culture and Cosmos* 1(2) (Winter–Autumn 1997): 35–48.

Notes to Chapter 1: Distant Echoes: Origins of Astrology

1   Jane Goodale, *Tiwi Wives: A Study of the Women of Melville Island* (Seattle and London: University of Washington Press, 1971), p. 146; see Chris Knight, *Blood Relations: Menstruation and the Origins of Culture* (New Haven and London: Yale University Press, 1991), p. 358.
2   I have taken the phrase 'sacred canopy' from Peter Berger, *The Sacred Canopy: Elements of a Sociological Theory of Religion* (New York: Anchor Books, 1969).
3   Edward Burnett Tylor, *Primitive Culture* (3 vols; New York: Harper Torchbooks, 1958 [London: Murray 1871]).
4   J.G. Frazer, *The Golden Bough: A Study in Magic and Religion* (London: Macmillan, abridged edn; 1971 [1922]).
5   Nicholas Campion, 'Prophecy, Cosmology and the New Age Movement: The Extent and Nature of Contemporary Belief in Astrology' (PhD thesis, University of the West of England, 2004), ch. 3; Charles Dupuis, *Mémoire sur l'origine des constellations, et sur l'explication de la fable* (Paris: Veuve Desaint, 1781); Charles Dupuis, *Was Christ a Person or the Sun? An Argument from Dupuis to Show that Christianity has its Origins in Sun Worship* (London: Holyoake and Co., 1857); Max Müller, *Introduction to the Science of Religion* (London: Longmans, Green and Co., 1873); Max Müller, 'Solar Myths', *The Nineteenth Century* (December 1885), pp. 900–22.
6   Tylor, *Primitive Culture*, vol. 1, pp. 378–90.
7   See Steven Mithen, *The Prehistory of the Mind: A Search for the Origins of Art, Religion and Science* (London: Orion, 1998).
8   Alexander Marshak, *The Roots of Civilisation* (Mt Kisco, N.Y. and London: Moyer Bell Ltd., 1991), p. 6.
9   A. Pannekoek, *A History of Astronomy* (London: George Allen and Unwin Ltd., 1961), pp. 19–20.

10   Barry Cunliffe, *Wessex to AD 1000* (New York and Harlow: Addison Wesley Longman, 1993), pp. 69, 110.

11   Claude Lévi-Bruhl, *How Natives Think* (Princeton: Princeton University Press 1985), esp. pp. 76–104.

12   Sean Kane, *Wisdom of the Mythtellers* (Peterborough, Ontario: Broadview Press 1997), esp. ch. 1.

13   David Abram, *The Spell of the Sensuous* (New York: Vintage, 1997), pp. 40–44.

14   Bartel van der Waerden, *Science Awakening*, vol. 2: *The Birth of Astronomy* (Leyden and New York: Oxford University Press, 1974), p. 3. See also the discussion in Nicholas Campion, 'The Inspiration of Astronomical Phenomena', in Nicholas Campion, (ed.), *The Inspiration of Astronomical Phenomena* (Proceedings of the Fourth Conference on the Inspiration of Astronomical Phenomena, sponsored by the Vatican Observatory and the Steward Observatory, Arizona, Magdalen College, Oxford, 3–9 August 2003; Bristol: Cinnabar Books, 2005), pp. xxviii–xxxix.

15   Ernst Cassirer, *The Philosophy of Symbolic Forms*, vol. 2: *Mythical Thought* (New Haven and London: Yale University Press, 1971 [1955]), p. 94.

16   Jacquetta Hawkes, *Man and the Sun* (London: Cresset Press, 1962), pp. 47–48.

17   R.G. Bednarik, 'Paleoart and Archaeological Myths', *Cambridge Archaeological Journal* 2(1) (1992): 27–57; Hugh Cairns, 'Aboriginal Sky-Mapping? Possible Astronomical Interpretation of Australian Aboriginal Ethnographic and Archaeological Material', in Clive Ruggles (ed.), *Archaeoastronomy in the 1990s* (Loughborough: Group D Publications, 1993), pp. 136–54 (143).

18   The work on lunar counters, inspired by Gerald Hawkins' theories about Stonehenge, was done by Alexander Marshak and published first in 'Lunar Notation on Upper Palaeolithic Remains', *Science* 146 (1964): 743–45. See also Marshak, *The Roots of Civilisation*. Marshak's theories have rarely been challenged though they are largely ignored by archaeologists. There are a few dissenting voices outside archaeology. For example, John Barrow prefers to see the notches, with no evidence, as a 'record of the hunter's skills' (see *Pi in the Sky: Counting, Thinking and Being* [London: Penguin Books, 1993], p. 31). For the difficulties in interpreting Palaeolithic art see the discussion in Bednarik, 'Paleoart and Archaeological Myths'.

19   Cairns, 'Aboriginal Sky-Mapping?', p. 143.

20   Marshak, 'Lunar Notation on Upper Palaeolithic Remains', p. 743.

21   See Richard Rudgley, *Lost Civilisations of the Stone Age* (London: Random House, 1998), pp. 156, 206–07; and Marshak, *The Roots of Civilisation*, pp. 333–36.

22   Knight, *Blood Relations*, p. 327, citing Karl Marx, *Grundrisse* (1857–59).

23   Goodale, *Tiwi Wives*, p. 146; cited in Knight, *Blood Relations*, p. 358.

24   M. Rappenglueck, 'The Pleiades in the "Salle des Taureaux" Grotte de Lascaux. Does a Rock Picture in the Cave of Lascaux Show the Open Star Cluster of the Pleiades at the Magdalenien Era (ca 15,300 BC)?', in C. Jaschek and F. Atrio Barandela, *Proceedings of the IVth SEAC Meeting 'Astronomy and Culture'* (Salamanca, Universidad de Salamanca 1997); Antequera Corregado Luz, 'Altamira: Astronomia y Religion en el Paleolitico', in Juan Antonio Belmonte Aviles (ed.), *Arqueoastronomia Hispanica* (Madrid, Spain: Equipa Sirius SS, 1994); Frank Edge, 'Taurus in Lascaux', *Griffith Observer* 61(9) (September 1997): 13–17. The Lascaux example is convincing, but we should be wary of liberal interpretations of visual evidence; Willy Hartner's argument that Mesopotamian seals as early as the fourth millennium showed images of Taurus and Leo are now regarded as too selective (see Willy Hartner, 'The Earliest History of the Constellations in the Near East and the Motif of the

Lion-Bull Combat', *Journal of Near Eastern Studies* 24(1–2) (January– April 1965): 1–16. For the context of cave art see David Lewis-Williams, *The Mind in the Cave* (London: Thames and Hudson, 2005).

25 See James L. Pearson, *Shamanism and the Ancient Mind: A Cognitive Approach to Archaeology* (Oxford: Altamira Press 2002).

26 As summarized in E.C. Krupp, *Beyond the Blue Horizon: Myths and Legends of the Sun, Moon and Stars and Planets* (New York and Oxford: Oxford University Press 1991), pp. 242–49.

27 R.D. Haynes, 'Astronomy and the Dreaming: The Astronomy of the Aboriginal Australians', in Helaine Selin (ed.), *Astronomy Across Cultures: The History of Non-Western Astronomy* (Dordrecht: Kluwer Academic Publishers 2000), pp. 53–90 (77–79); see also R.D. Haynes, 'Dreaming the Stars. Astronomy of the Australian Aborigines', *Interdisciplinary Science Review* 20(3) (1995): 187–97. For a broader context see Josephine Flood, *Archaeology of the Dreamtime: The Story of Prehistoric Australia and its People* (New Haven: Yale University Press, 1990).

28 B.A. Frolov, 'On Astronomy in the Stone Age', *Current Anthropology* 22(5) (October 1981): 585.

29 'Scientists Turn the Clock forward on Aboriginal Life', *The Times* (28 May 1998): 3.

30 Hugh Cairns, 'Discoveries in Aboriginal Sky-Mapping (Australia)', in John W. Fountain and Rolf M. Sinclair (eds), *Current Studies in Archaeoastronomy: Conversations Across Time and Space* (Durham, N.C.: Carolina Academic Press, 2005), pp. 523–38 (537).

31 For cognitive psychology see Steven Pinker, *How the Mind Works* (New York: W.W. Norton, 1997), and for an exposition of the theory of myth as the carrier of universal truth, see various of C.G. Jung's *Collected Works*, such as vol. 8, *The Structure and Dynamics of the Psyche* (trans. R.F.C. Hull; Princeton, NJ: Princeton, 1960), pp. 139–58.

32 William B. Gibbon, 'Asiatic Parallels in North American Star Lore: Ursa Major', *Journal of American Folklore* 77 (1964): 236–50; Owen Gingerich, 'The Origin of the Zodiac', in *The Great Copernicus Chase and Other Adventures in Astronomical History*, (Cambridge, Mass.: Sky Publishing Corporation and Cambridge University Press, 1992), pp. 7–12 (10). Also see Krupp, *Beyond the Blue Horizon*, esp. p. 239 and Joseph Campbell, *Historical Atlas of World Mythology*, vol. 1: *The Way of the Animal Powers*, part 2: *Mythologies of the Great Hunt* (New York: Harper & Row, 1988).

33 Roslyn M. Frank, 'Hunting the European Sky Bears: When Bears Ruled the Earth and Guarded the Gate of Heaven', in Vesselina Koleva and Dmiter Kolev (eds), *Astronomical Traditions in Past Cultures* (Proceedings of the First Annual General Meeting of the European Society for Astronomy in Culture, Smolyan, Bulgaria, 31 August–2 September 1992; Sofia: Institute of Astronomy, Bulgarian Academy of Sciences and National Astronomical Observatory, Rozhen), pp. 116–42; Roslyn M. Frank, 'Hunting the European Sky Bears: Hercules Meets Harzkume', in César Esteban and Juan Antonio Belmonte (eds), *Astronomy and Cultural Diversity: Proceedings of the 1999 Oxford VI Conference on Archaeoastronomy and Astronomy in Culture* (Tenerife: Oranismo Autonomo de Museos del Cablido de Tenerife, 2000), pp. 169–75; Frank M. Roslyn, 'Hunting the European Sky Beers: A Proto-European Vision Quest to the End of the Earth', in Fountain and Sinclair (eds), *Current Studies in Archaeoastronomy*, pp. 455–74.

34 Charles G. Leland, *The Algonquin Legends Of New England Or Myths And Folklore Of The Micmac, Passmaquoddy, And Penobscot Tribes* (Boston: Houghton, Mifflin and Co., 1884).

35 <http://www.clarkfoundation.org/astro-utah/vondel/songofstars.html> (accessed 20 March 2007).

36   Elizabeth Chesley Baity, 'Archaeoastronomy and Ethnoastronomy So Far', *Current Anthropology* 14(4) (October 1973): 389–449 (404, 410); James Mellaart, *Catal Huyuk: A Neolithic Town in Anatolia* (New York: McGraw-Hill, 1967).

37   Frolov, 'On Astronomy in the Stone Age'.

38   E.C. Krupp, 'Night Gallery: The Function, Origin and Evolution of Constellations', *Archaeoastronomy: The Journal of Astronomy in Culture* 15 (2000): 43–63.

39   *Ibid.*

40   Franz Cumont, *Astrology Among the Greeks and Romans* (New York: Dover Publications 1960 [1911]), p. 5. Respect for the priests was a feature of the early twentieth century. Dreyer concurred that the priests had sole control of the construction of the calendar and the 'worship of the moon and stars' (J.L.E. Dreyer, *A History of the Planetary Systems from Thales to Kepler* [New York: Dover Publications, 1953 (1906)], p. 1).

Notes to Chapter 2: Prehistory: Myths and Megaliths

1   Jacquetta Hawkes, 'God in the Machine', *Antiquity* 41 (1967): 174–80 (174).

2   Nikolai Bochkarev, 'Ancient Armenian Astroarchaeological Monuments: Personal Impressions of Metsamor and Carahunge'; available at <http://haldjas.folklore.ee/SEAC/ SEAC_teesid2.htm> (accessed 20 March 2007).

3   But for good, recent studies see, for example, Mary Blomberg, Peter E. Blomberg and Göran Henriksson, *Calendars, Symbols, and Orientations: Legacies of Astronomy in Culture* (Proceedings of the 9th Annual Meeting of the European Society for Astronomy in Culture [SEAC], The Old Observatory, Stockholm, 27–30 August 2001; Uppsala Astronomical Observatory Report, 59; Stockholm: SEAC, 2003); Vesselina Koleva and Dmiter Kolev (eds), *Astronomical Traditions in Past Cultures* (Proceedings of the 1st Annual General Meeting of the European Society for Astronomy in Culture, Smolyan, Bulgaria, 31 August–2 September 1992; Sofia: Institute of Astronomy, Bulgarian Academy of Sciences and National Astronomical Observatory, Rozhen, 1996); Clive Ruggles, with Frank Prendergast and Tom Ray, *Astronomy, Cosmology and Landscape* (Proceedings of the SEAC 98 Meeting, Dublin, Ireland, September 1998; Bognor Regis: Ocarina Books, 2001).

4   Tom Parfitt, 'Bronze Age Pyramid found in Ukraine', *The Guardian* (8 September 2006): 21.

5   See, for example, Alan Dundes (ed.), *The Flood Myth* (Berkeley, Los Angeles and London: University of California Press, 1988).

6   F. Pryor, *Seahenge: New Discoveries in Prehistoric Britain* (London: HarperCollins 2001). See also Mark Brennand, 'This is Why we dug Seahenge', *British Archaeology*, 78 (September 2004); available at <http://www.britarch.ac.uk/BA/ba78/feat5.shtml> (accessed 20 March 2007).

7   M. Edmonds, *Ancestral Geographies of the Neolithic: Landscape, Monuments and Memory* (London: Routledge, 2002), pp. 5–6.

8   Jude Currivan, 'Walking between Worlds – Cosmology Embodied in the Landscape of Neolithic and Early Bronze Age Britain' (PhD Thesis, University of Reading, 2003).

9   Sean Kane, *Wisdom of the Mythtellers* (Peterborough, Ontario: Broadview Press, 1997), p. 21.

10   J. Barnatt and M. Edmonds, 'Places Apart: Caves and Monuments in Neolithic and Earlier Bronze Age Britain', *Cambridge Archaeological Journal* 12(1) (2002): 113–29 (125); P. Davies and J.G. Robb, 'Scratches in the Earth: The Underworld as a Theme in British Prehistory

with Particular References to the Neolithic and Earlier Bronze Age', *Landscape Research* 29(2) (2004): 141–57; Caroline Malone, *Avebury* (London: Batsford/English Heritage, 1989), p. 76.

11 Edmonds, *Ancestral Geographies*, p. 83.

12 See the discussion in *ibid.*, p. 65.

13 *Ibid.*, pp. 62–63.

14 See Mircea Eliade, *The Sacred and the Profane* (New York: Harcourt Brace, 1959), including comments on, for example, pp. 10–11, 28, 117, 165, 202.

15 For the car-park post-holes and the best survey of the history and development of both Stonehenge and megalithic astronomy in the British Isles, see Clive Ruggles, *Astronomy in Prehistoric Britain and Ireland* (New Haven and London: Yale University Press, 1999).

16 J. McKim Mallville, Fred Wendorf, A.A. Mazaar and Romauld Schild, 'Megaliths and Neolithic Astronomy in Southern Egypt', *Nature* 392 (1998): 488–91.

17 *Ibid.*; see also the discussion in Lawrence H. Robbins, 'Astronomy and Prehistory', in Helaine Selin (ed.), *Astronomy Across Cultures: The History of Non-Western Astronomy* (Dordrecht: Kluwer Academic Publishers, 2000), pp. 31–52 (43–44); and Richard H. Wilkinson, *The Complete Temples of Ancient Egypt* (London: Thames and Hudson, 2000), pp. 16–17. See Béatrix Midant-Reynes, *The Prehistory of Egypt* (Oxford: Blackwell, 2000), for the prehistoric and climatic context.

18 Wilkinson, *The Complete Temples of Ancient Egypt*, p. 16.

19 Ronald A. Wells, 'Astronomy in Egypt', in Christopher Walker (ed.), *Astronomy Before The Telescope* (London: British Museum Press, 1996), pp. 28–41 (29).

20 For the Egyptian calendar see R.A. Parker, 'Egyptian Astronomy, Astrology and Calendrical Reckoning', in Charles Coulston (ed.), *Dictionary of Scientific Biography* (New York: Charles Scribner's and Sons, 1971), vol. 4, pp. 706–27 (706–07); see also R.A. Parker, *The Calendars of Ancient Egypt* (Oriental Institute of Chicago Studies in Ancient Oriental Civilisation, 26; Chicago: University of Chicago Press 1950), chs 1, 3.

21 Malville, *et al.*, 'Megaliths and Neolithic Astronomy', p. 490. See also A. Rosalie David, *The Ancient Egyptians: Religious Beliefs and Practices* (London: Routledge and Kegan Paul Ltd., 1982), p. 26, for speculation that an occupying people may have introduced the cosmic deities to the Nile Valley.

22 Frank Ventura, 'Evaluating the Evidence for Interest in Astronomy in the Temple Period of Malta (3600–2500 BCE)' (paper delivered at the second conference on the Inspiration of Astronomical Phenomena [INSAP II], Malta, January 1999); John Cox, 'The Orientations of Prehistoric Temples in Malta and Gozo', *Archaeoastronomy* 16 (2001): 24–37.

23 For the broad cultural sweep see Aubrey Burl, 'Pi in the Sky', in D.C. Heggie (ed.), *Archaeoastronomy in the Old World* (Cambridge: Cambridge University Press, 1982), pp. 141–68 (145); for the current chronology of construction at Stonehenge, see Ruggles, *Astronomy in Prehistoric Britain and Ireland*; and for earlier chronologies see R.J.C. Atkinson, *Stonehenge* (London: Hamish Hamilton, 1956), pp. 107–10. See also Euan MacKie, *Science and Society in Prehistoric Britain* (London: Paul and Elek, 1977), pp. 118, 126.

24 Diodorus Siculus, *Library of History* V.23. Although there is no proof that Diodorus was talking about Stonehenge, in the absence of other suitable candidates, it is widely accepted by most writers since William Stukeley (*Stonehenge: A Temple Restor'd to the British Druids* [London, 1740], p. 40) that he was. In fact in 1971 this assumption received the imprimatur of R.S. Newall's official guidebook, published by Her Majesty's Stationery Office.

25 The politics of the study of megalithic culture since the 1960s constitute an entire study all of their own, and it is impossible to understand any of the texts outside of this context. The fundamental divide is between astronomers who discern astronomical alignments in astronomical sites often with little regard for the archaeological evidence on the one hand, and archaeologists who reject such claims on the other, sometimes on the basis of the evidence but often because they clash with their, even now, entrenched beliefs that Neolithic people were too backward to measure even the simplest of astronomical patterns. This conflict has been well summarized by Clive Ruggles, who compares it to C.P Snow's famous 'two-cultures' thesis, in which the sciences and arts are in a state of permanent conflict (see Ruggles, *Astronomy in Prehistoric Britain and Ireland*, p. 6). The debate is further complicated by the intervention of neo-druids, New Agers, anarchists and advocates of ancient lost civilizations. For an analysis of Stonehenge, the most famous megalithic site, as a 'contested landscape' from the third millennium onwards down to the sometimes violent clashes which took place in the 1970s and 1980s, see Barbara Bender (ed.), *Landscape: Politics and Perspectives* (Oxford and New York: Berg Publishers, 1993); and Barbara Bender, *Stonehenge: Making Space* (Oxford and New York: Berg Publishers, 1998). For an introduction to the many cultural claims made upon Stonehenge since the seventeenth century see Christopher Chippendale, *Stonehenge Complete* (London: Thames and Hudson, rev. edn, 1994).

26 Stukeley, *Stonehenge*; Norman Lockyer, *Stonehenge and British Stone Monuments Astronomically Considered* (London: Macmillan, 1906).

27 Atkinson, *Stonehenge*, p. 181. The statement was repeated, as a trap for the unwary, in the 1979 edition.

28 Euan MacKie, 'Maes Howe and the Winter Solstice: Ceremonial Aspects of the Orkney Grooved Ware Culture', *Antiquity* 71 (1997): 338–59.

29 Barry Cunliffe, *Wessex to AD 1000* (New York and Harlow: Addison Wesley Longman, 1993), p. 111.

30 Caroline Courtauld, *In Search of Burma* (London: Frederick Muller, 1984), p. 55.

31 Aubrey Burl, *Great Stone Circles* (New Haven and London: Yale University Press, 1999), p. 121.

32 J.D. Scourse, 'Transport of the Stonehenge Bluestones: Testing the Glacial Hypothesis', in Barry Cunliffe and Colin Renfrew, *Science and Stonehenge* (Oxford: Oxford University Press, 1997), pp. 271–314.

33 An effort spread over several centuries of activity (see Chippendale, *Stonehenge Complete*, p. 210; and MacKie, *Science and Society in Prehistoric Britain*, p. 136). Of course, Stonehenge was not the only site on which work was required. According to Caroline Malone, writing for English Heritage, the construction of Silbury Hill sometime after Stonehenge I required perhaps three million man-hours, or 700 men working for 10 years while the ditch at Avebury may have required 156,000 man-hours, or three years' work for 100 men (Malone, *Avebury*, pp. 99, 116); also see MacKie, *Science and Society in Prehistoric Britain*, pp. 138, 141). Actually such estimates have an enormous margin of error. Malone reports other estimates varying from 650,000 to 1,540,000 man-hours for the excavation of the Avebury ditch and the erection of the sarsen stones together (Malone, *Avebury*, p. 111). The complex at Carnac in Brittany, which Alexander Thom argues was used to observe the moon, consisted of two rows of 1,600 stones extending for 1.6 miles. The largest stone nearby, which Alexander Thom argued was a lunar sightline (although others disagree), weighs 340 tons and would have stood 60ft tall (Alexander Thom and Archibald Stevenson Thom, 'Rings and Menhirs: Geometry and Astronomy in the Neolithic

Age', in E.C. Krupp (ed.), *In Search of Ancient Astronomies* (London: Penguin, 1984), pp. 39–76 (69).

34 Gerald Hawkins, *Stonehenge Decoded* (New York, Dorset Press, 1965); see also Gerald Hawkins, *Beyond Stonehenge* (New York, San Francisco and London: Harper & Row, 1973). See also discussion in Krupp (ed.), *In Search of Ancient Astronomies*, pp. 98–99; David Souden, *Stonehenge* (London: Collins and Brown, 1998), p. 126; Chippendale, *Stonehenge Complete*, p. 23; Ruggles, *Astronomy in Prehistoric Britain and Ireland*, pp. 3, 11, 205; Jacquetta Hawkes, *Man and the Sun* (London: Cresset Press, 1962), pp. 179–80.

35 Alexander Thom, *Megalithic Sites in Britain* (Oxford: Oxford University Press, 1967).

36 Fred Hoyle, 'Speculations on Stonehenge', *Antiquity* 40 (1966): 262–76; and Fred Hoyle, *From Stonehenge to Modern Cosmology* (San Francisco: W.H. Freeman and Co., 1972).

37 For the discussion of contested landscapes see Bender, *Landscape and Stonehenge*.

38 Most of the extensive discussion of the Nebra disc is on the web, and is either not in print or not yet accessible. But for one discussion of its significance, see Euan MacKie, 'New Evidence for a Professional Priesthood in the European Early Bronze Age?', in Todd W. Bostwick and Bryan Bates (eds), *Viewing the Sky Through Past and Present Cultures: Selected Papers from the Oxford VII International Conference on Archaeoastronomy* (Pueblo Grande Museum Anthropological Papers, 15; Phoenix: Pueblo Grande Museum, 2006).

39 Michael Hoskin, *Tombs, Temples and their Orientations: A New Perspective on Mediterranean History* (Bognor Regis: Ocarina Books, 2001).

40 Clive Ruggles, *Records in Stone: Papers in Memory of Alexander Thom* (Cambridge: Cambridge University Press, 1988), p. 25.

41 Cunliffe, *Wessex to AD 1000*, p. 111.

42 Aubrey Burl, *Prehistoric Astronomy and Ritual* (Prince Risborough: Shire Publications, 1997), p. 49; see also Aubrey Burl, 'Science or Symbolism: Problems of Archaeoastronomy', *Antiquity* 54 (1980): 191–200 (191).

43 Currivan, 'Walking between Worlds'.

44 See James Frazer, *The Golden Bough: A Study in Magic and Religion* (London: Macmillan, abridged edn, 1971 [1922]).

45 Burl, 'Pi in the Sky'.

46 Burl, 'Science or Symbolism'.

47 Aubrey Burl, ' "Without Sharp North": Alexander Thom and the Great Stone Circles of Cumbria', in Ruggles, *Records in Stone*, pp. 175–205 (202).

48 Stuart Piggott, *Ancient Britons and the Antiquarian Imagination* (London: Thames and Hudson, 1989), p. 118; Alex Gibson and Derek Simpson (eds), *Prehistoric Ritual and Religion* (Stroud: Sutton Publishing Ltd., 1998), p. 99.

49 MacKie, *Science and Society in Prehistoric Britain*, p. 226; Euan MacKie, 'Investigating the Prehistoric Solar Calendar', in Ruggles, *Records in Stone*, pp. 206–31 (230).

50 Clive Ruggles, 'Cosmology, Calendars and Society in Neolithic Orkney: A Rejoinder to Euan MacKie', *Antiquity*, 74 (2000): 62–74.

51 Burl, 'Pi in the Sky', p. 154.

52 Aubrey Burl, *Avebury* (New Haven and London; Yale University Press, 1979), p. 217.

53 Chippendale, *Stonehenge Complete*, p. 257.

54 Ruggles, *Astronomy in Prehistoric Britain and Ireland*, p. 155.

55 *Ibid.*, p. 155.

56 Clive Ruggles, 'Astronomy and Stonehenge', in Cunliffe and Renfrew (eds) *Science and Stonehenge*, pp. 203–29 (204).

57   Krupp, (ed.) *In Search of Ancient Astronomies*; for the alternative point of view, that around
      2000 BCE there was little sign of international trade, see Geoffrey Wainwright, *The Henge
      Monuments: Ceremony and Society in Prehistoric Britain* (London: Thames and Hudson,
      1989), p. 10.
58   Peter Beresford Ellis, 'Early Irish Astrology: An Historical Argument', available at <http://
      cura.free.fr/xv/11ellis1.html> (accessed 4 July 2007). See also Peter Beresford Ellis, *The
      Druids* (London: Constable, 1994).
59   Tony Paterson, 'Mysterious Gold Cones "Hats of Ancient Wizards"', *Sunday Telegraph* (17
      March 2002).
60   Garrett Olmsted, *The Gaulish Calendar* (Bonn: Dr Rudolf Habelt GmBh, 1992), pp. 90–131.
61   See the discussion in Stephen C. McCluskey, *Astronomies and Cultures in Early Medieval
      Europe* (Cambridge: Cambridge University Press, 1998), pp. 54–60.
62   Barry Cunliffe, *The Celtic World* (New York: Random House, 1988), p. 110: the calendar's
      nature is 'purely Celtic', and 'wholly Celtic in concept' (see also Cunliffe, *Wessex to AD 1000*,
      pp. 69, 110).
63   Ellis, *The Druids*, p. 237, citing Heinrich Zimmer, *Altindisches Leben: Die Cultur Vedischen
      Arier nach den Samhitach* (Berlin, 1879).
64   See Miranda Green, *The World of the Druids* (London: Thames and Hudson, 1997), p. 50:
      'Their astronomical observations would have been essential in making the calendrical
      calculations which were needed to establish the most auspicious dates to perform special
      rituals and ceremonies'; and p. 89: 'It is probable that the Coligny calendar was a Druidical
      device designed to help them in plotting predictions perhaps based upon astronomical
      observations'.
65   Cunliffe, *Wessex to AD 1000*, pp. 69, 110.
66   See Roy Rappaport, *Ritual and Religion in the Making of Humanity* (Cambridge: Cambridge
      University Press, 1999); and Robert Wallis, *Shamans/Neo-Shamans* (London: Routledge, 2003).
67   See the summary in Green, *The World of the Druids*, p. 11; and fuller discussions in Nora K.
      Chadwick, *The Druids* (Cardiff: University of Wales Press, 1966); and Ellis, *The Druids*.
68   Homer, *Iliad* 18.565–571.
69   See Chadwick, *The Druids*.
70   Julius Caesar, *The Conquest of Gaul* 1.1.
71   From the title of Jacobsen's description of the Mesopotamian cosmos (Thorkild Jacobsen,
      'The Cosmos as a State', in H. Frankfort, H.A. Frankfort, William A. Irwin, Thorkild
      Jacobsen and John A. Wilson, *The Intellectual Adventure of Ancient Man: An Essay on
      Speculative Thought in the Ancient Near East* (Chicago and London: Chicago University
      Press, 1946), pp. 125–84.

Notes to Chapter 3: The Mesopotamian Cosmos: The Marriage of Heaven and Earth

1   Dumuzi's prayer to Utu, the Sun God, *From the Great Above the Great Below* (in Samuel
     Noah Kramer and Diane Wolkstein, *Inanna, Queen of Heaven and Earth: Her Stories and
     Hymns from Sumer* [New York: Harper and Row, 1983], p. 72). The prayer probably dates
     to the third millennium BCE.
2   Sara L. Gardner, 'Scratching the Surface of Astronomy in the Land of the Bible: Archaeology,
     Texts, and Astronomy', in John W. Fountain and Rolf M. Sinclair (eds), *Current Studies in
     Archaeoastronomy: Conversations Across Time and Space* (Durham N.C.: Carolina Academic
     Press, 2005), pp. 393–411.

3   For Mesopotamian temples see Günter von Martiny, 'Zur Astronomischen Orientation Altmesopotamischer Tempel', *Architectura* 1 (1933): 41–45.

4   See W.G. Lambert 'Babylonian Astrological Omens and Their Stars', *Journal of the American Oriental Society* 107(1) (January–March 1987): 93–96.

5   *From the Great Above the Great Below* (see also the discussion in Kramer and Wolkstein, *Inanna, Queen of Heaven and Earth*, pp. xvi–xvii, 156–57).

6   For the following discussion see Thorkild Jacobsen, *The Treasures of Darkness: A History of Mesopotamian Religion* (New Haven and London: Yale University Press, 1976).

7   Alexander Heidel, *The Babylonian Genesis* (Chicago: University of Chicago Press, 1963); see also the recent translation in Benjamin Foster, *Before The Muses: An Anthology Of Akkadian Literature* (Bethesda, Md.: CDL Press, 2005).

8   Bartel van der Waerden, *Science Awakening*, vol. 2: *The Birth of Astronomy* (Leyden and New York: Oxford University Press, 1974), ch. 5.

9   Simo Parpola, 'The Asyrian Tree of Life: Tracing the Origins of Jewish Monotheism and Greek Philosophy', *Journal of Near Eastern Studies* 52(3) (July 1993): 161–208 (204); Jack N. Lawson, *The Concept of Fate in Ancient Mesopotamia: Of the First Millennium, Towards an Understanding of 'Simtu'* (Wiesbaden: Harrasowitz Verlag, 1994), p. 69.

10 For divine monarchy see Ivan Engnell, *Studies in Divine Kingship in the Ancient Near East* (Oxford: Blackwell, 1967); and Henri Frankfort, *Kingship and the Gods: A Study of Near Eastern Religion as the Integration of Society and Nature* (Chicago: Chicago University Press, 1978 [1948]).

11 Francesca Rochberg, *The Heavenly Writing: Divination and Horoscopy, and Astronomy in Mesopotamian Culture* (Cambridge: Cambridge University Press, 2004), p. 127.

12 Wayne Horowitz, *Mesopotamian Cosmic Geography* (Winina Lake: Eisenbrauns, 1998), p. 4. For accounts of Mesopotamian cosmology see W.G. Lambert, 'The Cosmology of Sumer and Babylon', in Carmen Blacker and Michael Loewe, *Ancient Cosmologies* (London: George Allen and Unwin Ltd., 1975), pp. 42–65; and Jacobsen, *The Treasures of Darkness*. See also Samuel Noah Kramer, *Sumerian Mythology: A Study of Spiritual and Literary Achievement in the Third Millennioum* BC (Philadephia: University of Pennsylvania Press, 1972 [1944]).

13 Samuel Noah Kramer, *The Sumerians, their History, Culture and Character* (Chicago and London: University of Chicago Press, 1963), pp. 122–23.

14 See Horowitz, *Mesopotamian Cosmic Geography*.

15 The effect of the sun's passage through the three paths was the division of the year into four seasons (*Mul Apin* Gap A 1–7 [in Hermann Hunger and David Pingree, *Mul Apin: An Astronomical Compendium in Cuneiform* (Archiv für Orientforschung, 24; Ferdinand Berger & Sohne: Horn, 1989), pp. 88–89]); Hermann Hunger and David Pingree, *Astral Sciences in Mesopotamia* (Leiden, Boston and Koln: Brill, 1999), p. 61; Ulla Koch-Westenholz, *Mesopotamian Astrology: An Introduction to Babylonian and Assyrian Celestial Divination* (Carsten Niebuhr Institute of Near Eastern Studies; Copenhagen: Museum Tusculunum Press, University of Copenhagen, 1995), pp. 24–25. The lists of the 36 stars which are divided between the three ways are preserved in three copies known to Assyriologists as 'astrolabes' but to the ancient scribes themselves as the 'three stars each', the earliest of which, the Assyrian 'Berlin' Astrolabe B, dates from the reign of the Assyrian Emperor Tiglath-Pileser I, around 1100 BCE (see Van der Waerden, *Science Awakening*, vol. 2, pp. 74–75). An alternative list of three sets of stars relating the heavens to the earth were grouped under Elam (the east, the way of Ea), Akkad itself (the way of Enlil), and Amurru

(the west, the way of Anu), suggesting that the system could be applied to geopolitical forecasting. If the astrologer knew which stars were emphasized by a particular planetary movement, he would know which country would experience the consequences (see the discussion in Francesca Rochberg-Halton, *Aspects of Babylonian Celestial Divination: The Lunar Tablets of Enuma Anu Enlil* [Archiv für Orientforschung, 22; Ferdinand Berger & Sohne: Horn, 1988], pp. 53–55). The sky then constituted both a guide to possible political events and action, and a vast mirror in which earthly possibilities were reflected in heavenly polarities.

16   *Enuma Elish* V.1–10 (in Heidel, *The Babylonian Genesis*); Horowitz, *Mesopotamian Cosmic Geography*, p. 115.

17   Jacobsen, *The Treasures of Darkness*, p. 131.

18   As one Assyrian astrologer reported of the moon: 'We kept watch on the 13th day; [we did not see the moon] and sun, there were clouds'; see Hermann Hunger, *Astrological Reports to Assyrian Kings* (Helsinki: Helsinki University Press, 1992), p. 82 (report 135).

19   A. Leo Oppenheim, *Ancient Mesopotamia: Portrait of a Dead Civilisation* (Chicago: University of Chicago Press, 1977), p. 204.

20   The argument was proposed by Thorkild Jacobsen, 'Primitive Democracy in Ancient Mesopotamia', *Journal of Near Eastern Studies* 2 (1943): 159–72. See also the discussion in Frankfort, *Kingship and the Gods*, pp. 221, 231–48; Oppenheim, *Ancient Mesopotamia*; the criticism in Stephanie Dalley (ed.), *The Legacy of Mesopotamia* (Oxford: Clarendon Press, 1998), p. 3; and the caution against sweeping generalizations in Francesca Rochberg-Halton, 'Elements of the Babylonian Contribution to Hellenistic Astrology', *Journal of the American Oriental Society* 108(1) (January–March 1988): 51–62 (52).

21   'The Mesopotamian king was not at one with the gods, inspired by their will, executing their counsels in his own divine decisions. He could maintain the natural harmony only by watching over the service of the gods and attuning the life of the community to such portents as were vouchsafed him as revelations of divine will' (Frankfort, *Kingship and the Gods*, p. 309); see also Engnell, *Studies in Divine Kingship*.

22   Jacobsen, *The Treasures of Darkness*, pp. 126–27; Kramer, *The Sumerians*, p. 123.

23   For a trenchant presentation of this theory see Theodor Adorno, *The Stars Down to Earth* (London: Routledge, 1994 [1953]).

24   For an authoritative account of the Mesopotamian calendar, though not its possible Palaeolithic origins, see Mark E. Cohen, *The Cultic Calendars of the Ancient Near East* (Bethesda, Md. CDL Press, 1993).

25   *Enuma Elish* V.12–24. It is unclear why Heidel translated the moon as feminine when all other authorities agree it was masculine; see E.A. Speiser, 'The Creation Epic', in J.B. Pritchard (ed.), *Ancient Near Eastern Texts Relating to the Old Testament* (Princeton: Princeton University Press, 1969), pp. 60–72.

26   Simo Parpola, *Letters from Assyrian Scholars to the Kings Esarhaddon and Assurbanipal*, part 1: *Texts* (Kevelaer: Verlag Butzon & Bercker and Neukirchen-Vluyn: Neukirchener Verlag, 1970), p. LXXIV; John van Seters, *In Search of History: Historiography in the Ancient World and the Origins of Biblical History* (New Haven and London: Yale University Press, 1983), pp. 96–97.

27   *Hamlet* I.v.211.

28   Seneca, *Naturales Quaestiones* III.xxvii.4.

29   Kramer, *The Sumerians*, p. 140.

30   Piotr Michalowski (ed.), *The Lamentation Over the Destruction of Sumer and Ur* (Winona Lake: Eisenbrauns, 1989), pp. 37–39 (lines 1–3, 5, 19, 30, 63).

31 Hunger, *Astrological Reports to Assyrian Kings*, pp. 52–53.

32 For the discussion of Mesopotamian astrology as scientific see Mogens Trolle Larsen, 'The Mesopotamian Lukewarm Mind: Reflections on Science, Divination and Literacy', in Francesca Rochberg-Halton (ed.), *Language, Literature and History* (New Haven, Conn.: American Oriental Society, 1987), pp. 203–26 (esp. p. 212); and Jean Bottéro, *Mesopotamia: Writing, Reasoning and the Gods* (Chicago and London: University of Chicago Press, 1992), p. 135.

33 Erica Reiner, *Astral Magic in Babylonia* (Philadelphia: American Philosophical Society, 1995), p. 9; see also C.J. Gadd, *Ideas of Divine Rule in the Ancient East* (Schweich Lectures of the British Academy, 1945; Munich: Kraus Reprint, 1980), p. 57. Bottéro (*Mesopotamia*, p. 133) pointed out that in extispicy Shamash was thought to write his messages directly onto the liver; the inference is that divine messages were written onto the sky in a similar fashion.

34 Gadd, *Ideas of Divine Rule*, p. 51; Bottéro, *Mesopotamia*, p. 125; Koch-Westenholz, *Mesopotamian Astrology*, pp. 9–10; Hunger and Pingree, *Astral Sciences in Mesopotamia*, p. 5; Oppenheim, *Ancient Mesopotamia*, p. 208; Cicero, *De Divinatione* I.vi. The retrospective division of divination into two types follows the division of astrology itself into two branches by Isidore of Seville, natural, which observed the planets' general influences, and superstitious, which relied heavily on the use of horoscopes for making precise judgements over such matters as future events and auspicious times for action; see Isidore of Seville, *The Etymologies* III.xxvii. This distinction was then adopted by cuneiform scholars in the nineteenth century (see Morris Jastrow, *Aspects of Religious Belief and Practice in Babylonia and Assyria* [New York: Putnam, 1911], p. 795; Rochberg-Halton, 'Aspects of Babylonian Celestial Divination', p. 5; and David Brown, *Mesopotamian Planetary Astronomy-Astrology* (Groningen: Styx Publications, 2000), p. 7, n. 16; citing R. French, *Ancient Natural History* (1994), where the two terms are changed to 'natural' and 'superstitious'.

35 Ulla Susanne Koch, *Secrets of Extispicy: The Chapter Multābiltu of the Babylonian Extispicy Series and Nisirti bārûti Texts mainly from Aššurbanipal's Library*, (Alter Orient und Altes Testament, 326; Münster: Ugarit-Verlag, 2005).

36 See the discussion in Bottéro, *Mesopotamia*, p. 135. See also Koch-Westenholz, *Mesopotamian Astrology*, pp. 13–19, 35, 38, 97; Christopher Walker and John Britton, 'Astronomy and Astrology in Mesopotamia', in Christopher Walker (ed.), *Astronomy Before the Telescope* (London: British Museum Press, 1996), pp. 42–67 (42–43); Hunger and Pingree, *Astral Sciences in Mesopotamia*, p. 6; Ivan Starr, *The Rituals of the Diviner* (Malibu: Undena Publications, 1983), p. 15; Van der Waerden, *Science Awakening*, vol. 1, pp. 50, 57. Unanswered questions include the unlikely possibility that the impossible omens were the result of scribal error and whether there was a progression from theory to observation over time, the theoretical omens representing an early form. There is, though, no reason why this should be so.

37 Brown, *Mesopotamian Planetary Astronomy-Astrology*, chs 3, 5, esp. pp, 105–12, 285.

38 P.J. Huber, 'Dating by Lunar Eclipse Omina with Speculations on the Birth of Omen Astrology', in J.L. Berggren and B.R. Goldstein (eds), *From Ancient Omens to Statistical Mechanics: Essays on the Exact Sciences Presented to Asger Aaboe* (Copenhagen: Copenhagen University Library 1987), pp. 3–13 (3). See also the discussion in Rochberg, *The Heavenly Writing*, pp. 270–71.

39 Reiner, *Astral Magic in Babylonia*, esp. pp. 13–15.

40 A. Leo Oppenheim, 'A Babylonian Diviner's Manual', *Journal of Near Eastern Studies* 33 (January–October 1974): 197–220 (204).

Notes to Chapter 4: Mesopotamian Astrology: The Writing of Heaven

1   From the Hittite *Removal of the Threat Implied in an Evil Omen* (in James B. Pritchard, [ed.], *Ancient Near Eastern Texts Relating to the Old Testament* [Princeton: Princeton University Press, 1969], p. 355).

2   Otto Neugebauer and H.B. van Hoesen, *Greek Horoscopes* (Philadelphia: American Philosophy Society, 1959), no. 137, p. 42. See also Pliny, *Natural History* VI.121–23; VII.103; Diodorus, *Library of History* 2.28.29–31; Simplicius, *De Caelo* 475B and the discussion in Franz Cumont, *Astrology Among the Greeks and Romans* (New York: Dover Publications, 1960 [1911]), p. 16.

3   Dan. 2.2–5, 10; 3.8; 4.7; 5.7.

4   Deborah E. Harkness, *John Dee's Conversations with Angels: Cabala, Alchemy and the End of Nature* (Cambridge: Cambridge University Press, 1999), esp. ch. 5.

5   See the summary of these arguments in Nicholas Campion, 'Babylonian Astrology: Its Origins and Legacy in Europe', in Helaine Selin (ed.), *Astronomy Across Cultures: The History of Non-Western Astronomy* (Dordrecht: Kluwer Academic Publishers, 2000), pp. 509–54. See also the discussion in David Brown, *Mesopotamian Planetary Astronomy-Astrology* (Groningen: Styx Publications, 2000), esp. pp. 246–48. At least one of the third-millennium tablets cannot be genuine because it records the sack of the Esagila, the temple of Marduk in Babylon, before it existed, by Shulgi, king of Ur (see C.B.F. Walker, 'Episodes in the History of Babylonian Astronomy' [lecture delivered to The Society for Mesoptamian Studies, Toronto, May 12, 1982], p. 22). On the other hand David Pingree regards these tablets as genuine ('Legacies in Astronomy and Celestial Omens', in Stephanie Dalley [ed.], *The Legacy of Mesopotamia* [Oxford: Clarendon Press, 1998], pp. 125–37 [125]).

6   P.J. Huber, 'Dating by Lunar Eclipse Omina with Speculations on the Birth of Omen Astrology', in J.L. Berggren and B.R. Goldstein (eds), *From Ancient Omens to Statistical Mechanics: Essays on the Exact Sciences Presented to Asger Aaboe* (Copenhagen: Copenhagen University Library, 1987), pp. 3–13 (3).

7   *Inanna, Lady of Largest Heart: Poems of the Sumerian High Pristess Enheduanna* (trans. Betty De Shong Meador; Austin: University of Texas, 2001).

8   *The Lady of the Evening*, in Samuel Noah Kramer and Diane Wolkstein, *Inanna, Queen of Heaven and Earth: Her Stories and Hymns from Sumer* (New York: Harper & Row, 1983), p. 101.

9   Kramer and Wolkstein, *Inanna, Queen of Heaven and Earth*, pp. 52–89. The story of Inanna's descent through the seven gates found a new appeal following the tablets' discovery and translation in the late nineteenth century, when the Irish playwright Oscar Wilde conflated Inanna with the New Testament temptress, Salome, and created the dance of the seven veils.

10 Giorgio Bucellati, 'The Descent of Inanna as a Ritual Journey to Kutha?', *Syro-Mesopotamian Studies* 4(3) (December 1982): 3–8.

11 Steve W. Cole and Peter Machinist, *Letters from Priests to the Kings Esarhaddon and Assurbanipal* (Helsinki: Helsinki University Press, 1998), p. 119 (§ 149).

12 Kramer and Wolkstein, *Inanna, Queen of Heaven and Earth*, pp. 154–55.

13 Ezek. 8.14–17.

14 Kramer and Wolkstein, *Inanna, Queen of Heaven and Earth*, pp. 52–53.

15 *Mul Apin* I i 38, I ii 13–15, II, i 7–8, II i 40–41 (Hermann Hunger and David Pingree, *Mul Apin: An Astronomical Compendium in Cuneiform* (Archiv für Orientforschung, 24;

Ferdinand Berger & Sohne: Horn, 1989); see also discussion in Hermann Hunger and David Pingree, *Astral Sciences in Mesopotamia* (Leiden, Boston and Koln: Brill, 1999), p. 73.

16 Hermann Hunger, *Astrological Reports to Assyrian Kings* (Helsinki: Helsinki University Press, 1992), p. 61 (report 102).

17 Thorkild Jacobsen, *The Treasures of Darkness: A History of Mesoptamian Religion* (New Haven and London: Yale University Press, 1976), p. 122.

18 *Ibid.*, p. 135.

19 Hunger, *Astrological Reports to Assyrian Kings*, p. 84 (report 130).

20 *Ibid.*, p. 136 (report 245).

21 Erica Reiner, *Astral Magic in Babylonia* (Philadelphia: American Philosophical Society, 1995), p. 16. See also the discussion in Bartel van der Waerden, *Science Awakening*, vol. 2: *The Birth of Astronomy* (Leyden and New York: Oxford University Press, 1974), p. 58; and Brown, *Mesopotamian Planetary Astronomy-Astrology*, p. 250. Also see Scott Noegel (ed.), *Prayer, Magic, and the Stars in the Ancient and Late Antique World* (Philadelphia: Pennsylvania State University Press, 2003).

22 Ditz Otto Edzard, *Gudea and His Dynasty* (Toronto: University of Toronto Press, 2003). See also Henri Frankfort, *Kingship and the Gods: A Study of Near Eastern Religion as the Integration of Society and Nature* (Chicago: Chicago University Press, 1978 [1948]), pp. 240–43, 255–80 and the discussion in Brown, *Mesopotamian Planetary Astronomy-Astrology*, p. 247. There is no question that Gudea's story includes several references to astrological divination, even though scholarly opinion is still divided: for example, Francesca Rochberg-Halton: 'Isolated references to celestial "signs" in Sumerian sources, such as the sign sent in the form of a bright star to Gudea for the building of Ningirsu's temple, do not constitute sufficient evidence to warrant speaking of the origins of celestial divination in a Sumerian milieu' (*Aspects of Babylonian Celestial Divination: The Lunar Tablets of Enuma Anu Enlil* [Archiv für Orientforschung, 22; Ferdinand Berger & Sohne: Horn, 1988], p. ix).

23 See the preliminary discussion in Rochberg-Halton, *Aspects of Babylonian Celestial Divination*, pp. 19–22; also Brown, *Mesopotamian Planetary Astronomy-Astrology*, p. 248 and further comments in Van der Waerden, *Science Awakening*, vol. 2, p. 48; Hunger and Pingree, *Astral Sciences in Mesopotamia*, pp. 7–8. It has been suggested that lunar eclipses may have been linked to the death of third-millennium Akkadian kings, but in the absence of any evidence, we really cannot say; see Ulla Koch-Westenholz, *Mesopotamian Astrology: An Introduction to Babylonian and Assyrian Celestial Divination* (Carsten Niebuhr Institute of Near Eastern Studies; Copenhagen: Museum Tusculunum Press, University of Copenhagen, 1995), p. 14.

24 Rochberg-Halton, *Aspects of Babylonian Celestial Divination*, p. 109 (tablet XII.17).

25 *Ibid.*, p. 108 (tablet XII.10).

26 Erica Reiner with David Pingree, *Babylonian Planetary Omens, Part 1, Enuma Anu Enlil, Tablet 63: The Venus Tablet of Ammisaduqa* (Malibu: Undena Publications, 1975).

27 For a detailed study of the planets in Babylonian astrology see Brown, *Mesopotamian Planetary Astronomy-Astrology*, ch. 2.

28 There is still considerable uncertainty concerning the accuracy of measurement of stellar positions in the second millennium, or indeed whether mathematical accuracy was considered to be important in itself; Bartel van der Waerden, 'Babylonian Astronomy II: The Thirty Six Stars', *Journal of Near Eastern Studies* 8(1) (January 1949): 6–26 (7). See

also Noel Swerdlow, *The Babylonian Theory of the Planets* (Princeton: Princeton University Press, 1998), Hunger and Pingree, *Astral Sciences in Mesopotamia*. Asger Aaboe has demonstrated how accuracy of observation was actually not necessary for the Babylonians to determine their relatively precise parameters for planetary measurements. Mathematical formulae for computing planetary positions were not devised until the third century BCE ('Observation and Theory in Babylonian Astronomy', *Centaurus* 24(1) (1980): 14–35).

29   See the discussion in Pingree, 'Legacies in Astronomy and Celestial Omens', p. 126.

30   Reiner and Pingree, *Babylonian Planetary Omens, Part 1*, p. 29.

31   Max Weber, *From Max Weber: Essays in Sociology* (ed. H.H. Garth and C. Mills Wright; London: Kegan Paul, Trench, Trubner & Co., 1947), p. 139.

32   Paul Ricoeur, *Time and Narrative* (Chicago: University of Chicago Press, 1985), vol. 2, p. 27.

33   For discussion see Francesca Rochberg-Halton, 'Elements of the Babylonian Contribution to Hellenistic Astrology', *Journal of the American Oriental Society* 108(1) (January–March 1988): 51–62 (52); and Hunger and Pingree, *Astral Sciences in Mesopotamia*, p. 5.

34   See the discussion in Ivan Starr, *The Rituals of the Diviner* (Malibu: Undena Publications, 1983), p. 15; Koch-Westenholz, *Mesopotamian Astrology*, p. 97.

35   See the discussion in Mogens Trolle Larsen, 'The Mesopotamian Lukewarm Mind: Reflections on Science, Divination and Literacy', in Francesca Rochberg-Halton (ed.), *Language, Literature and History* (New Haven: American Oriental Society, 1987), pp. 203–26 (208).

36   Brown, *Mesopotamian Planetary Astronomy-Astrology*, pp. 63–64, 75–81.

37   See Arthur O. Lovejoy, *The Great Chain of Being* (Cambridge, Mass. and London: Harvard University Press, 1936).

38   Rochberg-Halton, *Aspects of Babylonian Celestial Divination*, pp. 53–57; see also the discussion in Reiner, *Astral Magic in Babylonia*, p. 78.

39   Erica Reiner with David Pingree, *Babylonian Planetary Omens, Part 3* (Groningen: Styx Publications 1998), p. 43 (omens 28, 31, 35).

40   Swerdlow, *The Babylonian Theory of the Planets*, p. 3.

41   Hunger, *Astrological Reports to Assyrian Kings*, pp. 180–81 (report 320).

42   Simo Parpola, *Letters from Assyrian Scholars to the Kings Esarhaddon and Assurbanipal*, part 1: *Texts* (Kevelaer: Verlag Butzon & Bercker and Neukirchen-Vluyn: Neukirchener Verlag, 1970) (letter 289).

43   Richard I. Caplice, *The Akkadian Namburbi Texts: An Introduction* (Malibu: Undena Publications, 1974), p. 37; see also Hunger and Pingree, *Astral Sciences in Mesopotamia*, p. 6.

44   W.G. Lambert, *Babylonian Wisdom Literature* (Oxford: Oxford University Press, 1966), p. 113.

45   Hunger, *Astrological Reports to Assyrian Kings*, p. 55 (report 95); Parpola, *Letters from Assyrian Scholars to the Kings Esarhaddon and Assurbanipal* (letter 326).

46   Simo Parpola, *Letters from Assyrian and Babylonian Scholars* (Helsinki: Helsinki University Press, 1993), part 1, p. 217 (letter 278).

47   *Removal of the Threat Implied in an Evil.*

48   Parpola, *Letters from Assyrian Scholars to the Kings Esarhaddon and Assurbanipal*, part 1 (letter 292).

49   Rochberg-Halton, *Aspects of Babylonian Celestial Divination*, p. 15.

50   For this discussion see Samuel Noah Kramer, *The Sumerians: Their History, Culture and Character* (Chicago and London: University of Chicago Press, 1963), p. 123; Kramer and Wolkstein, *Inanna, Queen of Heaven and Earth*, pp. 15–19; Jack N. Lawson, *The Concept of*

Fate in Ancient Mesopotomia: Of the First Millennium, Towards an Understanding of 'Simtu' (Wiesbaden: Harrasowitz Verlag, 1994); A. Leo Oppenheim, *Ancient Mesopotamia: Portrait of a Dead Civilisation* (Chicago: University of Chicago Press, 1977), pp. 201–08.

51   Kramer and Wolkstein, *Inanna, Queen of Heaven and Earth*, p. 157.

52   *From the Great Above to the Great Below*, in *ibid.*, pp. 53, 61.

53   Frankfort, *Kingship and the Gods*, p. 189.

54   Reiner, *Astral Magic in Babylonia*, p. 23.

55   *Ibid.*, p. 114.

56   *Ibid.*, p. 71.

57   Cole and Machinist, *Letters from Priests to the Kings Esarhaddon and Assurbanipal*, p. 134 (§ 135).

58   Koch-Westenholz, *Mesopotamian Astrology*, pp. 44–50; Hunger and Pingree *Astral Sciences in Mesopotamia*, pp. 8–12; David Pingree, *The Yavanajataka of Sphujidhvaja* (Harvard Oriental Series, 48; Cambridge, Mass.: Harvard University Press, 1978), p. 614. See also Elizabeth Chesley Baity, 'Archaeoastronomy and Ethnoastronomy So Far', *Current Anthropology* 14(4) (October 1973): 389–449 (406, 417).

59   Asko Parpola, *Deciphering the Indus Script* (Cambridge: Cambridge University Press, 1997).

60   Richard L. Thompson, *Vedic Cosmography and Astronomy* (Delhi: Motilal Banarsidass, 2004).

61   K.V. Sarma, *Vedanga Jyotisa of Lagadha* (trans. and with notes by T.S.K. Sastry; New Delhi: Indian National Science Academy, 1985). *Rig Veda* 1.164.3, 11 (in Wendy Doniger O'Flaherty, *The Rig Veda: An Anthology* [New Delhi: Penguin, 1994]).

62   Sphujidhvaja *Yavanajataka* 73 (in Pingree, *The Yavanajataka of Sphujidhvaja*, vol. 2, pp. 174–76). For a mention, though not astrological details, in the Vedas, see *White Yajur Veda* XIV.19 ([trans. Ralph Griffith; Benares: E.J. Lazarus & Co., 1899], p. 125; available at <http://www.sacred-texts.com/hin/wyv/wyvbk14.htm> [accessed 20 September 2007]).

63   Joseph Needham, *Science and Civilisation in China*, vol. 3: *Mathematics and the Sciences of the Heavens and Earth* (Cambridge: Cambridge University Press, 1959), p. 242; Bradely E. Schaefer, 'Date and Place of Origin of the Asian Lunar Lodge Systems', in César Esteban and Juan Antonio Belmonte (eds), *Astronomy and Cultural Diversity, Proceedings of the 1999 Oxford VI Conference on Archaeoastronomy and Astronomy in Culture* (Tenerife: Oranismo Autonomo de Museos del Cablido de Tenerife, 2000), pp. 283–87.

64   David Pingree, 'Venus Omens in India and Babylon', in Rochberg-Halton (ed.), *Language, Literature and History*, pp. 293–315; David Pingree, 'Babylonian Planetary Theory in Sanskrit Omen Texts', in Berggren and Goldstein (eds), *From Ancient Omens to Statistical Mechanics*, pp. 91–99; see also Brown, *Mesopotamian Planetary Astronomy-Astrology*, p. 162.

Notes to Chapter 5:   The Assyrians and Persians: Revolution and Reformation

1   The earliest known interpretation of a birth chart, 29 April 410 BCE, from A.J. Sachs, 'Babylonian Horoscopes', *Journal of Cuneiform Studies* 6 (1952): 49–75 (54–57).

2   Hermann Hunger and David Pingree, *Mul Apin: An Astronomical Compendium in Cuneiform* (Archiv für Orientforschung, 24; Ferdinand Berger & Sohne: Horn, 1989). The extant tablets date from the eighth century, although may either have been compiled by 1000 BCE or be based on observations as far as back as 1350 BCE.

3   *Mul Apin* II.A 7 (in Hunger and Pingree, *Mul Apin*).

4   *Ibid.*, II.A 8.

5   The full text of *Enuma Anu Enlil* was excavated in the ruins of Ashurbanipal's library at the Assyrian capital, Nineveh. It consisted of around 6500–7000 *omina*, grouped into some 70 tablets, of which 13 are now available in translation or transliteration.

6   Hermann Hunger, *Astrological Reports to Assyrian Kings* (Helsinki: Helsinki University Press,1992), pp. 260–62 (reports 323, 324, 326).

7   See the discussion in Francesca Rochberg-Halton, 'Elements of the Babylonian Contribution to Hellenistic Astrology', *Journal of the American Oriental Society* 108(1) (January–March 1988): 51–62; Hermann Hunger and David Pingree, *Astral Sciences in Mesopotamia* (Leiden, Boston and Koln: Brill, 1999), p. 147. The *nisirti* were: sun–the Hired Man (Aries), moon–the Pleiades (which was broadened to become Taurus in the Hellenistic astrology), Venus–Anunitu (part of the Greek Pisces), Mars–Capricorn, Jupiter–Cancer and Saturn–Libra. In Hellenistic astrology these relationships were known as *hypsomata* or exaltations and given specific degrees (Dorotheus of Sidon, *Carmen Astrologicum* I.2; Ptolemy, *Tetrabiblos* I.19.

8   Rochberg-Halton, 'Elements of the Babylonian Contribution to Hellenistic Astrology', p. 53.

9   Francesca Rochberg, *The Heavenly Writing: Divination and Horoscopy, and Astronomy in Mesopotamian Culture* (Cambridge: Cambridge University Press, 2004), pp. 126–40.

10   The full list of these is given in *Mul Apin* (I iv 33–39). Hunger and Pingree reduce the list of constellations to 17, on the assumption that the Tails and the Swallow were the same group of stars: the Tails of the Swallow (Hunger and Pingree, *Astral Sciences in Mesopotamia*, p. 144; cf. p. 17).

11   For the association of the Hired Man with Dumuzi, see *Mul Apin* I i 43; Hunger and Pingree, *Mul Apin*, p. 30.

12   Ulla Koch-Westenholz, *Mesopotamian Astrology: An Introduction to Babylonian and Assyrian Celestial Divination* (Carsten Niebuhr Institute of Near Eastern Studies; Copenhagen: Museum Tusculanum Press, University of Copenhagen, 1995), p. 153.

13   A. Leo Oppenheim, 'Divine and Celestial Observation in the Last Assyrian Empire', *Centaurus* 14(1) (1969): 97–135. The letters from Assyrian scholars are found in Simo Parpola, *Letters from Assyrian Scholars to the Kings Esarhaddon and Assurbanipal*, part 1: *Texts*; part 2: *Commentary* (Kevelaer: Verlag Butzon & Bercker and Neukirchen-Vluyn: Neukirchener Verlag, 1970, 1983); Simo Parpola, *Letters from Assyrian and Babylonian Scholars* (Helsinki: Helsinki University Press, 1993); and the earlier edition by Robert H. Pfeiffer, *State Letters of Assyria: A Transliteration and Translation of 355 Official Assyrian Letters Dating from the Sargonid Period (722–625 BC)* (American Oriental Series, 6; New Haven: American Oriental Society, 1935). Most of the reports, both Assyrian and Babylonian were published by R. Campbell Thompson in *The Reports of the Magicians and Astrologers of Nineveh and Babylon in the British Museum* (2 vols; London: Luzac and Co., 1900) and in a new edition by Hunger, *Astrological Reports to Assyrian Kings*. Parpola (*Letters from Assyrian and Babylonian Scholars*, pp. xxv–xxvi) argues that, under the Assyrians, there was a small group of trusted Assyrian astrologers who were close to the emperor, and a larger group of Babylonians who were kept at arm's length.

14   See the account in Michael Baigent, *From the Omens of Babylon: Astrology and Ancient Mesopotamia* (London: Penguin, 1994), pp. 52–53.

15   Parpola, *Letters from Assyrian Scholars to the Kings Esarhaddon and Assurbanipal*, part 1, p. 9 (letter 12).

16 *Ibid.*, p. 43 (letter 65).

17 Leroy Waterman, *Royal Correspondence of the Assyrian Empire* (4 vols; Ann Arbor: University of Michigan Press, 1930–36) vol. 1, p. 457 (letter 659).

18 Thompson, *The Reports of the Magicians and Astrologers*, vol. 2, p. lxii (report 73).

19 Parpola, *Letters from Assyrian and Babylonian Scholars*; see also Waterman, *Royal Correspondence*, vol. 1, p. 337 (letter 477).

20 Wilfred Van Soldt, *Solar Omens of Enuma anu Enlil: Tablets 23(24)–29(30)* (Leiden: Nederlands Historisch-Archaeologisch Instituut te Istanbul, 1995) Tablet 29 III.17, 18.

21 For the reference to oral tradition see Parpola, *Letters from Assyrian Scholars to the Kings Esarhaddon and Assurbanipal*, part 1, p. 11, I.13.

22 Hunger, *Astrological Reports to Assyrian Kings*, pp. 249–50 (reports 443, 444, 448).

23 Ivan Starr, *Queries to the Sungod: Divination and Politics in Sargonid Assyria* (State Archives of Assyria, 4; Helsinki: Helsinki University Press, 1990), p. 94 (queries 81–82).

24 *Ibid.*, pp. 102–04 (query 88).

25 David Brown, *Mesopotamian Planetary Astronomy-Astrology* (Groningen: Styx Publications, 2000), p. 161.

26 Ptolemy, *Almagest* III.7.

27 For the best summaries of the relevant technical developments, see Hunger and Pingree, *Astral Sciences in Mesopotamia*; and Noel Swerdlow, *The Babylonian Theory of the Planets* (Princeton: Princeton University Press, 1998).

28 For the shift in the nature of astrological reasoning see Daryn Lehoux, 'Observation and Prediction in Ancient Astrology', *Studies in History and Philosophy of Science* 35 (2004): 227–46; and for the distinction between the measurement of planetary positions and assessment of their astrological significance, see Ptolemy, *Tetrabiblos* I.1.

29 Swerdlow, *The Babylonian Theory of the Planets*, p. 21.

30 A.J. Sachs, *Astronomical Diaries and Related Texts from Babylonia*, vol 1: *Diaries from 652 B.C. to 262 B.C.* (completed and edited by Herman Hunger; Vienna: Verlag der Osterreichischen Akademie der Wissenschaften, 1988), tablet 332.12, 21–24; see also Francesca Rochberg-Halton, 'The Cultural Locus of Astronomy in Late Babylonia', in *Die Rolle der Astronomie in den Kulturen Mesopotamiens* (Grazer Morganlandische Studien, 3; ed. Hannes D. Galter; Graz: RM-Druck & Verlagsgesellschaft m.b.H, 1993), pp. 31–46,

31 For moon-watching in the Assyrian period see Hunger, *Astrological Reports to Assyrian Kings*, pp. 74–76 (reports 116–23).

32 See the discussion in Brown, *Mesopotamian Planetary Astronomy-Astrology*, p. 162.

33 Koch-Westenholz, *Mesopotamian Astrology*, pp. 51–52.

34 Dan. 5.7.

35 For a full account see Mary Boyce, *A History of Zoroastrianism* (3 vols; Leiden and New York: Brill, 1983).

36 For this argument see Nicholas Campion, *The Great Year: Astrology, Millenarianism and History in the Western Tradition* (London: Penguin, 1994).

37 Bartel van der Waerden, *Science Awakening*, vol. 2: *The Birth of Astronomy* (Leyden and New York: Oxford University Press, 1974), ch. 5.

38 'About the Zoroastrians', fragment from Franz Cumont (ed.), *Catalogus Codicum Astrologorum Graecorum* (12 vols; Brussels: Lamertin, 1898–1953), VIII.3; Robert Hand (ed.) and Robert Schmidt (trans.), *The Astrological Records of the Early Sages in Greek* (Berkeley Springs, W.Va.: Golden Hind Press, 1995), p. 24 (records 120–22); Josephus, *Jewish Antiquities* I.2.3.

39 *The Bundahishn* 34.1 (E.W. West, *The Bundahishn, or Knowledge from the Zand* [n.p.:

Kessinger Publishing, 2004]), p. 640; Norman Cohn, 'How Time Acquired a Consummation', in Malcolm Bull (ed.), *Apocalypse Theory and the Ends of the World* (Oxford: Blackwell, 1995), pp. 22–37 (31–32). There were different variations on this theme.

40   Mt. 2.1–2.

41   Herodotus, *The Histories* I. For full discussion of Magian–Zorastrian doctrines see Richard Charles Zaehner, *The Teachings of the Magi* (Oxford: Oxford University Press, 1978).

42   Herodotus, *The Histories* I, VII.

43   *Ibid.*, VII.

44   *Ibid.*, VII.

45   *Ibid.*, VII.

46   Philo, *Every Good Man is Free* XI(74).

47   See Richard Charles Zaehner, *Zurvan: A Zoroastrian Dilemma* (Oxford: Clarendon Press, 1955).

48   *Hymns of the Atharva-Veda* XIX.53 (trans. Maurice Bloomberg; Delhi: Motilal Banarsidass, 2000 [1897], p. 224).

49   Bartel van der Waerden, 'History of the Zodiac', *Archiv für Orientforschung* 16 (1952–53): 216–30; Koch-Westenholz, *Mesopotamian Astrology*, p. 174. The development of the zodiac required the production of another form of astronomical document, the Almanacs, which survive for the years between 262 BCE and 75 CE; Rochberg-Halton, 'The Cultural Locus of Astronomy in Late Babylonia', p. 41; also see Robert Powell, *History of the Zodiac* (San Rafael: Sophia Academic Press, 2007). For a recent analysis of the zodiac as a measuring system see J.M. Steele and J.M.K. Gray, 'Babylonian Observations Involving the Zodiac', *Journal for the History of Astronomy* 28(4) (November 2007): 443–58.

50   Tablet VAT 4924; see Bartel van der Waerden, 'Babylonian Astronomy II: The Thirty Six Stars', in *Journal of Near Eastern Studies* 8 (January 1949): 6–26 (25) and Van der Waerden, *Science Awakening*, vol. 2, pp. 83, 122, 125.

51   Van der Waerden, 'History of the Zodiac', p. 224.

52   F.R. Stephenson, and C.B.F. Walker (eds), *Halley's Comet in History* (London: British Museum Publications, 1985), p. 24.

53   *Enuma Anu Enlil* 50.111.8a (in Erica Reiner with David Pingree, *Babylonian Planetary Omens, Part 2, Enuma Anu Enlil, Tablets 50–51* [Bibliotheca Mesopotamica, 4, fasc. 2; Malibu: Undena Publications, 1975], p. 41).

54   *Enuma Elish* II.27–32.

55   *Ibid.*, V.1–10; Wayne Horowitz, *Mesopotamian Cosmic Geography* (Winona Lake: Eisenbrauns, 1998), p. 115.

56   See Thorkild Jacobsen, *The Treasures of Darkness: A History of Mesopotamian Religion* (New Haven and London: Yale University Press, 1976), p. 109.

57   Erica Reiner with David Pingree, *Babylonian Planetary Omens, Part Three* (Groningen: Styx Publications, 1998), p. 49 (§§ 91–93).

58   Sachs, 'Babylonian Horoscopes', p. 68; See also Rochberg, *The Heavenly Writing*, pp. 202–08.

59   Sachs, 'Babylonian Horoscopes', pp. 54–57; Rochberg, *Babylonian Horoscopes*, pp. 51, 56–57.

60   Ptolemy, *Tetrabiblos* I.17.

61   Hunger and Pingree, *Astral Sciences in Mesopotamia*, p. 156.

62   Although we are limited to accidental finds, Neugebauer and van Hoesen noted that, when they were writing in 1959, there were only 20 birth charts surviving from a period which had yielded 1,800 astronomical tablets, suggesting that the birth chart may have

been a minority interest. See Otto Neugebauer and H.B. van Hoesen, *Greek Horoscopes* (Philadelphia: American Philosophical Society, 1959), pp. 161–62. The fragment of 369 BCE is classified by Rochberg as a birth note; see *Babylonian Horoscopes*, p. 143.

63   Sachs, 'Babylonian Horoscopes', pp. 57–58.

64   Plato, *Timaeus* 38C.

65   A.J. Sachs, 'The Lastest Datable Cuneiform Texts', in Barry L. Eichler (ed.), *Kramer Anniversary Volume: Studies in Honor of Samuel Noah Kramer* (*Alter Orient und Altes Testament* 25 [1976]: 379–98); see also the discussion in Rochberg, *The Heavenly Writing*, pp. 99–100.

66   Brown, *Mesopotamian Planetary Astronomy-Astrology*, p. 162.

Notes to Chapter 6: Egypt: The Kingdom of the Sun

1   The creator/sun god speaking as Re and Atum, spell 442 (O.R. Faulkner, *The Ancient Egyptian Coffin Texts*, vol. 2: *Spells 355–787* [Warminster: Aris and Phillips 1977], p. 79).

2   See the comprehensive account of Egyptian influence over the last two thousand years, especially on esoteric thought, in Erik Hornung, *The Secret Lore of Egypt: Its Impact on the West* (trans. David Lorton; Ithaca and London: Cornell University Press, 2001).

3   See the discussion in Jan Assmann, *The Mind of Egypt: History and Meaning in the Time of the Pharaohs* (trans. Andrew Jenkins; New York: Metropolitan Books, 2002), esp. pp. 204–07; cosmotheism was first used to describe the single ordered cosmos of the Greek and Roman Stoics, but Assmann broadened the term to include polytheistic societies in which the plurality of deities formed part of an ordered whole.

4   See Henri Frankfort, *Ancient Egyptian Religion* (New York: Harper & Row, 1948); Leonard H. Lesko, 'Ancient Egyptian Cosmogonies and Cosmology', in Byron E. Shafer, *Religion in Ancient Egypt* (Ithaca: Cornell University Press 1991), pp. 88–122; Françoise Dunand and Christiane Zivie-Coche, *Gods and Men in Egypt 3000 BCE to 395 CE* (trans. David Lorton; Ithaca: Cornell University Press, 2004), esp. ch. 2: 'Cosmogonies, Creation, and Time'.

5   For the broadest discussion of Egyptian political and religious cosmology see Henri Frankfort, *Kingship and the Gods: A Study of Near Eastern Religion as the Integration of Society and Nature* (Chicago: Chicago University Press, 1978 [1948]); and John Wilson, 'Egypt', in H. Frankfort, H.A. Frankfort, William A. Irwin, Thorkild Jacobsen and John A. Wilson, *The Intellectual Adventure of Ancient Man: An Essay on Speculative Thought in the Ancient Near East* (Chicago and London: Chicago University Press, 1946), pp. 31–124; see also Ivan Engnell, *Studies in Divine Kingship in the Ancient Near East* (Oxford: Blackwell, 1967). Rundle T. Clark, *Myth and Symbol in Ancient Egypt* (London: Thames and Hudson, 1959) provides an excellent introduction to religious cosmology while E.A. Wallis Budge, *From Fetish to God in Ancient Egypt* (Oxford: Oxford University Press, 1934) is a standard introduction to Egyptian religion. A. Rosalie David, *The Ancient Egyptians: Religious Beliefs and Practices* (London: Routledge and Kegan Paul Ltd., 1982) includes discussion of the social and functional aspects of religion (see esp. pp. 45–50); J.M. Plumley, 'The Cosmology of Ancient Egypt', in Carmen Blacker and Michael Loewe, *Ancient Cosmologies* (London: George Allen and Unwin Ltd., 1975), pp. 17–41 sets out the broad structure of Egyptian cosmology; see also Stephen Quirke, *Ancient Egyptian Religion* (London: British Museum Publications, 1992); and E.A. Wallis Budge, *Egyptian Magic* (London: Kegan Paul, Trench Trubner & Co., 1901).

6   For this claim see David, *The Ancient Egyptians*, p. 27.

7   Otto Neugebauer, *A History of Ancient Mathematical Astronomy* (3 vols; Berlin, Heidelberg and New York; Springer Verlag, 1975), vol. 2, p. 559.

8   O.R. Faulkner, *The Ancient Egyptian Pyramid Texts* (2 vols; Oxford: Oxford University Press, 1969; Warminster: Aris and Phillips, 2nd edn, 1993). The Pyramid Texts were inscribed on the inside of pyramids in a period of around 260 from the pharaoh Unas, last king of the Fifth Dynasty, who died around 2440 BCE, to those of the Sixth-Dynasty kings Teti, Pepi I, Mrenre and Pepi II, who died around 2180 BCE, as well as those of Pepi II's three queens and that of Ibi, who probably reigned in the First Intermediate Period (*c.*2175–1991 BCE).

9   O.R. Faulkner, *The Ancient Egyptian Coffin Texts*, vol. 1: *Spells 1–354*; vol. 2: *Spells 355–787*; vol. 3: *Spells 788–1186* (Warminster: Aris and Phillips, 1973, 1977, 1978).

10   E.A. Wallis Budge, *The Book of The Dead* (London: Kegan Paul, 1899); O.R. Faulkner, *The Book of the Dead* (London: British Museum Publications, 1985).

11   For this discussion see Jeremy Naydler, *Temple of the Cosmos: The Ancient Egyptian Experience of the Sacred* (Rochester, Vt.: Inner Traditions, 1996) and *Shamanic Wisdom in the Pyramid Texts: The Mystical Tradition of Ancient Egypt* (Rochester, Vt.: Inner Traditions, 2005).

12   Faulkner, *The Book of the Dead*, p. 11; Pyramid Texts utterance 662.1878.

13   I.E.S. Edwards, *The Pyramids of Egypt* (London: Penguin, rev. edn, 1988), p. 14; see also Robert Ritner, *Egyptian Magic* (Chicago: Chicago Oriental Institute, 1993).

14   Edwards, *The Pyramids of Egypt*, p. 7.

15   It was certainly believed that he was a historical figure and that his murder, dismemberment and resurrection were as real as the similar events in Christ's life are to Christians. He may have been first the king and then the god of the ninth Lower Egyptian *nome*, or district, possibly identified with a shepherd god, Andjeti (see the discussion in David, *The Ancient Egyptians*, pp. 72–73; and Edwards, *The Pyramids of Egypt*, p. 9, see also p. 5).

16   The worship of Isis and Osiris was to become one of the first salvation religions of the Roman Empire and its iconography would have been deeply familiar to the Christians of the first to fourth centuries. Indeed our only complete version of the Isis–Osiris legend is Plutarch's version, committed to writing in the first century CE, 'Isis and Osiris', *Moralia* V.26.

17   Mark Lehner, *The Complete Pyramids* (London: Thames and Hudson, 1997), p. 29. A work which straddles the territory between the academic and New Age is Jane B. Sellers, *The Death of the Gods in Ancient Egypt* (London: Penguin, 1992). She argues that the religious motif of the death and resurrection of Osiris is due to the constellation's periodic disappearance either due to the annual cycle, a reasonable hypothesis, or precession, a much more controversial one requiring a much greater period of continual observation than most historians would allow. However, regardless of any flaws in Seller's evidence, and the fact that she is influenced by modern writers such as Joseph Campbell as much as by the ancient evidence, and in spite of the protestations of Egyptologists, the evidence pointing to the Palaeolithic recognition of Orion and Ursa Major suggests that there is no objection in principle to her argument. (See pp. 204–05 and 196–97 for precession.)

18   David, *The Ancient Egyptians*, pp. 72–73.

19   Faulkner, 'The King and the Star Religion in the Pyramid Texts', *Journal of Near Eastern Studies* 25 (1966): 153–61 (161).

20   David, *Ancient Egyptians*, pp. 72–73.

21   Edwards, *The Pyramids of Egypt*, pp. 14, 16.

22   *Ibid.*, p. 16 (spell 405).

23   Faulkner, *Pyramid Texts*, utterance 606; see Edwards, *The Pyramids of Egypt*, p. 16.

24   Edwards, *The Pyramids of Egypt*, p. 8.

25   Faulkner, *Pyramid Texts*, utterance 488.1048–49.

26   Faulkner, *The Book of the Dead*, p. 41 (spell 15).

27   *Ibid.*, p. 41 (spell 15).

28   J. Viau, 'Egyptian Mythology', in Felix Guirand, *Larousse Encyclopaedia of Mythology* (trans. Richard Aldington and Delano Ames; London: Paul Hamlyn, 1959), pp. 8–48 (13).

29   The eye may also be Venus, see Rolf Krauss, 'The Eye of Horus and the Planet Venus: Astronomical and Mythological References', in John M. Steele and Annette Imhausen, *Under One Sky: Astronomy and Mathematics in the Ancient Near East* (Alter Orient und Altes Testament, 297; Munster: Ugarit Verlag, 2002), pp. 193–208.

30   Edwards, *The Pyramids of Egypt*, p. 6.

31   Herodotus, *The Histories* II.122–26.

32   Joyce Tyldesley, *The Private Life of the Pharaohs* (London: Macmillan, 2000), pp. 63–74.

33   J.H. Breasted wrote that 'the pyramidal form of the king's tomb was of the most sacred significance. The king was buried under the very symbol of the sun-god which stood in the holy of holies in the sun-temple at Heliopolis, a symbol upon which, they say ... he was accustomed to manifest himself in the form of a phoenix; and when in mountainous proportions the pyramid rose above the king's sepulchre, dominating the royal city below and the valley beyond for many miles, it was the loftiest object which greeted the sun-god in all the land and his morning rays glittered on its shining summit long before he scattered the shadows in the dwellings of humbler mortals below' (*Development of Religion and Thought in Ancient Egypt* [Philadelphia: University of Pennsylvania Press, 1972 (1912)], p. 72).

34   Virginia Trimble, 'Astronomical Investigation Concerning the So-Called Air-Shafts of Cheops' Pyramid', in *Mitteilungen des deutsches Akademie Berlin* 10 (1964): 183–87; Alexander Badawy, 'The Stellar Destiny of Pharaoh and the So-Called Air Shafts of Cheops' Pyramid' in *ibid.*, 198–206; see also I.E.S. Edwards, 'The Air Channels of Chephren's Pyramid', in William Kelly Simpson and Whitney M. Davies (eds), *Studies in Ancient Egypt, the Aegean and the Sudan: Essays in Honor of Dows Dunham on the Occasion of his 90th Birthday, June 1, 1980* (Boston: Museum of Fine Arts, 1981), pp. 55–57.

35   For a critique of the precise-alignment hypothesis, though not general orientations, see John J. Wall, 'The Star Alignment Hypothesis for the Great Pyramid Shafts', *Journal for the History of Astronomy* 38(2) (May 2007): 199–206.

36   J.A. Belmonte and Mosalem Shaltout, 'On the Orientation of Ancient Egyptian Temples: (1) Upper Egypt and Lower Nubia, *Journal for the History of Astronomy* 36(3) (May 2006): 273–98; J.A. Belmonte and Mosalem Shaltout, 'On the Orientation of Ancient Egyptian Temples: (2) New Experiments at the Oases of the Western Desert', *Journal for the History of Astronomy* 37(2) (May 2006): 173–92; Mosalem Shaltout, Juan Antonio Belmonte and Magdo Fekri, 'On the Orientation of Ancient Egyptian Temples: (3) Key Points in Lower Egypt and Siwa Oasis, Part 1', *Journal for the History of Astronomy* 38(2) (May 2007): 141–60; 38(4) (November 2007): 413–42.

37   Faulkner, *Pyramid Texts*, utterances 606.1688–89; 523.1231; see also the discussion in Edwards, *The Pyramids of Egypt*, p. 14.

38   Lehner, *The Complete Pyramids*, pp. 28–29.

39   *Ibid.*, p. 33.

40   E.C. Krupp, *Skywatchers, Shamans and Kings: Astronomy and the Archaeology of Power* (New York: John Wiley & Sons Inc., 1997), p. 289.

41   The Sirius connection has proved controversial because it was proposed by non-

Egyptologists Robert Bauval and Adrian Gilbert in *The Orion Mystery: Unlocking the Secrets of the Pyramids* (London: Heinemann, 1994), pp. 131–32. The Sirius hypothesis is reasonable but is bound up with controversy over Bauval and Gilbert's other theories. For the authoritative rebuttal of Bauval and Gilbert's work see Robert Chadwick, 'The So-Called "Orion Mystery" ', *KMT* 8 (1996): 74–83. See also Ian Lawton and Chris Ogilvie-Herald, *Giza: The Truth* (London: Virgin Publishing, 1999); and Kurt Mendellsohn, *The Riddle of the Pyramids* (London: Thames and Hudson, 1974), pp. 201–11.

42   William Flinders Petrie, *The Pyramids and Temples of Gizeh* (London: Fold and Tuer, 1883). See also the discussion Edwards, *The Pyramids of Egypt*, pp. 243–44.

43   One recent theory proposes that the two stars were Kochab in the Little Dipper and Mizar in the handle of the Big Dipper, but Alioth and Pherkad are other possibilities. For a general discussion see Edwards, *The Pyramids of Egypt*, pp. 245–48 and for specific studies see Otto Neugebauer, 'On the Orientation of Pyramids', *Centaurus* 24 (1980): 1–3; Steven C. Haack, 'The Astronomical Orientation of the Egyptian Pyramids', *Archaeoastronomy: Supplement to Journal for the History of Astronomy* 7 (1984): S119–S125; Kate Spence, 'Ancient Egyptian Chronology and the Astronomical Orientation of Pyramids', *Nature* 408 (16 November 2000): 320–24; Hugh Thurston, 'Aligning Giza: Astronomical Orientation of the Great Pyramid', *Griffith Observer* 65(9) (September 2001): 11–17; Juan Antonio Belmonte, 'On the Orientation of Old Egyptian Pyramids', *Archaeoastronomy: Supplement to the Journal for History of Astronomy* 26 (2001): S1–S20.

44   Trimble, 'Astronomical Investigation Concerning the So-Called Air-Shafts of Cheops' Pyramid'; see also the discussion in Krupp, *Skywatchers, Shamans and Kings*, p. 288.

45   Edwards, *The Pyramids of Egypt*, p. 278; Paul Jordan, *Riddles of the Sphinx* (Stroud: Sutton Publishing, 1998), p. 139; Krupp, *Skywatchers, Shamans and Kings*, p. 288.

46   Edwards, *The Pyramids of Egypt*, p. 278.

47   Lockyer's ideas were first published in 1890 in *Nature* (April–July 1891) and then in full in his *The Dawn of Astronomy* (London: Cassell and Co. Ltd., 1894) – see esp. pp xi–xii. Nissen's articles were published in the *Rheinisches Museum für Philologie*, 1885.

48   Lockyer, *Dawn of Astronomy*, p. xi.

49   *Ibid.*, p. 119.

50   E.C. Krupp, 'Light in the Temples', in Clive Ruggles, *Records in Stone: Papers in Memory of Alexander Thom* (Cambridge: Cambridge University Press, 1988), pp. 473–98 (477). See also Budge, *Egyptian Magic*, which was dedicated to Lockyer.

51   Richard H. Wilkinson, *The Complete Temples of Ancient Egypt* (London: Thames and Hudson, 2000), pp. 76, 78.

52   *Ibid.*, p. 79; see also Richard H. Wilkinson, *Symbol and Magic in Egyptian Art* (London: Thames and Hudson, 1994), pp. 60, 66, 69–71, 76.

53   Krupp, 'Light in the Temples'.

54   Krupp, 'Light in the Temples', p. 486, table 21.1.

55   *Ibid.*, p. 483; See also Wilkinson, *Complete Temples*, pp. 226–27; and Gregg de Young, 'Astronomy in Ancient Egypt', in Helaine Smith (ed.), *Astronomy Across Cultures: The History of Non-Western Astronomy* (Dordrecht: Kluwer Academic Publishers, 2000), pp. 475–508 (490), who gives 22 February rather than 18.

56   Krupp, 'Light in the Temples', pp. 497–98.

57   Belmonte, 'On the Orientation of Old Egyptian Pyramids'; Belmonte and Shaltout, 'On the Orientation of Ancient Egyptian Temples: (1)'; Belmonte and Shaltout, 'On the Orientaton of Ancient Egyptian Temples: (2)'.

58   Faulkner, *The Book of the Dead*, spell 15.

59   The classic study is still Budge, *Egyptian Magic*; see also Wilkinson, *Symbol and Magic in Egyptian Art*, p. 277.

60   Viau, 'Egyptian Mythology', p. 27.

61   Barbara Watterson, *Gods of Ancient Egypt* (Stroud: Sutton Publishing, 1999), p. 150.

62   See Jan Assmann, *Egyptian Solar Religion in the New Kingdom* (trans. Anthony Alcock; London: Routledge and Kegan Paul, 1995).

63   Viau, 'Egyptian Mythology', p. 31.

Notes to Chapter 7: Egypt: The Stars and the Soul

1   Description of the duties of the hour-watcher Harkhebi (Gregg deYoung, 'Astronomy in Ancient Egypt', in Helaine Selin [ed.], *Astronomy Across Cultures: the History of Non-Western Astronomy* [Dordrecht: Kluwer Academic Publishers, 2000], pp. 475–508 [492–93].

2   Otto Neugebauer, 'The Egyptian Decans', *Vistas in Astronomy* 1 (1955): 47–49; reprinted in Otto Neugebauer, *Astronomy and History: Selected Essays* (New York, Berlin, Heidelberg and Tokyo: Springer Verlag, 1983), pp. 205–09; Bartel van der Waerden, 'Babylonian Astronomy II: The Thirty Six Stars', in *Journal of Near Eastern Studies* 8(1) (January 1949): 6–26 (7–8); R.A. Parker, 'Ancient Egyptian Astronomy', in F.R. Hodson (ed.), *The Place of Astronomy in the Ancient World* (Transactions of the Royal Society, 276; London: Oxford University Press, 1974), pp. 51–65 (53–56); R.A. Parker, 'Egyptian Astronomy, Astrology and Calendrical Reckoning', in Charles Coulston (ed.), *Dictionary of Scientific Biography* (New York: Charles Scribner's Sons, 1971), vol. 4, pp. 706–27 (711).

3   Parker, 'Egyptian Astronomy', pp. 711, 715.

4   The coffin lids were decoded by A. Pogo, 'Calendars on Coffin Lids from Assyut', *Isis* 17 (1932): 6–24; see also Otto Neugebauer and R.A. Parker, *Egyptian Astronomical Texts* (Providence, R.I.: Brown University Press, 1969), pp. 105–74; Otto Neugebauer, 'The Egyptian Decans'; Dalgas H. Christiansen, 'Decanal Star Tables for Lunar Houses in Egypt?' *Centaurus* 35 (1992): 1–27; Kurt Locher, 'Egyptian Cosmology', in Norris Hetherington (ed.), *Encyclopaedia of Cosmology* (New York and London: Garland Publishing, 1993), pp. 189–94 (192–93): De Young, 'Astronomy in Ancient Egypt', pp. 482–86.

5   Neugebauer and Parker, *Egyptian Astronomical Texts*, pp. 118–39. See also Olaf E. Keper, 'The Astronomical Ceiling of Deir El-Haggar in the Dakhleh Oasis', *Journal of Egyptian Archaeology* 31 (1995): 175–95, and the discussion in De Young, 'Astronomy in Ancient Egypt', p. 496.

6   Parker, 'Ancient Egyptian Astronomy', p. 56.

7   Kurt Locher, 'The Decans of Ancient Egypt: Timekeepers for Worship, or Worshipped Beyond Time?', in John W. Fountain and Rolf M. Sinclair (eds), *Current Studies in Archaeoastronomy: Conversations Across Time and Space* (Durham N.C.: Carolina Academic Press, 2005), pp. 429–34.

8   Parker, 'Egyptian Astronomy', p. 711.

9   *Ibid.*, pp. 713–14.

10   Locher, 'Ancient Cosmology', p. 192 suggests that the coffin-lid diagrams contain errors and are therefore poor copies of an earlier model.

11   Herodotus, *The Histories* II.124.

12   Parker, 'Ancient Egyptian Astronomy', p. 51.

13   Otto Neugebauer, *A History of Ancient Mathematical Astronomy* (3 vols; Berlin, Heidelberg

and New York: Springer Verlag, 1975), vol. 2, p. 561; Neugebauer and Parker, *Egyptian Astronomical Texts*, vol. 3, pp. 183–202; Parker, 'Ancient Egyptian Astronomy', pp. 51, 58–59; Parker, 'Egyptian Astronomy', pp. 711, 718. See also the discussion in De Young, 'Astronomy', p. 506; Paul Jordan, *Riddles of the Sphinx* (Stroud: Sutton Publishing, 1998), p. 138; and Norman Lockyer's earlier and to an extent outmoded views in *The Dawn of Astronomy* (London: Cassell and Co. Ltd., 1894), chs 12, 37.

14   Parker, 'Ancient Egyptian Astronomy', p. 51.

15   Neugebauer, *Ancient Mathematical Astronomy*, vol. 2, p. 561.

16   Parker, 'Egyptian Astronomy', p. 718.

17   Virginia Lee Davis, 'Identifying Ancient Egyptian Constellations', *Archaeoastronomy: Supplement to the Journal for the History of Astronomy* 9 (1985): S103–S104; Kurt Locher, 'Probable Identification of the Ancient Egyptian Circumpolar Constellations', *Archaeoastronomy: Supplement to the Journal for the History of Astronomy* 9 (1985): S152–S153; José Lull, and Juan Antonio Belmonte, 'A Firmament Above Thebes: Uncovering the Constellations of Ancient Egyptians', *Journal for the History of Astronomy* 37(4) (November 2006): 373–92.

18   Davis ('Identifying Ancient Egyptian Constellations', p. S103) argues that the lion is Leo, Jordan (*Sphinx*, p. 138) disagrees. See also Kurt Locher, 'A Conjecture Concerning the Early Egyptian Constellation of the Sheep', *Archaeoastronomy: Supplement to the Journal for the History of Astronomy* 3 (1981): S63–S65 and Kurt Locher, 'The Ancient Egyptian Constellation Group of the Lion between Two Crocodiles and the Bird', *Archaeoastronomy: Supplement to the Journal for the History of Astronomy* 15 (1990): S49–S51.

19   Davis, 'Identifying Ancient Egyptian Constellations', p. S102.

20   Ronald A. Wells, 'Astronomy in Egypt', in Christopher Walker (ed.), *Astronomy Before The Telescope* (London: British Museum Press, 1996), pp. 28–41 (30).

21   Jan Assmann, *The Mind of Egypt: History and Meaning in the Time of the Pharaohs* (New York: Metropolitan Books, 2002), p. 301.

22   See Neugebauer and Parker, *Egyptian Astronomical Texts*, vol. 3, pp. 175–82 and plate 1, for Senmut's tomb; Parker, 'Egyptian Astronomy', p. 719; and the summary in De Young, 'Astronomy', pp. 506–07; see also Rolf Krauss, 'The Eye of Horus and the Planet Venus: Astronomical and Mythological References', in John M. Steele and Annette Imhausen, *Under One Sky: Astronomy and Mathematics in the Ancient Near East* (Alter Orient und Altes Testament, 297; Munster: Ugarit Verlag, 2002), pp. 193–208.

23   O.R. Faulkner, 'The King and the Star Religion in the Pyramid Texts', *Journal of Near Eastern Studies* 25 (1966): 153–61 (159–61).

24   Parker, 'Ancient Egyptian Astronomy', p. 60; 'Egyptian Astronomy', p. 719.

25   E.g., C. Jacq, *Egyptian Magic* (Warminster: Aris and Phillips, 1985), pp. 33–34.

26   E.C. Krupp, 'Light in the Temples', in Clive Ruggles, *Records in Stone: Papers in Memory of Alexander Thom* (Cambridge: Cambridge University Press, 1988), pp. 473–98 (497).

27   De Young, 'Astronomy', p. 492.

28   I.E.S. Edwards, *The Pyramids of Egypt* (London: Penguin, rev. edn, 1988), p. 278.

29   Thorkild Jacobsen, *The Treasures of Darkness: A History of Mesopotamian Religion* (New Haven and London: Yale University Press, 1976), pp. 126–27; Samuel Noah Kramer, *The Sumerians: Their History, Culture and Character* (Chicago and London: University of Chicago Press, 1963), p. 123; Joseph Campbell, *The Masks of God: Oriental Mythology* (New York: Viking, 1962), pp. 103–04.

30   De Young, 'Astronomy', p. 507.

31   Otto Neugebauer and H.B. van Hosen, *Greek Horoscopes* (Philadelphia: American

Philosophical Society, 1959), p. 42 (horoscope 137); see also De Young, 'Astronomy', p. 475 for Greek philosophers and Egypt.

32   See the accounts in James Breasted, *A History of Egypt* (New York: Bantam Books, 1964 [1905]), pp. 675–77, 485–88.

33   David Brown, *Mesopotamian Planetary Astronomy-Astrology* (Groningen: Styx Publications, 2000), p. 26.

34   See, e.g., Cyril Fagan, *Astrological Origins* (St Paul, Minn.: Llewellyn Publications, 1971).

35   De Young, 'Astronomy'; see Marshall Clagett, *Ancient Egyptian Science: A Sourcebook*, vol. 2: *Calendars, Clocks and Astronomy* (Philadelphia: American Philosophical Society, 1995), p. 490.

36   R.A. Parker, 'Ancient Egyptian Astronomy', pp. 51–52 and De Young, 'Astronomy', pp. 492–93. See also the discussion in Neugebauer and Parker, *Egyptian Astronomical Texts*, pp. 214–15.

37   De Young, 'Astronomy', p. 492.

38   Parker, 'Ancient Egyptian Astronomy', p. 52.

39   Parker, 'Egyptian Astronomy', p. 723.

40   *Ibid.*, p. 723.

41   Francesca Rochberg-Halton, *Aspects of Babylonian Celestial Divination: The Lunar Tablets of Enuma Anu Enlil* (Archiv für Orientforschung, 22; Ferdinand Berger & Sohne: Horn, 1988), pp. 49–57; Nicholas Campion, *The Great Year: Astrology, Millenarianism and History in the Western Tradition* (London: Penguin, 1994), pp. 84–94.

42   Text A, System II, 30–31: Parker, 'Egyptian Astronomy', p. 723.

43   Text A, System IV, 26–27: Parker, 'Egyptian Astronomy', p. 723.

44   Hephaestio of Thebes, *Apotelesmatics* I.21.

45   Text B, Column IX, 1–13: Parker, 'Egyptian Astronomy', p. 724.

46   Hephaestio of Thebes, *Apotelesmatics* I.21.

47   'Excerpt VI. Hermes to Tat', 2–10 (in Walter Scott [trans.], *Hermetica: The Ancient Greek and Latin Writings which contain Religious or Philosophic Teachings ascribed to Hermes Trismegistus* [4 vols; Boulder: Shambala, 1982]); see also Marcus Manilius, *Astronomica* 4.294–407; Diodorus Siculus, *Library of History* II.30–31 ('the decans were the "Judges of the Universe" '); and Firmicus Maternus, *Mathesis* IV.xxii.2–3, for astrological accounts of their use in the first and fourth centuries CE.

48   Parker, 'Egyptian Astronomy', pp. 719–21.

49   Julian, 'Hymn to King Helios' (in *Works*, vol. 1 [3 vols; trans. W.C. Wright; Cambridge, Mass. and London: Harvard University Press, 1913]); Van der Waerden, 'Babylonian Astronomy II', p. 26.

Notes to Chapter 8:   The Hebrews: Prophets and Planets

1   Amos 8.9; see also Isa. 13.10; 34.4; 61.19–20; 66.22–23.

2   For this and the following discussion see Sara L. Gardner, 'Scratching the Surface of Astronomy in the Land of the Bible: Archaeology, Texts, and Astronomy', in John W. Fountain and Rolf M. Sinclair (eds), *Current Studies in Archaeoastronomy: Conversations Across Time and Space* (Durham N.C.; Carolina Academic Press, 2005), pp. 393–411; for background see J. Edward Wright, *The Early History of Heaven* (Oxford: Oxford University Press, 2000), esp. pp. 60–61; and Ann Jeffers, *Divination and Prophecy in Israel and Palestine* (Leiden: E.J. Brill, 1996).

3   Beth Alpert Nakhai, *Archaeology and the Religions of Canaan and Israel* (Atlanta: American Schools of Oriental Research, 2001).

4   Judg. 5.20.

5   See Wright, *The Early History of Heaven*, esp. p. 63.

6   J. Glen Taylor, *Yahweh and the Sun: Biblical and Archaeological Evidence for Sun Worship in Ancient Israel* (Journal for the Study of the Old Testament Supplement Series 111; Sheffield: JSOT Press, 1993).

7   Gen. 2.6; 7.11–12; Job 26.11; Ps. 104.5.

8   Louis Jacobs, 'Jewish Cosmology', in Carmen Blacker and Michael Loewe, *Ancient Cosmologies* (London: George Allen and Unwin Ltd., 1975), pp. 66–86.

9   Gen. 1.26.

10 Exod. 26.30; Heb. 9.23–25.

11 Michael C. Astour, 'Political and Cosmic Symbolism in Genesis 14 and in its Babylonian Sources', in Alexander Altmann (ed.), *Biblical Motifs: Origins and Transformations* (Cambridge Mass.: Harvard University Press, 1966), pp. 65–112.

12 Isa. 66.1

13 Henotheism is the worship of one god, monotheism the belief in one god. The first commandment decrees that: 'You shall have no other gods before me', not 'there are no other gods' (Exod. 20.3). Some authors have found echoes of a Mesopotamian-style democratic divine assembly in the Hebrew heaven. Daniel 7.10 records that 'the court sat in judgment', while references to the council of the Lord occur in Jer. 23.18, 22 and Amos 3.7. For the early tradition of the cosmic state in Palestine see Lowell K. Handy, *Among the Host of Heaven: The Syro-Palestinian Pantheon as Bureaucracy* (Winona Lake, Ind.: Eisenbrauns, 1993); W.F. Albright, *Yahweh and the Gods of Canaan* (Winona Lake, Ind.: Eisenbrauns, 1990. See also Deut. 32.8–9, in which the 'Most High' allocates different peoples to the 'sons of God', with the Israelites being subject to the 'Lord'. Another reading of this passage has the Canaanite high god Elyon give Israel to Yahweh, a lesser god. The tradition of Yahweh as a lesser god was to have cosmological consequences and significance for astrology in the Gnosticism of the first centuries CE.

14 Ps. 19.1.

15 Job 8.7–10; see also Mt. 5.45.

16 Hab. 3.3–4.

17 *1 Enoch* 14.18.

18 See the various hymns to Amon and Aton in James B. Pritchard, (ed.), *Ancient Near Eastern Texts Relating to the Old Testament* (Princeton: Princeton University Press, 1969), pp. 365–71.

19 Amos 5.8; see also Job 9.8–9; 38.31.

20 For an excellent survey of astrological practices amongst the Jews, see J.W. McKay, *Religion in Judah under the Assyrians* (London: SCM Press, 1973), pp. 45–59. For a similar treatment of more classical Jewish traditions see Steven Fine, *Art and Judaism in the Greco-Roman World: Toward a New Jewish Archaeology* (Cambridge: Cambridge University Press, 2005).

21 See Mark S. Smith, *The Origins of Biblical Monotheism* (Oxford: Oxford University Press, 2001).

22 James Breasted, *Development of Religion and Thought in Ancient Egypt* (Philadelphia: University of Pennsylvania Press, 1972 [1912]); Sigmund Freud, *Moses and Monotheism* (trans. Katherine Jones; New York: Vintage Books, 1955).

23 Simo Parpola, *Letters from Assyrian and Babylonian Scholars* (Helsinki: Helsinki University Press, 1993), p. LXXIV.

24 For an up-to-date account of the Canaanite pantheon see Handy, *Among the Host of Heaven*.

25 Dan. 2.21.

26 Exod. 12.6–20; see also Lev. 23.5; Ezek. 45.21. If by any chance any believer was unable to observe Passover at the required time, they were obliged to begin their commemoration at the exact moment at which the full moon rose above the eastern horizon on the 14th of the second month (Num. 9.11).

27 Lev. 23.34, 39; Ezek. 45.25. According to later Jewish tradition all the patriarchs were either born in Nisan or Tishri, either at the spring or autumn festivals.

28 See the discussion on the relationship between Hebrew and Babylonian festivals in W. Oesterley, 'Early Hebrew Ritual Festivals', in Samuel Hooke (ed.), *Myth and Ritual: Essays in the Myth and Ritual of the Hebrews in Relation to the Culture Patterns of the Ancient East* (Oxford: Oxford University Press, 1933), pp. 111–46 .

29 See Millar Burrows, 'Ancient Israel', in Robert C. Dentan (ed.), *The Idea of History in the Ancient Near East* (New Haven: Yale University Press, 1983), pp. 99–131 (esp. pp. 112, 122).

30 Ezek. 8.14–15.

31 Gen. 8.22; Jer. 31.35–6. In the new world everyone will observe the festivals 'from new moon to new moon and from sabbath to sabbath' for ever (Isa. 66.22–2).

32 *1 Enoch* 18.14–20. *1 Enoch* 80.2–7 portrays an image of celestial collapse followed by agricultural and hence socio-economic breakdown prior to the apocalypse, the coming historical crisis: 'But in the days of the sinners the years will become shorter, and their seed will be late on the land and on their fields, and all things on earth will change and will not appear at their proper time ... And the moon will change its customary practice, and will not appear at its proper time'. See Piotr Michalowski (ed.), *The Lamentation Over the Destruction of Sumer and Ur* (Winona Lake: Eisenbrauns, 1989), p. 1: 'To overturn the (appointed time), to forsake the (preordained) plans'.

33 Num. 14.11, 22; Dan. 4.2–3.

34 Amos 8.9; see also Isa. 13.10; 34.4; 61.19–20; 66.22–23.

35 1 Kgs 8.12–13 ('The Lord has set the Sun in the Heavens, But has said that he would dwell in thick darkness, I have built thee an exalted house, a place for thee to dwell in for ever') has been used to argue that Solomon constructed the temple in Jerusalem after a solar eclipse (see F.J. Hollis, 'Suncult and Temple at Jerusalem', in Hooke [ed.], *Myth and Ritual*, pp. 87–110; see also Taylor, *Yahweh and the Sun*; and Mark S. Smith, 'The Near Eastern Background of Solar Language for Yahweh', *Journal of Biblical Literature* 109(1) (Spring 1990): 29–39.

36 Gen. 37.9. In Joseph's preceding dream (Gen. 37.7), his brothers' sheaves of corn bowed down before his sheaf. By inference there were therefore 12 sheaves in all, so the analogy may be with the natural seasonal cycle. Explicit solar imagery in connection with the number 12 occurs only in the much later apocryphal *Joseph and Aseneth*. In one section Joseph is presented as a typical sun god, riding a chariot pulled by four horses, wearing a golden crown decorated with 12 precious stones and emitting 12 rays; while in another he sends 12 men to prepare his coming to Heliopolis, the Egyptian city of the sun, at noon, the hour of the sun's upper culmination (*Joseph and Aseneth* III.1–2).

37 Exod. 15.27.

38 Num. 2.1–31; see also the discussion in Burrows 'Ancient Israel', p. 129. Ezekiel (48.30–35) converted the Hebrew camp into a sacred city, arranged as a quadrangle aligned to the cardinal points with 12 gates named after the 12 sons of Jacob, which by the first century CE became the model for the New Jerusalem in Rev. 21.12, 14. See also *1 Enoch* 33–36; 75–76;

2 Enoch 6.18. *1 Enoch* 72 gives a different system with six gates to the east and six to the west.

39   Aristotle, *Athenian Constitution* 8.3; C.A. Robinson, *Ancient History from Prehistoric Times to the Death of Justinian* (New York: Macmillan, 1951), p. 444.

40   Ezek. 8.16: 'At the door of the temple of the Lord, between the porch and the altar, were about twenty-five men with their backs to the temple of the Lord, and their faces towards the east, worshipping the sun towards the east'.

41   In the words of the probably first-century CE *Zadokite Document* (*Damascus Document* [CD]) x.15–16 (in Theodor H. Gaster, *The Dead Sea Scriptures* [New York: Anchor Books, 3rd edn, 1976], p. 83).

42   Deut. 17.2, 5–7.

43   Job 31.26–7.

44   Amos 5.25; Acts 7.43; *Zadokite Document* vii.9–viii.21; Gaster, *Dead Sea Scriptures*, p. 109, n. 29. Saturn is described as the star of the sun in R. Campbell Thompson, *The Reports of the Magicians and Astrologers of Nineveh and Babylon in the British Museum* (2 vols; London: Luzac and Co., 1900) (report 176). Kiyyun contains the initial letters of the Hebrew expression *Kitb Neb'im*, meaning 'writings of the prophets'. Veneration of Saturn may be connected to the celebration of the Sabbath on Saturday, although the day was not named until the Roman period (see Eric Zafran, 'Saturn and the Jews', *Journal of the Warburg and Courtauld Institutes* 42 [1979]: 16–27). The first-century CE *Testament of Solomon* 16.2–4, has Solomon sacrificing to Raphan and Moloch. Kaivân was a Babylonian name for Saturn, Kaimânu was the Persian; see Bartel van der Waerden, *Science Awakening*, vol. 2: *The Birth of Astronomy* (Leyden and New York: Oxford University Press, 1974), pp. 194–96.

45   Ulla Koch-Westenholz, *Mesopotamian Astrology: An Introduction to Babylonian and Assyrian Celestial Divination* (Carsten Niebuhr Institute of Near Eastern Studies; Copenhagen: Museum Tusculunum Press, University of Copenhagen, 1995), pp. 44–50; Hermann Hunger and David Pingree, *Astral Sciences in Mesopotamia* (Leiden, Boston and Koln: Brill, 1999), pp. 8–12; David Pingree, *The Yavanajataka of Sphujidhvaja* (2 vols; Harvard Oriental Series, 48; Cambridge, Mass.: Harvard University Press, 1978), vol. 2, p. 614; Elizabeth Chesley Baity, 'Archaeoastronomy and Ethnoastronomy So Far', *Current Anthropology* 14(4) (October 1973): 389–449 (406, 417).

46   1 Kgs 11.33. For worship of Venus as Ashtoreth under Solomon see also Gaster, *The Dead Sea Scriptures*, p. 71; See note on p. 71 for discussion of the worship of Ashtoreth under David.

47   Isa. 14.12–15.

48   Rev. 20.3.

49   1 Kgs 12.28–33.

50   2 Kgs 15.8.

51   2 Kgs 17.9–10, 16–17, 30.

52   Isa. 47.13–14.

53   2 Kgs 18.4.

54   2 Kgs 21.3–5, 21; 23.5–7, 11–12.

55   Jer. 10.2–3.

56   See Elias Bickerman, *The Jews in the Greek Age* (Cambridge, Mass. and London: Harvard University Press, 1988); and Elias Bickerman, *The God of the Maccabees: Studies on the Meaning and Origin of the Maccabean Revolt* (trans. Horst R. Moehring; Leiden: Brill, 1979). Also see W.F. Albright, *From the Stone Age to Christianity: Monotheism and the Historical Process* (New York: Doubleday, 2nd edn, 1957), p. 271.

57 These arguments are developed in detail in Kocku von Stuckrad, 'Jewish and Christian Astrology in Late Antiquity – A New Approach', *Numen* 47(1) (2000): 1–40.

58 Peder Borgen, *Early Christianity and Hellenistic Judaism* (Dulles, Va.: T&T Clark, 1998), esp. pp. 15–24.

59 *1 Enoch* 9.6–7.

60 *The Epochs of Time (The Ages of Creation* [4Q180]) fr. 1 (in Gaster, *The Dead Sea Scriptures,* p. 522).

61 See the discussion in Stuckrad, 'Jewish and Christian Astrology in Late Antiquity', pp. 9, 22, 25, 31.

62 Josephus, *Jewish Antiquities* I.2.3.

63 Philo, *On the Life of Moses* 2.133–5.

64 Philo, *On the Creation* 17, 18, 24, 39.

65 Philo, *On Providence* II.48–54.

66 Augustine, *Confessions* IV.3.

67 See the discussion in James H. Charlesworth, 'Jewish Interest in Astrology During the Hellenistic and Roman Period', *Aufstieg und Niedergang der Romischen Welt* 20(2) (1987): 926–56.

68 *Testament of Solomon* 18.

69 1 Kgs 4.29–34.

70 *Testament of Solomon* 1.1; 2.2–3.

71 In the *Theaetetus* Plato has Socrates announce: 'Evils, Theodorus, can never pass away; for there must always remain something which is antagonistic to good. Having no place among the gods in heaven, of necessity they hover around the mortal nature, and this earthly sphere. Wherefore we ought to fly away from earth to heaven as quickly as we can; and to fly away is to become like God, as far as this is possible; and to become like him, is to become holy, just, and wise' (Plato, *Theaetetus* 176).

72 *1 Enoch* 8–9.

73 *Treatise of Shem* 6.

74 Num. 24.17; for the following see Stuckrad, 'Jewish and Christian Astrology in Late Antiquity', pp. 29–40.

75 Num. 24.17; See John Joseph Collins, *The Scepter and the Star: The Messiahs of the Dead Sea Scrolls and Other Ancient Literature* (New York: Doubleday, 1995).

76 Lester Ness, *Written in the Stars: Ancient Zodiac Mosaics* (Warren Center, Pa.: Shangri La Publications, 1999), esp. ch. 1. See also Fine, *Art and Judaism.*

77 See the discussion in Stuckrad, 'Jewish and Christian Astrology in Late Antiquity', pp. 25–28.

78 From Num. 23.23: 'there is no enchantment against Jacob, no divination against Israel'.

Notes to Chapter 9: Greece: Homer, Hesiod and the Heavens

1 Homer, *Iliad* 18.565–71.

2 H.A.L. Fisher, *A History of Europe* (London: Fontana, 1979 [1935]), vol. 1, p. 13.

3 Edward Said, *Orientalism* (London: Penguin, 1985). The detail of Said's theory may be criticized but orientalism remains a persuasive critique of Western attitudes to the East.

4 Peter Kingsley, *Ancient Philosophy, Mystery and Magic: Empedocles and Pythagorean Tradition* (Oxford: Clarendon Press, 1995), p. 9; see also David Pingree, 'Hellenophilia versus the History of Science', *Isis* 83 (1991): 554–63; Jim Tester, *A History of Western*

Astrology (Woodbridge, Suffolk: Boydell Press, 1987), pp. 17–18; for discussion see J. Finkelstein, *The Ox That Gored* (Transactions of the American Philosophical Society 71(2); Philadelphia: American Philosophical Society, 1981).

5   For classic examples of the view or astrology as an irrational import from the East, see Franz Cumont, *Astrology Among the Greeks and Romans* (New York: Dover Publications, 1960 [1911]); and E.R. Dodds, *The Greeks and the Irrational* (Sather Classical Lectures, 25; Berkeley: University of California Press, 1951), esp. p. 245.

6   Bartel van der Waerden, *Science Awakening*, vol. 2: *The Birth of Astronomy* (Leyden and New York: Oxford University Press, 1974), p. 130.

7   Allan Chapman, *Gods in the Sky: Astronomy, Religion and Culture from the Ancients to the Renaissance* (London: Channel 4 Books, 2001), p. 77.

8   The rejection of Hellenophilia by cuneiform scholars was made powerfully in Finkelstein, *The Ox That Gored*. For a recent, comprehensive critique of the distorting effects of Hellenophilia on the history of astrology in particular, and astronomy and science in general, see Francesca Rochberg, *The Heavenly Writing: Divination and Horoscopy, and Astronomy in Mesopotamian Culture* (Cambridge: Cambridge University Press, 2004), esp. ch. 1.

9   Walter Burkert, *Babylon Memphis Persepolis: Eastern Contexts of Greek Culture* (Cambridge, Mass.: Harvard Univerisity Press, 2004), p. 66.

10   Typical is the view expressed by J.L.E. Dreyer (*A History of the Planetary Systems from Thales to Kepler* [New York: Dover, 1953 (1906)], p. 1): 'Astronomy may be said to have sprung from Babylon, but cosmology, distinct from mythological cosmogony, dates only from Greece'.

11   Walter Burkert, *The Orientalising Revolution: Near Eastern Influence on Greek Culture in the Early Archaic Age* (Cambridge, Mass.: Harvard University Press, 1992), p. 18.

12   Peter Gorman, *Pythagoras: A Life* (London: Routledge and Kegan Paul, 1979).

13   Otto Neugebauer, *A History of Ancient Mathematical Astronomy* (3 vols; Berlin, Heidelberg and New York: Springer Verlag, 1975), vol. 2, pp. 589–98.

14   Herodotus, *The Histories* II.

15   G.E.R. Lloyd, *Magic, Reason and Experience: Studies in the Origins and Development of Greek Science* (Cambridge, New York and Melbourne: Cambridge University Press, 1979), p. 234.

16   Jane Harrison, *Themis: A Study of the Origins of Greek Religion* (London: Merlin Press 1963).

17   Lucy Goodison, *Death, Women and the Sun* (Institute of Classical Studies, Bulletin Supplement 53; London: Institute of Classical Studies, 1989), p. 153.

18   Harrison, *Themis*, pp. 189–92.

19   Mary Blomberg and Goren Henriksson, 'Elements of Greek Astronomy and Relgion in Monian Crete', in John W. Fountain and Rolf M. Sinclair (eds), *Current Studies in Archaeoastronomy: Conversations Across Time and Space* (Durham N.C.: Carolina Academic Press, 2005), pp. 371–92 (379–83).

20   Florence Wood and Kenneth Wood, *Homer's Secret Iliad: The Epic of the Night Skies Decoded* (London: John Murray, 1999); see also Emmeline Mary Plunket, *The Judgement of Paris and Some Other Legends Astronomically Considered* (London: John Murray, 1908); Laurin R. Johnson, *Shining at the Ancient Sea: The Astronomical Ancestry of Homer's Odyssey* (Portland, Oreg.: Multnomah House Press, 1999).

21   See Robert Graves, *The Greek Myths* (2 vols; London: Penguin, 1960), vol. 2, pp. 103–57.

22   For theories that the zodiac was invented as a single exercise see Michael Ovenden, 'The Origin of the Constellations', *The Philosophical Journal* 3(1) (1966): 1–18; Richard Proctor,

Myths and Marvels of Astronomy (London: Longmans, Green and Co., 1891); Archie E. Roy, 'The Origins of the Constellations', *Vistas in Astronomy* 27 (1984): 171–97. See also criticism of these arguments in D.R. Dicks, *Early Greek Astronomy to Aristotle* (London: Thames and Hudson, 1970), pp. 163–65; and the discussion in E.C. Krupp, 'Night Gallery: The Function, Origin and Evolution of Constellations', *Archaeoastronomy: The Journal of Astronomy in Culture* 15 (2000): 43–63.

23   The original work in this area was conducted by Norman Lockyer, although his findings are probably as inaccurate as those for his later research on British megaliths; see *The Dawn of Astronomy* (London: Cassell and Co. Ltd., 1894); for a more recent study see Jean Richer, *Sacred Geography of the Ancient Greeks: Astrological Symbolism in Art, Architecture and Landscape* (Albany: State University of New York Press, 1994), ch. 17. Richer's work, though, is marred by an attempt to identify zodiacal patterns prior to the introduction of the Babylonian zodiac to Greece.

24   Cited in Erica Reiner, *Astral Magic in Babylonia* (Philadelphia: American Philosophical Society, 1995), p. 99; see also Plutarch, 'The Oracles at Delphi no Longer Given in Verse', *Moralia* V.28.400b and 'On the Decline of Oracles', *Moralia* V.29.416f–417a.

25   Plutarch, 'Isis and Osiris', *Moralia* V.26.357.

26   Herodotus, *The Histories* VI.106.

27   See Robert Parker, 'Greek States and Greek Oracles', in Richard Buxton (ed.), *Oxford Readings in Greek Religion* (Oxford: Oxford University Press, 2000), pp. 76–108; see also William R. Halliday, *Greek Divination: A Study of its Methods and Principles* (London: Macmillan, 1913); and J.S. Morrison, 'The Classical World', in Carmen Blacker and Michael Loewe, *Ancient Cosmologies* (London: George Allen and Unwin Ltd., 1975), pp. 87–114.

28   Plutarch, *Agis* (in *Lives* [2 vols; trans. John Langhorne and William Langhorne; London and New York: Frederick Warne and Co., 1890]).

29   Patrick Curry, 'Divination, Enchantment and Platonism', in Angela Voss and Jean Hinson Lall (eds), *The Imaginal Cosmos: Astrology, divination and the Sacred* (Canterbury: University of Kent, 2007), pp. 35–46 (35–36).

30   David Pingree, 'Legacies in Astronomy and Celestial Omens', in Stephanie Dalley (ed.), *The Legacy of Mesopotamia* (Oxford: Clarendon Press, 1998), pp. 125–37 (129). See also E. Burrows, 'The Constellation of the Wagon and Recent Archaeology', *Analecta Orientalia* 12 (1935): 34–40.

31   Homer, *Iliad* 18.565–71. Although the *Iliad* was not standardized in written form until considerably later, there seems no reason to question the antiquity of this verse.

32   Burkert, *The Orientalising Revolution*.

33   Bernard Goldman, 'An Oriental Solar Motif and its Western Extension', *Journal of Near Eastern Studies* 20(4) (October 1961): 239–47.

34   W.G. Lambert and P. Walcot, 'A New Babylonian Theogony and Hesiod', *Kadmos* 4 (1965): 64–72; see also the discussion in Nicholas Campion, *The Great Year: Astrology, Millenarianism and History in the Western Tradition* (London: Penguin, 1994), pp. 106–08.

35   Hesiod, *Homeric Hymns* III 'To Delian Apollo' 2–5 (in *The Homeric Hymns and Homerica, including 'Works and Days' and 'Theogonis'* [trans. Hugh G. Evelyn-White; Cambridge, Mass.: Harvard University Press, 1917]).

36   Hesiod, 'The Astronomy' 4 (in *The Homeric Hymns*); for a discussion of the text, see Graves, *The Greek Myths*, vol. 1, pp. 151–54; for a concise survey of theories of mythic structures see Robert A. Segal, *Myth: A Very Short Introduction* (Oxford: Oxford University Press, 2004), pp. 85–108.

37   Plutarch, *Theseus* (in *Lives*). See also Graves, *The Greek Myths*, pp. 336–37.

38   For Aratus see *Phaenomena* (trans. G.R. Mair; Cambridge, Mass. and London: Harvard University Press, 1927); for discussion and sources of Greek celestial deities see Theony Condos, *Star Myths of the Greeks and Romans: A Sourcebook* (Grand Rapids, Mich.: Phanes Press, 1997); and Chapman, *Gods in the Sky*.

39   Daryn Lehoux, 'Observation and Prediction in Ancient Astrology', *Studies in History and Philosophy of Science* 35 (2004): 227–46; and Daryn Lehoux, *Astronomy, Weather, and Calendars in the Ancient World: Parapegmata and Related Texts in Classical and Near-Eastern Societies* (Cambridge: Cambridge University Press, 2007); also see Robert Hannah, *Greek and Roman Calendars: Constructions of Time in the Classical World* (London: Duckworth, 2005), pp. 20–27.

40   Hesiod, *Works and Days* 668–69; see also the discussion in Campion, *The Great Year*, pp. 208–17.

41   Campion, *The Great Year*, pp. 151–60.

42   For Babylonian hemerologies see Reiner, *Astral Magic in Babylonia*, pp. 112–13.

43   For the role of *Works and Days* in the development of astrology, and its conceptual relationship to Babylonian astrology, see Lehoux, 'Observation and Prediction in Ancient Astrology'.

44   Hesiod, *Works and Days* 609–13.

45   *Ibid.*, 663–65.

46   *Ibid.*, 727–29.

47   Campion, *The Great Year*, pp. 134–35.

48   But, for an analysis of the farming calendar, see A.W. Mair, *Hesiod: The Poems and Fragments* (Oxford: Oxford University Press, 1908).

49   Hesiod, *Works and Days* 825–29.

50   For the relationship between religion and philosophy see Kingsley, *Ancient Philosophy, Mystery and Magic*; and Peter Kingsley, *In the Dark Places of Wisdom* (Inverness, Calif.: Golden Sufi Center, 1999).

51   See the discussion in Gregory Vastos, 'Theology and Philosophy in Early Greek Thought', *The Philosophical Quarterly* 2(7) (April 1952): 97–123.

52   Herodotus, *The Histories* II.109.

53   For an introduction to oracles see the discussions in Morrison, 'The Classical World'. On Apollo, Peter Kingsley, argues that he was not originally a solar deity: see *In the Dark Places of Wisdom*.

54   See the discussion in G.S. Kirk, J.E. Raven and M. Schofield, *The Presocratic Philosophers* (Cambridge: Cambridge University Press, 2nd edn, 1983), p. 92.

55   Herodotus, *The Histories* I.74.

56   Otto Neugebauer, *The Exact Sciences in Antiquity* (New York: Dover Publications, 2nd edn, 1969), pp. 42–43; see also A. Pannekoek, *A History of Astronomy* (London: George Allen and Unwin Ltd., 1961), pp. 98–99; and Hugh Thurston, *Early Astronomy* (New York: Springer Verlag, 1994), p. 110.

57   See Francesca Rochberg-Halton, *Aspects of Babylonian Celestial Divination: The Lunar Eclipse Tablets of Enuma Anu Enlil* (Archiv für Orientforschung, 22; Ferdinand Berger & Sohne: Horn, 1988), pp. 30–31.

58   For early Greek astronomy see Dicks, *Early Greek Astronomy to Aristotle*; Dreyer, *A History of the Planetary Systems from Thales to Kepler*; James Evans, *The History and Practice of Ancient Astronomy* (Oxford: Oxford University Press, 1998); Lloyd Motz and Jefferson Hane Weaver, *The Story of Astronomy* (New York and London: Plenum Press, 1995); Pannekoek, *A History of Astronomy*; David Furley, *The Greek Cosmologists* (Cambridge:

Cambridge University Press, 1987), vol. 1; and M.R. Wright, *Cosmology in Antiquity* (London: Routledge, 1995).

59 The argument is best made in Kingsley, *Ancient Philosophy, Mystery and Magic.*

60 Plutarch, 'Pericles' (in *Lives*). For Anaxagoras' cosmology see Edward Hussey, *The Presocratics* (London: Duckworth, 1983), pp. 133–41; and Kirk, Raven and Schofield, *The Presocratic Philosophers*, pp. 352–84.

61 For Anaximander's surviving fragments see Kirk, Raven and Schofield, *The Presocratic Philosophers*, pp. 100–42; see also Charles H. Kahn, *Anaximander and the Origins of Greek Cosmology* (New York: Hackett Publishing Co., 1960).

62 Kirk, Raven and Schofield, *The Presocratic Philosophers*, p. 135. As an example of the caution with which we should treat such claims, our source is the sixth-century CE writer Aetius, over 1000 years after Anaximander; see also Jonathan Barnes, *Early Greek Philosophy* (London: Penguin, 1987).

63 Kirk, Raven and Schofield, *The Presocratic Philosophers*, pp. 135, 154.

64 Ezek. 1.22.

65 Kirk, Raven and Schofield, *The Presocratic Philosophers*, p. 171 (fr. 174).

66 Simo Parpola, 'The Assyrian Tree of Life: Tracing the Origins of Jewish Monotheism and Greek Philosophy', *Journal of Near Eastern Studies* 52(3) (July 1993): 161–208 (esp. p. 204); Jack N. Lawson, *The Concept of Fate in Ancient Mesopotomia: Of the First Millennium, Towards an Understanding of 'Simtu'* (Wiesbaden: Harrasowitz Verlag, 1994), p. 69.

67 *The Bundahishn* I.1 (E.W. West, *The Bundahishn, or Knowledge from the Zand* (n.p.: Kessinger Publishing, 2004), p. 2. The Persian–Greek connection is now assumed by some scholars, such as Walter Burkert: see *Babylon Memphis Persepolis*, p. 66.

68 For this discussion as it pertains to the late-classical world see Polymnia Athanassiadi-Fowden and Michael Frede, *Pagan Monotheism in Late Antiquity* (Oxford: Oxford University Press, 2001).

69 Kirk, Raven and Schofield, *The Presocratic Philosophers*, p. 179 (fr. 186).

70 *Ibid.*, p. 201 (fr. 226).

71 *Ibid.*, p. 190 (fr. 204).

72 *Ibid.*, p. 188 (fr. 200).

73 *Ibid.*, p. 211 (fr. 247). Paraphrased by the nineteenth-century British astrologer, Alan Leo as 'character is destiny', Heraclitus' aphorism has long been a guiding principle of Western astrology.

74 See Hesiod, *Works and Days* 122. See the discussion in Shirley M.L. Darcus, 'Daimon as a Force in Shaping Ethos in Heraclitus', *Phoenix* 28 (1974), pp. 390–407.

75 Homer, *The Odyssey* II.556–58.

76 For Parmenides' fragments see Kirk, Raven and Schofield, *The Presocratic Philosophers*, pp. 239–62, and for discussion, Hussey, *The Presocratics*, pp. 78–106.

77 William Guthrie, *Orpheus and Greek Religion: A Study of the Orphic Movement* (Princeton: Princeton University Press, 1993); M.L. West, *The Orphic Poems* (Oxford: Oxford University Press, 1983); see also Liz Greene, 'The Influence of Orphic Beliefs on the Development of Hellenistic Astrology', *Culture and Cosmos* 9(1) (Autumn/Winter 2005): 21–44.

78 See Gaibor Betegh, *The Derveni Papyrus: Cosmology, Theology and Interpretation* (Cambridge: Cambridge University Press, 2004), p. 41 (col. 19) and ch. 5; and A. Laks, and G. Most (eds), *Studies on the Derveni Papyrus* (Oxford: Oxford University Press, 1997).

79 See the discussion in Mircea Eliade, *A History of Religious Ideas* (Chicago: University of Chicago Press, 1982), vol. 2, pp. 180–209; and Walter Burkert, *Ancient Mystery Cults* (Cambridge and London: Harvard University Press, 1987).

80 Plato, *Republic* I.364E.
81 Lynn Thorndike, *History of Magic and Experimental Science* (8 vols; New York: Columbia University Press, 1923–58), vol. 1, p. 282. Thorndike comments that Lucian's essay on astrology is widely regarded as spurious, although there is no evidence for this claim.
82 Plato, *Republic* X.612A.
83 For Pythagoras' life and teachings see Kenneth Sylvan Guthrie, *The Pythagorean Sourcebook and Library* (Grand Rapids, Mich.: Phanes Press, 1987); see also Gorman, *Pythagoras: A Life*.
84 Julius Caesar, *The Conquest of Gaul* I.1.
85 See the useful discussion in Liba Chaia Taub, *Ptolemy's Universe: The Natural, Philosophical and Ethical Foundations of Ptolemy's Astronomy* (Chicago and La Salle, Ill.: Open Court, 1993), pp. 138–40.
86 Aristotle, *Metaphysics* I.v.1–9.
87 William Shakespeare, *Troilus and Cressida* I.iii.109–10.
88 Kirk, Raven and Schofield, *The Presocratic Philosophers*, p. 287 (fr. 348); see also Denis O'Brien, *Empedocles' Cosmic Cycle: A Reconstruction From the Fragments and Secondary Sources* (Cambridge: Cambridge University Press, 1969).
89 Kirk, Raven and Schofield, *The Presocratic Philosophers*, p. 286 (frs 346–47).
90 See Kingsley, *Ancient Philosophy, Mystery and Magic*, esp. ch. 4.
91 See C.G. Jung's own account of his ideas in *Memories, Dreams, Reflections* (London: Fontana, 1967).
92 Aristotle, *De Anima* I.2.404b.
93 Harrison, *Themis*, p. 185.
94 Ioan Petru Culianu, *Psychanodia I: A Survey of the Evidence Concerning the Ascension of the Soul and its Relevance* (Leiden: E.J. Brill, 1983), p. 1.
95 Hippocrates, *Airs, Waters, Places* 2 (in *Works* [4 vols; trans. W. Jones and E. Witherington; Cambridge, Mass.: Harvard University Press, 1923], vol. 1); see also Mark J. Schiefsky, *Hippocrates on Ancient Medicine* (Leiden: Brill, 2004).
96 Hippocrates, *Airs, Waters, Places* 2.
97 Hippocrates, 'The Nature of Man' (in G.E.R. Lloyd [ed.], *Hippocratic Writings* [London: Penguin, 1983], pp. 260–61).
98 Hippocrates, *Airs, Waters, Places* 10.
99 Hippocrates, *On the Sacred Disease* I.297 (cited in Lloyd, *Magic, Reason and Experience*, p. 19).
100 Thurston, *Early Astronomy*, p. 111. See also below, p. 336. n. 23.
101 For the associations of months with deities in the Hellenistic period, after 300 BCE, see Charlotte Long, 'The Gods of the Months in Ancient Art', *American Journal of Archaeology* 93 (1989): 589–95 (591).
102 Louise Bruit Zaidman and Pauline Schmidt Pantel, *Religion in the Ancient Greek City* (trans. Paul Cartledge; Cambridge: Cambridge University Press, 1994), pp. 102–04; see also Hannah, *Greek and Roman Calendars*; and Elias Bickerman, *Chronology of the Ancient World* (London: Thames and Hudson, 1980), esp. pp. 22–37.

Notes to Chapter 10: Greece: The Platonic Revolution

1 Plato, *Theaetetus* 176.
2 'The Greek word *psyche* is conventionally and misleadingly translated by "soul". It is rather

life, or the cause of life, and in a human being sensation and perception, emotion and thought are all part of life if it is fully present' (F.H. Sandbach, *The Stoics* [Bristol: The Bristol Press, 1975], p. 82.

3 Augustine, *City of God* VIII.5–12.

4 See William Bell Dinsmoor, *The Architecture of Ancient Greece: An Account of Its Historic Development* (New York: W.W. Norton and Co., 1975).

5 Socrates' thought is scattered throughout Plato's dialogues. His discussion of the immortality of the soul is relevant for the development of Greek cosmology; see Plato, *Phaedo*. For a good recent discussion see C.C.W. Taylor, R.M. Hare and J. Barnes, *Greek Philosophers – Socrates, Plato, and Aristotle* (Oxford: Oxford University Press, 1999).

6 Plato, *Timaeus* 27–60; *Republic* X, see also VIII; *Laws* V.737–38, VI.771; *Phaedrus*; *Phaedo*; *Symposium*; *Epinomis*. There is some argument about the authorship of the *Epinomis*, which may have been written by Plato's secretary and student, Philip of Opus. However, the text is still included in editions of Plato's work and reflects his thought. See Leonardo Tarán, *Academica: Plato: Philip of Opus, and the Pseudo-Platonic Epinomis* (Philadelphia: American Philosophical Society, 1975). For the purposes of the development of Platonic cosmology from the fourth century BCE onwards, though, it makes no difference whether Plato or his student was the author. For a seminal and influential account of Plato's cosmology see F.M. Cornford, *Plato's Cosmology: The Timaeus* (London: Routledge, 2001 [1937]).

7 Plato, *Timaeus* 28C–29A, 41B, 42E.

8 Ps. 19.1.

9 Plato, *Timaeus* 38C.

10 Robin Waterfield, 'The Evidence for Astrology in Classical Greece', *Culture and Cosmos* 3(2) (Autumn/Winter 1999): 3–15.

11 Plato, *Epinomis* 987A–B.

12 Plato *Timaeus* 40C–D.

13 Plato, *Republic* VI.488.D.

14 Plutarch, *Pericles* (in *Lives* [2 vols; trans. John Langhorne and William Langhorne; London and New York: Frederick Warne and Co., 1890]). See also J.A.R. Munro, 'Thucydides on the Third of August, 431 B.C.', *The Classical Quarterly* 13(3–4) (July 1919): 127–28.

15 See the discussion in Frederick H. Cramer, *Astrology in Roman Law and Politics* (Chicago; Ares Publishers, 1996 [1954]), p. 9.

16 Hesiod, *Theogony* 371–73, 381.

17 Plato, *Timaeus* 38C–D.

18 Plato, *Epinomis* 987B–C. The question of Greek naming of the planets was dealt with exhaustively in Franz Cumont 'Les noms des planètes et l'astrolatrie chez les Grecs', *L'Antiquité Classique* 4(1) (1935): 5–43. The Platonic conversion of Babylonian to Greek deities became the standard, but there were other versions; see Charlotte Long, *The Twelve Gods of Greece and Rome* (Leiden and New York: Brill, 1987). By the first half of the third century BCE, the planets appear to have also all been given non-divine names, such as Phainon (Saturn), Phaeton (Jupiter), Pyroeis (Mars), Eospheros or Phosphoros (Venus) and Stilbon (Mercury) (See the discussion in Theony Condos, *Star Myths of the Greeks and Romans: A Sourcebook* [Grand Rapids, Mich.: Phanes Press, 1997], pp. 167–69).

19 Samuel Noah Kramer, *The Sumerians:Their History, Culture and Character* (Chicago: University of Chicago Press, 1963), p. 108.

20 Plato, *Epinomis* 987A–B, E.

21 Karl Popper, *The Open Society and its Enemies* (2 vols; London and New York: Routledge,

1945), vol. 1, p. 244, n. 1; see also p. 210, n. 5; Karl Popper, *The Poverty of Historicism* (London and New York: Routledge, 1986).

22 Plato, *Timaeus* 40E.

23 Mircea Eliade, *The Sacred and the Profane* (New York: Harcourt Brace, 1959).

24 Plato, *Republic* VI.509.

25 Plato, *Phaedo* 98A.

26 Plato, *Laws* VII.821B–D.

27 Plato, *Timaeus* 39E–40A, 55A–C. The structure was: fire = tetrahedron (pyramid), gods; air = octahedron, birds; water = icosahedron, fish; earth = cube, animals, including humans. A fifth solid, the twelve-sided dodecahedron, was considered to be the most perfect because it was closest to the sphere and used by God to decorate the universe, perhaps a reference to the zodiac.

28 Plato, *Timaeus* 35; *Republic* X.617B.

29 Plato, *Phaedo* 108E–109A, 110B.

30 Hesiod, *Theogony* 1.216–20.

31 Plato, *Republic* X.617C.

32 Plato, *Timaeus* 46D, 47A.

33 Cicero, *De divinatione* I.lv.125. See also the criticisms of the Stoic concept of fate in II.viii.20–ix.24.

34 Plato, *Timaeus* 28A; *Phaedo* 66A, 83A; *Theaetetus* 157.

35 Plato, *Symposium* 207C–208B.

36 Plato, *Phaedrus* 247C.

37 Plato, *Timaeus* 28A.

38 Plato, *Republic* VII.514–17.

39 Plato, *Phaedrus* 250 B–251B; *Republic* VII.518C–D, 519D.

40 Plato, *Timaeus* 42C–D, 47B–C; *Epinomis* 978D; *Republic* VII.529C–D; *Laws* XII.966E–967C.

41 Plato, *Phaedo* 66A.

42 Plato, *Republic* VII.517B; *Phaedrus* 250A–B.

43 Plato, *Laws* V.737E–738A.

44 Plato, *Phaedrus* 244–45.

45 Plato, *Phaedo* 75C–E.

46 *Ibid.*, 67A; see also 74A, 76A

47 *Ibid.*, 66C, 67A, 73B–74A, 83A; Plato, *Phaedrus* 240, 256A–B.

48 Plato, *Timaeus* 27C.

49 Plato, *Laws* VII.809C–D.

50 *Ibid.*, V.737E–738A, VI.771A–C; Plato, *Epinomis* 978E–979A. For the possible influence of 360-day years on the Greeks see Robert Hannah, *Greek and Roman Calendars: Constructions of Time in the Classical World* (London: Duckworth, 2005), pp. 25, 83–86.

51 Plato, *Timaeus* 22D, 39D; see Godefroid de Callatay, *Annus Platonicus: A Study of World Cycles in Greek, Latin and Arabic Sources* (Louvain-la-Neuve: Université Catholique de Louvain, 1996).

52 Plato, *Republic* VIII.546A–B; See also James Adam, *The Nuptial Number of Plato* (Wellingborough: Thorsons, 1985 [1891]) and *The Republic of Plato* (Cambridge: Cambridge University Press, 1902); Nicholas Campion, *The Great Year: Astrology, Millenarianism and History in the Western Tradition* (London: Penguin, 1994), pp. 242–46.

53 Paul Ricoeur, *Time and Narrative* (Chicago: University of Chicago Press, 1985), vol. 2, p. 23.

54 Plato, *Phaedrus* 249A–B.

55 *Hymns of the Atharva-Veda* XIX.53 (trans. Maurice Bloomberg; Delhi: Motilal Banarsidass, 2000 [1897]).

56 Plato, *Phaedrus* 246B–C.

57 *Hymns of the Atharva-Veda* XIII.40; for discussion of links between Platonic philosophy and India in general, see Thomas McEvilley, *The Shape of Ancient Thought* (New York: Allsworth Press, 2002).

58 See the discussion in Bartel van der Waerden, *Science Awakening*, vol. 2: *The Birth of Astronomy* (Leyden and New York: Oxford University Press, 1974), p. 147.

59 Ioan Petru Culianu, *Psychanodia I: A Survey of the Evidence Concerning the Ascension of the Soul and its Relevance* (Leiden: E.J. Brill, 1983).

60 Plato, *Timaeus* 41E–42A.

61 Plato, *Republic* X.620D–E; for a very useful discussion of the daimon see Hans Dieter Betz, 'The Delphic Maxim "Know Yourself" in the Greek Magical Papyri', *History of Religions* 21(2) (November 1981): 156–71.

62 This is not a view which would have been held by the Neoplatonic Philosophers of the third century CE onwards, who read Homer allegorically and referred to him as the 'divine theologian'. See Crystal Addey, 'Oracles and Divination in Late Antiquity: The Development and Integration of Religious Phenomena in Late Platonist Philosophy' (PhD Thesis: University of Bristol, forthcoming 2008).

63 G.S. Kirk, J.E. Raven and M. Schofield, *The Presocratic Philosophers* (Cambridge: Cambridge University Press, 2nd edn, 1983), p. 211 (fr. 247).

64 William Shakespeare, *Julius Caesar* I.ii.140–41.

65 Kirk, Raven and Schofield, *The Presocratic Philosophers*, p. 209 (fr. 93).

66 Plato, *Phaedrus* 246A, 253C–D.

67 Plato, *Republic* IV.443D.

68 See Bartel van der Waerden, *Science Awakening*, vol. 2, p. 147: 'It seems to me that we are here touching upon the deepest religious root of horoscope astrology. The soul comes from the heavens, where it partook of the circulation of the stars. It unites itself with a body and forms with it a living being. This explains how human character comes to be determined by the heavens.'

69 Plato, *Symposium* 207E.

70 Plato, *Republic* VIII.546A.

71 Plato, *Timaeus* 47E–48A.

72 Plato, *Republic* X.617E; see also X.619D; *Phaedrus* 249B.

73 Plato, *Phaedo* 82B–D.

74 *Nam* has been compared to necessity, although it has been suggested that the Greek words *moira* and *physis* are the only natural equivalents. For this discussion see A. Leo Oppenheim, *Ancient Mesopotamia: Portrait of a Dead Civilisation* (Chicago: University of Chicago Press, 1977), pp. 201–08.

75 Firmicus Maternus *Mathesis* I.VIII.2–3.

76 The fourth-century CE astrologer Julius Firmicus Maternus wrote: 'Mind settles into the frail earthly body and, thanks to its fleeting memory of sovereign soul, recognises what is taught and hands down to us all knowledge' (*Mathesis* I.IV.5). The theory of memory was influential in the Renaissance (see Frances Yates, *The Art of Memory* [London: Peregrine, 1978]) and remains a basis of progressive educational theory (see, for example, Rudolf Steiner, *Human Values in Education* [London: Rudolf Steiner Press, 1971]).

77 Aristotle, *Metaphysics* 1074a: after reviewing the theories of Eudoxus and Callippus, Aristotle defines a total of 55 'movers' (i.e., spheres) on which the planets rotate. See also

Aristotle, *On the Heavens* 292a and the discussion in W.K.C. Guthrie (trans.) *Aristotle: On the Heavens* (Cambridge, Mass. and London: Harvard University Press, 1921), p. 208.

78 Aristotle, *Metaphysics* 1074a, 1073a. Aristotle, was, though, critical of the Platonic theory of Ideas, or forms; see *Metaphysics* 1084.

79 Aristotle, *De Anima* I.2.404b.

80 Aristotle, *On Generation and Corruption*.

81 Aristotle, *Physics* I.v.188a.

82 See James Hillman, *The Soul's Code: In Search of Character and Calling* (London: Bantam Books, 1997), esp. ch. 1, 'In a Nutshell: The Acorn Theory and the Redemption of Psychology' and ch. 9, 'Fate'.

83 Aristotle, *Metaphysics* 1050a.12–14.

84 'Being born under a particular sign, or having a lot of planets or the ascendant placed there, doesn't automatically show that you are those things, that you have those qualities full-blown and ready to display in the shop window. It means that there is a reservoir of potential innate in you, something to strive toward. You grow into your chart, just as a seed grows into a full plant' (Liz Greene, *Astrology for Lovers*, London: Unwin Paperbacks, 1986).

85 Aristotle *Politics* 1.v.1254a 17.

86 Aristotle, *Metaphysics* XII.1074b; *On the Heavens* I.270b 1–12, II.292a.

Notes to Chapter 11: The Hellenistic World: The Zodiac

1 Aratus, *Phaenomena* 11–14.

2 For the transition of Babylonian astrology and astronomy to Greece, especially after the fifth century BCE, see e.g., Otto Neugebauer, 'The Survival of Babylonian Methods in the Exact Sciences of Antiquity and Middle Ages', in *Proceedings of the American Philosophical Society* 107(6) (December 1963): 528–35 (531); Francesca Rochberg-Halton, 'Elements of the Babylonian Contribution to Hellenistic Astrology', *Journal of the American Oriental Society* 108(1) (January–March 1988): 51–62 (52); Alexander Jones, 'Babylonian Astronomy and its Legacy', *Bulletin of the Canadian Society for Mesopotamian Studies* 32 (1977): 11–17; Alexander Jones, 'Evidence for Babylonian Arithmetical Schemes in Greek Astronomy', in *Die Rolle der Astronomie in den Kulturen Mesopotamiens* (Grazer Morganländische Studien, 3; ed. Hannes D. Galter; Graz: RM-Druck & Verlagsgesellschaft m.b.H, 1993), pp. 77–94; Alexander Jones, 'On Babylonian Astronomy and its Greek Metamorphoses', in F. Jamil Ragep and Sally P. Ragep (eds), *Tradition, Transmission, Transformation* (Leiden and New York: E.J. Brill, 1996), pp. 139–55; Alexander Jones, 'The Place of Astronomy in Roman Egypt', in Timothy D. Barnes (ed.), *The Sciences in Greco-Roman Society* (Edmonton, Alberta: Academic Printing and Publishing, 1994), pp. 25–51; David Pingree, 'Legacies in Astronomy and Celestial Omens', in Stephanie Dalley (ed.), *The Legacy of Mesopotamia* (Oxford: Clarendon Press, 1998), pp. 125–37. See also G.E.R. Lloyd, *Magic, Reason and Experience: Studies in the Origins and Development of Greek Science* (Cambridge, New York and Melbourne: Cambridge University Press, 1979), p. 226, on the danger of exaggerating connections between Mesopotamian and Greek cultures: 'The issue of the debt of Greek science to Egypt and Babylonia has been, since antiquity, an emotive topic; all too often it has been argued, by ancient and modern writers alike, either that the Greeks owed everything, or that they owed nothing, to Eastern wisdom, while fundamental questions relating to the processes of transmission, and the interpretation of what was transmitted, have been ignored. Thus the circumstances in which a metallurgical technique may be

transmitted from one culture to another are quite different from those of the transmission of a religious belief or myth, which differ in turn from those of an item of astronomical lore.'

3 The strict academic line is that theurgy properly developed with the Chaldean oracles, dated to the first or second century CE, probably the latter part of the second, and was founded by the oracles' writers, Julian the Chaldean and his son, Julian the Theurgist. However, theurgy, in the sense that it existed in the second century, is clearly evident in the second century BCE, and earlier traditions.

4 Lloyd, *Magic, Reason and Experience*, p. 266.

5 Jim Tester, *A History of Western Astrology* (Woodbridge, Suffolk: Boydell Press, 1987), p. 70; see also the analysis of 'strong' and 'weak' astrology in R.J. Hankinson, 'Stoicism, Science and Divination', in R.J. Hankinson (ed.), *Method, Medicine and Metaphysics: Studies in the Philosophy of Ancient Science (Apeiron* 21[2] [1988]), pp. 123–60.

6 Cicero, *De divinatione* I.iii.121

7 Diodorus Siculus, *Library of History* 17.112.2

8 Appian, *Roman History* II.9.58; cited in Frederick H. Cramer, *Astrology in Roman Law and Politics* (Chicago: Ares Publishers, 1996 [1954]), p. 11.

9 Francesca Rochberg, *Babylonian Horoscopes* (Philadelphia: American Philosophical Society, 1998); A.J. Sachs, 'Babylonian Horoscopes', *Journal of Cuneiform Studies* 6 (1952): 40–75.

10 Vitruvius, *De Architectura* IX.6.2.

11 Graham Shipley, *The Greek World After Alexander* (New York: Routledge, 2000), p. 205.

12 James Evans, *The History and Practice of Ancient Astronomy* (Oxford: Oxford University Press, 1998), pp. 121–25. However, Hypsicles did not acknowledge Babylonian astronomers in his text, the *Anaphorikos*.

13 Berossus, *Babyloniaca*; Seneca, *Naturales Quaestiones* III.c.29.

14 Josephus, *Jewish Antiquities* 1.7.2.

15 Otto Neugebauer *A History of Ancient Mathematical Astronomy* (3 vols; Berlin, Heidelberg and New York: Springer Verlag, 1975), vol. 2, p. 609.

16 Robert Hand (ed.) and Robert Schmidt (trans.), *The Astrological Records of the Early Sages in Greek* (Berkeley Springs, W.Va.: Golden Hind Press, 1995), pp. 49–57.

17 As a example of the source problems we face in these centuries, Cramer (*Astrology in Roman Law and Politics*, pp. 14–15) accepts that Critrodemus lived in the third century BCE, Pingree (*The Yavanajataka of Sphujidhvaja* [2 vols; Harvard Oriental Series, 48; Cambridge, Mass.: Harvard University Press, 1978], vol. 2, pp. 424–25) suggests the first century BCE and Otto Neugebauer and H.B. van Hoesen, (*Greek Horoscopes* [Philadelphia: The American Philosophical Society, 1959], p. 186) conclude probably the late first century CE.

18 Hephaistio of Thebes, *Apotelesmatics* II.10. See also the discussion in Cramer, *Astrology in Roman Law and Politics*, pp. 14–15.

19 Otto Neugebauer, *The Exact Sciences in Antiquity* (New York: Dover Publications, 2nd edn, 1969), p. 168. Firmicus Maternus, *Mathesis* II, Praefatio.

20 Vitruvius, *De Architectura* IX.6.2.

21 Neugebauer and van Hoesen, *Greek Horoscopes*, pp. 14–16; see also the discussion in Roger Beck, *The Religion of the Mithras Cult in the Roman Empire: Mysteries of the Unconquered Sun* (Oxford: Oxford University Press, 2006), pp. 227–39; and Roger Beck, 'The Astronomical Design of Karakush, a Royal Burial Site in Ancient Commagene: An Hypothesis', *Culture and Cosmos* 3(1) (Spring/Summer 1999): 10–31.

22 E.C. Krupp, 'Bedroom Politics and Celestial Sovereignty', in John W. Fountain and Rolf M. Sinclair (eds), *Current Studies in Archaeoastronomy: Conversations Across Time and Space* (Durham, N.C.; Carolina Academic Press, 2005), pp. 412–27; see also the discussion

in Stanislaw, Iwaniszewski, 'Archaeoastronmical Analysis of Assyrian and Babylonian Monuments: Methodological Issues', *Journal for the History of Astronomy* 34(1) (February 2003): 79–93.

23 Hugh Thurston, *Early Astronomy* (New York: Springer Verlag, 1994), p. 111. Thurston only cites secondary sources, including Ptolemy's *Phases* which, of course, is almost 600 years later. Neugebauer, *History of Ancient Mathematical Astronomy*, pp. 294, 600, says only that Meton and Euctemon were using the sun's location at the solstices and equinoxes, approximately 21 March, 21 June, 21 September and 21 December, as markers. Ptolemy included extensive references to Euctemon. The mention of zodiac signs, though, may have been Ptolemy's own. See Ptolemy, *The Phases of the Fixed Stars*.

24 Plato, *Timaeus* 55C. R.G. Bury ([trans.], *Timaeus* [Cambridge, Mass. and London: Harvard University Press, 1931], p. 134, n. 1) assumes that the dodecahedron represents the zodiac signs and A.D. Lee (*Pagans and Christians in Late Antiquity* [London and New York: Routledge, 2000], p. 78), constellations.

25 See the discussion in D.R. Dicks, *Early Greek Astronomy to Aristotle* (London: Thames and Hudson, 1970), pp. 113–15. See also Charlotte Long, *The Twelve Gods of Greece and Rome* (Leiden and New York: E.J. Brill, 1987).

26 See the discussion by Robert Schmidt ('Translator's Preface', in Vettius Valens, *The Anthology: Book 1* [trans Robert Schmidt; Project Hindsight Greek Track, 4; Berkeley Springs, W.Va., Golden Hind Press, 1993], pp. xvi–xvii.

27 See the discussions in Dicks, *Early Greek Astronomy*, pp. 164–65 and Theony Condos, *Star Myths of the Greeks and Romans: A Sourcebook* (Grand Rapids, Mich., Phanes Press, 1997), pp. 19, 23.

28 See the 'Calendar or Register Attributed to Geminus', in Ptolemy, *The Phases of the Fixed Stars*.

29 Aratus, *Phaenomena* 342–52.

30 Aratus, *Phaenomena* 879–884. For the influence of Hesiod see 110–30 in which Aratus paraphrases Hesiod's five races.

31 Bradley E. Schaefer, 'The Latitude and Epoch for the Origin of the Astronomical Lore of Eudoxus', *Journal for the History of Astronomy* 35(2) (May 2004): 161–224. The Bear acquired meaning as the symbol of immortality in Egypt in the second and first centuries BCE; perpetually revolving around the pole, the constellation points to north and, in Old Kingdom celestial theology, immortality (see Excerpt VI: Hermes to Tat, 13 [in *Hermetica: The Ancient Greek and Latin Writings which contain Religious or Philosophic Teachings ascribed to Hermes Trismegistus* (trans. Walter Scott; Boulder: Shambala, 1982), vol. 1, p. 413]).

32 See the argument in Emma Gee, *Ovid, Aratus and Augustus* (Cambridge: Cambridge University Press, 2000). For Aratus' continuing influence in the Roman world see also D. Mark Possanza, *Translating the Heavens: Aratus, Germanicus, and the Poetics of Latin Translation* (Lang Classical Studies, 14; New York: Peter Lang, 2004).

33 See Condos, *Star Myths of the Greeks*; Mary Grant (trans.), *The Myths of Hyginus* (Lawrence, Kan.: University of Kansas Publications, 1960).

34 E.C. Krupp, 'Night Gallery: The Function, Origin and Evolution of Constellations', *Archaeoastronomy: The Journal of Astronomy in Culture* 15 (2000): 43–63.

35 Otto Neugebauer and R.A. Parker, *Egyptian Astronomical Texts* (Providence, R.I.: Brown University Press, 1960), vol. 3, pl. 47; See also the discussion in Marshall Clagett, *Ancient Egyptian Science: A Sourcebook*, vol. 2: *Calendars, Clocks and Astronomy* (Philadelphia: American Philosophical Society, 1995), pp. 472–76.

36 R.A. Parker, 'Egyptian Astronomy, Astrology and Calendrical Reckoning', in Charles Coulston (ed.), *Dictionary of Scientific Biography* (New York: Charles Scribner's Sons, 1971), vol. 4, pp. 706–27 (721–23).

37 Firmicus Maternus, *Mathesis* III.1.1–2, 9.

38 Vettius Valens, *The Anthology* I.2; see also Marcus Manilius, *Astronomica* 2.150–714 and Ptolemy, *Tetrabiblos* I.11–18.

Notes to Chapter 12: The Hellenistic World: Scepticism and Salvation

1 'Asclepius' I. 3c (in *Hermetica: The Ancient Greek and Latin Writings which contain Religious or Philosophic Teachings ascribed to Hermes Trismegistus* [trans. Walter Scott; Boulder: Shambala 1982], vol. 1).

2 F.H. Sandbach, *The Stoics* (Bristol: The Bristol Press, 1975).

3 Arthur O. Lovejoy, *The Great Chain of Being* (Cambridge, Mass. and London: Harvard University Press, 1936).

4 For a summary of Aristarchus' ideas see Hugh Thurston, *Early Astronomy* (New York: Springer Verlag, 1994), pp. 122–23; and for Lucretius, see Lucretius, *On the Nature of the Universe* V.

5 For the imaginative ability of the mind to rove through the heavens see Roger Miller Jones, 'Posidonius and the Flight of the Mind through the Universe', *Classical Philology* 21(2) (April 1926): 97–113. And see Marcus Manilius, *Astronomica* 876–78: 'The mind of man has the power to leave its proper abode and penetrate to the innermost treasures of the sky'.

6 Sandbach, *The Stoics*, esp. pp. 101–08.

7 Marcus Manilius, *Astronomica* 2.148–49.

8 Stephanie Dalley (ed.), *The Legacy of Mesopotamia* (Oxford: Clarendon Press, 1998), pp. 108–09; Alasdair Livingstone, *Mystical and Mythological Explanatory Works of Assyrian and Babylonian Scholars* (Oxford: Clarendon Press, 1986), pp. 71–79.

9 Sandbach, *The Stoics*, esp. p. 82.

10 Marcus Aurelius, *Meditations* V.47; see also IX.29; see Plato, *Republic* VII.516B.

11 Seneca, *Letters from a Stoic* XII, II.

12 *Ibid.*, CXXIII.17.

13 The issue of the dating of the corpus is a subject of some argument. The fifteenth-century notion that it was of immense antiquity, comparable to the Pentateuch, was challenged in the nineteenth century. A standard contemporary view is Scott's, that the texts display such a combination of Stoicism and Platonism that they can only have been composed once philosophers such as Posidonius had found a reconciliation between the two schools of thought after 100 BCE. There would then have been additions and insertions up to the third century, possibly later (see Scott, *Hermetica*, vol. 1, p. 9).

14 See the discussion in Brian P. Copenhaver, *Hermetica* (Cambridge: Cambridge University Press, 1992), p. xxiii.

15 Robert Hand, 'Introduction to the Liber Hermetis', in Hermes, *Liber Hermetis* (trans. Robert Zoller; Berkeley Springs, W.Va.: Golden Hind Press, 1993), pp. iii–xxxv (xv).

16 Gilles Quispel, 'Hermes Trismegistus and the Origins of Gnosticism', *Vigiliae Christianae* 46(1) (March 1992): 1–19.

17 Luther H. Martin, *Hellenistic Religions: An Introduction* (Oxford: Oxford University Press, 1987), p. 150.

18   Scott, *Hermetica*, vol. 1, p. 15.

19   For Christ as shepherd see Mt. 9.36; 1 Pet. 5.4; for Poimandres as the Stoic 'sovereign reason' see Ralph Marcus, 'The Name Poimandres', *Journal of Near Eastern Studies* 8(1) (January 1949): 40–43 (43).

20   Peter Kingsley, 'Poimandres: The Etymology of the Name and the Origins of the Hermetica', *Journal of the Warburg and Courtauld Institutes* 56 (1993): 1–24. Kingsley argues that Poimandres is linked to the Greek word *poimen* meaning shepherd; thus Poimandres may be shepherd of men (*andres*).

21   *Corpus Hermeticum* I.6 (in Scott, *Hermetica*).

22   *Ibid.*, VI.4a.

23   *Ibid.*, VI.3b.

24   *Ibid.*, I. 6.

25   *Ibid.*, I.18.

26   *Ibid.*, I.22–23.

27   *Ibid.*, I.25.

28   Morton W. Bloomfield, 'The Origin of the Concept of the Seven Cardinal Sins', *Harvard Theological Review* 34(2) (April 1941): 121–28.

29   *Corpus Hermeticum* XVI.17–19; Excerpt VII: Hermes to Tat.1. See also Asclepius 3b–4, I.10. For a summary see Garth Fowden, *The Egyptian Hermes: A Historical Approach to the Late Pagan Mind* (Princeton: Princeton University Press, 1986), p. 77.

30   *Corpus Hermeticum* XVI.17–19; for daimons see also Asclepius I.4–5.

31   *Corpus Hermeticum* XVI.13–14; see also Excerpt IIA: Hermes to Tat, 9–10.

32   The parts which feel desire and repugnance; see Scott, *Hermetica*, p. 271, n. 2; Plato, *Phaedrus* 246A, 253 C–D.

33   *Corpus Hermeticum* XVI.15–16.

34   *Ibid.*, XVI.17.

35   *Ibid.*, I.13a.

36   *Ibid.*, I.15–16; See also Excerpt XIV: Hermes to Tat, 1–2.

37   Asclepius, III.39–40c.

38   *Corpus Hermeticum* XII.18–20.

39   *Ibid.*, III.4.

40   *Ibid.*, XVI.13; see also IX.5.

41   Asclepius, II.19b.

42   *Ibid.*, III.35; See also IX.5, 7.

43   Plato, *Republic* X.611D–612A; *Phaedo* 68C, 67E, 77D, 82C–83A, 247B–C; *Phaedrus* 247 B–C.

44   Excerpt IIA, Hermes to Tat, 9.

45   See the discussion in Crystal Addey, 'Oracles and Divination in Late Antiquity: The Development and Integration of Religious Phenomena in Late Platonist Philosophy' (PhD Thesis: University of Bristol, 2008).

46   Plato, *Phaedrus* 249A–B.

47   Ptolemy, *Tetrabiblos* 1.3.

48   Hermes, *Liber Hermetis* VXIII.

49   *Corpus Hermeticum* I.19.

50   *Ibid.*, XIII.7b–12.

51   *Ibid.*, VI.5.

52   *Ibid.*, XVI.14–16.

53   *Ibid.*, XVI.15–16.

54 Excerpt VII. Hermes to Tat.3.
55 Asclepius, III.39–40c.
56 *Corpus Hermeticum* XVII.
57 Augustine, *City of God* V.5.
58 Cicero, *De natura deorum* II.47–62.
59 Cicero, *De divinatione* I.xxxix.85, II.vi.17–vii.18, II.xi.27, II.xiv.33–34, II.xliii–xlvii.
60 *Ibid.*, II.xi.27, II.xxiii.71.
61 *Ibid.*, I.xliii.95.
62 *Ibid.*, I.v.9, II.v.13.
63 *Ibid.*, I.vi12, xviii.34, xix.37, lv.124, lvi.127, II.iii.9, II.xi.25; Plato, *Phaedrus* 244.
64 Cicero, *De divinatione* I.i.2, xviii.36, xli.92.
65 *Ibid.*, I.lvii.131
66 *Ibid.*, I.xlii.93, liii.120, II.xlii.89.
67 Cicero is quite specific that by Chaldean he means Babylonian; he is not using the term as a generic description of astrologers (see *ibid.*, I.1.2 and W.A. Falconer [trans.], *De divinatione* [Cambridge, Mass. and London: Harvard University Press, 1929], p. 224, n. 1).
68 Cicero, *De divinatione* I.li.117, lii.118.
69 *Ibid.*, I.lv.125; see also the criticisms of the Stoic concept of fate in II.viii.20–ix.24.
70 *Ibid.*, I.lvi.127, 128.
71 Plutarch, *Plutarch* (in *Lives* [2 vols; trans. John Langhorne and William Langhorne; London and New York: Frederick Warne and Co., 1890], p. 150).
72 Cicero, *De divinatione* I.xlii.93.
73 *Ibid.*, I.xviii.34.
74 *Ibid.*, I.xxii.45.
75 *Ibid.*, I.xxiii.46.
76 Cicero, *Republic* VI.
77 Macrobius, *Commentary on the Dream of Scipio*.
78 Augustine, *City of God* V.3
79 Sextus Empiricus, *Against the Professors* V.47.
80 *Ibid.*, VI.64–67.
81 Manilius, *Astronomica*, 4.886–90, 893–95.

Notes to Chapter 13: Hellenistic Astrology: Signs and Influences

1 Marcus Manilius, *Astronomica* 4.877–79.
2 *Corpus Hermeticum* I.13a (in *Hermetica: The Ancient Greek and Latin Writings which contain Religious or Philosophic Teachings ascribed to Hermes Trismegistus* [4 vols; trans. Walter Scott; Boulder: Shambala, 1982]).
3 See the discussion in Robert Schmidt, 'Translator's Preface', in Vettius Valens, *The Anthology: Book 1* (trans. Robert Schmidt; Project Hindsight Greek Track, 4; Berkeley Springs, W.Va.: Golden Hind Press, 1993), pp. xvi–xvii (xvii).
4 For accounts of the technical procedures of Greek astrology see Roger Beck, *A Brief History of Ancient Astrology* (Oxford: Blackwell, 2007); George C. Noonan, *Classical Scientific Astrology* (Tempe, Ariz.: American Federation of Astrologers, 1984); Joseph Crane, *Astrological Roots: The Hellenistic Legacy* (Bournemouth: The Wessex Astrologer, 2007); and Mark Riley, 'Theoretical and Practical Astrology: Ptolemy and His Colleagues', *Transactions of the American Philological Association* 117 (1987): 235–56.

5   See the explanation and discussion in Vettius Valens, *The Anthology* I.4. The notion of rising constellations or zodiac signs was familiar much earlier. The Roman poet Ennius (237–169 BCE), referred to the moments when 'goat or scorpion … arise'; see Cicero, *Republic* I.xvii.30. We should also remember the use of rising decans in Egypt, dating back to the Old Kingdom.

6   Otto Neugebauer and H.B. van Hoesen, *Greek Horoscopes* (Philadelphia: American Philosophical Society, 1959), no 3, p. 17.

7   The passage is quoted in the late fourth-century work, the *Apotelesmatics* ('Outcomes'), by Hephaistio of Thebes, II.18. See also Antiochus of Athens, *The Thesaurus* 10.

8   Neugebauer and van Hoesen, *Greek Horoscopes*, p. 174.

9   The terminology can be confusing. In the Greek texts a zodiac sign can be a *zoidion*, an *oikos* (the root of the modern world ecology) or, confusingly, house, whereas a house was known as a *temple*, or *topos* (place). Initially, so-called 'whole-sign' houses were used in which the first degree of the house was the first degree of the zodiac sign containing the ascendant. Sometime in the classical period an alternative system came into use, eventually surpassing whole-sign houses, in which the ascendant was the first degree of the house. The meanings were: (1) life in its generality, (2) material prosperity, (3) brothers, siblings, (4) parents and patrimony, (5) children, good fortune, (6) illness, bad fortune, (7) marriage, (8) death, (9) travel, God, (10) honours, (11) friends, good daimon, (12) enemies, bad daimon. House systems were not always based on the diurnal circle – they could be based on mathematical constructions such as the Lot of Fortune (see Manilius, *Astronomica* III.43–159), or other considerations; see the discussion in Crane, *Astrological Roots*, ch. 7. There were conventionally 12 houses, and there are theories that they were derived from the 12 divisions of the sky used in Etruscan liver divination. Both Jack Lindsay (*Origins of Astrology* [London: Barnes and Noble, 1971]) and Roger Beck (*A Brief History of Ancient Astrology*) refer to this theory but it has never been fully investigated. There may have been an alternative system of 8 houses or, at least topics that might be dealt with in the horoscope. An apparent 8-house system is first attested in Manilius, *Astronomica*, though Goold argues that the 8 houses are just the first 8 of the 12 (G.P. Goold [trans.], *Marcus Manilius Astronomica* [Cambridge, Mass. and London: Harvard University Press, 1977], pp. lxi–lxii). See also Beck, *A Brief History of Ancient Astrology*, pp. 44–45.

10 See Ptolemy, *Tetrabiblos* I.17. The system was logical and symmetrical: the sun equated to one half of the zodiac from Leo to Capricorn and the moon to the other half from Aquarius to Cancer. Specifically, the sun ruled Leo and the moon Cancer. Each of the other planets then ruled over one sign in each half: Mercury over Gemini and Virgo, Venus over Taurus and Libra, Mars over Aries and Scorpio, Jupiter over Sagittarius and Pisces, Saturn over Capricorn and Aquarius. See also Manilius *Astronomica* 2.203–23, for variations.

11 Cicero, *De natura deorum* II.88.

12 Vettius Valens, *The Anthology* (ed. David Pingree as *Vettii Valenti Antiocheni Anthologiarium, libri novem* [Leipzig, 1986]); see the English translation (*The Anthology* [trans. Robert Schmidt; Project Hindsight Greek Track; Berkeley Springs, W.Va.: Golden Hind Press, 1993–2001); Alexander Jones, *Astronomical Papyri from Oxyrhynchus* (2 vols; Philadelphia: American Philosophical Society 1999); Neugebauer and van Hoesen, *Greek Horoscopes*.

13 The French historian Henri Bouché-Leclercq argued that *katarchic* horoscopes and birth charts were fundamentally opposed, theoretically and technically, the former being religious, the latter being embedded in Greek science (see *L'Astrologie Grecque* [Paris: Ernest Leroux, 1899], ch. 13). However, this theory has more to do with conventional nineteenth- and twentieth-century ideas that astrology represented some alien import

into Greece, and the argument breaks down when it is accepted that birth charts had no necessary connection with Greek scientific mentality.

14   Frederick H. Cramer, *Astrology in Roman Law and Politics* (Chicago; Ares Publishers, 1996 [1954]), p. 11.

15   David Pingree argued that the technical rules of interrogational astrology were developed in India, perhaps in the second century, on the basis of techniques for elections, and then transmitted to the West; see *From Astral Omens to Astrology From Babylon to Bikaner* (Rome: Istituto Italiano per L'Africa e L'Oriente, 1997), p. 16. He later suggested that the date may have been the fifth rather than the second century. The earliest textual evidence for interrogational astrology occurs in book V of Dorotheus of Sidon's *Carmen Astrologicum*, from either the first or second centuries, and again in the late fourth century in book III of Hephaistio's *Apotelesmatics*. Pingree argues that Dorotheus' text is a later Persian interpolation. However, Juvenal in the first century CE and Apuleius in the second century both talk about clients asking questions of astrologers; see Juvenal, *The Sixteen Satires* VI; and Lucius Apuleius, *The Golden Ass*. Pingree may be correct that certain interpretative rules were perfected in India, but it is unlikely that astrologers had no means of answering questions earlier.

16   Neugebauer and van Hosen, *Greek Horoscopes*, pp. 144–48 (nos L479, L483, L484).

17   Vettius Valens, *The Anthology* IV.4, 7.

18   Joanna Komarowska, 'The Lure of Egypt, or How to Sound Like a Reliable Souce', in Nicholas Campion, Patrick Curry and Michael York (eds), *Astrology and the Academy* (papers from the inaugural conference of the Sophia Centre, Bath Spa University College, 13–14 June 2003: Bristol: Cinnabar Books, 2004), pp. 147–58,

19   Dorotheus of Sidon, *Carmen Astrologicum* 'Introduction'. See also the brief discussion in Tamsyn Barton, *Ancient Astrology* (London: Routledge, 1994), pp. 26–27 and Firmicus Maternus, *Mathesis* II, Praefatio.

20   *Papyrus Cairo* 31222; R.A. Parker, 'Egyptian Astronomy, Astrology and Calendrical Reckoning', in Charles Coulston (ed.), *Dictionary of Scientific Biography* (New York: Charles Scribner's Sons, 1971), vol. 4, pp. 706–27 (725); see also G.R. Hughes, 'A Demotic Astrological Text', *Journal of Near Eastern Studies* 10 (1951): 256–64.

21   Beck, *A Brief History of Ancient Astrology*, p. 11; citing Zoroaster, *Geoponica* 1.10.

22   Hephaistio of Thebes, *Apotelesmatics* I.23.

23   Parker, 'Egyptian Astronomy', p. 725; Otto Neugebauer and R.A. Parker, 'Two Demotic Horoscopes', *Journal of Egyptian Archaeology* 54 (1968): 231–35. After Demotic script fell out of fashion, horoscopes were written in Greek, of which the latest example is set for 508 CE: see Alexander, *Astronomical Papyri from Oxyrhynchus*, vol. 1, pp. 5, 415.

24   Parker, 'Egyptian Astronomy', p. 725; Otto Neugebauer and R.A. Parker, *Egyptian Astronomical Texts* (Providence, R.I.: Brown University Press, 1960), vol. 3, pp. 217–55.

25   Pliny, *Natural History* II.iv.13.

26   *Ibid.*, II.v.14, 17, 20, 22–25; see also ix.54.

27   *Ibid.*, II.iv.12, vi.32–40; see also xvi.19.

28   Cicero, *De divinatione* I.i.2, I.xli.90–xlii.93.

29   *Ibid.*, I.vi.12; I.xliii.95.

30   Antiochus of Athens, *The Thesaurus*.

31   Already, by the fifth century, different manuscript traditions had emerged, on the basis of which the second-century original has to be reconstructed. See the introduction in W. Hübner (ed.), *Claudii Ptolemaei, Opera quae exstant omnia Volumen II, I: Apotelesmatika* (Stuttgart and Leipzig: B.G. Teubner, 1998).

32 For the best discussion of the intellectual context of Ptolemy's work see Liba Chaia Taub, *Ptolemy's Universe: The Natural, Philosophical and Ethical Foundations of Ptolemy's Astronomy* (Chicago and La Salle, Ill.: Open Court, 1993).

33 Ptolemy, *Tetrabiblos* I.1

34 See the discussion in Mark Riley, 'Science and Tradition in the *Tetrabiblos*', *Proceedings of the American Philosophical Society* 132(1) (1988): 67–84.

35 Ptolemy, *Tetrabiblos* III.12.

36 Dorotheus of Sidon, *Carmen Astrologicum* I.19.

37 Ptolemy, *Tetrabiblos* I.2. As Seneca wrote, 'tides are but the agency of fate': see *Naturales Questiones* III.xxviii.3.

38 Ptolemy, *Tetrabiblos* I.2.

39 Ptolemy, *Tetrabiblos* I.4.

40 Antiochus of Athens, *The Thesaurus* 8; see Ptolemy, *Tetrabiblos* III.12.

41 A.J. Sachs, 'Babylonian Horoscopes', *Journal of Cuneiform Studies* 6 (1952): 49–75 (68).

42 Manilius, *Astronomica* 2.926, 3.655, 4.258, 4.501, 4.143.

43 Ptolemy, *Tetrabiblos* II.4–8.

44 *Ibid.*, I.3.

45 *Ibid.*, I.3.11.

46 *Ibid.*, I.3.

47 See Patrick Curry, 'Divination, Enchantment and Platonism', in Angela Voss and Jean Hinson Lall (eds), *The Imaginal Cosmos: Astrology, Divination and the Sacred* (Canterbury: University of Kent, 2007), pp. 35–46.

48 Firmicus Maternus, *Mathesis* I.VII.1–6.

49 Ptolemy, *Tetrabiblos* 1.2.4, 8.

50 Asclepius, III.39; Manilius, *Astronomica* 880–81. I am not suggesting that the writer of the Asclepius, Manilius and Ptolemy all shared the same idea of 'seed' but that there were common themes being developed in different ways.

51 Ptolemy, *Tetrabiblos* I.3.12.

52 *Ibid.*, 1.2.

53 *Ibid.*, 1.3.

54 Manilius, *Astronomica* IV.883–85.

55 Ptolemy, *Almagest* I.1.

56 *Ibid.*

57 Ptolemy, *Tetrabiblos*, 1.2. 7, 9.

58 Ptolemy, *Almagest* I.3.

59 Ptolemy, *Harmonics* III.96.27; see also 97.16.

60 *Ibid.*, II.12–13.

61 Ptolemy, *Tetrabiblos* III.13 (trans. F.E. Robbins; Cambridge, Mass. and London: Harvard University Press, 1940). See also the translation in Ptolemy, *Tetrabiblos* (vol. 3; trans. Robert Schmidt; Cumberland, Md.: Golden Hind Press, 1996), II.14.

62 See the discussion in F.H. Sandbach, *The Stoics* (Bristol: The Bristol Press, 1975), esp. pp. 60–61.

63 Ptolemy, *Tetrabiblos* III.13.

64 *Ibid.*, I.18, II.3

65 Otto Neugebauer, *A History of Ancient Mathematical Astronomy* (3 vols; Berlin, Heidelberg and New York: Springer Verlag, 1975), vol. 2, p. 596.

66 Pliny, *Natural History*, II.xvii.81.

67 Ptolemy, *Tetrabiblos* I.10

68 Vettius Valens, *The Anthology* VII. Valens complained: 'Whether the ancients, though knowing the workings of prognostication, jealously concealed it because it was a matter for boasting and hard for human nature to understand, or whether, not grasping what nature was articulating as a gift because of necessity she had to box it up, they nevertheless wrote in a riddling manner, I cannot say ... However, it being surely the case that those men either so wished it or that they were so unable, even so, in mentioning the chief of them below, I am astonished that his meaning is so twisted and hard to catch'.

69 Aries, Leo and Sagittarius = fire, Taurus, Virgo and Capricorn = earth, Gemini, Libra and Aquarius = air and Cancer, Scorpio and Pisces = water. But we should note George Noonan's clarification that earth, air, fire and water, are not 'elements; but primary bodies out of which all other bodies are assumed to be made'; see Noonan, *Classical Scientific Astrology*, p. 47. The system of sign–element correspondences also occurs in Antiochus of Athens, *The Thesaurus* I.3. It is uncertain, though, whether this is Antiochus' own work or an insertion in the early seventh-century paraphrase by Rhetorius.

70 Vettius Valens, *The Anthology* V.6.

71 *The Homeric Hymns*, 'Hermes', lines 13–14, 254, 541.

72 *The Homeric Hymns*, 'Hermes', line 538.

73 Vettius Valens, *The Anthology* I.1.

74 *Ibid.*, I.1.

75 See, for example, Margaret Hone, *The Modern Textbook of Astrology* (London: L.N. Fowler, 4th edn repr. 1973), pp. 24–31.

76 Augustine, citing Varro, in *City of God* VII.19; Bartel van der Waerden, *Science Awakening*, vol 2: *The Birth of Astronomy* (Leyden and New York: Oxford University Press, 1974), p. 195.

77 Ben Jonson, *Diana* I. 1.

78 Vettius Valens, *The Anthology* I.1; Ptolemy, *Tetrabiblos* I.4; see also III.4 for the moon and mothers.

79 Plutarch, 'Isis and Osiris', *Moralia* V.367.

80 Manilius, *Astronomica* 2.651–54, 673–96.

81 Firmicus Maternus, *Mathesis*, III.vi.1, 4.

82 See James Evans, 'The Astrologer's Apparatus: A Picture of Professional Practice in Greco-Roman Egypt', *Journal for the History of Astronomy* 35(1) (February 2004): 1–44; Tamsyn Barton, *Ancient Astrology*, pl. 13.

83 Suetonius, *The Twelve Caesars* 31.1; Acts 19.19.

84 Hans Dieter Betz, *The Greek Magical Papyri in Translation, Including the Demotic Spells* (Chicago: Chicago University Press, 1992); *Papyri graecae magicae* VII. 284–99 (ed. K. Preisendanz; Berlin, 1928).

85 Betz, *The Greek Magical Papyri*; *Papyri graecae magicae* VII. 795–845, 846–61, 862–918.

86 Juvenal, *The Sixteen Satires* VI.l.565–68.

87 Joan Breton Connelly, *Portrait of a Priestess: Women and Ritual in Ancient Greece* (Princeton: Princeton University Press, 2007).

88 Juvenal, *The Sixteen Satires* VI.1.555–56.

89 Marinus of Samaria, *The Life of Proclus* 28.

90 Evans, 'The Astrologer's Apparatus'.

91 Josèphe-Henriette Abry, *Les tablettes astrologiques de Grand (Vosges)* (Lyon: University Jean Mill-Lyon III, 1993).

92 Neugebauer and van Hoesen, *Greek Horoscopes*, pp. 18, 156 (nos 15/22, L497), see also the discussion on pp. 163–64; and, for the origin of planetary and zodiacal symbols,

Otto Neugebauer, 'Demotic Horoscopes', *Journal of the American Oriental Society* 63(2) (April–June 1943): 115–27 (123–25).

93   Betz, *The Greek Magical Papyri*, p. 312.
94   Plato, *Timaeus* 47C.

Notes to Chapter 14: Rome: The State, the Stars and Subversion

1   Firmicus Maternus, *Mathesis* I.v.9.
2   For a recent discussion of Rome's developing views of its own history, see Denis Feeney, *Caesar's Calendar: Ancient Time and the Beginnings of History* (Sather Classical Lectures, 65; Berkeley: University of California Press, 2007).
3   Cicero, *De divinatione* I.xviii.42.
4   *Ibid.*, II.xlvii.99.
5   Firmicus Maternus, *Mathesis* II.xxx.4–5. Firmicus still allowed himself to discuss general indicators of imperial status: see for example II.ii.20.
6   Cicero, *Republic* I.xvii.30. See also II.xiii.30, citing Democritus from Ennius: 'No one regards the things before his feet, But views with care the regions of the sky'.
7   Frederick H. Cramer, *Astrology in Roman Law and Politics* (Chicago: Ares Publishers, 1996 [1954]), p. 45.
8   Cicero, *Republic* I.xvi.25.
9   Quoted in *ibid.*, I.lviii.132.
10 Cato, *De Re Rustica* 1.5.4.
11 Cicero, *De divinatione* I.lvi.128.
12 Valerius Maximus, 1.3.3, writing in 31 CE: see Cramer, *Astrology in Roman Law and Politics*, p. 96.
13 Jack Lindsay, *Origins of Astrology* (London: Barnes and Noble, 1971), p. 217; Cramer, *Astrology in Roman Law and Politics*, pp. 61–63.
14 Plutarch, *Sulla* xxxvii.1 (in *Lives* [2 vols; trans. John Langhorne and William Langhorne; London and New York: Frederick Warne and Co., 1890]).
15 Frank McGillion, 'The Influence of Wilhelm Fliess' Cosmobiology on Sigmund Freud', *Culture and Cosmos* 2(1) (Spring/Summer 1998): 33–48.
16 Mary Beard, John North and Simon Price, *Religions of Rome* (2 vols; Cambridge: Cambridge University Press, 1998), vol. 2, p. 219.
17 Cicero, *De divinatione* II.xlvii.99.
18 Diodorus, *Library of History* 36.5.1–4.
19 See Cramer, *Astrology in Roman Law and Politics*.
20 Petronius, *The Satyricon* 39.
21 Juvenal, *The Sixteen Satires* VI.552–89.
22 Lucius Apuleius, *The Golden Ass*.
23 Manilius, *Astronomica* II.509–11.
24 *Ibid.*, IV.547–554.
25 *Ibid.*, I.801–11.
26 Firmicus Maternus, *Mathesis* 2.xxx.4–5.
27 Manilius, *Astronomica* I.801.
28 Suetonius, *The Twelve Ceasars*, 'Augustus' 94. See also Dio Cassius, *Roman History* xlv.1.5. Jack Lindsay (*Origins of Astrology*, p. 218) points out that the dates of Augustus' birth and the debate do not match (See pp. 218–20 for background on Nigidius).

29 Suetonius, *The Twelve Caesars*, 'Augustus' 94; Dio Cassius, *Roman History* i.2–3

30 Manilius, *Astronomica* I.759–63.

31 Dio Cassius, *Roman History* xlv.6.5–7.2; see also John T. Ramsey and A. Lewis Licht, *Caesar's Comet: The Comet of 44 BC and Caesar's Funeral Games* (Atlanta: Scholars Press, 1997). See also Lindsay, *Origin of Astrology*, p. 219 for Nigidius Figulus' argument that the death of heroes is linked to the appearance of constellations.

32 Pliny, *Natural History* II.xxii.92–94, xxx.99.

33 Suetonius, *The Twelve Caesars*, 'Augustus' 94.

34 Manilius, *Astronomica* 2.509–11.

35 Hesiod, *Works and Days* 12–28. For the manipulation of myth, time and the calendar by both Augustus and Julius Caesar, see Feeney, *Caesar's Calendar*.

36 Virgil, *Eclogues* VI.

37 Virgil, *Eclogues* VI.48–59.

38 Claudia Rousseau, 'An Astrological Prognostication to Duke Cosimo I de Medici of Florence', *Culture and Cosmos* 3(2) (Autumn/Winter 1999): 31–59.

39 Cicero, *De natura deorum* 173.

40 Berossus, *Babyloniaca*; Seneca, *Naturales Quaestiones* III.c.29.

41 Lindsay, *Origins of Astrology*, p. 219.

42 Pliny, *Natural History* VII.xvi.73. If we accept the standard chronology that Jesus was born in 4 BCE, his ministry would have begun in 27 BCE, at the age of 30, i.e., when he had completed one generation according to Heraclitus, or one lunar phase according to the *Epinomis*.

43 Tacitus, *Annales* VI.xx; see also Dio Cassius, *Roman History* LV.11, LVII.15. For fragments of Thrasyllus' lost work, see Robert Hand (ed.) and Robert Schmidt (trans.), *The Astrological Records of the Early Sages in Greek* (Berkeley Springs, W.Va.: Golden Hind Press, 1995), pp. 57–60.

44 *Catalogus Codicum Astrologorum Graecorum* VIII.3 (12 vols; ed. Franz Cumont; Brussels: Lamertin, 1989–53); see James Herschel Holden, *A History of Horoscopic Astrology* (Tempe, Ariz.: American Federation of Astrologers, 1996), pp. 26–27 for an English translation of fragments of the *Pinax*.

45 Tacitus, *Annales* VI.xxi; see also Dio Cassius, *Roman History* LVII.19.

46 Suetonius, *The Twelve Caesars*, 'Tiberius' 14.

47 Cramer, *Astrology in Roman Law and Politics*, p. 10.

48 Suetonius, *The Twelve Caesars*, 'Tiberius' 14.

49 Tacitus, *Annales* II.xxvii; see also Dio Cassius, *Roman History* LVII.15

50 Tacitus, *Annales* II.xxvii.

51 Thrasyllus' relationship with the royal dynasty of Commagene is accepted by some writers, such as Holden (*Horoscope Astrology*, p. 28) but questioned by others; see the discussion in Lindsay, *Origins of Astrology*, pp. 261, 280–81.

52 Holden, *Horoscopic Astrology*, p. 28 assumes the prefect of Egypt was also the astrologer; Lindsay (*Origins of Astrology*, pp. 270, 280–81, doubts it. Lindsay speculates though, that Balbillus was denounced in Revelation as the character who gives life to the image of the beast: see Rev. 13.11–18.

53 See the English translation in Holden, *Horoscopic Astrology*, pp. 28–30.

54 Suetonius, *The Twelve Caesars* 19; see 22 for Caligula as a 'monster'.

55 Dio Cassius, *Roman History* LX.26.1–5.

56 Tacitus, *Annales* XII.xxii; see also Suetonius, *The Twelve Caesars*, 'Claudius' 26.

57 Tacitus, *Annales* XII.lii.

58   *Ibid.*, XII.lii, Dio Cassius, *Roman History* LXI.33.3
59   Suetonius, *The Twelve Caesars*, 'Claudius' 29, 36.
60   *Ibid.*, 46.
61   Seneca, *Apocolocyntosis Divi Claudii.*
62   Dio Cassius, *Roman History* LXII 5.2–6.2.
63   Tacitus, *Annales* XVI.xiv.
64   Dio Cassius, *Roman History* LXI.2.1–2; Tacitus, *Annales* XIV.ix.
65   Tacitus, *Annales* XIV.ix; see also XII and the discussion in Josèphe-Henriette Abry, 'What was Agrippina Waiting For', in Günther Oestmann, H.K. von Stuckrad and D. Rutkin (eds), *Horoscopes and History* (Berlin and New York: Walter de Gruyter 2005), pp. 37–48.
66   Suetonius, *The Twelve Caesars*, 'Nero' 36.
67   Suetonius, *The Twelve Caesars*, 'Nero' 40; see also Tacitus, *Annales* XII, V.xiii.
68   Tacitus, *Annales* I.xxii.
69   Tacitus, *Annales* I.lxxxvi, Dio Cassius, *Roman History* LXIII.7.1.
70   Dio Cassius, *Roman History* LXII.4.3; Tacitus, *Annales* II.lxii.
71   Suetonius, *The Twelve Caesars*, 'Vitellius' 9.
72   Dio Cassius, *Roman History* LXIV.8.1.
73   *Ibid.*, LXV.9.2.
74   *Ibid.*, LXIV.14.2–3.
75   *Ibid.*, LXIV.11.1–2.
76   Tacitus, *Annales* V.xiii.
77   Dio Cassius, *Roman History* LXV.8.1–2, LXV.9.2, LXVI.17.1–2.
78   *Ibid.*, LXVI.17.1–2.
79   Suetonius, *The Twelve Caesars*, 'Domitian' 14–15.
80   Dio Cassius, *Roman History* LXVII.15.5–6.
81   Suetonius, *The Twelve Caesars*, 'Domitian', 16.
82   See Lindsay, *Origins of Astrology*, pp. 309–12. Hadrian's horoscope is included in Otto Neugebauer and H.B. van Hoesen, *Greek Horoscopes* (Philadelphia: American Philosophical Society, 1959), pp. 90–91 (no. L76).
83   Dio Cassius, *Roman History* LXXVII.11.1–2, 13.3–4.
84   *Ibid.*, LXXVI.16.5.

Notes to Chapter 15: Christianity: A Star out of Jacob

1   Mt. 2.1–2.
2   See the argument in Mary Ely Lyman, 'Hermetic Religion and the Religion of the Fourth Gospel', *Journal of Biblical Literature* 49(3) (1930): 265–76.
3   For discussion of the Hellenistic context of early Christianity see Peder Borgen, *Early Christianity and Hellenistic Judaism* (Dulles, Va.: T&T Clark, 1998). For a conventional view of St Paul's Christianity see John Ziesler, *Pauline Christianity* (Oxford: Oxford University Press, 1983), but for a more radical perspective, which examines Paul's context within Gnostic currents, see Elaine Pagels, *The Gnostic Paul: Gnostic Exegesis of the Pauline Letters* (Philadelphia: Trinity International, 1970).
4   Jn 1.1; for a broader discussion see Martin Hengel, *The 'Hellenization' of Judaea in the First Century after Christ* (London: SCM Press, 1989); J. Rendel Harris, 'Stoic Origins of the Prologue to St. John's Gospel', *Bulletin of the Sir John Rylands University Library* 6 (1921): 439–51.

5   *Corpus Hermeticum,* the 'Poimandres' 6–7 (in *The Corpus Hermeticum: The Divine Pymander in XVII Books: The Second Book, Poemander* [trans. John Everard from Ficino's Latin translation; London, 1650]; available at <www.levity.com/alchemy/corpherm.html> (accessed 20 September 2007).

6   Acts 27.3

7   See the discussion in Kocku von Stuckrad, 'Jewish and Christian Astrology in Late Antiquity – A New Approach', *Numen* 47(1) (2000): 1–40.

8   Mk 8.18–21.

9   Lester Ness, *Written in the Stars: Ancient Zodiac Mosaics* (Warren Center, Pa.: Shangri La Publications, 1999).

10 Ptolemy, *Tetrabiblos* II.3; see also I.18.

11 Exod. 15.27.

12 Acts 6.2.

13 Num. 2.1–31.

14 *War Rule* II; see also John Allegro, *The Dead Sea Scrolls* (Harmondsworth: Penguin, rev. edn, 1961). The writers of the Dead Sea Scrolls described a system in which overall authority was vested in three priests, probably imitating the priestly triumvirate around Moses: Aaron, Eleazar and Ithmar. The three elders are also mirrored in the equivalent function of John, Peter and James who were described by Paul as pillars of the Jewish-Christian church (Num. 3.4; Gal. 2.9).

15 *Manual of Discipline* ii.1–6.

16 *Ibid.,* viii.1–19. See also *The War of the Sons of Life and the Sons of Darkness* ii.1–6; *War Rule* II.

17 Rev. 21.6.

18 Augustine, *City of God* XV.20.

19 That is, 3+4=7, 3×4=12.

20 For seven stars see Rev. 1.17; 3.1

21 Rev. 12.1; 22.2.

22 Rev. 6.12–13; 8.10.

23 For recent Christian perspectives see William Barclay, *The Gospel of Matthew* (Daily Study Bible; Edinburgh: St Andrews Press, 1975); R.T. France, *Matthew* (Tyndale New Testament Commentaries; Intervarsity Press, Leicester, 1985).

24 See the discussion in J.C. Greenfield and M. Sokoloff, 'Astrological and Related Omen Texts in Jewish Palestinian Aramaic', *Journal of Near Eastern Studies* 48(3) (1989): 201–14.

25 '4Q318: A Divination Text (Brontologion)', in Michael Wise, Martin Abegg and Edward Cook, *Dead Sea Scrolls* (London: Harper Collins, 1996), pp. 303–05; see also Florentino Garcia Martinez, *The Dead Sea Scrolls Translated: The Qumran Texts in English* (Leiden, New York and Cologne: E.J. Brill, 1994), pp. 451–54.

26 4Q186, 'The Horoscope of the Messiah', in G. Vermes, *The Dead Sea Scrolls in English* (Harmondsworth: Pelican, 1962), p. 270.

27 Bayard Dodge, *The Fihrist of al-Nadim: A Tenth-Century Survey of Muslim Culture* (2 vols; New York: Columbia University Press, 1970), vol. 2, p. 777.

28 For recent books on the Star of Bethlehem see David Hughes, *The Star of Bethlehem Mystery* (London, Toronto and Melbourne: J.M. Dent and Sons, 1979); Mark Kidger, *The Star of Bethlehem: An Astronomer's View* (Princeton: Princeton University Press, 1999); Percy Seymour, *The Birth of Christ: Exploding the Myth* (London: Virgin Publishing Ltd., 1998). See also the bibliography at <http://www.phys.uu.nl/~vgent/stellamagorum/stellamagorum.htm> (accessed 20 September 2007).

29   Michael R. Molnar, *The Star of Bethlehem: The Legacy of the Magi* (Rutgers University
      Press: New Jersey, 1999); see also Michael R. Molnar, 'The Magi's Star from the Perspective
      of Ancient Astrological Practices', *Quarterly Journal of the Royal Astronomical Society*
      36 (1995): 109–26; Michael R. Molnar, 'Firmicus Maternus and the Star of Bethlehem',
      Culture and Cosmos 3(1) (Spring/Summer 1999): 3–9; Michael R. Molnar, 'The Evidence
      for Aries the Ram as the Astrological Sign of Judea', *Journal for the History of Astronomy*
      34(3) (August 2003): 325–27.
30   Suetonius, *The Twelve Caesars*, 'Nero' 40; see also Tacitus, *Annales* XII.
31   Ignatius of Antioch, *To the Ephesians* 19.3.
32   Augustine, *Contra Faustum Manichaeum* 2.5, cited in Jim Tester, *A History of Western
      Astrology* (Woodbridge, Suffolk: Boydell Press, 1987), pp. 111–12.
33   Acts 1.6; see also Mt. 24.36, 44; 25.13; Mk 13.32; Lk. 22.36.
34   1 Thess. 5.2.
35   Mk 13.24–5.
36   Mk 13.32–3; almost identical words are used in Mt. 13.29–36 and Lk. 21.25–33.
37   Acts 2.19–21.
38   Mt. 27.51.
39   Demetra George, 'Manuel I Komnenos and Michael Glycas: A Twelfth-Century Defence
      and Refutation of Astrology: Part 2', *Culture and Cosmos* 6(1) (Spring/Summer 2002):
      23–43 (30); citing *Letter to Polycarp* 7.
40   Lynn Thorndike, *The Sphere of Sacrobosco and its Commentators* (Chicago: University of
      Chicago Press, 1949), p. 142; see also p. 117.
41   Num. 24.17.
42   *The Epochs of Time* (*The Ages of Creation* [4Q180]) fr. 1 (in Theodor H. Gaster, *The Dead
      Sea Scriptures* [New York: Anchor Books, 3rd edn, 1976]), p. 522.
43   Rev. 22.16.
44   'Everything written about me in the law of Moses and the prophets and the psalms must
      be fulfilled' (Lk. 24.44); Christ 'was destined before the foundation of the world' (1 Pet.
      1.20).
45   'He destined us in love to be his sons through Jesus Christ, according to the purpose of his
      will' (Eph. 1.5).
46   George, 'Manuel I Komnenos and Michael Glycas', p. 28.
47   As Jim Tester put it: 'If we look for the attitude of the early Church, of the first two centuries
      or so, to astrology, we find very little evidence of any "attitude" '; *A History of Western
      Astrology*, p. 55.
48   Mt. 5.34.
49   Lk. 10.17.
50   Mt. 24.34; see also Lk. 21.33; 2 Cor. 5.1; Rev. 21.1, 23.
51   2 Cor. 5.17.
52   1 Thess. 5.2.
53   Acts 17.28.
54   1 Cor. 15.40–41.
55   *Catechism of the Catholic Church* 1994, 2116; available at <http://www.christusrex.
      org/www1/CDHN/ccc.html> (accessed 4 March 2007).

Notes to Chapter 16: Rome: The Imperial Heaven

1   Plotinus, 'On Whether the Stars are Causes', *Ennead* II.3.12.32–33.
2   I am careful in following Roger Beck in referring to the mysteries of Mithras, rather than the conventional, modern Mithraism, on the grounds that an 'ism' implies an ideology rather than a practice (see Roger Beck, *Planetary Gods and Planetary Orders in the Mysteries of Mithras* [Leiden and New York: E.J. Brill, 1988]; see also Roger Beck, *The Religion of the Mithras Cult in the Roman Empire: Mysteries of the Unconquered Sun* [Oxford: Oxford University Press, 2006]; Ugo Bianchi [ed.], *Mysteria Mithrae* [Proceedings of the International Seminar on the 'Religio-Historical Character of Roman Mithraism, with particular Reference to Roman and Ostian Sources'; Leiden: E.J. Brill, 1979]; Walter Burkert, *Ancient Mystery Cults* [Cambridge and London: Harvard University Press, 1987]; Manfred Clauss, *The Roman Cult of Mithras* [trans Richard Gordon; Edinburgh: Edinburgh University Press, 2000]; Franz Cumont, *The Mysteries of Mithra* [New York: Dover Publications, 1956 (1903)]; John R. Hinnells [ed.], *Mithraic Studies* [Proceedings of the First International Congress of Mithraic Studies; 2 vols; Manchester: Manchester University Press, 1975]; Payam Nabarz, *The Mysteries of Mithras: The Pagan Belief That Shaped the Christian World* [Rochester, Vt.: Inner Traditions, 2005]; Michael P. Speidel, *Mithras-Orion: Greek Hero and Roman Army God* [Leiden: E.J. Brill, 1980]; David Ulansey, *The Origins of the Mithraic Mysteries: Cosmology and Salvation in the Ancient World* [New York and Oxford: Oxford University Press, 1989]).
3   See Robert Graves, *The Greek Myths* (2 vols; London: Penguin, 1960), vol. 1, pp. 336–37.
4   Jerome, *Letter* 107.2; available at <http://www.newadvent.org/fathers/3001107.htm> (accessed 4 March 2007).
5   Beck, *Planetary Gods and Planetary*, p. 1.
6   Ptolemy, *Tetrabiblos* I.4.
7   *Ibid.*, II.3.
8   See Gaston H. Halsberghe, *The Cult of Sol Invictus* (Leiden: E.J. Brill, 1972); and the discussion in John Ferguson, *The Religions of the Roman Empire* (London: Thames and Hudson, 1972), pp. 44–56.
9   Stephen C. McCluskey, *Astronomies and Cultures in Early Medieval Europe* (Cambridge: Cambridge University Press, 1998), p. 41.
10 Cumont, *The Mysteries of Mithra*, p. 89.
11 For a history of Neoplatonism and its antecedents back to the Hellenistic period, see Giovanni Reale, *The School of the Imperial Age: A History of Ancient Philosophy* (Albany: State University of New York Press, 1990). For a good, recent summary of the main currents of Neoplatonic thought, see R.T. Wallis, *Neoplatonism* (London: Duckworth, 1995). For parallels, and therefore possible connections, between Neoplatonism and Indian thought, see R. Baine Harris (ed.), *Neoplatonism and Indian Thought* (Norfolk, Va.: International Society for Neoplatonic Studies, 1982); see also Crystal Addey, 'Oracles and Divination in Late Antiquity: The Development and Integration of Religious Phenomena in Late Platonist Philosophy' (PhD Thesis: University of Bristol, forthcoming 2008).
12 Harris, *Neoplatonism and Indian Thought*.
13 Plotinus, 'On Whether the Stars are Causes', *Ennead* II.3.
14 *Ibid.*, II.3.7.
15 *Ibid.*, II.3.9.
16 *Ibid.*, II.13.1–3.

17 *Ibid.*, II.3.9, 14. See also 'On Matter', *Ennead* II.4.1: 'what is called "matter" is said to be some sort of "substrate" and "receptacle" of forms'.
18 Plotinus, 'On Whether the Stars are Causes', *Ennead* II.3.8.
19 *Ibid.*, II.3.15.
20 *Ibid.*, II.3.15, 9–11.
21 Plotinus, 'On Whether the Stars are Causes', *Ennead* II.3.7.5–7
22 Plotinus, 'Against the Gnostics', *Ennead* II.9.
23 See Iamblichus, *On the Mysteries*.
24 See the discussion in Lynn Thorndike, *History of Magic and Experimental Science* (New York: Columbia University Press, 1923), vol. 1, pp. 298–321.
25 Iamblichus, *On the Mysteries* I.1.
26 For a reliable discussion of Iamblichus' cosmology, see Gregory Shaw, *Theurgy and the Soul: The Neoplatonism of Iamblichus* (University Park, Pa.: The Pennsylvania University Press, 1995).
27 Iamblichus, *On the Mysteries*.
28 *Ibid.*, I.18.
29 *Ibid.*, IX.1–10.
30 Iamblichus, *On the Mysteries* X.4.
31 David Pingree, 'The Horoscope of Constantinople', in *Prismata* (Festchrift for Willy Hartner; Wiesbaden: Franz Steiner Verlag, 1977), pp. 305–15 (305–06); also Michael Grant, *The Emperor Constantine* (London: Phoenix, 1998), p. 181: 'Constantine, being highly superstitious, did not actually proceed against the art, and duly consulted astrologers himself (for example, in 326–8)'.
32 Proclus, 'To the Sun' in Marinus of Samaria, *The Life of Proclus* (trans. Kenneth Guthrie; Grand Rapids, Mich. Phasnes Press 1986, pp. 65–66).
33 Marinus of Samaria, *The Life of Proclus* 37.
34 Averil Cameron, *The Later Roman Empire* (London: Harper Collins, 1993), p. 75.

Notes to Chapter 17: Christianity: The Triumph of the Sun

1 Tertullian, *The Prescription of Heretics*.
2 This argument was developed by F.M. Cornford (see esp. *Mystery Religions and Pre-Socratic Society* [4 vols; Cambridge: Cambridge University Press, 1923]); see also the discussion in William Guthrie, *Orpheus and Greek Religion: A Study of the Orphic Movement* (Princeton: Princeton University Press, 1993), ch. 6.
3 1 Cor. 10.32; 2 Cor. 6.14–15.
4 Tatian, *Oratio ad Graecos* 8.
5 Tertullian, *Idolatry* 9.
6 Hippolytus, *Refutation of all Heresies* IV.I–XXVII; Sextus Empiricus, *Against the Professors*, V.95–103.
7 Athanasius, *Easter Letter* 39.1 [367 CE].
8 Plato *Laws* 715e–716a; Clement of Alexandria, *Exhortation to the Greeks* 6.
9 Clement of Alexandria, *Exhortation to the Greeks* 2.
10 Clement, *The Recognition*, book X, ch. IX, in Alexander Roberts and James Donaldson (eds), in *The Ante-Nicene Christian Library*, (Edinburgh: T&T Clark, 1847).
11 Jerome, *Letter* 107.4.
12 1 Cor. 1.22–23.

13 See the discussion in Alan Scott, *Origen and the Life of the Stars: A History of An Idea* (Oxford: Clarendon Press, 1994), p. 107.

14 Gen. 1.14.

15 Origen, *Philocalia* XXIII.14.

16 *Ibid.*, XXIII.19.

17 *Ibid.*, XXIII. 8.

18 *Ibid.*, XXIII. 15.

19 Scott, *Origen and the Life of the Stars*, pp. 130–31.

20 Origen, *Contra Celsum* VIII.66–67.

21 Scott, *Origen and the Life of the Stars*, pp. 160–61.

22 Plato, *Phaedrus* 256D.

23 James M. Robinson (ed.), *The Nag Hammadi Library in English* (Leiden and New York: E.J. Brill, 1988); for Catholic attacks on Gnosticism see Irenaeus, *Against Heresies*; Tertullian *Against Heretics* and *Against Marcion*; Hippolytus *Refutation of all Heresies*. See also Giovanni Filoramo, *A History of Gnosticism* (Cambridge, Mass. and Oxford: Harvard University Press, 1990); Charles W. Hedrick and Robert Hodgson (eds), *Nag Hammadi Gnosticism and Early Christianity* (Peabody, Mass.: Hendrickson, 1986); Hans Jonas, *The Gnostic Religion: The Message of the Alien God and the Beginnings of Christianity* (Boston: Beacon Press, 2nd edn, 1963); Elaine Pagels, *The Gnostic Gospels* (Harmondsworth: Penguin, 1979); Horace Jeffrey Hodges, 'Gnostic Liberation from Astrological Determinism: Hipparchan "Trepidation" and the Breaking of Fate', *Vigiliae Christianae* 51(4) (1992): 359–73. The Nag Hammadi library includes fragments of Plato's *Republic* and the Hermetic Asclepius.

24 'Do you not know that your body is a temple of the Holy Spirit within you, which you have from God? (1 Cor. 6.19); 'Yet among the mature we do impart wisdom, although it is not a wisdom of this age or of the rulers of this age, who are destined to pass away. But we impart a secret and hidden wisdom of God, which God decreed before the ages for our glorification' (1 Cor. 2.6–7). For discussion see Elaine Pagels, *The Gnostic Paul: Gnostic Exegesis of the Pauline Letters* (Philadelphia: Trinity International, 1970); Walter Schmithals, *Paul and the Gnostics* (trans. John E. Steely; Nashville: Abingdon Press, 1972).

25 Lk. 12.56.

26 Jn 3.12; Mt. 13.11.

27 *The Apocryphon of John* x–xi (in Robinson, *The Nag Hammadi Library*).

28 *The Teachings of Silvanus* 92–93, 97 (in Robinson, *The Nag Hammadi Library*).

29 Jude 13.

30 *The Teachings of Silvanus* 96, 98, 101–102 (in Robinson, *The Nag Hammadi Library*).

31 *Pistis Sophia* I (trans. Carl Schmidt and Violet Mcdermott; available at <http://www.gnosis.org/library/psoph1.htm> (accessed 21 March 2007); Alexandra von Lieven, 'Gnosis and Astrology: "Book IV" of the Pistis Sophia', in John M. Steele and Annette Imhausen, *Under One Sky: Astronomy and Mathematics in the Ancient Near East* (Alter Oient und Altes Testament, 297; Munster: Ugarit Verlag, 2002), pp. 223–36.

32 Gilles Quispel, 'Hermes Trismegistus and Tertllian', *Vigiliae Christianae* 43(2) (June 1989): 188–90.

33 Mt. 12.45.

34 Irenaeus, *Against Heresies* I.XV.6.

35 Plotinus, 'Against the Gnostics', *Ennead* II.9.1–3.

36 Henry Chadwick, *The Early Church* (The Pelican History of the Church, 1; Harmondsworth: Penguin, 1986), pp. 125–28.

37 Robert Milburn, *Early Christian Art and Architecture* (Aldershot: Scolar Press, 1988), pp. 39–41.

38 Polymnia Athanassiadi-Fowden and Michael Frede, *Pagan Monotheism in Late Antiquity* (Oxford: Oxford University Press, 2001).

39 Mt. 13.43.

40 Saint Basil, *Exegetic Homilies* 6.

41 See the discussion in Averil Cameron, *The Later Roman Empire* (London: Harper Collins, 1993), pp. 68–69.

42 *Codex Theodosianus*; available at <http://www.ucl.ac.uk/history/volterra/texts/cthconsp.htm> (accessed 20 March 2007).

43 See the discussion in Jim Tester, *A History of Western Astrology* (Woodbridge, Suffolk: Boydell Press, 1987), p. 55.

44 *The Complete Canons of the Synod of Laodicea in Phrygia Pacatiana*, Canon 36, <http://reluctant-messenger.com/council-of-laodicea.htm> (accessed 28 November 2007).

45 For further discussion see A. Bouché-Leclercq, *L'Astrologie Grecque* (Paris: Ernest Leroux, 1899), ch. 16. In Bouché-Leclercq's opinion, the church councils were careful to condemn fatalistic astrology, implicitly laying the way open for an astrology of moral choice.

46 Augustine, *City of God* V.21.

47 For which the best introduction remains John B. Morrall, *Political Thought in the Medieval World* (Toronto: University of Toronto Press, 1980).

48 See the summary of Manichaean cosmology in Jonas, *The Gnostic Religion*.

49 Augustine, *Confessions* V.7.

50 Augustine, *City of God* VIII.3.

51 *Ibid.*, VIII.6–12; see also II.7.

52 Augustine, *Confessions* III.8.

53 *Ibid.*, 4.3, 7.6.

54 *Ibid.*, III.6; Augustine, *City of God* V.30.

55 Augustine, *City of God* V.1–7.

56 *Ibid.*, V.1.

57 *Ibid.*, VII.15.

58 Augustine, *Confessions* IV.3; *City of God* V.7.

59 Augustine, *City of God* XII.4.

60 For the 'life-world', see David Abram, *The Spell of the Sensuous* (New York: Vintage, 1997), pp. 40–44.

61 Augustine, *Confessions* IV.16.

62 Augustine, *City of God* VIII.2.

63 Augustine, *De Genesi ad litteram* II.ix.20; see Marina Smyth, *Understanding the Universe in Seventh-Century Ireland* (Woodbridge: Boydell Press, 1996).

64 Augustine, *City of God* V.10–11.

65 *Ibid.*, V.6.

66 Athanasius, *Easter Letter* 39.1.

67 John Chrysostom, *Homilies on First Corinthians* 4.11.

68 Origen, *Philocalia*, XXIII.15; Saint Basil, *Exegetic Homily* 6.8.

69 See Kocku von Stuckrad, 'Jewish and Christian Astrology in Late Antiquity – A New Approach', *Numen* 47(1) (2000): 1–40.

70 See for example <http://www.pathlights.com/theselastdays/tracts/tract_22a.htm> (accessed 20 September 2007).

71 For this and the general blurring of boundaries between solar religion and Chrstianity, see Chadwick, *The Early Church*, pp. 125–29.

72 Mal. 4.2.

73 Zeno of Verona, 'XXXVIII. Tractatus de XII signis ad neophitos', in *Zenonis Veronensis Tractatus* (Corpus Christianorum, 22, Ternhout: Brepols, 1971), pp. 105–06.

74 Lester Ness, *Written in the Stars: Ancient Zodiac Mosaics* (Warren Center, Pa.: Shangri La Publications, 1999), p. 113.

75 For Harran see Tamara Green, *The City of the Moon God: Religious Traditions of Harran* (Leiden: E.J. Brill, 1992).

76 Otto Neugebauer and H.B. van Hoesen, *Greek Horoscopes* (Philadelphia: American Philosophical Society, 1959), p. 147; David Pingree, 'Historical Horoscopes', *Journal of the American Oriental Society* 82 (1962): 487–502.

77 Nicholas Campion, 'The Possible Survival of Babylonian Astrology in the Fifth Century CE: A Discussion of Historical Sources', in Günther Oestmann, H.K. von Stuckrad and D. Rutkin (eds), *Horoscopes and History* (Berlin and New York: Walter de Gruyter, 2005), pp. 69–92.

78 Tertullian, *The Prescription Against Heretics* XLIII.

79 Prudence Jones, *Northern Myths of the Constellations* (Cambridge: Fenris-Wolf, 1991).

80 See the discussion in Ronald Hutton, 'Astral Magic: The Acceptable Face of Paganism', in Nicholas Campion, Patrick Curry and Michael York (eds), *Astrology and the Academy* (papers from the inaugural conference of the Sophia Centre, Bath Spa University College, 13–14 June 2003; Bristol: Cinnabar Books, 2004), pp. 10–24.

81 Ronald Hutton, referring to the conversion of Britain in 'Do You Believe in Magic?' (Channel 4, 29 March 2003).

Notes to Afterword

1 Dionysius the Areopagite, *The Divine Names* VIII. 5.

2 For Dionysius and St Paul see Acts 17.34.

3 See the discussion in J.S.S. Evans, *The Age of Justinian* (London: Routledge, 1996), pp. 67–69.

4 Alan Cameron, 'The Last Days of the Academy at Athens', *Proceedings of the Cambridge Philological Society* 195 (1969): 7–29 (29).

5 Joseph Needham, *Science and Civilisation in China*, vol. 3: *Mathematics and the Sciences of the Heavens and Earth* (Cambridge: Cambridge University Press, 1959), esp. pp. 252–59; Hayashi Makoto, 'The Tokugawa Shoguns and Onmyōdō', *Culture and Cosmos* 10 (2006): 49–62 (52); Ikuyo Matsumoto, 'Two Mediaeval Manuscripts on the Worship of the Stars from the Fujii Eikan Collection', *Culture and Cosmos* 10 (2006): 125–44.

6 The history of Indian astronomy and astrology awaits a genuinely scholarly and comprehensive treatment. For a useful discussion see David Pingree, *Jyotiḥśastra: Astral and Mathematical Literature* (Wiesbaden: Otto Harrasowitz, 1981); and Archie E. Roy and Kripa Shankar Shukla, 'Main Characteristics and Achievements of Ancient Indian Astronomy in Historical Perspective', in *History of Oriental Astronomy* (ed. G. Swarup, A.K. Bag and K.S. Shukla; Cambridge: Cambridge University Press, 1987), pp. 9–22.

7 Sphujidhvaja, *Yavanajataka* 79.60–62 (in David Pingree, *The Yavanajataka of Sphujidhvaja* [2 vols; Harvard Oriental Series, 48; Cambridge, Mass.: Harvard University Press, 1978], vol. 2, pp. 190–92).

8   David Pingree, *Vrddhayanajataka of Minarāja* (Gaekwad's Oriental Series, 162, 163; Baroda: Oriental Institute, Maharaja Sayajirao University of Baroda, 1976).

9   Pingree, *Jyotihśastra*, pp. 71–78, 84–85, 107–09.

10   M. Ramakrishna Bhat, *Varāhamira's Brhat Samhita* (2 vols; Delhi: Motil Banarsidass 1981), p. ix.

11   The standard text is Thomas McEvilley, *The Shape of Ancient Thought* (New York: Allsworth Press, 2002); see also R. Baine Harris (ed.), *Neoplatonism and Indian Thought* (Norfolk, Va.: International Society for Neoplatonic Studies, 1982).

Bibliography

Aaboe, Asger, 'Observation and Theory in Babylonian Astronomy', *Centaurus* 24(1) (1980): 14–35.

Abram, David, *The Spell of the Sensuous* (New York: Vintage, 1997).

Abry Josèphe-Henriette, *Les tablettes astrologiques de Grand (Vosges)* (Lyon: University Jean Mill-Lyon III, 1993).

——'What was Agrippina Waiting For?', in Günther Oestmann, H.K. von Stuckrad and D. Rutkin (eds), *Horoscopes and History* (Berlin and New York: Walter de Gruyter, 2005), pp. 37–48.

Adam, James, *The Nuptial Number of Plato* (Wellingborough: Thorsons, 1985 [1891]).

——*The Republic of Plato* (Cambridge: Cambridge University Press, 1902).

Addey, Crystal, 'Oracles and Divination in Late Antiquity: The Development and Integration of Religious Phenomena in Late Platonist Philosophy' (PhD Thesis: University of Bristol, forthcoming 2008).

Adorno, Theodor, *The Stars Down to Earth* (London: Routledge, 1994 [1953]).

Albright, W.F., *From the Stone Age to Christianity: Monotheism and the Historical Process* (New York: Doubleday, 2nd edn, 1957).

——*Yahweh and the Gods of Canaan* (Winona Lake, Ind.: Eisenbrauns, 1990).

Allegro, J.M. *The Dead Sea Scrolls* (Harmondsworth: Penguin, rev edn, 1961).

Antiochus of Athens, *The Thesaurus* (trans. Robert Schmidt; Berkeley Springs, W.Va.: Golden Hind Press, 1993).

Appian, *Roman History* (4 vols; trans. Horace White; London and New York: Harvard University Press, 1912–28).

Apuleius, Lucius, *The Golden Ass* (Harmondsworth: Penguin, 1984).

Aratus, *Phaenomena* (trans. G.R. Mair; Cambridge, Mass. and London: Harvard University Press, 1927).

Aristotle, *De Anima* (trans. Hugh Lawson-Tancred; London: Penguin, 1986).

——*Athenian Constitution* (trans. H. Rackham; Cambridge, Mass. and London: Harvard University Press, 1931).

——*On Generation and Corruption* (Kila, Mont.: Kessinger Publishing, 2004).

——*On the Heavens* (trans. W.K.C. Guthrie; Cambridge, Mass. and London: Harvard University Press, 1921).

——*Metaphysics* (2 vols; vol. 1, trans. Hugh Tredennick; vol. 2, trans. Hugh Tredennick and G. Cyril Armstrong; Cambridge, Mass. and London: Harvard University Press, 1933).

——*Physics* (2 vols; trans. F.M. Cornford and P.H. Wickstead; Cambridge, Mass. and London: Harvard University Press, 1930).

——*Politics* (trans H. Rackham; Cambridge, Mass. and London: Harvard University Press, 1943).

Assmann, Jan, *Egyptian Solar Religion in the New Kingdom* (trans. Anthony Alcock; London: Routledge and Kegan Paul, 1995).

——*The Mind of Egypt: History and Meaning in the Time of the Pharaohs* (trans. Andrew Jenkins; New York: Metropolitan Books, 2002).

Astour, Michael C., 'Political and Cosmic Symbolism in Genesis 14 and in its Babylonian Sources', in Alexander Altmann (ed.), *Biblical Motifs: Origins and Transformations* (Cambridge, Mass.: Harvard University Press, 1966), pp. 65–112.

Athanassiadi-Fowden, Polymnia and Michael Frede, *Pagan Monotheism in Late Antiquity* (Oxford: Oxford University Press, 2001).

Atkinson, R.J.C., *Stonehenge* (London, Hamish Hamilton, 1956).

Augustine, *City of God* (trans. Henry Bettenson; Harmondsworth: Penguin, 1972).

——*Confessions* (trans. R.S. Pine-Coffin; Harmondsworth: Penguin, 1961).

Badawy, Alexander, 'The Stellar Destiny of Pharoah and the So-Called Air Shafts of Cheops' Pyramid', *Mitteilungen des deutsches Akademie Berlin* 10 (1964): 198–206.

Baigent, Michael, *From the Omens of Babylon: Astrology and Ancient Mesopotamia* (London: Penguin, 1994).

Baity, Elizabeth Chesley, 'Archaeoastronomy and Ethnoastronomy So Far', *Current Anthropology* 14(4) (October 1973): 389–449.

Barclay, William, *The Gospel of Matthew* (Daily Study Bible; Edinburgh: St Andrews Press, 1975).

Barnatt, J. and M. Edmonds, 'Places Apart: Caves and Monuments in Neolithic and Earlier Bronze Age Britain', *Cambridge Archaeological Journal* 12(1) (2002): 113–29.

Barnes, Jonathan, *Early Greek Philosophy* (London: Penguin, 1987).

Barton, Tamsyn, *Ancient Astrology* (London: Routledge, 1994).

Barrow, John, *Pi in the Sky: Counting, Thinking and Being* (London: Penguin Books, 1993).

Bauval, Robert and Adrian Gilbert, *The Orion Mystery: Unlocking the Secrets of the Pyramids* (London: Heinemann, 1994).

Beard Mary, John North and Simon Price, *Religions of Rome* (2 vols; Cambridge: Cambridge University Press, 1998).

Beck, Roger, 'The Astronomical Design of Karakush, a Royal Burial Site in Ancient Commagene: An Hypothesis', *Culture and Cosmos* 3(1) (Spring–Summer 1999): 10–31.

——*A Brief History of Ancient Astrology* (Oxford: Blackwell, 2007).

——*Planetary Gods and Planetary Orders in the Mysteries of Mithras* (Leiden and New York: E.J. Brill, 1988).

——*The Religion of the Mithras Cult in the Roman Empire: Mysteries of the Unconquered Sun* (Oxford: Oxford University Press, 2006).

Bednarik, Robert G., 'Paleoart and Archaeological Myths', *Cambridge Archaeological Journal* 2(1) (1992): 27–57.

Belmonte, Juan Antonio, 'On the Orientation of Old Egyptian Pyramids', *Archaeoastronomy, Supplement to the Journal for History of Astronomy* 26 (2001): S1–S20.

Belmonte, J.A. and Mosalem Shaltout, 'On the Orientation of Ancient Egyptian Temples: (1) Upper Egypt and Lower Nubia', *Journal for the History of Astronomy* 36(3) (2006): 273–98.

——'On the Orientation of Ancient Egyptian Temples: (2) New Experiments at the Oases of the Western Desert', *Journal for the History of Astronomy* 37(2) (May 2006): 173–92.

Bender, Barbara, *Stonehenge: Making Space* (Oxford and New York: Berg Publishers, 1998).

Bender, Barbara (ed.), *Landscape: Politics and Perspectives* (Oxford and New York: Berg Publishers, 1993).

Berger, Peter, *The Sacred Canopy: Elements of a Sociological Theory of Religion* (New York: Anchor Books, 1969).

Berossus, *Babyloniaca* (ed. Stanley Mayer Burstein; Malibu: Undena Publications, 1978).

Betegh, Gaibor, *The Derveni Papyrus: Cosmology, Theology and Interpretation* (Cambridge: Cambridge University Press, 2004).

Betz, Hans Dieter, 'The Delphic Maxim "Know Yourself" in the Greek Magical Papyri', *History of Religions* 21(2) (November 1981): 156–71.

Betz, Hans Dieter (ed.), *The Greek Magical Papyri in Translation*, vol 1: *Texts* (Chicago: University of Chicago Press, 1992).

Bhat, M. Ramakrishna, *Varāhamira's Brhat Samhita* (2 vols; Delhi: Motil Banarsidass, 1981).

Bianchi, Ugo (ed.), *Mysteria Mithrae* (Proceedings of the International Seminar on the 'Religio-Historical Character of Roman Mithraism, with particular Reference to Roman and Ostian Sources'; Leiden: E.J. Brill, 1979).

Bickerman, Elias, *Chronology of the Ancient World* (London: Thames and Hudson, 1980).

——*The God of the Maccabees: Studies on the Meaning and Origin of the Maccabean Revolt* (trans. Horst R. Moehring; Leiden: Brill, 1979).

——*The Jews in the Greek Age* (Cambridge, Mass. and London: Harvard University Press, 1988).

Blacker, Carmen and Michael Loewe, *Ancient Cosmologies* (London: George Allen and Unwin Ltd., 1975).

Blomberg, Mary and Goren Henriksson, 'Elements of Greek Astronomy and Relgion in Monian Crete', in John W. Fountain and Rolf M. Sinclair (eds), *Current Studies in Archaeoastronomy: Conversations Across Time and Space* (Durham, N.C.: Carolina Academic Press, 2005), pp. 371–92.

Blomberg, Mary, Peter E. Blomberg and Göran Henriksson, *Calendars, Symbols, and Orientations: Legacies of Astronomy in Culture* (Proceedings of the 9th Annual Meeting of the European Society for Astronomy in Culture [SEAC], The Old Observatory, Stockholm, 27–30 August 2001; Uppsala Astronomical Observatory Report, 59; Stockholm: SEAC, 2003).

Bloomfield, Morton W., 'The Origin of the Concept of the Seven Cardinal Sins', *Harvard Theological Review* 34(2) (April 1941): 121–28.

Bochkarev, Nikolai, 'Ancient Armenian Astroarchaeological Monuments: Personal Impressions of Metsamor and Carahunge'; available at <http://haldjas.folklore.ee/SEAC/SEAC_teesid2.htm> (accessed 20 March 2007).

Borgen, Peder, *Early Christianity and Hellenistic Judaism* (Dulles, Va.: T&T Clark, 1998).

Bottéro, Jean, *Mesopotamia: Writing, Reasoning and the Gods* (Chicago and London: University of Chicago Press, 1992).

Bouché-Leclercq, A., *L'Astrologie Grecque* (Paris: Ernest Leroux, 1899).

Boyce, Mary, *A History of Zoroastrianism* (3 vols; Leiden and New York: Brill, 1983).

Breasted, James, *Development of Religion and Thought in Ancient Egypt* (Philadelphia: University of Pennsylvania Press, 1972 [1912]).

——*A History of Egypt* (New York: Bantam Books, 1964 [1905]).

Brennand, Mark, 'This is Why we Dug Seahenge', *British Archaeology* 78 (September 2004); available at <http://www.britarch.ac.uk/BA/ba78/feat5.shtml> (accessed 20 March 2007).

Brown, David, *Mesopotamian Planetary Astronomy-Astrology* (Groningen: Styx Publications, 2000).

Bucellati, Giorgio, 'The Descent of Inanna as a Ritual Journey to Kutha?', *Syro-Mesopotamian Studies* 4(3) (December 1982): 3–8.

Budge, E.A. Wallis, *The Book of The Dead* (London: Kegan Paul, 1899).

——*Egyptian Magic* (London: Kegan Paul, Trench Trubner & Co., 1901).

——*From Fetish to God in Ancient Egypt* (Oxford: Oxford University Press, 1934).

Burkert, Walter, *Ancient Mystery Cults* (Cambridge, Mass. and London: Harvard University Press, 1987).

——*Babylon Memphis Persepolis: Eastern Contexts of Greek Culture* (Cambridge, Mass.: Harvard University Press, 2004).

——*The Orientalising Revolution: Near Eastern Influence on Greek Culture in the Early Archaic Age* (Cambridge, Mass.: Harvard University Press, 1992).

Burl, Aubrey, *Avebury* (New Haven and London: Yale University Press, 1979).

——*Great Stone Circles* (New Haven and London: Yale University Press, 1999).

——'Pi in the Sky', in D.C. Heggie (ed.), *Archaeoastronomy in the Old World* (Cambridge: Cambridge University Press, 1982), pp. 141–68.

——*Prehistoric Astronomy and Ritual* (Prince Risborough: Shire Publications, 1997).

——'Science or Symbolism: Problems of Archaeoastronomy', *Antiquity* 54 (1980): 191–200.

——' "Without Sharp North": Alexander Thom and the Great Stone Circles of Cumbria', in Clive Ruggles, *Records in Stone: Papers in Memory of Alexander Thom* (Cambridge: Cambridge University Press, 1988), pp. 175–205.

Burrows, E., 'The Constellation of the Wagon and Recent Archaeology', *Analecta Orientalia* 12 (1935): 34–40.

Burrows, Millar, 'Ancient Israel', in Robert C. Dentan (ed.), *The Idea of History in the Ancient Near East* (New Haven: Yale University Press, 1983), pp. 99–131.

Cairns, Hugh, 'Aboriginal Sky-Mapping? Possible Astronomical Interpretation of Australian Aboriginal Ethnographic and Archaeological Material', in Clive Ruggles (ed.), *Archaeoastronomy in the 1990s* (Loughborough: Group D Publications, 1993), pp. 136–54.

——'Discoveries in Aboriginal Sky-Mapping (Australia)', in John W. Fountain and Rolf M. Sinclair (eds), *Current Studies in Archaeoastronomy: Conversations Across Time and Space* (Durham, N.C.: Carolina Academic Press, 2005), pp. 523–38.

Callatay, Godefroid de, *Annus Platonicus: A Study of World Cycles in Greek, Latin and Arabic sources* (Louvain-la-Neuve: Universite Catholique de Louvain, 1996).

Cameron, Alan, 'The Last Days of the Academy at Athens', *Proceedings of the Cambridge Philological Society* 195 (1969): 7–29.

Cameron, Averil, *The Later Roman Empire* (London: HarperCollins, 1993).

Campbell, Joseph, *Historical Atlas of World Mythology*, vol. 1: *The Way of the Animal Powers*, part 2: *Mythologies of the Great Hunt* (New York: Harper & Row, 1988).

——*The Masks of God: Oriental Mythology* (New York: Viking, 1962).

Campion, Nicholas, 'Babylonian Astrology: Its Origins and Legacy in Europe', in Helaine Selin (ed.), *Astronomy Across Cultures: The History of Non-Western Astronomy* (Dordrecht: Kluwer Academic Publishers, 2000), pp. 509–54.

——*The Great Year: Astrology, Millenarianism and History in the Western Tradition* (London: Penguin, 1994).

——'The Possible Survival of Babylonian Astrology in the Fifth Century CE: A Discussion of Historical Sources', in Günther Oestmann, H.K. von Stuckrad and D. Rutkin (eds), *Horoscopes and History* (Berlin and New York: Walter de Gruyter, 2005), pp. 69–92.

——'Prophecy, Cosmology and the New Age Movement: The Extent and Nature of Contemporary Belief in Astrology' (PhD thesis: University of the West of England, 2004).

Campion, Nicholas (ed.), *The Inspiration of Astronomical Phenomena* (Proceedings of the Fourth Conference on the Inspiration of Astronomical Phenomena, sponsored by the Vatican Observatory and the Steward Observatory, Arizona, Magdalen College, Oxford, 3–9 August 2003: Bristol: Cinnabar Books, 2005).

Caplice, Richard I., *The Akkadian Namburbi Texts: An Introduction* (Malibu: Undena Publications, 1974).

Cassirer, Ernst, *The Philosophy of Symbolic Forms*, vol. 2: *Mythical Thought* (New Haven and London: Yale University Press, 1971 [1955]).

Catalogus Codicum Astrologorum Graecorum (12 vols; ed. Franz Cumont; Brussels: Lamertin, 1989–53).

Cato and Varro, *De Re Rustica* (trans. H.B. Ash and W.D. Hooper; Cambridge, Mass.: Harvard University Press, 1979).

Chadwick, Henry, *The Early Church* (The Pelican History of the Church, 1; Harmondsworth: Penguin, 1986 [1967]).

Chadwick, Nora K., *The Druids* (Cardiff: University of Wales Press, 1966).

Chadwick, Robert, 'The So-Called "Orion Mystery" ', *KMT* 8 (1996): 74–83.

Chapman, Allan, *Gods in the Sky: Astronomy, Religion and Culture from the Ancients to the Renaissance* (London: Channel 4 Books, 2001).

Charlesworth, James H., 'Jewish Interest in Astrology During the Hellenistic and Roman Period', *Aufstieg und Niedergang der Romischen Welt* 20(2) (1987): 926–56.

Charlesworth, James H. (ed.), *The Old Testament Pseudepigrapha* (2 vols; New York: Doubleday, 1983–85).

Chippendale, Christopher, *Stonehenge Complete* (London: Thames and Hudson, rev. edn, 1994).

Christiansen, Dalgas H., 'Decanal Star Tables for Lunar Houses in Egypt?' *Centaurus* 35 (1992): 1–27.

Cicero, *De Divinatione* (trans. W.A. Falconer; Cambridge, Mass. and London: Harvard University Press, 1929).

——*De Natura Deorum* (trans. H. Rackham; Cambridge, Mass. and London: Harvard University Press, 1933).

——*Republic* (trans. C.W. Keyes; Cambridge, Mass. and London: Harvard University Press, 1927).

Clagett, Marshall, *Ancient Egyptian Science: A Sourcebook*, vol. 2: *Calendars, Clocks and Astronomy* (Philadelphia: American Philosophical Society, 1995).

Clark, R.T. Rundle, *Myth and Symbol in Ancient Egypt* (London: Thames and Hudson, 1959).

Clauss, Manfred, *The Roman Cult of Mithras* (trans. Richard Gordon; Edinburgh: Edinburgh University Press, 2000).

Clement of Alexandria, *Works* (2 vols; trans. G.W. Butterworth; Cambridge, Mass. and London: Harvard University Press, 1919).

Codex Theodosianus; available at <http://www.ucl.ac.uk/history/volterra/texts/cthconsp.htm> (accessed 20 March 2007).

Cohen, Mark E., *The Cultic Calendars of the Ancient Near East* (Bethesda, Md.: CDL Press, 1993).

Cohn, Norman, 'How Time Acquired a Consummation', in Malcolm Bull (ed.), *Apocalypse Theory and the Ends of the World* (Oxford: Blackwell, 1995), pp. 22–37.

Cole, Steve W. and Peter Machinist, *Letters from Priests to the Kings Esarhaddon and Assurbanipal* (Helsinki: Helsinki University Press, 1998).

Collins, John Joseph, *The Scepter and the Star: The Messiahs of the Dead Sea Scrolls and Other Ancient Literature* (New York: Doubleday, 1995).

Condos, Theony, *Star Myths of the Greeks and Romans: A Sourcebook* (Grand Rapids, Mich.: Phanes Press, 1997).

Connelly, Joan Breton, *Portrait of a Priestess: Women and Ritual in Ancient Greece* (Princeton: Princeton University Press, 2007).

Copenhaver, Brian P., *Hermetica* (Cambridge: Cambridge University Press, 1992).

Cornford, F.M., *Mystery Religions and Pre-Socratic Society* (4 vols; Cambridge: Cambridge University Press, 1923).

——*Plato's Cosmology: The Timaeus* (London: Routledge, 2001 [1937]).

Coulston, Charles (ed.), *Dictionary of Scientific Biography* (14 vols; New York: Charles Scribner's Sons, 1970–76).

Courtauld, Caroline, *In Search of Burma* (London: Frederick Muller, 1984).

Cox, John, 'The Orientations of Prehistoric Temples in Malta and Gozo', *Archaeoastronomy* 16 (2001): 24–37.

Cramer, Frederick H., *Astrology in Roman Law and Politics* (Chicago; Ares Publishers, 1996 [1954]).

Crane, Joseph, *Astrological Roots: the Hellenistic Legacy* (Bournemouth: The Wessex Astrologer, 2007).

Culianu, Ioan Petru, *Psychanodia I: A Survey of the Evidence Concerning the Ascension of the Soul and its Relevance* (Leiden: E.J. Brill, 1983).

Cumont, Franz, *Astrology Among the Greeks and Romans* (New York: Dover Publications 1960 [1911]).

——'Les noms des planètes et l'astrolatrie chez les Grecs', *L'Antiquité Classique* 4(1) (1935): 5–43.

——*The Mysteries of Mithra* (New York: Dover, 1956 [1903]).

——*Oriental Religions in Roman Paganism* (New York: Dover Publications, 1956).

Cumont, Franz (ed.), *Catalogus Codicum Astrologorum Graecorum* (12 vols; Brussels: Lamertin, 1898–1953).

Cunliffe, Barry, *The Celtic World* (New York: Random House, 1988).

——*Wessex to AD 1000* (New York and Harlow: Addison Wesley Longman, 1993).

Cunliffe, Barry and Colin Renfrew, *Science and Stonehenge* (Oxford: Oxford University Press, 1997).

Currivan, Jude, 'Walking between Worlds – Cosmology Embodied in the Landscape of Neolithic and Early Bronze Age Britain' (PhD Thesis: University of Reading, 2003).

Curry, Patrick, 'Divination, Enchantment and Platonism', in Angela Voss and Jean Hinson Lall, (eds), *The Imaginal Cosmos: Astrology, Divination and the Sacred* (Canterbury: University of Kent, 2007), pp. 35–46.

Dalley, Stephanie (ed.), *The Legacy of Mesopotamia* (Oxford: Clarendon Press, 1998).

Darcus, Shirley M.L., 'Daimon as a Force in Shaping Ethos in Heraclitus', *Phoenix* 28 (1974): 390–407.

David, A. Rosalie, *The Ancient Egyptians: Religious Beliefs and Practices* (London: Routledge and Kegan Paul Ltd., 1982).

Davies, P. and Robb, J.G., 'Scratches in the Earth: The Underworld as a Theme in British Prehistory with Particular References to the Neolithic and Earlier Bronze Age', *Landscape Research* 29(2) (2004): 141–57.

Davis, Virginia Lee, 'Identifying Ancient Egyptian Constellations', *Archaeoastronomy: Supplement to the Journal for the History of Astronomy* 9 (1985): S103–S104.

De Young, Gregg, 'Astronomy in Ancient Egypt', in Helaine Selin (ed.), *Astronomy Across Cultures: the History of Non-Western Astronomy* (Dordrecht: Kluwer Academic Publishers, 2000), pp. 475–508.

Dicks, D.R., *Early Greek Astronomy to Aristotle* (London: Thames and Hudson, 1970).

Dio Cassius, *Roman History* (9 vols; trans. E. Cary; Cambridge, Mass. and London: Harvard University Press, 1914–27).

Diodorus Siculus, *Library of History* (12 vols; trans W.H. Oldfather, C.L. Sherman, C.B. Welles, Russell M. Greer and F.R. Walton; Cambridge, Mass. and London: Harvard University Press, 1933–46).

Dionysius the Areopagite, *The Divine Names and The Mystical Theology* (trans. C.E. Holt; London: SPCK, 1920).

Dinsmoor, William Bell, *The Architecture of Ancient Greece: An Account of Its Historic Development* (New York: W.W. Norton and Co., 1975).

Dodds, E.R., *The Greeks and the Irrational* (Sather Classical Lectures, 25; Berkeley: University of California Press, 1951).

Dodge, Bayard, *The Fihrist of al-Nadim: A Tenth-Century Survey of Muslim Culture* (2 vols; New York: Columbia University Press, 1970), vol. 2.

Dorotheus of Sidon, *Carmen Astrologicum* (ed. and trans. David Pingree; Leipzig: BSG B.G. Teubner Verlagsgesellschaft 1976); English edn (Nottingham: Ascella Books, 1993).

Dreyer, J.L.E., *A History of the Planetary Systems from Thales to Kepler* (New York: Dover Publications, 1953 [1906]).

Dunand, Françoise and Christiane Zivie-Coche, *Gods and Men in Egypt 3000 BCE to 395 CE* (trans. David Lorton; Ithaca: Cornell University Press, 2004).

Dundes, Alan (ed.), *The Flood Myth* (Berkeley, Los Angeles and London: University of California Press, 1988).

Dupuis, Charles, *Mémoire sur l'origine des constellations, et sur l'explication de la fable* (Paris: Veuve Desaint, 1781).

——*Was Christ a Person or the Sun? An Argument from Dupuis to Show that Christianity has its Origins in Sun Worship* (London: Holyoake and Co., 1857).

Edge, Frank, 'Taurus in Lascaux', *Griffith Observer* 61(9) (September 1997): 13–17.

Edmonds, M., *Ancestral Geographies of the Neolithic: Landscape, Monuments and Memory* (London: Routledge, 2002).

Edwards, I.E.S., 'The Air Channels of Chephren's Pyramid', in William Kelly Simpson and Whitney M. Davies (eds), *Studies in Ancient Egypt, the Aegean and the Sudan: Essays in Honor of Dows Dunham on the Occasion of his 90th Birthday, June 1, 1980* (Boston: Museum of Fine Arts, 1981), pp. 55–57.

——*The Pyramids of Egypt* (London: Penguin, rev. edn, 1988).

Edzard, Ditz Otto, *Gudea and His Dynasty* (Toronto: University of Toronto Press, 2003).

Eliade, Mircea, *A History of Religious Ideas* (Chicago: University of Chicago Press, 1982), vol. 2.

——*The Sacred and the Profane* (New York: Harcourt Brace, 1959).

Ellis, Peter Beresford, *The Druids* (London: Constable, 1994).

——'Early Irish Astrology: An Historical Argument'; available at <http://cura.free.fr/xv/11ellis1.html> (accessed 4 July 2007).

Engnell, Ivan, *Studies in Divine Kingship in the Ancient Near East* (Oxford: Blackwell, 1967).

Evans, J.S.S., *The Age of Justinian* (London: Routledge, 1996).

Evans, James, 'The Astrologer's Apparatus: A Picture of Professional Practice in Greco-Roman Egypt', *Journal for the History of Astronomy* 35(1) (February 2004): 1–44.

——*The History and Practice of Ancient Astronomy* (Oxford: Oxford University Press, 1998).

Everard, John (trans.), *The Corpus Hermeticum; The Divine Pymander in XVII Books, The Second Book, Poemanders* (London, 1650); available at <www.levity.com/alchemy/corpherm.html> (accessed 20 September 2007).

Fagan, Cyril, *Astrological Origins* (St Paul, Minn.: Llewellyn Publications, 1971).

Faulkner, O.R., *The Ancient Egyptian Coffin Texts*, vol. 1: *Spells 1–354*; vol. 2: *Spells 355–787*; vol. 3: *Spells 788–1186* (Warminster: Aris and Phillips, 1973, 1977, 1978).

——*The Ancient Egyptian Pyramid Texts* (2 vols; Oxford: Oxford University Press 1969; Warminster: Aris and Phillips, 2nd edn, 1993).

——*The Book of the Dead* (London: British Museum Publications, 1985).

——'The King and the Star Religion in the Pyramid Texts', *The Journal of Near Eastern Studies* 25 (1966): 153–61.

Feeney, Denis, *Caesar's Calendar: Ancient Time and the Beginnings of History* (Sather Classical Lectures, 65; Berkeley: University of California Press, 2007).

Ferguson, John, *The Religions of the Roman Empire* (London: Thames and Hudson, 1972).

Filoramo, Giovanni, *A History of Gnosticism* (Cambridge, Mass. and Oxford: Harvard University Press, 1990).

Fine, Steven, *Art and Judaism in the Greco-Roman World: Toward a New Jewish Archaeology* (Cambridge: Cambridge University Press, 2005).

Finkelstein, J., *The Ox That Gored* (Transactions of the American Philosophical Society 71(2); Philadelphia: American Philosophical Society, 1981).

Fisher, H.A.L., *A History of Europe* (London: Fontana, 1979 [1935]).

Flood, Josephine, *Archaeology of the Dreamtime: The Story of Prehistoric Australia and its People* (New Haven: Yale University Press, 1990).

Foster, Benjamin, *Before The Muses: An Anthology Of Akkadian Literature* (Bethesda, Md.: CDL Press, 2005).

Fountain, John W. and Rolf M. Sinclair (eds), *Current Studies in Archaeoastronomy: Conversations Across Time and Space* (Durham, N.C.: Carolina Academic Press, 2005).

Fowden, Garth, *The Egyptian Hermes: A Historical Approach to the Late Pagan Mind* (Princeton: Princeton University Press, 1986).

France, R.T., *Matthew* (Tyndale New Testament Commentaries; Intervarsity Press: Leicester, 1985).

Frank, Roslyn. M., 'Hunting the European Sky Bears: When Bears Ruled the Earth and Guarded the Gate of Heaven', in Vesselina Koleva and Dmiter Kolev (eds), *Astronomical Traditions in Past Cultures* (Proceedings of the First Annual General Meeting of the European Society for Astronomy in Culture, Smolyan, Bulgaria, 31 August – 2 September 1992; Sofia: Institute of Astronomy, Bulgarian Academy of Sciences and National Astronomical Observatory, Rozhen, 1996), pp. 116–42.

——'Hunting the European Sky Bears: Hercules Meets Harzkume', in César Esteban and Juan Antonio Belmonte (eds), *Astronomy and Cultural Diversity: Proceedings of the 1999 Oxford VI Conference on Archaeoastronomy and Astronomy in Culture* (Tenerife: Oranismo Autonomo de Museos del Cablido de Tenerife, 2000), pp. 169–75.

——'Hunting the European Sky Bears: A Proto-European Vision Quest to the End of the Earth', in John W. Fountain and Rolf M. Sinclair (eds), *Current Studies in Archaeoastronomy: Conversations Across Time and Space* (Durham N.C.: Carolina Academic Press, 2005), pp. 455–74.

Frankfort, Henri, *Ancient Egyptian Religion* (New York: Harper & Row, 1948).

——*Kingship and the Gods: A Study of Near Eastern Religion as the Integration of Society and Nature* (Chicago: Chicago University Press, 1978 [1948]).

Frazer, J.G., *The Golden Bough: A Study in Magic and Relgion* (London: Macmillan, abridged edn, 1971 [1922].

Freud, Sigmund, *Moses and Monotheism* (trans. Katherine Jones; New York: Vintage Books, 1955).

Frolov, B.A., 'On Astronomy in the Stone Age', *Current Anthropology* 22(5) (October 1981): 585.

Furley, David, *The Greek Cosmologists* (Cambridge: Cambridge University Press, 1987), vol. 1.

Gadd, C.J., *Ideas of Divine Rule in the Ancient East* (Schweich Lectures of the British Academy, 1945; Munich: Kraus Reprint, 1980).

Gardner, Sara L., 'Scratching the Surface of Astronomy in the Land of the Bible: Archaeology, Texts, and Astronomy', in John W. Fountain and Rolf M. Sinclair (eds), *Current Studies in Archaeoastronomy: Conversations Across Time and Space* (Durham, N.C.: Carolina Academic Press, 2005), pp. 393–411.

Gaster, Theodor H., *The Dead Sea Scriptures* (New York: Anchor Books, 3rd edn, 1976 [1956]).

Gee, Emma, *Ovid, Aratus and Augustus* (Cambridge: Cambridge University Press, 2000).

George, Demetra, 'Manuel I Komnenos and Michael Glycas: A Twelfth-Century Defence and Refutation of Astrology: Part 2', *Culture and Cosmos* 6(1) (Spring/Summer 2002): 23–43 (30).

Gibbon, William B., 'Asiatic Parallels in North American Star Lore: Ursa Major', *Journal of American Folklore* 77 (1964): 236–50.

Gibson, Alex and Derek Simpson (eds), *Prehistoric Ritual and Religion* (Stroud: Sutton Publishing Ltd., 1998).

Gingerich, Owen, 'The Origin of the Zodiac', in *The Great Copernicus Chase and Other Adventures in Astronomical History* (Cambridge, Mass.: Sky Publishing Corporation and Cambridge University Press, 1992), pp. 7–12.

Goldman, Bernard, 'An Oriental Solar Motif and its Western Extension', *Journal of Near Eastern Studies* 20(4) (October 1961): 239–47.

Goodale, Jane, *Tiwi Wives: A Study of the Women of Melville Island* (Seattle and London: University of Washington Press, 1971).

Goodison, Lucy, *Death, Women and the Sun* (Institute of Classical Studies Bulletin Supplement, 53; London: Institute of Classical Studies, 1989).

Gorman, Peter, *Pythagoras: A Life* (London: Routledge and Kegan Paul, 1979).

Grant, Mary (trans.), *The Myths of Hyginus* (Lawrence, Kans.: University of Kansas Publications, 1960).

Grant, Michael, *The Emperor Constantine* (London: Phoenix, 1998).

Graves, Robert, *The Greek Myths* (2 vols; London: Penguin, 1960).

Green, Miranda, *The World of the Druids* (London: Thames and Hudson, 1997).

Green, Tamara, *The City of the Moon God: Religious Traditions of Harran* (Leiden: E.J. Brill, 1992).

Greene, Liz, *Astrology for Lovers* (London: Unwin Paperbacks, 1986).

——'The Influence of Orphic Beliefs on the Development of Hellenistic Astrology', *Culture and Cosmos* 9(1) (Autumn–Winter 2005): 21–44.

Greenfield, J.C. and M. Sokoloff, 'Astrological and Related Omen Texts in Jewish Palestinian Aramaic', *Journal of Near Eastern Studies* 48(3) (1989): 201–14.

Gregory, John, *The Neoplatonists* (London: Kyle Cathie, 1991).

Guthrie, Kenneth Sylvan, *The Pythagorean Sourcebook and Library* (Grand Rapids, Mich.: Phanes Press, 1987).

Guthrie, William, *Orpheus and Greek Religion: A Study of the Orphic Movement* (Princeton: Princeton University Press, 1993).

Haack, Steven C., 'The Astronomical Orientation of the Egyptian Pyramids', *Archaeoastronomy: Supplement to Journal for the History of Astronomy* 7 (1984): S119–S125.

Halliday, William R., *Greek Divination: A Study of its Methods and Principles* (London: Macmillan, 1913).

Halsberghe, Gaston H., *The Cult of Sol Invictus* (Leiden: E.J. Brill, 1972).

Hand, Robert, 'Introduction to the Liber Hermetis', in Hermes, *Liber Hermetis* (trans. Robert Zoller; Berkeley Springs, W.Va.: Golden Hind Press, 1993), vol. 1, pp. iii–xxxv.

Hand, Robert (ed.) and Robert Schmidt (trans.), *The Astrological Records of the Early Sages in Greek* (Berkeley Springs, W.Va.: Golden Hind Press, 1995).

Handy, Lowell K., *Among the Host of Heaven: The Syro-Palestinian Pantheon as Bureaucracy* (Winona Lake, Ill.: Eisenbrauns, 1993).

Hankinson, R. J., 'Stoicism, Science and Divination', in R. J. Hankinson (ed.), *Method, Medicine and Metaphysics: Studies in the Philosophy of Ancient Science* (*Apeiron* 21, no. 2), 1988, pp. 123–60.

Hannah, Robert, *Greek and Roman Calendars: Constructions of Time in the Classical World* (London: Duckworth, 2005).

Harkness, Deborah E., *John Dee's Conversations with Angels: Cabala, Alchemy and the End of Nature* (Cambridge: Cambridge University Press, 1999).

Harris, R. Baine (ed.), *Neoplatonism and Indian Thought* (Norfolk, Va.: International Society for Neoplatonic Studies, 1982).

Harris, J. Rendel, 'Stoic Origins of the Prologue to St. John's Gospel', *Bulletin of the John Rylands University Library* 6 (1921): 439–51.

Harrison, Jane, *Themis: A Study of the Origins of Greek Religion* (London: Merlin Press, 1963).

Hartner, Willy, 'The Earliest History of the Constellations in the Near East and the Motif of the Lion-Bull Combat', *Journal of Near Eastern Studies* 24(1–2) (January– April 1965): 1–16.

Hawkes, Jacquetta, 'God in the Machine', *Antiquity* 41 (1967): 174–80.

——*Man and the Sun* (London: The Cresset Press, 1962).

Hawkins, Gerald, *Beyond Stonehenge* (New York, San Francisco and London: Harper & Row, 1973).

——*Stonehenge Decoded* (New York: Dorset Press, 1965).

Haynes, R.D., 'Astronomy and the Dreaming: The Astronomy of the Aboriginal Australians', in Helaine Selin (ed.), *Astronomy Across Cultures: the History of Non-Western Astronomy* (Dordrecht: Kluwer Academic Publishers, 2000), pp. 53–90.

——'Dreaming the Stars: Astronomy of the Australian Aborigines', *Interdisciplinary Science Review* 20(3) (1995): 187–97.

Hedrick, Charles W. and Robert Hodgson (eds), *Nag Hammadi Gnosticism and Early Christianity* (Peabody, Mass.: Hendrickson, 1986).

Heidel, Alexander, *The Babylonian Genesis* (London and Chicago: Chicago University Press, 1963).

Hengel, Martin, *The 'Hellenization' of Judaea in the First Century after Christ* (London: SCM Press, 1989).

Hephaistio of Thebes, *Apotelesmatics* (2 vols; Project Hindsight Greek Track, 6; trans. Robert Schmidt; Berkeley Springs, W.Va.: Golden Hind Press, 1994–98).

Heraclitus, *Fragments* (4 vols; trans. W. Jones and E. Withington; Cambridge, Mass. and London: Harvard University Press, 1923).

Hermes, *Liber Hermetis* (trans. Robert Zoller; Berkeley Springs, W.Va.: Golden Hind Press, 1993).

Hermetica: The Ancient Greek and Latin Writings which contain Religious or Philosophic Teachings ascribed to Hermes Trismegistus (4 vols; trans. Walter Scott; Boulder: Shambala, 1982).

Herodotus, *The Histories* (trans. Aubrey de Sélincourt; Harmondsworth: Penguin, 1972).

Hesiod, *The Homeric Hymns and Homerica, including 'Works and Days' and 'Theogonis'* (trans. Hugh G. Evelyn-White; Cambridge, Mass.: Harvard University Press, 1917).

——*The Poems and Fragments* (trans. A.W. Mair; Oxford: Oxford University Press, 1908).

——*Theogony and Works and Days* (trans. Dorothy Wender; Harmondsworth: Penguin, 1972).

Hillman, James, *The Soul's Code: In Search of Character and Calling* (London: Bantam Books, 1997).

Hinnells, John R. (ed.), *Mithraic Studies* (2 vols; Proceedings of the First International Congress of Mithraic Studies; Manchester: Manchester University Press, 1975).

Hippocrates, *Hippocratic Writings* (ed. G.E.R. Lloyd; London: Penguin, 1983).

——*Works* (4 vols; trans. W. Jones and E. Withington; Cambridge, Mass.: Harvard University Press, 1923).

Hodges, Horace Jeffrey, 'Gnostic Liberation from Astrological Determinism: Hipparchan "Trepidation" and the Breaking of Fate', *Vigiliae Christianae* 51(4) (1992): 359–73.

Holden, James Herschel, *A History of Horoscopic Astrology* (Tempe, Ariz.: American Federation of Astrologers, 1996).

Hollis, F.J., 'Suncult and Temple at Jerusalem', in Samuel Hooke (ed.), *Myth and Ritual, Essays in the Myth and Ritual of the Hebrews in Relation to the Culture Patterns of the Ancient East* (Oxford: Oxford University Press, 1933), pp. 87–110.

Homer, *Iliad* (trans. Robert Fagles; London: Softback Preview, 1997).

——*Odyssey* (trans. Robert Fagles; New York: Penguin 1997).

Homeric Hymns (trans. Apostolos N. Athanassakis; Baltimore: Johns Hopkins University Press, 1976).

Hone, Margaret, *The Modern Textbook of Astrology* (London: L.N. Fowler, 4th edn repr., 1973).

Hornung, Erik, *The Secret Lore of Egypt: Its Impact on the West* (trans. David Lorton; Ithaca and London: Cornell University Press, 2001).

Horowitz, Wayne, *Mesopotamian Cosmic Geography* (Winona Lake: Eisenbrauns, 1998).

Hoskin, Michael, *Tombs Temples and their Orientations: A New Perspective on Mediterranean History* (Bognor Regis: Ocarina Books, 2001).

Hoyle, Fred, *From Stonehenge to Modern Cosmology* (San Francisco: W.H. Freeman and Co., 1972).

——'Speculations on Stonehenge', *Antiquity* 40 (1966): 262–76.

Huber, P.J., 'Dating by Lunar Eclipse Omina with Speculations on the Birth of Omen Astrology', in J.L. Berggren and B.R. Goldstein (eds), *From Ancient Omens to Statistical Mechanics: Essays on the Exact Sciences Presented to Asger Aaboe* (Copenhagen: Copenhagen University Library, 1987), pp. 3–13.

Hübner, W. (ed.), *Claudii Ptolemaei, Opera quae exstant omnia Volumen II, I: Apotelesmatika* (Stuttgart and Leipzig: B.G. Teubner, 1998).

Hughes, David, *The Star of Bethlehem Mystery* (London, Toronto and Melbourne: J.M. Dent and Sons, 1979).

Hughes, G.R., 'A Demotic Astrological Text', *Journal of Near Eastern Studies* 10 (1951): 256–64.

Hunger, Hermann, *Astrological Reports to Assyrian Kings* (Helsinki: Helsinki University Press, 1992).

Hunger, Hermann and David Pingree, *Astral Sciences in Mesopotamia* (Leiden, Boston and Koln: Brill, 1999).

——*Mul Apin: An Astronomical Compendium in Cuneiform* (Archiv für Orientforschung, 24; Ferdinand Berger & Sohne: Horn, 1989).

Hussey, Edward, *The Presocratics* (London: Duckworth, 1983).

Hutton, Ronald, 'Astral Magic: The Acceptable Face of Paganism', in Nicholas Campion, Patrick
    Curry and Michael York (eds), *Astrology and the Academy* (papers from the inaugural
    conference of the Sophia Centre, Bath Spa University College, 13–14 June 2003; Bristol:
    Cinnabar Books, 2004), pp. 10–24.
Hymns of the Atharva-Veda (trans. Maurice Bloomberg; Delhi: Motilal Banarsidass, 2000
    [1897]).
Iamblichus, *On the Mysteries of the Egyptians, Chaldeans, and Assyrians* (trans. Thomas Taylor;
    Frome: Prometheus Trust, 1999 [1821]).
Inanna, Lady of Largest Heart: Poems of the Sumerian High Pristess Enheduanna (trans. Betty
    De Shong Meador; Austin: University of Texas, 2001).
Irenaeus, *The Third Book of Irenaeus Against the Heresies* (trans. Henry Dean; Oxford: Oxford
    University Press, 1880).
Isidore of Seville, *The Etymologies* (trans. Stephen A. Barney, W.J. Lewis, J.A. Beach and Oliver
    Berghof, Cambridge: Cambridge University Press, 2007).
Iwaniszewski, Stanlslaw, 'Archaeoastronmical Analysis of Assyrian and Babylonian
    Monuments: Methodological Issues', *Journal for the History of Astronomy* 34(1) (February
    2003): 79–93.
Jacobs, Louis, 'Jewish Cosmology', in Carmen Blacker and Michael Loewe, *Ancient Cosmologies*
    (London: George Allen and Unwin Ltd., 1975), pp. 66–86.
Jacobsen, Thorkild, 'The Cosmos as a State', in H. Frankfort, H.A. Frankfort, William A. Irwin,
    Thorkild Jacobsen and John A. Wilson, *The Intellectual Adventure of Ancient Man: An Essay
    on Speculative Thought in the Ancient Near East* (Chicago and London: Chicago University
    Press, 1946), pp. 125–84.
——'Primitive Democracy in Ancient Mesopotamia', *Journal of Near Eastern Studies* 2 (1943):
    159–72.
——*The Treasures of Darkness: A History of Mesopotamian Religion* (New Haven and London:
    Yale University Press, 1976).
Jacq, C., *Egyptian Magic* (Warminster: Aris and Phillips, 1985).
Jastrow, Morris, *Aspects of Religious Belief and Practice in Babylonia and Assyria* (New York:
    Putnam, 1911).
Jeffers, Ann, *Divination and Prophecy in Israel and Palestine* (Leiden: E.J. Brill, 1996).
Johnson, Laurin R., *Shining at the Ancient Sea: The Astronomical Ancestry of Homer's Odyssey*
    (Portland, Oreg. Multnomah House Press, 1999).
Jonas, Hans, *The Gnostic Religion: The Message of the Alien God and the Beginnings of
    Christianity* (Boston: Beacon Press, 2nd edn, 1963).
Jones, Alexander, *Astronomical Papyri from Oxyrynchus* (Philadelphia: American Philosophical
    Society, 1999), vols. 1–2.
——'Babylonian Astronomy and its Legacy', *Bulletin of the Canadian Society for Mesopotamian
    Studies* 32 (1977): 11–17.
——'Evidence for Babylonian Arithmetical Schemes in Greek Astronomy', in *Die Rolle der
    Astronomie in den Kulturen Mesopotamiens* (Grazer Morganländische Studien, 3; ed. Hannes
    D. Galter; Graz: RM-Druck & Verlagsgesellchaft m.b.H 1993), pp. 77–94.
——'On Babylonian Astronomy and its Greek Metamorphoses', in F. Jamil Ragep and Sally P.
    Ragep (eds), *Tradition, Transmission, Transformation* (Leiden and New York: E.J. Brill, 1996),
    pp. 139–55.
——'The Place of Astronomy in Roman Egypt', in Timothy D. Barnes (ed.), *The Sciences
    in Greco-Roman Society* (Edmonton, Alberta: Academic Printing and Publishing, 1994),
    pp. 25–51.

Jones, Prudence, *Northern Myths of the Constellations* (Fenris-Wolf: Cambridge, 1991).

Jones, Roger Miller, 'Posidonius and the Flight of the Mind through the Universe', *Classical Philology* 21(2) (April 1926): 97–113.

Jordan, Paul, *Riddles of the Sphinx* (Stroud: Sutton Publishing, 1998).

Josephus, *The Antiquities of the Jews*, in *Works* (trans. William Whiston; n.p.: Hendrickson Publishers, 1987 [1736]).

Julian, *Works* (3 vols; trans. Wilmer Cave Wright; Cambridge, Mass. and London: Harvard University Press, 1913).

Julius Caesar, *The Conquest of Gaul* (trans S.A. Handford; Harmondsworth: Penguin, 1951).

Jung, C.G., *Collected Works*, vol. 8: *The Structure and Dynamics of the Psyche* (trans. R.F.C. Hull; Princeton, N.J.: Princeton, 1960).

——*Memories, Dreams, Reflections* (London: Fontana, 1967).

Juvenal, *The Sixteen Satires* (trans. Peter Green; London: Penguin, 2004).

Justin Martyr, *Writings of Justin Martyr* (ed. Alexander Roberts and James Donaldson; Ante-Nicene Christian Library; Edinburgh: T&T Clark, 1877).

Kahn, Charles H., *Anaximander and the Origins of Greek Cosmology* (New York: Hackett Publishing Co., 1960).

Kane, Sean, *Wisdom of the Mythtellers* (Peterborough, Ontario: Broadview Press, 1997).

Keper, Olaf E., 'The Astronomical Ceiling of Deir El-Haggar in the Dakhleh Oasis', *Journal of Egyptian Archaeology* 31 (1995): 175–95.

Kidger, Mark, *The Star of Bethlehem: An Astronomer's View* (Princeton: Princeton University Press, 1999).

Kingsley, Peter, *Ancient Philosophy, Mystery and Magic: Empedocles and Pythagorean Tradition* (Oxford: Clarendon Press, 1995).

——*In the Dark Places of Wisdom* (Inverness, Calif: Golden Sufi Center, 1999).

——'Poimandres: The Etymology of the Name and the Origins of the Hermetica', *Journal of the Warburg and Courtauld Institutes* 56 (1993): 1–24.

Kirk, G.S., J.E. Raven and M. Schofield, *The Presocratic Philosophers* (Cambridge: Cambridge University Press, 2nd edn, 1983).

Kleist, James A. (trans.), *The Epistles of St. Clement of Rome and St Ignatius of Antioch* (New York and London: Newman Press, 1946).

Knight, Chris, *Blood Relations: Menstruation and the Origins of Culture* (New Haven and London: Yale University Press, 1991).

Koch, Ulla Susanne, *Secrets of Extispicy: The Chapter Multābiltu of the Babylonian Extispicy Series and Nisirti bārîti Texts mainly from Aššurbanipal's Library* (Alter Orient und Altes Testament, 326; Münster: Ugarit-Verlag, 2005).

Koch-Westenholz, Ulla, *Mesopotamian Astrology: An Introduction to Babylonian and Assyrian Celestial Divination* (Carsten Niebuhr Institute of Near Eastern Studies; Copenhagen: Museum Tusculanum Press, University of Copenhagen, 1995).

Koleva, Vesselina and Dmiter Kolev (eds), *Astronomical Traditions in Past Cultures* (Proceedings of the 1st Annual General Meeting of the European Society for Astronomy in Culture, Smolyan, Bulgaria, 31 August – 2 September 1992; Sofia: Institute of Astronomy, Bulgarian Academy of Sciences and National Astronomical Observatory, Rozhen, 1996).

Komarowska, Joanna, 'The Lure of Egypt, or How to Sound Like a Reliable Souce', in Nicholas Campion, Patrick Curry and Michael York (eds), *Astrology and the Academy* (papers from the inaugural conference of the Sophia Centre, Bath Spa University College, 13–14 June 2003; Bristol: Cinnabar Books, 2004), pp. 147–58.

Kramer, Samuel Noah, *Sumerian Mythology: A Study of Spiritual and Literary Achievement in the Third Millennioum* BC (Philadephia: University of Pennsylvania Press, 1972 [1944]).

——*The Sumerians: Their History, Culture and Character* (Chicago: University of Chicago Press, 1963).

Kramer, Samuel Noah and Diane Wolkstein, *Inanna, Queen of Heaven and Earth: Her Stories and Hymns from Sumer* (New York: Harper & Row, 1983).

Krauss, Rolf, 'The Eye of Horus and the Planet Venus: Astronomical and Mythological References', in John M. Steele and Annette Imhausen, *Under One Sky: Astronomy and Mathematics in the Ancient Near East* (Alter Orient und Altes Testament, 297; Munster: Ugarit-Verlag, 2002), pp. 193–208.

Krupp, E.C., 'Bedroom Politics and Celestial Sovereignty', in John W. Fountain and Rolf M. Sinclair (eds), *Current Studies in Archaeoastronomy: Conversations Across Time and Space* (Durham, N.C.: Carolina Academic Press, 2005), pp. 412–27.

——*Beyond the Blue Horizon: Myths and Legends of the Sun, Moon and Stars and Planets* (New York and Oxford: Oxford University Press, 1991).

——'Light in the Temples', in Clive Ruggles, *Records in Stone: Papers in Memory of Alexander Thom* (Cambridge: Cambridge University Press, 1988), pp. 473–98.

——'Night Gallery: The Function, Origin and Evolution of Constellations', *Archaeoastronomy: The Journal of Astronomy in Culture* 15 (2000): 43–63.

——*Skywatchers, Shamans and Kings: Astronomy and the Archaeology of Power* (New York, John Wiley & Sons Inc., 1997).

Krupp, E.C. (ed.) *In Search of Ancient Astronomies* (Harmondsworth: Penguin, 1984).

Laird, Edgar, 'Christine de Pizan and Controversy Concerning Star Study in the Court of Charles V', *Culture and Cosmos* 1(2) (Winter–Autumn 1997): 35–48.

Laks, A and G. Most (eds), *Studies on the Derveni Papyrus* (Oxford: Oxford University Press, 1997).

Lambert, W.G., 'Babylonian Astrological Omens and Their Stars', *Journal of the American Oriental Society* 107(1) (January–March 1987): 93–96.

——*Babylonian Wisdom Literature* (Oxford: Oxford University Press, 1966).

——'The Cosmology of Sumer and Babylon', in Carmen Blacker and Michael Loewe, *Ancient Cosmologies* (London: George Allen and Unwin Ltd., 1975), pp. 42–65.

Lambert, W.G. and P. Walcot, 'A New Babylonian Theogony and Hesiod', *Kadmos* 4 (1965): 64–72

Larsen, Mogens Trolle, 'The Mesopotamian Lukewarm Mind: Reflections on Science, Divination and Literacy', in Francesca Rochberg-Halton (ed.), *Language, Literature and History* (New Haven, Conn.: American Oriental Society, 1987), pp. 203–26.

Latour, Bruno, *We Have Never Been Modern* (Cambridge, Mass.: Harvard University Press, 2006 [1991]).

Lawson, Jack N., *The Concept of Fate in Ancient Mesopotomia: Of the First Millennium, Towards an Understanding of 'Simtu'* (Wiesbaden: Harrasowitz Verlag, 1994).

Lawton, Ian and Chris Ogilvie-Herald, *Giza: The Truth* (London: Virgin Publishing, 1999).

Layton, Bentley, *The Gnostic Scriptures: Ancient Wisdom for the New Age* (Anchor Bible Reference Library; New York: Doubleday, 1995).

Lee, A.D., *Pagans and Christians in Late Antiquity* (London and New York: Routledge, 2000).

Lehner, Mark, *The Complete Pyramids* (London: Thames and Hudson, 1997).

Lehoux, Daryn, *Astronomy, Weather, and Calendars in the Ancient World: Parapegmata and Related Texts in Classical and Near-Eastern Societies* (Cambridge: Cambridge University Press, 2007).

——'Observation and Prediction in Ancient Astrology', *Studies in History and Philosophy of Science* 35 (2004): 227–46.

Leland, Charles G., *The Algonquin Legends Of New England Or Myths And Folklore Of The Micmac, Passmaquoddy, And Penobscot Tribes* (Boston: Houghton, Mifflin and Co., 1884).

Le Roy, Louis, *Of the Interchangeable Course or Variety of Things in the Whole World* (London: n.p., 1594).

Lesko, Leonard H., 'Ancient Egyptian Cosmogonies and Cosmology', in Byron E. Shafer, *Religion in Ancient Egypt* (Ithaca: Cornell University Press, 1991), pp. 88–122.

Lévy-Bruhl, Lucien, *How Natives Think* (Princeton: Princeton University Press, 1985).

Lewis-Williams, David, *The Mind in the Cave* (London: Thames and Hudson, 2005).

Lieven, Alexandra von, 'Gnosis and Astrology: "Book IV" of the Pistis Sophia', in John M. Steele and Annette Imhausen, *Under One Sky: Astronomy and Mathematics in the Ancient Near East* (Alter Orient und Altes Testament, 297; Munster: Ugarit-Verlag, 2002), pp. 223–36.

Lindsay, Jack, *Origins of Astrology* (London: Barnes and Noble, 1971).

Livingstone, Alasdair, *Mystical and Mythological Explanatory Works of Assyrian and Babylonian Scholars* (Oxford: Clarendon Press, 1986).

Lloyd, G.E.R., *Magic, Reason and Experience: Studies in the Origins and Development of Greek Science* (Cambridge, New York and Melbourne: Cambridge University Press, 1979).

Locher Kurt, 'The Ancient Egyptian Constellation Group of the Lion between Two Crocodiles and the Bird', *Archaeoastronomy: Supplement to the Journal for the History of Astronomy* 15 (1990): S49–S51.

——'A Conjecture Concerning the Early Egyptian Constellation of the Sheep', *Archaeoastronomy: Supplement to the Journal for the History of Astronomy* 3 (1981): S63–S65.

——'The Decans of Ancient Egypt: Timekeepers for Worship, or Worshipped Beyond Time?', in John W. Fountain and Rolf M. Sinclair (eds), *Current Studies in Archaeoastronomy: Conversations Across Time and Space* (Durham, N.C.: Carolina Academic Press, 2005), pp. 429–34.

——'Egyptian Cosmology', in Norris Hetherington (ed.), *Encyclopaedia of Cosmology* (New York and London: Garland Publishing, 1993), pp. 189–94.

——'Probable Identification of the Ancient Egyptian Circumpolar Constellations', *Archaeoastronomy: Supplement to the Journal for the History of Astronomy* 9 (1985): S152–S153.

Lockyer, Norman, *The Dawn of Astronomy* (London: Cassell and Co. Ltd., 1894).

——*Stonehenge and British Stone Monuments Astronomically Considered* (London: Macmillan, 1906).

Long, Charlotte, *The Twelve Gods of Greece and Rome* (Leiden and New York: E.J. Brill, 1987).

——'The Gods of the Months in Ancient Art', *American Journal of Archaeology* 93 (1989): 589–95.

Lovejoy, Arthur O., *The Great Chain of Being* (Cambridge, Mass. and London: Harvard University Press, 1936).

Lucretius, *On the Nature of the Universe* (trans. R.E. Latham; Harmondsworth: Penguin, 1981).

Lull, José and Juan Antonio Belmonte, 'A Firmament Above Thebes: Uncovering the Constellations of Ancient Egyptians', *Journal for the History of Astronomy* 37(4) (November 2006): 373–92.

Luz, Antequera Corregado, 'Altamira: Astronomia y Religion en el Paleolitico', in Juan Antonio Belmonte Aviles (ed.), *Arqueoastronomia Hispanica* (Madrid: Equipa Sirius SS, 1994).

Lyman, Mary Ely, 'Hermetic Religion and the Religion of the Fourth Gospel', *Journal of Biblical Literature* 49(3) (1930): 265–76.

McCluskey, Stephen C., *Astronomies and Cultures in Early Medieval Europe* (Cambridge: Cambridge University Press, 1998).

McEvilley, Thomas, *The Shape of Ancient Thought* (New York: Allsworth Press, 2002).

McGillion, Frank, 'The Influence of Wilhelm Fliess' Cosmobiology on Sigmund Freud', *Culture and Cosmos* 2(1) (Spring–Summer 1998): 33–48.

McKay, J.W., *Religion in Judah under the Assyrians* (London: SCM Press, 1973).

MacKie, Euan, 'Investigating the Prehistoric Solar Calendar', in Clive Ruggles, *Records in Stone: Papers in Memory of Alexander Thom* (Cambridge: Cambridge University Press, 1988), pp. 206–31.

——'Maes Howe and the Winter Solstice: Ceremonial Aspects of the Orkney Grooved Ware Culture', *Antiquity* 71 (1997): 338–59.

——'New Evidence for a Professional Priesthood in the European Early Bronze Age?', in Todd W. Bostwick and Bryan Bates (eds), *Viewing the Sky Through Past and Present Cultures: Selected Papers from the Oxford VII International Conference on Archaeoastronomy* (Pueblo Grande Museum Anthropological Papers, 15; Phoenix: Pueblo Grande Museum, 2006).

——*Science and Society in Prehistoric Britain* (London: Paul and Elek, 1977).

Macrobius, *Commentary on the Dream of Scipio* (trans. W.H. Stahl; New York: Columbia University Press, 1990 [1952]).

Makoto, Hayashi, 'The Tokugawa Shoguns and Onmyōdō', *Culture and Cosmos* 10 (2006): 49–62.

Mallville, J. McKim, Fred Wendorf, A.A. Mazaar and Romauld Schild, 'Megaliths and Neolithic Astronomy in Southern Egypt', *Nature* 392 (1998): 488–91.

Malone, Caroline, *Avebury* (London: Batsford/English Heritage, 1989).

Manilius, Marcus, *Astronomica* (trans. G.P. Goold; Cambridge, Mass. and London: Harvard University Press, 1977).

Marcus Aurelius, *Meditations* (trans. Maxwell Staniforth; Harmondsworth: Penguin, 1964).

Marcus, Ralph, 'The Name Poimandres', *Journal of Near Eastern Studies* 8(1) (January 1949): 40–43.

Marinus of Samaria, *The Life of Proclus* (trans. Kenneth Guthrie; Grand Rapids, Mich.: Phasnes Press, 1986).

Marshak, Alexander, 'Lunar Notation on Upper Palaeolithic Remains', *Science* 146 (1964): 743–45.

——*The Roots of Civilisation* (Mt Kisco, N.Y. and London: Moyer Bell Ltd., 1991).

Martin, Luther H., *Hellenistic Religions: An Introduction* (Oxford: Oxford University Press, 1987).

Martinez, Florentino Garcia, *The Dead Sea Scrolls Translated: The Qumran Texts in English* (Leiden, New York and Cologne: E.J. Brill, 1994).

Martiny, Günter von, 'Zur Astronomischen Orientation Altmesopotamischer Tempel', *Architectura* 1 (1933): 41–45.

Maternus, Julius Firmicus, *Mathesis* (trans. Jean Rhys Bram as *Ancient Astrology: Theory and Practice*; Park Ridge, N.J.: Noyes Press, 1975).

Matsumoto, Ikuyo, 'Two Mediaeval Manuscripts on the Worship of the Stars from the Fujii Eikan Collection', *Culture and Cosmos* 10 (2006): 125–44.

Mellaart, James, *Catal Huyuk: A Neolithic Town in Anatolia* (New York: McGraw-Hill, 1967).

Mendellsohn, Kurt, *The Riddle of the Pyramids* (London: Thames and Hudson, 1974).

Michalowski, Piotr (ed.), *The Lamentation Over the Destruction of Sumer and Ur* (Winona Lake: Eisenbrauns, 1989).

Midant-Reynes, Béatrix, *The Prehistory of Egypt* (Oxford: Blackwell, 2000).

Milburn, Robert, *Early Christian Art and Architecture* (Aldershot: Scolar Press, 1988).

Mithen, Steven, *The Prehistory of the Mind: a Search for the Origins of Art, Religion and Science* (London: Orion, 1998).

Molnar, Michael R., 'The Evidence for Aries the Ram as the Astrological Sign of Judea', *Journal for the History of Astronomy* 34(3) (August 2003): 325–27.

——'Firmicus Maternus and the Star of Bethlehem', *Culture and Cosmos* 3(1) (Spring/Summer 1999): 3–9.

——'The Magi's Star from the Perspective of Ancient Astrological Practices', *Quarterly Journal of the Royal Astronomical Society* 36 (1995): 109–26.

——*The Star of Bethlehem: The Legacy of the Magi* (New Jersey: Rutgers University Press, 1999).

Morrall, John B., *Political Thought in the Medieval World* (Toronto: University of Toronto Press, 1980).

Morrison, J.S., 'The Classical World', in Carmen Blacker and Michael Loewe, *Ancient Cosmologies* (London: George Allen and Unwin Ltd., 1975), pp. 87–114.

Motz, Lloyd and Jefferson Hane Weaver, *The Story of Astronomy* (New York and London: Plenum Press, 1995).

Müller, Max, *Introduction to the Science of Religion* (London: Longmans, Green and Co., 1873).

——'Solar Myths', *The Nineteenth Century* (December 1885): 900–22.

Munro, J.A.R., 'Thucydides on the Third of August, 431 B.C.', *The Classical Quarterly*, 13(3–4) (July 1919): 127–28.

Nabarz, Payam, *The Mysteries of Mithras: The Pagan Belief That Shaped the Christian World* (Rochester, Vt.: Inner Traditions, 2005).

Nakhai, Beth Alpert, *Archaeology and the Religions of Canaan and Israel* (Atlanta: American Schools of Oriental Research, 2001).

Naydler, Jeremy, *Shamanic Wisdom in the Pyramid Texts: The Mystical Tradition of Ancient Egypt* (Rochester, Vt.: Inner Traditions, 2005).

——*Temple of the Cosmos: The Ancient Egyptian Experience of the Sacred* (Rochester, Vt.: Inner Traditions, 1996).

Needham, Joseph, *Science and Civilisation in China*, vol. 3: *Mathematics and the Sciences of the Heavens and Earth* (Cambridge: Cambridge University Press, 1959).

Ness, Lester, *Written in the Stars: Ancient Zodiac Mosaics* (Warren Center, Pa.: Shangri La Publications, 1999).

Neugebauer, Otto, 'Demotic Horoscopes', *Journal of the American Oriental Society* 63(2) (April–June 1943): 115–27.

——'The Egyptian Decans', *Vistas in Astronomy* 1 (1955): 47–49: reprinted in Otto Neugebauer, *Astronomy and History: Selected Essays* (New York, Berlin, Heidelberg and Tokyo: Springer Verlag, 1983), pp. 205–09.

——*The Exact Sciences in Antiquity* (New York: Dover Publications, 2nd edn, 1969).

——*A History of Ancient Mathematical Astronomy* (3 vols; Berlin, Heidelberg and New York; Springer Verlag, 1975).

——'On the Orientation of Pyramids', *Centaurus* 24 (1980): 1–3.

——'The Survival of Babylonian Methods in the Exact Sciences of Antiquity and Middle Ages', *Proceedings of the American Philosophical Society* 107(6) (December 1963): 528–35.

Neugebauer, Otto and R.A. Parker, *Egyptian Astronomical Texts* (Providence, R.I.: Brown University Press, 1960).

——'Two Demotic Horoscopes', *Journal of Egyptian Archaeology* 54 (1968): 231–35.

Neugebauer, Otto and H.B. van Hoesen, *Greek Horoscopes* (Philadelphia: American Philosophical Society, 1959).

Noegel, Scott (ed.), *Prayer, Magic, and the Stars in the Ancient and Late Antique World* (Philadelphia: Pennsylvania State University Press, 2003).

Noonan, George C., *Classical Scientific Astrology* (Tempe, Ariz.: American Federation of Astrologers, 1984).

O'Brien, Denis, *Empedocles' Cosmic Cycle: A Reconstruction From the Fragments and Secondary Sources* (Cambridge: Cambridge University Press, 1969).

Oesterley, W., 'Early Hebrew Ritual Festivals', in Samuel Hooke (ed.), *Myth and Ritual: Essays in the Myth and Ritual of the Hebrews in Relation to the Culture Patterns of the Ancient East* (Oxford: Oxford University Press, 1933), pp. 111–46.

Oestmann, Günther, H.K. von Stuckrad and D. Rutkin (eds), *Horoscopes and History* (Berlin and New York: Walter de Gruyter, 2005).

O'Flaherty, Wendy Doniger, *The Rig Veda: An Anthology* (New Delhi: Penguin, 1994).

Olmsted, Garrett, *The Gaulish Calendar* (Bonn: Dr Rudolf Habelt GmBh, 1992).

Oppenheim, A. Leo, *Ancient Mesopotamia: Portrait of a Dead Civilisation* (Chicago: University of Chicago Press, 1977).

——'A Babylonian Diviner's Manual', *Journal of Near Eastern Studies* 33 (1974): 197–220.

——'Divine and Celestial Observation in the Last Assyrian Empire', *Centaurus* 14(1) (1969): 97–135.

Origen, *The Philocalia of Origen* (trans. George Lewis; Edinburgh: T&T Clark, 1911).

——*Works* (ed. G.W. Butterworth; Cambridge, Mass.: Harvard University Press, 1936).

Ovenden, Michael, 'The Origin of the Constellations', *The Philosophical Journal* 3(1) (1966): 1–18.

Pagels, Elaine, *The Gnostic Gospels* (Harmondsworth: Penguin, 1979).

——*The Gnostic Paul: Gnostic Exegesis of the Pauline Letters* (Philadelphia: Trinity International, 1970).

Pannekoek, A., *A History of Astronomy* (London: George Allen and Unwin Ltd., 1961).

Papyri graecae magicae (ed. K. Preisendanz; Berlin, 1928).

Parfitt, Tom, 'Bronze Age Pyramid found in Ukraine', *The Guardian* (8 September 2006): 21.

Parker, R.A., *The Calendars of Ancient Egypt* (Oriental Institute of Chicago Studies in Ancient Oriental Civilisation, 26; Chicago: University of Chicago Press, 1950).

——'Ancient Egyptian Astronomy', in F.R. Hodson (ed.), *The Place of Astronomy in the Ancient World* (Transactions of the Royal Society, 276; London: Oxford University Press, 1974), pp. 51–65.

——'Egyptian Astronomy, Astrology and Calendrical Reckoning', in Charles Coulston (ed.), *Dictionary of Scientific Biography* (New York: Charles Scribner's Sons, 1971), vol. 4, pp. 706–27.

Parker, Robert, 'Greek States and Greek Oracles', in Richard Buxton (ed.), *Oxford Readings in Greek Religion* (Oxford, Oxford University Press, 2000), pp. 76–108.

Parpola, Asko, *Deciphering the Indus Script* (Cambridge: Cambridge University Press, 1997).

Parpola, Simo, 'The Assyrian Tree of Life: Tracing the Origins of Jewish Monotheism and Greek Philosophy', *Journal of Near Eastern Studies* 52(3) (July 1993): 161–208.

——*Letters from Assyrian and Babylonian Scholars* (Helsinki: Helsinki University Press, 1993).

——*Letters from Assyrian Scholars to the Kings Esarhaddon and Assurbanipal*, part 1: *Texts*; part 2: *Commentary* (Kevelaer: Verlag Butzon & Bercker and Neukirchen-Vluyn: Neukirchener Verlag, 1970, 1983).

Paterson, Tony, 'Mysterious Gold Cones "Hats of Ancient Wizards" ', *Sunday Telegraph* (17 March 2002); available at <http://www.telegraph.co.uk/portal/main.jhtml?_DARGS=/core/lowerHeaderBarWideFrag.jhtml> (accessed 21 March 2002).

Pearson, James L. *Shamanism and the Ancient Mind: A Cognitive Approach to Archaeology* (Oxford: Altamira Press, 2002).

Petrie, William Flinders, *The Pyramids and Temples of Gizeh* (London: Fold and Tuer, 1883).

Petronius, *The Satyricon* (trans. J.P. Sullivan; London: Penguin, 1986).

Pfeiffer, Robert H., *State Letters of Assyria: A Transliteration and Translation of 355 Official Assyrian Letters Dating from the Sargonid Period (722–625 BC)* (American Oriental Series, 6; New Haven: American Oriental Society, 1935).

Philo, *Works* (trans. C.D. Yonge; Peabody, Mass.: Hendrickson, 1993).

Piggott, Stuart, *Ancient Britons and the Antiquarian Imagination* (London: Thames and Hudson, 1989).

Pingree, David, *From Astral Omens to Astrology From Babylon to Bikaner* (Rome: Istituto Italiano per L'Africa e L'Oriente, 1997).

——'Babylonian Planetary Theory in Sanskrit Omen Texts', in J.L.L. Berggren and B.R. Goldstein (eds), *From Ancient Omens to Statistical Mechanics: Essays on the Exact Sciences Presented to Asger Aaboe* (Copenhagen: University Library, 1987), pp. 91–99.

——*Jyotiḥśastra: Astral and Mathematical Literature* (Wiesbaden: Otto Harrasowitz, 1981).

——'Hellenophilia versus the History of Science', *Isis* 83 (1991): 554–63.

——'Historical Horoscopes', *Journal of the American Oriental Society* 82 (1962): 487–502.

——'The Horoscope of Constantinople', *Prismata* (Festchrift for Willy Hartner; Wiesbaden: Franz Steiner Verlag, 1977), pp. 305–15.

——'Legacies in Astronomy and Celestial Omens', in Stephanie Dalley (ed.), *The Legacy of Mesopotamia* (Oxford: Clarendon Press, 1998) pp. 125–37.

——'Venus Omens in India and Babylon', in Francesca Rochberg-Halton (ed.), *Language, Literature and History: Philological and Historical Studies Presented to Erica Reiner* (New Haven: American Oriental Society, 1987), pp. 293–315.

——*Vṛddhayanajataka of Minarāja* (Gaekwad's Oriental Series, 162, 163; Baroda: Oriental Institute, Maharaja Sayajirao University of Baroda, 1976).

——*The Yavanajataka of Sphujidhvaja* (2 vols; Harvard Oriental Series, 48; Cambridge, Mass.: Harvard University Press, 1978).

Pinker, Steven, *How the Mind Works* (New York: W.W. Norton, 1997).

Plato, *Epinomis* (trans. W.R.M. Lamb; Cambridge, Mass. and London: Harvard University Press, 1929).

——*Laws* (2 vols; trans. R.G. Bury; Cambridge, Mass. and London: Harvard University Press, 1934).

——*Phaedo* (trans. H.N. Fowler; Cambridge, Mass. and London: Harvard University Press, 1914).

——*Phaedrus* (trans. H.N. Fowler; Cambridge, Mass. and London: Harvard University Press, 1914).

——*Republic* (2 vols; trans. Paul Shorey; Cambridge, Mass. and London: Harvard University Press, 1937).

——*Republic* (trans. H.D.P. Lee; Harmondsworth: Penguin, 1971 [1955]).

——*Symposium* (trans. W.R.M. Lamb; Cambridge, Mass. and London: Harvard University Press, 1914).

——*Theaeteus* (trans. Benjamin Jowett; Indianapolis: The Library of Liberal Arts, 1949).

——*Timaeus* (trans. R.G. Bury; Cambridge, Mass. and London: Harvard University Press, 1931).

Pliny, *Natural History* (10 vols; trans H. Rackham and D.E. Eichholz; Cambridge, Mass. and London: Harvard University Press, 1949–62).

Plotinus, *Enneads* (trans. A.H. Armstrong; Cambridge, Mass. and London: Harvard University Press, 1966).

Plumley, J.M., 'The Cosmology of Ancient Egypt', in Carmen Blacker and Michael Loewe, *Ancient Cosmologies* (London: George Allen and Unwin Ltd., 1975), pp. 17–41.

Plunket, Emmeline Mary, *The Judgement of Paris and Some Other Legends Astronomically Considered* (London: John Murray, 1908).

Plutarch, *Moralia* (trans. F.C. Babbit; Cambridge, Mass. and London: Harvard University Press, 1936), vol. 5.

——*Lives* (2 vols; trans. John Langhorne and William Langhorne; London and New York: Frederick Warne and Co., 1890).

Pogo, A., 'Calendars on Coffin Lids from Assyut', *Isis* 17 (1932): 6–24

Popper, Karl, *The Open Society and its Enemies* (2 vols; London and New York: Routledge, 1957 [1945]).

——*The Poverty of Historicism* (London and New York: Routledge, 1986).

Possanza, D. Mark, *Translating the Heavens. Aratus, Germanicus, and the Poetics of Latin Translation* (Lang Classical Studies, 14; New York: Peter Lang, 2004).

Powell, Robert, *History of the Zodiac* (San Rafael: Sophia Academic Press, 2007).

Pritchard, James B. (ed.), *Ancient Near Eastern Texts Relating to the Old Testament* (Princeton: Princeton University Press, 1969).

Proclus, 'Five Hymns' (trans. Thomas Taylor, in Marinus of Samaria, *The Life of Proclus* [trans. Kenneth Guthrie; Grand Rapids, Mich.: Phanes, 1986).

Proctor, Richard, *Myths and Marvels of Astronomy* (London: Longmans, Green and Co., 1891).

Pryor, F., *Seahenge: New Discoveries in Prehistoric Britain* (London: HarperCollins, 2001).

Ptolemy, *Almagest* (trans. G.J. Toomer; Princeton: Princeton University Press, 1998).

——*Harmonics: Translation and Commentary* (trans. Jon Solomon; Leiden: E.J. Brill, 2000).

——*The Phases of the Fixed Stars* (trans. Robert Schmidt; ed. Robert Hand; Berkeley Springs, W.Va.: Golden Hind Press, 1993).

——*Tetrabiblos* (trans. J.M. Ashmand; London: Foulsham, 1917).

——*Tetrabiblos* (trans. F.E. Robbins; Cambridge, Mass. and London: Harvard University Press, 1940).

——*Tetrabiblos* (4 vols; trans. Robert Schmidt; [vols 1–3 ed. Robert Hand]; Cumberland Md.: Golden Hind Press, 1994–98).

Quirke, S., *Ancient Egyptian Religion* (London: British Museum Publications, 1992).

Quispel, Gilles, 'Hermes Trismegistus and the Origins of Gnosticism', *Vigiliae Christianae* 46(1) (March 1992): 1–19.

——'Hermes Trismegistus and Tertllian', *Vigiliae Christianae* 43(2) (June 1989): 188–90.

Ramsey, John T. and A. Lewis Licht, *Caesar's Comet: The Comet of 44 BC and Caesar's Funeral Games* (Atlanta: Scholars Press, 1997).

Rappaport, Roy, *Ritual and Religion in the Making of Humanity* (Cambridge: Cambridge University Press, 1999).

Rappenglueck, Michael, 'The Pleiades in the "Salle des Taureaux" Grotte de Lascaux: Does a Rock Picture in the Cave of Lascaux show the Open Star Cluster of the Pleiades at the Magdalenien Era (ca 15,300 BC)?', in C. Jaschek and F. Atrio Barandela, *Proceedings of the IVth SEAC Meeting 'Astronomy and Culture'* (Salamanca: University of Salamanca, 1997).

Reale, Giovanni, *The Schools of the Imperial Age: A History of Ancient Philosophy* (Albany: State University of New York Press, 1990).

Reiner, Erica, *Astral Magic in Babylonia* (Philadelphia: American Philosophical Society, 1995).

Reiner, Erica, with David Pingree, *Babylonian Planetary Omens, Part 1, Enuma Anu Enlil, Tablet 63: The Venus Tablet of Ammisaduqa* (Malibu: Undena Publications, 1975).

——*Babylonian Planetary Omens, Part 2, Enuma Anu Enlil, Tablets 50–51* (Bibliotheca Mesopotamica, 4, fasc. 2; Malibu: Undena Publications, 1981).

——*Babylonian Planetary Omens, Part Three* (Groningen: Styx Publications, 1998).

Richer, Jean, *Sacred Geography of the Ancient Greeks: Astrological Symbolism in Art, Architecture and Landscape* (Albany: State University of New York Press, 1994).

Ricoeur, Paul, *Time and Narrative* (Chicago: University of Chicago Press, 1985), vol. 2.

Riley, Mark, 'Science and Tradition in the *Tetrabiblos*', *Proceedings of the American Philosophical Society* 132(1) (1988): 67–84.

——'Theoretical and Practical Astrology: Ptolemy and His Colleagues', *Transactions of the American Philological Association* 117 (1987): 235–56.

Ritner, Robert, *Egyptian Magic* (Chicago: Chicago Oriental Institute, 1993).

Robbins, Lawrence H., 'Astronomy and Prehistory', in Helaine Selin (ed.), *Astronomy Across Cultures: the History of Non-Western Astronomy* (Dordrecht: Kluwer Academic Publishers, 2000), pp. 31–52.

Robinson, C.A., *Ancient History from Prehistoric Times to the Death of Justinian* (New York: Macmillan, 1951).

Robinson, James M. (ed.), *The Nag Hammadi Library in English* (Leiden and New York: Brill, 1988).

Rochberg, Francesca, *Babylonian Horoscopes* (Philadelphia: American Philosophical Society, 1998).

——*The Heavenly Writing: Divination and Horoscopy, and Astronomy in Mesopotamian Culture* (Cambridge: Cambridge University Press, 2004).

Rochberg-Halton, Francesca, *Aspects of Babylonian Celestial Divination: The Lunar Eclipse Tablets of Enuma Anu Enlil* (Archiv für Orientforschung, 22; Ferdinand Berger & Sohne: Horn, 1988).

——'The Cultural Locus of Astronomy in Late Babylonia', in *Die Rolle der Astronomie in den Kulturen Mesopotamiens* (Grazer Morganlandische Studien, 3; ed. Hannes D. Galter; Graz: RM-Druck & Verlagsgesellchaft m.b.H, 1993), pp. 31–46,

——'Elements of the Babylonian Contribution to Hellenistic Astrology', *Journal of the American Oriental Society* 108(1) (January–March 1988): 51–62.

Rousseau, Claudia, 'An Astrological Prognostication to Duke Cosimo I de Medici of Florence', *Culture and Cosmos* 3(2) (Autumn/Winter 1999): 31–59

Roy, Archie E., 'The Origins of the Constellations', *Vistas in Astronomy* 27 (1984): 171–97.

Roy, Archie E. and Kripa Shankar Shukla, 'Main Characteristics and Achievements of Ancient Indian Astronomy in Historical Perspective', in G. Swarup, A.K. Bag and K.S. Shukla (eds), *History of Oriental Astronomy* (Cambridge: Cambridge University Press, 1987), pp. 9–22.

Rudgley, Richard, *Lost Civilisations of the Stone Age* (London: Random House, 1998).

Ruggles, Clive, 'Astronomy and Stonehenge', in Barry Cunliffe and Colin Renfrew (eds) *Science and Stonehenge* (Oxford: Oxford University Press, 1997), pp. 203–29.

——*Astronomy in Prehistoric Britain and Ireland* (New Haven and London: Yale University Press, 1999).

——'Cosmology, Calendars and Society in Neolithic Orkney: A Rejoinder to Euan MacKie', *Antiquity* 74 (2000): 62–74.

——*Records in Stone: Papers in Memory of Alexander Thom* (Cambridge: Cambridge University Press, 1988).

Ruggles, Clive (ed.), *Archaeoastronomy in the 1990s* (Loughborough: Group D Publications, 1993).

Ruggles, Clive with Frank Prendergast and Tom Ray, *Astronomy, Cosmology and Landscape* (Proceedings of the SEAC 98 Meeting, Dublin, Ireland, September 1998; Bognor Regis: Ocarina Books, 2001).

Sachs, A.J., *Astronomical Diaries and Related Texts from Babylonia*, vol. 1: *Diaries from 652 B.C. to 262 B.C.* (completed and edited by Herman Hunger; Vienna: Verlag der Osterreichischen Akademie der Wissenschaften, 1988).

——'Babylonian Horoscopes', *Journal of Cuneiform Studies* 6 (1952): 49–75.

——'The Lastest Datable Cuneiform Texts', in Barry L. Eichler (ed.), *Kramer Anniversary Volume: Studies in Honor of Samuel Noah Kramer* (*Alter Orient und Altes Testament* 25 [1976]: 379–98).

Said, Edward, *Orientalism* (London: Penguin, 1985).

Saint Basil, *Exegetic Homilies* (trans. Agnes Clare; Washington, D.C.: The Catholic University of America Press, 1963).

Sandbach, F.H., *The Stoics* (Bristol: The Bristol Press, 1975).

Sarma, K.V. *Vedanga Jyotisa of Lagadha* (trans and with notes by T.S.K. Sastry; New Delhi: Indian National Science Academy, 1985).

Schaefer, Bradley E., 'Date and Place of Origin of the Asian Lunar Lodge Systems', in César Esteban and Juan Antonio Belmonte (eds), *Astronomy and Cultural Diversity, Proceedings of the 1999 Oxford VI Conference on Archaeoastronomy and Astronomy in Culture* (Tenerife: Oranismo Autonomo de Museos del Cablido de Tenerife, 2000), pp. 283–87.

——'The Latitude and Epoch for the Origin of the Astronomical Lore of Eudoxus', *Journal for the History of Astronomy* 35(2) (May 2004): 161–224.

Schiefsky, Mark J. *Hippocrates on Ancient Medicine* (Leiden: E.J. Brill, 2004).

Schmidt, Robert 'Translator's Preface', in Vettius Valens, *The Anthology: Book 1* (trans Robert Schmidt; Project Hindsight Greek Track, 4; Berkeley Springs W.Va.: Golden Hind Press, 1993), pp. xvi–xvii.

Schmithals, Walter, *Paul and the Gnostics* (trans. John E. Steely; Nashville: Abingdon Press, 1972).

'Scientists Turn the Clock forward on Aboriginal Life', *The Times* (28 May 1998): 3.

Scott, Alan, *Origen and the Life of the Stars: A History of an Idea* (Oxford: Clarendon Press, 1994).

Scourse, J.D., 'Transport of the Stonehenge Bluestones: Testing the Glacial Hypothesis', in Barry Cunliffe and Colin Renfrew, *Science and Stonehenge* (Oxford: Oxford University Press, 1997), pp. 271–314.

Segal, Robert A., *Myth: A Very Short Introduction* (Oxford: Oxford University Press, 2004).

Selin, Helaine (ed.), *Astronomy Across Cultures: the History of Non-Western Astronomy* (Dordrecht: Kluwer Academic Publishers, 2000).

Sellers, Jane B., *The Death of the Gods in Ancient Egypt* (London: Penguin, 1992).

Seneca, *Apocolocyntosis Divi Claudii* (trans W.H.D. Rouse; Cambridge, Mass. and London: Harvard University Press, 1969).

——*Letters from a Stoic* (Harmondsworth: Penguin, 1969).

——*Naturales Quaestiones* (trans. John Clarke; London: Macmillan, 1910).

——*Naturales Questiones* (2 vols; trans. T.H. Corcoran; Cambridge, Mass.: Harvard University Press, 1971).

Sextus Empiricus, *Against the Professors* (trans. R.G. Bury: Cambridge, Mass. and London: Harvard University Press, 1933).

Seymour, Percy, *The Birth of Christ: Exploding the Myth* (London: Virgin Publishing Ltd., 1998).

Shaltout, Mosalem, Juan Antonio Belmonte and Magdo Fekri, 'On the Orientation of Ancient Egyptian Temples: (3) Key Points in Lower Egypt and Siwa Oasis, Part 1', *Journal for the History of Astronomy* 38(2) (May 2007): 141–60; 38(4) (November 2007) 413–42.

Shaw, Gregory, *Theurgy and the Soul: The Neoplatonism of Iamblichus* (University Park, Pa.: The Pennsylvania University Press, 1995).

Shipley, Graham, *The Greek World After Alexander* (New York: Routledge, 2000).

Shuttle, Penelope and Peter Redgrove, *The Wise Wound* (New York: Bantam Books, 1990).

Smith, Mark S., 'The Near Eastern Background of Solar Language for Yahweh', *Journal of Biblical Literature* 109(1) (Spring 1990): 29–39.

——*The Origins of Biblical Monotheism* (Oxford: Oxford University Press, 2001).

Smyth, Marina, *Understanding the Universe in Seventh-Century Ireland* (Woodbridge: Boydell Press, 1996).

Souden, David, *Stonehenge* (London: Collins and Brown, 1998).

Sparks, H.F.D. (ed.), *The Apocryphal Old Testament* (Oxford: Clarendon Press, 1984).

Speidel, Michael P., *Mithras-Orion: Greek Hero and Roman Army God* (Leiden: E.J. Brill, 1980).

Speiser, E.A., 'The Creation Epic', in J.B. Pritchard (ed.), *Ancient Near Eastern Texts Relating to the Old Testament* (Princeton: Princeton University Press, 1969), pp. 60–72.

Spence, Kate, 'Ancient Egyptian Chronology and the Astronomical Orientation of Pyramids', *Nature* 408 (16 November 2000), pp. 320–24.

Starr, Ivan, *The Rituals of the Diviner* (Malibu: Undena Publications, 1983).

——*Queries to the Sungod: Divination and Politics in Sargonid Assyria* (State Archives of Assyria, 4; Helsinki: Helsinki University Press, 1990).

Steele, J.M. and J.M.K. Gray, 'Babylonian Observations Involving the Zodiac', *Journal for the History of Astronomy* 28(4) (November 2007): 443–58.

Steele, John M. and Annette Imhausen, *Under One Sky: Astronomy and Mathematics in the Ancient Near East* (Alter Orient und Altes Testament, 297; Munster: Ugarit-Verlag, 2002).

Steiner, Rudolf, *Human Values in Education* (London: Rudolf Steiner Press, 1971).

Stephenson, F.R. and C.B.F. Walker (eds), *Halley's Comet in History* (London: British Museum Publications, 1985).

Stuckrad, Kocku von, 'Jewish and Christian Astrology in Late Antiquity – A New Approach', *Numen* 47(1) (2000): 1–40.

Stukeley, William, *Stonehenge: A Temple Restor'd to the British Druids* (London: n.p., 1740).

Suetonius, *The Twelve Caesars* (trans. Robert Graves; Harmondsworth: Penguin, 1957).

Swerdlow, Noel, *The Babylonian Theory of the Planets* (Princeton: Princeton University Press, 1998).

Tacitus, *Histories and Annales* (trans. Clifford H. Moore; Cambridge, Mass.: Harvard University Press, 1925).

Tarán, Leonardo, *Academica: Plato: Philip of Opus, and the Pseudo-Platonic Epinomis* (Philadelphia: American Philosophical Society, 1975).

Tatian, *Oratio ad Graecos* (trans. Molly Whittaker; Oxford: Clarendon Press, 1982).

Taub, Liba Chaia, *Ptolemy's Universe: The Natural, Philosophical and Ethical Foundations of Ptolemy's Astronomy* (Chicago and La Salle, Ill.: Open Court, 1993).

Taylor, C.C.W., R.M. Hare and J. Barnes, *Greek Philosophers – Socrates, Plato, and Aristotle* (Oxford: Oxford University Press, 1999).

Taylor, J. Glen, *Yahweh and the Sun: Biblical and Archaeological Evidence for Sun Worship in Ancient Israel* (Journal for the Study of the Old Testament Supplement Series, 111; Sheffield: JSOT Press, 1993).

Tester, Jim, *A History of Western Astrology* (Woodbridge, Suffolk: Boydell Press, 1987).
Tertullian, *The Prescription Against Heretics* (trans. Peter Holmes); available at <http://www.
earlychristianwritings.com/text/tertullian11.html> (accessed 20 March 2007).
Thom, Alexander, *Megalithic Sites in Britain* (Oxford: Oxford University Press, 1967).
Thom, Alexander and Archibald Stevenson Thom, 'Rings and Menhirs: Geometry and
Astronomy in the Neolithic Age', in Ed Krupp (ed.), *In Search of Ancient Astronomies*
(London: Penguin, 1984), pp. 39–76.
Thompson, R. Campbell, *The Reports of the Magicians and Astrologers of Nineveh and Babylon
in the British Museum* (2 vols; London: Luzac and Co., 1900).
——*Semitic Magic: Its Origins and Development* (London: Luzac and Co., 1908).
Thompson, Richard L., *Vedic Cosmography and Astronomy* (Delhi: Motilal Banarsidass, 2004).
Thorndike, Lynn, *History of Magic and Experimental Science* (8 vols; New York: Columbia
University Press, 1923–58), vol. 1.
——*The Sphere of Sacrobosco and its Commentators* (Chicago: University of Chicago Press,
1949).
Thurston, Hugh, 'Aligning Giza: Astronomical Orientation of the Great Pyramid', *Griffith
Observer* 65(9) (September 2001): 11–17.
——*Early Astronomy* (New York: Springer Verlag, 1994).
Treatise on the Bright Fixed Stars (trans. Robert Schmidt; ed. Robert Hand; Berkeley Springs,
W.Va.: Golden Hind Press, 1993).
Trimble, Virginia, 'Astronomical Investigation Concerning the So-Called Air-Shafts of Cheops'
Pyramid', *Mitteilungen des deutsches Akademie Berlin* 10 (1964): 183–87.
Tyldesley, Joyce, *The Private Life of the Pharaohs* (London: Macmillan, 2000).
Tylor, Edward Burnett, *Primitive Culture* (3 vols; New York: Harper Torchbooks, 1958
[London: Murray, 1871]).
Ulansey, David, *The Origins of the Mithraic Mysteries: Cosmology and Salvation in the Ancient
World* (New York and Oxford: Oxford University Press, 1989).
Valens, Vettius, *The Anthology* (ed. David Pingree, as *Vetii Valenti Antiocheni Anthologarium,
libri novem* [Leipzig, 1986]).
——*The Anthology* (trans Robert Schmidt; Project Hindsight Greek Track; Berkeley Springs,
W.Va.: Golden Hind Press, 1993–96).
Van der Waerden, Bartel, 'Babylonian Astronomy II: The Thirty Six Stars', in *Journal of Near
Eastern Studies* 8(1) (January 1949): 6–26.
——'History of the Zodiac', *Archiv für Orientforschung* 16 (1952–53): 216–30.
——*Science Awakening*, vol. 2: *The Birth of Astronomy* (Leyden and New York: Oxford
University Press, 1974).
Van Seters, John, *In Search of History: Historiography in the Ancient World and the Origins of
Biblical History* (New Haven and London: Yale University Press, 1983).
Van Soldt, Wilfred, *Solar Omens of Enuma anu Enlil: Tablets 23(24)–29(30)* (Leiden:
Nederlands Historisch-Archaeologisch Instituut te Istanbul, 1995).
Vastos, Gregory, 'Theology and Philosophy in Early Greek Thought', *The Philosophical
Quarterly* 2(7) (April 1952): 97–123.
Ventura, Frank, 'Evaluating the Evidence for Interest in Astronomy in the Temple Period of
Malta (3600–2500 BCE)' (paper delivered at the second conference on the Inspiration of
Astronomical Phenomena (INSAP II), Malta, January 1999).
Vermes, G., *The Dead Sea Scrolls in English* (Harmondsworth: Pelican, 1962).
Viau, J., 'Egyptian Mythology', in Felix Guirand, *Larousse Encyclopaedia of Mythology* (trans.
Richard Aldington and Delano Ames; London: Paul Hamlyn, 1959), pp. 8–48.

Virgil, *Eclogues, Georgics and Aeneid* (2 vols; trans. H.R. Fairclough; Cambridge, Mass.: Harvard University Press, 1916).

Vitruvius, *De Architectura* (trans. F. Granger; Cambridge, Mass.: Harvard University Press, 1954).

Wainwright, Geoffrey, *The Henge Monuments: Ceremony and Society in Prehistoric Britain* (London: Thames and Hudson, 1989).

Walker, C.B.F., 'Episodes in the History of Babylonian Astronomy' (lecture delivered to the Society for Mesopotamian Studies, Toronto, May 12, 1982).

Walker, Christopher and John Britton, 'Astronomy and Astrology in Mesopotamia', in Christopher Walker (ed.), *Astronomy Before the Telescope* (London: British Museum Press, 1996), pp. 42–67.

Wall, John J., 'The Star Alignment Hypothesis for the Great Pyramid Shafts', *Journal for the History of Astronomy* 38(2) (May 2007), pp. 199–206.

Wallis, R.T., *Neoplatonism* (London: Duckworth, 1995).

Wallis, Robert, *Shamans/Neo-Shamans* (London: Routledge, 2003).

Waterfield, Robin, 'The Evidence for Astrology in Classical Greece', *Culture and Cosmos* 3(2) (Autumn–Winter 1999): 3–15.

Waterman, Leroy, *Royal Correspondence of the Assyrian Empire* (4 vols; Ann Arbor: University of Michigan Press, 1930–36).

Watterson, Barbara, *Gods of Ancient Egypt* (Stroud, Gloucestershire: Sutton Publishing, 1999).

Weber, Max, *From Max Weber: Essays in Sociology* (ed. H.H. Garth and C. Mills Wright; London: Kegan Paul, Trench, Trubner & Co., 1947).

Wells, Ronald A., 'Astronomy in Egypt', in Christopher Walker (ed.), *Astronomy Before The Telescope* (London: British Museum Press, 1996), pp. 28–41.

West, E.W., *The Bundahishn, or Knowledge from the Zand* (n.p.: Kessinger Publishing, 2004).

West, M.L., *The Orphic Poems* (Oxford: Oxford University Press, 1983).

White Yajur Veda (trans. Ralph Griffith; Benares: E.J. Lazarus & Co., 1899; available at <http://www.sacred-texts.com/hin/wyv/wyvbk14.htm> (accessed 20 September 2007)).

Wilkinson, Richard H., *The Complete Temples of Ancient Egypt* (London: Thames and Hudson, 2000).

——*Symbol and Magic in Egyptian Art* (London: Thames and Hudson, 1994).

Wilson, John, 'Egypt', in H. Frankfort, H.A. Frankfort, William A. Irwin, Thorkild Jacobsen and John A. Wilson, *The Intellectual Adventure of Ancient Man: An Essay on Speculative Thought in the Ancient Near East* (Chicago and London: Chicago University Press, 1946), pp. 31–124.

Wise, Michael, Martin Abegg and Edward Cook, *Dead Sea Scrolls* (London: Harper Collins, 1996).

Wood, Florence and Kenneth Wood, *Homer's Secret Iliad: The Epic of the Night Skies Decoded* (London: John Murray, 1999).

Wright, J. Edward, *The Early History of Heaven* (Oxford: Oxford University Press, 2000).

Wright, M.R., *Cosmology in Antiquity* (London: Routledge, 1995).

Yates, Frances, *The Art of Memory* (London: Peregrine, 1978).

Zaehner, Richard Charles, *The Teachings of the Magi* (Oxford: Oxford University Press, 1978).

——*Zurvan: A Zoroastrian Dilemma* (Oxford: Clarendon Press, 1955).

Zafran, Eric, 'Saturn and the Jews', *Journal of the Warburg and Courtauld Institutes* 42 (1979): 16–27.

Zaidman, Louise Bruit and Pauline Schmidt Pantel, *Relgion in the Ancient Greek City* (trans. Paul Cartledge; Cambridge: Cambridge University Press, 1994).

Ziesler, John, *Pauline Christianity* (Oxford: Oxford University Press, 1983).

Zeno of Verona, 'XXXVIII. Tractatus de XII signis ad neophitos', in *Zenonis Veronensis Tractatus* (Corpus Christianorum, 22; Ternhout: Brepols, 1971).

Index